TREATMENT
OF THE
OBSESSIVE
PERSONALITY

TREATMENT
OF THE
OBSESSIVE
PERSONALITY

Leon Salzman, M.D.

NEW YORK   JASON ARONSON   LONDON

CONTENTS

Part II
THE OBSESSIVE STATE AND OTHER SYNDROMES

Part III
TREATMENT

Part IV
CASE STUDY: THE OBSESSION TO KILL

PREFACE

In the decade or so since *The Obsessive Personality* first appeared, interest in the obsessional disorder has been on the increase, particularly among therapists seeking effective techniques for dealing with these elusive and resistant behavioral manifestations. Though an abundance of papers have been published in the interim, especially by advocates of behavior modification techniques, none of these contributions have diminished the importance of psychodynamic formulations regarding the etiology and treatment of this disorder. Flooding, imagery, thought stopping, and the like, all of them designed to reduce the incidence and intensity of rituals, obsessions, and phobias, have been useful in only a few cases, and then only for short periods. Often it has proved necessary to supplement these techniques with insight-oriented psychotherapy in order to deal effectively with the distress occasioned by the characterological behavior disorders inevitably accompanying these rituals and obsessions.

More important, behavioral approaches have not significantly advanced our understanding of why these defensive techniques develop in one individual and not in another, or why in some they are extremely incapacitating while in others they are adaptive, economical, and productive. Adherents of these techniques have offered no coherent or cogent theory beyond their standard focus on learning theory and habit formation; instead they concentrate on eliminating these habits by desensitization, either in small steps or by implosive flooding techniques, which are in actuality only desensitization on a grand scale. Such therapies miss the very essence of the obsessional disorder. By completely disregarding the reasons for its incorporation in human activity they tacitly discourage any theoretical attempt to comprehend the development of these symptoms. Their techniques stress behavior change by reducing the avoidance elements in obsessional behavior and in so doing reduce the patient to an object of manipulation and authoritarian control. The underlying factors that determine and influence behavior are neglected and in effect denied.

Yet the obsessive-compulsive personality type is today's most prevalent neurotic character structure. In earlier years the hysterical personality was more widely studied, perhaps because Freud used the hysteric as a paradigm in his conceptualization of psychoanalysis. The theories that followed upon Freud's naturally tended to be elaborations of concepts based on the hysterical disorders, and so it is hardly surprising that hysterical phenomena seemed to predominate in psychoanalytic practice. There is now good reason, however, to believe that the obsessional defensive mechanism is the most widely used technique whereby man achieves some illusion of safety and security in an otherwise uncertain world. In spite of advances prolonging life and reducing the risk of disease and the threat of natural catastrophe, there is increasing uncertainty regarding ultimate survival in the atomic age. Complex technologies determine daily routines and decrease the measure of personal control individuals have over their lives. Insecurity and anxiety over both present and future uncertainties demand increasingly elaborate obsessional maneuvers if any illusion of control over one's destiny is to be maintained.

The obsessional style serves a positive and constructive role in one's living until it gets out of hand; then the illusion-sustaining mechanisms and perfectionistic patterns prevent rather than facilitate action. Ultimately, refusal to acknowledge the reality limitations of being human will lead the individual to deny all reality and become psychotic. The value of the obsessive-compulsive defense for the maintenance of adequate functioning in the human being has been stressed by behavioral scientists of every stripe. Man's physical deficiencies and mental limitations leave him susceptible to profound uncertainties and inevitable feelings of helplessness and insecurity. Not only does he have limited control over the forces of nature; he is equally incapable of controlling his intellectual and emotional responses. He is often at the mercy of the "out-of-awareness" ideas and impulses that propel him into action. The existential problems that face him constantly and the knowledge of his limited span of existence and eventual certain death are things he can do little about — except construct illusions.

Besides the realistic and inevitable problems that confront the entire human race, many people suffer the additional burden of increased insecurities and uncertainties consequent upon untoward early experiences or traumatic events. The uncertainties of childhood, produced by inconsistent and sometimes malevolent family situations, can only compound the widespread insecurity occasioned by financial crises or economic and political disasters. These personal and social difficulties further complicate man's inevitable human frailties and frustrate his attempts to control his existence.

Under these circumstances the obsessive-compulsive technique is an attempt, through fantasized or realistic devices, to maintain in a person the illusion that he exercises greater control over his functioning than is in fact the case. The obsessional technique,* through its elaborate devices of avoiding commitments and decisions, never exposes the individual to realizing the possibility of failure; thus he avoids any awareness of imperfection, fallibility, or humanness. The attempt at omniscience and omnipotence, coupled with an elaborate set of verbal defenses, sometimes gives the individual the illusion that he possesses the superhuman power to guarantee his future. If the verbal devices fail, then the ritual — with its magical possibilities of overcoming human limitations — attempts to achieve such guarantees. Finally, if all else fails, the individual can, by developing phobias, absolutely avoid any encounter with situations or objects that endanger his sense of control.

But such phrases as *he is obsessed,* in common parlance, describe simply a tendency to be devoted, intense, and preoccupied with a matter. The dictionary defines *obsession* as an "abnormal preoccupation with an idea or feeling"; it does not specify the point at which preoccupation becomes abnormal. This I propose to do in the following pages. Devotion to an idea or cause, with persistent efforts to actualize it, is not automatically abnormal or obsessive. Doubting and being unable to commit oneself do not necessarily indicate obsessive living. Being scrupulously clean or passionately orderly with perfectionistic desires does not imply an obsessional concern with order. Yet such manifestations *might* indicate neurosis. As the expression *to be obsessed* has taken on a pejorative meaning and implies some mental disorder, its use can both discourage and

---

* In this book the term *obsessional* will for reasons of convenience often be used in place of *obsessive-compulsive.*

disparage some quite sincere and creative efforts. We must therefore be clear about the healthy and pathological elements of dedication, as well as the degree of preoccupation possible before it interferes with productive living. To do a masterful job in any area, from carpentry to astronomy, requires a dedication that insists on the highest performance. This involves total participation in the doing and may demand the totality of an individual's time and effort. This is not obsessional behavior and may be entirely contrary to it. It may be a freely selected activity to which one commits one's skills and interests. This stands in direct contrast to the obsessional preoccupation, in which one is "imprisoned," unable to shift and change, and fearful lest any involvement or commitment leave one vulnerable and endangered. It is interest by default, even though at times it may be strong enough to result in many useful products. It is the negative of the creative process.

Freud describes the condition masterfully in the following way:* "Obsessional neurosis is shown in the patient's being preoccupied with thoughts in which he is in fact not interested, in his being aware of impulses in himself which appear very strange to him and in his being led to actions the performance of which give him no enjoyment, but which it is quite impossible for him to omit. The thoughts (obsessions) may be senseless in themselves, or merely a matter of indifference to the subject; often they are completely silly, and invariably they are the starting-point of a strenuous mental activity, which exhausts the patient and to which he only surrenders himself most unwillingly. He is obliged against his will to brood and speculate as though it were a question of his most important vital problems. The impulses which the patient is aware of in himself may also make a childish and senseless impression; but as a rule they have a content of the most frightful kind, tempting him, for instance, to commit serious crimes, so that he not merely disavows them as alien to himself, but flies from them in horror and protects himself from carrying them out by prohibitions, renunciations and restrictions upon his freedom. At the same time, these impulses never — literally never — force their way through to performance; the outcome lies always in victory for the flight and the precautions. What the patient actually carries out — his so-called obsessional actions — are very harmless and certainly trival things, for the most part repetitions or ceremonial elaborations of the activities of ordinary life. But these necessary activities (such as going to bed, washing, dressing or going for a walk) become extremely tedious and almost insoluble tasks. In different forms and cases of obsessional neurosis the pathological ideas, impulses and actions are not combined in equal

* Freud, *Standard Edition* 16; pp. 258–260.

proportions; it is the rule, rather, that one or other of these factors dominates the picture and gives its name to the illness, but the common element in all these forms is sufficiently unmistakable.

"Certainly, this is a crazy illness. The most extravagant psychiatric imagination would not, I think, have succeeded in constructing anything like it; and if one did not see it before one every day one would never bring oneself to believe it. Do not suppose, however, that you will help the patient in the least by calling on him to take a new line, to cease to occupy himself with such foolish thoughts and to do something sensible instead of his childish pranks. He would like to do so himself, for he is completely clear in his head, shares your opinion of his obsessional symptoms and even puts it forward to you spontaneously. Only he cannot help himself. What is carried into action in an obsessional neurosis is sustained by an energy to which we probably know nothing comparable in normal mental life. There is only one thing he can do: he can make displacements, and exchanges, he can replace one foolish idea by another somewhat milder, he can proceed from one precaution or prohibition to another, instead of one ceremonial he can perform another. He can displace the obsession but not remove it. The ability to displace any symptom into something far removed from its original conformation is a main characteristic of his illness. Moreover it is a striking fact that in his condition the contradictions (polarities) with which mental life is interlaced emerge especially sharply differentiated. Alongside of obsessions with a positive and negative content, *doubt* makes itself felt in the intellectual field and little by little it begins to gnaw even at what is usually most certain. The whole position ends up in an ever-increasing degree of indecision, loss of energy and restriction of freedom. At the same time, the obsessional neurotic starts off with a very energetic disposition, he is often extraordinarily self-willed and as a rule he has intellectual gifts above the average. He has usually reached a satisfactorily high level of ethical development; he exhibits over-conscientiousness, and is more than ordinarily correct in his behaviour. You can imagine that no small amount of work is needed before one can make one's way any distance into this contradictory hotchpotch of character-traits and symptoms. And to begin with we aim at nothing whatever else than understanding a few of the symptoms and being able to interpret them."

Recently, in the process of clearing away a large accumulation of notes, unpublished articles, and early drafts of books, I came across a completely transcribed case of an obsessional neurotic whose treatment had been included as part of a research project studying "change of subject." It was a case successfully terminated in 1953, and every hour had been recorded and transcribed for the research group. As I reread the transcript it struck me as eminently suitable for inclusion as a full-length case study in this revised and updated version of my earlier book. It not only documented the enormous difficulties encountered in treating these disorders but also contained *in nuce* the theories I was to develop and put forward some fifteen years later. This review of the case a full quarter century later was most instructive to me, and I was convinced it would so serve any therapist who finds himself constantly faced with the arduous and often discouraging task of treating this condition.

Unfortunately, in the intervening twenty-five years we have not moved very far in the elaboration of the genetic and structural elements underlying obsessional defense techniques; nor have any new hypotheses surfaced during this period. There have been a few developments along the lines of viewing these behaviors as cognitive elements, but basically the theories presented in this book — psychodynamic formulations developed out of Freud's epochal contributions — retain their wide applicability.

Leon Salzman, M.D.
August 1979

PART I

CHARACTERISTICS OF THE OBSESSIVE PERSONALITY

CHAPTER 1

Theories of Obsessive Behavior

Current conceptions of the etiology and therapy of mental disorders are of surprisingly recent origin. Although our medical understanding dates back to 3000 B.C., our knowledge of mental functioning is less than two hundred years old. Each year brings forth a vast collection of books, articles, and research reports that cast doubt on older theories and suggest alternative explanations to the hitherto cherished formulations. This process is healthy because we have not yet arrived at final statements about most mental disorders. Our biochemical, anatomical, histological, and genetics research has expanded our knowledge in a geometric progression. Fifty years ago our microscopes were capable of 1,000 to 1,200 enlargement with the use of oil-immersion lenses. Today we can achieve 750,000 enlargement with the electron microscope. This advance symbolizes the revolution of knowledge and makes it essential that we review all physical theories of human functioning from a more recent perspective.

HISTORICAL PERSPECTIVES

Until Sigmund Freud began his investigations of hysteria and other neurotic states, psychiatric knowledge was largely limited to the classification of mental disorders by similarity of symptoms. These classifications often differed markedly from one author to another and were rarely precise enough to enable comparative studies. Etiological classifications were rare, and explanations of man's behavior — both normal and abnormal — were primitive and animistic. Abnormal behavior was often thought to be caused by a disorder of the bodily humors, hereditary factors, or invasion of witches or other ungodly creatures. The explanations varied according to the prevailing theological or philosophical conceptions of man. In later centuries, scientific considerations began to influence such theories, but the most widespread interpretations were teleological and assumed to represent some expression of God's will and design. The therapy for these disorders reflected these views and consideration for the individual's feelings.

Until the medical sciences accepted Semmelweiss's observations regarding the spread of puerperal fever by the physician's dirty hands, they could not recognize the necessity for cleanliness prior to introducing a hand into the vaginal canal. When Pasteur and the germ theory prevailed, such a therapeutic regime became routine. Practice follows theory or empirical evidence. Until a theory is confirmed in the laboratory or by objective findings, it should remain open to exploration or alteration. When our theory was primitive, treatment appears to us to have been brutal, ignorant, and destructive. In psychiatric terms, as our knowledge increased our sensitivity, our treatment became less punitive and more compassionate. Measures such as rest, occupational and recreational therapies, and exhortative and interpretive approaches were initiated.

Freud, who grew up in the late nineteenth and early twentieth centuries, assimilated and reflected all the prevailing sociological and scientific thinking. Consequently, his theories were heavily influenced by the mechanical theories in physics and the instinct theories in biology. Energy as a mechanical force dominated the physiological sciences, and the medical sciences reflected these physical notions. It was a period of extensive discovery of the etiology of man's physical disorders, and the Helmholtzian application of physical theory was thought to be the mode of comprehending mental behavior. All mental activity was to be comprehended in the language of physiology and energy mechanics.

That Freud's theories were couched in the language of energy (libido) and mechanics (cathexis, countercathexis, repression, etc.), as well as in instinctual notions of human motivation, is only natural. The sexual nature of libido became a prime issue in his theoretical formulations, even though his final instinct theory involved the Eros-Thanatos dualism. Freud endeavored to distinguish libido from adult sexual activity; however, he was never fully successful in this area, so that even today the distinctions are blurred or disregarded by many of the most sophisticated psychoanalytic theorists and therapists. As this matter bears on the etiology of obsessive-compulsive behavior I want to examine it briefly.

Although it is clear to all that the child, for example, cannot conceptualize adult sexual behavior, many psychoanalytic practitioners assume that three-to five-year-old children do in fact comprehend the adult role of the genitals. Through some inheritance of this complex biological interaction they must understand it because of their expectation of a threat to their genitals when they perceive them as being used in an adult fashion with mother to arouse the fury of father. Thus, they reflect Freud's view that the oedipal problems grow out of sexual interest toward the parent of the opposite sex, causing fear of castration in boys. This implies that some knowledge of the sexual function of the genital exists in the child, who until now has been aware only of its urinary function. To explain this knowledge we must assume that the Lamarckian theory of acquired characteristics is a valid theory of inheritance, even though it has been roundly rejected from all quarters. The child is too young and his cortex too immaturely developed to conceive of his acquiring this information in any other way. According to Max Schur, "Freud occasionally let his imagination run far afield as he did, for example, with the outline of a study on the application of psychoanalysis to the neo-Lamarckian theory of the inheritance of acquired characteristics."* Schur maintains that "Freud adhered stubbornly to this belief throughout his life." Ernest Jones provides further insights: "Next comes an extraordinary part of the story which provides us with a baffling problem in the study of the development of Freud's ideas and also in that of his personality. eg ... A stranger might almost suppose that Freud was ignorant of the doctrine of natural selection, which is assuredly out of the question. Before Darwin the only previous explanation of evolution that had any vogue was Lamarck's doctrine of the inheritance of acquired characteristics"† — a doctrine completely discredited for more than half a century, as Julian Huxley makes clear: "With the knowledge that has been amassed since Darwin's time it is no longer possible to believe that evolution is brought about through the so-called inheritance of acquired characteristics." In spite of innumerable similar strictures, Freud remained from beginning to end what one must call an obstinate adherent

---

* Max Schur, *Freud — Living and Dying* (New York: International Universities Press, 1972), pp. 312–313.
† Ernest Jones, *Life and Work of Sigmund Freud*, Vol. 3 (New York: Basic Books, 1957), pp. 310–313.

of this discredited Lamarckism. Freud wrote to Karl Abraham on November 11, 1917, concerning his ideas on this subject: "the idea is to put Lamarck entirely on our ground and to show that the 'necessity' that according to him creates and transforms organs is nothing but the power of unconscious ideas over one's own body. ... This would supply a psycho-analytic explanation of adaptation. ..." * We must then either assume some Lamarckian inheritance regarding the genital apparatus or concede that a great deal of confusion, extrapolation, and fuzzy thinking surrounds the libido theory and its implications for the explanation of the role of regression to the anal-sadistic phase of psychosexual development and as a key explanatory concept for obsessive-compulsive disorders.

This confusion has particular significance to a theory of obsessive-compulsive behavior when it is postulated that the obsessive mechanism is a defense against sexual or aggressive impulses.

Until our understanding could replace the theological explanations, man's behavior was considered directed by God's will and part of man's nature. It was thought to be preformed through inborn instinctual patterns of behavior. While man possessed a will that distinguished him from other animals, and was capable of exercising choice, it was assumed that he also functioned through an elaborate set of instinctual patterns. Instinct, which was an adequate and valid description of animal behavior, was utilized without any alteration and applied to human beings to explain their social and cultural patterns as well as their biological behavior. Freud used instinct as an explanation for man's motivated behavior, behavior that was designed to fulfill many of his innermost needs. Thus, in socialization man was of necessity forced to restrain and control much of his "natural" behavior because his attempts to fulfill his instinctual needs could endanger himself and others. In an oversimplified way, the defenses — which are patterned activities designed to achieve this purpose — constitute the essence of neurosis or psychosis.

The problem of controlling the instincts (sex and aggression) that are pressing for fulfillment constitutes the core of the neuroses and is particularly evident in obsessive-compulsive behavior. Where the intrusive, undesired thoughts and behavior often relate to destruction, hostility, and sexuality, Freud, in adopting an instinct psychology, seemed able to comprehend large areas of human activity (both normal and abnormal) that previously were completely unintelligible. He could understand both the purpose and significance of a piece of behavior and develop a motivational psychology of human behavior.

---

* *A Psycho-Analytic Dialogue: The Letters of Sigmund Freud and Karl Abraham 1907-1926* (New York: Basic Books, 1965) pp. 261-262.

Motivation involves the understanding of behavior in either its short- or long-range goal of fulfilling some need of the organism. Such behavior is neither random nor purposeless; it derives from particular needs or interests. These needs can often be identified without difficulty, even though long-range goals are at times difficult to unravel — both for the individual himself and for the onlooker. Except in special circumstances, human behavior has some goal toward which the individual moves with some efficiency or else is interrupted and deviated by a variety of factors. Man's needs differ at various periods of his own development as well as in different sociological circumstances. Freud emphasized the biological needs (instincts) of man and hypothesized that the cultural developments were devices to deal with these basic biological demands. Later theorists — such as Horney, Alexander, Sullivan, and others — emphasized man's cultural needs and saw them as independent developments growing out of man's psychological needs for intimacy, relationships, involvement, and interpersonal interaction, rather than as avenues for his biological requirements.

A significant advance in the understanding of animal and human behavior was the introduction of the concept of *adaptation*. While this notion was implicit in many of Freud's ideas, the recognition of the role of culture in personality development required the incorporation of the idea of adaptation in theories of personality. Defenses such as rationalization, sublimation, reaction-formation, and projection not only were devices to deal with the pressures of instinctual demands but also were some ways of functioning in the face of pressing anxieties. They prevented serious personality disorganization and disintegration and allowed the individual to cope with his anxieties in an adaptive fashion. Although in the long run such measures were maladaptive and resulted in neuroses or psychoses, the immediate effect was to prevent disruption of the functioning organism. In this way the concept of adaptation enhanced and broadened motivational concepts even while the psychological theories were instinct-oriented.

While some personality theorists are still reluctant to utilize adaptational frameworks, the group of psychoanalysts called ego psychologists, cultural psychoanalysts, or post-Freudian psychoanalysts has adopted a motivational-adaptational view of human behavior. Man is viewed as an animal who has largely abandoned his instincts in his capacity to learn to cope with internal and external demands. The ego as it confronts the culture has become the main object of study. Thus, all aspects of the culture — social, economic, and political — have come within the purview of the behavioral scientist. Although an individual needs to deal with his inner biological demands, he must also adapt and adjust to his culture and its idiosyncratic value systems, ideals, goals, demands, and expectations. These needs have differed at various times just as the biological demands differ at particular chronological epochs in an individual's own development. Some ego theorists such as Harry Stack Sullivan and Erik Erikson have drawn up timetables for the developmental cycle describing the tasks of personality development at those epochs. Regardless of one's convictions about the role of instinct in human development, recognition of the effects of the environment in which it must unfold is essential to any comprehensive theory of human development.

The concept of adaptation filled a large gap in understanding the function of a particular piece of behavior in the total functioning of the individual. It is possible to recognize that many devices, techniques, and maneuvers (both physiological and psychological) are moves to *defend* — that is, to protect or overcome dangers or threats of danger to the existence of the individual. They modify the behavior of the organism in the direction of adapting to the situation without succumbing to it. Some of these activities are simple and straightforward; they meet the threat directly in an effort to deal with it. Generally they are more subtle, less specific, and ultimately symbolized partial solutions which we call neuroses. These techniques are the result of a long evolutionary process, and the particular pattern of adaptation an individual adopts is based on many unknown factors.

As man evolved beyond the pressure for survival to higher levels of functioning, the dangers to his existence became more subtle and less involved with simple physiological necessities. Ultimately, man was no longer exclusively or predominantly occupied with fulfilling his basic survival needs (except as this still exists in underdeveloped areas of the world). These challenges have been largely overcome by man's intelligence in providing ways to increase and sustain his physiological requirements.

Once basic physiological needs are provided for, man is then confronted with needs that are specifically human and which grow out of his emergence from his animal existence. These needs are the result of man's capacity for self-consciousness and his ability to project himself into the future and recognize his limited powers and capacities as well as his ultimate demise. As a result of these developments, security as a psychological issue becomes a prime need and major motivating force in human behavior. Man's security needs derive from his awareness of his separateness and his need for human interaction. Feelings of isolation and imposed or imagined threats to his feeling acceptable as a person stimulate a specifically human reaction called *anxiety*. In a greater or lesser degree this response is familiar to every human being; it has its origin in infancy as a consequence of the infant's need for contact and tenderness as well as food and shelter. While generally speaking the infant's physiological and psychological needs are automatically supplied by the environment, anxiety will nevertheless be experienced because fulfillment cannot be indefinitely guaranteed. However, unless the infancy is a particularly stressful one, the role of anxiety in human development becomes more prominent during childhood and in the juvenile years. Being acceptable becomes a more significant concern for the juvenile, and a great deal of activity occurs, the purpose of which is designed to avoid, prevent, or overcome anxiety. Anxiety is a most painful and distressing feeling, and it must be dealt with. In addition to physiological reactions such as sweating, tachycardia, palpitation, and breathlessness, there is the overwhelming distress caused by a feeling of impending doom and destruction, accompanied by agitation and restlessness. Such a state can be tolerated only for short periods of time before panic supervenes. Anxiety cannot be dealt with directly, since the sources are usually unknown. The individual therefore develops a number of psychological responses (defenses) to deflect, diminish, or remove the anxiety. The obsessional defense is particularly useful and is thus widely utilized. Since the anxiety reaction is ultimately caused by some human incapacity, the obsessional defense that attempts to create an illusion of power and control may temporarily dissipate the anxiety. As will be shown this defense is especially suited to dealing with man's feeling of powerlessness, which is a realistic appraisal that can leave him feeling threatened both by nature and by other humans. If he cannot accept the realities of his limited powers and capacities he will feel endangered in a world he cannot control. The obsessional defense is an adaptative device to deal with such feelings, and to the extent that some of it is used by all mankind, the defense is universal. When the anxieties and feelings of powerlessness are minimal, the obsessional defenses are minimal. As the anxieties increase, the need for greater defenses becomes more insistent and the obsessional defenses become more severe — sometimes overshadowing all other activities of the individual.

OBSESSIVE-COMPULSIVE DYNAMISM

Several elements are invariably present and constitute the obsessive-compulsive dynamism, including the following:

1. An idea or behavior that is insistent and intrusive into one's consciousness and is accompanied by anxiety

2. Behavior or thought that persists beyond the need for and/or in spite of voluntary action

3. The presence of anxiety and somatic distress because of the ego-alien nature of such thoughts

4. Insight into the illogical and unreasonable nature of the thought or action, which does not alter the behavior.

The obsession is a persistent, ritualized thought pattern, whereas the compulsion is a persistent ritualized behavior pattern. The obsessive dynamism can be identified in the personality structure prior to the presence of noticeable ritualized behavior. There is, in fact, no necessary or expected relationship between obsessional personality traits and obsessional symptoms congealed into a neurosis. Obsessive traits are commonplace whereas the obsessive neurosis is comparatively infrequent.

Obsessive character structures were described by Freud as orderly, stubborn, and parsimonious; others have described them as being obstinate, orderly, perfectionistic, punctual, meticulous, parsimonious, frugal, and inclined to intellectualism and hair-splitting discussion. Pierre Janet described such people as being rigid, inflexible, lacking in adaptability, overly conscientious, loving order and discipline, and persistent even in the face of undue obstacles. They are generally dependable and reliable and have high standards and ethical values. They are practical, precise, and scrupulous in their moral requirements. Under conditions of stress or extreme demands, these personality characteristics may congeal into symptomatic behavior that will then be ritualized.

When present, the rituals are dramatic and pathognomonic. The combination of character traits described above is also easily identified. As the purpose and adaptive functions of the variety of personality traits and the ritual are better understood, it will be seen that they all subserve the need of achieving control of oneself and the environment.

It was evident to many people long before Freud that such bizarre behavior has great meaning to the person. In more recent years the adaptive function of such behavior has come to be recognized and acknowledged as being of great utilitarian value in a culture that honors productivity and the work ethic. It has become obvious that the insistent, preoccupying thoughts that cannot be eliminated so fill the attention of the individual that it is scarcely possible for any other thought process to take place. In this way the obsessive thought serves the purpose of distracting attention away from a more significant and possibly more distressing one. This is more easily understood when the obsessive thought is a pointless rumination or an endless speculation about philosophical or religious matters. The distracting or controlling function of such a thought is more difficult to recognize when the thought itself is extremely upsetting and seemingly significant. Such obsessive thoughts may center around aggressive wishes against significant people or blasphemous or morally repugnant ideas that cannot be eliminated from one's mind. In either case, the obsessive preoccupation may be total, claiming the individual's entire interest and thus preventing any other thought processes. The sudden appearance of highly repugnant thoughts is so bizarre and alien to the person's manifest personality that it immediately distracts him from anything else that might be going on at the time. The occurrence of such fantastic instrusions has provided considerable support for the concept of an unconscious and the notion that ideas and feelings outside of immediate awareness can nevertheless significantly influence behavior. Instrusive thoughts that involve screaming obscene words at inappropriate times or places suggest that the individual wants to become the focus of public attention. It seems to contradict the notion that the obsessive thought is designed to distract the individual from public notice and crucial concerns. However, the same basic process is operative when regardless of how extreme or revolting an obsessive thought might be to the individual it is still much less distressing than the idea it is covering up. Freud called this process *displacement* and assumed that the obsessive symptom was always distracting the individual from essential concerns. However, these preoccupying thoughts and ruminations are often the very essence of the person's concerns. Ruminations about death, philosophical, and moral issues or hypochondriacal preoccupations about one's health are attempts to control one's destiny and to guarantee one's future. It seems to me that it is the need for total control that more accurately describes the entire range of obsessive activity, rather than the simple technique of displacement.

Freud's explanation of the obsessive-compulsive behavior pattern was most illuminating. He emphasized the meaning of symbols in their function of dealing with hostile and unacceptable sexual feelings. Freud postulated that there was a constant and insistent threat of these impulses to break into awareness and that the obsessional defenses restrain and prevent such eruptions and effectively limit the anxiety that might occur. However, the rigidity of the overdeveloped superego requires not only defenses of displacement or reaction-formation but also undoing as a means of a penitent reversal of the feared hostile thought or action. According to Freud, the symptom originated during the anal-erotic period of psycho-sexual development and was therefore directly related to bowel-training experiences. Sandor Rado put more emphasis on the repressed rage and the adaptive purpose of the symptom in attempting to counteract and undo the repressed rage.

The symptoms oscillate between rage and atonement, which are often expressed in magical terms. Karen Horney and Harry Stack Sullivan placed more emphasis on the attempts to overcome feelings of helplessness and insecurity. More recent theorists such as Ernest Gebstattel view the symbols in terms of distorted concepts of time and space, death and existence. Erwin Strauss sees the obsessive mechanism as a technique for dealing with feelings of decay and disgust. The conditioning theories postulate the symptomatology as a conditioned response to anxiety. Association with anxiety-provoking stimulus to obsessional thinking creates anxiety. The compulsion is a conditioned capacity to reduce the anxiety created in obsessional thinking and becomes firmly established, since it can relieve anxiety temporarily.

Freud's view of the essential nature of the obsessive-compulsive disorder as relating to toilet training has influenced a large number of behavioral scientists. It involves the notion of a child's battling with his parents about the necessity for withholding his urine and feces until the proper time and place. If the parents' efforts are begun too early and are too extreme, the child may respond with hostile feelings and active rebellion, which may be dealt with by obsessive mechanisms. Freud contended that such a development accounted for the widespread presence of obsessive behavior patterns in childhood, which may be manifested in an obsessive-compulsive neurosis in later years. There is currently considerable disagreement about Freud's emphasis on the anal-erotic aspects of such formulations. In addition to the conflicting evidence over the bowel-training struggle, there are many obsessives in whom all the elements of control seemingly affect all areas of their living except the anal function. Meyer Gross and Fritz Redlich disagree about the origin of the "battle of the chamber pot." However, the widespread prevalence of obsessive behavior in children can be readily understood as a factor of the child's helplessness and vulnerability and the need for order and control in dealing with his insecurities. The child is also engaged in a struggle for self-expression and maintaining an identity. This struggle takes place on all fronts and in relation to problems of acculturation as well as to toilet training.

Although the factors suggested by many theorists can be identified in the obsessive-compulsive mechanism, the overriding purpose of the behavior is to attempt to achieve some security and certainty for the person who feels threatened and insecure in an uncertain world. The possibility of controlling oneself and the forces outside oneself by assuming omniscience and omnipotence can give one a false illusion of certainty. Therefore, the main ingredient is control. This notion is neither novel nor essentially different from what has been expressed by previous investigators. Both

Freud and Sullivan highlighted this very element, and it is only the matter of emphasis that makes it a useful approach.

Freud saw the obsessive-compulsive mechanism as a device for dealing with unacceptable hostile or sexual impulses. He felt that such people control the expression of these impulses by using displacement, reaction-formation, condensation, and symbolization as defenses against them. The symptom, he thought, was a compromise of "doing" the forbidden wish and at the same time "undoing" it. However, not only sexual or hostile impulses need to be controlled but also the tender, friendly, or stupid and unworthy thoughts and feelings. In my view, the obsessive-compulsive dynamism is a device for preventing any feeling or thought that might produce shame, loss of pride or status, or a feeling of weakness or deficiency — whether such feelings are hostile, sexual, or otherwise. I see the obsessional maneuver as an adaptive technique to protect the person from the exposure of any thought or feeling that will endanger his physical or psychological existence. This extends Freud's views and does not require the postulate of an instinct or libido theory.

Viewing the obsessive-compulsive dynamism in this light will enable one to recognize its function in the normal person as well as in the neurotic or psychotic. It will also help one to understand the role it plays in compulsive states such as phobias (compulsive avoidance), obesity (compulsive eating), alcoholism (compulsive drinking), kleptomania (compulsive stealing), and others. This view will clarify the relation of obsessions to paranoid states and other delusional systems in which stereotyped and rigid ways of perceiving the world are the essential issues.

OBSESSIVE-COMPULSIVE NEUROSIS

The term *obsessive-compulsive neurosis* refers to a wide variety of phenomena that may be manifested at any time in a person's life. It refers to thoughts, feelings, ideas, and impulses that an individual cannot dispel in spite of an inner desire to do so. The compelling nature of the activity — even though it may be illogical, undesirable, and unnecessary — is the central issue. Generally such thoughts or feelings are alien to the individual's usual attitudes and are experienced as being somewhat strange, even outrageous, sometimes disgusting, and, at times, frightening. Their presence is embarrassing and quite distressing. It is an intriguing development — particularly in the face of current notions of free will and freedom of choice — because despite all the wishes, desires, and active opposition of the person, he is forced by some internal pressure to concern himself with a variety of experiences that may be distasteful or frightening. It is considered a neurosis rather than traits or personality manifestations when it becomes disruptive and unproductive and produces anxiety not relieved by the compulsive rituals designed to alleviate that anxiety. The distress can be severe enough to immobilize the individual and impair all his functioning.

CHAPTER 2

The Obsessive Style

REVIEW OF OBSESSIONAL DYNAMICS

What extraordinary phenomena obsessions and compulsions are! Ideas, thoughts, or insistent demands for action that are entirely alien to his conscious mind or his moral or ethical standards — like an army of psychic demons or sophisticated electronic rays from outer space — overcome an individual. He can neither expel nor terminate these thoughts, and all conscious efforts to do so only aggravate and enhance these intruders. In fact, invasion by demons was the explanation for this phenomenon for many years, until Freud first suggested an explanation based on the recognition of unconscious feelings and attitudes which reside in the individual himself rather than forces which intrude from the outside. During the Christian era, prior to Freud's formulations, such experiences were viewed as possession states in which devilish, anti-God forces overcame and took hold of a person's being and controlled his thoughts and behavior.

How can obsessional thoughts overtake the human brain, an exquisitely equipped organ capable of developing a technology that can land men on the moon? How is it that the control of man's mind through his own efforts flounders miserably in the face of these intrusive thoughts? So pervasive and malignant can they become at times that their presence can tie up a person to the extent that his intellectual skills are reduced to elaborate rituals of cleansing, grooming, and the like, leaving no time for culture, leisure, or freedom from anxiety and pain. Yet in spite of the adhesive persistence of thoughts, they rarely get carried into action, since they are defenses or distractions and ways of avoiding confrontation with more threatening ideas or attitudes that will humiliate and totally undermine the individuals's security. These intrusive thoughts and obsessive ideas are defined as "Ideas, emotions and impulses which occupy consciousness, irrespective of the subject's desire, intruding themselves at inopportune times and occupying consciousness to the exclusion of other ideas. Compulsions, which are aspects of the same dynamic issue but manifested in action, are defined as behavior which is compelled by unknown sources and while the individual is fully aware of how foolish, inappropriate and illogical these ideas and actions are, he cannot alter them."*

Whether they are present, stored in an area of the mental apparatus called the unconscious, or simply outside the immediate fringe of awareness and subject to focal attention by some mysterious process in the individual, obsessional ideas can exert profound effects on behavior by demanding full attention all the time in the most severe cases or by distracting usual activities by an insistent intrusiveness in other cases. The obsessional individual cannot identify the source without help or guidance, since the thoughts are alien, unacceptable, and grossly discordant with his public personality patterns of thinking, and behaving. He therefore describes them as outside of his own self and as unwelcome intruders into his functioning.

So overpowering are these tendencies that no act of will, determination, or effort can terminate them, nor can drugs, electroshock treatment, or lobotomies — even though these treatment modalities can reduce some of the anxiety that accompany these thoughts. Only an investigation of the origin of these forces, coupled with a committed intention to change, will reduce or eliminate them. Although behavior-modification techniques may alter some of the compulsive behavioral phenomena, they cannot influence the underlying personality structure that requires such drastic security measures.

Overpowering feelings, thoughts or pressures to think or behave in ritualized ways are consistent and dramatic features of human behavior. These persistent feelings are called *obsessions*, and when they are expressed

*Leland E. Hinsie, M.D., and Robert Jean Campbell, M.D., *Psychiatric Dictionary,* (New York: Oxford University Press, 1970).

in behavioral acts, they are called *compulsions.* Clearly, the same psychic mechanisms are at work, manifesting themselves in either action or thought.

How can we understand the behavior of a bright, highly educated person who spends two hours cleaning the kitchen after drinking a single cup of coffee, for fear of contaminating some aspect of it in defiance of a dietary law? How can we comprehend the behavior of a person who, in order to be relieved of severe and intense anxiety, needs to shower from six to eight continuous hours before going out into the world? Consider the scrupulous person who feels that ten "Hail Marys" are inadequate and must do a hundred, or the individual who cannot eliminate a phrase or a tune from his mind to the point of being unable to proceed with his daily living. These phenomena are the essence of the compulsive ritual, regardless of the variety and content; they consist of absolute, demanding, and preemptive action over which the individual has no influence or control. Such rituals are terminated by fatigue or when the ludicrousness of the process becomes apparent to the individual. If the rituals are prematurely terminated or prevented from being expressed, severe anxiety or panic may ensue.

In the presence of obsessions a person is overwhelmed with persistent thoughts that cannot be extruded, eliminated, or denied, and they may interfere with his functioning in ways that completely tie up his living and prevent him from performing or pursuing other reasonable tasks and goals that are essential to his well-being. This is truly an extraordinary phenomenon which distinguishes man the animal from man the Homo sapiens. The awareness of the nature of the demands that are being made and the inability to be free to choose or to alter such demands are paramount features of this disorder. Instincts are physiochemical built-in indicators and organizers of animal behavior and are beyond conscious or willful choice. However, very few instincts determine man's behavior, and — except for those basic functions controlled by the paleocortex — his behavior, concerns, interests, values, and ideals are within his deliberate and conscious choice. Obsessions and compulsions interfere and, at times, absolutely prevent such choices because their imperious demand, the source of which the individual cannot identify, must be acknowledged and pursued. These intrusive thoughts, which are clearly unsolicited, can determine and influence one's behavior. They are the clearest evidence of the presence of what is called the *unconscious,* or the out-of-awareness elements in human mentation and activity. In fact, compulsions and obsessions are evasive, relentless efforts to give a person an illusion of power by strength and control; he must achieve a state of perfection which can sustain the illusion of invincibility and omnipotence.

The obsessive-compulsive aspect of human behavior becomes a disorder only when it is excessive and becomes the dominating feature in a person's living. Prior to a scientific understanding that allowed for a rational explanation, abnormal behavior was often thought to be caused by a disorder of the bodily humors, hereditary factors, or an invasion of malevolent or other ungodly forces. The explanations varied according to the prevailing theological or philosophical conceptions of man. In later centuries scientific considerations began to influence such theories, but the most widespread interpretations were still teleological and explained such behavior as representing some expression of God's will and design.

The concept of possession was a very understandable explanation, since the individual often behaved as if he were overcome by something so alien to him that it could not possibly arise from inside himself. However, with the advance of understanding and the recognition of the presence of the unconscious, such intrusions could be recognized as arising solely inside the individual — that is, from the unconscious. The unconscious has been viewed as a repository for experiences which are not immediately available to recall but which can be resurrected by the use of free-association techniques or some other focusing techniques (hypnosis, meditation, etc.). With the development of this concept the notion of ideas, thoughts, and impulses being present but not immediately aware to the person was no longer alien to our understanding.

Rituals, which are the dominating feature in obsessional or compulsive manifestations, are only the more obvious, inscrutable, and confusing aspects of man's need to adjust to the realities of his existence. These rituals attempt to control one's own deficiencies in an uncertain world.

The elements that go into the obsessional way of living relate to the matter of exerting sufficient control over one's life or the external world so that one can maintain the illusion of functioning with a degree of safety and security in the face of the realities of the actual situation. Since uncertainties always exist in the real world, this need is present in all of us in varying degrees. We must all take risks in being alive. It is never clear when one leaves one's home in the morning that one will, in fact, be back at night. Yet we make appointments for dinner or the theater and we work under the assumption that no accident will interfere and that no cataclysmic catastrophe will take place. In this sense we are acting as naive, trusting, unsophisticated individuals who are seemingly unaware of life's threats and dangers. While this may be so, the only way we can function with any degree of continuity is to operate on the fairly certain hypothesis that our daily living will not be marred constantly by catastrophes. These uncertainties go largely unattended and are out of awareness, yet they are forever present in the real world. The assumptions we make about the orderliness and the continuity of life permit us to engage in planning and functioning without the constant need to try to eliminate all potential dangers and hazards. In many respects we use minor rituals to permit us to function; they may consist of religious rituals, with prayers to assure some security about tomorrow, or the magic of certain superstitions or gimmicks. Some live by astrological charts or other means which permit them to go along with some expectations of security. In most of us there are unrecognized magical devices or other rituals to permit us to avoid getting caught up with the examination and review of all possible risks.

Obsessional persons utilize these same operations in more intensive ways. Their devices and rituals are more manifest to themselves and others and can become so extreme that the persons are unable to function. We describe them as either suffering from an *obsessional personality* or an *obsessional neurosis.* The spectrum of obsessional functioning depends on the severity of the need and the number of rituals or other devices the individual may utilize. As the defenses become overriding, a person may form patterns of behavior which are congealed and enduring. The obsessive personality, then, is manifested by meticulous, overly cautious, fearful and phobic behavior. Such obsessive individuals are afraid to risk new adventures or to go into new situations where the issues are unclear. They always take exaggerated precautions with regard to every move in their lives. When obsessional patterns begin to impair the individual's effectiveness and become somewhat bizarre and excessive, we call such behavior an obsessional neurosis. Picture someone who spends two hours of preparation before leaving the kitchen to make certain that all boxes are in order, all counters spotlessly clean, and all floors immaculate, or the housekeeper who goes over the living room rug for hours for fear a particle of dust has been left behind. These are manifestations of obsessive doubting, which prevents a person from ever feeling certain. No matter what the obsessional does, it is never fully and completely done; it is never perfect. The doubting is enormously incapacitating in such a person's life.

Obsessional persons may be bright, capable of understanding complicated, highly technical issues, or philosophically astute with high I.Q.'s and still incapable of alternating trivial, nonsensical items of thought or behavior. Such persons strive to achieve; they often claim an omniscience and omnipotence of superhuman proportions and feel humiliated by their inability to manage their thoughts. In order to effectively attempt to control one's living and guarantee one's safety, it is essential to be fully cognizant and aware of the threats and dangers to one's living. Therefore, the obsessive individual tries to be knowledgeable and fully conversant in all areas of human functioning — a super-expert. He attempts to focus on intellectual attainments and achievements at the cost of all other aspects of living, in the hope that he will be able to identify all the dangers and threats and to know enough about them so that they can be avoided. The omniscient tendency helps sustain the fiction that in his perfection he has achieved absolute security. We see this in some of the rituals such as ultra-cleanliness (hand-washing or cleaning compulsion) and neatness, and in the expectation of perfection, which tends to serve as a pseudosecurity for the notion that all the danger can be warded off. The need to know everything will often lead to an enormous accumulation of information, which seems to be unrelated to the issues of living with other human beings. For the obsessive person, technical proficiency in his occupational skills is very enhanced but his ability to deal with humans is very deficient.

An obsessional can never make a mistake or admit an error. One can achieve this by keeping the issues open, procrastinating about decisions and maintaining an aura of doubt which says, "I'm not sure yet or I haven't made up my mind yet," so that one cannot be found making a mistake. The tendency to procrastinate is often severely incapacitating because it causes endless delays unless there is clear support from an authority that supports the position. The indecisiveness prevents the obsessional from taking a position even on matters with which he is well acquainted. This may give others the impression that he is uninformed when, in fact, he is trying to be totally informed. The position, as it seems to others, is that the obsessional person is unprepared to commit himself to any statement, cause, or idea because of some wishy-washy tendency. In fact, he has considerable contempt and disgust for his inability to take a stand or commit himself while priding himself on his insistence on making decisions only when he is completely informed.

The inability to make a commitment, with its accompanying risks of loss of control and the possibility of error, is a major feature of the obsessional disorder. It is responsible for the feeling of being alienated, uninvolved, and on the fringe of living. It prevents an individual from feeling part of the scene in which he functions. It is this feeling, rather than the presence of rituals or other striking obsessional symptoms, that pushes the obsessional patient into treatment. Some commitment must be made and concessions and compromises arrived at in order to function in the real world. Depending on the situation the obsessional may feel pride in his unwillingness to make a premature decision or have contempt and disgust for himself when his indecisiveness prevents action and allows others to win the acclaim of society. It is only when Darwin faced possible prior publication by a colleague that he overcame his obsessional indecisiveness and put *The Origin of the Species* into the hands of the publishers. What a tragedy it would have been for Darwin had he continued to procrastinate because he felt he did not yet have all the facts and data to absolutely confirm his thesis!

IMPEDIMENTS TO THERAPY

The inability to make a commitment prevents an obsessional from taking a stand that might not always turn out to be right. He may use many tactics and devices to manage and justify his procrastinating indecisiveness. One way is through displacement, or the tendency to focus on the unessential or lesser significant issues in living. This enables him to remain unaware of those areas of functioning in which he may lose control. Displacement may result in compulsive avoidance or distraction, which will manifest itself in every aspect of his living — in his communications, in his functioning with himself and others, and at work. For example, the communicative process is one of obfuscation, rather than clarification, and it is singularly notable that the obsessional moves away from clarity because clarity may force him to recognize his weakness. Because of the feeling of danger in such an awareness, he may become severely anxious or panicky. Thus, the communicative process is typically complicated by distraction, evasion, and multiple sidetracking. He must be certain that he covers all issues in order to be perfect and not leave anything out. This leads him to go into endless details about an event, taking the focus away from the main issue and making it difficult to distinguish the essential from the nonessential and the relevant from the irrelevant.

The obsessional's lack of clarity is a major impediment in the therapeutic process. Clear communication and verbal exchanges, which it is hoped will bring into awareness elements that the neurotic process itself strives to becloud, are required. The tendencies toward preciseness, orderliness or extreme disorderliness and the insistence upon maintaining such rigid control of oneself that feelings are never expressed also run counter to the very essence of therapeutic requirements. These must be taken into account in the therapy of such a person and must be overcome as part of the treatment technique; the therapist cannot initially insist that the patient be capable of the communicative requirements of the psychoanalytic process.

The element of emotional flatness and the unwillingness to commit oneself to an endeavor are additional impediments, since therapy demands emotional interaction and a commitment to the process to the extent that the patient feels some trust and a willingness to engage in the relationship. Initially, the therapist is an unknown figure. The uneasy, distrustful, perfectionistic patient does not easily accept the therapist in spite of the therapist's qualifications and high repute. Doubts about being unable to be helped are an aspect of the obsessional's pervasive doubting about the world in general and the therapist in particular. The effect of pervasive doubting will become clear only late in therapy, which is the best one can expect. Yet the awareness of such doubting must be constantly in the forefront; otherwise therapist and patient will be fooled into thinking that because some contact and engagement occur and some insights have developed, change should take place. Disappointment follows on both sides when change does not occur in spite of all the intellectual formulations. Unfortunately, this happens even with highly trained and competent therapists if they fail to understand obsessional patients' difficulties in trusting as well as their uneasiness with new, unusual, or unexpected demands. Their patients remain tight, rigid, and unspontaneous. They are only comfortable with the known, the familiar, and the repetitive situations — all of which they have mastered. For them, therapy has the quality of a unique situation in which the therapist attempts to introduce a perspective through some novel view of a phenomenon which will allow the patient to see and illuminate a piece of behavior which heretofore was clouded with obsessive defenses and obfuscation. The obsessional patient is a wary and suspecting person who comes prepared with an agenda and a presentation in order to avoid a novel conclusion. His needs impede the therapeutic process, which calls for an open, unplanned, and free association of events and incidents in his life.

The patient's rigidity also manifests itself in his cold, calculating manner, which is often described in terms of being impassive and socially controlled. However, under the thin cloud of stolidity is a steaming cauldron of unexpressed feelings and emotions — which may come out in the form of obsessional thoughts and compulsive rituals, as frightening to others as they are alien and shocking to the patient. The cold, calculating manner, the overconcern about technical aspects of living, and the unwillingness to allow feelings to emerge become marked impediments to interpersonal relationships with others. In a marriage they may produce many difficulties with being intimate, both sexually and otherwise. For many of these individuals the performance of the sex act is proper, adequate, and even technically perfect, albeit lacking in feeling, emotions, warmth, or tenderness. They often appear to be a competent fornicating machine to their partners, rather than someone engaged in a loving involvement.

Obsessional individuals may function adequately and effectively at a job and are usually successful because of their dedicated overzealousness in their need to achieve perfection. They are viewed as good, competent workers but usually not as intimate friends or companions. Their need to do a perfect job may interfere with performing tasks on time and may require extra amounts of work at home. The day-to-day living tends to be humorless and without joy. They pay their bills on time and try to display no weakness and to be viewed by others as responsible in all regards. However, the responsibility will be regarded as irresponsibility when the procrastinating, indecisive tendencies appear and prevent them from making a decision. Tasks may never actually be performed, and others may think they are avoiding efforts to live up to their commitments when, in fact, they are trying to live up to them too well and to do the job perfectly.

While the picture I've drawn may seem unflattering, I must point out that obsessional individuals are not without charm and often have a good sense of humor in spite of their need for certainties and guarantees in their living. As there are enough areas of functioning that allow some freedom, they do make companionable friends and marital partners and do live out their lives — often with financial and material success — even though their anxieties may be mitigated by drugs, alcohol, or excessive activity.

The human infant arrives in a state of absolute helplessness and total dependence upon his environment. Although his capacities to function independently enlarge as he matures physically and psychologically, he is never in full control of the forces which act upon him from the inside or the outside. Some of his physiological functions are autonomic and thus totally beyond his control, just as are some of the forces of nature. In order to experience a minimum of security and a measure of certainty, man constructs a number of myths about his powers and skill in influencing these forces.

Jules Masserman has called them the *Ur*-defenses*, and they are persistent myths about man's competence, the goodwill of other humans, and the magic of his omnipotence. He described three such myths, including a presumption of personal invulnerability, power, and immortality; a hopeful faith in humanity; and a wishful myth of a transcendental order and perfect servant. These personal myths have been used since man developed a cortex capable of visualizing his own self. His structuralizing involved attempts to insure order and consistency in his universe and were often unreasonable. As they were rigidly held and had magical connotations, the devices could be called obsessive mechanisms.

In children these techniques consist of magical, repetitive acts, which the child feels will prevent dangerous consequences from occurring if the rituals are carried out precisely. In adults such behavior is called superstitious and irrational; the magical quality involved is readily evident. The greater the extent of fear and uncertainty, the more prevalent will be the magical superstitions and rigid rules of behavior designed to control or master these uncertainties. Kurt Goldstein, in his studies of brain-injured people, noted the subjects' attempts at understanding the environment through extreme measures of orderliness and routinized activity.

---

* Jules Masserman, "Faith and Delusion in Psychotherapy (The Ur-defenses of Man)," *American Journal of Psychiatry* 110 (1953): 324-333.

Obsessional mechanisms are omnipresent, but in some people they will be more pronounced and will characterize the major ways of dealing with their needs, therefore playing an integral part in their personality structure. Such people's behavior will be predictable and consistent in their reactions to various needs and circumstances. Yet, not all the characteristics of the obsessional way of life are present in all obsessional individuals.

Nor will we find that obsessional patterns of functioning are necessarily dysjunctive or conjunctive, constructive or destructive to healthy productive living. Much will depend on the intensity and rigidity of these patterns and areas of living to which they are applied. In the obsessive-compulsive neurosis, such tendencies become extreme and maladaptive.

The primary dynamism in all instances will be manifested as an attempt to gain control over oneself and one's environment in order to avoid or overcome distressful feelings of helplessness and powerlessness.

The concern about the possibility of losing control by being incompetent or insufficiently informed, or by taking risks without identifiable guarantees and certainty, stimulates much anxiety. The realization of one's humanness — with its inherent limitations — is often the basis for considerable anxiety which requires obsessive attempts at greater control over one's living.

Fear of loss of control is commonly symbolized in the physical sense, as in fainting or going crazy. One will resort to the extremes of shouting and screaming or engage in other undisciplined activities. Phobias often develop around these situations, in which the person fears he will lose control of himself in giddiness, fainting, swaying feelings, collapsing, or possibly dying. The phobias may involve heights, open spaces, enclosed spaces, or a hundred other specific issues, but essentially in every instance the fear is that of going out of control. The problem of control in the obsessive person is complicated by his tendency to deal in extremes, so that unless he feels he has total control he tends to experience total *lack* of control. He experiences the possibility of loss of control as so painfully humiliating, frightening, and dangerous that phobic avoidances are common. (The relation of phobias to the obsessional states will be described in a later chapter.)

RESPONSIBILITY OF BEHAVIOR

Obsessional thinking and behavior tend to avoid closure and postpone action on the grounds that one must accumulate more knowledge and facts before acting. However, to achieve control over one's living and to guarantee one's existence, one must acquire a knowledge of all the possibilities that may occur. This will permit one to anticipate and be prepared for anything confronted in the course of living. In this way the person can control all the factors involved and achieve the most favored outcome. The striving for omniscience through emphasis on intellectuality is an integral part of the obsessive process and is a major goal. The obsessional can be comfortable only when he feels he knows everything or is engaged in the process of trying to know everything. He is convinced not only that this is absolutely necessary but also that it is often possible, even in the face of his intellectual grasp of the impossibility of achieving the goal. He demands of himself that he be capable of anticipating his own reactions and the emotional responses of others by rational and logical means. He requires that he be able to control the uncontrollable. Thus, he expects to know how he will be feeling several days hence so that he can plan properly. He expects his decisions or opinions to be acceptable to everyone, even to those who disagree with him or do not know him. He expects to know in advance that his plans will be ideal and agreeable to all. Such expectations often serve to immobilize him and to prevent him from making any plans. He rationalizes the immobility by insisting that he wants only to plan most effectively and to suit everyone. He will say, "If it cannot be done perfectly, then why do it at all?" This statement has a flavor of righteous and conscientious living and is often rewarded with praise and support. The truth, however, is that it is not based on a moral injunction but on a compelling need to guarantee the outcome of the endeavor — which is hardly ever possible. It is, in fact, compulsive behavior and not simply conscientious and responsible behavior.

THE NEED FOR OMNISCIENCE

Rather than face an awareness of the impossibility of being omniscient and acknowledging his human limitations, the obsessional concludes that if only he knew more and tried harder he could achieve these goals. The solution is to become more perfect, and thus even more obsessional. In this respect obsessional living tends to stimulate the need for more obsessional defenses. This becomes one of the major burdens in therapy since the patient hopes to reduce his anxiety by improving his obsessional neurosis instead of abandoning it. The demands for omniscience, available only to the gods, prevent him from enjoying the rewards of limited potentialities that are available to humans. Even with a total understanding of all the relevant factors in an event he cannot take into account accidental circumstances and the indeterminacy which is an inescapable part of our physical universe. Such expectations lead to a futile impasse, and an enormous amount of time and energy is expended in fruitless efforts to overcome such obstacles.

The obsessional attempts to absorb every piece of information in the universe. Nothing seems irrelevant or unrelated to his interest, since every piece of information may have some value on some future occasion. In attempting to absorb it all, he succeeds in absorbing less than he is capable of, since his activities are laden with tension and uneasiness. Reading a novel or technical book becomes a challenge and a chore, since every detail must be noted regardless of its significance. He does not read to understand the author's point of view or the theme of the book; instead, he reads to memorize every single idea. Therefore it takes him an inordinately long time to read a book, resulting in an accumulation of unread books. This happens even when he limits his reading to a specialized area of concern or professional interest. He quickly finds himself with an accumulated pile of books, newspapers, magazines, and clippings — which are put aside to be read later. As the unread material accumulates, nothing may be discarded for fear something important will be missed. This same issue is involved in the collecting and saving of newspapers, magazines and other material that needs to be read, absorbed, memorized or at least scrutinized. Such behavior leads to mountains of unread materials, which either are tossed out in one sweep or become a permanent part of the "mess." It soon becomes clear that all this accumulation cannot be dealt with, and it is then either moved out of sight or dismissed in one grand cleaning gesture. This vicious circle can be interrupted only by a decision to risk losing some potentially significant information by more selective or directed reading. Although it is a decision that all of us must make, it is extremely difficult for the obsessional. Eventually, circumstances and the sheer accumulation of material force him to make a decision. His desk is then cleared so that the vicious circle can begin all over again.

The need to know everything often interferes with his valid interest and desire to keep up with developments in his professional areas of interest. An economist who reads extensively could easily be sidetracked by insisting that every phase of human activity is related to economics and therefore should be on his reading list. Meanwhile, the literature on economics continues to pile up unread in his library. This may produce a superficial, dilettantish involvement in all developments in the arts and sciences and often gives others the impression that he is a profound scholar with a deep knowledge of all fields. While his knowledge may indeed be varied, his erudition is superficial. The intelligence and energy he expands would result in notable achievements if channeled and directed to limited areas.

In the search for omniscience there is a singular incapacity to separate the relevant from the irrelevant, since everything is considered relevant to the obsessional's global demands. This incapacity serves to impede any progress toward intensive exploration of one particular area. The obsessional is often a scholar of great repute when he manages to establish some boundaries in his work. It is this type of researcher who undertakes the most tedious and rigorous tasks in relatively obscure areas of human concern, which may result in significant discoveries. However, these discoveries occur when the research goes beyond the search for data for the personal security of the researcher and aims at an increased control over nature. Even in these circumstances the obsessional's productions differ qualitatively from the explorations of the relatively free and unrestrained researcher who is curious about himself and nature and is also interested in increasing his control over it. Unlike the obsessive, who is *driven* to such activity, the free researcher may be dedicated, but he is motivated more by the pleasure in his adventures than by the decrease in anxiety. Even though there are no pure cultures of "free" or "compulsive" scientists or artists, such a distinction provides some clues about creativity and productivity — which, although they may coexist, are not synonymous.

The creativity of a genius need not derive from neurotic sources; more often it arises from curiosity and a capacity for originality and novelty that is anathema to the obsessive person. In fact, obsessional qualities may seriously impair the creative process and limit the potential genius. Many creative individuals have an astonishing capacity for surmounting their neurosis, and they would be moumental contributors if they were not being harrassed by their rigidities.

The difference between the work of the creative person and that of the obsessional is determined by the motive source of the intense and energetic productions of each. In both there is a capacity for tedious, painstaking activity. One functions out of the positive pleasures of the utilization of his skills, while the other is in search of absolutes and perfection in order to achieve security. For both the rewards may be status, recognition, and financial success, but one will be content and contemplative while the other will need constant reassurances. Both kinds of activity may benefit mankind, but the commitment of the noncompulsive person holds greater promise for meaningful discoveries. He concerns himself with transcending the known and exploring the unknown. This activity is not solace seeking, anxiety avoiding, or pushed on by never-ending doubts and the need for certainties. The obsessional's work may actually *provoke* anxiety and may involve matters which have no possibilities of solution.

When the compulsive is forced to act, he will often refuse to take full responsibility for the consequences because he was not in full accord with the plan and therefore should not be held accountable for the outcome. In this way, the compulsive justifies any failure of his activities by placing the blame on others who forced him to act. This tendency was quite troublesome to a young obsessional who had great difficulty making dates in advance, since he was not quite certain how he would feel when the day of the date arrived or whether he would want to be with that particular girl at that time. He found it virtually impossible to buy theater tickets in advance, as he could never be sure of what he would feel like doing when that day came or with whom he would like to do it. He maintained that he did not wish to be committed to advance arrangements, so that he could feel free to do whatever he wished when he wished to do it. Since the ultimate effect is actually to limit his choice to whatever is available at the last minute, it is clearly a spurious claim. When he was certain of what he wanted to do and with whom he wanted to do it, he would discover that the girl was already committed to a date with someone else or that the theater tickets were not available. Thus, he ended up with the least desirable girl and at the least desirable place, or he spent the evening alone. As his social life began to dwindle, he was forced to make dates in advance. Then he would invariably wish that he had made a date with someone else, and the evening would therefore always end badly. He would conclude that he should not have made the date in advance in the first place.

The inability to relinquish or compromise, or to take a chance, impairs the effectiveness of the person's capacity for full and mature living. Dating becomes a challenge instead of a pleasant, enjoyable experience. The person senses that there is something amiss in the way he organized his living, but he seems able to do very little about it. Instead, he justifies his behavior with intellectual and philosophical rationalizations. He prefers to present a picture of a thoughtful person who examines issues in depth, instead of acknowledging that his demands for omniscience make action and decision difficult.

Excursions into Philosophy

Philosophizing can often provide the way to avoid action and to forgo decision. While it may be a prelude to action, philosophizing often becomes a substitute for living, rather than a design for better living. It avoids taking sides, helping to sustain the aura of omniscience.

Philosophizing provided the impetus for the growth of many seminal ideas in the sciences as well as in the arts. Aristotle, Plato, Descartes, Marx, Whitehead, and many other intellectual giants broadened the horizons of man in every direction. For the obsessional, however, philosophizing becomes perverted into a justification for inaction and a demonstration of infallibility. The obsessional will become intensely involved in philosophical considerations of abstract justice, "truth," and other issues about which final statements cannot be made. The preoccupation with the most minute elements of experience, when examined in a formal fashion, has been the source of profound advances in man's enlightenment, but it can also be a justification for inaction. The obsessional's philosophizing is generally directed at distracting and obfuscating rather than focusing and clarifying. He has a tendency to fractionate or dissect every experience with compulsive rigidity, a process that confuses rather than enlightens. His verbal skills serve mainly to blur understanding.

The obsessional insists on arriving at ultimate truths in all matters. He claims a purity of intellectual pursuit, maintaining that unless certainty can be established, final statements must be avoided. This device is defensive particularly when the certainty he demands is in areas where the possibility of it is remote or unattainable and where such a search may seriously impair the possibilities for real discovery. Such unrealistic demands are obstacles, rather than challenges, to uncovering the laws of man or nature.

Although the obsessional's philosophizing is sometimes fruitful, it most often leads only to a dead end by concerning itself with questions that have no meaning or that have no real answers (for example, speculations about the number of fairies on the head of a pin). In the search for ultimate truths, one may exhibit intellectual integrity, but in the obsessional, the rigidity of the search may be disrupting and digressing rather than creative. While he is seemingly pressing for truth in an uncompromising manner, he is more often launched on a rigid, inflexible program without any realistic comprehension of the obstacles that such demands impose on an investigation.

A preoccupation with ultimate and total truths and abstract concepts of justice is often combined with a rigid set of standards. Exaggerated expectations of the behavior of others and supermoralistic requirements of one's own behavior often pose a caricature of human functioning, so that the obsessional may insist on truth under all circumstances without taking cognizance of the impossibility of establishing such criteria. It becomes truth for truth's sake alone and not an honest awareness of the benefits to be derived from adhering to the truth. It is a slogan and defense rather than a recognition of the virtue of integrity in human relationships. This applies also to his expressed goal of knowing all.

For example, the obsessional husband may insist on telling his wife everything (including his fringe thoughts) about every girl he admires or feels a fleeting interest in, yet he expects his wife to admire his honesty and not be discomfited by his disclosures. He expects his wife to support this caricature of honesty; anything else would indicate that he and his wife have a less-than-perfect relationship, since they agreed from the beginning to tell each other everything. Though the obsessive person expects to be rewarded for his confessions, he, in turn, cannot accept or tolerate similar confessions from his mate.

The abstract concepts of honesty, integrity, truth, and intellectual curiosity have compulsive qualities and are often responsible for a great deal of damage in interpersonal relationships. Such a firm position often puts others on the defensive and forces them to justify their own more limited concepts of virtue and openness. It is always simpler to defend an extreme thesis when one refuses to recognize the realistic limitations of it. Virtue is then entirely on one's own side and total lack of it on the other. The rigidity of the obsessional often poses moralistic problems in this very way. Questions are resolved on the basis of global formulations. Each instance is judged not in its own right and setting. The rigid rules are applied indiscriminately and unselectively, without any qualifying considerations of the particular situation or circumstance. There is no element of choice in deciding the questions individually, but rather a compulsive necessity to behave in rigid, circumscribed and stereotyped ways. What often appears to be a strong, decisive, and affirmative action is the product of precisely the opposite — an uncertain, uneasy, wavering indecisiveness that requires rigid and inflexible rules to overcome. Consequently, what may seem to be a positive, affirmative, and moral set of values is simply the compulsive's need to appear perfect and omniscient. Such needs are manifestations of great uneasiness about one's integrity and honesty and serve as a device for diminishing activity. Such a rigid position prevents a decisive response by an automatic reaction, which is always on the side of the angels, even when the circumstances may dictate a more human response.

The philosophical acceptance of high moral standards can become a way of avoiding the responsibility for one's behavior. It is as if one's verbalized standards are enough and one need not be concerned about maintaining them in one's actual living. In this regard society often cooperates, so that the admission of sin in a church confessional may be enough expiation for the behavior. Similarly, the magic words "I'm sorry" may be sufficient to absolve one from the consequences of one's behavior. It is small wonder that serious concern about responsibility is lacking in so many people. Such verbalisms are particularly common in obsessional living, where the words *magic* and *undoing* are widely used. Omnipotence of thought and wishes coupled with the feelings of being pushed and compelled to act enables the obsessional to avoid taking responsibility for his thoughts and actions. The expectation of privileged exemptions from responsibility by the use of expiating formulas may not be shared by the community or the obsessional's friends and may produce serious conflicts.

At times the recognition of limitations or the admission of a deficiency may appear to be an honest confrontation with one's humanness. It may, however, also be a device for claiming exemptions from the consequences of one's behavior. The disarming admission of one's imperfections is a claim for tolerance with regard to an inadequate performance, which further limits the demands to be made of one. In addition, it is further evidence of the obsessional's superiority; he is "big" enough to admit his failings.

The obsessional is a master in this ploy, and the admission of not knowing everything enhances his superiority and confirms his infallibility. He manages the double bind very successfully by being right when he is right and merely human when he is wrong. At the same time he forces others into a double bind of "wrong when they do and wrong when they don't." The double-bind element is widespread in the obsessional's life and is forced onto most people with whom he has to deal. Because of his need to be decisive but never wrong, he is forced to take stands in which whatever he does must be correct. In practice this is very difficult, unless he can force others to approve his behavior no matter what choice is made. Although he avoids direct and open negotiations, he demands that the relationship with him be intimate in spite of the absence of intimacy. He generally succeeds in such relationships for varying periods of time, when the other person has something to gain from keeping the relationsip intact. This is the case with one's wife, husband, friend, or relative, where the need to be considerate, gentle, or tolerant requires a variety of double-talk that is pervasive even if it is not identified by the participants. In overt or, more commonly, in covert distortions, confusions and evasions of direct contact, the individual gets involved in double binds that may be quite incapacitating. It often becomes an integral part of the obsessional's living and is the inevitable result of trying to realize opposite goals and objectives, to fulfill contradictory needs and desires, and to achieve omniscience.

Omniscience of Thought

The obsessional's striving for omniscience is frequently reflected in a characteristic development called *omniscience of thought*. It is an aspect of the tendency to overemphasize the rational, gnostic elements in the obsessional's living. In such thinking (which is also operative in some psychotics) one has the conviction that one's thinking is capable of effecting changes in other people as well as in events. When this phenomenon is present, the person feels that he may be responsible for some cataclysm or significant event at a great distance because he may have thought about the possibility of its happening. Specifically, even when such a possibility is positively excluded, the person may feel responsible for the death of another simply because he may have wished the other dead at some time. It is an overestimation of his intellectual capacity and its magical possibilities that permits him to confuse thinking with achieving. It is this quality that often frightens the obsessional when he has aggressive or hostile thoughts and presumes that they can effect injury on others. Many ritualistic acts of undoing are designed to prevent the damage from occurring. Magic is undone by more potent magic. The grandiosity implicit in such assumptions prevents him from recognizing that thinking is a prelude to action and not synonymous with it. When the failure to distinguish the process of thinking from the act of achieving occurs in the extreme, we have the typical grandiose delusion that occurs in schizophrenia and in the manic-depressive states.

At times the accidental coincidence of an obsessional thought with some event may precipitate a psychosis by confirming the grandiosity about which heretofore the obsessional had no firm convictions. This type of reasoning, which relates cause and effect to the temporal contiguity of events, characterizes a phase of human cognitive development and has been called *parataxic thinking*. It is a normal development that goes beyond the infant's conceptions of cause and effect. It precedes the comprehension of logical relationships between events and their causes. In parataxic thinking, before a youngster comprehends the nature of lightning or the reasons for anger in another person, he attributes the cause to something that may have immediately preceded it. If a mother is angry when her child asks a question, the child may assume the mother's anger results from the question instead of from the quarrel she had with a neighbor a few minutes earlier. In extreme forms parataxic thinking is the dominant cognitive mode of paranoid mechanisms.

It is possible to exert some influence on others by one's thoughts or gestures (or other actions that are the outgrowth of one's thoughts) when the other person is in close range or is able to perceive these manifestations of one's thinking. Gestures, minimal physical changes in voice, syntax, or eye contact can convey significant feeling states. However, unless one accepts the possibility of extrasensory perception, it must be assumed that the person who takes responsibility for events beyond the limits of perception or under circumstances in which thinking can have no effect is making magical and grandiose assumptions about the power of his thinking.

Obsessional omnipotence of thoughts and the self-fulfilling prophecy of some neurotics seem to have some things in common. However, there are also great differences. Through his grandiosity the obsessional may assume to be influencing events elsewhere; the person who subtly and "unwittingly" stimulates others to influence the outcome he has already predicted is producing the so-called self-fulfilling prophecy. The latter refers to a widespread tendency in some neurotics who anticipate that they will be rejected, for example, and who covertly behave toward others in ways guaranteed to produce rejection.

If an accident should befall the victim of an obsessional's hateful feelings, he may assume total guilt for the event. Although such guilt may not have achieved delusional proportions — because there is still an awareness of the irrational nature of it — it may produce a good deal of expiating behavior. The obsessive person is overwhelmed by feelings of guilt and may assume blame and responsibility for events because he can never really resolve the doubt about the possibility of his being responsible. This factor plays a large role when confessions are made in major criminal cases under circumstances that clearly indicate that the confession is false. Compulsive doubting coupled with omniscience of thought and perfectionistic demands for certainty leave the obsessional so uncertain that his confessions are misread as evasions and accepted as fact. Such confessions, which stem from compulsive tendencies, are often accepted by the courts — even though the evidence is far from convincing.

It is curious that the thoughts involved in the omnipotent concerns of the obsessional are almost always unfriendly and malevolent. He is rarely concerned about the favorable or friendly effects his thoughts have on others. This is a core issue in understanding the obsessional's dynamics, since the defenses of displacement and isolation refer to dangerous feelings that often are of a tender and dependent nature. Awareness of tenderness is immediately and automatically avoided by a consciousness of unfriendly or antagonistic feelings. It is these thoughts that get caught in magic operations disguising the original warm and accepting feelings.

The feeling of the omnipotence of one's thought is almost universally present in early childhood and in the juvenile period and is associated with rituals which attempt to undo the possible damage one's thoughts may inflict. Primitive man's conviction of the power of his thoughts is closely related to magical rites and the superstitions that still plague modern man. Magic, as well as many religious practices, is based on the belief that devotional thinking can produce significant happenings. This belief is often coupled with ritualistic practices to guarantee the effect of one's thinking.

When bizarre, unconventional, and extreme claims are made about the power of one's thoughts, they become delusional and part of a mental illness. At these times responsibility is assumed for events that often have not taken place or that have occurred accidentally or coincidentally. Hurricanes, epidemics, and even wars can become the sole responsibility of the obsessional. A phobic avoidance of weapons or other destructive implements, for example, may be the result of an obsessional's fear that his hostile wishes will force him into extreme behavior. Phobias are thus intimately related to obsessional thinking, providing the tactics for avoiding dangerous places, things, or people.

Intrusive "Homosexuality"

Homosexual thoughts often occur as intrusive elements in many obsessional people when there are no behavioral manifestations whatsoever. Like other intrusive thoughts, they are distracting and preoccupying and not necessarily factual issues that might be carried into action. The person will interpret these fantasies as evidence of latent or repressed homosexual desires. He frequently interprets these intrusions as representing actual wishes rather than symbolic or metaphorical statements about his weakness or inadequacy. The psychiatrist, too, often falls into this trap. Such thoughts may not necessarily be wishes; they may be defensive devices designed to distract and displace attention from a significant problem. While Freud also noted this factor, many psychiatrists and psychoanalysts tend to apply the oversimplified notion of wishful thinking to all motivated behavior. They tend to interpret thoughts as literal issues and neglect Freud's most essential contribution, which involves the role of defenses in dealing with unacceptable thoughts and wishes. An expressed desire may actually be a rationalization, reaction-formation, or obsessional substitution for its opposite. Homosexual thoughts may, in fact, be a displacement for uneasy heterosexual wishes. When the therapist simplistically or routinely overlooks the defensive role of intrusive thoughts such as homosexual concerns, he strengthens an area of doubt in the obsessional about his strength or prowess or, in the case of a woman, about her femininity. The occurrence of this type of thinking does not support the theory of latent homosexuality. Instead, it emphasizes the tendency of the neurotic as well as the normal person to utilize cultural symbols and conventional biases to express the doubts and convictions of his feelings of unworthiness and to draw on all conventional attitudes in a manner that reinforces his neurotic system.

It is, in fact, rare indeed to find an obsessional who puts intrusive thoughts into action, whether it be hostile, destructive, or outrageous. Murder, suicide, shouting obscene words, or just losing control in public places rarely occurs. Likewise, obsessional concerns about homosexuality are rarely pursued or actualized. The intrusive homosexual thoughts may symbolize nonsexual conflicts and concerns regarding competition and fear of one's capacity in nonsexual areas. As suggested, these thoughts most often represent doubts about one's heterosexual capacities in the face of the obsessional demands that he perform the sex act perfectly every time. These obsessive thoughts are also likely to appear in the male obsessive who may have difficulty in prolonging the sex act and controlling his ejaculation. The expectation of perfect control prevails in the obsessional's sex life as it does everywhere else. Consequently there is no consideration given to the psychological and physiological effects of abstinence, fatigue, or other debilitating conditions that tend to produce rapid ejaculation. The obsessional maintains that the possibility of prolonging intercourse and maintaining an erection is limitless and that the failure to do so is the result of weakness and unmanly behavior. One obsessional was determined to produce an orgasm in a woman who had never been able to achieve one. He prolonged intercourse until he was exhausted or until it was physically painful to his partner. In spite of this, he felt that he was a failure and assumed that were he a better man, he would have been successful. The compulsive sexual behavior of some men — like the Don Juan type or the insatiable sex seeker who pushes his intercourse to extreme lengths — may be attempts to cover up doubts about their manliness or to prove their individual worthiness by their sexual prowess. A fifty-year-old artist would have intercourse for hours at a time before ejaculating and would repeat such prolonged sexual contact 10 to 15 times in one week. Another young male who occasionally had homsexual contacts required that his wife have an orgasm regardless of the time it would take, which might run into many hours. He was compelled to have intercourse whether he wished to or not, to prove his worthiness.

The obsessional demands that he transcend his biological limits and maintain his erection or postpone ejaculation entirely at his will. His inability to do so may produce intrusive doubts about his masculinity. Interpretation of the obsessive concerns about homosexuality in this light is a liberating one, in contrast to the unfortunate tendency to view such doubts as evidences of wishful thinking implying homosexual or latent homosexual interest.

Control of Emotions

If one demands total control of oneself, it is imperative that the emotions be held in check and that the person has a cognitive understanding of the issues involved in living. Since feelings are not entirely within conscious control, it is even more important that a rigid guard be placed over the obsessional's feelings and emotions.

All emotional responses must be dampened, restrained, or completely denied. Since he approaches life in an intellectualized fashion, the obsessional tries to appear unmoved by disturbing or rewarding experiences. He tries to examine each situation as a rational event, insisting that only by putting emotional reactions aside can one be fair and accurate. Such an ideal goal, however, is rarely possible — man's emotional responses are mostly autonomic and beyond conscious control. Since intellectual reactions are entirely under control, it is not hard to understand why the obsessional person places such great emphasis on intellectuality. Yet, he does not or cannot always use his intellectual resources to enlighten or clarify his living.

Man's emotional responses are ontogenetically much older and more primitive than his intellectual development. They arise in the thalamus in the midbrain, whereas the forebrain or cerebral cortex is the center of intellectual activity. This physiological fact helps us understand a large portion of the obsessional's desire to isolate or eliminate his emotional responses. As he cannot always control his emotions, he may "get involved" or become committed to people or things too strongly to suit his protective needs. He would prefer to eliminate feelings entirely from his life; because he cannot achieve this end, he uses the techniques of displacement, isolation, and compartmentalization — which characterize obsessive behavior.

Displacement refers to the defense process by which strong feelings are attached to less significant or meaningless activities, thereby removing them from significant areas of living. In such circumstances, for example, a strong, unacceptable reaction may be displaced from a parent, child, or close friend onto some food fad, distant relative, or political ideology. Such displacement is a means of isolating or distorting feelings and may give a bizarre appearance to an obsessional's behavior. He may appear to be uninvolved emotionally with significant people or events while grossly overinvolved with minutiae. *Isolation* and *compartmentalization* are closely related to displacement, and their function is to make the feelings unavailable at a particular moment or to have them so unrelated to events that they cannot participate in associations, relationships, or significant decisions.

In the obsessional neuroses, whatever emotional elements may be present appear to be attached to unessential or irrelevant issues in the person's life. In this way, he is able to avoid a confrontation with his true feelings and become involved in areas of living that he can control while *appearing* to be uninterested in those areas that he cannot control. He does not accept emotional responses, when they occur, as normal accompaniments to living. When they do occur, they are justified by extensive rationalizations that make them appear to be reasonable and logical.

The obsessional's efforts to control his emotions may result in a paucity of emotional displays, but they cannot eliminate the enormous ground swells of feeling which are stored up. These untapped emotional sources may periodically burst out, either in minor ways such as slips of the tongue or other parapraxes or in explosive, major eruptions. At times the obsessional is quite aware of the presence of these underground forces that he keeps under such strict control. He justifies controlling his behavior by pointing to the intensity of these feelings. He insists that he must keep his feelings in check because they are too explosive to be let out. At a certain point, this undoubtedly becomes true, since the vicious circle that characterizes neurotic development allows for an accumulation of feelings because of a need to control one's feelings. After a while, the accumulation may be so great that the expression of such feelings might be excessive even if the stimulus were minimal. It is this feature that tends to be exaggerated in psychodynamic hypotheses about obsessional behavior when they are viewed exclusively as techniques for controlling unacceptable hostile or aggressive behavior. One notes the presence of angry, hostile, or destructive thoughts and assumes that the rituals are attempts to control these feelings. The positive or tender feelings are not noted by the psychiatrist as being dangerous or threatening to an individual. However, what the obsessional really wishes to avoid is the expression of *any* feelings — tender or hostile. The freer expression of tender feelings might actually stimulate positive responses from others, rather than rejection. For the obsessional such reactions might be more "involving" and thus more dangerous than hostile ones.

It is not the expression of feelings that is actually dangerous but the failure to express them and the tendency to store them up. Emotional expression in general allows for a more direct and responsive reaction from the other person, thereby permitting a proper and realistic appraisal of one's situation. Like everything else in the obsessional's life, however, the expression of his emotions is also a matter of all or none. The middle road, with its possibilities of moderate reactions with moderate responses, appears impossible for him.

Magic of Language

Like thoughts, language is a magical tool to influence and control the environment of people as well as things. The power of the verbal gesture, which seemed to be so successful in the early years, is vastly overestimated now. In his need to control others, the obsessional seems to retain the dramatic power of his earliest verbalizations as a child and their capacity to influence the adult. In addition, the success of the verbal gesture in minimizing punishment and expiating guilt attests to its magical power. Such verbal maneuvers generally have their origins in the childhood era, when speech development takes place. The molding of sounds into speech and comprehensible words is generally met with great enthusiasm and delight by the parents. These early productions greatly influence others, and one begins to note the power of language in interpersonal relationships. The addition of a vocabulary and skill in utilizing words to assuage and control others and the magical formulas of "I'm sorry," "I didn't mean it," or "Excuse me!" becomes part of the child's verbal armamentarium and are magically successful in relieving the child of punishment, guilt, and responsibility for his behavior.

The recital of a formula that conveys remorse, regret, or the desire to change works so well that it subsequently gets automatized and is a substitute for a program of action. Eventually, the formulas may become divorced from action and are pure verbal productions that evoke all the desirable effects without any motor activity. Words and thoughts become obsessional devices in which their omnipotence becomes a substitute for active and responsible effort. The devices are incorporated into the character structure of the person, who entertains magical expectations of massive achievement and guilt-expiation through rhetoric and verbal production that bypass any need for *doing*.

Language can also be used to confuse and distort whenever necessary, either as a protective or adaptive measure. One may wish to avoid direct or incriminating statements while appearing to communicate in an intimate framework. The obsessional has developed this capacity into an art. Aside from the exaggerated need for being precise and accurate, the obsessional has an uncanny skill in leading any exchanges into blind alleys, irrelevancies, and often far from the original intent of the communication. There is a tendency toward subtle changes of subject and emphasis on the nonessential, with an involvement in side issues, which are generally initiated by anxiety. This verbal juggling seems to occur when the obsessional senses, in the course of the communication, that he is at fault or that his esteem may be lessened. Verbal magic and rituals are therefore very prominent in this disorder.

The obsessional's security at times requires that he avoid actual trial and possible failure, which can produce humiliation. On the other hand, he thinks he can achieve great successes through declamation and oratorical promises without actual trial and confrontation. The use of words to escape living and to confuse and obfuscate is an indirect heritage from early years, fortified by the compelling achievements of words in later years. The patient's extensive use of such verbal maneuvers must always be brought to his attention, and he must be helped to see the function this plays in the illness.

In addition to the voluminous verbal outpourings or the change of subject before a point has been established, the obsessional may use autistic symbolism, tonal devices, or the specious requirements of preciseness and accuracy, which require so much qualification and detail that the whole point of the communication is overshadowed and lost. The linguistic and rhetorical skill he develops through the years becomes a prime tool in his encounters with others. He uses it to justify all his excesses and to make his perfectionistic drives seem reasonable and wholesome. The more extreme his position becomes, the more facile are his explanations. It often requires great skill and marked attentiveness and persistence to keep the obsessional's verbal meanderings and rhetorical ploys in some manageable context — which can be most enlightening to the patient when it is demonstrated.

Since the obsessional views most of his activities as a challenge to his omniscience, every encounter is a contest that he must win. This is also true of his verbal exchanges in therapy, which are rarely viewed as simple communications. They are challenges that turn into debates in which the communicative intent is lost in the struggle to prove his omniscience. This becomes a real problem in the therapeutic process if every interpretation, observation, question, or comment is viewed as either criticism or a challenge to the obsessional's omniscience. Since he requires that he already know all, he cannot accept even a valid statement from the therapist without some initial objection or qualification. In this way he proves he cannot be pushed around and that in the long run he does know more than the therapist does.

Simply to accept an observation or interpretation without some challenge is viewed as a weakness and a defect. It is an admission of not knowing everything. He develops great skill in taking from others — in the guise of doing it for the other person's sake or in accepting it as a token of generosity (since he does not really need what he is taking). This device allows him to maintain his perfectionistic state and his grandiosity by proving that he is not unyielding or rigid, but open to new knowledge and new insights.

The precise and exhaustive manner of speaking that characterizes obsessional reporting is still another reflection of his personal striving for perfection. His passion for accuracy and completeness is an effort to eliminate all doubts and uncertainties and place him beyond criticism. Therefore his narratives are filled with minutiae and no detail is left out. These tales seldom get to the point without prodding, as the fear of being inaccurate or of making an error requires every kind of qualification to cover all contingencies. The narratives thus become dull and tedious and often waste a great deal of time; such devices are also a way of controlling others by forcing their attention and distracting them from essential issues.

While such devices may appear to be a simple matter of a person's inability to be appropriately selective, careful observation will reveal that the insistence on total detail requires great skill and demands high intellectual capacity. It often demands an intricate knowledge of a variety of matters that others often bypass in the interest of time and economy. The passion for detail in speech may reflect itself in a meticulous attention to dress and in other patterns of behavior. It leads to the precise categorizing of ideas and things so that they can be readily available to buttress one's verbal encounters. Thus, detail and order facilitate control over one's activities.

DOUBTING, PROCRASTINATION, AND INDECISION

A most effective way of supporting an illusion of infallibility and perfection is to avoid any challenges or tests that might expose one's deficiencies and errors. One can avoid a test or postpone the inevitable awareness of uncertainties through endless procrastination and indecision. When a decision can no longer be postponed, an element of doubt can then be introduced, so that one need not be entirely responsible for the consequences of the decision. Such pervasive vacillating and indecision — accompanied by gnawing, inconclusive doubting — characterizes the obsessive state. At one time the disorder was known as *mania de doute* because doubt is often the most pronounced feature of the illness.

Unless one can be absolutely certain about one's choice or decision, one stands the risk of being wrong. This, for the obsessional, is synonymous with being held weak, fallible, and defenseless. Until one can make a final, fully completed, and perfect product, it is best to keep it from the view of others, lest they see the imperfections. Therefore,examination papers are held onto until the last possible moment in order to make changes, or manuscripts are not submitted until the final deadline date. Such delays are designed to put off the possibility of adverse judgment, but they are rationalized as a desire to do the finest job possible. Once a task is finished or a paper submitted, it is beyond correction and amplification. If completion is postponed until a deadline forces one to turn in a paper, one can rationalize by insisting that if only there were more time, any imperfections could have been corrected. In addition, the experience is used to support and justify more procrastination, as criticism may be the stimulus for considerable anxiety, which, in turn, will require more defensive patterns and more indecisiveness. The issue may be as trivial as a reluctance to make a date with the hairdresser in case something more important should turn up or as significant as not accepting a job offer because a better one may appear in the future. It may involve not committing oneself to a purchase, relationship or idea because all the data are not in and a mistake might be made. Although in general one would applaud such behavior, the pervasive quality of indecision is most distressing even to the most organized and obsessional individual. The indecisiveness may have disastrous consequences if no action is taken when action is required.

Decisions cannot be postponed indefinitely. Sooner or later one must decide on the make of a car, the brand of a cigarette, or one's career and one's mate, to say nothing of an endless series of trivial decisions in everyday life. Being forced by circumstances to make a choice, the obsessional may deny the deficiencies inherent in such decisions and blame others if they go wrong. He may behave as though he is entirely disinterested in such trivial matters and considers himself beyond criticism. joining his potential detractors by disparaging the choice he made and thus being unable to enjoy it. On the other hand, the rigid and unreasonable advocacy of his choice makes him incapable of recognizing its real defects and thereby learning from experience and avoiding the same error in the future. Any decision, minor or major, rarely gives him pleasure. It only serves to increase his anxieties and leaves him wishing frequently that he could become more perfect.

Doubting, too, plays a role in the procrastinating. When one is forced to make a decision, one can always maintain that since he had doubts about it, he should therefore not be held fully accountable for the decision. Therefore, whatever decision he makes, the obsessional feels that perhaps the alternative would have been better. The activity or issue is often lost sight of when the proper outcome becomes far more important than the activity itself. This is particularly noticeable in sports, when the fun of playing takes second place to winning. Instead of being relaxing, the activity is overladen with tension and obsessional safeguards.

Doubting thus becomes a useful device in sustaining one's omniscience by not committing oneself without reservations and thereby risking a failure. By maintaining an atmosphere of doubt, one can easily shift sides to come out with the correct position. Therefore, to avoid error, firm decisions should be avoided.

The obsessional's indecisiveness is also supported by an elaborate pseudopride with which he views himself as being objective, honest, and wishing only to examine all the issues involved in making a decision. This, of course, can prolong a decision indefinitely. However, the "examination" does not represent a valid quest but rather a compulsive need to avoid commitment and closure. It allows the obsessional to convey an atmosphere of open-minded flexibility in his desire to avoid quick judgments without an adequate exploration of the facts. It soon becomes evident, however, that what appears to be judicious scrutiny is really a compulsive need to keep the lines open for fear of making a decision.

To illustrate, a restaurant menu carries multiple choices and a diner must finally decide on one item. The anguish of this choice can often be identified in many people who would like to have a sample of everything or at least more than one or two dishes. The obsessional is particularly distressed by the need to choose. He wants to have both the lobster and the steak and knows that he cannot order both. Here the issue is not one of making an error but of making the best possible choice. To order one item only to discover that the other is preferable would be a blow to his pride and omniscience. A compulsive eater or obese person may resolve this dilemma by ordering both. The indecisive obsessional, however, will keep on trying to decide until the last possible moment. He will make a choice, perhaps change it, and possibly change it a third time. When the waiter departs, the obsessional begins to doubt his choice and wishes he could change it, but embarrassment prevents him from doing so. When his dinner arrives he will then find reasons for justifying his indecisions, or he may exaggerate the quality of his choice. Either way, he cannot fully enjoy the dinner because he is annoyed over his doubts and procrastinations.

Although the preceding description may be somewhat exaggerated, one can notice how frequently it occurs to a lesser extent. Could it be that the Chinese restaurant has become so universally popular because of the custom of serving many dishes passed around in family style, so that one can get a bit of every dish? This surely is the most acceptable style of eating for a severe obsessional unless others at the table allow him a portion of their order, which he covets because it is not his.

The same considerations apply to the most diverse and significant decisions in the obsessional's living, sometimes in a more covert fashion. In both the obese compulsive eater or the compulsive drinker (alcoholic), the difficulty of making a choice is exemplified in the "which one" category as well as the "whether or not" category. Choice is impossible, and the compulsion is called an addiction. This is particularly true in eating (obesity) or noneating (anorexia) addictions or other addictions where physiological dependence is not a factor. It is also the case with compulsive gambling, masturbation, and the like where choice or the exercise of will is no longer possible because the compulsive behavior is beyond free choice.

Doubting, which serves to fortify the indecisiveness, often comes to play a prominent role and overshadows all other elements in the obsessional's living. At times it may be so severe that the person doubts that he has really taken a breath or performed a task that, in fact, he may have completed only a moment ago. This may lead to the kind of behavior which has come to be the hallmark of compulsive behavior — compulsive handwashing, a tendency to recheck doors to see that they are locked, and the like.

These well-described phenomena were presumed to be evidence of the person's hostile intentions toward others (for example, in rechecking the locked door or turning off the gas). The handwashing compulsion or the need to check up on one's mate was presumed to represent guilt feelings that were being dealt with by expiatory or *undoing* activities. Although such factors may be present, it is clear that the element of doubt in these instances may be the compelling factor that requires the activities to be repeated endlessly and often in circumstances in which hostility plays no role whatsoever. The behavior represents an all-pervasive aura of doubt and uncertainty that does not permit the person to have any conviction of having completed a task; the rechecking is an attempt to achieve some degree of certainty about the matter.

The latter explanation clearly accounts for the repetitive, ritualized behavior of a young man who had to review the contents of his pockets repeatedly before leaving for work in order to be certain that he had not left anything behind. He checked his wallet, pen and pencil, glasses, handkerchief, notebook, and small change and keys. No sooner had he finished his inventory than he would need to recheck it, and then again before leaving the house, and yet again in the car, and another time finally on arriving at the office before he could abandon the review for the rest of the day. There was no element of hostility in this ritual, merely a fear of making a mistake. Likewise, doubt was the issue in the behavior of a young lady who insisted on checking her lights, switches, and electric plugs repeatedly to make certain they would not set off electrical fires. After one survey of her apartment she would need to repeat it endlessly until some accidental factor or shortage of time forced her to stop.

Frequently, the doubts about all aspects of living, including who one is and what one desires, may paralyze all action. If one feels that his behavior, however trivial, may have disastrous consequences, it is understandable why action must be delayed or abandoned. The obsessional remains immobile and passive and abandons all pretense of making choices. He acts only when circumstances force him to, and then he feels the decision was made by default and not by choice. This allows him to disown the action if it is embarrassing to him. He blames fate or the circumstances that have denied him control of the behavior.

Psychodynamics of Doubting

Freud thought that the obsessional's doubts were extensions of his ambivalence and incapacity to love. He maintained that the obsessive doubts his own capacity to love because of the existence of hateful feelings toward the loved person. These doubts, Freud concluded, then spread to all the obsessional's activities and relationships because ambivalent feelings exist throughout nature. While it is clear that the obsessive person is often incapable of loving another, it is an aspect of his ambivalence and doubting and not the result of it. It is the feeling of danger in committing himself and abandoning doubts about another that prevents the obsessional from falling in love. Being in love means being concerned about the feelings and reactions of another person, who is not entirely under his control. In surrendering one's freedom in a committed loving relationship, the feelings of rejection or unacceptability are particularly painful and threatening. One must therefore be certain that one's partner is an ideal choice, free of petty critical evaluations of him, and that nobody else is better suited to him. Being at the judgment of others is anathema, and so he must be beyond doubt in his selection.

In one sense ambivalence is the experience of wanting and not wanting at the same time. After a while, it begins to stimulate doubts and uncertainties about one's integrity and honesty, but it results from the inability to commit oneself, which stimulates further doubts about oneself and others. It becomes a vicious circle that continues to expand unless interrupted by therapy. In the therapeutic process, the doubting expresses itself also as an incapacity to love and an avoidance of involvement with the therapist in a warm, tender relationship. Anger, hostility, and unfriendliness are more easily expressed and acknowledged because they encourage distance. Whenever the patient feels some warmth or intimacy for the therapist, he will immediately counter it with doubts about its purpose. He derogates it by thinking that the tender feelings must be devices to entrap or deceive the therapist, or else it may get labeled as latent homosexuality by the patient (or therapist). In this way, the doubting serves to prevent intimacy instead of being the result of it. Certain elements in traditional psychoanalytic theory tend to support this view by suggesting that tender feelings are defensive reaction-formations against hostility. If the patient acts in a friendly manner or expresses warm feelings toward the therapist, he is asked to explore the underlying feelings, implying that tenderness is a defensive response rather than a primary feeling. This is widespread application of the concept of an aggressive instinct and the primary role of hostility in human affairs. Consequently, ambivalence is fostered and tenderness is viewed as a defense, so that the doubts that are already predominant in an obsessional's neurotic structure are reinforced by the therapist's own doubts about the expressed feelings of the obsessional. The doubting must be viewed as a defensive rather than a reasonable response to uncertainty. All decisions, particularly those involving human relationships, must have an element of uncertainty that healthy functioning must accept. Risks must be taken to get ahead with living. This the obsessional cannot easily accept.

Sullivan viewed obsessional doubting as a response to the need to avoid clarity and understanding. He felt that certainty was a menace to the obsessional in the communicative process. The obsessional needs to distract, confuse, and cloud up communication; he tends to get into a panic when he begins to establish some clear line of understanding or come to a definite point of view. Sullivan assumed that the doubts were designed to obscure issues and to keep the environment at a distance by demanding advice or assistance, which usually alienated the other person or set him off at a distance, preventing any real involvement. Doubt does seem to serve this purpose along with the others already mentioned. However, the confusion created by the doubting is secondary to its role of avoiding error and the recognition of imperfection. To avoid being wrong, one must never take a firm stand and must always be ready to take either side.

Commitment also implies assuming some responsibility for the outcome of behavior. When the obsessional hedges on the issue of his responsibility, the wavering interferes with the maximum success of his endeavors. It often seems that the disregard of the outcome of an activity enhances and improves it by reducing the anxiety connected with it. However, a total lack of concern or involvement in a project will reduce the enthusiasm for the task and thereby impair the performance. It is clear that in terms of performance, an uncommitted attitude may be less destructive to the outcome than the tense, preoccupied, anxious activity of the obsessional. In the face of a decision that cannot be avoided, the obsessional may assume the role of a disinterested spectator in order to allow the activity to proceed more effectively. However, he cannot divorce himself completely from the outcome, and his obsessional patterns are quickly manifested.

Extent of Doubts

When the doubts begin to reach psychotic proportions, the obsessional may become uncertain about whether he has internal organs or whether he really exists — which, in turn, may produce massive delusions, misidentification, and confusion as to the very existence of people or places. Some schizophrenics' delusional denial of members of their immediate families, geographical and historical landmarks, and other facts is also related to the severity of the patients' doubts about themselves and their environment. Therefore, they cannot permit any definite opinions or decisions about such matters as long as the doubts persist. Similarly, the nihilistic delusions of the depressed person — in whom we find the denial of the existence of large areas of his universe including his internal organs — are also the result of profound doubting.

The issue of doubting is also reflected in the problem of free will and free choice. While pretending to make a choice, the obsessional is actually being forced by his neurosis to act in the way he does. Free choice is possible only when one is prepared to accept all the possible results of his decision and take the risks of failure. It is no longer freedom if choice is limited only to enterprises that have certain and absolute outcomes. Choice is eliminated, since only one path is permitted. Unless doubting is abandoned as a major element in decision making, freedom of choice does not exist. At the outset of therapy, the obsessional cannot make a free choice about either getting treatment or the need for change; therefore, the therapist cannot require or expect that such a patient be without doubts about his motivation and desire for change. Clarity, conviction, and free choice regarding his desires, interests, and motivation can only appear as therapy proceeds.

Rigidity

The patient's rigidity is manifested in his posture and muscular tonus as well as in the persistent, ritualized, inflexible, and single-minded style of thinking and acting. There is no real exchange or response to the ideas of the other person. Whatever concessions or techniques are employed, he expects agreement on his terms alone. He is frequently described by others as being stubborn, headstrong, willful, and determined to get his way. He is unable to shift his attention and interest to allow for any change of subject in his conversations. He certainly cannot allow his attention to wander or to permit spontaneous thoughts to occur. His rigidity makes it difficult for him to move; but once in motion in a particular direction, it is difficult to stop or deflect him.

Rigidity, or the fixed pursuit of a course of action, can be a guarantee of a certain outcome if the path has already been tried successfully. Rigidity characterizes the ritual, which is a stereotyped activity that permits no variation or alteration. By an absolute adherence to known and guaranteed patterns of thinking or behaving, the obsessional feels that he greatly enhances the possibility of a favorable and safe outcome.

This rigidity or stability of purpose is extremely useful in the performance of tasks that require intense concentration. However, it interferes with originality by avoiding novelty in one's living. If a person must focus on facts or intellectual data, he frequently misses the emotional tone or quality of a situation. This is particularly true in interpersonal or social situations when the facts of an event are often subordinate to the nonverbal communication by gesture, glance, and other somewhat covert signals. The rigidities of the obsessional are observable in every aspect of his living, since the adherence to prescribed rules or established patterns of behavior provides an inner security.

Such pervasive rigidity seems to be contradicted by the ambivalent attitudes which the obsessional displays. However, he is rigid about his instabilities as well and may thus resist inflexibly any effort to alter his more extreme ambivalent attitudes. Under these circumstances, rigidity about not taking sides preserves the myth of intellectual and moral integrity and his "open mind."

Ambivalence

Ambivalence is a quality evident in all people. Everyone at one time or another will have mixed and at times opposite feelings toward the same person. In psychiatry, however, the term has taken on a special meaning. It was first used by Bleuler to describe the contradictory feelings noted in schizophrenia; the patient exhibits marked fluctuations in his feelings of love and hate, which may coexist in varying proportions toward the same person. Freud, too, was impressed with this phenomenon and explained it on the basis of unconscious feelings which are inconsistent with conscious ones. Freud assumed that when a person outwardly professed love but belied it by his actual behavior (which conveyed hate), his hateful feelings could be unconscious. Freud believed that marked ambivalence was the basis for severe conflict and personality disorganization, as in the neuroses and psychoses.

It is naive and idealistically visionary to conceive of absolute and unconditional feelings of love or trust toward another person in the realistic world of denials, frustrations, limitations, and disappointments. As the infant and child are required to conform to the requirements of the culture in which they live, discipline replaces permissiveness and demands are made of the child, which he may not completely accept or enjoy. In addition, he inevitably faces some disappointments, disapprovals, and punishments — as well as rewards, satisfactions, and tenderness — from the significant people in his life. In this way, ambiguous and mixed feelings of love, trust, hate, and distrust become tied up with the same person, without necessarily producing conflicts. These contradictory feelings toward the same person often present problems in terms of the qualities of good mother or bad mother, preventing the individual from seeing the parent as a whole integrated person. This process is described as *splitting* and in extreme manifestations is presumed to be a characteristic feature of some personality disorders.

The obsessional, however, is unable to tolerate ambiguities and unpredictable responses. He has great difficulty with the ambivalent feelings he recognizes in himself and others. To be certain of how others feel about him, he must either have absolute power over the other or be unaware of the other's negative feelings. He could also be so committed to a relationship of love and trust with another that he might have no doubts about that person's feelings. Since the obsessional has great reluctance to commit himself fully, he finds himself trapped in a contradictory goal of trying to eliminate ambivalence but at the same time maintaining it; this produces great tension in his relations with others. He generally manages this dilemma by having immoderate views about people or things. In this way he may have extreme and absolute feelings but also be able to shift to the opposite extreme, thus managing to maintain ambivalent but absolute attitudes. He may even consider this a virtue and an example of his flexibility. However, it is really a way of not acknowledging ambivalences.

Ordinarily, we try to acknowledge and to a certain extent accept the failings and deficiencies in others, particularly in those we love. We may be critical and resentful at times, but we do not reject such persons completely if they should let us down or if they fail to recognize or reciprocate our tender approaches. As long as the overall feeling is one of positive interest and affection, we are able to accept temporary feelings of disapproval or disappointment toward and from these persons. The obsessional cannot tolerate such uncertainties; he views ambivalent feelings or tolerant attitudes as weak or dishonest. He has contempt for what he calls a compromise with deficiencies and demands of himself that he maintain firm, fixed attitudes without qualifications or reservations. Thus, the awareness of ambivalent feelings leaves the obsessional feeling weak and threatened. When he notes such ambivalences, his guilt and anxiety are related to the hostile elements in these feelings and to the self-derogatory attitudes that are then stimulated in him, since, as I indicated earlier, he is extremely reluctant to acknowledge tender elements in his ambivalence.

Freud tended to overemphasize the hostile issues as the focal concern in ambivalence; he believed that the hostile feelings accounted for the guilt and self-derogation that resulted. However, hostility is not the only element that produces guilt; ambivalence in interpersonal relationships is also related to the cultural attitudes about loyalty and dedication toward those who support us as well as one's intolerance toward ambiguities and ambivalence. Freud was greatly influenced by his own cultural back-ground, in which children were expected to behave properly and to respect their parents without any show of defiance or rebellion. Ambivalence was not tolerated and a display of anger or hostility toward parents was quickly followed by stern punishment. However, covert ambivalence flourished while outward demonstrations of unfriendly attitudes were discouraged. Freud was describing a situation that was widely prevalent in the middle and upper classes of some cultural groups. Child-rearing practices and child-parent relationships, however, have been vastly altered in the intervening years. Some cultures have become permissive and have allowed children to express their negative feelings as well as their positive ones toward adults. Mildly hostile gestures have been encouraged in other cultures. At one time, permissiveness was presumed to be the basis for later securities, whereas at another time (and based on later findings) the setting of limits and discipline was presumed to be the basis for developing healthy adults. Cultural practices vary. Demand feeding of infants was followed by more scheduled feedings, and each program was supported by most authoritative statements and held to be the certain road to sound mental growth. The prevailing trend over the past forty years, however, has been to encourage the child to express his negative feelings toward adults, as it is assumed that such feelings inevitably occur in the course of a child's development and that it will be less damaging for the child to express them than to suppress them.

Certainly when ambivalences are accepted guilt feelings are lessened. This development not only finds some rationale in present psychological understanding of human behavior but also is in accord with the freedom of expression encouraged in democratic societies. It reflects the notion that love or affection should be earned and not simply expected or demanded by an authoritarian figure who has the physical power to enforce such a demand.

The requirement of total loyalty and devotion and a parental insistence of absolute love and affection can only create conflict and anxiety. This is particularly true when such demands are made by parents in a family situation in which a minimum of tenderness and love is present. The contradictory and hypocritical family situation is particularly conducive to developing an obsessional problem in the children. Joseph Barnett has emphasized this matter in his theoretical descriptions of the cognitive disorder he feels characterizes obsessional processes. When a child grows up in a family where deeds and verbalizations are discrepant and where the child's expectations are not the same as those of the parents, he develops an innocence and ignorance of the real world. It is from such a family background that obsessional patterns are most likely to develop as a means of coping with the ambivalent feelings that inevitably occur. As demands for absolute devotion are most likely to come from parents who are themselves obsessional, it is easy to visualize how, without the need for a constitutional explanation, children become obsessional. Doubts, guilts, and uncertainties stirred up by the child's mixed feelings are often dealt with by denying or being selectively inattentive to one segment of these feelings, giving a spurious notion of resolving the ambivalence. (This process is often called *repression*.) At other times obsessional rituals and preoccupations are widely used to distract the child from disturbing ambivalences. If such defenses work, the child may seem to have firm and positive feelings, but he feels divided or at war with himself.

When the child is entirely dependent on adults and is therefore insecure and vulnerable, too rigid demands for control of his behavior (as well as his sphincter) may cause him to develop severe anxieties, which he attempts to limit by obsessional ritualistic patterns and rigid standards of performance. Compliance is often the price the child must pay to guarantee acceptance and to prevent rejection.

It is small wonder that early childhood is normally "loaded" with obsessional behavior patterns. If the situation is extreme, a neurosis may develop to allow the child to deal with the expectation of complete rejection. The amount of obsessional patterns present in childhood is an index to the degree of struggle of the dependent child in an unreasonably demanding environment. In families in which dissidence is forbidden and perfection is demanded, obsessional rituals and phobias will be more common. If the family situation encourages outspoken feelings and allows for the child's deficiencies, such symptoms may be minimal.

The relationship of obsessional developments to ambivalent attitudes has put the emphasis on the need to control hostility. However, ambivalence goes beyond hostility and may develop out of the discrepancy between the infant's idealized conception of all-giving parents and the parents who demand more controlled and socialized behavior. Ambivalent attitudes occur simultaneously with, and are not the causative agents in, obsessional developments. The inevitable disciplinary measures required in bowel training, achieving cleanliness in eating, dressing oneself, and the like may provide ample opportunities for feelings of anger and disappointment toward the adults who previously were completely permissive and accepting. The same background for the production of obsessional defenses produces ambivalent feelings; the guilt which follows reflects not only the hostile feelings that are felt but also the inability to fulfill the adult demands and requirements.

In later years, the obsessional's recognition of ambivalent attitudes is looked on as weakness; he demands positive, "black or white" attitudes on all questions. This applies not only to feelings about people but also to matters of taste or preferences in such areas as music and art. Clearly, it is not weak or dishonest to suspend judgment or to have mixed feelings on issues where absolute determinations cannot be made, as in matters of aesthetic taste. On some occasions, it may be the essence of integrity to avoid extreme positions. But the demand for absolutes and certainties does not necessarily imply conviction. The obsessional requirement insists on absolute judgments when only aesthetic preferences are possible. Although the obsessional's directness and unequivocating opinions may convey the impression of honesty and forthrightness, they also convey the picture of an opinionated, rigid individual.

Ambivalence, ambiguity, and uncertainty are unavoidable ingredients in human existence. To function effectively and without undue anxiety, one must recognize this existential fact. The obsessional who tries to overcome these issues through perfectionistic and superhuman achievements is doomed to fail.

Much mischief has been produced by the notion that ambivalence involves feelings of love and hate and that the resolution of the ambivalence would result in the cure of many neurotic problems, including the obsessive-compulsive neuroses. It leads to the simplistic notion of "letting out anger" or "screaming" at one's mother as a way of resolving the ambivalent feelings toward her. Such expressive therapies that relate neuroses exclusively to pent-up hostilities may give temporary relief in explosive tantrums, but in the long run they complicate the already convoluted and confused situation.

Ambivalence is the natural outcome of human development and produces difficulties only when absolute and rigid attitudes are demanded of one. It is then that guilt feelings and feelings of unworthiness are experienced, together with expectations of rebuke and rejection. Therefore these feelings must be kept under control and out of awareness, even though they may represent wholesome and independent responses to people or events.

Closely related to the problem of ambivalence is its opposite — the tendency to think and feel in extremes or to react in an all-or-none manner. As the obsessional is concerned about this tendency, he justifies his demand for absolute control on the basis of preventing these extreme responses from occurring. The exaggerated feelings he experiences are often the result of his incapacity to allow minimal reactions to be expressed. Since he lives in extremes, his expectation in relinquishing some control is to respond in the extreme — that is to feel completely out of control — and this is completely unacceptable to the obsessional (as it is for anyone else). The heart of the matter is whether human reactions and responses need to be "all or none." The obsessional views all situations and experiences only in extremes. Any compromise or acquiescence is viewed as weakness. He despises the indecisiveness in himself and insists that he must always be firm and definite. The pattern seems to derive from the desire to convey a picture of a firm, integrated, and positive person, which the obsessional wants very much to be.

In the atmosphere of all or none, tenderness cannot be given in a total sense, since it is already viewed as a weakness and as giving in to someone else — which leaves one vulnerable. Like the other characteristics of the obsessional described above, these extremes do not occur all of the time. They are, however, sufficiently present to be consistent elements in the personality structure.

All or None

Much of the symptomatology of the obsessional state — such as the subject's meticulousness or sloppiness, dependent or independent attitudes, and absoluteness or pervasive doubting — is related to the tendency to respond in extremes. Any in-between attitude is viewed as weakness. Being average or ordinary is contemptible, and mediocrity is the disgraceful acceptance of one's limitations. The obsessional therefore sees people as either exceptional or ordinary. There is no room for anything in between.

When the obsessional is forced by circumstances to recognize his limitations and to acknowledge that he is, after all, a mortal human and not a superman, he may become quite depressed. Why does he react so violently to the notion that he is only human? On one level he does wish to be like everyone else, but on another level he has a need for absolute control and certainty with guarantees that he be a superman. To him, an ordinary person is weak, helpless, unable to control the universe — someone who is pushed around and forced to yield to the control of others. The obsessional cannot acknowledge the fact that everything is not all black or white and that not everyone is either totally in control or controlled entirely by someone else. Most people function more or less independently while at the same time they are dependent on others. The obsessional equates normality with stupidity. For him, anything less than perfection is mediocrity, which is intolerable. He cannot recognize that acknowledging one's limitations enables one to achieve realistic goals. With his extreme all-or-none philosophy, the obsessional may have expansive but impossible goals, which he then makes little effort to achieve. His goals usually remain on an idealized and verbalized level, mostly unrealized. His failure to achieve them is often rationalized as being caused by the interference from others.

"Mediocre" is the derogatory label he applies to most hardworking, successful (or unsuccessful) people. Some other people are idealized, glamorized, and exaggerated far beyond the reality of the situation. These idealized images can rarely withstand close inspection, and when reality sets in, these persons are the ones who are treated with venom and exceptional bitterness. Such shifts can occur very quickly when a single or minimal flaw is discovered in the idealized figure. This problem presents itself regularly in therapy when the idealized therapist is seen as perfect, flawless, calm, and completely in control. This view can be radically reversed if the therapist displays a flaw, however insignificant. He may forget a name or an incident, make a grammatical error, or express an opinion the patient feels is mundane or trivial. He is instantaneously toppled from his throne without any consideration of the circumstances. Excuses, explanations, or accidental circumstances are unacceptable. The therapist is no longer the ideal, a superman. Unless this is observed, noted, and dealt with, it can produce a prolonged treatment situation in which the patient overtly is cooperative and compliant but covertly feels superior, condescending, and contemptuous of the therapist and the process. The patient must be confronted with regard to this exaggerated demand and expectation of others.

To be acknowledged as a leader, beyond fear of danger or criticism, is rarely possible. Yet this is what the obsessional insists on being, since he feels that some have achieved this (for example, a president or a king) and therefore it should be available to him. Accidents of fate, birth, or genius do not exist; for him everything is possible. In spite of these professed beliefs, the obsessional is reluctant to take the initial steps toward, or to assume any risks in arriving at, these goals. He cannot run for office if there is a danger of defeat. He will not gamble unless all the odds are in his favor. He will buy only two sweepstake tickets, but he will be furious if he loses. While his demands are at one extreme, his willingness to accept the risks and challenges to achieve these goals are at the opposite one. Hoping to win a Pulitzer prize for writing or a Nobel prize for scientific achievement, he will produce the brilliant plot or develop the ingenious scientific experiment, but he will not carry the program to fruition. Instead, the rewards of victory will be enjoyed in fantasied parties and receptions that will make it even more difficult to pursue the drudgery of the task, since the achievement has already been acknowledged.

The problem of extremes characterizes all the neuroses, even though it is particularly noticeable in obsessional states. All neurotic symptoms appear to be exaggerated responses, extreme activities, or overcompensated defensive developments. This phenomenon is not yet clearly understood. The parallel in the external world or in the organisms is that of adaptive techniques overcoming physical deficiencies. Animals lay millions of eggs to guarantee the survival of some; the plant kingdom abounds with excesses to assure minimal survival. In the same way, the leukocytes respond in excessive amounts to invading organisms as the repair apparatus overacts to insure results. In addition, there are parallels to the all-or-none reaction in the obsessional state that resemble the response of the nerves, which appear to react in this fashion. The tendency to overreact, which is evident in obsessional behavior, is an intrinsic part of the tendency of living matter to approach all dangers and threats as serious, even if they are trivial. The full force of the counterattack or defense may be brought into action to overcome the attack. The obsessional often acts if he is unable to distinguish the serious from the trivial danger, or else he magnifies all the dangers in order to be invulnerable to any kind of attack.

GRANDIOSITY

A significant outcome of the tendency to deal in extremes is the development of grandiose attitudes toward oneself. This is the obsessional's response to his attempts at omniscience and omnipotence. It is likely that he looks on himself covertly as a superperson, even while he feels helpless and impotent. Because he sees himself as someone who is striving for perfection, or believes that he has already achieved it, he has a grandiose view of himself. Often he expects others to acknowledge his grandiose self and is offended or angered when that does not occur. These claims are not based on reality achievements, but on fantasized and introspective appraisals of himself. It is not the expectation resulting from a realistic appraisal of his capacities and capabilities but an outgrowth of the high standards and impossible demands he makes on himself. It is his unwillingness to settle for anything less than the best that makes him feel superior to others and is frequently responsible for arrogant and contemptuous attitudes toward those who will settle for "second best."

In spite of his arrogance and grandiose contempt for others, he feels also that he is inferior to others and therefore unsafe, producing what Karen Horney has described as *false pride*. It is a pseudoesteem or neurotic esteem, based on an exaggerated standard, rather than a true pride based on actual achievements. As has already been indicated, his perfectionistic demands often result in notable feats of scholarship. His devotion to a task and his desire to know everything frequently result in achievements of great competence. Even under these circumstances, however, he remains dissatisfied and critical of his realistic achievements, which never seem able to satisfy his strivings for absolute perfection. The realistic basis for pride is lost in his own disparagement and disappointment and in his failure to achieve absolute success. This picture presents a difficult therapeutic problem because the obsessional esteem in the patient's neurotic achievements prevents the growth of a valid esteem. He tends to belittle his small therapeutic gains and yearns only for superhuman, impossible achievements.

A striking illustration of this situation was that of a highly competent but seriously obsessional physician who became greatly upset when he could not diagnose every disorder that was brought to his attention. While he read all the current literature in his specialty, he was dissatisfied because he could not keep up with all the other specialties as well. The need for absolute and certain diagnoses led him to prescribe costly and often unnecessary laboratory studies to eliminate even the slight possibility of the most remote disorders. He could never accept obvious evidence for simple and common diseases, but felt impelled to rule out all possibilities of exotic and rare diseases. In addition, he felt that he should be expert in all the subspecialities, and would refer patients to other specialists only with the greatest reluctance and with feelings of failure.

The doctor's patients would occasionally interpret his meticulous and exhaustive studies as evidence of concern, interest, and great competence. More often, however, other interpretations were made that were less flattering, as patients would note that much of his uneasiness seemed stimulated by his doubts and requirements for perfection. They noted his lack of concern for the costs involved in the tests prescribed or for the discomfort of the extensive studies he ordered. Most of his patients became critical of his obsessive indecision and pervasive doubts in spite of the enormous amounts of time and devotion he gave to each patient. Secretly, he felt that he was the best and most careful doctor in the world. He thought of himself as a twentieth-century William Osler and secretly claimed that if he were given enough time he could diagnose every human disorder that appeared before him. Consequently, if a patient became critical or dissatisfied, he was deeply offended and very surprised. He could not entertain the slightest possibility that his claims were extreme or that his conception of himself was grandiose. Instead he prided himself on being precise and concerned only with the patient's welfare. He could never admit that he had made an error in diagnosis or that an incomplete diagnosis was the result of his deficiency or incomplete knowledge of the voluminous detail of the medical sciences. Instead, he always blamed the pressure of circumstances, which did not permit him enough time; the technical deficiences of the laboratory; or the demands of the society for quick patient turnover. He had to insist on repeated tests with the feeling that ultimately the answer would turn up. If he discovered a lesion, particularly a potentially cancerous growth, he felt guilty for not having discovered it earlier, regardless of when it might have occurred. The possibility that the lesion had not existed at the prior examination never relieved him of the obsessional demand that he should have somehow predicted or anticipated the lesion. Such episodes would reinforce his overzealousness. Instead of acknowledging man's inability to anticipate or predict everything, he refused to make final statements on the possibility of the presence of a lesion, as such would indicate that it just might have been present in previous examinations. This increased his indecisiveness and doubting.

Another example of this type of grandiosity was manifested by a man who was quite annoyed with his wife when she refused to countenance his open liaison with another woman. He could not understand her resistance to inviting this woman to live with them. He felt that if his wife really loved him she would readily support such an arrangment, since he really needed both women and felt that he was entitled to it because he was such a valuable member of mankind that ordinary rules should not apply to him. After his wife obtained a divorce he offered her the same arrangement in his new household. He could not see that his demand was grandiose and egocentric.

For the obsessional, always being in the right (exempt from criticism) is not a grandiose claim. It appears to be a resonable expectation of someone who deserves it. He feels that his high ideals and exceptional standards merit only the highest rewards. Therefore, he should be free from criticism because he tries to be perfect, and he should not be criticized if he fails to attain perfection. Since this does not ordinarily occur, a great deal of resentment and grievance is felt by the obsessional. This pattern of grandiose development, with its claims for exemption from human responsibility, is the cause for many complications that occur in compulsive states, such as obesity, addictions, and kleptomania. In these conditions, the individual acts as if he were beyond human limitations or restraints. He insists that calories do not affect his weight or that he can steal without ever being apprehended. The kleptomaniac maintains that he is entitled to what he takes and that he is not doing his "all" if he fails to steal when the opportunity presents itself, as his goals are worthy and exemplary. Likewise, the compulsive gambler or alcoholic insists that he can stop at any time and that the human frailties that beset a gambler or alcoholic are alien to him. He can hold his drink or stop gambling any time he wishes to. Their grandiosity maintains and sustains their addictions, in addition to being responsible for its development.

It is inevitable that the grandiosity of the obsessional will be challenged directly or indirectly by the notable successes and achievements of others in comparable age groups. This is particularly upsetting to the obsessional, as he can no longer deny such achievements. He will attribute others' successes to their being richer, more opportunistic, without his integrity, and other such factors. He will maintain that he could have done as well if he had really wanted to or if he had sacrificed his principles. More and more rationalizations are required as times goes by, as are more obsessional symptoms to overcome the realistic differences. The illusion of grandiosity is not maintained by realistic achievement but by a denial of the realistic limitations.

RITUALS

The obsessional's need for absolute control requires an omniscience and omnipotence impossible to achieve. Reality constantly intrudes itself into his life in spite of all his efforts to deny it. Therefore, he may call on superhuman sources of strength and power in order to overcome any human limitations. The efficacy of magic is presumed to be enhanced by a ritualistic performance, which is precisely defined by the magic maker and passed on to future generations. The belief in magic and the possibility of influencing others through verbal formulas or ritualistic behavior has been practiced since the beginning of man. While magic was more prominent in the daily routine of primitive man, it still plays a role in the activities of modern man, in his religious practices, obsessional activities, or both. It was more prevalent when man's control over nature was severely limited by his lack of comprehension and knowledge; his dependence upon magic was great and it played an intrinsic role in his culture. As man's knowledge increased, his need for magic in its primitive forms decreased and was manifested in more artful and sophisticated ways. However, in times of crisis and stress, it may still dominate an individual's behavior. This is what takes place in a subtle and symbolic way in the obsessional mechanisms. Rituals and the belief and dependence on magic are common accompaniments of obsessive processes and may be the most prominent elements in the obsessional neurosis. The ritual is an attempt to control the individual's behavior by focusing his attention on the ritual, thereby distracting interest away from other matters. In addition, it may be a symbolic performance in which the individual controls those elements he feels may go out of control.

In a more general sense the ritual is an attempt to gain some control over a superhuman agent by a direct appeal in which the action is presumed to be satisfying some desire of a god. It may be simply expiatory or supplicatory when repetitive formulas or placating sacrifices will influence the gods in one's behalf to perform the action desired. This is the essence of any ritual as it is peformed by the most primitive or the most sophisticated religious systems.

Primitive man, when exposed to real threats to his physical existence, had few resources to deal with these dangers. The rituals were as varied as the dangers man faced, and there were malevolent as well as benevolent powers to appeal to. The rituals developed from the needs of a group, which were largely determined by geographical factors. The advent of monotheism simplified ritualistic practices by focusing on one godhead, although patron saints for particular needs were retained. Some rituals could be carried out by the individual himself, whereas others required the intercession of an especially gifted holy man, who would make contact that ordinary mortals presumably could not. Some rituals have remained unchanged as they passed through primitive magic, paganism, polytheism, monotheism, and throughout the developments in science. Others became more refined and rationalized. The scientific advances that increased man's understanding of nature have been accompanied by a decrease in the use of rituals and magic. The overwhelming influence of religious systems of all kinds has diminished as man's grasp of the world and of himself has increased.

Freud viewed religion in some part as an obsessional symptom because of the extensive use of rituals in religious practice. I think it is more correct to say that the use of obsessional mechanisms is widespread in religious practice but that religion is a more complex sociological and anthropological development than mere rituals or obsessional practices. Religion expresses a deep desire for significance, relationship meaning and transcendence. It goes beyond the obsessional's desires for certainty and security.

Rituals still persist in many disguised forms even today (and in all superstitious beliefs) because man is still unable to control nature, nor is his knowledge complete. Despite all the monumental advances in science and technology, man is still handicapped in his control of energy sources and the cataclysms of nature. The knowledge of his physiology and the functioning of his inner world are still in a primitive state. Because of the finiteness of his existence, both in longevity and cerebral capacity, it is likely that he will never reach a point where he can exercise total control over himself or the universe. It is therefore not surprising that he continues to have large numbers of ritualistic practices and magical assumptions in areas such as the possibility of life after death, the existence of heaven, control over all disease, or life on other planets. As knowledge expands, science replaces ritual. Cloud seeding begins to replace the rain dance. However, in areas totally beyond man's control, only the acceptance of his limitations will permit him to abandon superstition and ritual. It is in this connection that the relationship of ritual to obsessional behavior becomes evident. The persistence of rituals in spite of man's scientific advances owes largely to man's insecurity and uncertainty, which still prevail. Reason, logic, and knowledge are still not sufficiently developed to permit man to function comfortably in the face of human deficiencies; thus, ritual in the obsessional mechanism is pervasive.

Obsessional Rituals

Obsessional rituals are as variable as the elaboration of man's imagination. However, they usually have some relevance to the particular needs of the individual and may frequently be symbolic dramatizations of the particular problems the individual is attempting to resolve. Like religious rituals, they consist of a series of repetitive activities that must be precisely performed; otherwise anxiety ensues. The individual may have some rational explanation of his behavior, or else he may be aware of the nonsensical nature of the behavior and yet be unable to stop it. It cannot be terminated by reasoning or persuasion, as its origin is not intellectual and therefore cannot be altered by "clear thinking." While the ritual may be meaningless intellectually, its function as an agent of control has emotional roots and can be understood only in these terms.

At times the meaning of the ritual may be obvious and its adaptive purpose clear. If one has obsessional preoccupations about murder or destruction, the ceremonious avoidance of knives or rituals involving measures for the control of one's anger are easily understood. On the other hand, some rituals are incomprehensible in their entirety. For example, a young man was compelled to walk 12 paces north and 5 paces east ten times while repeating the word "aroribus."

Doubting is an integral part of many rituals. For instance, the obsessional must go back and try the door handle to make certain it is really closed, or recheck the gas-stove jets to make sure they are turned off, or rewash his hands to guarantee their cleanliness. These are not illustrations or admissions of human frailty but compulsive efforts at perfection. Originally, Freud utilized such examples to emphasize the underlying hostility or the aggressive impulses that lay behind the obsessional ritual. He felt the ritual implied that the obsessional covertly wished to burn his house down and was overtly trying to avoid this by rechecking the door or the gas range. The obsessional's inclinations toward violence needed to be checked by his avoidance of knives or other dangerous instruments. However, many rituals have nothing to do with violence or sex. With the young man who checked and rechecked his pockets' contents, the ritual was a matter of control and certainty. Such rituals are more common in the obsessional, although they are not so dramatic as those that are clearly involved with the avoidance or control of violent or sexual impulses. Rechecking is a way of overcoming the doubts and uncertainties about an action.

The patient who must pick up all the matches he sees, wherever they may be, is rechecking to absolve himself of any responsibility for a conflagration that might occur and for which he might be blamed. Ordinarily, a person washes his hands with the expectation that he will do a reasonably good job at it, but not so the obsessional. He might express it as follows: "If I wash again, I will reduce the risk of germs, so washing again and again will reduce the risks altogether. But two hours of hand washing is all I can spare, since I must also dress perfectly, eat perfectly, etc., which will make further washing impossible." One patient spent seven hours, fifty-one minutes, and twelve seconds by his stopwatch (his latest time, a reduction from twelve hours and twenty-six minutes) making absolutely certain about his cleanliness and redoing the entire procedure if he deviated in any way from his ritual. Paradoxically, he showered only once in three or four weeks. His toilet and shaving procedures were equally long and tedious, yet he could not alter them, even though he reduced his toilet activity to three hours from four and his showering to two hours and forty-two minutes. The termination of these rituals is often the result of outside pressures, since the doubting that produces the symptom prevents a firm decision to terminate it. At times, the rituals become so extensive that they exclude all other activities; ultimately the routine demands of living require their termination. The ritual is designed to achieve certainty, and the fact that this is impossible to achieve is the sad fact of the obsessional illness.

One type of ritual has attracted a great deal of attention from psychiatrists for many years: the ritualized avoidance reactions we call *phobias*. They enable a person to control his living to the extent that he eliminates the possibility of anxiety that may occur in certain situations in which he feels vulnerable and in which he may lose control. In this way, the phobia is precisely the same as other rituals.

Rituals are often dramatic and striking elements in the obsessive-compulsive neurosis, particularly when they are bizarre and carried out in public. However, rituals of all sorts play a significant role in everyone's life in that they are economical ways of managing one's life. Each of us has a particular way of going to bed, a particular routine for the morning ablutions, and a wide variety of stereotyped and repetitive ways of performing many routine activities. Such "rituals" do not necessarily involve the avoidance of anxiety except as they routinize the regular activities of one's existence, avoiding the requirements of choice or decision. They are analogous to reflex action except that they are learned and are capable of modification when necessary. It is this element that distinguishes such rituals from obsessional rituals, which are required to cope with potential dangers, and, if changed or interrupted, will result in severe anxiety. The impeded or interrupted obsessional ritual will cause feelings of restlessness, uneasiness, and apprehensiveness in the neurotic — a reaction that accompanies the feeling that one may get out of control. Thus, if the danger of losing control is experienced as being very great, the reaction to interrupting the ritual may be overwhelming.

The compulsive ritual that consists of a series of motor acts is identical to the relentless repetitive and persistent thoughts of the obsessive process. It also controls by taking over the central interest of the individual, thereby diverting his attention. It is a very successful device and can be so oppressive at times in its demand for attention that the individual is unable to do anything else. At other times it may be present, even though the person is actually performing other activities that require his interest. At such times he is obviously unable to give his full attention to the matter at hand.

Freud assumed that every ritual was accompanied by an *undoing* because the obsessional's ambivalence was involved. Freud described it as "a kind of negative magic ... in which the individual's second act abrogates or nullifies the first in such a manner that it is as though neither had taken place whereas in reality both have done so." * The undoing not only preserves the ambivalence but also is an expiating activity. However, this interpretation of Freud stems from his notion that obsessional rituals develop from aggressive or sexual impulses. In his examples, the undoing can be an effort to restore the balance. If, however, the ritual is the result of a need to deal with weakness or an illusion of helplessness, an appeal for help to a superior being may be experienced as humiliating for someone who must always be strong and powerful. The undoing element may therefore deny the weakness in the appeal and restore the feeling of omniscience and omnipotence. The extent of the undoing element in the ritual will be determined by the obsessional's need to maintain face and the illusion of strength in spite of his illness. Some are unwilling to face any awareness of their helplessness if the attitude of the culture toward weakness is highly condemnatory and such ritualistic appeals for help may require an undoing element. On the other hand, the ritual itself may be viewed as an aspect of the obsessional's power rather than as a weakness.

The undoing is also an aspect of the obsessional's doubting tendency;

* Sigmund Freud, *The Problem of Anxiety* (New York: W.W. Norton, 1936), p.33.

even in this instance he cannot fully commit himself to the ritual. The undoing may need to be part of the ritual as an expression of the uncertainty of one's use of it. Undoing, however, is not necessarily a part of every ritual, nor does it seem to be an essential element in it.

CHAPTER 3

Commitment, Sex, and Marriage

DEPENDENCY

The obsessional's attempts to be in complete control of himself and others is endangered by his dependency needs. He would prefer to achieve an independence that would free him entirely from needs that he cannot fulfill for himself. However, totally independent living in a physical and psychic sense is an impossibility for man.

Dependency is a natural state that characterizes both living and nonliving matter; it is an essential quality in man's existence. Whether a person's relationships are parasitic, symbiotic, cooperative, or collaborative, he depends on other humans as well as on nature. Yet he must balance his dependency with a measure of self-sufficiency and a capacity for independent behavior that will enable him to be creatively adaptive.

At times, because of some physiological defect or psychological "warp," an individual has a greater-than-normal need of others and is more dependent upon them. When this occurs, a great deal of trust must be present in a relationship or else security is decreased instead of increased. Unless one can be certain that his dependent needs do not stimulate resentment in others, there is always the danger of feeling rejected or abandoned. Such doubts can sometimes be assuaged if one is in a position of strength and able to demand absolute loyalty from the person on whom he is dependent. Generally, however, the dependent person is in doubt about his status and position and avoids a total commitment to the relationship. In this way he can fill his dependent needs but still be free to move elsewhere if his dependency is threatened. A commitment means the abandonment of total independence for a state of mutual interdependency.

Being dependent is interpreted by the obsessional as being out of control and under the influence and control of someone else. This extends not only to his intimates, on whom he can feel almost comfortably dependent, but also to inanimate objects such as an automobile or a TV set. He may refuse to acknowledge his dependency on the forces of nature and react with anger, frustration, or exaggerated feelings of helplessness when, for example, changes in the weather interfere with his plans. At such times he is forced to acknowledge his dependency and he may be forced to alter his plans and his freedom of action. If such circumstances continue for a long period of time, a breakdown may occur in his obsessional adjustment. This may be the case when a hitherto integrated obsessional pattern begins to crumble with the birth of a child, which forces a limitation on the freedom of action of the parents. This was the situation in a twenty-four-year-old patient who was severely obsessional with numerous rituals all designed to sustain marked feelings of uncertainty and create an illusion of superman grandiosity. He was caught on a superhighway during a snowstorm and could not proceed to his destination. In the twelve-hour delay until the road could be cleared, he became actively delusional and psychotic, insisting he had a message for the president on how to achieve world peace.

The most striking and debilitating difficulties occur when the obsessional is unwilling to acknowledge his dependency on the proper functioning of his body and its limitations. He resents the fact that his energies are limited or that he cannot engage in exercise or play without some rest even while he is intellectually aware of the limitation. He may resist going to sleep; to do this would be to acknowledge the limitations of his physiology and would also mean giving up control. For this reason many obsessionals have difficulty in falling asleep, though they usually sleep soundly once they do.

They also resent having to limit their eating and drinking and become furious if their excessive indulgence produces some gastric distress. They may refuse to wear a coat or rubbers; weather should not determine their actions. They make impossible demands on other people as well as on their material possessions. Cars should not break down, airline schedules should not be altered, and gadgets should always function perfectly. The obsessional is angered when such events occur and feels them to be impositions on him. He cannot accept accidental events as part of human existence, and he is resentful of them. He may be even more incensed at his inability to control or prevent these accidental occurrences than at the inconvenience they may cause.

In addition to man's very limited control of natural forces and his own life span, he cannot control the time and circumstances of his birth or the historical, political, social, and economic events that preceded his birth. At best, he has only minimal influence over them during his own lifetime. The obsessional flatly refuses to accept this situation, even though he is forced to live under these realistic limitations. He will deny the existence of such issues and will act as if he can live forever, or else maintain the myth that his death is solely the result of his own choice.

A commonplace observation of obsessionals is their intention that they neither feel nor look their age. They insist on being young forever, and while they acknowledge aging in others, they will not identify it in themselves. Their forgetfulness, breathlessness, and getting fatigued are attributed to all sorts of physical ailments other than simple aging.

Dependency on people is even more difficult for him than dependency on objects. He deprecates peoples' usefulness or minimizes his need of them. When this is not possible, he will try to rationalize his dependency by claiming that he is fulfilling the other person's needs and that actually it is the other person who is dependent on him. At all times, however, he resents and criticizes the part of himself that requires help and is dependent on others.

Marriage is difficult for the obsessional not only because of the degree of commitment required but also because of the inevitable dependencies that are a part of marriage. Unwittingly, he comes to depend on his partner and his family in a way that is highly satisfying but difficult to accept. Marriage serves to avoid loneliness and often produces satisfying emotional exchanges. It may be so rewarding that he cannot consider abandoning it and therefore feels trapped and resentful toward his partner. An awareness of this dependency may account for a great deal of the derogation and contempt he expresses toward marriage and his mate. By such means he can minimize his feelings of dependency. He will criticize his wife at the same time as he will covertly lean on her for most of his needs. He may tyrannize his partner in order to maintain an illusion of power and independence. Thus, he may appear to be "boss" or in control when he is the one who is more dependent.

This dependency-independency struggle manifests itself in a tug of war for domination and control that is regularly present in obsessional households. It is not long before the obsessional begins to feel that those he is dependent on — whether a marital partner, colleague, or friend — are malevolent exploiters while he is a generous benefactor.

Every human activity requires some measure of commitment, and the degree of commitment is often determined by the individual's ability to be dependent. The word *commitment* implies a person's emotional and intellectual involvement in a project or relationship in which one's concern and interest is strong enough to make it a significant and meaningful activity. It is synonymous with the French word *engagement*. In recent years the philosophical explorations of the Existentialists have focused more attention on this aspect of human functioning. We can often permit ourselves to be totally committed in activities in which we have complete control, where we feel safe and secure from the powers of others to humiliate or hurt us. Fantasizing is such an activity, and many people commit themselves to it with gusto and enthusiasm. On the other hand, since most activities are carried on with other people, we are subject to others' needs and desires as well as our own and cannot control the activity completely to suit our own interests. In such situations, commitment may be tentative and conditional unless we can feel secure and trustful about the outcome.

It is a truism that one derives benefits from an experience in proportion to what one puts into it. Therefore the rewards that can be expected from an activity will depend upon the degree of commitment to it. Indifference, which is the antonym of commitment, reduces the possibilities of personal satisfaction in any activity. For some, frenzied activity and spurious enthusiasms cover up boredom, and the difficulties of real commitment. Total commitment is difficult for anyone; it requires a feeling of total security.

Most of us, however, put enough into an activity or relationship that we are committed to the extent that we can be. We therefore enjoy and grieve as our fortunes expand or diminish. Since we take responsibility for the failures, we take pride in the achievement. Commitment involves a stake in the relationship. The obsessional has great difficulty in achieving such relationships, since he cannot abandon control or relinquish his escape routes. His commitment is tenuous and conditional, permitting him to run when the going gets rough. Thus, he maximizes his control over his life by limiting his commitments, but at the same time he tends to minimize his satisfactions in living.

In extreme states of insecurity and feelings of danger, which are characterized by flightiness and extreme distractibility, there is the absence of commitment. Such a state is often called *manic excitement*. When the obsessional cannot avoid a commitment, he will try to protect himself against the risks of involvement. This may involve prolonged investigation, and although it may serve a valid purpose by supplying necessary facts about a situation, it may discourage others from becoming involved with him. If he is forced to become involved, the commitment is often hedged with doubts, procrastinations, and loopholes, and even this degree of engagement may be postponed as long as possible.

An obsessional commitment is often made by default. For example, failure to act on a deadline produces effects that are equivalent to a commitment to some action or inaction. If one procrastinates about a down payment on a house, the house may be sold and the problem of whether to buy is settled by default. This kind of a decision leaves the obsessional dissatisfied and not fully committed to the project. While he resents being pushed and forced by circumstances, he will often remove himself completely from making the decision by using cards, ouija boards, astrology, tea leaves, and other supernatural devices. A mistake or an unsatisfactory decision can then be blamed on fate, and he can feel justifiably aggrieved that fate never plays him a good turn. While such involvements may appear to be commitments, they lack the vital interest and dedication that comes from making a personal choice. Under circumstances of default, involvement is tentative, hesitant, and ambivalent. At times the obsessional may cast all caution aside and make an impulsive and rapid decision, claiming that time did not permit a careful examination of all the factors. This is another way of avoiding a full commitment.

Such was the case with a severely obsessive young man who studied the specifications of all the new model automobiles in order to make the best possible purchase. This process was so involved and became so prolonged that by the time the survey was finished the new model arrived and he had to begin his survey all over again. This sequence continued for a few years until need finally forced him to make a choice. He then purchased the first car he saw on a used-car lot, a car which lacked all the engineering qualities he had until then considered absolutely essential. He took no responsibility for this choice, claiming that he was forced into the decision by the automobile industry and the therapy.

Thus, the obsessional rarely commits himself to a person or task even when his interest is very urgent. The dilemma of involvement without commitment is particularly emphasized in those professions where decisive actions cannot be avoided. The obsessional tends to become involved in sideline activities, such as sports, or in unrelated business ventures in which he allows himself total participation, since his security does not depend exclusively on that activity.

It is his fear of commitment that accounts for so much of the obsessional's indecisiveness. A young executive who was involved in a foreign financial activity was pushed into an obsessional panic when he was asked to choose between a post in Western Europe or one in Asia. He was a bright and energetic person who was, however, quite obsessive. His decision had to serve too many contradictory requirements, and he examined each alternative, balancing one against the other in an attempt to predict every possible consequence. When he leaned toward one choice, the other immediately began to look better. He drew up charts, tables, and balance sheets, but when the deadline was reached he made his choice on frivolous grounds. No sooner was it made than he began to regret not having made the other. As he felt that his choice had to be the perfect one, it was viewed as a life-and-death issue. One can understand the agony and anguish involved in making such a commitment.

MARRIAGE AND THE OBSESSIONAL

The marriage commitment is particularly difficult for the obsessional because it involves interpersonal issues as well as legal sanction. Since it is possible to achieve some degree of control over things through intelligence or know-how, the obsessional can manage some power in his dealings with objects or ideas. Emotions and feelings enter into the relationships with one's fellowman, and these elements are much harder to control; the degree of control over interpersonal relationships is always far less than is possible in nonpersonal relationships. The commitments are always partial and contingent and, if possible, have an escape route. When no legal or social ties bind the relationship, there is always a threat of dissolution from one moment to the next.

While marriage has legal binds, the marriage commitment may still be minimal. As times goes on, however, the obsessional comes to enjoy the commitment if the atmosphere offers some security. The marriage commitment may even encourage greater closeness. The early days of an obsessional marriage can be extremely difficult, but if the marriage survives, it may prove quite therapeutic. However, the demands for perfection and the critical and derogating behavior that the obsessional brings to a marriage may prove too much to withstand. This is especially so when only a minimum of warmth and affection is present. The obsessional's insistence on "honesty" leads him to tell all, regardless of its effect on his partner; unless some enduring qualities are present to override such arrogance, disaster may very likely occur. As the obsessional has difficulty in admitting a mistake or acknowledging a failure, he may postpone dissolving the marriage, so that in the long run it may work out after all, and in such a case delay may be efficacious.

When both partners are obsessional, the complications are increased geometrically. This is not an uncommon situation; in spite of the well-known aphorism that opposites attract, only an obsessional can feel comfortable with another obsessional. The courtship is characterized by cautious restraint (which pleases both partners), and the decision to marry is followed by many postponements and delays accompanied by uncertainties and uneasiness on both sides. As long as the demands on each other are minimal and neither partner feels trapped, all goes well and the marriage may work out. These marriages are punctuated by frequent and dramatic power struggles, in which each obsessional partner is striving to gain the advantage. A draw is the most frequent outcome. The relationship is characterized by minimal commitment on each side, while each partner demands maximal commitment from the other. Often when the relationship is moving along nicely, one partner may pull away to avoid the possibility of too intense an involvement. As one pulls away, however, the other pushes harder in order to be reassured. Such pressures are interpreted as power ploys and produce further withdrawal in the partner. The situation produces the typical neurotic spiral wherein the fear of rejection requires gestures of reassurance but instead produces further rejection. At one point the rejected individual gives up and may make no further demands. At that time the partner stops withdrawing and may proceed to demand assurances, since he is not being pursued. This temporarily breaks the vicious circle and if the marriage provides some benefits, these limited demonstrations of need and affection may be the only tender moments the couple has.

Such seesaw movements are quite common, and the symbiotic balance is maintained because there is some commitment, even though it is minimal. There is a covert agreement of limited involvement in the marriage, and each partner pursues his own interests and desires, although they share the common responsibilities. While pursuing their individual needs, they occasionally call on each other to fill those satisfactions that require a partner. Mingling and companionship are part of this agreement, and each partner knows the limits and extents of these boundaries. Failure to respect these rights and limits is a frequent cause of marital difficulties in such situations. Intimacy is achieved to a limited degree, and as the years roll by, the boundaries of the commitment to one another may even be extended.

Marriages such as these are generally loaded with elaborate book-keeping systems to make certain that one partner does not give or get more than the other. Accounting of contributions — whether of time or money or who did the dishes last — is generally accurately recorded in the account book or the memory of each partner. Concessions, compromises, sacrifices, and contributions need to be equalized so that neither partner is taken advantage of. Love, affection, and gifts are also handled in this way;

to give too much affection might be read as too great an involvement. Besides, one partner might presume that such displays are evidence of unconditional commitment, so that he will take advantage of the other. If one gives too much, the partner may interpret this as coming from a great need, which would indicate a weakness. One needs to keep his partner in doubt as to how he stands in the relationship, in order to exercise some degree of control over it. This is how the obsessional limits the danger when closeness cannot be avoided. To play it safe, he must be able to detach himself quickly from the relationship, should it become necessary.

These marriages are often conditional in every sense, and the marriage was probably made possible in the first place because the partners agreed in advance that if all did not go well they could get a quick and easy divorce. This type of agreement limits the commitment at the outset, and while it may be necessary in order that the marriage take place, it provides the basis for the later dissolution.

Such relationships are continually under tension and consist of a multitude of games in a tug-of-war to establish a degree of safety and security by having some measure of control over the other person. Love is the main piece of equipment, and it is used in a variety of ways to gain and hold the advantage. The goal is to guarantee one's own security and to fulfill one's own needs without offending or alienating the other person by withholding too much. A proper balance must be struck, and this requires great skill in the art of gamesmanship. By giving enough to stir up expectations and a promised return, but not too much so as to imply that one is "gone" and available, the obsessional hopes to maintain a fine balance that will ensure a stable relationship while retaining sufficient autonomy to dissolve it without too great stress or pain.

The obsessional hopes and expects that he will advance his strivings for perfection and absolute control in his marriage. His wife will overcome his own deficiencies. She should be free, spontaneous, warm, tender, decisive, and secure. She should have social graces and the ability to charm all the people that he would tend to alienate. If, however, she does have these qualities, he tends to criticize and derogate her and her petty concerns. On her side, his high standards and perfectionistic demands, as well as his grandiose conceptions of himself, have undoubtedly led her to the hope of some fulfillment through his presumed strength and power, which, she assumes, will lead him to the pinnacle of success. Such hopes and unrealistic expectations are doomed to disappointment and create much dissension in the marriage because each partner is able to claim honestly that he or she made no promises and that the expectations came from the other's own neurotic demands.

Such a situation of unrealistic expectations produced continuing crises in a marriage where the obsessional partner, who was bright, perfectionistic, and ambitious led his wife to expect high levels of achievement — an ambassador if not a college president. However, his obsessional indecisiveness, arrogant contempt for climbing the ladder, and expectations of being propelled to the top by the magical recognition of his talents never permitted him to use his real capacities. A persistent atmosphere of disappointment and resentment prevailed, and only in therapy was this dilemma revealed to both parties.

When very rigid and uncompromising obsessionals marry, there are few possibilities for success. Every marriage, regardless of how overt the understanding of limited commitment, requires some "give and take" and the necessity of abandoning total control of the partner. Unless one is prepared for some compromise, the partner will reach a point beyond which he will refuse to go. At this point the marriage will dissolve, since the demand to be right will overcome even the minimal rewards of marriage. It then becomes a game of "chicken," and fatal results ensue when neither partner will give way. Disaster can be averted only when one partner is prepared to acknowledge that a stubborn refusal to compromise endangers both partners. When obsessionals marry, the difficulty ultimately reflects the limitations of a commitment that minimizes the responsibility for the success of the marriage.

An interesting situation ensues when a hysteric and an obsessional marry, as they often do. The spontaneous, open, and freely expressed emotionality of the hysteric looks very attractive to the obsessional. Likewise, the quiet, reserved, controlled, but well-informed obsessional fills the gaps for considered judgments and decisions, in contrast to the hysteric's impetuous leaps into activity. To the extent that the characterological patterns are not extreme, the mix works very well. However, it can be too fragile and tenuous when the obsessional begins to criticize the histrionic, hypocritical, or superficial emotional displays of the hysteric, whose effervescence and charm is belittled and derogated. The obsessional's serious and intense behavior is valued, and the pervasive critical atmosphere that results can destroy the original symbiotic relationship.

SEX BEHAVIOR AND THE OBSESSIONAL

While the particular patterns of sex behavior may vary in each obsessional, depending on his idiosyncratic experiences and background, they are also influenced to a greater or lesser extent by the typical characterological attitudes involved in the obsessional defense. The need for perfection and the resistance to any involvement or commitment, coupled with an uneasiness about receiving or giving tenderness, greatly influences his sexual behavior. The issue of control and the fear of loss of control, which are essential elements in the sex act and in the obsessional system, are responsible for many complications in the obsessional's sex life.

Although Freud assumed that a normal sex life was incompatible with neurosis, it is surprising how often the obsessional person, with either mild or severe symptoms, manages a satisfactory sexual adjustment. He can often perform the sex act well and in conformity with the latest sex manuals and acceptable sex practices. Due consideration is given to the partner, according to the latest psychiatric theories. The act itself, however, is stilted, unspontaneous, and routinized. Experimentation is avoided or carried out according to a program. While this approach may be entirely satisfactory for the male partner, it may be unsatisfactory for the woman. At other times, it may be mutually enjoyable, as in the quest for a perfect performance, much care is given to the needs of the female.

The sexual enlightenment that followed Freud's discoveries encouraged the female to expect and demand some satisfaction from the sex act while promoting a series of notions that could increase difficulties. For the female, orgasm became a realizable goal, and as a result of her newly acquired knowledge, it was assigned as a responsibility of the male. This, however, was only the first step toward a perfect sex act. Mutual and simultaneous orgasm was also expected. Since it is already difficult for the obsessional female to achieve an orgasm, the expectation of simultaneous orgasm as a usual outcome is generally impossible to fulfill.

In addition to these complications, the assumption of two types of orgasm in the female (vaginal and clitoral), and the notion that one was more mature and therefore more desirable, was also popularized by psychoanalytic theory. This assumption was not based on psychological evidence but was the result of applying the libido theory to the female. This postulate was necessary, in order to make the elaborate psychosexual development scheme for the male fit the pattern of sexual development for the female. Finally, the tendency to view the male as the active sex partner and the female as the passive sex partner has encouraged doubts about one's sexual potency and adequacy when one's desires and interests run counter to this assumption.

While the notion of orgasm for the female is a justifiable expectation, the insistence on the simultaneous orgasm is an idealized notion encouraged by the overzealous and mistaken view of the possibilities of psychoanalytic therapy. This has placed a burden on both partners; they should achieve this desirable goal or else feel that each has failed and that the relationship must be bad. However, even under the best of circumstances, simultaneous orgasm is not common. In spite of the obsessional's capacity to control his ejaculation in order to achieve the ideal orgasm for his wife, such perfect timing is often impossible and cannot be expected to occur every time.

The assumption of dual orgasms (vaginal and clitoral), however, has produced even more mischief and distress, not only in obsessional marriages but also in every other kind. This notion is popularly interpreted as an orgasm achieved only by the use of the penis in the vagina. If any other stimulation is used, such as a finger or other kind of friction on the clitoris, it is considered a clitoral orgasm and therefore both imperfect and immature. The obsessional female already has enough difficulties in letting go, and requires a great deal more clitoral stimulation than is usually necessary. The failure to achieve orgasm with or without manual manipulation may not only make the woman feel inadequate but may also leave a feeling of failure in the male who has been unsuccessful in producing an orgasm for her.

"Recent studies of female sexual behavior also fail to support this notion of a clitoral and vaginal orgasm. After an extensive examination of the factors, it is clearly a physical impossibility to separate the clitoral from the vaginal orgasm as demanded by psychoanalytic theory."* Masters and Johnson agree completely with this formulation. Orgasm appears to be the result of the stimulation of the highly sensitized clitoris in the female and the glans penis in the male. Although one means of stimulating these organs may be preferred over another, orgasm results from such stimulation. The presence of the penis in the vagina is a convenient arrangement for the mutual stimulation of both clitoris and penis. Since there is a growing conviction that sex activity is a process to be enjoyed and practiced in whatever manner is conducive to the greatest mutual enjoyment, provided no physiological or psychological damage results to either partner, the manner of stimulating both the glans penis and clitoris — whether by means of the mouth, finger, or vaginal insertion — should not be viewed in terms of either normality or maturity. While there is a preferred posture to insure procreation, a more enlightened attitude toward sex should avoid assigning priorities to particular methods of achieving sexual satisfaction.

The obsessional male or female, in his or her striving for perfection, is thus easily subjected to the cultural descriptions of normality, masculinity, and femininity and can be pushed into unrealistic and invalid pursuits. Consequently, the concept of double orgasm, which has questionable

* M.S. Sherfy, "Evolution and Nature of Female Sexuality," *Journal of the American Psychoanalytic Association* 14 (1966): 28–129.

validity, has complicated and aggravated the obsessional's sex life. Instead of being an occasion of intimacy and potential pleasure, sex becomes a test and trial of his adequacy. Efforts involving the use of the hands or the mouth to improve the possibility of pleasure are considered evidence of immaturity or perversity. The concern about producing an orgasm for the woman often results in premature ejaculation as a result of the tension involved in the efforts to prolong the sex act. Premature ejaculation is also the result of anxiety, which produces a loss of control in the male. In contrast to the female, where anxiety and tension interfere with the relaxation required for an orgasm, the male responds by ejaculating too quickly.

The presence of anxiety severely handicaps the sexual activities of obsessional couples. The anxiety is generally described as *performance anxiety* and is attributable to the unrealistic expectations and demands for a superior performance or the intolerance for a less-than-perfect performance. Premature ejaculation is a common sexual dysfunction in obsessionals when the demands produce anxiety that interferes with adequate control. *Ejaculatio tarda* is another possible disorder in the male obsessional when his requirements produce such intensity and compulsive control that he cannot relax sufficienty to allow sphincter action to occur.

The Element of Control

The need to be in control at all times, even during the sex act, prevents the woman from allowing something to happen to her. Instead, she must manage her own orgasm and do it herself. The sex act ordinarily proceeds with a gradual increase in tension of the entire musculature, particularly in the pelvic area. The orgasm is a climax of a release of tension and relaxation of the musculature. Ejaculation in the male is the result of a spasmodic contraction of the urethral musculature followed by muscular relaxation. Therefore, at some point, the female must let go, or abandon control, just as the male ultimately abandons control to allow ejaculation to occur. It is an instance of human functioning; in order to allow some activity to proceed, one must give up trying to force it to happen. The physiology of sphincter action most clearly demonstrates this paradox: The tension produced by active efforts to force open a sphincter tends to close it even more tightly. To allow the sphincter to open, one must relax and give up the forcing. Thus, anxiety about one's physiological functions may increase the tension and prevent the relaxation required to allow orgasm to occur. In trying desperately to achieve orgasm during intercourse, the obsessional female will generally manage it only after her husband has ejaculated; then, with manual massage of her clitoris, accompanied by extensive fantasizing in which the entire sexual performance is under her control, orgasm can be achieved.

Interestingly, when the issue of control is not crucial, such as in fleeting relationships or if intimacy is entirely lacking, the sex act may be far more successful. This explains the contradictory situation in which the sex act can be far more satisfactory with paramours, prostitutes, or single encounters than with one's own wife. The use of alcohol or other relaxants will also enhance the possibilities of enjoyment for the woman as well as the man.

In general, however, the need to control influences the male's performance far less than the female's. Control over his ejaculation may improve the possibility of orgasm in the female, providing he does not get too anxious about it and thereby bring on premature ejaculation. The treatment of premature ejaculation or anorgasm in the female follows directly on these matters; the patients are taught to relax by taking the focus off the orgasm and onto the pleasure of the activity. It becomes "fun and games" rather than a desperate challenge to confirm one's capacities and competence.

The assignment of specific and limited behavioral qualities to each sex — such as activity as a male requisite and passivity as a female attribute — has played special havoc with the sex life of the obsessional. This notion has been widely accepted, and only in recent years has it been shown that the female, instead of being a passive recipient, plays an active participating role in the sex act. She is more than a mere receptacle, and her sexual organs, particularly the vaginal canal, play an active role in drawing and transporting the sperm up into the uterus. However, the prevailing conception of sexual roles — which requires that the male be the aggressive initiator of the sex act while the female wait patiently to be invited — has greatly aggravated role problems for obsessional couples because control is considered entirely the prerogative of the male and activity or initiative on the part of the female is regarded as unfeminine and immature. The lusty and sexy female has needed to inhibit her passion or suffer critical condemnation, whereas the withdrawn, inactive female has been supported by the cultural prejudices toward passivity. Any of her inclinations toward active involvement during or before the sex act had to be restrained. Similarly, the male who might need some reassurance from a supportive or expressive wife was forced to be the initiator and active participant. Any interest in allowing his wife to be more active might be judged as unmasculine. This pattern could also be related directly to the notion of "who is on top" in the sex act. This matter is significant for the obsessional;

therefore, a positional variation could be the basis for considerable distress in this type of person. However, reversing positions in the sex act can frequently provide greater satisfaction for the female by allowing her more freedom of motion and better control of her movements during coitus, and physiologically, it enhances the possibility of achieving orgasm. For the male, reversing positions can also be a most enjoyable variation, provided he does not view it as "feminine." However, popular prejudice — initiated and encouraged by scientific misconception — has interfered with this variation of sex activity and has produced fear and guilt with the implication that the position is indicative of homosexual tendencies. Such labels discourage experimentation and exploration. For the obsessional who is already burdened with problems, prohibitions of this type increase his difficulties. The female is prevented from enhancing her possibilities for achieving orgasm, while the male is prevented from the beneficial abandonment of some control in the sex act.

Mutuality and "Guarantees"

Sex should be mutual activity in which each participant feels free to be both active and passive, giving and receiving — without concern as to who is doing the giving or receiving at each moment. Since the goal is pleasure, "who is on top" is significant only in terms of whether it is pleasureable for that couple. The obsessional's reticence about sex is the outcome of his problems in other areas of living. Since he is already insecure and restrained, the conventional notions of masculinity and femininity throw additional burdens on his sex activities.

Added to the burden of producing or achieving orgasm is the obsessional's need for guaranteed performances, which require rigid sexual patterns in which curiosity and experimentation are dangerous. Unless he can have some assurances, either personal or cultural, that his excursions will not produce rejection or loss of esteem, he will not attempt them. He must secure, if possible, control over his performance. This requirement often leads him to make appointments for his sex activity, thus preventing spontaneous demands or refusals; such arrangements may be made days or hours in advance. They need not be verbal, and generally such arrangements are made by signals tacitly acknowledged by both partners. This eliminates the possibility of a direct refusal or rejection, as the signals need not be acknowledged. While such arrangements minimize the risks of being rejected, they also reduce the spontaneous quality of sex, which can be a source of great pleasure. Instead, the act becomes more like a business deal — routinized and properly executed — than a response to passion or love. The sexual patterns of obsessionals are inevitably influenced by the partial involvement and commitment of the partners.

The impasse about sex is overcome when the sex needs of one partner become so strong that he will yield and make a gesture of surrender, which will allow intercourse to take place. After a passage of time, however, grievances begin to accumulate again and the need to exert control takes the upper hand. This forces the partner to become defensive, and the vicious circle is set up again.

This drama was reenacted regularly in the life of a young obsessional couple who played out their roles with almost total lack of awareness. Sex was a game in which each partner awaited a signal from the other before proceeding. After a respectable waiting period following the previous sexual episode, the man would look increasingly hurt and neglected, hoping to force his wife to make a positive gesture that would then allow him to take a more definitive step to initiate sex activity again. The wife, in turn, would delay the gesture as long as possible, waiting until her husband's pained demeanor would make her feel guilty. She would then give the signal, by way of taking a shower or going to bed early.

The husband was almost totally preoccupied with sex and whether he could succeed in getting his wife to agree. While his pride and manliness were at stake, his notion that he was thoughtful and considerate of his wife was his justification for not taking the initiative by direct action. She, in turn, would try to postpone agreement as long as possible. Her role was always that of the martyr who agreed in order to please him, although her real aim was that of appeasing her guilt. Sex was never discussed between them, and therefore neither partner knew for sure what the game or the rules were.

The situation would proceed as follows: Upon arrival from work, the husband would scrutinize his wife for gestures of friendliness that he could interpret as a sexual invitation. In order to avoid his tendencies to misinterpret her gestures, she would have to be careful not to be too warm or accepting. Instead, she might announce a new symptom of some physical discomfort or regale him with stories about how tired she was or how much work she needed to do. This was invariably interpreted (and not always correctly) as a notice of evasion. At first he would find this mildly irritating, but after a few days it would visibly annoy him. If she would question him at these times, he would deny being angry. As he got more annoyed, however, he would avoid all friendly gestures. This would be the signal to her that sex was necessary to forestall further difficulty with him, and she would proceed to give him some sign announcing her intention and permitting him to be sure about the acceptance of his advances. As there were long delays and a continuing "trial" of his potency, the sex act invariably terminated in premature ejaculation, followed by a long session of manual manipulation to enable her to achieve an orgasm. Intercourse occured only when the two were annoyed, guilty, angry at each other, or sexually starved. It was small wonder that the sex act was not pleasurable for them.

On other occasions when the tug-of-war became tiresome and both partners were more friendly, sex activity would be agreed on long in advance and preparations that exaggerated the significance of the occasion would be made. Sex for them was never the outgrowth of spontaneous warmth, friendliness, or lustful desire. Instead of an occasion for romantic fun, it became a great event designed to deal with many issues.

This tug-of-war was directly related to the inability of either partner to relinquish control of the marriage in general and sex in particular. There was too much at stake in maintaining the position of a strong, controlled, and uncomplaining partner whose love was so great as to outweigh the inadequacy of the sex performance. Each had to be firm and resolute and not expose his or her need for the other, for fear of being hurt, rejected, and despised as a weakling. The inability to let go and deal with sex as an experience rather than a therapeutic event was manifest in the woman's incapacity to have an orgasm except after prolonged manipulation, which produced so much weariness that she could no longer exert any control. She resented not being able to have an orgasm by herself and of having to be dependent upon her husband. Most often her orgasm would be achieved when clitoral manipulation was accompanied by fantasies of being overwhelmed and having control taken away from her. Again the issue of control, so central to the obsessional disorder, interfered strikingly with the sex life of this couple.

One of the remarkable benefits from psychotherapeutic work with both the husband and wife was the marked improvement in their sex life. The release of the need to control and recognition of the mutually destructive patterns enabled them to enjoy sex and make it an experience of pleasure, mutual exchange, and commitment. The husband could prolong the act before ejaculating, and his wife's orgasms became more frequent. Sex was not avoided, and for the first time in their marriage, they began to look forward to intercourse as a more spontaneous experience.

As has been suggested earlier, the obsessional has no conviction of the possibility of obtaining tenderness gratuitously; he feels it must be earned through good works. While the development of tender, loving relationships requires both activity and concern, it cannot be achieved exclusively through deliberate promotion and calculated effort. Warmth and intimacy grow out of tender exchanges implicit in meaningful relationships. One can not buy, nor can one demand, tenderness from another through exploitation or by barter. It often comes without being asked and can be achieved when one is simply available and friendly. The obsessional can neither comprehend nor believe this in spite of much evidence to the contrary in his marriage. The uncertainty and distrust of his likableness makes him suspicious of any tenderness that comes spontaneously to him; if it is unearned, he cannot accept it comfortably. When it occurs in this way he responds with contempt for the giver, whom he feels must be weak and a sucker. He may also become suspicious of the giver's motives, feeling that the tenderness is a device to manipulate and control him. This makes marital exchanges extremely difficult.

Since the other person's tender activities are viewed with caution and suspicion, every move must be countered by a gambit in which one tries to get the advantage and the control over the relationship. The experience of tenderness is viewed as a move in an ongoing struggle. In the struggle, strong negative feelings are generally not openly expressed. Such feelings, however, can accumulate and become so overwhelming that the obsessional feels guilty and expects retribution. The guilt feelings may produce exaggerated displays of affection and interest, which may take on a begging and obsequious tone. This type of behavior may make him angry at himself as well as with his partner because he views it as weak and as evidence of being under the control of the other person. It kindles his destructive fantasies and sets the vicious circle into motion again.

The obsessional person may rationalize this reaction by implying that the hostility and destructiveness come from the other person and that his reaction is a response to it. He justifies his behavior by implying that the other person, if permitted, would overwhelm and disintegrate him, and therefore it is necessary for him to actively oppose and overcome the opponent. In sex or outside it, the obsessional's capacity for tender exchanges is seriously hampered; he operates in the borderlands of uncertainty as to how he stands with regard to other people — even in a marriage that seems to be proceeding well or in sex activity that is pleasurable.

TIME AND THE OBSESSIONAL

It is most significant that while the obsessional insists on total freedom to remain uncommitted and to do whatever he pleases, he demands such commitments from others. At the same time, his notions of freedom are absolute and extreme, and he cannot acknowledge any form of restraint. His apparent freedom and his choices are rigidly determined, however. The notion of being free as a justification for failing to become involved is spurious. His attitudes toward time illustrate his resistances to being committed to the present and thus the allure of the future.

Since time moves relentlessly onward, uninfluenced by man, it offers special burdens to the obsessional. He approaches it as an enemy to be fought and overcome, or dismissed as playing no role in his life. He will often behave as if he had an eternity in which to live and his projects and activities were not bounded by time at all. His plans therefore take no account of the realistic limitations of his life span, and his projects may encompass programs that require several lifetimes to fulfill.

It is preferable for him to maintain the illusion of absolute freedom and lack of involvement by excluding time as a realistic limitation on his life and regarding it as an enemy of all his plans and programs. Failure to take into account the element of time permits his plans to be so elaborate and time-consuming that he may never begin the projects. It is as if the obsessional would be admitting a weakness or a deficiency if he had to acknowledge his dependency on time. Disregarding the realistic presence of time permits the obsessional to disregard normal sleep rhythms or schedules for eating and to be irresponsible with regard to his appointments. As there is always enough time to do everything, the obsessional is invariably late (unless he is scrupulously on time) because he can do just one more thing before departing for his appointment. He is always astonished and remorseful when the tasks can not be completed in his overburdened time frame.

On the other hand, his devotion to decisiveness and precision forces him to be scrupulously prompt and to be intolerant of deviations by others. Such attitudes do not owe either to respect for time or to a recognition of its values; the obsessional is painfully aware of the future as an extension of the present, since he is constantly preoccupied with guaranteeing the future. The "new" is significant only as it may play a role in guaranteeing the tomorrow. The present does not seem to exist for itself; it is often without meaning or significance and must be tolerated or "killed" in order to arrive at the guaranteed and perfect future.

Since he rarely considers the element of time as a factor in his activities, the obsessional organizes it poorly and has little ability to estimate its passage accurately. Long periods of time may be experienced as a few moments, and invariably the estimate of passed time is incorrrect. To overcome a persistent tendency to be late, one patient set his watch ahead. Instead of proceeding according to his reset watch, he would allow for extra time and would usually underestimate it. He would then be later than he would have been had he not reset his watch. This tendency to underestimate the actual passage of time is almost always present in obsessionals.

Because his focus of interest is on the future, the obsessional's awareness of the present may be superficial and cursory; therefore, his recall may be inadequate, sketchy, and, at times, fallacious. Since the past is a collection of "presents," the obsessional's ability to recall his past is limited and uncertain. Therefore, if the therapeutic process rests heavily on an accurate recall of the past, the obsessional presents many difficulties in this respect. Freud made this discovery very early in his research, when he discovered that most of his obsessional patients who described sexual assaults — which became the dynamic for the cause of obsessional neurosis had, in fact, never experienced them. This discovery created a crisis in his theorizing, and he entertained the possibility of abandoning his research because it seemed to be based on falsehoods. After correspondence with his friend Fliess, he reexamined the situation and made a much more significant observation — that is, the effect of fantasy on the mental life. It became clear that what we imagined or fantasized to have occurred in our life was more significant than an actual event. At this time, Freud abandoned the traumatic theory of causation of the obsessional and hysterical neuroses.

While the construction of the remote past may be distorted, the same problems pertain to the obsessional's recall of the recent past. His recollections are mainly in intellectual terms, and he has great difficulty in identifying the emotional elements in these experiences. As the focus is on the future, he cannot clearly understand that the past is a guide to the present, thereby influencing his future. He appears to derive little benefit from past experiences and gets only temporary reassurance from the success of earlier performances. He has, therefore, little reverence for the past and its usefulness to his living.

Unless the present is an exact replica of the past, which it never can be, the obsessional feels a new challenge and a threat in each experience in spite of having resolved a similar situation in the past. There is little carry-over from his success in the past. This is evident in the phobic states, wherein prior confrontation and successful encounter with a phobic situation does not necessarily eliminate a repeated problem in the future. The past tends to become a clutter of irrelevant experiences except as it documents and fortifies the obsessional's neurotic needs and programs.

Because of the obsessional's disregard for time, he soon discovers that he does not have enough time to complete even the most modest project. His commitments to a task are seriously disrupted because he has no real involvements with the element of time. In order to asssemble a record player, for example, he may insist on first becoming an expert in electronic speakers and amplifiers. This turns into an impossible task for which enough time is never available. When the day is over, many tasks are still not completed and he is dissatisfied because time has run out and he must go to bed. Sleep is invariably postponed because he refuses to abandon his activities. There is never enough time to work or enough time to rest.

Insomnia is related to the problem of giving up and abandoning controls; it is quite prevalent in obsessional individuals. The insomniac becomes tense and uneasy when he feels he is falling asleep. He attempts to regain control, but to get to sleep he must slowly relinquish it; as soon as he does he becomes more alert in order to regain it. This goes on until fatigue overcomes him and he can no longer stay awake.

Comparisons

The obsessional's view of time is unlike that of the hysteric, who is more actively concerned with time in the here and now. For the hysteric, the present performance — with its possibilities for influencing the immediate environment — occupies his focus of interest. Tomorrow is an abstraction that is of no concern to him now; he is interested in the effect his performance is achieving at this moment. Prospective considerations, planning, foresight, and utilization of past experiences for the present to determine the future are alien to the hysterical individual and the hysterical performance.

For the depressed person, on the other hand, time exists only as it transpired in the past. The present has no value and the future is without possibility. Time has stopped. It has no significance for him except as it was, and the passage of time is a burden that he cannot surmount.

The preoccupation with the past, in the depressions, leads to a stagnation and an absence of planning for the future. For the obsessional, planning and programming for the future occupies the bulk of his time. The hysteric neither looks to the past nor plans for the future; he counts only the next moment of his existence.

The hysteric's style of living characterizes other immature types of personality — notably the psychopath, who emphasizes the distrust of past and future in favor of what is now available. His philosophy is "a dollar now is better than two in the future." This type of orientation is related to a great distrust of the future; the person hasn't the confidence in his own ability to anticipate a favorable future or else is convinced of a malevolence that will deny him any future possibilities. Therefore, he must grab all he can right now — not to do so is inconceivable. There is only a limited capacity to postpone gratification of all kinds, since there is a strong suspicion that it will not be available later. Only the present moment has any reality for such a person. This is strikingly true for some obese people who must eat all they can at each meal as if no food will be available at the next meal. They are unable to postpone any gratification, as they have no confidence that the future will be able to provide for them. They have no conviction that what they do not eat now will be available later.

Erwin Strauss, an Existential psychiatrist, has viewed the obsessional process as a failure to deal with time as a realistic accompaniment of living. The obsessional person is preoccupied with decay and disintegration. Everything is viewed in relation to the future, since the past has no reality and the present is dead or already decaying. The obsessional has a great need to deny death and acts as if it will never occur. While he abhors death, he finds the notion of a timeless eternity equally frightening. Death, decay, destruction, and violence — anything dealing with uncontrollable elements of human existence — must be kept out of awareness. Strauss believes that the obsessional develops many rituals in order to maintain the dissociation of these unacceptable ideas. Since the obsessional is not able to deny entirely the evidences of death and decay around him, he often has a compulsive fascination with them.

The compulsive need to deny death as a reality often leads to a reckless disregard of danger; the person may push himself beyond the boundaries of normal exertion. He may expose himself to dangers that others would ordinarily protect themselves from. Unlike the mature person, he cannot utilize an understanding of the past as a guide to more adequate performance in the present as a solid basis for his future existence. He therefore cannot benefit from experience, nor does he respect past performances as evidences of present capacity.

CHAPTER 4

The Obsessive Spectrum

Every human is limited in his capacity to influence each aspect of his existence. Sometimes he may be irritated when physical incapabilities or limitations prevent him from doing all that he might wish to do or when the natural obstacles are too difficult to overcome. It is only when a person attempts to achieve superhuman goals that his human frailties become a valid issue. A wide variety of devices are employed to evade or deny such limitations. Belief in eternal life or reincarnation and the delusion of omnipotent control are attempts to evade this kind of awareness.

Such tendencies are omnipresent. Many of the measures employed can be recognized as aspects of the obsessional syndrome. The degree of uneasiness and uncertainty that one experiences will range from feeling endangered at all times to a state of relative ease and security in which only the gross, existential dangers — such as the awareness of one's ultimate death — need to be dealt with. While the use of obsessional patterns is found in all human behavior, it will vary according to one's need for guarantees and certainties. There is, therefore, a broad spectrum of obsessional behavior ranging from the normal (that is, the amount that enables one to function without undue anxiety) to that which pervades a person's living, whether or not it impedes that living or impairs his performance. If it is present in greater amounts and manifests itself in distressing or incapacitating symptoms, it is called *neurotic*. This means that the obsessional patterns are sufficiently encompassing and determinative that they interfere with constructive and productive living.

Why are some individuals less secure than others in an emotional sense? What factors determine the sense of danger and threat that permeates the life of such people? These are the focal questions in all psychiatric formulations because the defense mechanisms that are utilized in one's living are attempts to deal with feelings of insecurity and threats to one's psychic integrity. Does the obsessional defense have some specificity? For instance, why do some people utilize the hysterical mode of dealing with anxiety while others tend to become obsessional? This is a difficult and elusive problem, involving the matter of choice of symptoms in neurotic and psychotic disorders. Clearly, constitutional factors play a role in this choice, as do the parental patterns that become the emotional environment of the growing individual.

Some theorists, namely Freud and those who subscribe to the libido theory, postulate that the choice of symptoms is related to the degree of maturation or fixation of the libido at a particular stage of psychosexual development. Thus, disturbances at an oral phase of development will produce a variety of symptoms and syndromes different from fixation at an anal or genital stage. External factors play a role in this process, and the real threats posed by racial, political or economic factors are also involved. It is a complex issue in which monocausal explanations have no place. Yet there are some factors that can be related more clearly to one type of defense than to another.

If the obsessional pattern is heavily involved with control, it would tend to be present in situations in which the infant or child found himself unable to handle the demands made on him. For example, a child whose early experiences of being able to please or manipulate adults through his repertoire of assorted behavioral devices might develop feelings of personal power — the capacity to control and influence the world around him. This would be in contrast to the child who is unable to please, manipulate, or influence significant adults regardless of what he does or how hard he tries. Although this may be attributable to the rigidity or neurotic tendencies of his parents, he is left with feelings of doubt and uncertainty about his capacities and may develop an obsessional personality or an obsessive neurosis at some time in his life. The first child will tend to have fewer obsessional patterns in his living.

Growing up in contradictory households where parental demands are contrary to their own behavior is very conducive to developing obsessional patterns, since the management of such situations is beyond rational control. Such parents present their children with double binds, leaving them feeling helpless and powerless.

The need to defy, control, or comply as an expression of self-esteem and self-worth comes to play a vital role in the developmental situation, depending on the amount of freedom, coercion, or manipulation coming from the significant adults. If the pressures are extreme, the individual may need to defy or rebel in order to express his own self-esteem. The defiance may become automatic or compulsive and be detrimental to the growing personality. It can produce a rigid, negativistic person, instead of one with a strong sense of will. Some of these issues are part of many theories that center around the process of bowel training or discipline in general as related to the origin of the obsessional disorders. The role of early patterning in obsessional behavior is undoubted, as is the influence of the parental figures and their own obsessional difficulties. It is conceivable that severe obsessional problems in the child can only develop in households where one or both parents are obsessional.

DEVELOPMENTAL FACTORS

Many observers have noted that particular developmental stages in human growth tend to be more closely related to obsessional development than others. Freud stressed bowel training. Certainly the matter of control is an essential ingredient in bowel training, as it is in all sphincter activity. The periods during which the outside world may make excessive or extreme demands in terms of fulfilling the cultural modes may stimulate obsessional patterns, tending to promote or accelerate any already-existing doubts and apprehensions about oneself. Infancy, where greater freedom is permitted, is followed by the childhood, juvenile, and adolescent epochs — where the greatest acculturation occurs. During these periods of development, one must learn to function with the smaller social unit (family) and with the larger units of society. The person must learn to control his sphincter and his clumsy, unruly, and uncleanly traits, as well as his manners, etiquette, style of dress, and the like. The stages of juvenile conformity or the patterning of social or sexual behavior to conform with adult demands may also be the impetus for obsessional developments. Therefore, phobias and other obsessional manifestations may be more prominent at certain periods of development than at others.

Brief excerpts from the early experiences of several severe obsessionals illustrates the relationship of parental demands. A patient, as a child, had a physical defect, which required cautious concern from the parents. At the age of four the patient lost an eye in an unfortunate accident. In her anxiety to protect the child's good eye, his mother was excessively vigilant about all his physical activities. She felt comfortable about him only when he was at home studying. Consequently, academic achievement was stressed far beyond everything else. Nothing less than the best in his class was acceptable. The constant preoccupation with caution and safety in what was pictured for him as a potentially dangerous world made him unable to deal with the universe without a host of phobias and rituals. These began at an early age and continued throughout his life. When he reached eighteen, he had a widespread obsessional neurosis, which impaired his effectiveness in spite of exceptional mathematical skills. His anguish in trying to buy an automobile was described in chapter 3. His tardy, irresponsible, and indecisive tendencies produced occupational complications, which required psychoanalytic treatment.

He had an overpowering need to be in absolute control of himself and the universe at every moment in order to guarantee his safety and maintain his delusion of omnipotent control. He had grown up in an atmosphere charged with danger at every moment, and it was this feeling of ever-present threat that determined his neurotic need to establish guarantees and certainties in his living, rather than any particular trauma or specific series of events.

Another young lady, whose parents demanded perfection, would respond to her grades at school by insisting they could be better. If she had received an A, why not an A+? Nothing was good enough, and she felt herself a failure unless she could be certain that she was the best. While managing to achieve that status in elementary school, it was more difficult in secondary school. Her obsessional defenses finally cracked while at college, where she had a nervous breakdown during the preparation for her first final exam.

Although the beginnings of the obsessional defense mechanisms can often be fixed around the stage associated with the development of sphincter control or traced to a response to ambivalent attitudes toward one's parents, it is also associated with a general atmosphere of doubt and uncertainty about one's ability to modify or influence the environment to satisfy one's needs. The history of obsessional development is as varied as one's environment and the personality of one's parents. The consistent theme in all obsessionals is the presence of anxieties about being in danger because of an incapacity to fulfill the requirements of others and to feel certain of one's acceptance. Sexual complications in the early years —

which were also presumed to play a role in the etiology of the obsessional state — can rarely be identified. In fact, as mentioned earlier, Freud abandoned his notion that obsessional difficulties were the result of an active sexual assault on the child. However, the obsessional frequently does experience sexual problems in his adult life, and he views them as evidence of his incapacity to function in an effective manner.

It is evident that all reasonably effective human beings want to live in an atmosphere in which their skills and intelligence can afford them some guarantee of the outcome of their activity. All humans are motivated to some extent by the expectation of success in achieving their goals. They exercise foresight by using the hindsight of experience and the benefits derived from it. Their plans are based on minimizing risks by foreseeing possible complications and difficulties. However, most people are also aware that not all possible dangers or potential risks and complications can be anticipated and overcome. Unforeseen changes, unexpected complications, accidental, coincidental, and cataclysmic events can always occur, and they often demand an alteration in one's plans. In general, such complications are met and dealt with, and plans are not abandoned simply because everything cannot be accurately anticipated. Because of these ever-present potential complications and the human incapacity to fully control and influence them, man has always needed some devices — rational or irrational — to allow him to proceed with projects where the outcome is uncertain. These devices would minimize his uncertainties and permit a greater optimism than the facts would allow. As man could not affect these unforeseen difficulties directly, he utilized magical devices, delusions of omnipotent controls, rituals, and the whole gamut of techniques described in earlier chapters to give him the illusion of greater control than he possessed.

If this picture of the role of obsessional techniques is valid, it would follow that as man's security increased, his use of obsessional devices would diminish. One would expect a decrease of obsessional practices as man's grasp of the universe extended. Instead, there are evidences of the widespread use of obsessional techniques in all cultures. Certainly the manifestations are more manifest when they are culturally encouraged and are less in evidence when they are derided by the culture. At all times, however, the amount of obsessional practice in each individual varies widely according to his own personal and idiosyncratic experiences. A wide spectrum of obsessional behavior will be found, depending upon the individual's personal security and based on his intellectual and emotional development and the awareness of his powers and its limitations.

At one extreme is a minimum of obsessional patterns, ones that are barely noticeable under ordinary circumstances. At the other extreme, the patterns are so pervasive and bizarre as to interfere with productive living. In the first extreme, which we may call *normal*, obsessional defenses may even enhance one's performance. In the opposite extreme they may produce neurotic or psychotic behavior and may seriously impair one's capacity for living. Between these two extremes are the "more or less" obsessional defenses, which are sometimes identified as a cluster of personality patterns called *obsessional personality*. The total population may be roughly classified into three groups: (1) normal utilization of obsessional defenses (2) obsessional personality structure and (3) obsessional neurosis.

In spite of the widespread presence of the obsessional behavioral pattern there is a tendency among social scientists and behavioral scientists in some cultures to use the term *obsessional* as a pejorative label. Even when the value of such behavior is held in high esteem — such as in neatness or orderliness — it becomes derogatory if it is labeled *obsessional*. The term may also be used to belittle someone else's performance when one feels either envious or competitive toward him. In this way the term is often used as a critical one and the behavior associated with is is derided or condemned. Often, the psychiatrist, psychologist, or social worker, in misplaced zeal, identifies and labels symptoms with the notion that identification is itself therapeutic. There is a tendency to view the ability to supply labels as evidence of one's skill as a therapist.

This type of labeling, however, can be both destructive and unprofitable for the patient; it may produce anxiety which will require further obsessional defenses. In addition, when the defensive obsessional patterns which have been valuable to the individual's integration are merely spotlighted and labeled, they may no longer be effective and the hitherto stable equilibrium may be prematurely and unwisely disrupted. The utilization of obsessional defenses varies not only from person to person but may even vary in the same person at different times. As the situation changes and the pressure increases, obsessional patterns in the same individual may become more and more extensive; and while these patterns were originally within manageable limits, they may become sufficiently widespread to blossom into an obsessional neurosis. Once the patterns become this severe, they generally tend to become more and more extensive and more and more incapacitating. This is the typical vicious circle of the neuroses, in which some of the attempts to relieve the distress of the neurotic involvements only produce further anxiety and more neurotic reactions to the anxiety. While this is true of any neurotic development, it is particularly true for the obsessional neurosis.

If additional burdens and stresses are placed on the obsessional neurotic, there can be a further disintegration of functioning, with the resulting development of a schizophrenic reaction. While this particular development is fortunately not common, it does form the basis for a plausible theory regarding the origin of schizophrenia.

NORMAL OBSESSIONAL BEHAVIOR

The designation of *normal* obsessional behavior may appear contradictory; however, it is preferred only because the word *obsessional* is usually used as if it always implies pathologic changes, even though it may well include the multitude of obsessional patterns that serve constructive and adaptive purposes in human functioning. The difficulty arises when we try to define the criteria for identifying obsessional behavior that can be considered well within the range of normal behavior. Can we be certain that it is useful or productive, in contrast to the neurotic's obsessional patterns? How do we know when the normal obsessional patterns become sufficiently extensive so that we can now call them an obsessional personality structure?

While the differentiation is not particularly significant for theoretical reasons, it has much value in enabling the therapist to clarify his own thinking about which patterns should become the target for study and possible elimination and which should be left undisturbed. This is not a decision to be made by the therapist alone, but one for the patient as well, and it is intimately related to the value of the pattern in the individual's total living. However, such a determination is often beyond the scope of the individual, as at the outset the obsessional does not want to eliminate his obsessional patterns at all; rather, he wishes to improve and perfect them so that they will be invulnerable. He wants to change only to the extent of overcoming his distress at his failure to achieve his superman status. He wants a better neurosis — one without anxiety while he retains all his neurotic patterns. It is the responsibility of the therapist to highlight the destructive aspects of such patterns of behavior and to reduce their role in the patient's life.

It is clear that obsessional behavior can increase one's efficiency and effectiveness in performing certain tasks. The tenacity that characterizes the obsessional often enables him to pursue his goals with single-minded dedication. An awareness of the limit of this dedication may help to decide which patterns require psychiatric scrutiny and which, even if peculiar, should not be tampered with.

For example, in the anxiety not to throw anything away lest it yield information, the obsessional may actually accumulate collections of historical, esthetic, or commercial value. Many of these collections are rationalized on the basis that the items may be needed at some future time, and since one never knows when that might be, it is safer to save everything and throw nothing away. This may result in collections of such items as buttons, strings, and bric-a-brac. Occasionally, a hard-to-get item will be included. Usually it would be more useful and perhaps even more economical to get rid of the old and buy a new one when the need arises. However, the obsessional cannot chance this. His collections are attempts to guarantee that his needs will always be fulfilled. To throw something away is an irreversible act and one that carries a certain amount of risk.

Occasionally, this tendency to accumulate can be productive and can become the basis for a career or a trade. Unless it is unmanageable and begins to interfere with one's living, it should not be labeled neurotic or even noted with the pejorative term *obsessional*. It might be viewed as odd, and if it is excessive enough to be noticed, it might evince some concern in the person himself. Ordinarily, however, the collecting tendency is a part of the person's life that produces some clutter and some periodic annoyance but does not become severe enough to be unmanageable. The person still has some choice; he may often recognize the excesses and may even begin to limit this tendency in many areas.

One patient had to buy every book that dealt with his profession. His library became too large for his small apartment, and under extreme pressure from his wife, they moved to a larger apartment. However, the new apartment soon became overloaded as well. He had to buy every new book to make sure he did not miss any new developments in his field. While owning these books, he could not keep up with the reading; thus, most of them remained untouched or were examined in a cursory fashion. Under treatment, the symptoms improved, as he began to abandon the need to know everything in order to feel minimally competent.

The matter can also be considered from the point of view of the purpose of the collecting, particularly as to what underlies or motivates the collector. Clarification is important, in order to determine whether some therapeutic intervention may be necessary. The criteria of adaptation, which can be applied, are very useful in recognizing whether the tendency is incapacitating or not. On the other hand, the person who collects on the assumption that the articles may have some value in the future differs from the person who collects because he cannot give anything up. The latter acts as if the supplies of everything in the universe are limited, and to abandon anything means to lose it forever. This type of person is a hoarder, and he may collect anything and everything. His anxiety arises from a different order of concern than that of the obsessional. The hoarder's collections are often purposeless and meaningless in contrast to those of the obsessional. The latter may discard the objects as soon as they have served their purpose; the hoarder can never give up anything. The hoarder's total preoccupation is collecting; the obsessional collects to achieve perfection and omniscience.

Obsessional collecting, however, is not far removed from hoarding and can easily become a total preoccupation. The distinction is qualitative as well as quantitative, and the same gradation can be seen in other obsessional patterns as well. For example, the concern for preciseness and accuracy can be a great asset in those professions or crafts in which faultless behavior is both necessary and possible. It is highly valued in the field of mathematics and in science in general, as well as in certain industrial laboratory processes. In these activities the dedication to, and the obsession with, absolute accuracy may enhance a person's professional status. However, while these characteristics are virtues under some circumstances, they may become pitfalls and serious obstacles when the desired accuracy is unobtainable. Since this is the situation in most areas of human knowledge, one must be prepared to compromise with the ideal in terms of what is attainable. When one is unable to accept anything short of perfection and becomes anxious, ineffective, and disorganized unless perfection can be achieved, he presents obsessional behavior that, in the extreme, is neurotic and self-defeating.

The obsessional researcher will find himself greatly handicapped, particularly in the social sciences, if he tries to apply absolutes when only approximations are possible. He may find himself being more congenial to the mathematical or measurable aspects of his research project than to the broader intuitive and speculative aspects of the problem. The insistence on preciseness when only approximations are possible may often produce such severe anxieties that the effectiveness of a brilliant worker can be reduced to a point where his skill becomes a handicap. The withdrawn or autistic obsessional can often find a suitable outlet for his fantasizing and delusional thinking if he focuses it on painting, dancing, composing, or acting.

In the more practical aspects of living, obsessional patterns can impose many obstacles. While philosophizing and keeping an open mind are admirable goals, there are frequent occasions when rapid decisions must be made without the intellectual consideration of all possible issues. The indecisive obsessional tends to be clumsy, inept, and ineffective in his routine living. He may move slowly and cautiously, delaying all his living while he considers alternative actions.

For truly creative activities one must achieve a balance. Some questions are held open and at the same time answers may be suggested even before all the data are accumulated. To the extent that one is restrained from committing oneself or taking wild leaps without proper guarantees, one might be handicapped in such enterprises. Creativity is characterized by intuitive and premature excursions into areas in which there are no road maps or prior pathways.

The indiscriminate demand for complete certainty can be the cause of an enormous waste of time and energy in tracking down all the factors involved in a phenomenon. The obsessional's ability to be precise and to respect order and routine can make him an asset to any organization. On the other hand, his rigid, inflexible way of operating can quickly irritate and antagonize the less rule-bound, freewheeling worker. It is clear that in the normal utilization of obsessional patterns some patterns are useful (that is, productive and adaptive) and others are not. Simply to label a characteristic obsessive or compulsive does not ordinarily convey its positive or constructive elements. However, in delineating the group of normal utilizers of obsessional defenses from the group we say possesses obsessional personality and the *obsessional-neurotic group*, we must take into account the adaptive as well as the maladaptive aspects of the behavior. What are the distinctions of the obsessional personality group as opposed to the obsessional-neurotic group?

The scientific worker who has obsessional patterns can function effectively and constructively if his working conditions are ideal. If his anxiety increases he may have some difficulty in continuing, but he can still make the necessary decisions to proceed with his job. At this time he might be classified in the obsessional personality group. Although he is more distressed than the nonsymptomatic scientist, he is not nearly so handicapped as the obsessional neurotic who can no longer take effective action. Here the capacity to make a decision is disrupted by the demands for absolute certainty, which is not achievable. Panic and disorganization may follow.

OBSESSIONAL PERSONALITY

Differentiating between manifestations of obsessional traits of behavior and an obsessional personality is a matter of consistency and the extent of the pattern's involvement with the individual's total life. While admittedly such a distinction is extremely difficult to make, it is nevertheless worth the effort. The label *obsessional personality* refers to a widespread, fairly cohesive set of obsessional traits in a person whose anxieties are noticeable. Such behavior patterns are fixed and durable, and one can predict with some degree of accuracy the individual's response to certain stimuli. The consistency of behavior suggests more integrated functioning than is generally found in the occasional bits of obsessional behavior that might occur in any personality structure — such as the hysterical, the schizoid, or the psychopathic personality.

A further distinction between the obsessional personality and the obsessional neurotic is in the area of differing functional capacity. As long as the individual remains productive — though he might be given to fairly extensive rituals or other obsessive behavior — he is not necessarily neurotic. The label *neurotic* refers not only to a clinical syndrome characterized by specific, definable limits but also to behavior that becomes maladaptive or runs counter to the community's standard for what is acceptable. The individual might behave strangely or impress some people as being odd, but as long as he is integrated and functioning effectively (strictly speaking), he is not neurotic in the public eye. For example, a middle-aged man who held a high financial post in a municipal government was involved in endless rituals and obsessional thinking. His favorite preoccupation during World War II was to work out techniques for helping servicemen sublimate their sexual needs. He had devised a sublimation dance in which every male had two females. He also had a project for solving the housing shortage by proposing spatial housing. This was an ingenious proposal in which rockets would be used not only to propel the materials to build the apartments outside the pull of gravity but also to project the inhabitants from the earth to their homes in outer space and back. While he was fully occupied with plans for these programs, his colleagues were unaware of the bizarre nature of his inner life. It was not until he had decided to present these ideas to the President that he himself became aware of the peculiarity of his thoughts. He functioned effectively at his job, and only when his anxieties became extreme did he need to see a psychiatrist. It was quite clear, at that time, that he was a severely obsessional neurotic, bordering on and periodically regressing into, schizophrenia.

A less severe case involved a graduate student who had spent ten years finishing his doctoral requirements. His inability to finish his thesis grew out of his efforts to include everything, so that each new publication, study, or research in his field required him to revise his report. While his friends viewed him as a scholarly man who was intellectually honest and precise, he was compelled to pursue this endless goal for fear of being rejected because of an inadequate or incomplete thesis. Endless rationalizations, justifications, referential blaming of others, and moralistic and self-aggrandizing explanations were elaborated. However, he managed to function reasonably well as a parent and teacher, but his career was always in jeopardy because of his interminable procrastinating, indecisiveness, and perfectionistic drives.

It is common to find severely obsessional persons functioning effectively in settings in which their "queerness" and unconventional attitudes may be noticed by all. Either because of the sympathetic goodwill of the management and colleagues or because of such people's value to the organization — where they are generally regarded as good workers — they are maintained on the job. It is only when some extreme untoward event occurs or some personal crisis unfolds to aggravate their obsessional patterns that these obsessionals may be dismissed.

Such an instance was true in the case of an electronics engineer who was a totally undisciplined worker. He would arrive at and depart from his plant according to his own schedule, and on many occasions he would work through the night. He was meticulously precise and had some hand-washing compulsions as well as a total inability to settle for anything less than a perfect performance at the job. While his lack of discipline tended to disrupt the laboratory routine, the management was extremely sympathetic and even managed to increase his hourly rate in order to bring his salary up to a reasonable level. Periodically, his preciseness and passion for order would resolve some hitherto unsolvable circuitry problem. However, as his undisciplined behavior began to be too disruptive and his unique qualities less available because of his absence from the job, he was urged to see a psychiatrist.

Shortly after his marriage his performance became more erratic and unreliable. As his work behavior became more extreme, his performance on the job became markedly disruptive and maladaptive. What heretofore had been considered merely odd and queer was now labeled an obsessional neurosis that required therapy.

Another example is that of a mathematician whose job did not require him to punch a time clock or to follow a set routine. However, he was expected periodically to file a report on the current status of his project. He worked in a large "think" factory with a great number of brilliant scientists and technicians. While he was considered unusually talented and was respected by his superiors, he began to grow panicky about his failure to complete a report that was six months overdue. His indecisiveness and procrastination made it impossible for him to complete the task. Though such difficulties were evident in every aspect of his life, he had managed to have a fairly successful career until he was hired by this high-level scientific laboratory. His anxiety about perfect performances interfered with what he was capable of doing; as his panic increased, his level of performance decreased. He came to therapy on his own volition, finally acknowledging that his indecisiveness was too extreme to be rationalized even as scientific caution. Although he managed to postpone his job crisis through repeated promises, his inability to get the report written finally resulted in his being asked to resign.

Manifestations of "more-than-normal" obsessiveness may be subtle or obvious, and there may be recognizable rituals of a sufficiently bizarre nature that the person may be known as an oddball, a queer fellow, or an eccentric. In the obsessive personality, the rituals may be minimal and known only to the person's intimates, or they may be sufficiently evident to others. At times, the obsessional's preoccupations may not be noticed as unusual on casual contact and may reveal a piece of obsessional behavior only after a long acquaintance. While the obsessional personality is consistent in using obsessional techniques, the individual retains some flexibility and can function without the undue anxiety that would incapacitate the obsessional neurotic.

OBSESSIONAL NEUROSIS

As the obsessional personality's anxiety increases because of external demands or inner stress, the patterns tend to become more extensive and prominent. The extension of obsessional processes is related to the increasing anxiety as well as to the capacity of the existing patterns to deal with them. While heretofore many of his preoccupations or bizarre bits of behavior could be kept isolated or under control, he now can no longer maintain such control, and gradually his activities may be dominated by his compulsions. The islands of activity outside of compulsive pressure tend to become smaller, and his rituals may be more evident and less answerable to justification or rationalization. His obsessional activities may become so preoccupying that he has little time for the more routine activities in his living. His work suffers as well as his personal life, and the efforts to isolate his difficulties are less successful. Even though his disabilities are becoming more public — possibly obvious to any bystander — there still remain some successful modes of functioning (except for the most severe neurotic), which often allow him to keep at his job and to remain outside of the mental hospital. However, as the rigid adherence to his obsessional demands begins to alienate him from his professional colleagues or family unit, the necessity for some psychiatric intervention becomes clear.

A young electronics and mathematical student performed excellently as a computer technician. He was highly regarded in spite of the irritations caused by his meticulous concern for details, even the most irrelevant ones. When his company began to fail, his duties became less necessary and his obsessional difficulties, which heretofore were adaptive, became severely incapacitating. His washing routine grew to seven hours from one hour, with the explanation that dirt was omnipresent and dangerous. His toilet and eating rituals began to occupy most of his waking day, and he had to quit his job to permit them to be completed. The skin complications resulting from excessive washing forced him to see a physician, who referred him to a psychiatrist. From an obsessional personality he moved into a neurosis, which was induced by a change in the economic picture of his computer concern.

Yet the question of therapy is still unclear. When does obsessional behavior require psychiatric intervention? In the extremes the answer is obvious. However, more often the question can be answered only after a consideration of the effects of these patterns on others as well as on the patient. When his effectiveness at his job is grossly impaired or when the symptoms produce sufficient social problems, the need for treatment may become quite evident to his associates. At other times the obsessional preoccupations and hypochondriacal concern with somatic difficulties may be so debilitating that the person himself seeks some relief from these inner torments.

A historian who periodically had overwhelming fears of dying managed to forestall psychiatric therapy until an anxiety attack in the middle of the night brought him to a cardiac ward and a psychiatric consultation. The absence of any physical changes and the awareness of his obsessive preoccupation with his health and physical functioning convinced him of the need for psychotherapy, even though he did not give up his expectations of doom and death. He taught, played tennis, and lived a full and active intellectual life in spite of his severe obsessional patterns. The whole range of symptoms — from overintellectualizing and perfectionistic, meticulous, and controlled behavior to a procrastinating indecisiveness — was present. Doubting was his most pervasive and intimidating pattern.

Another obsessional neurotic, an actress, sought therapy when her intense excessive perfectionistic demands forced her to rehearse her roles to such an extent that her performances became stereotyped and full of tension. From an accomplished actress she had become a tense, fearful, and overly rigid individual who had difficulty in getting roles. Depression and periodic manic attacks forced her into therapy where the underlying obsessional personality was clearly revealed.

Another young lady was for years a conscientious, dedicated, and intense researcher before her obsessional behavior began causing her great difficulties. She was highly regarded at her job, and not until she became involved with a lover did her preoccupation with making certain that she had eliminated all danger of fire and the like begin to dominate her life. Pressure from her boyfriend and her own intense intellectual curiosity led her to seek psychotherapy.

The obsessional often resorts to therapy on his own, in spite of the blow to his pride in such an admission of vulnerability and imperfection. His request for assistance is an admission of imperfection and is made with great reluctance. His awareness of increasing anxiety in the face of some minor crisis and the ensuing panicky expectation of doom makes him fearful of a possible breakdown in his obsessional defenses. At other times he comes to therapy because he feels ineffective, harrassed by his compulsions, and not free to make choices or decisions in any area of his life. He recognizes that he is not utilizing his potentialities and that too much energy goes into the planning and programming of his life. He feels incapable of enjoying himself, and too alienated from his family and friends. He may acknowledge that he has no real commitments, even though he may work most intensely and conscientiously. He feels that something is wrong, which he cannot clearly verbalize, and that he is not getting out of life what is possible, both personally and professionally. Or the bizarre nature of his rituals may become so discomforting and embarrassing that he wishes to eliminate them. It is these subjective factors that are largely responsible for his seeking therapy and not pressures from the outside. He has a feeling of loss of identity or a feeling of never having had one, and he hopes that therapy will help him find it. The identity problems that characterize obsessional living are the basis for the large numbers of people visiting psychiatrists in the last three decades. The feeling of unproductiveness, coupled with an uncertainty of what one is or wishes to be, is a characteristic complaint. These factors, rather than severe anxieties, are the main instigators for therapy, as the obsessional defenses are very successful in maintaining anxiety at a low level.

Many obsessional neurotics and people with obsessional personalities come to therapy because of psychosomatic difficulties. Ulcers, colitis, and cardiovascular complications are common; the patients, after a thorough examination by an internist, are often informed that their problems are functional and require psychiatric care. This is extremely difficult for them to accept, since it not only implies a weakness but also means that treatment will be long and arduous and will require their participation.

A young man of thirty-nine was referred for therapy by his general practitioner after prolonged study of cardiac complaints for a period of three years, with repeated EKG studies, blood and kidney tests, and innumerable X rays. The heart condition began when the patient awoke one evening with palpitations and a feeling of pain in his chest. He immediately assumed that he had heart disease and would not move until the arrival of the doctor, who confirmed the patient's worst suspicions by saying that he had a heart murmur. For three years he cut down his activity to a minimum, gave up all sports (in and out of doors), and became preoccupied with observing his heart action under all sorts of circumstances. Prior to this difficulty, however, he had many other troubles because of his indecisive procrastinations. He had numerous phobias, which involved closed spaces, open spaces, automobiles, bridges, elevators, and others. His life was enormously circumscribed by rituals of all sorts, particularly relating to his health, and he had cut out all social relationships, both male and female, because they might be a drain on his heart. He insisted that he had heart disease and that he could die at any moment. The thorough medical study, which unfortunately served to fix many of his obsessional preoccupations, proved negative, and his physician decided that the tachycardia was psychological in origin and that the murmur had no physiological significance. The young man visited a psychiatrist but could not accept the psychological explanation of his condition. His obsessional difficulties were clearly manifest to the psychiatrist, but they did not impress the patient or his physician; it was only the somatic complaints that produced the referral.

It was easier for the patient to accept therapy for some medical or physiological need than for psychological difficulties. This is understandable when we recognize that the obsessional person believes that physical illnesses are outside of his control but that mental illnesses are entirely within his control; therefore, it is his own fault or weakness that produces it. This is patently false once we recognize that the nature of the obsessive-compulsive processes are entirely outside of the individual's control. Heart disease is thought to occur without the person's intervention, and he is able to believe that he has done nothing to bring it about. Emotional problems, however, are assumed to be the result of a lazy, undisciplined, and selfish concern for himself. While this attitude has a grain of truth, it is exaggerated in the typical obsessional style; physical illness is therefore considered good, and mental illness bad. The physician can do something for his patient in treating a physical illness, but in a mental illness the patient must do it himself; and the treatment is slow, painstaking, and without magical cures. This may account for the obsessional's ready acknowledgment of physical illnesses in contrast to his reluctant recognition of emotional problems. It also explains why many obsessional patients may come to therapy for their ulcers or colitis but will not see the need for getting help for their extreme indecisiveness or procrastination.

To summarize, all people use obsessional techniques in their living. The extent to which these defenses take over the person's total living or interfere with one's productivity or make one appear to be odd and curious will determine the label applied. It is not only the extent of the activities which are involved in obsessional behavior but also the capacity of the rest of the organism to isolate that behavior and still function effectively. As one's adjustment and adaptation become less successful and the obsessional living more noticeable, the label of *obsessional neurosis* becomes applicable. Therapy is determined not by label or the presence of obsessional behavior but by the extent to which the person's living is blocked, both subjectively and objectively.

PART II

THE OBSESSIVE STATE AND OTHER SYNDROMES

CHAPTER 5

Phobias

To fulfill the goal of maintaining absolute control over oneself and others, one must have the power, intelligence, or ability to predict the future, or one must avoid any situation in which loss of control may occur. I have described the various techniques utilized by the obsessional personality to attempt total mastery through either intelligence or magic. The other alternative — that of avoiding anything that threatens loss of control — is called a *phobia*. The individual absolutely avoids a situation that is a symbolic representation of the potential danger; he does not avoid the actual danger itself. In this way the phobia is one of the most powerful techniques of defense in the obsessional personality structure.

Phobias attracted the attention of the earliest medical practitioners, but it is only recently that meaningful explanations have been suggested for their presence. The Greeks described many phobias, such as agoraphobia and claustrophobia, with the names indicating the object of the phobia. Freud became interested in phobias quite early in his career and revised his conception of them many times. In 1895 he wrote a paper on the relationship between obsessions and phobias. In this paper he distinguished between the two by indicating that in phobias the emotional state is always one of morbid anxiety, whereas in the obsessions other emotional states, such as doubt and anger, may occur in the same capacity as fear does in the phobias. He also pointed out that the origin of the phobia was fear and the source was derived from the symbols of unconscious fantasies and conflicts. Freud stated that "combinations of a phobia and an obsession proper may co-exist, and that indeed this is a very frequent occurrence."* While he maintained this distinction, Freud confused these two categories at various times, classifying them under the rubric of hysteria or the anxiety neuroses. In the famous study of Hans, who had a phobia when he was five years old, Freud emphasized that phobias belonged with the anxiety neuroses because there was a similarity between the psychological structure of phobias and that of hysteria. The function of the phobia as an avoidance technique was evident in its very essence. It was this issue that was spotlighted when Freud considered phobia a hysterical phenomenon, yet he continued to link phobias with obsessions and, at times, considered them almost synonymous. An excerpt from his *Interpretation of Dreams* highlights this attitude: "I had an opportunity of obtaining a deep insight into the unconscious mind of a young man whose life was made almost impossible by an obsessional neurosis. He was unable to go out into the street because he was tortured by the fear that he would kill everyone he met. He spent his days in preparing his alibi in case he might be charged with one of the murders committed in the town. It is unnecessary to add that he was a man of equally high morals and education.... After his father's painful illness and death, the patient's obsessional self-reproaches appeared — he was in his thirty-first year at the time — taking the shape of a phobia transferred on to strangers. A person, he felt, who was capable of wanting to push his own father over a precipice from the top of a mountain was not to be trusted to respect the lives of those less closely related to him; he was quite right to shut himself up in his room."† Freud could have added that in this case the phobia was a device to exert and to guarantee the necessary control that would obviate the dangers involved in the patient's going out into the streets. In this brief vignette Freud indicated his psychodynamic theory of phobias and obsessions and gave an inkling of the two disorders' close association.

   The obsessional preoccupations and ritualistic behavior of this patient were a means of controlling the aggressive impulses which had unconscious roots in his hatred of his father. Both the phobia and obsessive devices were attempts to control dangerous and undesirable impulses of a sexual or aggressive nature. While Freud emphasized sexual and aggressive impulses

---

* S. Freud, "Obsessions and Phobias: Their Psychical Mechanism and Their Aetiology," *Standard Edition* 3, pp.81–82.

   † S. Freud, "The Interpretation of Dreams," *Standard Edition* 4, p. 260.

in the development of phobias, *any* "out-of-control" impulses that would be a threat to the integrity of the individual can be involved. They need not necessarily be hostile or aggressive impulses. A phobia may develop around tender impulses, power drives, or the need to maintain pride and self-esteem. Loss of control and concern about humiliating and threatening consequences which might result are the factors that produce a phobia. The danger of loss of control does not necessarily involve hostile feelings. Rather, the fear of losing control is in itself the threat of being humiliated and made to feel worthless. It is a public display of inadequacy and imperfection rather than a fear of violence that provides the phobic state.

The phobia, by an absolute injunction, prevents an individual from confronting any situation, place, or person that is potentially capable of producing anxiety and that may temporarily put the individual out of control. It is a ritualized avoidance reaction, which, like all rituals, attempts to exert some control over nature through the agency of magic. The phobia is a ritual of "no doing" or inaction, while the obsessive-compulsive syndrome involves some doing or positive activity to maintain control, thus avoiding the intolerable humiliation which comes from the awareness that he is a mere mortal and is imperfect.

AVOIDANCE REACTIONS

The phobia prevents the person from coming into contact with the kind of situation or thing that may put him out of control. However, avoidance reactions must be distinguished from other avoidance tendencies which are prominent in nature; that is, not all avoidance reactions are phobias. For example, in the typical conditioned responses in man and animals, certain objects or experiences are avoided because of a prior unpleasant experience. These avoidance reactions are specific, literal, and devoid of any content other than the anticipated pain or displeasure based on previous experience and reinforced by subsequent ones. This is implicit in the learning process. It is a physiological response and part of the inherent self-preservation mechanism. Such a response may be reflex in nature or secondarily conditioned. One experience with a cactus plant or one whiff of ammonia may produce a strong avoidance reaction. On a lesser scale, food reactions and other sensory experiences may condition the person against further contacts.

Other avoidance reactions may not be conditioned by repetitive experiences, but may occur under single, dramatic, and traumatic circumstances—perhaps under circumstances of severe stress, as in times of war. The effect might be a sudden and dramatic avoidance of certain elements in that experience. Such occurrences have been confused with phobias in the past and have even been mistakenly labeled as such. These are conditioned responses, whether operant or nonoperant, as opposed to the phobia, which is a defensive reaction based on emotional elements in the experience. The need to distinguish between these responses is not a semantic game or even only a theoretical concern; it is of great practical importance.

An example concerns a pilot who, during a bombing mission, underwent severe danger and was exposed to intense, fear-provoking stimuli. Consequently, he developed extreme fear on approaching a plane, looking at a plane, or even thinking about flying. This pilot's reaction was based on an actual danger in a situation which produced such discomfort that he refused to confront a similar situation again. The object avoided was directly involved in the experience. There was no symbolism or transformation of the elements involved. It was a rational and comprehensible outcome of an intense experience of anxiety, which, while its manifestations resembled a phobia in many ways and may have even been a prelude to a phobic reaction, was acutally a simple avoidance reaction based on conditioning. The phobia, on the other hand, is a more complicated phenomenon that invariably involves some symbolic transformation and deals with psychic dangers as opposed to physical dangers. Often the avoided dangers may be vague and entirely unrelated to the phobic objects.

If the avoidance reaction described above began to spread so that elevators, heights, and crowds all began to be involved (not just airplanes), it would then move into the realm of the phobia. This often occurs when the realistic avoidance reaction produces a sense of shame or humiliation and begins to involve psychic defensive reactions as well as physiological ones. For example, avoidance of white-hot objects is not considered a phobia. It is an elementary protective reaction. Similarly, the avoidance of deep water when one is a poor swimmer and has recently had to be rescued from drowning would not be called a water phobia. However, if such an experience should produce a total avoidance of bathing and spread to other symbolic situations in which breathing may be interfered with, it might then become a phobia and not a simple avoidance reaction.

There is some inclination to attempt to make a distinction by implying that the simple avoidance reactions are based on conscious factors, whereas the phobia is involved with unconscious elements; however, this is neither satisfactory nor correct. Phobias may originate and persist in the face of clear knowledge of the factors involved. An elevator phobia is not the result of the possibility of physical danger involved in a falling elevator but is related to the necessity of being able immediately to get clear of other people when one becomes anxious. The anticipation of panic is related to the need to move swiftly when anxiety supervenes, and even the seconds or fraction of a second in going from one floor to the next is too long. In addition, there is the apprehension that the elevator might get stuck and not open at all. This reaction is reminiscent of the nightmare in which one is unable to move and to be in control of one's activities at all times.

In all such phobias the element of danger is not the issue. The panic and humiliation which might ensue if the person does go out of control are the basic content of the phobic avoidance; thus, the relationship to the phobic object is symbolic rather than literal, and it represents a more generalized psychic danger rather than a specific physical danger.

Phobias often appear quietly and without any precipitating event. They also occur under circumstances in which the relationship of anxiety in connection with the phobic object may not be evident. It is easy to understand the avoidance of airplanes after a dangerous or unpleasant flight. The avoidance of elevators and open spaces or other varieties of phobias is often difficult to understand. The phobia cannot be comprehended on rational grounds, even though rational explanations might be made for its existence. In addition, the phobia may not specifically involve a particular element in the situation but may generalize to include a total event or class of things. Phobias may involve single elements, such as flowers or brown elevators with a capacity of six occupants. Generally, however, the phobia involves broader categories, such as open spaces which include flowers, trees, streets, or buildings. In addition, the phobia tends to involve similiar objects or situations which have emotional factors in common. A phobia of elevators, for example, may also include phobias of narrow spaces or mechanical objects which are not connected to the outside or other noticeable escape routes. The phobia involves an idea or a content of experience rather than the object itself. The phobic object has symbolic significance; it is this factor that distinguishes it most clearly from simple avoidance reactions.

Unlike phobias, avoidance reactions have a high rate of cure. Simple avoidance reactions can be influenced with comparative ease by drugs, reconditioning, or hypnotic techniques. Phobias, on the other hand, are extremely difficult to influence, even with extensive therapy. The additional dimension of psychic involvement (over and above the somatic response) complicates the therapy most emphatically. It is this difference which accounts for the discrepant claims for some therapeutic approaches with regard to curing phobias. Exaggerated claims of cures are based on the failure to distinguish between true phobias and simple avoidance reactions.

In addition to the difficulty of distinguishing between the simple avoidance reaction and the phobia, there is a tendency to use the terms *fear, phobia*, and *anxiety* as synonyms. While they are clearly related and can coexist side by side, they are not identical. Fear is defined by Webster as "a painful emotion marked by alarm, awe, or anticipation of danger." It is not synonymous with phobia, which is defined as "as irrational or persistent fear of a particular object or objects." Fear can be present with or without a phobia; a phobia invariably contains an element of fear. In spite of the fact that in his psychiatric dictionary Leland Hinsie defines 211 phobias in terms of fear only, fear is not a phobia. Hinsie's definitions range from fear of air, animals, and anything new to fear of weakness, wind, women, work, and writing. This elaborate list attests only to early ignorance of the subject and the presumption that each item represented a different disorder; it simply identifies the phobic object without clarifying its significance in the dynamics of phobias.

The distinction between fear and anxiety is difficult to make, and presently there is no consensus about the distinction. Freud made it in terms of conscious and unconscious derivatives. Others, such as Kurt Goldstein and Harry Stack Sullivan, see the difference as qualitative and maintain that anxiety is experienced when the psychological intregrity of the organism is at stake, while fear is experienced when the physiological integrity of the organism is at stake. This distinction applies to the difference between the simple avoidance reactions, where the threat is physiological, and the phobias, where the threat is psychological.

ANXIETY AND OTHER FACTORS

Anxiety is described as a warning signal or a feeling of apprehension in response to some danger, often of an unknown source. While anxiety is an invariable accompaniment of the phobic states, a successful phobia can often disguise its presence. Like fear, anxiety is not synonymous with phobia; it can be manifested in many ways other than by a phobia. On the other hand, anything can become a phobic object, and the particular object does not give any clues about the source of the anxiety. For example, a phobic state may develop around public appearances or about performing before audiences (stage fright). The issue need not be a particular place or event or a specific fear or anxiety, but rather the broad spectrum of feeling under scrutiny by a critical or unfriendly audience. This response could take place not only in a theater but also at parties or luncheons with one or two people. The apprehension is not that of a physical danger but of being humiliated or laughed at, of making a fool of oneself by inadequate or uncontrolled behavior. It is the individual's pride system which is at stake, not his physical well-being.

A phobia develops when a person utilizing the obsessive-compulsive defense is faced with a situation in which he feels he cannot maintain control. If there has been a similar threat of possible loss of control on a previous occasion, a guaranteed way of dealing with this possibility is to avoid such situations permanently. The phobic state achieves this avoidance, since mere anticipation or fantasy of the situation will produce sufficient anxiety to ward off any participation in it. Consequently, it is a most potent technique for control; indeed, it is infallible. One need never encounter a particular difficulty if there is a permanent injunction against ever facing it.

THE SPREAD OF PHOBIAS

Phobias have a characteristic tendency to spread. A phobia which involves large groups may gradually extend to smaller and smaller groups, so that ultimately the person can function only when he is alone. The spread is along symbolic lines as well as in terms of the superficial content of the phobia. Such a spread has been explained by the conditioned reflex theorists as *stimulus generalization*, or conditioning at a higher level of integration. However, the tendency for the phobia to spread can be better understood on the grounds that similar psychic dangers in various situations may be included in the total phobia. Insisting on an aisle seat or one next to a door in a theater or in other large halls is a partial solution to the fear of enclosure or lack of quick exit. The anxiety of being kept in an elevator even for seconds or being unable to get through a crowd immediately involves an inability to take the consequences of ordinary living—where one cannot always do immediately what one wishes. The phobic person demands immediate and absolute relief, whether it be in the form of a tranquilizer or a rapid, evasive action. Like those of an over-indulged child, his needs must be fulfilled at once. The phobia is a way of making certain of this fulfillment; through the phobia, life becomes organized in such a way as to guarantee that one will not be uncomfortable, even for the briefest moment.

Once a phobia begins, continued public exposure causes it to spread. One young woman developed a writing phobia, which began in a bank. Soon she was unable to sign her name in a department store and then in a restaurant; she finally reached the point where having to hold a cup or anything would cause hand tremors and uneasiness. While the spread of her phobia reduced the chances of exposing her lack of control, it also limited her dealings with others, so that she could eat only in the presence of her immediate family.

Phobias can develop around an infinite variety of situations or objects. The limitless possibilities of anything becoming a phobic object have produced an extremely large list of phobias — from generalized ones such as school phobias to discrete ones such as phobias about blue horses or four leaf clovers. The term *school phobia,* for example, generally implies a fear of, or a resistence to going to, school. It gives us no clue as to whether the phobic object is the school bus, the driver, the teacher, the desk, other pupils, or the brown dog who prowls about the school. For a clearer understanding of the phobic process, it is important to recognize that in speaking of a school phobia one is not describing a specific condition but a generalized situation in which a specific factor operates. To treat such situations, it is necessary to determine the precise factors which produce the phobic response. These factors are invariably symbolic representations of some aspect of the broader situation.

In the years prior to a dynamic understanding of the phobic process it was believed that each phobia had a separate etiology and dynamic function. Freud adopted this view of the phobic state even though he felt that the phobic object always symbolized some sexual fear. More recently the theory of phobias has assumed a less specific etiology.

If a person has a great fear of his hostile or aggressive feelings, it is not surprising that any phobia he might develop would involve dangerous weapons or access to the hated persons should he feel that under some circumstances he might lose control of himself. In the same way a person who fears exposure of his weaknesses or imperfections or his inability to exert absolute control may develop phobias about situations in which these deficiencies might be exposed. Thus, the significance of a phobia may be the same even if the phobic objects are different. Some theorists have pointed out that the phobic object may be related to inner conflict; however, it may also have nothing to do with such a problem.

The phobia, however, does begin in the sensory context of a critical attack of anxiety, and the symbolic associations may or may not be made with the original unconscious sources of fear. The phobic object, however, is distinctly related to the sensory context of the critical anxiety situation and does not, in itself, constitute the symbolism or the significance of the underlying fear. All phobias have the same dynamic and functional significance. The phobic object or situation is an accidental or coincidental accompaniment of a severe state of anxiety, when the person has experienced the possibility of going out of control. The context of the phobia is then woven around the situation when the anxiety occurred. The fact that certain situations are conducive to setting off severe anxieties about loss of control — such as heights, elevators, closed spaces, or dangerous weapons — accounts for the high incidence of such objects in the phobic states. Certain situations, such as stage appearances or social settings, may be the frequent objects of phobias, as in these circumstances severe anxieties about being out of control may also arise.

In therapy the phobic object is of a secondary role. What must be analyzed and clarified is the fear of losing control, which first manifested itself in an atmosphere where, for some reason, the person experienced a panic or some severe anxiety. The analysis of the basic character structure, which is the obsessive-compulsive character structure, is the main therapeutic thrust.

The dynamics of the phobic state are illustrated in an obsessional individual who had an intense fear of losing control and of being uncertain what might happen should he faint on a strange street. He began to avoid the streets of large cities, and soon the streets of smaller cities as well. Finally, his phobia extended to the streets of his own city. This patient's phobia began when he was in his early twenties and was attending college in a Midwestern town. One evening, while on his way home from a movie, he was picked up by a police cordon in an area where a burglary had been committed. Since he had some difficulty proving that he had been in the movie at the time the crime was committed, he was held in custody for several hours. Afterwards, he was fearful whenever he was on the streets alone; he felt powerless to protect himself. His apprehension became an overpowering obsession, and whenever he was out alone he would need a witness to make him more comfortable. For a time these phobic fears diminished. Following a short-lived romance with a young woman at a summer resort, his phobic fears became severe enough to require treatment.

His behavior at the time was indicative of his character structure, which made his phobias comprehensible. He met the young lady on the night of his arrival at the resort. She seemed to like him, and he became very enthusiastic about his conquest, fantasizing a major romance and possible marriage. She seemed to reciprocate most of his feelings but suggested moving a bit more cautiously. When she seemed to be too friendly toward other guests, he became irritated and infuriated and began to feel abused and taken advantage of. One evening he decided that he was through paying her bar bill while she flirted with other men. Although he said nothing to her about this, he sulked, acted hurt, and lost all his previous animation and enthusiasm. She wondered what was happening, but he could not tell her what he really felt because it seemed extreme even to him.

On the following day she was quickly put off by his hurt, accusing attitude and began avoiding him. This served to justify his suspicions, but as she withdrew, he made some tentative attempts to win her back. However, he was already too angry, too certain that she was a tease, and too annoyed when she did not apologize for her behavior of the previous evening. During the next few days she avoided him, and he became morose and jealous as he watched her enthusiastic and joyful encounters with others. He finally cut his vacation short.

He was extremely upset over this event and his phobia returned with increased strength. It was at this point that he came for therapy. Exploration of his behavior at the summer resort clearly showed that he was imperious, grandiose, and egocentric. He could not share the girl with her friends nor could he tolerate her friendly behavior toward others. In spite of their short acquaintance he demanded that she should devote herself exclusively to him, since he had committed himself to her. He tried to control and direct her behavior according to his program and his needs. He could not make the demand openly, however; and when she behaved in a friendly fashion toward others, he felt rejected although she obviously liked him and was as friendly toward him as she was toward her other acquaintances. It was this aspect of her personality which had attracted him to her in the first place, though it also made him anxious. His perfectionistic demands required that a woman be charming and attractive, with many friends and admirers, yet focus her attention exclusively upon him. While he might have clarified the situation by telling her how he felt, he would also have revealed his weakness which was loneliness and a fear of competition. He hoped to convey his demands by hurt looks and a sulking, scolding attitude, as though through some magical mind reading or thought transference she would know what produced his distress. His withdrawal changed the hitherto pleasant relationship into a tense and uneasy one, which was hardly worth her pursuing. Her behavior then served to confirm his distortions and proved what he inevitably expected and what his actions generally caused to happen.

The whole incident was a clear example of his insistent need to maintain control over his relationships so that they would proceed according to his plans. He could not take chances; he had to know, even before it was possible, that he was in complete control. This kind of person expects an absolute commitment from others in order to feel certain of their loyalty.

His phobia made no sense to him whatsoever, particularly since it was reactivated following his summer holiday. His ambivalent feelings toward his mother as well as his aggressive attitudes were explored in relation to his phobias. The problem of guilt and the fear of exposure of his unconscious needs to steal were also explored with regard to the initial experience at age twenty. While these issues had some relevance, the consistent element in the early experience as well as in his later experiences was the factor of fear of losing control. At age twenty it was the fear of being out of control on the streets, unable to defend himself and without friends to support him should he faint or become ill. Moreover, it would be humiliating and intolerable to convey to others that he felt anxious on the streets or in crowds. He recognized that in the presence of people whom he had no need to impress or those with whom he felt in complete control, he felt no anxieties when confronted with such situations. But in the presence of others the condition was aggravated—especially when he wanted these others to acknowledge his strength and worldliness. All his phobias were direct representations of his overwhelming concern with fainting and losing control, about which he envisaged the most humiliating and dangerous consequences.

In his sex life, the lack of control manifested itself in his inability, most of the time, to delay orgasm longer than a few seconds, and he would frequently ejaculate prior to entrance. This was also a great source of distress to him and had begun to produce phobic avoidance of intercourse in order to prevent this failure. This vicious circle — refraining from intercourse to avoid exposing his prematurity — leads to such infrequent sexual contacts that when intercourse does take place the excitement is too great to permit control of the orgasm, further aggravating the anxiety which stimulates the production of the phobia. Because of his increasing concern about his premature ejaculation and impotence, he began to have fantasies of intercourse with young girls, with whom he would feel entirely in control. At times these fantasies became very pressing and frightening, and yet they were the only means by which he could visualize successful, prolonged intercourse.

His so-called perverted interests were directly related to his difficulties in controlling his living in both sexual and nonsexual matters. He was therefore attracted to situations and people where his power to control was clear and manifest. This is frequently the basis on which an adult contemplates activities with young children, sexual or otherwise. In this way the adult can feel superior, better informed, and clearly the master of the situation. In sexual terms this is undeniably true, since children usually have either no knowledge of sexual matters or so little that they are less informed and experienced than an adult. Thus, there is no possibility of humiliation, criticism, or of feeling inferior to the child—even though such a relationship may be most vicious and destructive.

CLINICAL TYPES AND THE OBSESSIONAL STATE

Phobias occur in obsessional characters — either as part of an obsessive-compulsive neurosis or as the prominent symptom when the obsessional way of life is secondary. The presence of a phobia indicates that the obsessional mechanism is not serving its purposes, and the phobic state intervenes to guarantee avoidance and absolute control in threatened areas of the personality structure. There are four clinical possibilities in the relationship of obsessional states to phobias:

1. Obsessional state without phobias
2. Obsessional state with mild phobic symptoms
3. Obsessional state with moderate phobic symptoms
4. Obsessional state with severe phobic symptoms

Without Phobic Symptoms

In this state one finds the classical situation of an obsessional disorder, which may be characterized by manifestations of doubting, indecision, or compulsive acts. There are no phobic avoidance symptoms that are crystallized out of the matrix of the generally distracting and avoiding tendency of the obsessional mechanism. While there is considerable anxiety about engaging in any activity or initiating any project, there is no specific bar or obstacle aside from a generalized unwillingness to commit oneself. The reluctance to make decisions or to select alternatives often presents the picture of a person avoiding involvements, but these avoidance reactions are not yet sufficiently organized to constitute phobias.

Under such circumstances the obsessional patterns are sufficiently potent and successful in warding off severe anxiety attacks without the necessity of imposing absolute safeguards, as in the phobias. This does not mean that the person is healthier, or even that he functions more efficiently. It does imply that the obsessional technique is capable of exerting enough control to make other techniques unnecessary. This may mean that the person is actually less effective; that is, it may be more efficient to isolate one area of living and close it off to further experiencing and to allow the rest of the person's living to go relatively untouched than to be subject to the generally inhibiting and depressive effect of obsessional doubting and indecisiveness and to minimize all involvements.

With Mild Phobic Symptoms

In this state we find the obsessive-compulsive neuroses with one or more phobic problems, all secondary to the main issues. The phobias frequently relate to the content of the obsessions or the compulsions. For example, the obsessional preoccupation may involve murder, and the individual may have a marked phobia regarding knives and guns. In most instances the phobias involve the issue of losing control in particular areas in which the person may have had an experience that endangered his control.

Generally, the phobias do not occupy the central role in the therapy and often may go unnoticed as part of the patient's problem. Therapy centers on the obsessive-compulsive problem, and the phobia frequently disappears without any focus being directed to it.

With Moderate Phobic Symptoms

In this group the phobic manifestations of the person's difficulties often predominate, and the emphasis of therapy tends to be on the phobic problems rather than on the underlying obsessional state. More often than not, the phobias force the person into therapy; he may be unaware of his obsessional problems. Such patients are often categorized as phobic, and they prove quite resistant to hypnosis, conditioning, or other therapies designed exclusively to alter the phobic manifestations. It is these cases that illustrate the very close relationship of phobias to the obsessional state.

Such was demonstrated in a patient who came to therapy for what was described as an occupational phobia. While working, he experienced a sudden, rapid rise in pulse, accompanied by fear of fainting; he was forced to terminate the conference he was engaged in. After this incident he avoided all conferences. In the precipitating episode, the patient thought he was having a heart attack and subsequently was obsessionally preoccupied with his cardiac state for many years. In addition to this phobia, he also had phobias about bridges, enclosed spaces, and tunnels of all sorts. As time went on he developed a speaking phobia whenever he was called upon to give a prepared address. When called upon unexpectedly, he could function very well and could speak quite persuasively.

Prior to the fainting spell he had experienced other difficulties in his job, since he always had to do it perfectly. He would prepare his work with exceptional thoroughness. This tendency annoyed some people at work, who considered it unnecessary and excessive. His life was organized around being a dedicated man of integrity, who was beyond reproach in both his private and professional life. He took on total reponsibility for the fate of his clients and their problems and had great difficulty distinguishing between doing the best he could for them and filling *all* their needs. Many people thought highly of him, since his successes outweighed his defeats by far. He spent an inordinate amount of time trying to satisfy his need always to be certain and correct.

The fainting spell occurred when a colleague introduced an argument which he had not anticipated; he was taken unaware. He immediately became very tense, excited, and extremely restless. His pulse became very rapid and he felt a sudden pain in his chest. It is relevant that the unexpected argument was neither significant nor crucial. However, because it was unexpected, it could not be dealt with in the ideal and perfect fashion.

Characteristically, his phobias were those of control. Since he could never achieve absolute certainty, clarity, and wisdom in every situation, his phobias avoided the challenge and the discovery of his human frailties. At the same time he felt weak and cowardly for avoiding them. He could dissipate these feelings by fantasizing that, if it weren't for the phobias, he could achieve the hero role and perform perfectly. This patient's problems arose directly out of his obsessional difficulties. As the obsessional problems were gradually clarified, many of the phobias were entirely resolved, while others showed marked improvement.

Another example is that of a forty-five-year-old man whose major problem — like that of the woman described earlier in the chapter — was a writing phobia, which had its beginnings when he had to sign his name to a contract in the presence of other people. On that occasion he was in the spotlight and began to get uneasy about the possibility of losing his composure and shaking visibly, which would have been humiliating for him. By pleading illness he avoided the actual trial, but thereafter he could not sign his name at banks, department stores, or even at home in the presence of friends or strangers. His pride prevented him from informing anyone except his wife. The major focus in this phobia was the issue of displaying a tremor, which would betray his nervousness. The writing phobia gradually extended to a phobia about socializing wherever drinks were to be served, including luncheons, cocktails, and dinners. His social life became restricted because of the agitation produced in anticipation of such engagements. The phobias served a vital purpose for him and at the same time were unacceptable to him. He felt ashamed and disappointed in himself for not being able to overcome these weaknesses. He was a very bright person who could not tolerate any situation in which he was second-best or less well informed than anyone else. Socializing was difficult for him apart from the tremors, as he could never know in advance whether he could measure up to all the people he might encounter. He was afraid that if he did not know everything, others would find him dull. His emphasis was entirely on intellectual achievement, and although he recognized the impossibility of competing with everyone about everything, he actually expected always to be the best. Anything less than this was unacceptable to him because to be less than perfect meant to be humiliatingly ordinary. Although he wanted his phobias eliminated, he did not want to alter his perfectionistic goals and his requirement of omniscience. The phobias directly intervened at times when he felt he was in danger of appearing human and therefore limited and imperfect. His obsessional problems were manifest in his demands for perfection, control, and guarantees of the future and in specific matters such as his meticulous concern for his own person and affairs and his obsessional ruminations, preoccupations, and rituals.

With Severe Phobic Symptoms

In this category one finds the phobic condition so much in the foreground that the underlying obsessive-compulsive patterns are frequently either in the background or completely hidden. It is under these circumstances that one is led to a separate category called *phobic states*, where phobias appear to be the sole problem that requires treatment. The content of the phobias may be varied and diffuse and, at times, may not give any clues to the underlying obsessive-compulsive state, which is invariably present.

For example, a particularly severe phobia about animals prevented a very prosperous businessman from entering any house or establishment until he was assured that there were no animals on the premises. This phobia was closely related to a dirt phobia which necessitated his washing his hands dozens of times during the day and changing his clothes three or four times a day. The phobic issues were so incapacitating that the compulsive hand-washing ritual was considered secondary and unimportant. These phobias alternated with other strong phobic reactions to particular places and things, but essentially the problem centered about the issue of germs, dirt, and other noxious elements.

This man was an extremely successful entrepreneur who managed very large financial deals. He sought help only from banks. He felt he could trust no one, as others would inevitably let him down. He was a lone operator who was convinced of his invincible capacity and afraid that at any moment he might not be able to meet his financial obligations and would thus lose everything. He was in a constant state of tension, preoccupied with ways of guaranteeing his next payments and making certain of his future. He could enjoy neither his money nor his possessions because of his constant concern as to whether any of it would be there tomorrow. Every restaurant bill, charity drive, or legitimate demand was scrutinized with great care to guard against his being victimized. Objectively, his financial situation was most secure, but he directed all his efforts to making certain that tomorrow would be exactly like today. He had no interest in the tendencies he displayed toward omnipotence or omniscience and saw the whole difficulty as a peculiarity of his phobias, which he wanted to eliminate.

The phobic problem was certainly central both in his thoughts and in the limitations in his living, while the obsessional difficulties were in the background. The phobias expressed his insistence on a purity and perfection that were impossible to achieve. His extensive hand washing was designed to guarantee his health. The animal phobia was a concern focused on preventing the passage of organisms from animal hosts. Any contact, even the most remote, would require washing and a change of clothes. This is an extreme form of control, representing an attempt to dictate to the world what contacts it should make with him and what it should keep out of his range. It was often evident that the germ phobia was a device to distract him from his greater concern, namely, the need to have a guaranteed financial structure to demonstrate to the world, and particularly to his father, that he was invincible and unassailable. To fail meant that he would be totally rejected by all and expelled from the human race as inadequate and imperfect.

The phobia is thus an excellent technique of defense against anxiety. The anxiety is clearly related to personality characteristics which are in danger of being exposed or destroyed. They may involve covert hostilities, or fear of being weak and dependent, or they may cover the entire range of human conflict. The underlying character structure which is organized to maintain a rigid control against exposure of acknowledgment is the obsessive-compulsive dynamism, which is ideally set up to serve this purpose. Under circumstances in which the obsessive-compulsive dynamism is not sufficiently intact, the phobia, with its absolute avoidance, guarantees against exposure by never permitting the situation to develop. Consequently, the phobia becomes a technique for absolute control, and unless it becomes too diffuse or widespread, it serves its purpose well. It is, however, qualitatively different from the simple avoidance reactions that serve the same purpose of protecting the person from known sources of danger. The phobia arises in response to a severe and critical anxiety attack in which some psychological need, defense, or conflict is brought dangerously near to being exposed or going out of control.

The setting or sensory accompaniments determine the phobic object in which the real danger may or may not be symbolically represented. The phobic object may be entirely accidental or coincidental and may involve the sensoria in auditory, kinesthetic, or visual senses. The symbolism and setting frequently combine, and the spread of the phobia is determined both by sensory contiguity and by symbolic associations possible in the new setting. The phobia is, in essence, an avoidance technique established through the defensive capacities of the human psyche to prevent the destruction of the integrity of the organism. However, it is the neurotic integration and, consequently, the necessity for symbolism and other devices to represent both unconscious and out-of-awareness needs and conflicts that are essential. Recognition of the origin of the phobia from an obsessive-compulsive disorder makes it clear that the ultimate resolution of the phobia rests on clarifying the obsessive-compulsive difficulty.

CHAPTER 6

Depression

In the preceding chapters the obsessional mechanism has been described as a defense against feelings of powerlessness and helplessness. What happens when the obsessional devices fail to serve their purpose and the person is forced to acknowledge his weakness and his incapacity to control all the aspects of his living? A number of possibilities confront him, ranging from the need to extend or expand his obsessional defenses to a total breakdown of his integrative capacities. A frequent outcome of the failure of an obsessional defense is a depressive reaction. In this framework depression is not viewed as a specific defense or a syndrome but rather as a response to the breakdown of a defense mechanism.

Until very recently depression has been described as a disease entity. This fact is related to the historical development of psychiatric theory out of the medical tradition of separate disease entities with differing etiologies. While this procedure was entirely rational for disorders in which the pathological changes were demonstrable and the causative agents identifiable, attempts to use such criteria with mental disorders proved inaccurate and misleading. Except where the etiology was clear and established (for example, GPI caused by syphilis or senile arteriosclerosis), attempts to establish disease entities out of symptom complexes have been unsuccessful.

A great advance in psychiatric nomenclature took place when the hundred or more presumed functional disorders were classified under these major headings: the neuroses and the psychoses which consisted of the schizophrenic and manic-depressive disorders. While this step encouraged the movement away from discrete disease entities, it still maintained the notion of a single disease with a specific cause and treatment. This tendency still plagues psychiatric theory and therapy and has resulted in serious errors in appraising the value of certain therapeutic measures, such as shock or drug therapy. In addition, it has led to a search for etiological agents, which has sidetracked psychiatric research for a long time. It has also been responsible for much mischief in statistical studies of the therapeutic results of psychotherapy, as it presumes to deal with established and clear-cut disease entities. The recent changes in the *Diagnostic Statistical Manual* (DSM III) reflects these newer under-standings, and the category of neuroses has largely been replaced by the label *disorder*. This is a giant step forward, but it still retains the medical disease philosophy.

Some of the presumed disease entities may simply be reaction modes or adaptive techniques designed to cope with certain intrapsychic or environmental stresses. Recent contributions to psychiatric theory have approached mental illness from this latter framework, which emphasizes the adaptive activities of human behavior. Such a viewpoint focuses on the needs of the individual and the processes and activities that are set into motion to fulfill these needs. If the needs are excessive, extreme, or distorted, the behavior that is organized to fill them may be maladaptive and may fail to satisfy the individual's productive requirements. Such responses are called neurotic or psychotic, and they constitute a wide range of reaction types called *defense mechanisms*. At times, these mechanisms cluster into large reaction types suited to deal with particular demands of the organisms. While they may resemble disease entities because their manifestations are similar, they do not constitute separate syndromes with specific etiology, pathology, or therapeutic management.

The understanding of depression has suffered from this historical development, particularly since it has been viewed as a disorder based upon physiological or biochemical causes. Despite the consistent biochemical changes in amine and ketosteroid metabolism, as well as in salts such as potassium chloride, depression cannot be viewed as a disorder of metabolism. Since it is such a widespread phenomenon and is present to degrees in almost everyone, it is more likely to be a response of the organism to some external stimulus which registers in a biochemical fashion in the cells. Depression is not something one *has*, but rather it is something that is *happening* in a person in relation to another person. The chemical changes are probably secondary.

This likelihood is most strikingly manifested by the massive reactions in voodoo death, when "the word" can produce adrenal insufficiency and death and when forgiveness from the chief can produce an immediate and striking improvement in the dying person. This reaction is certainly psychological and represents a reaction to disapproval or total rejection in a social setting in which such beliefs are held. It is, incidentally, a dramatic representation of the power of words and provides a major clue to the efficacy of psychotherapy in the depressive disorder, as with other psychological disorders.

CONCEPTS OF DEPRESSION

Freud's earlier classifications of the mental disorders were strongly influenced by Kraepelin. In spite of their more dynamic explanation, Kraepelin's writings supported the notion of depression as being a distinct disease entity with a specific etiology and therapy. Since Kraepelin, however, there has been a recurring tendency to link depression with the obsessional state. Premorbid obsessional personality traits are particularly common in involutional depression.

Freud's formulation was related to the libido theory and stated that depression was the result of the loss of an ambivalent loved object. He felt that the individual introjected the lost object and that the hostility manifested in this disorder resulted from the expression of the person's feeling toward the hated aspects of the lost object. This interpretation was useful in explaining many observable manifestations of the depressive reaction, both neurotic and psychotic. It emphasized the elements of hostility and the loss of a valued object, which resembled the process of mourning. It was particularly useful in increasing the understanding of suicide, and it served to draw some focus away from the physiological theories which emphasized biochemical and hormonal elements. However, in retaining the disease concept, the viewpoint discouraged the exploration of depression as an adaptive reaction which attempted to restore some lost possession — whether it be a person or thing. Later theorists such as Edith Weigert, Karen Horney, and Sandor Rado helped to expand the earlier dynamic formulations, although they disagreed about the omnipresence of hostility and its major role in the depressive process. The emphasis on oral factors in the disorder, as highlighted by Karl Abraham, was also discounted. While Freud focused on the lost object (which referred to a person), Rado viewed the loss in terms of a loss of love and saw the depressive reaction as an attempt to restore that loss.

The concept of depression presented here proposes that depression is a reaction to a loss *and* a maladaptive response in attempting to repair the loss. It is not seen as a disease but as a potential in all personality structures when a loss is experienced as leaving one totally helpless and impotent. It is in this respect that its relationship to the obsessional mechanism is manifested, and it is under these circumstances that the obsessional mechanisms break down because of internal or external stresses.

A variety of defensive responses may occur in the wake of a failing obsessional defense—for example, schizophrenia, paranoid developments, and other grandiose states, as well as depression. At present it is extremely difficult to determine why one response occurs and not another. However, it is clear that the depressive reaction is commonplace because the obsessional mode of behavior is universal. The depressive reaction may be mild or severe, with the same wide spectrum as noted in chapter 4. When it occurs in the normal obsessional or in those with any other neurotic disorder or personality type, it is the failure of the obsessional defense to maintain the standards or values considered by the individual to be essential. Depression follows the conviction or apprehension that the value, person, or thing deemed necessary may actually be lost or no longer available.

These values or persons are not necessarily realistic nor are the demands reasonable. They are invariably extreme and excessive and form part of the obsessive-neurotic value system in which the requirements for perfection and omniscience are essential ingredients. While the obsessional system is intact, the illusion of omniscience and perfection can be maintained. However, a crisis, a sudden disease, or some unexpected event may stir up the individual's apprehension about his ability to maintain these standards. If the concerns continue and the apprehension becomes a conviction, depression may supervene.

The relationship of the obsessional dynamism to depression is frequently portrayed in a dramatic form in the involutional depressions that arise in retired or incapacitated people. The precipitating factor is the forced recognition that one's previous productivity and capacity has become limited. This exacerbates any prior obsessional or perfectionistic traits, obsessional preoccupation, doubting, or procrastination, coupled with depressive reactions about not being able to live up to one's previous standards.

A prototype of this situation is represented by a sixty-two-year-old lawyer who had been very successful in his profession and who had had to slow down his pace for the previous five years because of a heart attack. Although he had been the organizer of a very successful law firm, he had over the previous few years become increasingly depressed, with feelings of worthlessness and despair. He was, in his own words, a perfectionist who was dedicated to his job and would not settle for anything but the best. He had few other interests and tried to acquire *all* the knowledge about his particular specialty. He was inflexible in his demands upon himself and simply had to keep up with the best. Though he had achieved a large measure of success and was happily married, he was a tense anxious person.

In trying to slow down at work, he began to feel less adequate than his colleagues, and guilty about not earning his way. He needed extra assurances about his output and his usefulness to the firm, while his colleagues tried to relieve him of difficult problems. He began to notice that he tired more easily and could not keep up with the younger staff in long-winded conferences, which involved extensive drinking. He could not accept the realities of the aging process and was humiliated when he felt tired. He was compelled to try to prove that his efficiency was as high as ever, even though he was aware of physiological limitations.

As he slowly began to feel depressed, he began wondering whether the firm would drop him in spite of his having participated in its founding. He felt he was a failure and wondered if he had a right to burden others. He began to develop some paranoid ideas. His sex life was less active, and he wondered if his wife would also abandon him. At this point, his depression was still mild, but it was clear that it would not be long before he might be involved in suicidal preoccupations or even in possible attempts at suicide.

The picture he described was directly related to his inability to accept the inevitable consequences of physiological aging, with its psychological accompaniments. By activity, success, and continuous acknowledgment from others, he could avoid the full recognition of his failing capacities. The heart attack forced this recognition upon him, along with a recognition of his dependence upon others. He was forced to admit that being sixty-two years of age was different from being forty. As the recognition of his increasing limitations was forced upon him, he became depressed, despaired of the future, and saw no reason for his existence. He concluded that he would have to go out and get a new batch of clients to prove that he was as good as ever, but he realized that this was not possible. He could not recognize that aging is inevitable and must be dealt with as a fact of life.

It is abundantly clear that a heretofore successfully adapted obsessional individual was, under forced circumstances of aging and disease, unable to accept his human predicament. This man could react only with despair, hopelessness, and depression.

Depression is, of course, hardly confined to older people! The demand for perfection often causes a student to become depressed if he fails to maintain his demands for A grades in all subjects. His presumed failure convinces him of his fallibility, and his depression is a response to the feeling of loss of standards and values.

A third-year medical student attempted suicide when he received only a passing grade in one subject. Up to that time he had only gotten top grades, and he viewed this occasion as the beginning of his decline. He was a severe obsessional who could not accept any compromise with his requirements of perfection and expected total rejection from his family in the face of what he considered a shameful grade. Only when the whole network of his compulsive demands and expectations was explored could he relinquish his superman requirements and continue in his training.

As another illustration, a person who receives a promotion and an increase in authority may react with a contradictory depressive response. At such times his neurotic expectation to be loved by all may be shattered by the realization that his promotion requires him to be a disciplinarian and perhaps an unpopular figure. The object or value that is supposed to be lost is considered essential; it may be the cornerstone of the neurotic integration, which is endangered if it is lost.

Depression occurs only in response to the neurotic elements in a person's personality and is often the key that allows us to see these elements. The loss of real things tends to produce a determined effort to replace what has been lost. Depression is the neurotic's maladaptive response, which attempts to force the return of the lost object or value.

CASE ILLUSTRATIONS

The situation of depression as a reaction increasing obsessional demands was dramatically portrayed in an extremely bright and ambitious young man. His expectations far exceeded his realistic potentials, leading to several severe depressive reactions while at college. In the early part of his marriage, he became depressed when he felt that his wife was losing interest in him, and this caused him to seek psychoanalytic therapy. During the treatment process he went into another severe depression, which permitted us to study the process's development in detail. It began after he became the director of a national organization, which was faltering until he began making a notable success of it. He inaugurated a large fund drive, and he functioned most effectively, even though his standards were extremely high and he was overly dedicated and conscientious. As the fund drive grew more elaborate and the deadline for a major event in the drive was approaching, he became overwhelmed by the details. He tried to handle every phase of the venture himself and demanded that every activity be perfectly executed. He wanted guarantees that the gala evening that was planned would come off perfectly. As evidence began to accumulate that it would be successful and as more prominent persons became involved, he became more depressed instead of being reassured. The participation of all these important people made it even more imperative that it be successful, and he demanded further guarantees that all would go perfectly.

As the day approached he became increasingly agitated and preoccupied. His restlessness and insomnia were stimulated by a constant reexamination of all the plans. All the minutiae became major issues, and every phase had to be scrutinized anew to prevent some disaster from occurring. What had begun as a successful venture, which he was handling effectively, turned into a nightmare of fear and danger. He saw himself on trial, as if the event would determine his entire future standing. Its significance was enormously exaggerated. He saw himself in the spotlight, critically appraised by all — which justified his concerns and perfectionistic strivings. He became self-critical and self-derogatory and had crying spells, with demands for reassurance about impossible matters. His physical processes slowed down, which aggravated his depression further until he was no longer able to get to the office. Although he withdrew several weeks before the event, it still came off well. He felt guilty about his failure to complete the project, but he received much acclaim for its success. His depression now quickly lifted. The whole incident was strikingly similar to a depression he suffered several years earlier when he was learning to drive. His expectations about his driving skill after a few lessons made the driver's test so distressing that he abandoned it for fear he would look ridiculous. Since he did not feel completely in control of the car and anticipated a debacle, he gave up driving altogether.

On both these occasions his depression was directly in response to the increasing obsessional demands which he made on himself. As he became aware of this he was overwhelmed by feelings of failure and tragedy, and his illusionary requirements of omnipotence and perfection began to be shattered. Despair and hopelessness were the result. The understanding and the resolution of the depressive process strengthened his feelings of esteem and lessened his obsessional requirements. This was facilitated by his recognition of the success of the venture, which was the result of his own efforts and which succeeded without guarantees of perfection.

Comments

The effect of a loss of a highly esteemed value or person upon one who is not involved in a neurotic personality structure is different from depression; it is more like the process of mourning. The individual quickly attempts to reorganize his personality structure without the lost value or person. While some grief normally accompanies this process, there is a reasonable effort to replace the loss or substitute something else. This is contrary to Freud's view that mourning and melancholia are similar, with the exception that the loss in depression or melancholia is unconscious while in grief or mourning it is conscious. It seems to me, however, that this distinction is not valid; in depression, too, the loss may often be conscious.

Mourning and depression are similar with respect to the emotion of unhappiness, which is prominent in both states. Mourning is a constructive process which follows a loss in which the relationship was primarily one of tenderness and love. Mourning is also a process of repair, which enables the person to sever and terminate his relationship. In this process his esteem for the lost person may be enhanced, and he may benefit from an intensified identification with him. The mourner's personality may be reintegrated at a higher level of maturity, and the experience may ultimately be productive.

Melancholia, on the other hand, is a destructive process in which the person refuses to relinquish the lost person and to accept the loss as a reality. It is experienced as abandonment, and the person feels helpless and impotent. There is a marked diminution in self-esteem, with self-derogatory and self-deprecatory accusations. The individual senses an attack on his pride, and he feels worthless and self-destructive. He resents the loss and feels antagonistic toward those who have deprived him. This often results in considerable hostility, overtly expressed as threats or attacks (both verbal and physical) or covertly expressed in the form of nagging, demanding, pleading, and clinging. This behavior is part of the depressed person's effort to repair the loss by forcing others to return what has been lost. The demands are generally made upon those who are closest and most intimate with the depressed person. Ultimately, the demands may extend to the whole environment in an attempt to force people to restore or reinstate the former condition. This is essentially a *power* operation and a struggle to control the behavior of others. The behavioral manifestations may be mild or severe, overt or covert, passively sullen or actively clinging, or accusing and demanding. They are essentially energetic efforts at restoring what has been lost. The self-destructive tendencies are the most powerful weapons in this effort.

In view of the central role played by control and power in the obsessional mechanism, we should expect to find a close relationship of the depressions with the obsessional states. This similarity has been noted by a great many personality theorists, beginning with Freud and Karl Abraham and including Karen Horney, Harry Stack Sullivan, Franz Alexander, and Sandor Rado. Their descriptions of the depressive personality are almost identical to those of the obsessive-compulsive personality. Franz Alexander noted the similarity and attempted to make some distinction between the two. He described the depressive personality as a warm and practical one which showed preferences for concrete rather than abstract thinking. The compulsive, on the other hand, was described as being inclined toward abstract thinking and remaining largely detached from his fellow man. However, such distinctions are not sufficiently specific to warrant typing separate personality structures. The compulsive personality is often practical and frequently concrete, while the depressive's warmth is often like the compulsive's strong attachments at the extremes of feeling. It is likely that what has been described as a separate depressive personality is actually an obsessional personality that tends toward depressive reactions.

The depressive person is one who has exceptionally high standards and who cannot accept any compromises. He is egocentric and overreacts to frustration and denial. His relationship to others is characterized as one of exploitative dependency, in which he controls and manipulates others. He tends to deal in extremes of good and bad (black and white) and fails to see the total person, who is a mixture of both. He is serious, dedicated, and determined to achieve perfection in all things. He feels that he has failed to fulfill his own expectations of himself, as well as his parents'. However, he maintains his level of existence by an illusion that he is achieving a perfect performance. When he is forced by circumstances to acknowledge some deficiency or failure in his system of values, he feels humiliated by the notion that he has lost status and esteem in the eyes of others. This is accompanied by feelings of hopeless despair and depression. This description is a precise parallel of the descriptions of obsessionals who react with despair to any awareness of imperfections. When the failure is extreme and presumed to be irreparable, a severe depression may ensue. If the obsessional feels that total rejection may follow some failure on his part to maintain absolute control at all times, depression may also follow. As the excessive and exaggerated standards of the obsessional defense can rarely be maintained, it is inevitable that frequent depressions will occur — ranging from the mild to the severe forms.

ONSET OF DEPRESSION

Depression not only results from the failure to maintain excessive standards but also may result when one anticipates that weakness or deficiencies will prevent one from even approximating such standards. The situation may be transient and may be relieved when some evidence of acceptability or some success in an unrelated area temporarily restores the illusion of perfection. Since the obsessional person has inconsistent and fleeting feelings of self-worth, he cannot appraise his capabilities with validity; hence, his assets are easily overlooked in moments of temporary difficulty and despair.

Such a situation is very common in neurotic states, particularly in the obsessional personality. It may also occur in other personality structures in which obsessional factors are significant, the frequency being directly related to the amount of obsessional defenses in the person's personality patterns.

It is this view of the dynamics of depression that enables us to see why such reactions are so widespread. Since we all utilize obsessional defenses, it is small wonder that most of us experience frequent and minor depressions in the course of living. At times it is quite evident that the issue of standards is related to the onset of depression — for example, when minor or trivial events trigger the reaction. When an extreme reaction takes place because one has received a lower-than-expected grade, it is evident that the response cannot be fully understood in terms of this event alone. It would be better understood if one could realize the severe condemnation and utter contempt the person feels for himself because he failed to fulfill his demands. His response is so marked that he anticipates total rejection and severe censure from others. When success brings on a depression, the same factors are at work. The person who has a depressed reaction to success aspires to higher standards and values than those expressed in his new status. His underlying feelings of inadequacy and his demands for a perfect performance in his new position leave him with feelings of uncertainty and incapacity to achieve them. If the apprehension is great enough, it may bring on a depression. Success in such instances is not regarded as a mark of achievement but rather as a test and a challenge toward further achievement. Thus, success produces tension and uneasiness instead of a comfortable feeling of recognition and acknowledgment.

The concept of depression considered here demonstrates that it is more than a faulty process of past learning; it is caused by a severe overreaction to a failure to achieve goals and values which may be excessive and impossible. While this tendency derives from one's past characterological development, it is provoked by present events and future anticipations. If this is so, the treatment of depression must focus on the here and now, rather than becoming obsessively preoccupied with the past.

DYNAMICS OF DEPRESSION

Freud's description of depression, amplified by Karl Abraham and others, focused on the hostile elements in the process — that is, the tendency to express one's anger toward the ambivalent, introjected love object. This produced the typical picture of the depression, with guilt, self-accusations, and self-destructive tendencies. Suicide was held to be the extreme instance of the depressive tendency toward self-hatred. These explanations required the death-instinct and libido hypotheses.

From the adaptational point of view (without recourse to earlier theories), depression is a reparative process which supervenes when a person feels he has lost something vital to his psychic integration. The reaction of despair and depression is the result of the anticipated rebuff and the expectation of total rejection as a consequence of this loss. With this framework in mind, the other elements in depression become more understandable. The hostile, demanding, and clinging behavior is related to this desperate attempt to regain the lost object from those felt to be responsible for taking it away or capable of restoring it. The depressed person pleads, begs, demands, cajoles, and attempts to force the environment to replace or restore the object.

At first, the tenacious and demanding behavior stirs up sympathy, pity, and sometimes even empathy in others. But as these reactions do not restore what has been lost, the demands increase and then produce resentment and anger toward the depressed person. The end result is an annoyed and distressed individual who generally feels guilty, even though he has tried his best to please and appease the depressed person. The annoyance soon turns to noticeable irritation and finally to anger. At this point the depressed individual may actually be rejected; this confirms his grievances, producing hostility and justifying his accusations against the environment.

Unlike the above-described agitated type of depressive, who hopes that by evoking guilt reactions he can stir up some activity in his behalf, the silent, retarded depressive is immovable and uncommunicative; he conveys a silent rebuke and reproach to the environment. He may refuse to eat or to participate in any activities whatsoever. The passive, seemingly demanding attitude is actually a most potent device in inciting large amounts of guilt and activity. All efforts of friends, relatives, and other helpers are received with only slight appreciation because they fail to fulfill the depressed person's demands. There is always a note of criticism about the limitations and inadequacy of what is being done for him. One soon begins to feel that it is impossible to satisfy the depressed individual and begins to resist his demands. The immediate family and friends are the first to be alienated, even though they begin by being the most understanding. This situation soon spreads to others, often including the physician and psychiatrist.

Then the depressive's hostility becomes more evident, and a vicious circle is quickly established. His hostile attacks stimulate counterattacks; he is accused of being insatiable, greedy, and ungrateful — which only increases his hostility. Much of the symptomatology of the depressed person reflects an attempt to regain control of himself by desperately trying to regain the lost object. The typical obsessional picture, with its devices and techniques for achieving control, can be clearly seen in the behavior of the depressed individual.

Within this framework the problem of suicide and some of the contradictory elements in the older theories of depression can be clarified. While it has been known for some time that suicide is particularly prevalent in depressive states, it is not directly proportional to the depth of the depression or the extent of the expressed or repressed hostility. As a matter of fact, suicide often occurs when the depression is at a minimum or moving toward some resolution. It also seems to occur when the overt hostility is greater than the covert hostility, in contradiction to the theoretical presumption. On the other hand, suicide is directly related to the degree of despair and the feeling of hopelessness about being able to restore one's esteem in the face of expected condemnation from the community. The threat of such action is therefore greatest as one goes into or out of a depression — that is, when the despair about reconstructing one's former status and integration is greatest. Suicide seems unrelated to the amount of hostility; instead, it seems directly related to feelings of hopelessness. Oversimplified notions of suicide as a means of embarrassing others or expressing hostility toward them no longer seems tenable.

COMMENTS ON TREATMENT

The solution to the dilemma created by the conflict between pleading for help and rejecting it as being "patronizing" lies in giving help judiciously and wisely, with a view to stimulating the greatest feeling of esteem without stirring up major resentments. This requires some knowledge of the depressive's behavior patterns, so as not to respond unwisely to his neurotic and contradictory demands.

The demand to be entirely independent underlies much of the depressive's behavior. The depression is an appeal for a meaningful relationship and is, in essence, a cry for love which cannot be made openly and unashamedly. Such a person has difficulty in developing a loving relationship through care, concern, interest, and affection. He has the obsessional conception that love means being weak and giving in. He tries to force love through demands that produce guilt feelings in others. While others may initially respond with loving concern, the continued ungrateful attitude of the depressed person ultimately changes the love to irritation and anger. Anger and frustration may also occur in the therapeutic situation as a result of such maneuvers. It may become very difficult for the therapist to restrain his own hostility.

Coercive, insistent demands and angry rebukes antagonize the environment. This is precisely what takes place in the obsessional mechanism. However, the obsessional's loss is not experienced as real; therefore, the dynamic patterns are still concerned with maintaining control rather than retrieving a loss. There are no demands and rebukes for restoration of control, as the obsessional individual still believes that he is maintaining control. It is when there is a *conviction* of loss — whether real or imagined, conscious or out-of-awareness — that the depressive maneuver supervenes in the obsessional's attempt to replace the loss.

The relationship of mania to depression — which is manifest in manic-depressive disorders and related states — can also be more clearly understood in the context of the depression's being related to the obsessive-compulsive dynamism. At times the depressive maneuvers appear to produce a restoration of the lost object or value. This, however, is not real or valid; it is impossible to replace the lost object or to restore the impossible requirements of the individual. The feeling of success is magical — an illusionary fulfillment not visible to others. The depressed person's reaction to such an event is one of joy and satisfaction — which in an extreme state is called *mania*, since it confirms his belief in his magical powers and his capacity to control and manipulate the world for his purposes. While such a reaction is generally short-lived, it is a state of euphoria in which all forms of power and skills are artificially assumed, and the person acts as if he were possessed of omnipotent and omniscient qualities. He claims the capacity to achieve anything and everything. It is a state of exaggerated grandiosity in which there is a limitless view of one's physical and mental capacities. However, failure to recognize one's limitations (even in the manic state) can also bring about a depression, as in the cyclic disorders of depression and mania. Mania may relate to the omnipotence and magical powers that the obsessive-compulsive seeks.

A striking example of the relationship of depression, mania, grandiosity, and paranoid developments occurred in a young lady who, after thirteen years of a rather stormy marriage, was finally faced with the possibility of divorce. While this issue had been raised previously, she was certain at those times that her husband would not leave her. On the last occasion he informed her in clear and decisive terms that he was separating on a permanent basis. Her initial reaction was one of depression, with pleas, promises, and resolves to change. When this had no effect upon him, she became hyperactive and set about visiting friends and planning for her future. During this period she insisted that her husband really did love her and would ultimately return. She developed delusional ideas about how much her husband loved her, and cited evidence to substantiate it. Any evidence to the contrary was denied and she insisted that what had transpired was in the nature of a test. Her manic behavior, which persisted for several days, was characterized by increasingly grandiose delusions, culminating in a paranoid outburst while she was in a beauty parlor.

On the day which preceded this outbreak, she assumed that all the neighbors were on guard, in order to make certain that she got all the sleep she needed. She felt that she was a privileged special person and the object of everyone's concern and interest. At the beauty parlor, however, she became abusive and violent, accusing her hairdresser of trying to humiliate and destroy her status in the eyes of her husband. Her behavior became so extreme that she required hospitalization at this time. This delusional system disappeared, within days, when she began to accept realistically the estranged situation; she then began to plan how she would win her husband back. She was amused, horrified and curious about her delusional ideas but could not adequately explain how they developed.

If depression is related to the obsessive dynamism, the responsiveness of depressions to physiological therapies must also be accounted for. Because electric shock therapy and drug convulsants produced effects which either injured the patient or made him fearfully resistive, he viewed such treatment as punishment. This attitude coincided with the theory of depression which implied that such people are guilty and self-destructive. Shock therapy was viewed as relieving the superego of its harshness, permitting the depression to be resolved. This is an appealing view, even though the insulin therapies (unlike metrazol and ECT) are neither painful nor distressing. Too, the use of tranquilizers, psychic energizers, and placebos — which produce little or no distress yet prove valuable — casts serious doubts on such an interpretation. It has never been clearly established where the value of such dissimilar physiological approaches lies. The tranquilizing drugs, with their mildly euphoric effect, and the psychic energizers, which improve the patient's physical condition, are also beneficial in the treatment of depressive states.

It is generally agreed that it is necessary to produce a confused state before benefit can be derived from many physiologically based procedures. Such confusion is also produced by the tranquilizing drugs. While a severe confused state may not be essential, what does seem necessary is a disorganization of the individual's existing value systems. The high standards which have been unfulfilled and the resulting low esteem and self-derogatory accusations are disrupted by these approaches, allowing the individual to reorganize his value systems in a less rigid and extreme fashion. The temporary loss of memory induced by these procedures also permits such a value reorganization, either on a pre-illness basis or on an even more moderate and realistic one. This reorganization, with its reduced demands on the person, results in a rapid amelioration of the depressive symptomatology.

When psychotherapy assists in a reorganization of the distorted values of a depressed person, it also facilitates resolution of the difficulty. Shock and drug therapies, by producing confusion, memory defects, or some reduction of the tension involved in maintaining false ideals, can accelerate this process.

In spontaneous recoveries which occur by merely changing the individual's environment, a reorganization of the value system can also be noted. The change of geography, of the interpersonal setting, or of the usual routine of the depressed person often permits him to appraise his value system in the new setting and to discover its false or neurotic basis.

Aside from the physiological approaches, therapy for depression must take into account the factors noted in the relationship of depression to the obsessive-compulsive disorders. The therapeutic problem centers on the recognition of false value systems and the underlying neurotic supports which have been lost, rather than on the issue of hostility and its expression. The power techniques of the person must be exposed for their true intent and purpose, and the possibility of establishing a new value system must be introduced. Invariably, the lost object is an exaggerated, overly idealized value or goal which was incapable of ever being actualized in the first place. A revision of such goals will reduce the necessity for maintaining control over the environment, thus eliminating the fear of being rejected or isolated. What is accomplished in the physiological therapies can be more permanently and usefully produced through a psychotherapeutic process that gives full consideration to the dynamics involved. Such a project will undoubtedly serve the patient more effectively because it will not only relieve the depression but will also open up the entire obsessive-compulsive problem for consideration. In view of the high rate of remissions produced by such physiological resolutions, the somewhat slower results produced by the psychotherapeutic process may, in the long run, prove more efficient and economical.

CHAPTER 7

Breakdown of the Obsessive Defense

The obsessional defense pattern is excellently suited to providing someone with a feeling of security in a world in which uncertainty is inevitable. However, critical situations — which may be caused by disease, social upheavals, catastrophic events, or accidental circumstances — may be sufficiently severe that the obsessional integration can no longer be maintained. Crises such as these may be the result of wars, the death of significant people in one's life, demands beyond one's capacity made by others or oneself, or physical changes in the course of one's development. Such changes are common in the aging process; they are particularly significant during adolescence, when marked psychological and physiological demands are made on the individual. The maturation of the gonads during this period produces physiological tensions which are entirely beyond one's control and usually push the person toward sexual intimacy. At the same time, social and cultural pressures may require the youth to become independent and make vocational decisions, as well as achieve some heterosexual intimacy of a sexual and nonsexual nature. Some of these pressures may be controlled and managed by the individual, while others are sufficiently powerful to demand conformity. Adolescence, therefore, is an era of great turmoil and decision; any obsessional patterns which have been successful until then may break down. One begins to feel weak, powerless, and incapable of handling all the demands. It is no surprise that the adolescent era has such a high percentage of schizophrenic episodes.

If lustful needs are very great and the person's skill in making contact with the opposite sex is not adequate, the youth may experience a good deal of difficulty unless he can control such needs. Obsessional defenses are most commonly utilized to control these desires and to keep the person's anxieties to a minimum. His ability to do so will depend on his own capacities and on the availability and quality of sex partners. Therefore, we may find that in some adolescents a minor event may produce a major breakdown, while in other individuals the most traumatic events seem to be handled with considerable ease. The capacity is directly related to the experience and self-esteem established prior to adolescence. The success of obsessional patterns will depend on the extent to which they have been needed to support the security structure prior to adolescence, so that the increased strain will not cause the structure to collapse. Harry Stack Sullivan developed this point of view most effectively, demonstrating how the breakdown of obsessional defenses may result in a schizophrenic disintegration of the personality structure.

The variety of psychological defenses which a person utilizes in order to deal with anxiety will rarely dissipate the anxiety entirely. A neurosis is essentially a collection of such defenses, constituting a personality structure which attempts to minimize and deflect the anxiety. The success of these defensive tactics depends on the severity of the realistic issues which the individual must meet and the strength of his resources outside the neurotic tendency. The obsessional defense, when functioning efficiently, is capable of handling large amounts of anxiety unless it dislocates the person's life or alienates him from others to the extent that it may stimulate even more anxiety.

The obsessional's desire to overcome his feelings of powerlessness and to guarantee his future existence by a firm determination to know everything cannot really succeed because the neurosis can provide only an illusory solution. His failure to achieve omniscience — which would eliminate anxiety — must be defended either by denial or by a variety of devices which serve to minimize his awareness of this deficiency. The phobia is often the technique used to maintain an illusion of perfection by avoiding the areas that would expose these deficiencies. It allows one to maintain an illusion of omnipotence on the assumption that one could manage everything if exposure to the threatening experiences were avoided. The deficiency is never confronted and therefore does not need to be acknowledged.

Ordinarily, an individual attempts to minimize his anxiety through judicious planning or by restraining his demands and expectations, thereby avoiding the need to test his resources. The obsessional also tries to avoid challenges, particularly when he has no guarantee of success. However, this is not always possible, and such challenges may produce exacerbation of the existing obsessional patterns or initiate new ones. The presence of an obsessional technique demands a greater display of one's omnipotence — which, in turn, forces the person to recognize his limitations, thereby stimulating more obsessional tactics. This process produces the typical neurotic cycle, in which the presence of anxiety stirs up defenses which produce more anxiety.

This vicious circle can be interrupted if one is willing to accept being human — which means to be prepared to accept uncertainty. As long as one insists on absolute control, he will be unable to disrupt the obsessional way of life because the world continues to be potentially destructive. The obsessional device is more comforting to him and appears more reasonable than a recognition of his human limitations. It is this seemingly obvious choice which makes the obsessive pattern so adhesive and explains why the obsessive clings to his defenses with such tenacity, even while he recognizes their paradoxical value.

When the obsessional defenses are no longer capable of dealing with the demands on the inside or outside of the person, several possible developments may ensue. It has already been demonstrated that a depression may follow a failure to sustain the obsessional's illusions of his capacities. Under other circumstances there could be an increase in one's activities, with agitated efforts to overcome the demands and avert a breakdown. The agitated behavior may be associated with an increase and extension of the obsessional patterns; this development could produce mania if unrestrained and panic if unsuccessful. Should a panic occur and continue unchecked, schizophrenic disintegration of the personality structure may follow. Sullivan emphasized this sequence of events in the beginnings of schizophrenia. In his classical study of schizophrenia, Bleuler noted that compulsive ideas occur regularly in schizophrenia and manifest themselves early in the illness. It is notable that in adolescence the obsessional illnesses frequently precede the development of schizophrenia.

Some recent theorists have hypothesized that obsessional defenses are an attempt to prevent a schizophrenic disintegration of the ego. This notion implies that a neurosis is an attempt to immunize an individual against a possible psychotic breakdown. This view has less support, however, than the concept that mental illness is a part of a broader spectrum extending from normal to psychotic, with the neurotic development somewhere near the middle. The latter concept emphasizes the more prevalent notion that these disorders are different from the normal only quantitatively, not qualitatively; they are simply exaggerations of tendencies prevalent in all people.

TYPES OF DEFENSES

In the spectrum of mental illness the type of defense constitutes the symptoms of the neurosis or psychosis. One could hypothesize that certain defenses are related to certain mental illnesses or that one type of defense may be exclusively present in a particular nosological category. This view is implied in the psychosexual theory of development, according to which such zonal qualities as the oral (intake, incorporation, etc.) are responsible for such defenses as introjection and sadistic incorporation, in contrast to the anal (expulsive, retentive, etc.), which produce such obsessional defenses as displacement and paranoid externalization. This notion has been expressed by many psychiatrists and psychoanalysts, but I believe it is not a valid theoretical assumption. It would be incorrect to say that the obsessional type of defense implies a greater degree of personality disorganization than does the hysterical defense, simply because it utilizes more extreme techniques. Exactly the opposite situation may be true. Yet this notion has sometimes led to a snobbish glorification of the obsessional schizophrenic defense.

It was thought that the introspective, highly sensitized obsessional had greater capacities for self-understanding, as well as for understanding others. This attitude led some researchers to assume that the schizophrenic had particular talent for interpreting dreams and other symbolic or unconscious productions. The extravagant, dramatic hysteric was viewed as being overly concerned with the outer world in contrast to the obsessional, who was more preoccupied with his inner world.

The type of defense and the symptoms which are developed in a particular neurosis or psychosis are closely related to constitutional factors as well as to the problems the person has to deal with in his life. It may be a matter of utilizing the same defenses which he observes in his parents or developing suitable defenses to deal with his parents' personality traits. For example, if the situation is extremely threatening, the technique of denial or dissociation may be utilized to allow for simple survival. On the other hand, the obsessional parent who makes demands upon his children for absolute performances and perfect achievements will be fostering obsessional patterns in the children, who will have to cope with these demands.

Some defenses involve the utilization of physiological mechanisms or somatic sources for influencing or shaping the environment. Some defenses allow the organism to function more effectively temporarily, by focusing away from painful or significant issues. Sublimation, suppression, repression, denial, and selective inattention — among other devices — function in this way. In general, most personality types use all three modalities of defense organization, even though one may be more prominent and more influential in controlling the person's behavior. The style or characterological patterns of behaving have produced the nosological labels in the categories of character disorder, but we rarely find pure types and the descriptions for our classifications are generally a stereotyped collection of all the qualities found in the character structures of the described type. Obsessionals are not always meticulous, and hysterics are not always theatrical; yet a need for certainty is far more in evidence in obsessionals and a superficial overt emotionality is more easily noted in the hysteric.

By reducing anxiety, obsessive defenses may accelerate learning to a certain extent, but in the long run they tend to interfere with the learning process. The defense which enables a person to appear to others the opposite of what he really feels is called a *reaction-formation.* A highly competitive person may appear to himself and to others to be a most cooperative individual, entirely disinterested in competitive struggles. This defense enables him to function in situations in which some cooperation is necessary, but it interferes with the process and inevitably disrupts it because the competitive strivings manifest themselves in covert and accidental ways when the person cannot identify his true interests; he cannot confront them or deal with them and they subtly defeat his goals in the long run. Reaction-formations are generally not used for major personality constituents. If the issues are more significant, and more drastic consequences could result from an awareness of such needs or tendencies, more rigorous defenses, such as denial, may be needed.

Denial

In *denial,* a person does not recognize a personality trait which is unacceptable to him, even though it is obvious to others and is brought to his attention. Denial is accomplished in a variety of ways, but the most effective device is that of selective inattention. By selective inattention, one fails to notice or fails to respond and thereby makes no memory impact of a perceptual event. It is as if it never happened, even though we can perceive the event and store it in our memory bank. This accounts for the discrepant reports often given by people viewing the same event. Such denials deal with relatively minor occurences; massive denials in terms of total situations can be produced by repression.

The obsessional also uses other devices — namely substitutions utilizing magic and rituals, which are defenses fostering illusions of power and strength by denying the realities of existence up to a point. When the realities are completely denied and the person takes up an entirely new, unreal existence, he is manifesting a psychosis. This may occur when a previously denied or dissociated feeling or impulse is brought forcibly to a person's awareness. His inability to accept it may produce panic and a disintegration of his personality structure.

In the psychotic defense, when one takes on a new identity, one strives to document his new self by a denial of the facts relative to his old self. While adducing proofs regarding his new identity, he may deny his family, friends, and backgrounds and not even acknowledge that he is in a mental hospital. The new identity may be tenaciously supported in spite of extensive intellectual assaults and the absence of any confirmation from the environment. Such delusions are quite common in psychotic states.

However, the type of defense employed does not determine the presence or absence of mental illness, even though defenses can be graded according to their closeness or distance from reality. We may find evidence of obsessional substitution, denial, and fantasies bordering on delusions in people who are functioning quite effectively, whereas the psychotic patient who is severely withdrawn may be rationalizing in a way reminiscent of healthy, unneurotic living. It is not the type of defense employed, but the extremes to which that defense is used. All the defenses are used by most people — ranging from the normal to the psychotic. Some defenses may be more prominent than others because they are more extensively utilized and become the dominant personality traits. Diagnostic categories have often reflected these main defenses and have given a label to the disorders involved. Such a label does not mean, however, that what is named is the only defense that is being employed. The diagnosis of hysteria in a person need not mean that other defensive techniques are not also present. The obsessional device present in all personality types is called obsessional living or obsessional neurosis only when it dominates the personality picture. All categories of mental illness contain several defenses, with one predominating. One can identify the obsessional defenses in hysterias, anxiety states, psychosomatic disorders, and manic-depressive and schizophrenic disorders. Whatever the diagnosis, however, its role is similar to what has already been described.

Some Mistaken Notions

While the severity of a mental illness is often closely related to the major defensive technique employed, there is no hierarchy of illness beginning with hysteria and progressing to schizophrenia. An hysterical illness may be completely disruptive and incapacitating, while an ambulatory or intermittent schizophrenic may be functioning at a rather high level of adjustment — perhaps higher than that of the hysteric. It is this mistaken notion that has produced the concern that the obsessional neurotic who is functioning adequately may regress into a nonfunctioning schizophrenic if he is improperly treated. Similarly, it has been suggested that the resolution of a schizophrenic disorder would regularly produce an obsessional disorder which, if maintained, would immunize the person against schizophrenia. While such back-and-forth swings do occur, they do not occur because of their hierarchical relationship. Generally speaking, the obsessional pattern of living rarely disintegrates for the worse and only with the utmost skill and activity can it be altered for the better. Usually it is quite stable and is an effective development which may be disorganized only in the face of extreme circumstances. It is because the obsessional pattern has such stability that therapy is most difficult. The very nature of the defense, with its capacity for distraction, emotional isolation, denial, grandiosity, and doubting, makes it difficult to undermine the obsessional defense. Only when the patient can be made to feel that some benefit can be derived from any change can we hope to achieve it.

However, there is some validity to the idea that a neurosis may protect the individual against a psychotic breakdown, since the longer one has managed to function effectively with a neurosis the less likely is a psychotic breakdown to occur in later years, when the demands on one's living have lessened. This is not always true, however, in the obsessional neurosis — when aging is accompanied by the actual lessening of one's physical and mental capacities — a fact the obsessional cannot accept. The accompaniments of aging, with its diminution of psychological and physical capacities, can and do aggravate the obsessional disorder.

A predominantly obsessional illness can become, particularly in the later years, an involutional depression or a schizophrenic illness with delusions and hallucinations. Usually such people may have been functioning successfully until the crisis of aging overtook them. This would suggest that a neurosis does not necessarily ward off a psychosis. Some compulsive symptoms — particularly anorexia, compulsive gambling, or kleptomania — are accompanied by such grandiose feelings of exemption or freedom from responsible consequences to their behavior that the psychotic or unrealistic elements seem glaring even in the face of their ability to function effectively. In addition, the tendency in younger people to move back and forth — from an obsessional neurosis to a withdrawn schizophrenic state — also negates the notion of the immunizing power of a neurosis.

Possible Regressions

Is there a particular kind of obsessional neurosis which tends to regress into schizophrenia? While there is little support for the notion that certain kinds of obsessions are more likely to precede schizophrenia, it has been noted by some that when somatic preoccupations are prominent or hypochondriasis is extreme there is a greater likelihood for schizophrenia to supervene. A shift in the patient's preoccupation with dirt or feces to his bowels and its activities can be the center around which psychotic delusions may develop. These delusions may involve the feeling of being poisoned or of having no intestines because they were destroyed by some malevolent influence. A variety of delusions may focus around the feces. Or the obsessional's preoccupation with his heart and its functioning and his uneasy vigilance lest the cardiac rate change may be the prelude to a delusion concerning the heart. The intense anxiety surrounding this matter may actually alter the cardiac action, which may presage a psychosis.

In the transition from obsessionalism to schizophrenia, many features of these two syndromes can be noted and identified, and it can be seen that they seem to serve the same purposes. The grandiosity of the obsessional is dealt with as a reality in the schizophrenic illness, and the omniscient demands in the obsessional state become expressed as being God or some other metaphoric superman. Phobic avoidance in the obsessional is manifested as total withdrawal and emotional isolation during the psychotic episode. The obsessional distractions of obfuscation and other complicated verbal operations can be recognized in the schizophrenic in his neologisms, autistic activity, and alienation of thought and feeling. The prevailing feeling of danger, threat, anticipated humiliation, and rejection is often translated as a paranoid system when a psychosis develops.

Often, the resulting psychosis appears to be an extreme extension of the previous obsessional symptoms. The individual can no longer manage, and what was previously odd but functional now appears "crazy" and therefore totally unacceptable, maladaptive, and disruptive.

Under certain circumstances an extension of the obsessional patterns can lead to paranoid developments which, in turn, may become delusional and become part of a schizophrenic development. The uneasy, uncertain, obsessional person who scrutinizes every individual and event for evidence of criticism, contempt, or rejection sees every contact as a possible source of danger. He is set for attack and it is no wonder he often sees it coming. Since he must always be on top, correct, and omniscient, every minor failure will be viewed with alarm and will be accompanied by his feelings that the community will be pleased at his failure and will humiliate him. This is an ideal setting for the development of paranoid ideas —

particularly when feelings of anger and hostility are also involved. The development of paranoid feelings which include expectations of malevolence from others inevitably follows the tendency to distort events and experiences, so that one is always a victim. When one expectantly scrutinizes the behavior of others for evidence of reassurance, approval, or criticism, one does not take sufficient account of the possibility that the other person may be in some distress and may be focused on his own needs. This can mistakenly be interpreted as displeasure with, or disapproval of, the obsessional. Such a capacity for distortion arises from the obsessional's excessive need for approval and the assumption that everything that happens has relevance for him.

The obsessional person is unaware that he cannot always win the approval of others; thus, any gesture from others, the significance of which is not clearly evident, is often viewed as expressing disapproval. He does not explore or inquire about this particular gesture — which may owe to indigestion or some other cause quite unrelated to him. The simple and regular explanation is that he is being criticized and disliked. This explanation also satisfies the obsessional's feeling of specialness and his expectation of being envied by others. He assumes the other person has reason to dislike him because he is so clever, capable, and successful and that consequently the other person would like to knock him down and humiliate him. From this point of view of being special it is but a short step to the grandiosity of the psychotic, which is a regular part of the paranoid system.

Grandiosity — the ultimate effect of striving for omniscience, omnipotence, and the fulfillment of superhuman ideals — is an integral part of the obsessional disorder. While the obsessional proclaims his modesty and readiness to be satisfied with small achievements, his strivings and behavior belie this position. It is clear that he can be satisfied only with superhuman achievements. This is grandiosity in action, even though there is some embarrassment and denial when the obsessional is confronted with the full implication of such demands. The grandiosity of the paranoid state, on the other hand, is unashamedly expressed and aggressively defended, even though it consists of precisely those elements present in the obsessional state. Obsessional rituals and preoccupations are often indistinguishable from psychotic, ritualistic performances, and they appear to serve the same purpose. While the obsessional ritual may be explained as silly and meaningless but necessary nonetheless, the schizophrenic makes no explanation for such behavior or else insists on its rationality and evident appropriateness.

In spite of these similarities, there is no direct continuum of obsessional neurosis into schizophrenia or vice versa, even though the schizophrenic may have an underlying obsessional personality structure. This situation was demonstrated in a young man whose life was filled with obsessive ritualistic practices involving yogalike exercises and hand-washing rituals as well as word games. He was immersed in "doing good" for all, while neglecting many essentials in his life. Periodically, however, under the stress of criticism at the job or difficulties with his wife or friends, he would express delusions of being God and would plan to carry out some dangerous mission to prove this. The effect was only to produce damage to his professional standing. Instead of carrying out the dangerous missions, he would either admit himself or permit himself to be admitted to a mental hospital where, after a brief period of psychotherapy, he would temporarily abandon his delusions and return to the community. While such events might suggest an obsessional moving in and out of schizophrenia, the picture is essentially that of a psychotic individual who manages to keep his psychosis in control. This person demonstrates the close relationship of the obsessional defense with the schizophrenic illness, rather than the notion that one disorder regularly moves into the other.

Another example of the relationship between the obsessional personality structure and schizophrenia (and particularly the development of a paranoid delusion) is that of a young lady whose attempts to achieve Godlike perfection occasionally took on messianic proportions in her soul-saving activities. She was enormously energetic and usually effective. Most of her activities were constructive up to the point where she would meet some opposition or criticisms. Then her activity would become more tense and frenetic, and her previously guarded behavior would be less restrained and would become antagonizing and frightening to the community. She had some rituals, many compulsive patterns, and a great deal of preoccupation with being invulnerable, imperturbable, and invincible. On one occasion some mild restraints imposed on her behavior by others provoked a number of paranoid delusions in which she insisted that she was being followed by television cameras and was in danger of being killed. At this point she sought therapy, and hospitalization was avoided. Her obsessive patterns began to unfold dramatically during therapy, and this took the focus away from her paranoid tendencies. Her activities at home, socially, and at her job were severely obsessive, and her schizophrenic tendencies became manifest only during the therapy sessions. In general, she functioned quite effectively as a somewhat unusual woman who related to everyone in a sticky, obsessional fashion.

On one occasion during therapy, I had the opportunity to observe the development of a transient, paranoid delusion in this patient. This patient's capacity for introspection and the insight which she obtained from therapy allowed her to examine this incident in detail. One day, after finishing her teaching job, she noticed that a car seemed to be following her car. She concluded that the two men in the car were trying to force her to the side of the road and kill her. As she ruminated about this she began to panic and to elaborate a detailed, paranoid delusion. She related this brief psychotic development several days later in her therapy hour. After this hour she wrote me a letter from which I quote: "I knew I hadn't pin-pointed the cause of discomfort during the hour with you. I kept at it as I returned home. The time I saw the two men pulling out in their car, as I got into mine, was in the afternoon. As I was closing up my desk I looked at a box full of pencils and ballpoint pens, etc. — probably 25 assorted ones or so. We're always running out of pencils at our house. I remember using one of the pens for record-taking, wanting to put it in my purse, and saying to myself: 'the discomfort you'll feel about this won't be worth the convenience of taking it.' It wasn't that I felt it would be missed, or that anyone would care ... but that STEALING would register in my mind. As I was closing up, I rummaged through the box and took two pencils — middle size, somewhat beat up ones ... put them in my purse. Now as I walked toward my car this came back vividly, and I felt a sudden relief which made me feel this was the direct cause of the feeling 'they're going to get me,' which occurred, timewise, not more than a half-hour later. As I thought of symbols, I burst out laughing, asking myself out loud, 'But why did you have to take TWO of them?' I hope you can help me answer that question — or rather, why did I *have* to take even one?"

As we explored the letter and all her feelings in connection with it, the following issues became clear: (1) She felt guilty about not behaving perfectly and not being in control of herself; (2) she could not resist getting something for nothing — an integral part of her grandiosity; and (3) her perfectionism and self-righteousness could not allow her to take even one badly beat-up pencil, and her rigid intolerance to any human frailty expected that her action would be followed by severe and immediate punishment.

When it was suggested that perhaps her taking the pencils did not merit such extreme consequences, her reply was, "Then you think it's all right to be a thief?" As will be indicated in chapter 9, the obsessional's response to an attempt to focus on his humanness elicits the extreme reaction suggesting that the therapist has no standards at all. To suggest that it is human to pilfer a pencil implies that stealing is justified. The obsessional deals in absolutes at both extremes; thus, one pencil makes him a thief. However, as our discussion proceeded, she could relate the superhuman demands she made on herself with her expectations of retribution. At this understanding, her anxiety and paranoid feelings dissipated. She could relax and acknowledge that the initial repression of the incident and her ability to finally look at it removed the stored-up suspiciousness of others and her own feelings of phoniness, lack of integrity, and guilt — which followed such a minor breach in her behavior. This incident enabled her to understand many of her previous delusional systems.

While the schizophrenic reaction does follow the breakdown of an obsessional defense, these changes are not necessarily stages in the same illness. The defensive structure evident in the psychosis can often be recognized in the obsessional dynamisms, but this is characteristic of all mental mechanisms which, in the extreme, participate in the psychoses. The obsessional neurosis, on the other hand, is closely related to schizophrenia, and the therapy of each can be enhanced through the understanding of both.

CHAPTER 8

Addictive States

Grandiosity is the assumption of an exalted, superior state which is beyond realistic possibility or actuality. While it is related to a feeling of high esteem and worth, it is qualitatively different. It is an illusory conception of strength, unjustified by actual or potential achievement. It is a defensive and adaptive development which arises out of certain psychological needs and is found regularly in psychopathological developments. Its characteristic presence in the obsessional neurosis casts some light on its adaptive role in the psychological problems of obesity, alcoholism, narcotic addiction, compulsive gambling, masturbation, and kleptomania.

This is not to say that grandiosity is the only feature or even the most salient one in these disorders. It does, however, highlight the obsessional and compulsive issues and the grandiose consequences of the compulsive patterns of perfection, omnipotence and omniscience. It is as if the need for certainty and absolutes is achieved in the grandiose presumption of exemption, privilege, and superhuman potentiality. Grandiosity also plays a major role in nonaddictive disorders, such as paranoia and psychopathic personality, where this feeling of specialness and certainty is fulfilled either in thought or action.

In all these conditions the common thread of grandiosity is to be found when the individual tends to assume a privileged status. In each instance the grandiose feelings are expressed in terms of being exempt from the consequences of one's behavior and not being subject to the laws of nature, and these feelings account for the excesses in the person's activity. It is a short step from compulsively needing to be universally capable, never deficient, and all-knowing to feeling superhuman.

DEVELOPMENT OF GRANDIOSITY

Omnipotent feelings have been described by many behavioral scientists as a usual accompaniment of certain periods of development, particularly infancy. Sigmund Freud, Sandor Ferenczi, Sandor Rado, and other personality theorists conceived of infancy as a period of unlimited power and influence during which the infant manages to get everything he wants with no limitations or restrictions. This has been called *primal omnipotence*, from which later feelings of grandiosity may develop. This assumption presupposes that the infant feels truly powerful and effective during the first year of his existence, when his needs are automatically fulfilled or when his slightest effort is met with unlimited fulfillment. While it is true that under certain fortunate circumstances the infant may have a coterie composed of mother and "assistant mothers," as well as other significant adults who will cater immediately to his every need, the infant generally is in a most precarious position, dependent on the goodwill and attentive benevolence of the environment. What can be observed is that the infant is helpless and completely incapable of filling any of his own needs except oxygen intake, provided he is suitably placed on his back. Otherwise he is entirely dependent upon others.

It seems more reasonable, therefore, to speculate about the infant's feelings of *insecurity* rather than his feelings of omnipotence. One could emphasize the constant state of jeopardy he is in, and his readiness to fall into severe states of anxiety, anaclitic depression, apathy, and panic. Rather than considering it a state of euphoria, one can find more evidence of potential panic, danger of asphyxiation, a potential for starvation, and an incapacity to communicate these feelings of apprehension. The cry, which is often a most potent force in mobilizing attention to the infant's needs, can also produce the opposite effect when it is either misunderstood or when it falls on already distraught and anxious ears. Therefore, while the problems of omnipotence and grandiosity may have some roots in very early experiences, it is doubtful that there is a direct relationship. The experiences of early infancy and childhood may serve to enhance the adult's security and feeling of power and esteem if that stage was a successful period of development without too many thwarts or traumas. Such experiences could be reflected in the adult as comfortable feelings of self-worth, self-esteem, and self-respect. Grandiosity is the negation of real self-esteem; it denies one's real assets and demands impossible, superhuman attributes to overcome one's doubts.

The ability to influence the environment and to fulfill one's needs may develop valid feelings of esteem and power and may be the beginning of a stable and solid self-system. Difficulties during infancy, rather than unlimited gratification, may be the cause of the grandiosity that may develop in later life. Grandiosity may be the result of a thwarted and unsuccessful infancy during which one can manage to infuence adults only with great difficulty, and consequently always feeling himself to be on the edge of danger.

The feelings of uncertainty and threat because of neglect or malevolence require extreme measures to overcome. Omnipotent feelings may develop in order to establish certainties and to protect and guarantee one's existence. This is the early history of the future obsessional, whose need for control by an omnipotent, omniscient, and ritualistic pattern of living emphasizes the uncertain, contradictory, and inconsistent relationships of those early years. Grandiosity and omnipotence are adaptive devices designed to deal with the apprehension of extreme threats. Such threats are most distressing during the periods of greatest dependency and realistic powerlessness, such as in infancy and childhood. As the person's actual powers and skills increase, his dependency may diminish, as may his need for special protective devices. If, however, his early patterns of dependency and insecurity are extreme, the development of his self-esteem may lag and he may remain helpless and dependent throughout his life.

There are some fortunate people whose early experiences leave them with a comfortable feeling of power and strength, derived from their ability to deal effectively with their needs. While they may be dependent in some matters, they can also satisfy their needs independently of others. Such people are confident and self-sufficient, but they are not grandiose. They are aware of their limitations and they are prepared to admit their deficiencies. Their goals and expectations are realistic. They do not swing from supreme confidence to profound self-derogation. Instead, they appear to have an ongoing, steady feeling of comfortable self-assurance, which permits them to meet each new occasion with open curiosity rather than with dread and evasion. This state is called healthy self-assertion, or self-esteem, and it must be distinguished from grandiosity, which is a neurotic or psychotic defensive development. Healthy self-confidence, however maligned by the less fortunate, is a source of constructive energy, as opposed to endless obsessional procrastinations and evasions (no matter how flamboyant the grandiosity).

ADDICTIVE DISORDERS

Grandiosity is a very notable element in the addictive disorders, such as alcoholism, obesity, and drug addiction.* While the issue of grandiosity does not constitute the entire problem, it plays a major role in the fantasy life of these individuals. The alcoholic or drug addict has a compulsive necessity to drink or take drugs and an incapacity to exert any reasonable control over his behavior in these areas. To this extent the condition is related to the obsessive-compulsive syndrome, wherein the issue of control is the essential feature. Once it is established, the addiction problem has a physiological basis as well as a psychological one. However, the underlying personality that lends itself to addictions is that of the obsessive-compulsive. The problem of control and the need to handle the anxieties that result from loss of control can be recognized as the overriding issue in people suffering from addictive disorders. While depression, anxiety, and a host of other psychological problems may be present, obsessional difficulties are omnipresent. The alcoholic, for example, is regularly described as a dependent person with a variety of obsessional symptoms, whose failure to control his impulses results in the excessive intake of alcohol. This enables him to overcome the recognition of his incapacity and to resort to the illusory power and fulfillment of his fantasy life. The same obsessional patterns which are successful in nonaddicts seem to fail periodically in addicts. They are forced to recognize their limitations and incapacities, which are ordinarily covered over by their obsessive technique. When this happens they may be sufficiently distressed to start drinking.

However, they may also begin an addictive debauch — whether it be drugs, food, or alcohol — when these techniques are successful. At such times, the person may become excited and overjoyed and may react in the extreme to his achievement. This may develop into a euphoric grandiosity which allows him to indulge in his excesses and feel exempt from the

* In an illuminating article on addiction, Henry A. Davidson noticed the marked similarity of addiction to the compulsive neuroses. He was referring to the mounting tension in addicts, which seems to be relieved only by taking the addictive medication: "Psychologically, it seems strikingly similar to a compulsive (neurotic) reaction. The kleptomaniac or pyromaniac will tell you, 'I get no pleasure out of stealing (or setting fires) but I have a mounting unendurable tension (or anxiety) which can be relieved in this way.'" Thus, he pointed out that addiction is not an escape but a search for a better life. (H. A. Davidson, Confessions of a goof ball addict, *American Journal of Psychiatry* 120 [1963]: 8).

consequences. Whether the anxiety is caused by failure or success, the addict is compulsively drawn to the object of his addiction. The recognition of an incomplete capacity to control oneself and the environment becomes an occasion for tossing over all controls and going to the opposite extreme — the binge.

It is a commonplace that alcoholics cannot moderate their drinking. It is all or nothing. This is precisely the obsessional problem. After abandoning all controls and getting lost in alcoholic binges or drug reveries, the illusory superman can be revived in the grandiose fantasies of the intoxicated state. After an alcoholic bout, the alcoholic experiences great remorse and guilt, which produce the inevitable resolution to abandon the addiction. Since the underlying compulsion is untouched, the resolution has no chance of succeeding. The inability to honor his resolution only reinforces the awareness of his inability, producing more drinking. The grandiose patterns that ensue not only serve temporarily to reinstate the illusion of superhuman capacity for control but also serve to deceive the person into believing that he *can* exert the necessary control whenever he decides to do so. This feeling of privilege and exemption from human frailties and natural laws plays a prominent role in the alcoholic addictive state. The alcoholic always insists that he can drink and that he can stop. This is simply a grandiose statement, with all the deception and illusion conveyed by such claims. The alcoholic may secretly believe his grandiose claims of his superior capacities and skills. He may even demonstrate it in his contempt for himself and others, before and during his alcoholic bout. He may admire his cleverness in deceiving others and feel he can outwit them in the never-ending hunt for the bottle. He is only emphasizing the grandiose view of himself and his exemption from being human. He cannot understand why others fail to believe in his superior status. The addiction or the compulsion to take alcohol or drugs, which ultimately produces a somatic or physiological craving after prolonged use, thus has its origins in a psychological deficit.

Sandor Rado described addiction in the following manner: "Addiction begins when use of a drug occurs at a time of acute distress from a serious physical illness or some point of chronic distress that may have been produced by a variety of causes (psychiatric disorder, physical incapacity, misfortune, etc.). The distressed and helpless patient craving for miraculous help has been sensitized to the pleasure effect of the narcotic drug. His intoxication (which he seeks to hide knowing that society condemns the misuse of narcotics) is the expression of his *exalted* feeling that with the help of the drug he has at long last brought about the longed-for change in his life." * The drug deals with anxiety by erasing it,

* S. Rado, *Psychoanalysis and Behavior* (New York: Grune and Stratton, 1962).

narcotizing it, and temporarily removing the realities of a distressing and intolerable situation. This is one of the most widespread techniques for dealing with anxiety in all cultures, through the ages. However, alcoholism and drug addiction, even though widespread, represent only a small proportion of those who take drugs or alcohol. The essential difference lies in the way an individual drinks and the way he controls it. Once the person gets beyond the possibility of choice and is forced to drink by pressures which he can neither control nor identify, then we see the compulsive drinker or addict. The problem manifests itself in the alcoholic or drug addict who secretly maintains large numbers of omnipotent and omniscient fantasies and many openly expressed superiority feelings, in addition to an uncontrollable impulse to drink or take drugs. The contrast between the addicts' magical and superman expectations and the extreme degradation in which they often find themselves following a binge produces such humiliation and guilt that they make resolutions to abandon the addiction — without notable success.

In another context, Rado stated that "the grandiose conception of self is the factor that makes the craving uncontrollable. The addict believes that 'nothing can happen to me.' Though his powers of reasoning and judgment appear to be otherwise unimpaired, he believes unshakably in his personal invulnerability and immortality. His image of himself as an omnipotent and indestructible giant must be clinically described as a thinly veiled narcotic delusion of grandeur." Other authors conclude that addiction occurs in individuals who are predisposed to the response of grandiosity, through retention of primordial feelings of the omnipotent self.

Some obsessionals who are prone to addiction do not drink at all or only very sparingly, when drinking happens to be part of their "not to" compulsion. They fear that if they drink at all, they may go to extremes. Thus, they build pride around their capacity to limit their drinking and to "hold their liquor well." However, their grandiose claims, which are not always maintained, periodically produce sufficient humiliation to require narcotizing and hence the addict's binge. Clearly this is not the entire picture, but in a complete understanding of the addict the central role of grandiosity needs to be recognized.

COMPULSIVE GAMBLING

The issue of grandiosity is also evident in the compulsive gambler, who periodically engages in gambling sprees and cannot control his participation even at the risk of jeopardizing his family relationships, his profession, and even his life. When he becomes involved in a game he has no choice but to continue until he is either broke or has "broken the bank." His participation is compulsive, and he cannot freely choose to leave the game. A typical obsessive-compulsive personality lies behind such behavior, and the individual's grandiose expectations are that he will win everything and lose nothing. He never expects to lose and always assumes that he can risk anything because he is protected and privileged and will ultimately win. Such attitudes are strikingly similar to those of the alcoholic or drug addict, who does not expect to be influenced unduly by the whiskey or the drug and insists that he can control the intake if he wishes. The gambler also insists that he can control his risks. Like the alcoholic, he may risk his home and his job in his uncontrollable orgy of gambling. In spite of the evidence that he can lose, since he frequently does, he moves into each game with the conviction that he is certain to win. While he is abashed after each orgy, his shame and humiliation do not restrain his compulsion.

The anxiety which sets off the compulsion to gamble is often a feeling of despair and hopelessness about oneself and one's fortunes and the impossibility of achieving some success through ordinary channels. The gambler cannot accept the slow climb to status but hopes to achieve it in one magical moment, without the necessary output of energy. It will all be achieved through the magic of immediate fulfillment. Such anxieties prompt him to risk his fortune and his status to achieve that magical moment which must surely come. He can exert no limits upon himself except those that are imposed by others. He is not gambling to make money. Like the alcoholic who frequently does not enjoy his drinking, he often does not enjoy the sport. His gambling is an obsessive device to relieve anxiety and to reassure himself of his special, privileged position. That it fails to do so only leaves him with the certainty that it will succeed the next time. During the game he is triumphant and about to actualize his grandiose claims and privileged self. Like the alcoholic and drug addict, he is caught in a web of obsessive necessity from which he cannot escape except through a recognition of the basic problem.

COMPULSIVE MASTURBATION

There are many other compulsive pieces of behavior that might not get to the attention of others because they are private and do not involve antisocial activities. Yet they are equally as demanding and distressing as other addictions. Compulsive masturbation, for example, can become extremely disconcerting in its imperious demands upon the individual. It is quite different from the masturbatory activity in which most people indulge. Under the circumstances of a compulsion, masturbation may need to take place many times a day. When the pressure mounts and the person must masturbate to relieve the tension, he may need to do so even under unfavorable or dangerous circumstances. The person cannot resist or postpone the act.

The compulsive masturbater rarely masturbates to relieve sexual tension. He is himself fully aware of this, as the impetus to masturbate is infrequently stimulated by erotic fantasies. The need generally arises for unknown reasons and cannot be resisted. The individual is compelled to masturbate and while this may relieve his tense state temporarily, it often leaves him even more tense and uncomfortable.

The grandiose elements associated with this compulsion are often expressed in the fantasies that accompany the act. When masturbation is a substitute for normal sex activity, the individual, being uncertain about his potency, may avoid the test of heterosexual activity and thus be able to maintain the grandiose illusion about his great sexual prowess. This symptom, like other compulsions, does not have any specific significance. Rather it reflects a general obsessive-compulsive personality structure, despite the classical psychoanalytic formulation which describes compulsive masturbation as "serving the purpose of protecting a passive-dependent ego from the separation anxiety caused by active sadistic phallic impulses by using the penis as a fetishistic representation of the phallic mother."

The type of compulsion that is found in an individual has some reference to his earlier experience as well as to his genetic endowment. However, the problem of the *choice* of compulsion — like the choice of symptoms in general — is still largely an unsolved one.

OBESITY

While the compulsive elements in certain types of obesity are very evident, in others they may not be so obvious. Assessment is difficult because such individuals generally engage in their compulsive eating orgies in secret. Unlike the alcoholic or the drug addict, the obese person rarely displays antisocial or obnoxious behavior. Psychologically, he is an addict, and the psychological aspects of his addiction are similar to those of the alcoholic or drug addict. Like many alcoholics, compulsive eaters are "secret imbibers" and publicly eat so little that one is often astonished at their obesity. This tends to support the popular justification of the fat man who says he suffers from glandular trouble. While the obese person is delighted to accept this label from his friends, who never see him overeat, he knows full well where the trouble lies, even though he may also insist on a glandular diagnosis from his physician. While he strenuously avoids a direct confrontation with his addiction and hopes for magical cures with pills, exercise, diets, or hypnosis, he is, on another level, fully aware of the compulsive nature of his overeating.

Compulsive eaters are not simply overeaters; neither are they people who are chronically but slightly overweight. Such excesses are conscious and deliberate even if they are recognized as having undesired results. They accompany expansive feelings or a readiness to indulge despite untoward consequences. Such overeating may be an outlet for depressed or lonely feelings where the compulsive syndrome is not present. Compulsive eaters are also strikingly different from those who overeat because of a metabolic disorder or a thyroid deficiency. The overeating problem currently plagues a large number of Americans and citizens of other affluent countries. This situation is the result of eating and drinking in excess of the metabolic possibilities of the individual, so that there is a gradual accumulation of weight. The compulsive eater is one who is *driven* and who is incapable of limiting or controlling his intake of food, so that he becomes grossly overweight. He is compelled to eat in the same way that the alcoholic or the drug addict has no choice in his addiction. The compulsive eater is pressed, not by taste or hunger, but by inner drives that he can neither understand nor control. Unlike the eater who eats too much because he likes and enjoys his food, the compulsive eater often stuffs and gorges to a point of illness. Ordinary overeating is often associated with festive events in the midst of jolly company — good food and drink in an atmosphere of good fellowship and companionship. The atmosphere adds to the enjoyment and may increase the intake of food. The compulsive eater, on the other hand, eats in secret and eats whatever is at hand — feeling somewhat sly and guilty, yet unable to abandon his misadventure. The eating proceeds in a ritualistic fashion, and sometimes he may read while eating in order to avoid recognizing his excessiveness. Generally, he proceeds to eat everything at hand in an ordered fashion, and the eating ritual is like other rituals of the compulsive syndrome. It is carried out without understanding, purpose, or need and may have some meaning in a magical context.

Excessive eating has always been heavily loaded with moralistic and derogatory connotations, and the victims were and still are labeled pigs and gluttons and considered sinful in a Christian theology. Overeating was considered abusing one's person and was thought to be one of the cardinal sins. While obesity in females did not always involve social disapproval in terms of aesthetics, as it has in recent years in Western culture, it has usually been recognized as a medical hazard and a handicap. However, it was not considered a psychological problem similar to touching, dressing, or performing other acts as compulsive rituals. Overeating was considered the consequence of weakness, sinfulness, and inadequate self-control, whereas a hand-washing ritual might be quickly identified as abnormal mental behavior. Moralistic attitudes toward obesity have clouded the understanding of the obsessional factors involved and have therefore hampered therapy.

Obesity is neither a moral problem nor a matter of a healthy resolve and a weak will. The compulsive eater is an addict. The occasions for his addictive binges are invariably involved with anxiety — whether or not it is manifested — and are frequently initiated by hurt pride, humiliation, and feelings of rejection or isolation. These feelings are generally the outcome of a failure to live up to the person's own grandiose expectations of himself rather than the expressed disappointment of other people. Under such conditions, he may engage in eating bouts of unrestrained and unlimited proportions. He will often eat until he is physically exhausted. Since he is ashamed of the quantity consumed, he prefers to eat secretly and in isolation. Often he will repress or simply forget the eating binge, especially when it may take place at odd times such as in the middle of the night. His denial may at times be so extreme as to suggest a schizophrenic dissociation process. The loneliness and emptiness of the compulsive eater are suggested by his symbolic attempt to swallow everything in order to fill this emptiness. Nothing must be left over, as if it would no longer be available if it were not eaten at that moment. He seems to be stocking up on caloric reserves as if the world would soon be emptied of nourishment with no possible replacement. Coupled with this attitude is the related feeling of being entitled to all that is around and the fear of being cheated and taken advantage of. This feeling is sometimes related to early deprivation experiences but more often to grandiose expectations and claims in which the person sees himself as being worthy of total fulfillment. Similar to the competitive and envious person who watches what other people get to make certain that he is not short-changed, the obese person may overeat to make sure that he does not get cheated. The eating may often take place in an atmosphere of rebellion, in which he feels that he is entitled to special rewards for having been previously denied. The rebelliousness may be in response to praise if the person interprets the praise as insufficient, phony, or tricky. One 300-pound patient regularly overate when her husband told her that she looked fine and was losing weight. She felt that his remarks were phony and were designed to mislead her, since she knew she was still overeating. Her husband did not know her true secret inner life, and she felt hopeless about his capacity to see through her even when she did not divulge that inner life.

The capacity for self-deception and the delusional distortions of the self-image of the obese person can be striking phenomena. Calories don't count if someone else does not see them being consumed. In this way obese people can convince themselves that they have eaten sparsely. The self-deception is aided by the grandiose assumption that, for them, excess carbohydrates are not stored as fat. They may express astonishment at this biochemical fact, even though they are fully aware of it on another level of conceptualization.

One 350-pound patient who came for treatment because of marital problems looked at herself in the nude regularly, noting her slim and graceful lines and openly admiring her lovely figure. She claimed that she ate very little at mealtimes and could not understand her overweight. Her husband was convinced that she did not overeat except on infrequent occasions, when he would inadvertently awaken early in the morning to find his wife gorging on huge sandwiches, cokes, cakes, and candies. This happened with far greater frequency than he was ever aware of. The defense of denial may often reach psychotic proportions. Such people feel that they live prudent, mildly uncontrolled lives. Hilde Bruch has noted in her classic studies on obesity that the self-image of the obese person is often that of a thin person who will starve unless he continues to eat. It is the converse of the anorexia nervosa patient who is extraordinarily thin and refuses to eat because his self-image is that of an obese person who will become grossly ugly unless he controls his food intake. At times the obese person may have a delusion of being denied nourishment by a hostile world or of being destroyed by worms which demand a constant intake of food. The schizophrenic qualities of the disorder are often clearly manifest, and the element of denial is often a crucial factor in the therapy of obesity, as it is with alcoholics.

The underlying character structure of the obese person is like that of other addicts. The compulsive incapacity to control the food intake is related to the overall problem of control in other areas of living. Such people are pressed by their uncertainties and feelings of helplessness and impotence; they display a wide variety of obsessive symptoms. They are caught up in attempts at perfection and invulnerability and have a need at all times to control their own actions as well as those of others. For example, one moderately obese compulsive eater refused to acknowledge her approaching menopause. She said that she was not ready for it and had not decided she wanted it yet. She was desperately searching for approval, and while her activity was directed toward controlling others, she tried to justify her behavior by insisting that she was just a puppet in the hands of her husband. There was no real conviction about losing weight, since she had not yet decided that she was fat. Thus, she denied her overeating except at rare moments of self-awareness which fitted into her grandiose conception of omnipotence and superiority.

This patient had many phobias and somatic obsessional preoccupations. Her communication difficulties were classically obsessional. She obscured all her statements with qualifications and needed to explain each one, so that she never got to the point of her story. She was evasive, distracting, and indecisive. Although she wanted very much to lose weight and reestablish some of her earlier attractiveness, she maintained that she could not exert the proper degree of self-control to achieve it.

Her usual indecisiveness made her swing back and forth in her resolve to diet, and at times of stress she would overeat as a rebellious gesture against her husband. At the bottom of her difficulty was the grandiose picture of herself, which would not allow her to admit that she could not control her overeating. As a superior, godlike person, she expected that she should be loved for what she was and should not need to conform to any conventional ideas of beauty. She considered herself exempt from caloric issues and insisted that the foods that made others fat should not bother her. She never related the issues of calorie count to weight because she considered herself superhuman and beyond the natural laws of digestion.

The same issue was demonstrated in a 285-pound compulsive eater who was tall and had attractive features but was gross in her appearance. Her compulsive eating was complicated by a tendency toward stealing. She was a marked manipulator whose activities were invariably involved in controlling others, yet she appeared to be entirely at the mercy of others.

Her eating was done in secret and in the evenings, and she was mainly unaware of the quantity of her intake. On these occasions she gorged herself, although she was extremely restrained in the presence of her family. In this way she engaged their sympathy, since they were impressed by her sparse appetite and felt her obesity was not her fault. She was rigid, stubborn, and rebellious. To avoid being pushed around she went to the opposite extreme of refusing to budge an inch once she made up her mind. At other times, she refused to make a decision for fear she might be pushed to change it. Her eating problem was tied up with her capacity for denial, and, at times, she was firmly convinced that she was not fat. Every positive comment from her husband was translated as affirmation of her attractive figure, even though she could not really trust or believe him. She managed to force him to compliment her, but when he did she became angry and overate because she felt his comments were not freely given. While her obesity forced her into treatment, she came only upon the insistence of her husband. She did not deal with her obesity for a long time after she began therapy. She directed her communications to many other areas. During this period she unwittingly managed to expose the whole range of her obsessional symptoms, which made her overeating understandable. In addition to her obesity, she had a compulsion to steal.

Relationship to Kleptomania

The patient just discussed managed to avoid mentioning the stealing and to deny it as part of her living until she was arrested, even though her need to shoplift anything portable was ever-present. While the things she took did not have any utilitarian or intrinsic value, she justified her behavior by a Robin Hood fantasy of stealing from the rich to help the poor. She was quite well off financially and could comfortably fill all the needs of her family. Her stealing was rationally unmotivated and could be understood only in terms of her inability to pass up anything that she could get for nothing. If it was there to be had, she felt she was entitled to it. She never considered the consequences of her behavior because it never occurred to her that she would get caught. She secretly viewed herself as a superhuman person whose grandiose self could outwit and outmanipulate anyone in the world. Thus, she had never even considered the possibility of being caught.

She felt that shoplifting was a virtue and a positive achievement and that it would be cheating her family not to steal. She viewed this as her job, just as her husband had his job. It was an extraordinary defense, typical of many compulsive justifications in which the compulsion is visualized as a virtue. In this instance, however, it had antisocial consequences.

Kleptomania raises the question of why some compulsions direct the person to antisocial acts, whereas others produce effects which are destructive only to the individual involved. The compulsion itself is amoral and is the result of a defensive process. The direction of the compulsion and its acceptability by the culture is determined by the ethos of that culture and is not innate in the symptom itself. The compulsion to peep (voyeurism) or the compulsion to expose oneself may have severe consequences in one culture and be relatively unnoticed in another. The compulsion's origins may have some basis in the mores of the culture, but the person himself may not respond to his acts as being immoral. On the other hand, some compulsions which may not antagonize or be abhorrent to the culture may be entirely unacceptable to the person himself. This is true, for example, of compulsive eating or obsessive preoccupations of a hostile or sexual nature. While it involves moral issues, the compulsion can be understood only in psychological terms — even though our ability to treat some compulsions is often thwarted by the legal consequences of the behavior.

For the patient just described, stealing was her contribution to the household, and she felt proud, rather than contrite and ashamed. While she recognized the distortions in her explanation and the compulsive nature of her stealing, she was extremely reluctant to connect her kleptomania with her compulsive eating. Yet she could see similarity in her grandiose expectations of exemption and special privilege in both areas. She felt guilty about both her eating and stealing only when they were brought to her attention. Her rationalization that she was serving others and the denial and evasiveness are familar defenses against anxieties. However, the relationship to anxiety is neither simple nor direct. It is not that she stole or overate when she became noticeably anxious or upset; it was frequently the opposite. The relationship is a much more subtle one and concerns the uncertainty of her acceptability and desirability — which may be stirred up by many things, including praise and compliments. Her compulsive symptoms derived from her needs to prove, justify, and document a superior and omnipotent self which would guarantee her future security.

Thus, on the one occasion when she was apprehended, she did not appear crushed or chastised; rather, she considered it an unexpected error in her usual impregnable and grandiose self. She thought it was the result of carelessness caused by a headache and that it would not happen again. At the time of her apprehension she attempted to evade the responsibility for her behavior by telling the authorities that she was not stealing, but was gathering material for a short story. This fantasy was sufficiently reworked, so that when she related it she more than half believed it. She also maintained that her shoplifting was a creative task, which, when she wrote her account of it, would be a boon to humanity for which she should be rewarded. So certain was she of her immunity that she never really expected the storekeeper to prosecute. She simply did not see the event as a crime but only as a mistake.

When the trial date was set, rather than feeling restrained, she went on a shoplifting binge. Instead of trying to impress the court with spotless behavior before the trial, she was determined to get as much as possible before it became known publicly that she had shoplifted. She dealt with the incident as a minor error and continued trying to rework the plot so that she would end up as a heroine in the eyes of her family, although she actually took great care that they should learn nothing about the matter.

As a result of this incident and of my active interest in her during this period, the therapeutic work advanced considerably. We managed to explore the intricacies of her obesity as well as the kleptomania. She was able to examine her grandiosity in a most direct way and described several occasions that she had previously forgotten. The first was an early experience when she had played God and in an authoritarian manner relieved a neighboring woman of witches and ghosts. The neighbor treated her with great awe from then on. The patient then began to believe in her omnipotence and on several occasions tried to take over a hospital ward and cure a friend. She finally had to be asked to leave, as she was disrupting the hospital routine by countering the doctor's orders. She recognized that these grandiose assumptions were related to her need to be omniscient and omnipotent, as her early life had been one of marked uncertainty about herself and her future. She was able to see the connection between this occasion and her secret expectations of Godlike exemption from the natural laws of biology or the social laws concerning stealing. She became aware that her inability to recognize any danger or guilt was a result of her grandiosity; she also began to see the realistic consequences of her behavior on herself and her family.

As a result of her therapy, she began to have only occasional temptations to steal, particularly when the items were small and could be considered necessary. However, she managed to restrain these feelings most of the time. Her stealing became less compulsive and she had some choice in the matter. An understanding of risk, danger, guilt, and similar factors began to enter into her calculations, and she would have to decide between the danger of being caught and the pleasure of getting away with it. She was still less motivated by moral considerations than by practical ones and still had some doubt about whether she did or did not have a right to steal. While her grandiose state was punctured, it did not disappear. The automatic, unplanned, and unprogrammed stealing had, on the whole, diminished, even though she still had strong feelings of invulnerability and of the capacity to pull off the perfect job. After several years' therapy, she moved to another city. Though her kleptomania was much reduced, her obesity was not. It was as if practical necessity of a more dramatic kind took precedence over the cosmetic aspects of her problem.

From the point of view of the problem related here, however, the patient demonstrated very clearly the relationship between grandiosity and particular symptoms such as kleptomania and obesity. The connection lies in the concept of the compulsive drive, in which compulsive behavior is directly related to grandiosity. From this point of view, the problem of grandiosity is considered more essential to the therapeutic process than the previously held relationships of kleptomania or obesity to sexual problems. The symbolic significance of stealing as a sexual transformation is not borne out in the observations of this woman. Her sexual difficulties appeared to have no relation to her kleptomania.

ANOREXIA NERVOSA

Anorexia nervosa, which frequently results in life-endangering situations because of malnutrition, is the syndrome of compulsive noneating. Whether because of a distorted body image or the unreasonable fear of overeating, there is a compulsive necessity to limit food intake. Such individuals often keep a meticulous record of their weight, balancing every ounce gained with a reduction of intake to lose it. They may weigh themselves a dozen or more times a day. While they were generally presumed under the category of hysterical disorders because of their flamboyant theatrics, the overall patterns more closely resemble the obsessional dynamisms and the overconcern with control and preoccupation with somatic issues. Frequently, there is a close association to the problem of obesity and there may be a wide fluctuation from overweight to underweight and from binge eating to starvation.

One young lady of twenty-one would lose or gain from 50 to 100 pounds over several months' time. While not grossly overweight, she would overindulge in sweets, ice cream, and other junk foods. Her boyfriend on one occasion intimated that she was putting on too much weight and this set into motion a period of anorexia which reduced her weight to under 90 pounds and seriously endangered her life. When forced to eat, she would vomit at the earliest convenience. She became totally preoccupied with the problem of weight and calories. She established a rigid pattern of overeating — vomiting and gradual loss of weight until threatened with hospitalization, when she would begin to eat to excess until concerns of obesity triggered the vomiting pattern again.

She was a perfectionist in her schoolwork, appearance, and dating behavior. Her demands for total control and minute management of her physical state produced profound disgust and humiliation when she went out of control. The ensuing anxiety was dealt with by unmanageable eating binges. She could not pass a bakery or supermarket without buying sacks of candy, cakes, and soft drinks. At these times, she was convinced of her capacity to limit the intake and vowed not to vomit. However, at the first bite her resolutions dissolved and her addiction took over finally, resulting in vomiting and forced starving.

Another example is a laboratory technician from a family of research scientists who were preoccupied with nutritional issues. She functioned very well with a multitude of obsessional traits — namely, perfectionistic and superman demands on her intellectual capacities. She was controlled, emotionally flat, indecisive, and rigid, with many compulsive rituals. Her first date stirred up concerns about germs, dirt, and contamination, and she began to doubt her capacity to keep the young man interested in her. She focused on her appearance and weight and began to weigh her foods precisely as well as herself. She tyrannized her household, demanding absolute quiet for her studying. Any footsteps would result in a torrent of abuse against her parents. She began to lose weight steadily, insisting that this was the only way of avoiding the ugliness of obesity. Anemia and general weakness and fatigue brought her into treatment.

This patient claimed an unrefutable contention to deal with her problem in spite of all evidence to the contrary. Her somatic preoccupations extended beyond her weight, and her contempt for others was conveyed in her grandiose disdain for other professionals.

Anorexia nervosa is the exact mirror image of obesity — one extreme to another. I believe the problems, issues, dynamics, and treatment are identical except that the life-endangering quality of anorexia must first be treated before the compulsive issues can be dealt with. While conditioning therapies can be useful, anorexia nervosa should not be viewed exclusively in that light. It is a compulsive problem, and tactics which assume volitional control and management are doomed to failure. Anorexia, like obesity, is a displacement of other pressing problems that must be identified and dealt with.

PARANOID STATES

Many problems, namely the psychopathic personality addictions and paranoia, could be better understood when the issue of grandiosity is taken into account. This is particularly relevant to conceptualizing the psychodynamics of the paranoid state. The omnipotent and grandiose tendencies that are consistently present in the paranoid state were explained by Freud as reflecting the result of the paranoid's feeling of being especially selected for malevolence and attention. This feeling of specialness and significance is then enhanced to a grandiose state. In this connection, Freud said: "The development of megalomania is thus attributed by the textbooks to a process which ... we may describe as 'rationalization.' But to ascribe such important effective consequences to a rationalization is, as it seems to us, an entirely unpsychological procedure."* In this view, the paranoid state precedes the development of grandiosity and is responsible for it. This concept is quite superficial and, as Freud himself recognized, an "unpsychological procedure" with which to explain such a significant development. This is particularly true when one recognizes that grandiosity occurs quite commonly in situations other than paranoid development. A more generalized theory of grandiosity not only should explain the condition's development in paranoids but also should be capable of explaining its role in other psychiatric disorders.

* S. Freud, "Psycho-analytic Notes on an Autobiographical Account of a Case of Paranoia (Dementia Paranoides)," *Standard Edition* 12, pp. 48–49.

We find paranoid ideation in practically everyone except the most secure and mature individuals. However, when a true paranoid development occurs, the special sense of privilege and being superhuman is reflected in the feeling of grandiosity which becomes delusional and can be part of a schizophrenic disorder. There is much evidence that the grandiosity which develops out of the obsessional disease is responsible for the paranoid development. The response of the community to the exaggerated claims and demands of the grandiose paranoid is rarely friendly or compliant and, in fact, is usually angry and rejecting. The soil from which the grandiose feelings develop was already nourished with doubts, fears, and uncertainties. Thus, the unfriendly, rejecting, and at times hostile reaction of the environment tends to provoke and stimulate paranoid ideas. Such a response may be sufficiently humiliating, infuriating, and damaging to the grandiose structure to encourage the development of a feeling of conspiracy or malevolence which can become organized into a plot. Thus, rather than the paranoid state being based on a repressed homosexual wish (as Freud postulated) and the grandiosity being a secondary development which explains the delusion, my view suggests that grandiosity is primary and is an outgrowth of an obsessional defense system and that paranoid developments result from the realistic rejections or frustrated feelings of failure to achieve the grandiose claims. The paranoid state results from profound insecurities and low self-esteem. The superhuman or messianic claims of the grandiose individual stimulate rebuff and rejection, even if they result, in some instances, in the form of cults with many followers.

Several case histories demonstrate the effects of the community response to an individual's claims on the development of paranoid ideas. An obsessional young lady in a grandiose excitement claimed to be one of the four best writers in the English language. She based this claim on an unfinished manuscript, which had been years in the making and which realistically supplied no basis for such an appraisal. She was an extremely insecure person, overburdened by a succession of phobic and compulsive rituals. Under great stress she would become quite excited and would openly express many of her grandiose claims, which she secretly nourished even while derogating herself.

Another patient took me to task for assuming that his boss, who was an outstanding authority in his field and twenty years the patient's senior, was necessarily better informed about the job than the patient was. The patient felt that the realistic situation did not necessarily prove this contention because no one yet knew what he, the patient, was capable of. He refused to take into account the factors of experience, additional education, and background. All the patient offered was the remote — but "correct" (in the strictest sense) — notion that he still might be better at the task if he were magically and suddenly transported into it. His insistence in the face of numerous rational factors was an instance of his grandiosity. While it would be truly reassuring for the patient to recognize that he *might* achieve his boss's position in due time and that it would be impossible to expect to be in it at this stage of his development, he preferred to consider the situation in the most farfetched ways in order to maintain his grandiosity. He explained the boss's position in terms of politics, accident of birth, and a collusion of immoral and unfair practices.

Another example illustrates the relation of obsession and paranoia, including grandiosity. This case deals with a forty-five-year-old man who grew up the middle child of three sons. He was treated with special care but was also derided because of his physical inadequacies. His household was chaotic and completely hypercritical. The Christian virtues were expounded and emphasized, while the father made his living in periodic illegal ventures. From a very early age, the patient experienced severe anxieties in his family relationships and spent most of his time trying fruitlessly to impress his family with his capacity and skill. He soon outshone his family in intellectual pursuits, but this failed to stimulate their admiration and respect. In early childhood he developed many phobias and compulsive ritualistic behavior patterns, which elicited the family's derision. At first he followed the family design for his career but soon abandoned it for a career in science. Although he felt successful, his financial reward was small.

He began therapy when he was almost immobilized by a complicated succession of compulsive rituals, ranging from washing routines to activities surrounding his work life. All his work had to be letter-and-comma perfect, so that he might redo it dozens of times. These rituals, when interspersed with obsessional preoccupations arising from past incidents and recent events, made his life an impossible hurdle. He could work only against the greatest odds and at times could do nothing at all except to perform the obsessional demands made upon him.

With regard to the issue of grandiosity, he became very angry on an occasion when he assumed that I thought a piece of research which had won a prize was better than the one he had submitted. His rationalization regarding his failure to win the prize consisted essentially in tearing down the winning project, with which he was not even familiar, and accusing the judges of being ignorant and prejudiced. He recognized his inability to accept any kind of second-best position, and after some discussion he appeared to accept the observations about his obsessional demands. Several weeks later, however, he expressed great anger and annoyance and insisted that the therapy was trying to sell him on the notion of grandiosity when everything was clearly a matter of his being factually superior. He introduced more evidence of the prize winner's shortcoming and tried to prove that in this instance he should have won. He accused me of siding with his enemies and pushing him around. He not only defended his grandiose claims but expressed great disappointment and anger that the overvalued judgment of himself was not accepted by others.

We explored his rationalizations and other defensive devices, which were designed to force me and others to accept his point of view. It became clear that his intense need to win and his inability to accept any other judgment but his own were involved in this crisis. I added in the course of our exploration that it was clear that his failure to win was neither shameful nor disappointing. While it certainly would have been preferable if he had won, it would not necessarily make him more acceptable. Therapy was not judging his talent but examining his way of life. It finally became clear to him that he could not admit defeat in this instance because he felt I expected him to win and would reject him and dispose of him as a patient unless he was superior and outstanding. His failure to win the prize would be interpreted as an indication of his mediocrity. This incident was very revealing to the patient. It demonstrated his grandiosity and his defenses against it and illuminated the obsessive pattern and its adaptive function very clearly.

PSYCHOPATHIC PERSONALITY

Grandiosity is also related to a character disorder called *psychopathic personality*. In these people, however, addictive qualities in their behavior are more easily demonstrated. Earlier explanations involved the contradiction of a person who feels no guilt or suffers no remorse and yet is looking for punishment. This interpretation required the hypothesis of a death-instinct or the concept of an unconscious feeling of guilt. Yet the psychopathic personality moves about in the community in every walk of life, often very successfully, and is brought before justice by society only when he commits illegal acts. The type of behavior that constitutes the core of this illness is related to the inability of such individuals to make any deep, meaningful relationships, even when they are often actively involved in social affairs. They do not get emotionally involved in positive terms, and they exploit every relationship they have. They seem conscienceless, devoid of shame and remorse, and appear to feel no guilt for any of their antisocial behavior. When apprehended they may make fervent pleas for forgiveness or promise never to repeat such behavior but invariably they do repeat it. They seem not to benefit from either punishment or previous experiences. For these reasons they sometimes appear stupid, though they generally have high I.Q.'s and are usually clever and brilliant operators. They trade on their charm and capacity to deceive and are extremely successful in taking advantage of the human propensity to get something for nothing.

Generally these people appear to function well — without anxiety and seemingly without difficulty or distress. They appear to have no manifest delusions or to give other evidence of psychoses. While their relationships are cold, calculated, and without real feeling, they seem to be intense and involved. Such individuals have always posed an unusual problem for psychiatrists. They seem to be quite normal, even when their behavior has been illegal, reproachful, or openly hostile and deceitful. One psychiatrist has described them as wearing "masks of sanity."

There have been various attempts to explain the psychopathic personality's behavior by the notion of a deficient superego or conscience. It was assumed that because their repetitive behavior made it certain they would be apprehended by the authorities, this was an indication of their desire to be caught and punished. While all agree that such people do not seem to benefit from punishment, some theorists hold the "deficient superego" view and explain it by either the death-instinct or the unconscious need for punishment. However, they do not clarify why someone pushes himself into getting punishment when he can neither benefit from it nor enjoy it. Other explanations for such behavior are in order.

One notion about the psychopath is that he does not experience anxiety. While it is generally agreed that anxiety is not ordinarily manifested by such a person in a direct way, it is clear not only that he is capable of experiencing anxiety but also that the anxiety can be sufficiently severe to warrant the most stringent defenses in order to cope with it. The psychopath's anxiety is usually expressed in indirect ways, such as in hectic, compulsive behavior — especially when he feels himself in danger of being discovered or exposed. When one would expect outbursts of anxiety — that is, when he is actually discovered, apprehended, or convicted — he seems to display the least anxiety. It is as if, at these times, he utilizes the defense of denial against his anxiety. Keeping this in mind, many things seem understandable about the psychopath.

The psychopathic personality, like all other psychiatric syndromes, is the consequence of a series of defensive maneuvers designed to adapt to certain conditions of existence. There are many data to suggest that the personality of the psychopath may result from extreme conditions of almost total rejection and indifference in the early years. In the atmosphere of cold, detached, and undoubtedly egocentric parents, the child manages through some psychological defenses to avoid psychosis and even death. Consequently, the child develops such characteristics as result from survival under the most extreme circumstances — cunning, egocentricity, distrust, and emotional fluidity. In addition, he develops a collection of techniques to charm and exploit others for his own use, with no consideration for their feelings. Thus, the syndrome could be visualized as an adaptive development in which the person tries to get what he can, using guile and cunning, at the least cost to his own feelings. He behaves as though the world owes him a living. What he can achieve by trickery and deceit is valued as highly as achievements obtained by effort and hard work. Often even greater pride is taken in achievements which are the result of deceit, even when they may require more effort than more conventional behavior. It is as though the illegal and dangerous nature of an activity carries special rewards. Rebellion and nonconformity are elements in this behavior, but the atmosphere of getting something for nothing by activity which is not designed to achieve the usual results is most appealing to the psychopath. He wishes to avoid being a "sucker like everyone else." Only unusual paths are valued, even if they are illegal or bizarre.

The psychopath's need for a guaranteed avoidance of anxiety is very strong. He achieves his goal with the technique of denial, through which he refuses to acknowledge his distress overtly. While cunning and trickery are useful devices to achieve illegal goals, intelligence and a clear awareness of the weaknesses of other humans are also essential. The complicated efforts to achieve easy rewards often require a highly developed intellectual capacity and always a skilled understanding of the ways of society and the weaknesses of man and the temptations to which he is subject. With such techniques the psychopath's life proceeds with maximum security.

Such characteristics are an essential part of the obsessive-compulsive personality. The psychopathic personality is a compulsive and perfectionistic one, and it strives for omniscience and omnipotence in order to guarantee existence. Unlike the obsessional, however, the person's anger and rebellion appear greater and more overt. Many psychopaths, however, enjoy full and successful careers because the particular medium they choose to express their psychopathy is not looked upon as illegal — for example, a fringe political or religious group.

The psychopath has a grandiosity which expands and prospers under success and which remains untouched when failure occurs. It leads him to view himself as exempt from natural causes and events and permits him to engage in the most extreme and arrogant kinds of behavior. He believes that he is invulnerable and much too clever to be caught by the police. He feels he is able to carry out the perfect crime or the faultless swindle. He has contempt for the police as well as for his victim, and it is this attitude which leads him to excesses of behavior and eventual exposure. He invariably overestimates his cunning and underestimates the capacities of the police and all others. Most of his failures arise out of foolish and arrogant errors and not from unconscious wishes for punishment. What appears to be unconscious guilt or the need for punishment is a grandiose presumption of immunity and a certainty of exemption and privilege. Psychopaths are always surprised, annoyed, and disappointed when caught. They insist that the incident was an accident. It is in this sense that they do not appear to benefit from punishment. Prison or punishment is considered an interim period; the next time he will execute his plans more efficiently. His intellectual capacity, which might win him success in almost any undertaking, is put to use in trying to get something for nothing. His intellectual skills are not freely used but are tied to the compulsive performance of shady activities.

For a short period of time I had occasion to deal with a thirty-two-year-old male psychopath who had already spent eighteen years in jail for a variety of minor crimes, mainly stealing. The last time that I saw him, he had broken into a parsonage and had stolen the poor box. He had been released from prison only fifteen days before this incident and was on his way home. He was a very bright man, with an I.Q. of over 130, and had been a teacher during his last prison term. He had gone into the parsonage and had managed to find the money; but on his way out he tripped over a chair, and the resulting clatter brought the police. The robbery was unplanned and was done on the spur of the moment. He felt that he had taken every precaution in selecting this target and in not making any commotion or drawing attention to himself. However, he said he did not need to plan any of his crimes; stealing was easy and all the odds were on the side of the thief. He never expected to get caught. He stated that he learned from each crime how to do it better the next time, but he suggested that he might not be around long enough to be really perfect. He described a compulsive need to steal that manifested signs usually associated with alcoholism. His grandiose fantasies all involved being more clever than the authorities and secretly expecting this to be acknowledged by them. His previous imprisonments had no effect whatsoever upon him except to justify his grievances and to polish up his plans for further jobs.

The grandiosity of the psychopath is one level removed from the grandiose delusions in all psychoses, in which the individual attempts to actualize his grandiosity and insists that he is the exalted, privileged, and exempt individual. Many of the phenomena associated with the psychoses, including suicide, can often be understood as the result of grandiose illusions through which the person feels immune from the laws of nature and expects no consequences from his extreme behavior. Grandiosity often accompanies the manic state. In such cases, the exuberant, intensely overactive, and, at times, creative performances frequently lead the person to presume powers he does not possess. These fantasies are the direct result of an enormous output of energy, which may produce an unusual amount of activity. The person misconstrues quantity for quality and assumes a competence far beyond his resources. The grandiosity is not a rationalization for his uniqueness; rather, it is his mania which manifests itself in a plethora of performances that resemble a massive skill that is misinterpreted by the patient. The grandiosity becomes a defense against the doubts and uncertainties that lie a mere fraction below the surface. It can easily be punctured and deflated, leaving the manic hurt, angry, irritable, and frequently depressed.

In the schizophrenic psychoses we find a variety of backgrounds for the grandiose states that may be involved in the illness. At times they are part of a paranoid development in which the initial problem appears to be a grandiose development designed to deal with a severely damaged ego structure and a failing self-esteem. Such a possible failure endangers the person with feelings of disintegration and humiliation. The grandiose state may be the bulwark that prevents panic and utter destruction. The grandiose presumptions are rarely shared by the community and are generally scoffed at. This stimulates the conviction of a malevolent, destructive environment that requires caution and extreme vigilence and may quickly lead to a paranoid state in which malevolence is expected and anticipated and is finally openly expressed in words and behavior. On the other hand, grandiosity may be the outcome of a catatonic withdrawal during which the person is engaged in an assortment of world-shaking fantasies and delusions. The alternative is either annihilation or hebephrenic deterioration. The severely low self-esteem which produces a schizophrenic withdrawal often demands a massive reorganization by means of a grandiose elaboration which brings the person to the opposite extreme: an omnipotent giant guaranteed against all the threats and anxieties of living. Three vignettes highlight this issue.

GRANDIOSITY AND SCHIZOPHRENIA

Following a severe depression, a minister became hypermanic and began working fourteen to sixteen hours a day, visiting his parishioners, lecturing, preaching, and covering an enormous amount of territory in his parish. This sudden increase in zeal and devotion made him decide that he had made contact with Christ, and he began to believe that he had been chosen for great work. His grandiosity expanded to the point of assuming that he was eternal and without illness or disease. He threw away his glasses and claimed that he no longer needed any sleep. The exhaustion and near-blindness which followed soon led to some paranoid elaborations about the envy of his fellow clergymen. The paranoia soon became more prominent, and his behavior became hostile rather than benevolent; he required hospitalization.

A young woman decided that she was a writer of great note. This followed a series of growing crises about her writing, which was not proceeding very well. She decided that she was being recorded all the time in order that her pearls of wisdom be captured. She soon began suspecting everyone — particularly her husband, who, she felt, was derogating her. The grandiose delusions produced a series of embarrassing situations which necessitated removing her from her friends. Her grandiosity subsided under tranquilizing drugs and psychoanalytic therapy that was directed at exploring the necessity for such a massive defensive system.

Following a trip to New York, a young man was slowly becoming alienated and isolated from his family and friends. On his trip he had begun to ruminate about the Cold War and had decided upon a solution. It was a complicated, typically obsessive program, which he was determined to bring to the President immediately. The grandiose response followed a growing deterioration in his mental condition and a great deal of anxiety about it. He was becoming fearful of having a mental breakdown, and his grandiose solution was an attempt at reconstruction that overshot the mark.

PART III

TREATMENT

CHAPTER 9

Therapy of the Obsessive Personality

The problems implicit in the therapy of obsessional states all derive from their characteristic defenses which in most regards are antithetical to the therapeutic task. These defensive tactics are such that they militate against the very essence and requirements of the therapeutic process. The psychotherapy of emotional disorders, as initiated and expanded by the work of Sigmund Freud and the schools of psychoanalytic psychodynamic therapies that followed, requires basic agreements with the patient in order for the process to proceed. Many of these requirements are inimical to the obsessional defensive structure — which tends, therefore, to make the process of therapy difficult, arduous, tedious, and sometimes unrewarding. On the other hand, the intricacies and extraordinary variety of tactics that characterize the human brain are all played out in this disorder, and it is a fascinating and rewarding encounter if one is willing to be free, flexible, and open to the intricacies of these maneuvers, in order to effectively counter them. Consequently, treatment of the obsessional is a difficult but rewarding endeavor.

The essential task in the therapy of the obsessive-compulsive disorders or in dealing with the obsessional dynamisms in other personality disorders is that of conveying insight and initiating learning and change without getting caught in the *obsessional tug-of-war*. This term describes obsessional behavior which in all its varied aspects attempts to limit learning from experience and to maintain a rigid style of functioning that avoids novelty and change. Many of these tactics stimulate hostility in others and prevent the collaborative efforts needed in the psychotherapeutic enterprise.

As with all neurotic difficulties, the work lies in the identification, clarification, and, finally, alteration of the defensive patterns which maintain the neurosis. Such progress becomes possible when the patient's self-esteem or ego strength becomes sufficiently strengthened to withstand the major assaults against his defenses. While the problems that brought about the obsessional defenses are comparatively easy to uncover, the defensive structure which develops around these issues is most difficult to unravel. At times the particular issues of the patient are obvious and are plainly stated in his obsessional ruminations or his compulsive rituals. For example, a ritualistic avoidance of knives may be a clear statement within the awareness of the patient that he has some uneasiness about losing control of his hostile impulses. Thus, the identification of the problem — which is the fear of loss of control of his hostile impulses — is simple enough. However, it is soon evident that it is not a fear only of injuring someone else that is involved but rather a generalized uneasiness and uncertainty about the possibility of losing control in general or of being unable to control oneself at all times. The fear of loss of control is the central conflict, which gets displaced onto a variety of issues — hostility being an obvious one, since it is difficult to understand how tenderness, if uncontrolled, may produce dangerous or threatening situations. Such a development is more subtle, complex, and irrational.

It is paradoxical that in the attempts to clarify an obsessional's life, the issues become more complicated and confused. Ordinarily, increasing one's knowledge of a particular problem helps to focus on the relevant components. In dealing with the obsessional, however, new issues and qualifications of the old ones tend to broaden the inquiry. It often appears as though the patient were deliberately confusing the situation by introducing new issues when there is a real danger of clarifying something. By introducing more details and qualifications he wants to assure greater accuracy; he is trying to be precise and to avoid making errors. The additional factors are generally raised as he gets close to seeing his responsibility or failure in some activity. Before he is ready to accept an observation about some matter in which he played a responsible role, he tries to involve every possibility outside himself. Therefore, it looks as if he does this purposefully, as these new factors often lead the investigation into a cul-de-sac from which no fruitful return is possible.

In order to obtain some value from such a development once it has occurred, the therapist must go back to the beginning of the exchange and retrace it carefully, noting where the extraneous or vaguely relevant matters were introduced by the patient. It is only rarely that this sort of unraveling can take place outside of therapy. Ordinarily, one is left with a feeling of hopelessness and helplessness when one gets caught in a conversation which appears to be moving in one direction and suddenly shifts just as one approaches the destination. Attempts to retrace the path generally lead to further digression. Usually, the other party simply withdraws altogether. It is this activity that causes the obsessional to be referred to as "slippery" or "elusive" — it is so hard to pin him down.

In therapy it is imperative that such communication entanglements be worked through so that the patient can see exactly what he does and how he defeats attempts at understanding. He must recognize that while he may not do this deliberately, it nevertheless occurs frequently and regularly. The therapist must retrace the conversation and point out every new digression as it develops. He must resist all temptations to follow every lead and every rationalization; he must stick to the point in following through this particular gambit. Recording sessions can be very useful in this regard, but the compulsiveness of the therapist may outweigh the advantages gained by the patient, who can hear just how he frustrates clarity even while he is searching for clarification.

It is inevitable that the therapist will occasionally get caught in the flypaper of the obsessional's way of life, and he must recognize it as quickly as possible so as to avoid as much of it as he can. The patient gets a sense of power out of these exchanges, in which his verbal gymnastics serve to frustrate the therapist.

The situation just considered is illustrated by the following vignette: A patient expressed irritation at her husband because he became abusive about the driver in front of him. Her husband countered by saying that the driver was a poor one who was endangering himself as well as others. Besides, he asked, why did she always defend the other person and attack him? She stated that her concern was with his behavior because he was her husband. He charged her with being an appeaser and with failing to criticize others even when it was deserved. He referred to another occasion when, at a party, she had agreed with a guest who was obviously wrong in order to avoid a heated argument. She replied that she didn't want the party to break up — she was not just being an appeaser, she was just more socially adept than he was. At this he accused her of being a phony and of going overboard to be nice to others when she didn't really mean it. The issue had now moved from his irritable, egocentric behavior to her passive, compliant tendencies, and, if it did not get interrupted either by tantrums or sullen withdrawal by either of them, could extend far into the night, ranging from attack to counterattack as each one's sensitivities got touched upon. The ludicrousness of such an argument is more easily noted by an observer than by the participants.

It is clear in the preceding account that the subject was changed in the course of the exchange. At the outset, the husband was criticized, but when he counterattacked she was left defending herself. Generally, the patient's emotions are running so high and the need to win and overwhelm the other is so great that there is little chance of a logical or clear semantic analysis of the situation. When the partner also has some obsessional problems, the stickiness is compounded and only havoc can result. One can see how each step gets the original issue mixed in with additional issues until it is simply lost sight of.

It is necessary to face this aspect of the obsessional's difficulties early in the therapeutic work. The most effective way of countering it is by a slow, step-by-step unraveling process, as indicated above, wherein the actual side-stepping techniques are uncovered and brought to the patient's attention. The obfuscating tendencies can then be recognized and acknowledged. The flypaper entanglements refer to the tendency to get caught up in every distracting movement of the obsessional without recognizing its purpose at the same time. Only when the therapist discovers that he is now far removed from the original communication or report of an anxiety experience of great relevance does he experience the quality of being entangled and unable to extricate himself. All efforts to do so produce more engulfments and accusations of being defensive, confused, or incompetent. It leaves the therapist feeling impotent and helpless.

THERAPEUTIC ALLIANCE

The patient must have a minimum of trust in the therapist and a willingness to accept the role of patient for the process to begin. The readiness to admit the need for help does not mean a total acceptance of another's ability to provide such help. The obsessional's excessive standards for himself and others coupled with his contempt and disdain for anything but the best require an idealized image of the therapist and the process, which is impossible to fulfill. To overcome the initial uneasiness the therapist must be fantasized as perfect, infallible, and free from anxiety or deficiency. Unless this romanticized and exaggerated notion is exposed, it will soon perish in a disappointed recognition of the therapist's humanity.

The therapist must also be alert to his expectations of the patient and his capacity to fulfill the therapeutic contract. While there are many formal requirements for the doctor-patient relationship, such as keeping appointments, paying the fees, and saying whatever comes to mind — all of which can be agreed upon in advance — there are some requirements which cannot be met so easily, in view of the nature of the neurotic or psychotic process. The obsessional patient will try to follow the formal requirements scrupulously. However, the more pervasive tendencies of omniscience and omnipotence, the characteristic doubts, the grandiose contempt, and the tendencies to distract will play havoc with the therapeutic process unless these matters are always kept in the forefront of the therapist's attention.

This type of patient does not deliberately sabotage the therapy; he is merely behaving as an obsessional. His behavior is not resistance, nor is it a need to defeat either the therapist or the therapy; it is merely another manifestation of obsessional behavior. The therapist cannot assume or take for granted that the patient will suddenly change and stop behaving like an obsessional simply because he has agreed to enter into therapy. It would be naive to expect that a neurotic who has difficulty in coming to grips with an issue or who procrastinates and is given to indecisiveness will be able to commit himself quickly to a process that demands total commitment and involvement.

It will be a long time before he will be able to verbalize his doubts about himself, the therapist, and the process. It is essential that he hold himself aloof and free of entanglement and commitment so that he can avoid being hurt and humiliated. He will need to know his therapist and experience a number of incidents with him before the more subtle safeguards can be dropped and the beginnings of trust can take place. It is inevitable that a person who must know everything and never be deficient or fallible will react to treatment as a challenge or a threat. In order to learn one must be receptive as well as motivated, which means to be free of the obstacles which interfere with learning. One must be able to listen with an open mind, without immediate denial or derogation of the material presented. Therapy is a learning process which requires the active interest and participation of the patient, and this is true whether one views the dynamics of cure as the result of insight, genetic reconstruction, resolution of transference neurosis, reconditioning, corrective emotional experience, or simple relearning. Therefore, not only is it necessary to motivate the patient to explore his way of living in order to discover the inappropriate patterns of behavior and their sources, but it is also necessary to interest and encourage him to take steps to change his way of life. This requires a therapist who can demand participation without challenging or stirring up the patient's opposition. The patient must acquire sufficient trust, self-esteem, and readiness to take some risks and face the possibility of failure.

UTILIZING INSIGHTS

All of the above-mentioned therapeutic requirements pose particular difficulties for the obsessional. In addition to his learning problems, he faces often insurmountable obstacles in attempting to try out new ways of functioning. Since most of the obsessional patterns of behavior arise from feelings of powerlessness and uncertainty, the patient finds it particularly threatening to try out new solutions unless he can have some guarantees and expectations of success. In spite of their unsatisfactory results, the old patterns are more familiar. There must be strong incentives to attempt new solutions.

Understanding that the obsessional needs to control and that the nature of the therapeutic relationship puts him in a dependent role, the therapist must acknowledge the patient's defiance and discomfort as a natural outcome of his neurotic demands. Because of these dependency problems, the therapeutic relationship should not be of an authoritarian type if it is to succeed. However, the very structure of the psychoanalytic situation tends to encourage a development in which the therapist is the leader, the teacher, and the person who has an "in" on what's happening. The patient is the pupil who is forced to depend on the ministrations of the magic man who sets the rules of the game. Such an atmosphere may tend to produce an outwardly compliant attitude with an inwardly resistive and negativistic defense.

The obsessional ordinarily proceeds only by being forced — by either circumstances or strong pressures — to overcome his indecisive ruminations. While he needs pushing, he nevertheless resents it and insists that he be allowed to act on his own, free from compulsion. Therefore, the therapist may be caught in a double bind if he takes a strong hand to forestall the controlling tendencies of the patient while allowing sufficient space for maneuvering so that the patient is permitted to decide on matters for himself. For any useful work to grow out of the therapeutic relationship, the prevailing atmosphere must be one of freedom — with a lack of compulsion and authority, with a minimum of rules and rituals, and with a maximum of exchange, in which the rights and limits of both parties are clearly understood. For the patient to perceive clearly his patterns of operation, the therapeutic atmosphere must not parallel the life experiences of the obsessional. In every respect the treatment behavior of the obsessional must be understood in its contradictory aspects, in order to maintain the cooperation and participation of the patient.

The patient must not be viewed as a stubborn ingrate who is arrogant and contemptuous, and if only he would behave right, all would be well.

The understanding that the compulsive behavior is beyond his control and therefore not available to volitional change must limit the therapist's expectation that knowledge will undo the compulsion. At the same time the patient must make efforts to understand the reasons for his continued need for guarantees and certainty that interferes with attempts to change his behavioral patterns. This paradoxical and contradictory situation must be fully explored in the therapy.

The ultimate goal in therapy is to effect a change in the patient's living, not merely to induce insight. Insight is only the prelude to change; it provides the tools for the alteration in one's patterns of living. But the therapist must also assist the patient in utilizing his new understandings. This demands an approach which is less rigid and less tied up in traditional methodology. The therapist must feel free to be of active assistance in the process. Obsessional patterns which are heavily involved with ritualistic forms of behavior cannot be resolved by therapeutic measures which are just as overloaded with ritual. The therapist must be flexible enough to try novel approaches and techniques.

The process of therapy, therefore, can only be described in general terms that leave room for considerable variation and flexibility in specific instances. Broad tendencies and characteristic maneuvers of both the patient and therapist can be discussed because the nature of the obsessional defense produces particular technical problems. However, detailed exchanges and specific interventions will vary with each patient and therapist.

The detailed case history that follows in part 4, chapters 11–15 will allow the reader to sit in on the author's therapeutic handling of a particular obsessional nerosis. However, it is not suggested that the reader react precisely the same way as the author did. Rather, this account should encourage the reader to explore his own reactions within the framework of the general therapeutic principles in dealing with obsessional problems.

Not every obsessional patient will present all the characteristics described in earlier chapters. Some elements will be more obvious and will play a more important role in one patient or be of secondary importance in another. It is the therapist's job to recognize the main themes in each case, as well as the subsidiary themes. Therapeutic emphasis must be placed on the major mechanisms but at the same time should not minimize the lesser patterns.

GENERAL PRINCIPLES

Since the therapist should not have a preconceived program but rather some general open hypotheses, his reaction to the patient must avoid stereotypical attitudes or responses. For example, if one hypothesizes that obsessional behavior controls hostile or aggressive impulses, it follows that the expression of such feelings should be encouraged. The therapist in noting instances of hostile feelings or attitudes might insist on the verbalizations of these feelings. At times, this technique may be unsuccessful, but at other times it may produce strong negative responses with a stubborn insistence that the patient does not feel hostile. At other times the therapist may interpret friendly responses as reaction-formations, insisting that the patient become aware of the true underlying feelings. Such exchanges often lead to contention and power plays in which one or the other must yield — most often the patient in his concern about not alienating the therapist. At times the therapist may become annoyed or, if he does not feel irritated, pretend to be in order to stir up manifest expressions of hostility.

While role-playing may be valid under certain conditions, it is not useful and may be dangerous in the therapy of obsessional states. A prior decision to avoid all intellectual discussions in therapy is also unwise, since it resembles so closely the obsessional's tendency to make resolutions or plans to replace spontaneous responses. Such a decision should come out of the experiences in the process of therapy.

The patient's persistent intellectualization which the therapist knows is not the salient issue cannot artificially or prematurely be avoided until the relationship will sustain the therapist's attempts to do so. One cannot say, "It's all too intellectual. Tell me how you feel about your wife (or someone else)." The patient will become annoyed and will respond with a sharp reply that he is doing the best he can and besides he has no feelings toward his wife. Instead, one approaches the matter by suggesting that while his descriptions are useful and accurate, they leave out a major dimension — that is, how he felt about it all.

A spontaneous bit of irritation or anger in response to a specific event can meaningfully advance the therapy. But a prescription for the therapist to express hostility in order to encourage the patient's hostile feelings or a program of provocative silence to stimulate the patient's anger may be quite detrimental. Such controlled responses are easily identified by the patient and seen as a contrived attempt to test his reactions. He may respond in a way which is expected to win approval or he may become discouraged because he feels manipulated and "on trial" instead of being engaged in a collaborative enterprise.

The obsessional person has considerable difficulty in being spontaneous or direct in the expression of his feelings. A spontaneously provoked response by the therapist can be very efficacious in stimulating the patient's spontaneity, although this type of approach requires a highly responsive therapist and a greater involvement and participation by him in the process. It means that the therapist must take some risks with regard to exposing some of his own weaknesses and deficiencies. As well as being able to maintain some objectivity and separateness, he must respond in human terms to the interpersonal exchanges to demonstrate to the patient that being human, fallible, and admitting to deficiencies need not result in rejection or humiliation. Instead of rejecting the therapist, the patient may have heightened respect for him — which can be an important learning experience for the patient and may encourage him to try it too. Such an approach to a patient is both difficult and uncomfortable for the therapist, but it is more interesting and fruitful for both therapist and patient.

The use of humor and sarcasm in the therapy of the obsessional can be most effective too; it requires becoming involved with the patient's tendencies toward extremes and his difficulty in dealing lightly with any issues. A most effective technique in this respect is to highlight the patient's extreme positions by pressing still further, which has the effect of slapstick exaggeration and often points up the pretentiousness of the patient's superstandards. Exclamations such as "God, did you really do that or say that?" or "how could you?" in a good-humored way can quickly mobilize patient participation. Such exclamations are viewed as friendly and empathic and create closeness and cooperation.

When the patient demands that every detail be precisely accurate or that impossible goals be achieved, one can agree that this might be possible if the patient were indeed a combination of God, Einstein, Shakespeare, and General MacArthur. The effective use of this type of sarcasm may be more successful than hours of patient explanation and clarification. The obsessional's latent sense of humor is one of his unused capacities and to bring it out into the open and help him use it can be a most rewarding experience. The use of humor and spontaneous laughter can often break through a communication impasse.

The therapist's attempts at humor, however, are not invariably met with warm acceptance. The patient may just as frequently counter the therapist's efforts with condescending jibes and contemptuous ridicule. He may deprecate the humor and derogate the therapist's intelligence and skill by insisting that "making light of serious matters" displays an immature mind. A defensive therapist may become annoyed or hurt, but the patient's reactions can be seen as further evidence of the patient's intense seriousness and inability to touch lightly on many matters which are not actually crucial to his existence. It is a laboratory demonstration of how the patient does react to attempts to make life more fun.

THE THERAPIST

While it is generally agreed that the sex of the therapist is not a significant factor in the therapy of obsessionals, the age, experience, and background are quite relevant and at times very significant. One factor is crucial: The therapist must not be so obsessional himself that he will inevitably get caught in a *folie à deux*, which can prolong therapy indefinitely if it manages to survive at all. A degree of obsessionalism can be an asset in all therapeutic endeavors. It encourages attentive concern and intellectual curiosity. When recognized by the therapist, his own obsessional qualities can enhance his ability to discover it in his patient. However, if too severe or unnoticed it can be an insurmountable handicap and is undoubtedly one of the major issues that prolong therapy in these disorders. This tendency is often coupled with passivity, which can only encourage the patient's passive resistances and indecisiveness. Passivity as a technical tool is too often viewed as the model for the ideal psychoanalyst. However useful it might be on other occasions, for the treatment of the obsessional it can be counterproductive.

A therapist who cannot get unlocked from the patient's struggles to control because he himself must always be in control either traps his patient into passive compliance and endless analysis or drives him away early by stirring up a great deal of hostility. Under such circumstances the patient and therapist may get into an obsessive bind in which the needs of each one may be satisfied at the high cost of permanent invalidism of the patient. While the obsessional patient will prefer a therapist who is older and very experienced, he will often end up with the opposite, a younger and less experienced therapist who is less of a threat to his omniscience and whom he thinks is more likely to be controlled and subdued.

To proceed successfully with the therapy of the obsessional, the therapist must be active, directive, and closely tuned to irrelevant communications so that they can be turned off as quickly as possible.

These distracting activities often occupy the bulk of therapy if allowed to continue and must be identified early in the work. How can the therapist know what is relevant and what is irrelevant? Except in the extremes, this is a difficult and complicated problem. The recipe for a cake, the number of cracks in the office ceiling, or the detailed description of occupational tasks can readily be identified as irrelevant to the therapeutic task at hand. The preoccupation with endless detail about one's early years, the school buildings, teachers, and empty accounts of earlier events may seem relevant but may well turn out to be evasive devices to forestall the examination of one's feelings and attitudes toward the teacher or other significant individuals.

One might say, "That is very interesting, but what happened between you and the teacher?" We now know enough about personality development and certain characterological disorders to be sure that certain matters are entirely irrelevant, others are relevant, and most are open to question. It is in this in-between area that the skill, intuition, and experience of the therapist are called upon in order to make judgments about the relevance of the communication.

The relevance of certain communications will, of course, be determined by the particular theoretical predilictions of the therapist. Some therapists consider all communication about the patient's earlier years as relevant, while others feel that such a focus is not always useful. Some insist that any reality concerns are out of place in analysis, considering useful only data that concern the transference. There are wide differences in viewpoints, depending on the therapist's theoretical position. However, it is universally agreed that the encouragement of certain details or topics tends to convey to the patient that some matters are of greater interest to the therapist, thereby encouraging their presentation.

Whatever the theoretical preference, certain issues are clearly irrelevant when they fail to advance the understanding of either the origin or the development of the personality defenses which characterize the disorder. Therefore, what is clearly relevant in all theoretical persuasions is material that touches on the dynamics of the obsessional state and the defense tactics which are an intrinsic part of it. Material which relates to anxieties (past or present), attempts at control, and preoccupations with guarantees and certainty is always pertinent and needs to be encouraged. The patient's evasive and defensive tactics must be brought into the open.

Material with emotional content usually has some degree of relevance in the therapeutic situation. However, the difficulty in deciding what is relevant should not allow the therapist to encourage undirected free association, which, in the obsessional, has a tendency to veer away from pertinent data. Neither should the notion that "everything is relevant" permit the therapist to allow treatment to continue endlessly because he is unwilling to narrow down the patient's communications. In a sense, everything can be shown to have a degree of relevance to everything else. However, it is no longer necessary to allow every therapeutic involvement to become a research project designed to prove such notions as determinism and unconscious motivation. Therapy is a practical contract directed at illuminating and alleviating behavioral disorders. Increasing knowledge of these disorders has enabled us to localize our inquiries, thereby giving us some clues as to what is pertinent and what is not. What may appear relevant during one session may be irrelevant in another. It is a judgment which can only be made in terms of material to be dealt with at a particular time; it must be decided upon in a specific situation.

In discouraging certain communications at particular times, however, one must be careful not to discourage it altogether. When the obsessive recital of dreams may, at one time, be avoiding currently unpleasant issues, this avoidance needs to be made known. Yet it should not be done in a way that would be entirely discouraging.

As suggested above, the obsessional has a great capacity to confuse the therapeutic process by producing irrelevant free associations or by constantly changing the subject or by having a sticky inability to change the subject. Great skill is called for on the part of the therapist to direct or control these tendencies. The therapist must be able to intervene actively and draw the focus of attention back to the significant matters. The defensive maneuvers may require frequent and repeated attention.

The therapist must always be aware of the limits of his patient's capacities to tolerate certain interpretations or observations; he must stop short lest he increase the anxiety and the defenses which ordinarily protect the patient against anxiety. This will limit the patient's capacities to observe and acknowledge the therapist's interpretations. When interpretations are seen as criticisms or as deflating the patient's esteem, the patient will react with even more elaborate defenses. On the other hand, the therapist's observations must not be too bland or else they may be easily overlooked.

Activity on the part of the therapist is an absolute essential from the beginning of the therapy to the end. Even a meager understanding of the dynamics of the obsessional state requires that the therapist not permit the techniques which defeat communication to continue for too long a time, although the therapist's activities must never be so intense as to overwhelm the patient or make him feel that the therapy is being run by the therapist. It does mean that the therapist must understand the obsessional's defense mechanisms of maintaining anxiety at a minimum, in order to facilitate learning and ultimately to resolve the obsessional patterns. Consequently, free association as well as the tendency toward endless detail and circumstantiality in the obsessive accounts must be controlled by the therapist. Passivity in the therapist can only lead to interminable analyses in an atmosphere that becomes more clouded and confused — often the reason for the long, fruitless analyses which characterized an early stage in the development of the methodology of psychoanalytic treatment of the obsessional.

TRANSFERENCE AND COUNTERTRANSFERENCE

The therapist is universally viewed as an authoritative figure who expects and demands maximum and perfect behavior. The patient feels that these demands are unreasonable and irrational and that the demands are more than he is capable of. The therapist clearly represents one parental figure who is more striking than the other and with whom there had been a relationship of some perverseness in terms of exaggerated expectations from the patient (which the patient felt to be far beyond his capacities). Often, both parents may be involved.

The therapist is seen as a critical, judging individual, with no respect for human frailties, who is sitting in judgment on every action of the patient. He is viewed as an unfriendly antagonist who must be overcome and exposed. At the same time, however, he must be impressed with the patient's skill and talents. These notions exist alongside those which aggrandize and idealize the therapist. He is put on a pedestal as being perfect and infallible and a model of controlled, spontaneous, passionate, and detached objectivity. He conforms to all the stereotypes and Hollywood versions of the romanticized psychoanalyst who is all-wise and all-understanding. Both these views put the patient at a distance and require him to behave properly and adequately.

It is only comparatively late in therapy that the patient can experience a collaborative interest on the part of the therapist and see him as a friendly helper rather than a caustic critic. Until then there is an ever-present atmosphere of suspicious uncertainty on the part of the patient and a readiness to hostility, which is generally well disguised in a superficially friendly and respectful demeanor. Such an atmosphere is easily punctured at the slightest rise of tension. This often makes the patient uneasy, so that he will strive to undo any damage that might have resulted from his anger and irritation. He tends to attribute to the therapist every deficiency which he despises in himself. His charges will range from his feeling that the therapist is a perfectionist, a procrastinator, and an indecisive person to ideas that he is a hypocrite and phony, whose standards are so flexible that they lack integrity. One can get a very clear view as to what ails the patient by examining his distorted views of the therapist.

Generally, the traits and attitudes attributed to the therapist are largely irrational and unjustified, but some of the characterizations may be more or less true. The therapeutic atmosphere may very well be one of an irrational authority who expects the rules to be followed simply because they exist and who demands certain behavior because it is good for the patient. The silent, passive, unseen therapist can easily exaggerate the authoritative atmosphere of the therapeutic setting and unnecessarily aggravate or rationally confirm the patient's defenses. Some of the elements of the classical techniques tended to do this very thing. The patient was put in an inferior, reclining role and was forced, by the rules of the game, to take over and proceed with the job. He received few, if any, answers to questions that might disturb him, and he was faced with a totally unreal situation in which he either accepted the rules or left.

Problems in the therapeutic situation are often crystallized in the rules for payment and absences, whether or not they are announced long in advance. Some therapists require a fixed contract in which all hours are paid for regardless of illness, occupational crises or vacation requirements. No accommodation is made for accidents, job requirements, or unexpected critical demands on the patient. This arrangement is rationalized on the grounds that the analyst has only a limited amount of time and that the patient must guarantee to fill it whether or not he can be present. This is not to say that the patient must not accept responsibility for the appointment; he must not absent himself for frivolous, escapist, or trivial reasons. However, in the treatment of an obsessional, a flexible, open attitude must prevail, and arrangements about cancellation and absences must be open to discussion and compromise, taking into account the therapist's needs and the patient's rights.

If flexibility is not part of the therapeutic atmosphere, the obsessional can easily accomodate to the rules and incorporate them into his rituals.

Therapy can thus become another ritual for the obsessional, rather than an experience in undoing his ritualistic symptoms. By following the rules rigidly and precisely and cooperating with every requirement of the process, the patient can often reinforce his neurosis, producing insuperable obstacles to its clarification and resolution. This can frequently result in the patient's achieving considerable insight but failing to gain any change in behavior or character structure as a result of the insight.

The therapist must be constantly aware that the obsessional's skill in deceiving himself and others and his secret demands for perfection, omniscience, and omnipotence reflect themselves in the relationship with him. Patients' apparent cordiality and conviviality in the face of an exchange in which they feel derogated must always be scrutinized, especially when the therapist is forced to make explanations or defenses of his interpretations. The cordiality is a thin veneer, and the underlying irritation and resentment must be brought into the open.

The *countertransference* phenomenon, or the reaction of the therapist to the patient, will vary considerably from therapist to therapist. The responses of the therapist, however, are of invaluable significance in the elucidation of the obsessional's way of life. The increased utilization of the countertransference phenomenon is one of the contributions of the post-Freudian psychoanalysts (this has been dealt with at length in my earlier book, *Developments in Psychoanalysis**).

---

* L. Salzman, *Developments in Psychoanalysis* (New York: Grune and Stratton, 1963).

The need for the therapist constantly to examine and occasionally to comment on his own feelings in response to some communication or the patient's behavior can bring the whole matter of emotions into the forefront of the work. The therapist may have some reaction to the patient's characteristic obsessional devices which can be identified or to some covert process in which the therapist has unwittingly been drawn into a defensive role. In the latter situation, he may feel particularly irritated at his own failure to be observant, a feeling which could be brought into the sessions. The way the therapist uses his reactions can be of great influence in the outcome of therapy. When he can be uninvolved in the sense of observing the patient's characteristic behavioral traits and identifying them, he can help the patient see what effect such behavior might have on others. At such times, the observations should be descriptive rather than critical and should convey goodwill and warm interest.

On the other hand, when the patient's behavior is irritating and particularly annoying or when it puts the therapist in a bind and stimulates his own anxieties about his deficiencies, the therapist's open responses will not be useful to the patient unless the therapist can acknowledge his own limitations and show the patient how the latter succeeded in drawing the therapist into his own neurotic net. In such an instance the therapist must be prepared to acknowledge his own defensive needs and his own tendency to justify himself and to be correct. He must also be able to express irritation and annoyance at the patient's undercover derogating and deriding activities. To be useful to the patient, such a procedure must be done in an atmosphere in which the emphasis is on the therapist's limitations and humanness, rather than on the patient's hostilities.

The tendency to focus on the hostile behavior of the patient serves only to distract the therapeutic process from its real task of investigating the sources of the patient's uncertainties and his need for guarantees in living. The therapist can always turn the discussion onto these matters when the patient is hostile, by expressing some curiosity about what the patient feels is being endangered that requires this hostile attack. In this way the hostility is seen only as a defense and not as a cause. It takes the focus off the hostility issue.

It is unfortunate that some psychodynamic theories stress the role of hostility as the etiology of obsessional behavior. This not only focuses on anger, but also gives permission for the therapist to be forever discovering the hostile elements in obsessional behavior, overlooking other key issues such as grandiosity, omniscient and omnipotent requirements, and anxieties about commitment, trust, and security. Too often, the therapist interprets the effect of the obsessional's behavior on others as its intent, thereby failing to indentify cause and consequence and encouraging more, rather than less, compliant and appeasing behavior. To tell a patient that he is hostile is to criticize, condemn, moralize, and implore him to behave better. To indicate that a patient's behavior produces a feeling of being attacked, demeaned, or deprecated suggests that the patient may be unaware of his hostility or that his efforts at communication misfire and stimulate reactions that are not intended. Such an attitude is more likely to encourage introspection than correction, with feelings of guilt and condemnation. Therapy must go beyond encouraging a patient to express his unexpressed hostile feelings or thoughts. It must discover the origin and adaptive purposes of such reactions if, in fact, they are present. Hostile attitudes are often defensive, rather than primal, and the therapist must go beyond the anger to look for the anxieties of being hurt, abandoned, or destroyed.

The therapist can use his reactions to initiate and accelerate insights by pointing out how the patient's behavior seems phony, hypocritical, or grandiose. Again, these reactions must be presented as an observation, rather than as a personal grievance or criticism. This can be done by wondering out loud whether others might not react in a similar way in response to many aspects of the patient's behavior. The use of a sharp or caustic comment or the single, well-intoned phrase can often simulate greater emotional response than the well-phrased intellectual formulation, which usually stirs up a defensive counterattack. The emphasis must be on comments or exclamations which will stir up feelings without humiliating the patient. The production of humiliation will sidetrack the inquiry. Sullivan employed his reactions with great skill in his work with obsessionals, and this undoubtedly accounted for much of his success with them.

The need for the active participation of the therapist has already been stressed. It must be emphasized that the possibility of involvement, exchange, and participation of the therapist can stimulate the patient to commit himself and make known his real feelings and attitudes. It can supply the needed experience in risking a relationship with a figure who will not be punitive or rejecting. The more involved the patient gets in the therapy, the clearer will his subtle and most closely guarded techniques come out into the open and be available for study. The more gross and obvious techniques will become evident early in therapy and will make it possible for changes to be made. However, the more elusive and intricate neurotic patterns which closely resemble nonneurotic behavior can become clear only in the intricacies of a relationship in which the patient allows himself some freedom to relax and let go. The best setting for such discoveries lies in the reactions of the therapist — usually called countertransference feelings — to the patient's behavior. The training of the therapist permits him to recognize these maneuvers and to bring them to the patient's attention, thus helping the patient to eliminate them from his living.

One must clearly distinguish between becoming truly involved and getting into arguments in order to win. Getting entangled in the flypaper tactics of the obsessional is not necessarily becoming more intimate or more involved. Any involvements or interactions of the patient and therapist should always be with regard to the therapeutic task. While quarreling indicates some involvement, it has no real place in the therapeutic process. The therapist must be aware that when he becomes active, certain safeguards must be applied so that activity does not turn into a repetition of the malevolent, authoritarian relationship which the patient had to deal with through his early experiencing.

The interaction characterized by the one-upmanship maneuver to maintain control of the therapeutic work can illustrate dramatically some of the pitfalls of an unaware or unsophisticated therapist. What is designed as a collaborative adventure can be changed into a struggle for control and position, and the therapeutic process can be viewed by some as a state of warfare. While it may be a struggle, it is not a war; the goal is not to win a battle but to communicate meaning and understanding to another, in order to help him deal with his problems in living. Transactional Analysis emphasizes these therapeutic gambits and can be very effective in resolving some of these problems if they do not get embedded in the win-or-lose portions intrinsic to many of the "games" that are played. An aware and skillful therapist can avoid these traps or, if he falls into them, can extricate himself by a skillful review of the tactics employed in the game.

If the therapist is unable to identify the patient's tactics of using double binds, semantic paradoxes, and verbal assaults — all devices used by obsessionals — therapy can very well develop into a state of war. The therapist must not lose sight of the fact that his job is to expose the tactics, not to beat the patient at his own game. Double binds are common occurrences in the obsessional's developmental history and in his own functioning, and one can easily be caught up in the game if one is not constantly on guard.

PAST VERSUS FUTURE

The obsessional is oriented toward the future, in order to guarantee that his living will be free of anxiety. Therefore, his interest in the past is generally meager, if not absent. At best, his recollection of his early years is distorted, and this period is frequently seen as a time when he was mistreated by one or both parents in a hypercritical and demanding fashion. His recollections of the more recent past are generally seen as a succession of occasions when he was taken advantage of and pushed around or was the object of discrimination by disrespectful people. Quite often, the therapist is fooled into thinking he is hearing a detailed and accurate review of some earlier historical event. The recollection seems so clear and lucid that it may be accepted in toto — as a fact. One needs to be very cautious in this regard and assume that every recollection has at least suffered some distortion, exaggeration, or convenient reconstruction.

The obsessional's tendency to distort the past as mentioned earlier, produced the crisis in Freud's theorizing that ultimately resulted in his greatest discovery. On the basis of the accounts of his obsessional patients — who described passive sexual assaults in their early years — Freud postulated that the obsessive disorder was caused by such sexual assaults. When, however, he attempted to validate these accounts, he discovered that they were untrue and were fantasies of the patient. He was then forced to acknowledge that either his theories were based on lies or he needed to explain such fantasized accounts in other ways. Freud resolved this difficulty when he recognized the power and significance of the imagination and the effect that thinking has on an individual's behavior. It became clear not only that actual events could produce widespread consequences but also that the person's imaginings or fantasies were capable of influencing his psychological history and behavior. Thus, the recollections of an individual may not be a major concern, as they are very likely to be distorted.

The obsessional's ability to reconstruct his early years is quite limited, as he has little interest in the past. His present behavior is related not only to his past experiences but also to the variety of defenses erected in the early years. The obsessional may have learned very little from his past experiences because his defenses prevented him from drawing any reasonable deductions from them. As a result, a successful experience or performance does not prevent anxiety about the next occasion. He approaches it with the same uneasiness and uncertainties, as though it had never happened before. Each occasion is a new trial in which he must prove himself over and over again.

Psychoanalytic therapy originally emphasized the need for a genetic reconstruction of the person's life, with emphasis on his libidinal development. It was assumed that the reconstructions would undo the repressions, which were the basis of the neurotic symptoms. However, much of the research on the therapeutic process and the ego psychological theories of personality development have raised doubts about the validity of this view. Whichever view may be correct, the possibility of an adequate or accurate genetic reconstruction of an obsessional's early life is highly questionable. Therefore, an emphasis on the past and the problem of the obsessional's distorted recollections make the usefulness of this aspect of therapy highly uncertain.

The most effective approach seems to be in the examination of recent events — particularly those events that occur in the ongoing relationship with the therapist. In this sense the transference and countertransference phenomena play their unique roles in advancing the therapeutic process by occurring in the actual moments of interaction of patient and therapist. They are therefore available for immediate examination. The emphasis on the *here and now* by many post-Freudian theorists finds its greatest reward in the treatment of obsessional disorders. The more recent conceptions of mental illness do not focus exclusively on the genesis of these disorders as libidinal deformations, nor do they conceive of the beginnings in relation to any specific trauma. The developments are seen as occurring in an atmosphere in which repeated experiences produce effects on the person in obvious or subtle ways. Therefore, discovering the actual origin or beginning of a symptom or personality characteristic seems of less value than a general recognition of the milieu or atmosphere of the household or the general attitudes of the parents.

In the ultimate development of the behavioral disorder, the conditioning effect of repeated experiences plays a major role, in addition to that of the initiating cause. In the adult years one deals with a problem the origin of which is only a single element in its continuation; the persistence of the faulty pattern is related to the process of conditioning and habit. Therapy must unravel the detailed and widespread defensive techniques which develop and penetrate into every aspect of the obsessional's life, as well as search for the origins of the symptoms. This requires a knowledge of the patient's present living in order that the therapist may see the subtleties and intricacies of his defensive processes. This is a most difficult task and comprises the bulk of the work in the therapeutic process. To achieve this the therapist must be prepared for a long and arduous job of repeating the same observations and interpretations frequently before they are truly recognized by the patient. It requires patience and understanding of the tenacious and persistent nature of the obsessional process.

One may find that the patient avoids present failures or recognized deficiencies, as they tend to expose too much of his feelings. In contrast, past angers can be described and experienced calmly, so that the actual value of their assessment in the therapeutic process is sharply reduced. Present emotional responses must be faced, and, as they are impinging on other responses, they can be usefully explored. As the exploration of such emotional experience is crucial to any useful work, stress on the here and now serves this purpose very well.

PROBLEMS OF CONTROL

Therapy requires a free, uncontrolling attitude toward one's thoughts and the ability to say aloud whatever may come to mind. Ordinarily, the obsessional tries to examine, appraise, and screen every thought before he utters it, in order to avoid exposing himself unfavorably. Thus, on the one hand his impulse is to censor anything that might make him appear in an unflattering light, while on the other hand he has a need to follow the therapist's instruction meticulously. In trying to do the latter he gets hung up on endless, detailed elaborations of each thought, which may unwittingly expose too much. The free flow of associations is also impeded by his difficulty in getting off a subject once it is started, thereby dwelling on what is no longer associative data but merely detailed bits of data. Any idea, thought, or attitude that happens to come to mind is simply worked to death. Both of these tendencies may succeed in controlling the content of the psychoanalytic hour.

The patient may frequently bring to the session a written or memorized agenda, which rigidly controls the content of the session and guarantees that nothing is left out and that nothing is inadvertently added. Fringe thoughts or ideas which occur in the course of the session are generally not permitted to interrupt or alter the prearranged presentation. The patient may unconsciously select and censor his thoughts in order to control the content of the interview. This must be brought to his attention — not as an aspect of his deceitfulness or failure to cooperate but as an impediment in the therapeutic process.

A patient who early in his therapy manifested overt and covert tendencies to try to run the therapeutic sessions by having an unwritten agenda wanted to take over the role of therapist. On one occasion, while this patient was deciding what was relevant to discuss, I pointed out that this was his method of controlling the sessions and that it would be preferable if he did not decide for himself unless the matter concerned something unquestionably irrelevant. He agreed and then went to the other extreme. He stated that he would therefore make no judgments of relevance at all; he wanted me to make the decision, so that he would not be accused of censoring any material. However, this could allow *him* to criticize or discount any judgments I might make. He was in effect saying, "Fine, I'll do what you say. But I'm letting you know that unless I run the show, I'll criticize it, or else take no responsibility for the consequences."

While insisting that he should not be asked to decide about the relevance of certain matters until he was much better informed, he still tried to run the process. I was trying to say that he should not control the process, but he was attempting to control it more effectively.

The tendency of some patients to stay rigidly on a topic and avoid fringe thoughts or associations might seem to indicate their efforts to avoid distraction. While this may be the case, it is also a way of avoiding unplanned or spontaneous reactions. That is, as one cannot predict the consequences of such reactions it is safer not to evoke them at all.

The problem of an agenda and the rigid adherence to a plan was exemplified in the behavior of an obsessional who became preoccupied prior to each session with concerns about *not* bringing an agenda to insure that he would freely present whatever came to mind. This was particularly true with regard to his concerns about his grandiose fantasies. If he were consciously concerned about some important matter, he could *not* bring it up as this would be preplanning. Therefore, important material would be postponed for long periods of time until it would be accidentally revealed.

Control of a situation can be direct or indirect, subtle and unwitting or calculated and obvious. The controlling tactics used by an obsessional, however, are rarely obvious to him, even though they may seem blatant and unmistakable to others. One image the obsessional has of himself is of someone who is under the influence of others, pushed and pulled by them. He sees himself a passive victim of the demands and requirements of others, and he feels himself to be helpless in the face of forces he must overcome. While he may see his helplessness, he generally does not recognize his defensive, controlling tactics and the striving for power involved in them. These elements must be drawn to his attention in the therapeutic process. To become aware of how he appears to others can help him understand why others react to him as they generally do.

One of the most effective techniques for controlling others is to put oneself entirely at the other's disposal and to abandon all pretense and plans for directing one's own life. While this appears to be a state of total dependency and can result in rejection, it may succeed in getting the other person to focus entirely on fulfilling the obsessional's needs. The risk of failure is present, but it is fairly safe to assume that in a middle-class Western culture such a display of total incapacity will stir up sympathy and help rather than open rejection. While it may overtly convey a total lack of control of the universe, covertly it serves to manipulate others through the emotional influence of helplessness. This type of "no control" is often a most effective device for exerting maximum control over others.

This personality trait manifests itself in the seemingly self-effacing, compliant person who presumes to do exactly what you want him to do. He follows all rules and procedures precisely. In therapy he will free-associate and will not withhold anything, following all instructions scrupulously. He will say anything and everything that comes to mind, including stock quotations, the number of cracks in the ceiling, the voluminous details of an exchange with the florist about how to care for African violets, and every last detail — inning by inning — of the baseball game. The overconforming literalness of this type of response tends to sabotage and interfere with the therapeutic process because it wastes so much time on what is clearly irrelevant and serves to distract from the relevant. When this is called to the patient's attention, he may respond with, "You told me to say everything that comes to my mind and not to censor any of it." In fact, these are the instructions he received. He is afraid not to say everything lest he leave out something important. If anything might be significant, his devotion to the total truth as well as his rigidity about the rules justify such detail.

The therapist must therefore be alert to who is controlling the interview and the therapy. It must always be very clear as to who is the doctor and who is the patient.

TUG-OF-WAR

In his relationships the obsessional invariably becomes involved in a tug-of-war when he attempts to one-up others, both in therapy and out. Since his security rests upon his always being right, even the most trivial exchange becomes a duel which he must win. In therapy he may have to have the last word with a routine question or comment, even if it may undo the whole hour's work or may cast doubt on the entire exchange. This is the effect of the familiar closing comment of many obsessionals — namely, "How am I doing?" or "Do you think I'm getting any better?" It is essential not to be drawn into answering the question but to indicate instead, while exiting from the office, that it should be discussed at the next session. It is most important to raise it at the next session if the patient forgets to, and it would not be surprising if he did forget. At another time the patient may challenge the therapist's capability in an attempt to put him on the defensive. This puts the therapist in an inferior role and requires him to explain his actions to another person who sits in judgment upon him. This technique is used in other personality configurations as well, but it is particularly common in obsessional relationships.

In the tug-of-war the patient tries to gain control by raising doubts about the validity of the process, the theory which underlies it, or the capacity of the therapist to utilize both. The patient not only may raise doubts about the concept of the unconscious or the validity of introspection but also may begin to attack psychotherapy as a pseudoscience and the practitioners as dupes or quacks. He may bring in the latest magazine, book, or newpaper attack on psychiatry or quote the prevailing detractor or antagonist to the psychotherapeutic methodology, whether it be valid or not. These attacks are generally timed to deal with the patient's feelings that the therapeutic situation is a hostile one and that the therapist is criticizing him and putting him in his place. The patient feels that he must counterattack and reassert his position. It is important at such times that the therapist does not get caught up with the patient's hostility and view it as if it were the primary issue. The patient is trying to establish some parity in a situation in which he feels himself to be inferior, and his hostility is a defensive device to overcome this supposed inferiority.

Hostile and aggressive feelings are often responsible for a great many of the obsessional's difficulties. However, the need to establish parity or even superiority may or may not involve feelings of hostility toward others. If his sense of control is endangered, as in a therapeutic situation in which he is forced to recognize his fallibility, the patient may very well react with anger and irritation and attack the therapist. The basis for such an attack can be clearly understood in terms of a need to control rather than as a reflection of some underlying "hostile core." The patient has great concerns about controlling his hostile impulses, as well as everything else, and it is therefore necessary to understand the causes of his hostility. In spite of the prevalence of hostile feelings in the obsessional, he has more difficulty in dealing with his tender impulses and his fear that they may get out of control and that he might be overly kind or loving. These reactions are even more dangerous than his hostile feelings because he sees them as weak, as giving up, and as losing the tug-of-war. Being tender means being a sucker or being taken advantage of; this feeling is untenable for him.

The struggle to be on top in the therapeutic situation may extend over long periods of time. Occasionally, it can be resolved early in therapy, but because it reflects the totality of the obsessional's character structure, it generally weaves in and out of the therapeutic process from beginning to end.

A patient spent several weeks exploring his objections to a statement I made and finally appeared with evidence to prove that I was wrong. He had difficulty understanding that I might have accepted his objections at the time I made the statement and that he need not have spent so much time researching his challenge. He felt I would defend my statement to death, just as he would have; he therefore needed support for his attack. In the interval, while he was accumulating data to counter my statement, he was subtly contemptuous of me, buoyed up by the knowledge that he had won the argument.

A comfortable capacity to admit errors and fallibility without any pretense of humility or virtue is an important quality in the therapist — not only to avoid the tug-of-war but also to demonstrate the possibility that one can be wrong and can survive without humiliation or anguish. There are many such opportunities in the course of therapy, and the therapist should not pass up any occasion to admit his error when he turns out to be wrong. Staging such an event, however, in order to give the patient such an experience, may create an atmosphere of trickery with regard to the therapist as well as to the process as a whole. One can be sure that enough situations will occur spontaneously, so that the therapist need not search for such opportunities.

It is obvious that the therapist cannot enter into the tug-of-war in order to overcome his "opponent." There are more significant issues involved which concern the elucidation and demonstration of the patient's insistent need to win or to be on top. He must be helped to see how this interferes with learning and relating effectively with people. To win in an immediate sense may often mean gaining control, but such control can be useless and ineffective. The tug-of-war, when it occurs in therapy, provides an opportunity for the obsessional patient to see in microscopic proportions how he functions in the world at large. Winning, which may supersede all other values for him, can be more costly than it is worth. Therefore, the tug-of-war is a most effective therapeutic tool if the therapist can use it skillfully. He should not avoid a challenge on the assumption that the patient may convert it into a battle but should grasp the chance to enlighten the patient about this tendency. If the therapist evades the challenge, he encourages the grandiose fantasies of the patient and strengthens his neurotic defenses. Intelligent confrontation and involvement — in which the therapist stands firm while yielding at opportune moments — can provide great enlightenment to the patient.

PROBLEMS OF PERFECTION

The desire to be perfect leads to a variety of complications in the therapeutic process, as therapy is basically a learning situation and the obsessive is unable to admit to deficiencies.

In order to learn, one must initially accept the premise that there is something to be learned. If the obsessional assumes a perfection and refuses to acknowledge gaps in his understanding, learning is extraordinarily difficult. His security rests on a presumed invulnerability based on his feelings of perfection and omniscience. He has the illusion that he can meet any challenge and can therefore be certain about his existence. An interpretation or observation which is unexpected, unfamiliar, or novel and which might challenge this conviction is denied, repressed, or overlooked. If it cannot be bypassed in these ways it is either minimized or rationalized as reflecting the therapist's jealousy or critical unfriendliness. At these times the patient views therapy as a battle; he feels he must defend himself against attack. This will occur in spite of his awareness of the need for therapy. He may even be aware of his unreasonable tendency to react as though attacked, yet he must still defend himself to maintain his illusion of perfection.

Such contradictory behavior is comprehensible when one recognizes that the obsessional's neurotic integration rests on the need to deny any deficiency or lack of knowledge about himself and the universe. Therefore he must resist or parry every observation which reflects on this matter. He may produce new data to cast doubt on the truth of any such observation made by the therapist. He will raise insignificant exceptions to question the validity of the interpretation. If the therapist's interpretation is convincing and cannot be evaded, the patient minimizes its value in order to make it more palatable and to reduce the shame of having to admit that he did not already know about the matter. Although he may accept the interpretation, he will move on quickly to other matters which, he says, are more important. Thus, the impact is reduced. At other times, while ostensibly agreeing with the interpretation, he will set up a barrage of highly intellectualized counterattacks to undermine or undo the interpretation.

After many qualifications and clarifications he may finally accept the interpretation but not without some belligerent counterattack. He may charge the therapist with running him down or with trying to destroy his self-esteem. Such an attack may put the therapist on the defensive and serve to tone down the interpretation, so that the real issue is evaded.

The patient may, at times, deny the observation only to discover it himself as a fresh and novel idea in succeeding hours. He will behave as if he figured it out all alone and will present it as a fascinating discovery. In doing this he can salvage the notion of his perfection and maintain the fiction of his flexibility. The patient's need to be perfect pushes him to present the most precise and extensive account of every event to be certain that nothing is left out. This produces an enumeration of the most minute details and accounts of minor and insignificant events. He will ramble on endlessly in his need to clarify and qualify every statement. Such endless detail may be rationalized as accurate reporting. One gets a clear impression, however, that the patient has no capacity to separate the relevant from the irrelevant. While this type of communication outside of therapy may be only boring and irritating, it is most important that in therapy the patient note the effect of such tendencies.

The patient attempts to retain the illusion of perfection by being doubtful or inattentive to interpretations. Since interpretations are the only way to advance a real understanding of the obsessional defenses, the patient's tendency to maintain his neurotic esteem and avoid what he considers a humiliating acceptance of shortcomings may prevent any movement in therapy. The undoing process often occurs even while the therapist is speaking. As he listens, the patient is already preparing his defenses, justifications, or counterattacks and is thus only partly paying attention to the therapist's statement. He may even feel superior by deciding that the interpretation does not go far enough and that the therapist is not so bright after all. Some patients literally hear nothing of what is said. They may often be able to identify exactly when they stopped hearing and began ruminating about some irrelevancy unconnected with the immediate exchange. This must be dealt with summarily, or valid and valuable exchanges can take place without any noticeable effect on the patient. The most brilliant observations or formulations can be wasted unless they are attended to; this requires that the therapist present them in a palatable fashion. The therapist's skill is manifested most clearly in his capacity to deal with this particular problem.

A particularly bright professor could identify exactly the moment that he would turn off listening and start preparing his offensive. On one occasion when he was describing his concerns about the worthiness of his lecture because he had failed to mention some unessential but interesting details, I suggested that he was again demanding the impossible of himself. I then focused on how this issue had appeared time and again and reminded him of his intolerance to forgetting names, even those he didn't care to remember. At this point he began to detail covertly, while I continued to talk, the names of all the people he had run into in the past week. It was an examination and he was testing his performance. He heard no more of what I was saying until a few moments later when he could tell me exactly what had happened.

The emphasis on intellectuality is another means of avoiding the potential humiliation of not being perfect. It prevents real involvements in any emotional exchange and thereby sidetracks the possibility of being influenced or affected by the therapist's interpretation or observation. Intellectualizing and philosophizing about life is a most successful device to avoid participating in it. The obsessional exhibits great skill in avoiding any involvement with the therapist, although he may talk extensively about involvement and the problems of transference and countertransference. He will even talk about feelings and emotions. However, it will be a succession of words drawn from an intellectual comprehension of the issues involved, devoid of any real emotional response. It is therefore necessary to focus on real feelings and to limit, as much as possible, such intellectual discussions. Obviously, they cannot be avoided entirely, but they can and should be minimized; and, whenever possible, their true function should be demonstrated to the patient.

Extremes

An aspect of perfection which poses innumerable therapeutic problems is the obsessional's tendency to think and live in extremes. For him, it is not a matter of being correct but of being perfect. His living is secure only when he can be assured of absolute safety, infallible prediction, and absolute certainty about his status — absolutes demanding superhuman attributes. The reaction to any discovery of inadequacy in therapy is one of extreme despair, discouragement, and feeling of failure.

Any attempt, therefore, to highlight these extreme demands in therapy and to portray the impossibility of fulfilling them may result in a countercharge that the therapist is supporting the opposite extreme and is trying to make the patient into an ordinary or mediocre person. Each time the therapist tries to point out that the demands for perfection are unachievable and only lead to despair and disappointment, he may be accused of having standards which are too low and of being too easily satisfied. At the beginning of therapy it is impossible for the patient to take a middle ground — that is, to do the best he can or to utilize the skills which he does have. He insists that this is not enough. As long as he must have absolute guarantees he cannot be satisfied with human uncertainties. He cannot see that to accept one's human limitations is an act of strength that accounts for some of man's great achievements. The need to reassert this constantly in the therapeutic exchanges results in the charge that therapy is attempting to reduce the patient's performance to a minimum. It is hard for the patient to accept the fact that being human does not mean being satisfied with the least output, or the utilization of only a fraction of one's capacities. The therapist must regularly interpret and demonstrate that the insistence on perfection produces the very results the patient abhors. Mediocrity is *not* the alternative to the superhuman expectations of the obsessional, although this is the only way he can see it. He sees the world in extremes because he lives that way and feels that unless he is pushed to act he will not perform at all. Therefore, when he is encouraged to relax or to limit his demands, he interprets this as encouragement to slacken his standards.

The tendency to see the world in extremes is the reason that some obsessionals fear to drink or take drugs. They feel that they would be unable to control themselves and would go to extremes; that is, they fear they would become alcoholics or drug addicts. They therefore go to the opposite extreme and never take a drink or use drugs, even aspirin. The drug issue also involves not wanting or needing outside help in filling some need — they can do it themselves. This often delays their visits to physicians when the situation justifiably requires it.

The therapist must help the obsessional patient to recognize that doing the best one is capable of is neither mediocre nor ordinary, but richly productive. To help the patient strive for a realizable goal which utilizes his highest skills and capacities is not a matter of compromise. One is not either a God or a shameful mortal. One can be proud and productive even while being restrained by human limitations.

If security is attainable only by being king, one cannot accept the role of prime minister, which is just as unsafe as being an ordinary citizen. This is the essence of the problem of extremes in the obsessional, and no amount of reassurance about the value of being second-best will suffice. Since the excessive demands owe to compulsive requirements, an intellectual clarification of the problem does not serve to reduce it, even though it paves the way for eventual change.

The dilemma of the extremes and the contradictory behavior resulting from them are reflected in the obsessional's inconsistent attitudes toward his need for others and his need to present himself as entirely independent and self-sufficient. The contradiction between his dependent and inde-pendent needs creates innumerable therapeutic crises and impasses, which need to be clarified by frequent interpretation and repetition. This is particularly highlighted in the phobic states when the obsessional requires the presence of another person in order to function at all. Although he insists on total independence, his phobia requires and therefore justifies his dependence. Independent and self-reliant behavior is preferred by the obsessional, as it helps sustain the illusion of a perfect, infallible, omniscient being. Total independence, however, cannot be achieved; the obsessional is forced to rely on others — for example, to marry or to go to a doctor. This reflects itself in the therapeutic process when the obsessional grudgingly admits that he is in need of treatment or insists that he is doing it for someone else. By going to a psychotherapist he is satisfying someone else's needs. He frequently reminds the therapist that while the therapy may be useful, it is not really necessary for him. But, he adds, since he is in treatment, why has it not overcome all the problems which he refuses to admit he had in the first place?

Whatever his reasons for being in therapy, what he really wants from therapy, on one level, is to become more perfect and to overcome the deficiencies which interfere with his achieving perfection. Being forced to acknowledge his deficiencies because of some crisis or unfortunate circumstance, he expects that therapy will now overcome them and will make him totally independent. However, he wants the therapy and the therapist to accomplish this. He is willing to acknowledge the expertness of the psychiatrist, to pay his fees, and to follow all the necessary instructions. In return, he expects the doctor to resolve the difficulties. The concepts of relationship, mutual endeavor, and collaboration are alien to him. As he doesn't really feel that he needs the therapist, he has no need to develop any relationship with him.

The obsessional is particularly incompetent in the area of interpersonal relationship. Relationship involves participation, which, in turn, implies some need or dependency as well as commitment and exchange that grow out of some trust in the relationship. The demand for self-sufficiency obviates and complicates all his attempts at forming relationships, and this becomes more aggravated as he grows older. Intimacy, either sexual or nonsexual, is largely foreign to him because he has had such limited experience with it, and nonsexual intimacy is what the therapeutic relationship requires.

Helping the obsessional gain insight into how he actually behaves requires not only the clear recollection of a recent event but also the elimination of the patient's doubts and uncertainties about such events. This does not mean a perfect reconstruction. It requires only enough recall to be able to illuminate the basis for the anxiety which stimulates obsessional processes. The here-and-now experience enables the therapist to pin down the facts of an event and the patient's feelings about it. His reaction to an event and his way of dealing with his anxieties are more easily ascertained when one explores a recent event that is uncluttered by the distortions, denials, or sheer forgetting permitted by the passage of time. For the obsessional, past events and hazy recollections are ideal opportunities to use powers of verbal manipulation and distortion. The patient finds it easier to restrict his communication to the past. It is easier for him to discuss angers, frustrations, or difficulties that occurred years ago. Because the emotional elements in the obsessional's life are generally constrained and under control, it is imperative that they be brought into focus with regard to his present attitudes and relationships, thereby forcing him to acknowledge the relevance to his present behavior and his responsibility for its effect on his present living.

PROBLEMS OF OMNISCIENCE

If the patient expects to know everything, he feels utterly humiliated when he is forced to acknowledge a new piece of information. The obsessional must accept new insights and points of view about his past and present living, and he must come to recognize that his preconceptions and distortions restrict and prejudice his present experiences. He must learn that he is not viewing the environment with fresh and open eyes. He must see that he cannot really learn unless he is able to observe what is actually happening. He must learn to learn by becoming aware of his tendency to see everything in the light of what he expects to find in the first place — that is, in light of the concept of the self-fulfilling prophecy, which plays a vital role in all neurotic processes. When one expects or anticipates rejection, hostility, or criticism, one can misconstrue or misinterpret a situation in this light. Consequently, one reacts by withdrawn irritation or outright hostility, thereby angering the other person and fulfilling the anticipated rebuff. If one is anxious and uneasy, an atmosphere of tension can be created, putting other individuals into an anxious or uncomfortable state. The obsessional can then interpret the other person's behavior as unfriendly. The uneasy expectation prevents him from actually discovering how the other person feels, and the tense atmosphere is interpreted as a rejection.

The inability to acknowledge limitations makes every observation, interpretation, or clarification a criticism and a challenge to the obsessional's omniscience. He cannot admit that there are things he does not know. He must challenge each observation at length, even while he may be aware that it is correct and useful. Most often, the patient's behavior is out of his awareness, and he automatically defends his position. His defensiveness may be manifested by his going on the offensive and saying that the interpretation is wrong or, if right, that it is too strong, poorly timed, and badly done because it came through as criticism and derogation rather than as a simple observation. He is on the attack and tries to embarrass the therapist and put him on the defensive. His need to be critical has enabled him to develop his skills in finding the weak and vulnerable areas in his opponent. Such maneuvers not only tend to weaken the therapist's observations but also serve to shift the focus from the patient's deficiencies to the therapist's weaknesses.

To minimize the patient's resistances to learning, the therapist's interpretations should not be presented as if they were obvious. Instead, they should be presented as curious and interesting observations on which the patient himself can elaborate. One should avoid saying, "From what you have said about the event, it is clear that your competitive need to excel must alienate others." Instead, it would be preferable to say, "What effect did you think your pushing John aside might have had on him?" or "How would you react in the face of a competitor who was pressing hard to beat you?" One should pose interpretations in the form of riddles in which the necessary ingredients for a solution can be supplied by the patient. In this way the patient makes the discovery which leads to some useful interpretations, and he does not have to resist the information. While this works very effectively for a while, the patient may soon catch on to the device and feel that it is an attempt to trick him. But even when discovered, it turns out to be more palatable than other techniques. As suggested previously, the patient may at other times hear an interpretation, deny it, and return several weeks later to announce that he has just discovered it himself. One cannot force or hurry understanding in such patients; one needs to repeat, over and over again. To make it more likely that the interpretation will take hold, the therapist must hold it back until the patient's life experiences are so clear and almost self-evident that the patient is ready to have the insight himself. Above all, the interpretation must not be made in an attacking or critical vein, such as, "How come you didn't see it?" (implying "You must have been stupid not to notice it!"). Often a preliminary statement noting why it would have been difficult for the patient to recognize it sooner can make a strong interpretation more palatable. Yet no amount of skill and maneuver can make an interpretation easy for the obsessional to take. He has to discover that he does not know everything, and this stirs up much resentment.

Some obsessionals who are able to limit the range of their interests may become bright, well informed, and highly proficient in their professional fields. Others, however, may have a superficial knowledge of many matters. Because they are aware of a lack of depth in many areas of knowledge, they avoid detailed discussions and prefer to keep matters on a surface level. If challenged in discussions, they make extreme and dogmatic statements in an effort to overwhelm their opponents and thereby terminate the discussion. Thus, they frequently take extreme positions which are difficult to defend, and they often find themselves supporting a point of view in which they do not believe. These complications generally arise when they are unwilling to admit to a lack of knowledge or an error and become entangled in a web of indefensible rationalizations.

This happens regularly in therapy when the obsessional faces someone who is better informed than he is on at least one subject. The therapist will have many opportunities to demonstrate such complications; because of their need to know everything, obsessionals will invariably stick their necks out, and the consequences can be quite humiliating to them. The therapist must exert great care not to get involved to the point of humiliation, but to interrupt the patient before he goes too far. Past experiences, both inside and outside of therapy sessions, can be used to document the therapist's presentation, instead of allowing the present situation to unfold completely. In this way the emotional encounter with the therapist can be used to advance the therapeutic process without stirring up too much resistance.

The patient may sometimes be eager to accept the therapist's observation and demonstrate his understanding, but he may leave no time for the amplification of the interpretation. He conveys the notion that he knew it all the time so "let's get on with it." He may, at times, even proceed to a statement about the therapist's great memory or his cleverness in understanding human behavior. This not only changes the focus of the exchange but also serves to stimulate the therapist's goodwill toward the patient. It is necessary on such occasions to examine this maneuver as well as the interpretation. The therapist must show the patient that the latter's readiness to receive the interpretation was intended as flattery to the therapist as well as evidence of the patient's own cleverness. The remark can then be seen as a maneuver in which the patient is actually shifting the focus from his behavior to the therapist's behavior.

In his omniscient strivings the patient may try to become informed about psychiatry in general and the therapist's professional orientation in particular. This fulfills the patient's need to know everything and also supplies him with ammunition to flatter or attack the therapist when a suitable occasion arises. As psychotherapy is still a young, growing science, it has many schisms and factions. Both organizationally and scientifically there are opposing points of view and, at times, bitter factional disputes. The patient may take advantage of this situation and adopt a superior attitude toward "petty, quarrelsome scientists who haven't been able to put their own houses in order." On the other hand, the patient may become an active partisan or proselyte of his own therapist's persuasion.

As he becomes well informed about the particular orientation of his therapist, the patient may color his observations and experiences, emphasizing those aspects he assumes to be of interest to his therapist and minimizing others. He soon learns that his therapist is particularly interested in sex or dreams, or recent versus past experiences. He may unwittingly slant his presentation to suit these interests. While this occurs more or less in all patients, it is particularly evident in the obsessional, who places great emphasis on intellectual skill and one-upmanship. In these situations, the omniscient strivings serve many purposes.

The emphasis on knowing also allows the patient to deal with the therapeutic process by the use of psychoanalytic jargon, which can result in an intellectual exercise that makes therapy an examination of psychoanalytic theory rather than of the patient's behavior. The patient attempts to deal with the therapist by impressing him with his brilliant observations — to be looked at in terms of theory rather than in terms of his own life. Too often, the therapist himself is guilty of substituting psychoanalytic jargon for comprehensible language. The obsessional patient can become quite expert in using this terminology to enter the "club," but it serves to evade a meaningful confrontation with his attitudes and behavior. Freud had this type of person in mind when he advised his patients against reading or becoming too familiar with psychoanalytic literature. He wished to avoid as much as possible any slanting of a patient's productions which would be stimulated by reading. He also wanted to forestall discussions about psychoanalysis that might be stimulated by such reading. Although this injunction still remains useful, it has become impractical because most patients have already become acquainted with psychoanalytic writings, either in popularized or professional forms.

In the service of pleasing the therapist and fortifying his theories, a patient may avoid discoveries or observations which he thinks may negate these theories. In his own search for certainty and in his skill at accumulating knowledge, the patient may not want to disturb the therapist's established systems. He needs to view the therapist as an idealized figure, in order to put his trust in him. To preserve this image, the patient may forego criticism and intellectual disagreement. He may even seek out evidence or distort observations in order to fortify the therapist's analytic orientation. Such activity must be dealt with by the therapist with dispatch and in a forthright fashion if the therapy is not to become a technical course or a mutual admiration society.

If the therapist is himself obsessional and requires such idealization, the therapeutic process reaches a stalemate. It may appear to be progressing well with few complications, but little therapeutic progress will be noted, and therapy may become an interminable process.

PROBLEMS OF GRANDIOSITY

The obsessional's grandiosity is often manifested in his arrogant and contemptuous behavior, even though it may be dressed in a cloak of modesty and humbleness. He may expose his snobbishness and haughty behavior by slips of the tongue, accidental oversights, or deliberate deletions.

One patient, while standing in a cafeteria line with his wife, had ordered two rare roast beef sandwiches. One turned out to be less rare than the other. The patient insisted that the less rare one was his wife's. This resulted in a rather heated argument about the restaurant and its defects. After he related the story during a therapeutic session, I asked him how he knew that the less rare sandwich (the least desirable one) was his wife's, since he had picked them both off the counter. He suddenly became silent and was dumbfounded when he realized that he had automatically taken it for granted that the better one was naturally for him. It was also striking that his wife did not make this observation but instead got into an argument about the restaurant and the poor service. The patient operated under the assumption that he was a privileged and special person whose desires were to be catered to at all times.

To maintain the illusion of superiority and to protect his grandiose conception of himself, the obsessional may limit his socializing to inferiors or to occasions when his superior feelings will go unchallenged. He may feel marked envy and anxiety in the presence of realistic status differences, and while he may yearn for relationships with higher-status individuals, he will either derogate them or discover some deficiency in them that allows him to eliminate them as potential friends. If they are rich, they may not be intelligent enough. If they are intelligent, he will insist that they are phony or pretentious. However, resolving the dilemma by limiting his relationships to inferiors leaves great areas of dissatisfaction because his own status is not sufficiently acknowledged by associating with such people.

In therapy, grandiosity manifests itself in a variety of ways; it needs to be identified whenever it appears. This issue often accounts for the aloofness and the failure to become involved in a relationship with the therapist. The patient remains distant but proper and does the job as it is outlined to him. Secretly, he feels superior and contemptuous of the therapist; he is "on" to what is happening. He feels smug and "above it all." He may catalog the therapist's deficiencies, storing them for use at a proper time. He may, for example, keep track of the time the sessions start, watching to see that he gets all the time he is entitled to and storing up evidence of the therapist's oversight. Such stored-up grievances are usually held as secret weapons and are revealed only under sufficient provocation. Meanwhile, they may be used to maintain secret feelings of superiority in his relationship to the therapist.

Such feelings may seriously interfere with the therapeutic work, not only because they are secret but also because they are used to discount or discard any formulations which the patient doesn't like. They help the patient remain on the outside, looking in. By feeling superior to what is going on, the patient remains uninvolved while he is supposedly participating in a mutual exchange. If the therapist fails to bring this into the open, documenting it well, it will seriously hamper the progress of therapy. If the therapist succeeds in exposing this technique to the patient, it will enhance the patient's respect for the therapist.

In this connection, a patient related an incident concerning his pregnant wife, who awakened in the middle of the night with a cramp and proceeded to wake him up. He became furious with her for awakening him, showing no concern about her pregnancy and suggesting that if she could not control her wakefulness she should sleep in another room. The following morning he recognized the arrogance of his attitude and felt quite remorseful. However, while relating the incident, he also reported his fantasy of how he thought I might behave under similar circumstances. In his fantasy he assumed that I allowed my wife to push me around, and he felt contempt for me because of this. When I called attention to the difficulties he had in making his tenderness for his wife evident, he fantasized that I was a softy who couldn't stick up for my rights. He was certainly remorseful about what he could recognize as arrogant behavior toward his wife, but he was unaware of his arrogance toward me during this exchange. I called his attention to this behavior and to how he felt toward me because he thought that I was taking his wife's side. He could then see his arrogance as it was expressed in various relationships.

The obsessional's grandiosity leads him to expect magical leaps and massive advances in therapy. He is impatient with small gains and expects every meaningful interpretation to be followed by great advances or total cure. There is often a profound disappointment when an illuminating exchange is followed by a repetition of the old pattern. When this happens, the patient criticizes the therapist and the psychotherapeutic theory as well as himself because he feels that he has failed to live up to his own grandiose expectations. As he can accept only total and complete restoration of his grandiose self through therapy, he cannot abide the slow, gradual process of learning and changing. This leads him to the frequent charge that the therapy is doing no good: "Nothing has changed" or "It's been a waste of time and money."

After acknowledging some advance when the patient recognizes that his somatic preoccupation is a way of dealing with doubts about his acceptability as a clever and creative person, he may begin to derogate himself for needing still to utilize obsessional techniques. He should be beyond that. His grandiosity, which requires automatic acknowledgment from others as to his brilliance, prevents him from appreciating the advances he is making in resolving his obsessional tendencies. The therapist must avoid trying to justify his work or blaming events on the patient's lack of cooperation. When progress is slow or absent, the therapist should not put the blame on the patient's resistance or resort to the concept of the negative therapeutic response. While many factors may be at work in the negative therapeutic reaction, it is clear that many therapeutic impasses or failures are also caused by the therapist's inadequate handling of the obsessional defense; this the therapist must face and take responsibility for. Therefore, failure cannot be said to be exclusively the fault of either the patient or the therapist. However, understanding of undue expectation, a need for magical solutions, and feelings of despair and disappointment when immediate success is not forthcoming is of particular significance in the treatment of obsessionals.

The therapist must show interest in the patient's charges that the work is not going well or that little progress is being made. He should not act as though such charges are entirely unjustified and as if he were always above reproach. Generally, one can find both rational and irrational elements in a patient's complaints, and when dealt with seriously, they offer an opportunity for the patient to examine his grandiose expectations and for the therapist to explore his own deficiencies. An admission of the slowness of the process and the limited success it has produced presents the patient with a view of the therapist's realistic goals in contrast to the patient's extravagant expectations. It may even be useful for the patient to recognize that because of the comparatively youthful state of the science of psychotherapy, the therapist is bound by limitations imposed by the science itself. This is a valuable learning experience for someone whose major difficulty lies in his reluctance to acknowledge any limitations caused by nature or biology. To have this acknowledged in a matter-of-fact way, without apologies, may be of great help in getting the patient to accept some limitations in his own existence. Such an exchange may well serve to increase the patient's respect for the therapist's honesty and integrity.

The obsessional's hope that psychotherapy will enable him to become perfect and invulnerable is an aspect of his expectations which often overshadows all of his goals. He hopes that psychotherapy will build up his resources so that he will never need to be dependent upon anyone and that it will strengthen his esteem so that he will never again need to be beholden. He hopes therapy will provide him with sufficient placidity and detachment that he need not be upset or distressed under any circumstances, even unfavorable ones. In short, he secretly hopes to repair his deficiencies and overcome his weaknesses and be made perfect — all as a result of therapy. When he discovers that, instead of making him a superman, therapy attempts to strengthen his humanness and get him to accept his imperfections, he is both angry and disappointed. Instead of an anxiety-free existence in a state of perfect living, he discovers that therapy will only help him to live with anxiety in an imperfect world in which he will have no ultimate control over his destiny. Such goals are so alien to him that he considers himself a failure for even approaching them. This produces the typical obsessional dilemma: As he becomes emotionally and psychologically more mature, he seems to feel that he is getting worse. However, as therapy progresses, he comes to realize that in the long run to accept his humanness will provide a more valid source of security. At this time, the patient's complaint that he is getting worse is often evidence of improvement — particularly when it is clear that getting worse means becoming less dependent upon his neurotic patterns. It is crucial that these factors be clearly explained to the patient, so that he can tolerate some temporary discomforts in order to gain the ultimate increase in his security.

CHAPTER 10

Therapeutic Tactics

The process of change for the obsessional is viewed as a potential source of danger which may leave him vulnerable and uncertain; therefore, he is reluctant to put new insights into action. It is not surprising that most of the obsessional's early attempts to move into new situations and relationships will be inclined to falter or fail. Since he has little confidence in his capacity to fulfill his extravagant expectations, he enters every new involvement with some apprehension and uneasiness. Thus, his involvements are tentative and uncertain, which prejudices the outcome in advance. He may abandon his efforts too early because he cannot see the project's being successful. If he continues the effort and completes it, he may feel that the situation did not yield as rich a reward as he expected from his new patterns of behavior. The new way of operating initially has more anxiety than the old, familiar way. Therefore, the therapist must be prepared for complaints and grievances about these experiments, which never come off to the full satisfaction of the patient.

One such patient could not hand in any reports at his job until he checked every reference twice and agonized over every grammatical alternative. He held up his reports until the last possible moment. This was accompanied by a variety of gastrointestinal symptoms. After some therapy he was able to hand in his reports after only one review. This greatly reduced the time involved, as well as his GI complaints. However, he became preoccupied with the errors he might have overlooked. Even when his supervisor complimented him on the task, he felt that it was not as outstanding as usual. In addition, he felt that while the work was accompanied by somewhat less anxiety, it was not much of an improvement. With repeated attempts at this report-writing pattern, the preoccupations lessened and the procedure became so much more acceptable that he soon began to act as if he had thought it all out and had achieved the change all by himself.

The position the therapist must take in these early efforts is to convey the notion that there are no guarantees in living and that every new experience contains some risks and may even turn out badly. While the therapist is trying to focus on the possible rewards and positive results of new adventures, he must avoid minimizing the risks or giving false guarantees of success. At times the therapist must make it clear that some risks must be taken and new behavior patterns must be tested for therapy to proceed. Obsessional ruminations and speculations produce no changes in outlook or in living; thus, a patient must be actively encouraged and assisted in new ventures.

One patient with a severe obsessional pattern and a phobia of public speaking managed to benefit from therapy by making considerable changes in his life. However, he could not risk speaking in public places, particularly when he would be scheduled in advance. On one occasion, after having managed to evade several speaking engagements, he called to tell me of his concern about the continuation of this symptom, which was interfering with his professional life. We agreed that he would accept the next engagement and make every effort to keep it. This time he took neither tranquilizers nor alcohol to help him through the anxiety, but with encouragement and support, he endured the considerable anxiety and gave his talk — which was not as successful as he had hoped it would be. However, he felt enormously relieved and was quite pleased with his accomplishment. He felt that he had finally licked his incapacitating phobic symptom. The willingness to endure some anxiety, which he had finally achieved, created the atmosphere for overcoming the demand for a perfect performance without anxiety or concern. While he undoubtedly continued to have minor bouts with this difficulty for some time, the symptom should not have greatly incapacitated him any longer.

OBSESSIONAL DEFENSES AND RESISTANCES

The therapy of the obsessional condition is hampered, at the outset, by the obsessional's need for perfection, which colors his communications. This problem is particularly difficult in psychotherapy, where verbal productions are an integral part of the process. Since the obsessional wants to be precise and clear, he introduces more and more qualifications in his presentation in order to be certain that the whole issue is presented in its fullest and completest form. This adds much confusion to the process, and instead of clarifying, it tends to obfuscate. While it may appear that the patient is deliberately being confusing, it must be understood that actually he is trying to be more precise and to avoid making any errors. The tendency to be distracted and to move off in tangents and endless clarifying details keeps the patient from getting to the point of his communication and makes it difficult to pin down an issue in order to illuminate it. The therapist must therefore often move in and direct the flow of communication. Because of the tendency to ramble and be distracted, the free-association process in the obsessional often serves to defeat its purpose. A rigid requirement to free-associate or to say everything that comes to mind will involve the therapy in endless trivia and irrelevance. The therapist must be active and energetic to prevent this development, and he must attempt to interrupt and focus on what is relevant whenever it becomes apparent to him.

It therefore follows that much of the therapeutic progress comes from the examination of events that can be explored in the immediacy of the therapeutic hours, especially in the transference relationship. While this is true in any therapeutic situation, whatever the disorder or personality style, it is crucial in the treatment of the obsessional, where recollections are pervaded with doubts that limit conviction about the interpretations. The endless bickering, qualifying, and uncertainty about any past event make it imperative that the patient see his distortions or other defensive activity under circumstances when doubts cannot be introduced or used to defeat insight.

Thus, the most effective technique for the therapy of obsessionals is the examination of recent events, or the here and now. This allows for the least distortions, so that the therapist and the patient can pursue an issue until some clarity and agreement can be reached.

It is difficult to avoid getting involved in a flypaper relationship or a tug-of-war with the patient, who reacts to what he experiences as control by attempting to put down the therapist or to minimize the value of the exploration. There is constant intrusion of the elements of doubting that the patient insists upon; this makes the material less meaningful. The obsessional's tendency to avoid feelings and to intellectualize also meets its greatest challenge in the exploration of recent events, since the past is fertile soil for distortion and manipulation. The obsessional demands certainty, even from the hazy uncertainty of the past. Current formulations are therefore most useful in developing insight into the patient's behavior patterns, especially since they are more available to some emotional reactions than are the intellectualized reconstructions of past emotional or traumatic experiences.

Since therapy requires a minimum trust in the therapist, a therapeutic alliance is difficult to develop. He tends to follow the formal requirements of the therapeutic process and secretly maintains doubts and contempt for the therapy. This is not a deliberate attempt to sabotage but merely a manifestation of the obsessional process. The therapist, therefore, cannot assume that the patient, even though he appears to be pursuing the therapeutic process, is in fact doing so. He may simply be doing the "right" thing. It is a long time before such patients can express their doubts and concerns about the process.

Their need to know everything and to admit no deficiency or ignorance presents numerous complications when therapy involves formulations and interpretations which require them to admit that they are, in fact, ignorant about many things — especially human relationships and interpersonal intimacy.

In order for the patient to accept new insights, there must be some motivation in seeing how it will benefit them, rather than visualizing the disasters that generally confront the obsessional when he feels helpless and not in total control of everything. This problem becomes acute when the patient is called upon to try out new insights in his living, since his needs for certainty and guarantees will strongly deter him from attempting new and untried pathways as solutions. Such a patient will report difficulties and failures in his attempts at change, and this tendency must be clarified to avoid becoming entrenched in his neurotic, circumscribed existence — which is experienced as safe because it is familiar. This issue will be noted over and over again in the therapy reported in this book, as it is apparent in the treatment of all obsessional patients. For example, a twenty-seven-year-old patient avoided dating because he felt he was clumsy and would fail to interest his date. After exploring this issue, he allowed himself to be brought into a foursome, and, finding the girl interesting and sexually provocative and desirable, he felt more justification in his unwillingness to make another date with her in his review of the evening. He felt only the potential danger of being rejected and not the positive potential in their mutual attraction. These and many other obsessional traits will unfold as the therapy proceeds and are major obstacles to therapeutic progress.

Not every obsessional patient presents all the obsessional characteristics. Some characteristics are more prominent than others; some patients relate to the need to be in major control by bringing in lists or agendas to the session, others will manifest severe rituals or phobias that occupy the forefront of the communication process. Other obsessionals are hampered mostly by their grandiosity and contempt for others, while still others are overwhelmed by their need for guarantees and certainties, which prevent them from taking any risks or accepting any new interpretations. The particular elements most prominent in the patient being treated should determine the general principles to be applied. Where intellectual discussions seem preeminent, the therapist must permit himself to be somewhat spontaneous in expressing some of his own feelings and, perhaps, encourage the expression of feelings from his patient by allowing and fostering the communication of his doubts and uncertainties. The therapist can encourage spontaneous behavior, which is so difficult for the obsessional, by becoming more involved with the patient and by taking some risks in exposing some of his own weakness so that he can enable the patient to recognize that human fallibility is not a cause for total rejection by others. In this connection it is important for the therapist to be aware of how he is being controlled or manipulated by the obsessional's tactics. The inevitability of being drawn in and being unable to find one's way after being caught in the sticky mesh of obsessional communication need be viewed not as a failure or a weakness of the therapist's technical skill but simply as an example of the enormous difficulties in seeing one's way into the process, and a review of such entrapments can be illuminating.

Rules for the therapy of the obsessional can only be drawn in a general way. Each occasion in the development of the interaction with the therapist must be seen in the light of the obsessional mechanisms and the therapist's tendencies to be fallible. This allows the process of therapy to be one that is determined not autocratically by the expert and his helpless patient but rather by two people who are attempting to explore an issue together. One person has skills which the other does not have; however, the therapist does not necessarily know all there is to know about the process.

MINIMIZING RISKS

Verbal speculation, a style of the obsessional, is an attempt to minimize the risks of failure; it often leads to more complications and greater insecurity. It can rarely overcome inaction. Real living in the face of real risks must be attempted through cautious encouragement by the therapist. The patient must not feel that failures will be viewed as disappointments by the therapist; therefore, the therapist must avoid becoming too identified with the success or failure of a project even while he warmly supports the project itself. This is often very difficult, as the patient tries to prove his worthwhileness by demonstrating his skill to the therapist; a failure, he feels, will be interpreted by the therapist as a disappointment. Therefore, while indicating interest in the outcome of an activity, the therapist should avoid conveying any notion that rejection or criticism would follow a failure. There must be nothing more at stake for the patient than the task at hand; he should not have a feeling of ultimate judgment or disappointment should it not turn out well.

While attempts at action are crucial to the successful outcome of therapy, they should not be made prematurely. There should be sufficient possibility of a successful outcome in an activity that has been heretofore avoided before the patient is encouraged to engage in it. This can be determined either through some decrease in anxiety or in a patient's willingness to abandon his perfectionistic goal. There must also be a sufficient background of experience to make the project a feasible one. A patient who has never attempted to date a person of the opposite sex should be cautioned about premature attempts to date and his expectation of having an easy and successful time. Premature attempts may result in disastrous failures, which then jeopardize the possibility of ultimately resolving the neurosis. Sometimes the patient will press for such activities and the resultant failure will be used as proof of the need to maintain his neurotic structure. The therapist must be alert to this maneuver and should forestall such adventures when they seem doomed to failure.

This was demonstrated by a severe obsessional who recognized that by not telling his business partner about some of his concerns he was jeopardizing their business; this was evident from examination of a number of occasions when he withheld his judgment on significant matters. However, he felt that I would be disappointed in him if he had another talk with his partner without telling him just how he felt, and he therefore pressed to do so. I informed him that I had no such expectation of him at this time and would feel no disappointment about it. However, I said that I was interested in his concerns about my reactions. This patient was pushing prematurely for a full revelation of all his difficulties, which would have doomed the partnership and endangered his own existence. It was quite feasible to wait until he was better prepared to deal with the difficulties that might ensue from such a revelation.

Many compulsive confessions which are often rationalized as the need to tell the whole truth in some abstract conception of honesty result in tragic consequences. An adolescent girl who was engaged to be married felt compelled to tell her fiancé that she had kissed another boy and then went into a deep depression when the engagement was terminated. Such premature or compulsive admissions or confessions in therapy are often called *acting out* and must be controlled by therapeutic intervention. This does not change the notion that the obsessional should be encouraged to action when he is ready for it and is not restrained by his obsessional need for guarantees.

Unless a patient is ready to attempt new ventures, it is unwise and unfruitful for the therapist to press the patient to make a decision; this would only produce further rationalizations and justifications for avoidance. Instead, the therapist must explore the question of the patient's caution and his demand for absolutes in his living. When the patient does make a decision, it should be an outgrowth of the consideration of these factors rather than of his need to comfort or please the therapist or to prove that he is capable of taking some action.

When an obsessional patient finally manages a new piece of behavior, he often sets it up in such a way as to minimize his responsibilities for a failure. Any failure is blamed on the therapist, who, the patient insists, forced him to do something he was clearly not ready to do. On the other hand, if such behavior is successful, the patient will assume full credit and ignore the role the therapist played in the matter. It is not particularly useful to clarify this situation too early or to emphasize the role of the therapy, as it may introduce too many extraneous factors, such as the need to take credit for the success. When the patient has experienced some real success in his new ventures and has a degree of self-assurance, the collaborative aspect of the work then needs to be emphasized in order to put the patient's grandiose tendencies in some perspective. The tendency to pass the responsibility for failure onto the therapist can lead to endless squabbles and unwarranted attacks on the therapist. The need of the patient to "pass the buck" should be noted, and full responsibility for any proposed action must be placed squarely on the patient's shoulders. While this will not remove the possibility of the therapist's being blamed, it does leave him free and able to state his position simply — without getting involved in a fruitless exchange of whose fault the failure is. The point in therapy is to encourage action and involvement; at the same time, it is important for the therapist to reduce the neurotic elements in his own involvement, even when he must get involved in order to clarify the "transfer-of-blame" distortions of the obsessional patient — particularly as they blend into paranoid ideas. Such involvements are invaluable sources of illumination of the obsessional defense and the tendency to transfer blame onto others.

PROBLEMS OF DOUBTING

The obsessional's persistent tendency to doubt and hence to procrastinate activity manifests itself throughout the therapeutic process and at times may defeat it. The patient may question each observation or interpretation and cast an aura of uncertainty over any exchange — especially if it is enlightening or disturbing to him. In short, the presence of doubt must be noted and dealt with throughout the entire therapeutic work.

Doubting also interferes with any effective action in the patient's current living. It prevents firm commitments; hence, the patient may put off an action, attempting to get the therapist to overcome such doubts and make the decision for him. If he succeeds in doing this, he still retains his doubts about the decision, secretly opposing it because he did not make the choice himself. He will covertly sabotage it; as a result, the effort will fail, proving that the choice was an error. Therefore, the therapist must be especially careful not to be drawn into this trap. Any attempt to eliminate the patient's doubts by a rational examination of the alternatives is clearly doomed to failure; the doubts do not arise as a result of some dilemma in which the alternatives are intellectual choices. It is not the rational or objective appraisal of the pros and cons of an issue which stimulates obsessional doubts about a choice. Therefore, the doubts cannot be resolved by a careful consideration of the situation. A cataloging or bookkeeping of all the issues would be endless and would increase the doubting instead of overcoming it. Every advantage on one side can be countered by an advantage on the other, as can the disadvantages. Such intellectual exploration of alternatives is a very successful device for avoiding a decision.

To deal with this obstacle in therapy it would be reasonable to assume that some insight into the origins and genetic history of the doubting might decrease its effect on the person's living. However, the attempt to explore the origins of the patient's doubting is generally fruitless; it does not arise as a result of single or multiple events in the past. Nor does it have any origins in a once-meaningful context which, if discovered, would clarify its origins. Such a search, if undertaken, would be obstructed by the very doubting itself — which would minimize any conviction about the discoveries that might be made.

Doubting is a baffling and overwhelming complication in the therapy of obsessionals. It makes every investigation uncertain and every statement or interpretation open to question. The doubts are often secretly maintained and brought out into the open only when necessary. Covertly they may be used to minimize the therapist's insights and to help the patient remain aloof and uninvolved with the therapist and the therapeutic process. The doubts create an atmosphere of tentativeness toward the whole process; therefore, they must be exposed early if therapy is to progress. However, as a device, doubting cannot be investigated as a fact in itself. This will result in getting the process bogged down in unproductive preoccupations and further doubting. It must be studied as a part of the patient's living, not as a separate item, and must be brought to his attention as it manifests itself in all his activities and relationships. As the doubting is a device to guarantee certainty and to avoid a decision when certainty is impossible, it will remain in the picture until the security needs of the patient are sufficiently enhanced that he can take some risks and accept some uncertainty.

The therapist must encourage the patient to arrive at decisions based on an *emotional* appeal of the alternatives as well as on an intellectual appraisal. Such a step follows from an awareness that all choices have emotional as well as intellectual sources and that choice cannot be solely an intellectual process. As decision making is already a burdensome problem for the obsessional, any encouragement to admit emotional factors into his living can be a most constructive prospect.

The therapist should encourage the patient to make any decision — even a poor decision is better than none at all. Moreover, he must help the patient to recognize that dreadful consequences need not follow an imperfect decision. The question, "Which alternative do you like?" has greater validity than, "Which alternative is the better choice?" The obsessional has difficulty in raising this question because his decisions must be correct rather than pleasing or satisfying. However, the consideration of which alternative would be least pleasurable or satisfying must enter the decision-making process, in addition to which is the correct alternative. This is clearly a most difficult problem for the obsessional, who feels that only intellectual considerations can guarantee the correctness of a choice. Emotions, he contends, are too easily pushed about by forces that cannot be controlled. Nevertheless, the patient must be encouraged to realize that emotional considerations must enter the decision-making process and that they are often the major ingredients. Many choices are matters of taste or preference rather than of economy or wisdom. There needs also to be a lightness and casualness in the patient's decision-making process — especially when such decisions do not touch on core issues or can be altered without major damage to the individual.

It is also evident that one can never assemble all the relevant factors in any situation in order to make a perfect choice. Alternatives can be so evenly matched that only the emotional factors of preference, prejudice, or pure feeling will be the final factor. On such occasions, the therapist, in encouraging the patient to make a choice, must be clear about his own predilections, prejudices, and inclinations in order to avoid covertly influencing the patient's decision.

Ultimately, doubting will come to play a less significant role in the therapeutic process as the patient's security and esteem are enhanced. The doubts are an adaptive technique and not elements of integrity in the obsessional's personality structure, and they should be distinguished from the real uncertainties that prevail in human existence. Not every uncertainty is a morbid doubt. In the therapy of the obsessional, this distinction becomes quite important because we wish to encourage valid uncertainties in contrast to the kind of insistence on certainty which requires morbid doubting.

The therapist must try to encourage real questioning while trying to eliminate the neurotic doubting. He must, however, avoid dealing with the doubts as if they represented valid and rational uncertainties. Therefore, a detailed examination of alternatives in every situation, which the obsessional will always insist upon, and the attempts to explore all the issues exhaustively to arrive at perfect decisions are an utter waste of time. It is not a matter of exposing the issues so that the patient can then see the facts which will allow him to decide and forgo his doubts; rather, there is a need to show him that the doubts are attempts to make infallible decisions regardless of the issues.

A Note of Caution

However, the fact must not be overlooked that many decisions and choices have realistic factors which need to be taken into account and that not all considerations of alternatives are instances of obsessional doubting. There are valid uncertainties owing to a lack of information, which must be acknowledged and recognized. Unless this is done we cannot communicate to the patient about his excesses which go beyond the legitimate task of exploring all the realistic alternatives. In addition, some uncertainties of the patient, such as whether he is really liked or what is it that he truly wants, must be viewed in a different light from doubts that arise in a situation in which the expectation of certainty and exemption from natural law is expected. Before one can convince the obsessional that this indecision is based on neurotic grounds and not on actual alternatives, and that his preoccupations and concerns are excessive and not in response to real issues, one must hear enough of the patient's account to consider all these possibilities. In this way the patient will be convinced that the realistic issues have been taken into account. This is especially important because while the therapist can quickly identify the concern as obsessional, the patient still believes it is based on fact and justified by circumstances. One must hear the story out even when it is quickly understood that the concerns are excessive and not responsive to the actual circumstances. After a while one can use a shortcut — saying, for example, "Now isn't that just like so and so, which was really your neurotic indecision, rather than a serious consideration of the alternatives?" The patient may agree, or he may be likely to say, "No, this is different." But we need to hear enough to show him that it is not different. One must have the patience to recognize that the obsessional learns slowly, if at all, and must hear repeated instances of a particular interpretation before he can really accept it.

PROBLEMS OF INDECISION

The indecision of the obsessional is closely related to his morbid doubts. As he requires certainty in every choice he must make and is unwilling to take any risks, it is understandable that he puts off making a decision until he can feel absolutely sure.

He must be very careful, since he presumes that every decision will tie him down permanently with no way out. This accounts for his tentative acceptance of the exchanges in the therapeutic process; nothing is seen or experienced with any degree of closure but remains open to alteration or reversal. Therefore, interpretations are rarely accepted with conviction or full agreement but are instead met with a qualifying, uncertain uneasiness. It is indecision which keeps the obsessive from coming into therapy early. Once in, however, he may remain endlessly and may be unable to leave unless an adequate handling of the therapeutic situation forces a change.

The usual instructions to forgo any decision during therapy and to postpone living until more valid decisions can be made play directly into the obsessional's neurotic pattern. The original injunction against taking a course of action during psychoanalytic therapy was designed to prevent premature or impetuous action during the discovery phase of therapy. It was sound advice and is particularly relevant for those character structures that are liable to make snap judgments or take precipitant action. However, this is not true of the obsessional unless he is so tormented by his indecisiveness that he terminates it by action in one way or another. Many obsesssionals who should benefit greatly from the psychotherapeutic process — which is the treatment of choice for this neurosis — find a haven for their neurosis and a reinforcement of their defenses because of inadequate or inept therapeutic handling in this regard. The obsessional prefers to take no action. Thus, psychotherapy, under certain conditions, can become an ideal culture for the enhancement of obsessional doubts and indecisions.

It is only in recent years that psychoanalysts have begun to recognize that the routine therapeutic techniques are not suitable for all types of character structures and sometimes need to be adjusted to the particular character-istics of the personality involved. The obsessional should be encouraged to arrive at conclusions and to make decisions which are the product of a reasonable and adequate exploration of the relevant factors. The technique for dealing with the patient's indecisiveness involves the need to clarify his quest for absolutes and certainties.

It must be recognized that the postponement of living in order to guarantee the best and wisest decision often takes a higher toll than making some decision, even if it is not the most perfect one. Imperfect decisions may be the best that one can reach at a particular time. The obsessional dresses up his indecision in intellectual rationalizations that imply strength rather than weakness and the virtues of honesty and integrity rather than fear and uncertainty. A helpful therapeutic atmosphere, therefore, would encourage movement and activity — both in and out of the therapeutic situation — and would cautiously advocate decisions in the patient's living. While therapy should always restrain premature or impulsive behavior, it should not encourage postponing activities on purely theoretical grounds.

A patient who got caught in an indecisive conflict over a professional choice is illustrative. She needed to decide between two geographical areas for her next assignment and had a reasonable amount of time in which to make the decision. After considering all the realistic differences which could be determined, she arrived at a tentative decision which was inconsistent with the emotional ties she had to these areas. She then reversed her decision. Having done this, she began to feel uneasy and more confident about her first choice. She was concerned about the frivolous way in which she had changed her mind. At this time her obsessional indecisiveness was in full swing, with her anxiety increasing as the final day arrived. She tried to explore every phase of the choice, taking into account which would be the better opportunity, which would offer the better climate, and which would have the larger number of museums, swimming facilities, travel opportunities, available boyfriends, and other advantages. Every consideration was explored, both relevant and irrelevant. The harder she tried, the more impossible it was for her to make a decision. Yet her choice did not have permanent consequences; she could shift if her preference turned out badly.

She exaggerated the significance of both the factors involved in the choice and the consequences. Everything involved in the choice was of the greatest seriousness; there was an absence of any lightness. She turned this moderately important decision into a laborious, life-or-death issue. As the final day approached, she began to get quite panicky. The emphasis which she placed on making the "right" decision helped her to see how this factor affected all the decisions in her life and why she had always been so indecisive. It finally dawned on her that success would come from work and achievement and not from the magic of the right choice.

Now a flood of new factors entered into her calculations, and she wished she could withdraw her decision. Her reaction was similar to the undoing of a ritual once it has been performed, which is associated with the uncertainty about the act once it has been performed. Therefore, there is the necessity to neutralize it for fear it may be the wrong act. In this case the patient could not rest with either choice, as she could not accept the possible disadvantages of either one.

I encouraged this patient to make some decision after we had fully explored the realistic differences in each alternative. I stressed the need for some choice, as it was not possible to foresee all the future advantages of either. I implied that there was no ideal decision, no matter how detailed or complete her consideration could be. She accused me of trying to force her to make premature decisions and of not being really interested in her career and her success. At the same time she acknowledged that if I pushed a particular choice, she would hold me responsible for any dissatisfactions she might find with it. I was most careful to indicate no preference, either covertly or overtly.

The tendency to doubt one's decision once it is made leads to the typical seesaw approach to decision making. As soon as one decides on a course of action the alternatives seem more interesting — and so on and so on, back and forth until fatigue or disgust ensues, or an ultimatum that forces a decision. In such instances, the therapist, after an initial survey of the alternatives, must restrict his observations to the question of the patient's need to make the perfect decision and not get involved in what that might be. The patient must recognize that all the pros and cons which he introduces as intelligent and rational steps in the decision-making process are actually attempts to avoid making a decision. They are measures designed to produce a perfect decision in order to prevent unfavorable consequences. As a perfect decision is impossible, the patient must acknowledge that any choice involves risks.

Too much of the obsessional's time is spent in preparation and in laying the groundwork for the expected success in some career. The success of the patient just discussed was delayed for many years because her preparations and academic work would shift from year to year so that she could cover all the possibilities. She developed a smattering of knowledge in many areas and an expertness in none. To specialize in one area she would have to eliminate another, and this she could not do. It took her a long time to realize that any decision would be to her advantage in the long run and would be better than spending her time trying to find the perfect one. Fortunately, time and circumstances often push these people into decisions which, once they are made, can be fruitfully exploited.

Because it is humiliating to face the weakness and ineffectiveness involved in procrastination, obsessionals easily transfer the blame for their indecisiveness onto wives, family, parents, community, and other targets. They rationalize their indecision by claiming that they cannot decide because they are either concerned with the best interest of others or they have been so thwarted in early years that making decisions is too difficult. It becomes part of the therapist's task to illuminate all these distracting techniques and to focus on the real issue — the patient's demand for omniscient, superhuman performance.

With regard to the patient's tendency to use the therapist for his decision-making processes and to make him his whipping boy when the decisions turn out badly, the therapist must make it clear time and again that he has no stake other than a professional concern and interest in the welfare of the patient and that he has no purpose or design directed at reducing the patient's goals or aspirations.

THERAPEUTIC ALLIANCE

While it is possible for some useful therapeutic work to take place when there is only a minimal amount of warmth between patient and therapist, progress is undoubtedly enhanced if there is more, rather than less, warmth in the therapeutic relationship. The positive attitudes of the patient for the therapist must be routinely utilized in the therapeutic process. In the treatment of the obsessional patient, this is particularly relevant because premature or clumsy disclosures of the therapist's feelings might impress the patient as a weakness of the therapist and an expression of his need to seduce the patient or take advantage of him. It could be viewed as an expression of the therapist's anxiety, for which the patient might feel contempt. Timing and an appropriate mode of expression are crucial elements in communicating such feelings to the patient. This is particularly necessary when the patient tries out new patterns of behavior. The therapist's interest can be a source of encouragement. As much of the therapeutic work deals with efforts to get the patient to reveal his true feelings and not only his intellectualized verbalizations, the therapist must set the tone and show the way by being frank and open about his feelings toward the patient.

While for some therapists the obsessive patient may be hard to like, one can generally find many likeable qualities. Some of the therapist's interest in changing his patient's way of life is the result not only of professional pride or status but also of warmth and affectionate feelings for the patient. Whenever change is attempted, it must come from the patient's interest in his own development and not because of gratitude toward the therapist or as a way of impressing him. It must emerge from a real desire to alter one's living and not just to please someone or to prove something. Change is encouraged and often promoted by an affectionate interest of one person toward another. This is one of the ingredients of a therapeutic relationship. The therapist's attitudes should reinforce the real aspirations of the patient by highlighting those neurotic elements which interfere with the attainment of achievable goals.

As he improves, the patient must be able — through his growing confidence in the therapist and an expanding trust in his own capabilities — to accept the risks and consequences of his new behavioral patterns. He must be able to face the possibility of his worst fears being realized — that he might feel humiliated or look weak and impotent in his new ways of functioning. He must be willing to abandon complete control of a project and allow a situation to develop on its own, often with no certainty of the outcome. Giving up control does not mean becoming apathetic or withdrawing: it means a more realistic acceptance of the world as it is, as a place where one must accept uncertainties in living. The resolution of an obsessional disorder should produce a more mature, more decisive and accepting, and less driven human being — not an emotionless, placid philosopher. The process can be assisted most dramatically by a warm and interested therapist who can inspire in his patient an intellectual grasp of the neurotic issues as well as of the real issues and encourage acknowledgement of feelings in a direct and open way.

RITUALS

The ritualistic behavior of the patient, whether it is in the form of a compulsive action or an obsessional rumination, must be dealt with in the same way as the doubting tendencies. The rituals represent attempts at achieving certainty or preventing the person from losing control in some significant area of his living. They involve not only aggressive or sexual impulses but also tender impulses. Attempts at understanding the precise meaning of the ritual may be an interesting intellectual exercise, but in general it will not advance the therapeutic process to any appreciable extent. The same problems which stem from investigating the origin of the doubting also apply in the instance of rituals.

While the symbolic meaning of a ritual can often be inferred from the various elements in it, an intellectual elucidation of the symbolic acts seldom, if ever, alters the ritual. The classical hand-washing ritual, for example, can be correctly interpreted as an attempt to be rid of dangerous germs or sexual contamination. It could also represent attempts to wash away the guilt or the symbolic blood of a fantasized victim. On the other hand, it could be a device for keeping the person preoccupied and thereby prevent him from getting on with his living. The particular ritual employed may be entirely accidental or coincidental and may have significance only in terms of the setting in which a severe anxiety attack may have occurred. The hand-washing ritual may be a device to avoid the recognition of the possibility of death and may have begun when the person was forced to face the early death of a friend because of some infectious disease. The proper interpretation of the ritual, however, does not influence its continuation; its real roots lie in deep-seated feelings of uncertainty about one's safety and security.

The understanding of the purpose of the ritual may be easy and readily accepted by the patient. He may often offer the correct explanation himself. Nevertheless, this rarely influences the course of the neurosis or the continuation of the ritual. At other times the ritual may be so autistic and complicated that its elucidation is impossible. Generally, the search for the origin of the ritual is not worth the time spent; it can be better explored in other contexts.

The existence of the ritual depends entirely on the individual's capacity to abandon his absolute needs in order to control his own feelings through magical performances. Intellectual clarifications and statements about the patient's wasting his time, energy, and skill in these rituals are to no avail. The patient is generally fully aware of all these facts. However, the serious complications resulting from the rituals may pressure the patient to end them, and he may press the therapist to exorcise them by direct intervention. Such demands often push the therapist to become preoccupied with the rituals themselves and may impede the ultimate and more significant therapeutic goal.

One way of evading the therapeutic relationship is for the patient to become preoccupied with descriptions and detailed explanations of the ritual. Unless the therapist can recognize the purpose and terminate these recitals, they may occupy the bulk of the therapeutic work. The presence of many rituals in a patient is some indication of the severity of the obsessional illness and generally implies a poor prognosis, while a paucity of rituals suggests a less severe personality disorder. In either case, the fate of the ritual is tied to the overall treatment progress, and the patient must be so informed right from the beginning.

The ritual will be abandoned when the patient's need for magic and ultimate control of himself and the universe is lessened. The therapist's handling of the ritual involves his ability to understand the role that it plays in the patient's life. When the patient persists in projecting it into the therapeutic process, it becomes the responsibility of the therapist to discourage repetition, with the explanation that it is more of a distraction than an aid to resolution of the illness. If the ritual is particularly incapacitating, one might try to attack it directly and attempt either to eliminate or alter it.

Behavior-modification procedures of various kinds can frequently terminate rituals. In doing this, however, one must be clear that the basis for the development of the ritual has been unchanged even though its presence may have been eliminated. The use of modeling implosion, thought stopping, or paradoxical intention can be effective in altering the ritual but not in altering the underlying obsessional characterological orientation.

RESOLUTIONS

For a long time the obsessional deals with therapy as if it were designed to improve his neurosis rather than to alter it. Even though the initial goal of becoming perfect through the therapeutic process may be abandoned, the patient will try for some time to overcome his compulsions, which are now viewed as "bad," or destructive, by replacing them with "good," or constructive, ones. When he discovers that the trouble is that he is compelled to be perfect, he will henceforth resolve never to be perfect. He simply alters all his previous extreme demands by resolving not to make any demands at all. As he functions by commands and great resolves, he simply shifts emphasis from a "bad" resolve to a "good" one. Because so much of obsessional behavior is the result of compulsion over which the obsessional has no choice, he attempts to deal with the compulsion through a countercompulsion. He now resolves to do the right thing. It is clear that this shift represents no essential change in the patient's personality or behavior, and this fact must be brought to his attention.

The patient justifiably insists that he can only overcome the power of his compulsions through resolve and action. The clue to this psychological bind lies in the patient's recognition that not all behavior is the result of conscious and deliberate decision and that the obsessional illness is itself proof of this. Therefore, he cannot overcome behavior that arises from unconscious sources by conscious intent. Instead of making new resolutions to overcome the compulsions, he should abandon all resolutions — conscious and otherwise. He must simply do the best he can instead of insisting on perfection. This is experienced by the patient as the advocacy of inaction and weakness. Instead, it is encouraging the patient (as in Zen) to let go and just allow an experience to happen rather than trying to make it happen. While the patient does not take to this program readily, he must learn to do so, as it is essential for the clarification of his disorder. It is in this regard that the variety of meditation and relaxation procedures are particularly useful in the therapy of obsessional disorders. These relaxation techniques can be encouraged either inside or outside of the therapeutic process, and, if wisely utilized as adjuvants and not as curative agents, they can accelerate the process of healing immeasurably.

The patient insists that to forgo the highest standards means that he will have to accept the lowest. It is the fear of nothingness, mediocrity, and total unconcern which forces him to cling to his rigid, extreme demands. Therefore, when it becomes clear to the patient that he should not feel he needs to do every job perfectly, he may resolve not to insist on perfection but to accept imperfection. With perfect control and using new rituals and variations of his obsessional technique, he will insist on imperfections. It is essential to point out to the patient at this juncture that he is substituting one compulsion for another. He must recognize and feel that what is needed is to see that one does not have to be perfect or to have compulsions about imperfections, but to be able to accept human limitations and to realize that one can only do the best one can. The obsessional patient will undoubtedly say, "What do you want me to do, settle for nothing and do a sloppy job?" He might also say that he cannot accept ordinary standards of mediocrity and accuse the therapist of trying to deflate and derogate him.

After considerable discussion, the patient may finally acknowledge his deep concern about abandoning any of his extreme needs, even though he recognizes the impossibility of attaining them. The therapeutic impasse at this point can be resolved only by indicating that it is not a question of "all or none" and that there are other alternatives aside from the extreme ones which the patient posits. The patient must be assured that the therapist has no demands to make on him other than to assist him in fulfilling his own realistic goals. The patient must be convinced that if he abandons his extremes, he will not be disappointed but rather will be pleased with the favorable developments that will follow. Indeed, it must be made clear to the patient that as the result of his greater esteem and security, which allow him to give up unrealistic goals for realizable projects, he can experience greater satisfaction.

DREAMS

The analysis of dreams in the therapy of the obsessional must take into account the previously discussed tendencies to evade and obfuscate the therapeutic process. It must also take into account the readiness of the patient to comply and win favor with the therapist by supplying dreams. Therefore, if the therapist puts undue stress on dreams or displays any special interest in them he may be flooded with dream material, which could, if one wished, take up all the time in therapy.

There are no particular characteristics of the obsessional dreams. The obsessional's dreams reflect the life problems and the emotional relationships of the patient with the therapist, friends, and others, just as all dreams do. They also utilize in the dreams the particular techniques of defense characteristic of the patient's waking life. As so much of the obsessional's life is preoccupied with problems of control, it will not be surprising to find that much of the dream material concerns itself with control.

The dreams need to be handled in the same way as are the dreams of other patients. The dream content should be examined in terms of the here and now and as it sheds light on the current living of the patient. The tendency to get deeply involved in understanding all the associations and every bit of detail can become a trap for the therapist. It can turn into an obsessional investigation in which the ultimate effect is to become distracted from the main pursuit. Because dreams can be very illuminating with regard to sources and unacknowledged feelings and attitudes, their use in the therapeutic process should not be discouraged. At the same time, they must be treated as simple data and dealt with in the same way as are other productions of the patient.*

The dream of a forty-two-year-old obsessional patient illustrates the points mentioned. She came into therapy because she felt that she was too controlling in her relationship with her daughter. She spent a considerable amount of therapeutic time complaining about her resentments and hostilities toward her own mother. At about her seventh hour, she reported a dream which occurred on the previous evening, after she had attended a movie with her husband and daughter. Only front-row seats were available in the theater, and she had indicated to her husband that she would prefer to return another time. Her daughter, however, preferred to stay. Without making any comment to his wife, the husband purchased the tickets and proceeded to enter the theater. Although angry and resentful toward her daughter, the patient made no comment either to her daughter or to her husband.

*The handling of dream material in general and obsessional dream material in particular is discussed in detail by Walter Bonime in *The Clinical Use of Dreams* (New York: Basic Books, 1962). This book is highly recommended to the reader.

In therapy on the following day the patient reported that she felt that she had overreacted to her daughter and that she had had the following dream: "I was in our house at Cape Cod with my family. Mother was there. Two uninvited guests arrived and I asked mother to fix the steaks. While I was bawling her out for not doing the steaks properly, I completely ruined the casserole dish I was making." While it was clear from her report about the movie and the dream that she had many problems in her relationship with her husband, mother, and daughter, the therapist's emphasis in the interpretation at that time was limited to her tendency to displace her anger to both her daughter and her mother and to avoid recognizing that in doing this she was damaging herself. This had been the focus of most of the reports during the first six sessions.

Her need to control her anger in the movie incident prevented any clarification of the relevant issues. At that time her anger was not an overreaction to her daughter. She was quite justified in being angry with her husband, who had paid no attention to her request and had disregarded her wishes completely. (This, incidentally, was her complaint about all the men in her life.) In the dream, too, she displaced her anger from the uninvited guests (whose identity could not be established) to her mother. She became angry with her mother for spoiling the steaks, rather than being angry with herself for ruining the family dinner (the casserole). Her tendency to displace her anger was the cause of the disaster; the casserole burned because she was preoccupied with the anger toward her mother.

Both the movie incident and the dream were rich sources of data in exploring many of this patient's problems of control and displacement of anger. In limiting the scope of the interpretations at that time, the patient could grasp the essence of her behavior and have a solid piece of insight with a convincing emotional response.

Another example was that of a thirty-five-year-old man who felt that he was overly competitive. This was how he accounted for his hostile and alienated relationships with both men and women. It was a formula and rationale for his socializing failures, but it did not influence his living in any respect. He reported a dream in which he found himself somewhat isolated at a party. He felt quite sorry for himself. But soon everyone left and he was alone with three attractive young ladies. He then became quite aggressive when the most attractive girl made overt sexual gestures toward him, to which he responded. He reported that it was a pleasant dream, even though he felt uneasy about his behavior.

The dream and the patient's association to it were explored from the point of view of current material which had been dealt with during previous therapy hours. The dream was seen as an instance of his tendency to avoid competition instead of seeking it out. When he was with the larger group, he isolated himself; when he was alone with the girls, he became aggressive and energetic. This interpretation opened up a new view of himself as a rather arrogant and egocentric person who avoided competition and felt entitled to get what he wanted. Instead of being competitive, he felt that he should automatically have exclusive possession of whatever he needed or wished. This grandiose view of himself, which he secretly held, was brought out into the open. It had been covered up by his picture of himself as a man with a great deal of humility and a tendency to be uneasy in his relationships. Actually, he felt resentful because his needs were not automatically filled and because he needed to exert some effort to get what he wanted. Some relevant factors revealed in the dream — such as the doubts about his masculinity, his notions of his desirability, and his anxieties about being rejected and humiliated — were bypassed for the moment.

To make the maximum use of a dream, its interpretation should be related to the material current in the therapy hours and restricted to a few major issues which can be explored sufficiently to provide some conviction about the validity of the interpretation. The dream reported in the full case study that follows in part 4, chapters 11–15, demonstrates in detail how a dream might be handled during the therapeutic work.

PHOBIAS

The treatment of the phobias is closely related to the therapy of the obsessional state, as the two disorders are dynamically similar. However, the phobia may be a minor element in the patient's problems or in the disability imposed by the phobia, or it may be so overwhelming as to demand the focus of the therapeutic process. In the usual course of events, the phobias accompanying the obsessional processes may either become less troublesome or disappear in the course of treatment, requiring no special handling. As the need to exert control over all of one's living diminishes and there is a growing capacity to accept the limitations in one's existence without having guarantees and certainties, the phobic symptoms also diminish. When this does not occur, we must then take some direct action and deal directly with the phobia.

It has been known for some time that understanding alone has been ineffectual in resolving phobias. It is a commonplace that while the patient may have adequate insight into the origin, symbolism, and function of his phobia, he is still unable to risk the initial venture into his phobic area of living. This fact has stimulated much discussion about the issue of intellectual versus emotional insight and particularly about the need for some *corrective emotional experience,* as Franz Alexander called it, to accompany the therapeutic process.

After some intellectual and emotional clarity about the phobic problem has been achieved, the major task is to encourage and assist the patient into entering and reexperiencing those areas of living which he has avoided. As the problem goes beyond mere fear, intellectual persuasion or sympathetic assurances will not suffice. As the phobia is more than a conditioned response to fear, "deconditioning" through reciprocal-inhibition techniques only serves to remove specific fears; it does not alter the phobic state. While great claims are made for this treatment technique, it is my belief that it influences "bad habits" rather than true phobias. As explained in chapter 5, the phobia is different from the simple avoidance reaction that results from a severe traumatic situation and it has overriding physiological concomitants; thus, the elucidation of the trauma, by hypnosis, will not alter its manifestations in phobias as it so dramatically does in avoidance reactions.

A combination of persuasive and encouraging techniques can be very fruitful. Once he has achieved sufficient insight, the patient must be directly encouraged and at times actively assisted to attempt to invade the phobic areas.

The use of phobia clinics where patients are encouraged and assisted in going out in the street (agoraphobics), or in entering airplanes (flying phobias), or in dealing with innumerable other phobic situations is understandably valid. These clinics are frequently very effective in their deconditioning effects. However, if such pressure for activity is not accompanied by sufficient understanding or support, the phobic problem may be exaggerated by the development of severe anxiety, which will reinforce the determination to resist change.

There are many possible ways of actively encouraging a patient to move into previously avoided areas. The therapist can use the potential in the positive transference which has developed in the course of treatment. Provided the patient has achieved some benefit from the therapeutic work in alleviating some of his obsessional difficulties, he may have some confidence in the possibility of change. At such times, he may be willing to risk anxiety in order to discover that the rewards for undoing the phobia may be greater than the anticipated anxiety. This is not an easy matter, and it may be necessary to call on the goodwill, trust, and confidence that the patient has developed in his therapist. Admittedly, this is a risky procedure for the therapist as well; if the maneuver fails, much work will need to be done to reverse the damage. Yet the therapist, as well as the patient, must take risks and must not expect guarantees or certainties.

The encouragement must be direct and energetic. While one should not minimize the risks, the positive possibilities must be highlighted. The support may, at times, involve accompanying the patient into the phobic area. On one occasion, I accompanied a patient with a phobia of open spaces into the street, walked with her a while, and then left her to return to the office alone. In some instances, tranquilizing drugs or even alcohol may be used to encourage the initial attempts. With some success, the way is opened for further attempts and finally for the abandonment of the phobia.

Posthypnotic suggestions can be used to induce a phobic person to explore a phobic area. However, in such an instance the relationship develops specifically around the treatment of the phobia and does not sufficiently recognize the obsessional elements in the symptom.

Some therapists utilize the phobic's need to control all his living by entering into the phobic way of life — taking over the running of the show and putting the patient in the background. This stimulates the patient's rebelliousness as well as his competitive needs, and he may abandon the phobia just to demonstrate his control. This is simply a manipulative device. While it may work, it only strengthens the obsessional patterns and may provide a greater source of difficulty at a later date.

In recent years, phenomenological analysts such as Viktor Frankl and H. O. Gerz have used a technique called *paradoxical intention* most successfully in the resolution of phobic states. This method takes into account the compulsive, unfree nature of the phobic avoidance. Against his will and free choice, the patient avoids a situation, place, or person, even while knowing it is absurd and irrational to do so. However, he must pursue the phobic demands because the threat of anxiety is so great. The paradoxical intention technique forces the patient to accept the phobia willingly and deliberately and to put it under voluntary control. This focuses on the absurdity of the symptom and also gives the person the possibility of controlling its manifestations by putting it squarely under his responsibility. While the paradoxical nature of a therapist's encouraging his patient to continue his symptom is most evident, the real issue is in terms of putting the action under the patient's choice and under his control.

Because many of the phobic symptoms are expressed through the autonomic nervous system, such feelings and functions are not under voluntary control. Therefore, when the patient tries to produce his symptom, as he is instructed to do, he usually fails. When he finds that he is unable to produce his symptom, it frequently disappears. This technique does not remove the symptom at once; it must be repeated over a long period of time because reconditioning is also involved in the permanent eradication of the phobia.

By encouraging the patient to get worse instead of better, he is freed from his symptom. The technique of paradoxical intention thus draws on the element of control and the issues of free will and choice. This treatment has also been applied to the obsessive states, particularly to compulsive rituals. The encouragement and insistence toward an exaggerated manifestation of the behavior often terminates such behavior, as it does the phobia. This technique is intended to supplement psychotherapy, not to replace it.

In summary, the treatment of phobias — in addition to providing insight and enlightenment — requires some direct encouragement through sympathy or persuasion to reexperience the phobic fear. The encouragement may be in terms of the personal and professional relationship of patient and therapist or through some device such as conditioning, posthypnotic suggestion, or paradoxical intention. In all instances success lies in the recognition that once a phobia develops, there must be some incentive to face anxiety, uncertainty, and discomfort through the helping presence of an interested, sympathetic helper.

TERMINATION

When the patient comes to therapy his goal is to achieve a state of anxiety-free living while retaining the same collection of personality traits that he had originally. During the course of therapy, the patient must recognize the extreme nature of his demands and accept some limitations of his expectations. It is hoped that he will be able to achieve some balance and compromise; instead of having to be a superman, he will be able to function as a fallible human being. This simplified picture of the therapeutic goal of treatment of the obsessional provides some clues as to guidelines in determining a termination date.

At the outset, the therapist must not have a set of ideal standards for his patient to meet. He should be able to express flexible and limited goals, to avoid getting involved in the same problems of perfection which are the patient's to begin with. While there is some pressure on the part of the patient to leave therapy and to function on his own, there is also great reluctance to give up the comfortable world of talk and move into the real world of action until he is absolutely certain that no insurmountable problems will occur. The patient will often insist on remaining in therapy, and the therapist will need to prod and push him into the world. In the obsessional neuroses we find the long, interminable analyses which have often become symbiotic relationships instead of doctor-patient ones. Termination plans cannot be left to the patient, as is often the case with other kinds of patients. Obsessional patients cannot be relied upon to raise the question or to press for termination on their own.

What are the criteria for assessing termination? There must first be a recognition that termination must be done gradually and experimentally and rarely in an absolute way. To begin with, the number of interview hours can be cut down, or their frequency can be reduced over a reasonable period of time. This will help the therapist to determine whether a date can be set for ultimate termination. Experimental reductions in therapy hours can begin when the patient becomes comfortable enough to accept some reverses in his living which heretofore have stimulated panic or severe anxiety. There should also be a reduction of tension in many areas of his living, coupled with a greater emotional involvement in all his relationships. There should be evidence of reduction in ritualistic behavior, and many of the obsessions which plagued the patient when he came to treatment should have become less tenacious or should no longer occur. There should be an increased capacity to enjoy life without having to fulfill certain demands all the time. But even these criteria should be flexible. The therapist must not get trapped into postponing or abandoning his plans to terminate because the patient experiences renewed anxiety when termination is under consideration. It must be clearly understood by both patient and therapist that anxiety attacks will occur throughout the life of the patient and that therapy is not a permanent guarantee against disturbed living.

When anxiety does occur, the therapist should not be stampeded into changing his arrangements and thus exposing his own demands for perfection, even though such a crisis may require some temporary acceleration of treatment. The decision to terminate cannot be made in terms of the fate of some particular symptom. This is especially true in the case of the psychosomatic symptoms, which are so common in the obsessional disorders. Gastrointestinal disorders, cardiovascular problems, and symptoms of all sorts may clear up in the course of therapy without any particular emphasis being placed upon them. Some symptoms, however, may continue no matter how successful the therapy is. Psychosomatic symptoms are usually the consequences of ever-present tension, which characterizes the obsessional picture. Ordinarily, as the tension diminishes, the somatic symptoms improve. If, however, the somatic problems have continued for too long a time, they may be irreversible and will continue after many other characterological problems are resolved. Therefore, their status should not, in general, determine the decision for termination.

After a formal termination, there should be ample opportunities for occasional visits and brief contacts at times of particular stress or crisis. It is hoped that in the process of therapy the patient will have developed sufficient skills in introspection (as opposed to preoccupation and rumination) that new problems can be approached in an analytic fashion, enabling him to proceed without resuming formal contacts.

Treatment of the obsessional patient is an extremely difficult task. Even minimal changes, however, are worth the investments of time and energy of both patient and therapist. Freedom from compulsions is often accompanied by a freeing of the individual's capacities, so that he becomes a more effectively functioning person. In contrast to his initial fears, the abandonment of his unreal standards and expectations leads to more creative productions rather than to a loose and unproductive existence. Freud's original conjecture was that obsessionalism was a neurotic problem which responded to psychoanalytic treatment; this belief has been amply documented in spite of the enormous difficulties and the extended time which is necessary. No other approach — including shock therapy, lobotomy, drugs, or the use of other devices — has detracted from the value of psychotherapy to this disorder. Psychotherapy is the treatment modality which can and does effectively reduce the enormous anguish and waste that is inherent in obsessionalism.

The therapy of the obsessional state involves illuminating and exposing the patient's extreme feelings of insecurity and uncertainty, which he tries to handle through the complicated patterns of defense already described in detail. As he comes to understand that his neurotic structure is a defense against recognizing these weaknesses, he can then begin to build a new security system. At therapy's inception, the obsessional defense cannot be abandoned because the individual is afraid of the consequences. As his esteem grows and the awareness of his strength increases, he can slowly risk abandoning such patterns, thereby freeing him to function on a more productive level. The goal is to move from superhuman expectations to human productiveness, and the latter can reach whatever limits the individual is capable of. When he recovers, his ambitions will no longer be sparked by his neurosis; rather, his achievements will be limited only by his capacities. The impossible goals which left him disappointed will be abandoned. An awareness of his valid capacities to produce may actually stimulate greater activity. In essence, the obsessional must learn that in abandoning rigid, inflexible patterns of behavior designed to control and protect himself, he can actually feel more secure and more capable and can be more productive as well.

A positive change in behavior was demonstrated by a severely obsessional patient who was dangerously depressed when he entered therapy. His standards were extreme and his goals were impossible, but his pride and his security system demanded that he hold on to both. His original crisis arose when he was unable to communicate his feelings toward his business partner; he felt crushed in his desire to liberate himself. After therapy had proceeded for some time, he began to feel sufficiently secure to attempt such a discussion. With great trepidation, but with a feeling of willingness to face the possible disastrous consequences, he undertook the discussion. To his surprise, the results were strikingly successful. There was great relief in the accomplishment; the successful outcome also cleared away a large number of problems which had persisted most of his life. Many of his paranoid characteristics disappeared. He could now recognize that many gestures which he had hitherto considered hostile were, in fact, friendly and complimentary. While not all his obsessional demands were cleared away, he had opened the first large hole in the defensive system. The results were very satisfying and marked the beginning of a successful resolution of a severe obsessional neurosis.

The goals and the treatment plan for the obsessional states can be summarized as follows:

1. To discover and elucidate the basis for the excessive feelings of insecurity which require absolute guarantees before action is pursued.

2. To demonstrate by repeated interpretation and encouragement to take action that such guarantees are not necessary and that they interfere with living. This requires active assistance in stimulating new adventures for the patient.

3. To realize that the foregoing is possible only when the patient can acknowledge that anxiety is universal and omnipresent and cannot be permanently eliminated from life. This means abandoning attempts at perfection and superhuman performance and accepting one's humanness with its limitations. It does not mean being mediocre, average, or without ambition; rather, it allows one to utilize all his assets and potentialities.

Such goals are achieved through the trust and intimacy that grow out of a relationship in which one is sincerely trying to be useful to another human being. However, it also requires skill and intelligence, and the treatment must follow techniques that may differ radically from the classical psychoanalytic model. It is important (1) to avoid strengthening the patient's obsessional tendencies, (2) to tailor one's techniques to counter such devices, and (3) to provide a learning experience which may enable him to alter his defensive patterns. An open, flexible technique with no rigid rules of procedure is demanded, as well as a therapist who is free to experiment and try out modifications in the therapeutic process.

PART IV

CASE STUDY: THE OBSESSION
TO KILL

CHAPTER 11

Initiating Therapy

INITIAL INTERVIEWS

One day in 1952 Mr. Jones arrived at my office with a disturbing, intrusive, and overwhelming notion. He made the following statement:

> I was feeling awkward, with some difficulty in expressing myself and in concentrating. I wondered what was wrong with me. After about a month of such disturbing feelings a frightening thought popped into my head as I was awakening one morning. The thought which suddenly appeared was, "You are going to kill your wife!"

Mr. Jones's treatment lasted fourteen months, interrupted by occasional business trips and vacation. Generally we managed three sessions a week. Our work produced some major changes in his way of living and in his severe obsessional personality structure, which was directly related to his symptoms and concerns.

When Mr. Jones first came to me for treatment he was disturbed about many developments in his life, especially with his job, where he experienced an increasing inability to deal adequately with his customers. He had great difficulty in concentrating and recalling early sales agreements and promises. The obsessional concerns about killing his wife, which were devastating to his peace of mind, climaxed considerable difficulties he was having with his wife and his parents. As I listened to his opening presentation, it was apparent that while his concern about killing his wife was a dominating preoccupation, he had a great many dissatisfactions with the way he had been living, the way he performed on his job, and the way he related to peers and superiors.

In 1950, two years prior to our first meeting, Mr. Jones first noticed some difficulty while moving from one city to another, where he had obtained a better job. About one month after the move, the thought of killing his wife kept intruding over and over again and was so overpowering and frightening that it greatly magnified all his other problems. His ability to concentrate was impaired: "My memory was practically nonexistent and my ability to communicate was greatly reduced. During that time my wife and I were arguing and I had a difficult time dealing with her. Anything I did seemed to disturb her and, likewise, I was disturbed by many things she did."

I soon learned that Mr. Jones's difficulties with his wife had begun prior to their move, although the problems seemed commonplace and not at all unusual. At the time of their move, his wife was experiencing a number of somatic difficulties, which made her irritable and disagreeable, and their differences began to escalate. She criticized him for being disinterested and unaffectionate and accused him of being more interested in his family than in her. She seemed to become more insecure about their relationship, and, after a number of bitter exchanges, he suggested that they might consider divorce. This suggestion evoked a violent reaction from her, and she said she would never consent to that. However, she suggested that he see a psychiatrist, which he did. His first experience with the psychiatrist produced some relief, although it was of brief duration. He realized that his resentments and hostile thoughts toward his wife were related in some way to his earlier resentments of the domination of his parents.

The intellectual insights he achieved were not sufficient to alter his behavior, nor did they illuminate the depths of his involvement and entrapment in a childish dependency on all dominating figures, parental and substitute. Although he was not freed from his excessive, hostile thoughts, these thoughts "no longer troubled him" as desperately as they used to." At this juncture, I tried to assess the extent of these thoughts.

Therapist: Now you say "thoughts." Were there others, aside from that one?

Mr. Jones: No, that was the central thought, the only one. But the other disturbing factors or conditions are not as apparent as my inability to think or remember.

Therapist: But the thought did remain the same?

Mr. Jones: Well, I thought the situation was gradually getting better and I would grow out of it. But as I said a few minutes ago, I found I wasn't growing out of it and I had trouble again with impaired memory and concentration.

At that time he found himself having outrageous and unacceptable thoughts about violence. As the treatment unfolded, it became clear that these thoughts were strongly opposed to his generally submissive, placating attitudes; he would become aware of anger and irritation, which he would immediately subdue and repress. While functioning successfully in his profession, he had become aware of the restraints and limitations which his preoccupation forced upon him, so that his degree of competence and performance was markedly reduced.

ESTABLISHING THE DIAGNOSIS

In the initial interview, we established the nature of his disorder, his reasons for coming, and a brief history of the development of his difficulty. At this point, I was already inclined to accept Mr. Jones for treatment. He seemed to be sufficiently intelligent and well-motivated, with some introspective skills and verbal facility. Since I was taping most of my interviews for a research project, I asked Mr. Jones if I could record our work and he agreed. The presence of the tape recorder was quickly accepted, and it affected the sessions only minimally at the outset. Later we were both unaware of its presence for the most part, except when the machine failed to function properly.

It is the psychiatrist's responsibility to the patient and society to hospitalize or at least immobilize those individuals who are dangerous to themselves or to others. Why did I feel calm in the face of a potentially homicidal situation and encourage Mr. Jones to remain at his home and to come to my office instead of recommending immediate hospitalization?

It is generally acknowledged that obsessional thoughts are rarely carried into action. If they are intense, they usually are protected by phobic avoidances, or else the need and capacity for control are so developed that the possibility of carrying such ideas into action is extremely remote. More to the point, however, is the recognition that such obsessive thoughts are not the dominant issues but actually serve the purpose of distracting attention away from the more significant and more distressing concern. This is more readily understood when the obsessive thought is a pointless rumination or an endless speculation about philosophical or religious matters. The distracting or controlling function of such a thought is more difficult to recognize when the thought itself is extremely upsetting and disturbing.

Obsessive thoughts may center around aggressive wishes against significant people or around blasphemous or morally repugnant ideas which cannot be eliminated from one's mind. In either case, the obsessive preoccupation may be total and may claim the individual's entire interest, thus preventing any other thought processes. The sudden appearances of highly repugnant thoughts are so bizarre and alien to the person's manifest personality that it immediately distracts him from anything else that might be going on at the time. Instrusive thoughts which involve screaming obscene words at inappropriate times or places suggest that the individual wants to become the focus of public attention. It seems to contradict the notion that the obsessive thought is designed to distract the individual from public notice and crucial concerns. However, the same basic process is operative when regardless of how extreme or revolting an obsessive thought might be to the individual, it is still much less distressing than the idea which it is covering up. This concept, which is called *displacement*, assumes that the obsessive symptom is always distracting the individual from essential concerns, yet these preoccupying thoughts and ruminations are often the very essence of the person's concerns, as he sees the problem.

Therefore, the presence of aggressive obsessional ideas need not cause the therapist to immediately take precautionary action or consider hospitalization, but this symptom *does* signal the need for treatment. In Mr. Jones's case, his concern about killing his wife had been present for at least two years, and its effect was to reduce concentration and effective action. There had been no danger to his wife, and our understanding of the dynamics of the obsessional personality gives us confidence that treatment can be carried on outside of a hospital.

If, however, the individual's capacity to function has deteriorated and the obsessions or compulsions prevent him from carrying on his necessary tasks for living, hospitalization may become necessary. If the hand washing produces severe dermatitis or the obsessional thoughts immobilize the person, he may need to be removed from his day-to-day routine. The dangers of homicide, however, are so remote that one can assume that the essence of the disorder is to keep one under control so that the obsession will succeed in maintaining a severe inhibition of all activities.

The obsessional situation must be distinguished from the psychotic states in which homicidal thoughts are heard as messages in the nature of orders or instructions to action. When this occurs, the individual is in a delusional state rather than an obsessional state; the auditory hallucinations are part of a schizophrenic process, generally of a paranoid type. Such a person, who may or may not perform a routine job efficiently, is an odd character who is isolated and will evidence his hallucinations and delusions in a variety of ways. When the hallucinations are part of a systematized paranoid delusional system, such an individual may become a serious menace to society by destroying property or killing people. He can be readily identified by a psychiatric interview and should be immediately hospitalized. He should not be treated as an outpatient, since serious risks are involved.

It was evident that Mr. Jones was not psychotic or delusional, and that he was not suffering from any paranoid systematized delusions or hallucinations. He was clearly in touch with reality, and his ideas and thoughts, although very distressing to him, did not represent gross distortions of perceptions or hallucinatory fantasies. He was suffering from an obsessive-compulsive neurosis, and I proceeded to make arrangements to see Mr. Jones in my office.

His life story did not unfold as a continuous narrative, but by a number of circuitous routes stimulated by free association. Some of his stored-up memories, which were activated by recent events, were trivial and others were significant or troublesome. During some long pauses or silences I might ask direct questions or encourage him to elaborate issues that seemed to me relevant at the time. Mr. Jones's verbalizations tended to be obtuse, unfocused, and indirect. However, there were considerable data that illuminated the psychodynamics of his obsessional defenses.

Mr. Jones had become increasingly distressed about his inability to be firm and assertive when he felt imposed upon and about his difficulty in communication. At these times he felt humiliated and experienced loss of pride and self-worth. He described it as follows: "The trouble began when I couldn't channel my thoughts into any topic or group of memories. I couldn't control my thought processes. I had a recurrence of the memory of two years ago [two years prior to our initial interview] when I wanted to kill my wife and then had to see a psychiatrist."

Prior to the latest appearance of these murderous thoughts, he had had numerous argumentative encounters with his wife. His frustrations, irritability, and controlled resentment appeared in spite of his awareness that she was truly troubled and distressed about her physical problems. He experienced her behavior as critical and withdrew, instead of confronting her with his disagreements. This was a characteristic response when he anticipated that confrontation would result in more criticism and deeper hurt. These arguments came in 1950, at the time he was involved in a major relocation because of a better job; the bulk of the household readjustment had fallen on his wife's shoulders.

In 1950 there was an air of tension and unexpressed resentment on both sides. At times Mr. Jones recognized his excessive demands and requirements; yet he could not seem to reduce them. During our first meeting he said, "I became aware of the fact that all my life I've had an exacting, uncompromising attitude towards everything. Everything had to be exact and perfect. Yes, I have been trying to get rid of that attitude ever since, and I felt reasonably successful in doing so." This was not borne out in subsequent events, as his inability to deal with excessive demands led to a series of obsessional symptoms.

During his period of difficulties in 1950, his ability to concentrate was greatly impaired and his memory was practically nonexistent, so that he could not participate in many conversations with his colleagues. Prior to that period, his difficulties with his wife were only differences of opinion of minor kinds; he had been irritable and distressed with her. "We had more than the usual number of disagreements or differences of opinion." She had back trouble, colitis, and arthritis, which made her uncomfortable and irritable, and she felt that her husband was growing away from her. He tried to reassure her, but at one point during this period he did say that they didn't seem to be suited to each other and wondered if she thought they should consider a divorce. This suggestion evoked a violent, hysterical reaction from her. It was at this time that she encouraged him to see a psychiatrist, as she felt he might be becoming mentally ill. He had expressed some hostility toward her because he felt dominated by her. He entered therapy for a brief period in 1950, and the unpleasant thoughts and most of the symptoms gradually disappeared until two years later, in 1952, when he began noticing that his memory and concentration were again impaired.

Mr. Jones felt distressed when he was unable to be firm or to react adequately when he felt imposed upon. He related an instance in which a surly person whom Mr. Jones had been trying to correct became resentful. Mr. Jones had great difficulty communicating his annoyance. In reporting this incident the patient used typical obsessional circumlocutions: "Well, it seems that the situation was entailed, or which should entail, I guess, are the ones which are particularly deserving. But regardless of whether there was an aggressiveness involved, the impairment of memory involved and the ability to concentrate is closed and that's accompanied by a feeling of tension and pressure in which I know I can think and reason better than I think I'm doing or have been able to for the last two years. It's annoying and frustrating to be experiencing this continual feeling in which I cannot make the appropriate reply to pressures put on me. ..."

Mr. Jones had difficulty recalling other incidents in which such frustrations occurred, but his inability to express his irritability led him to withdraw rather than face up to it. This happened particularly with his wife during the time of their move in 1950. It was an important occasion, since there was considerable tension about the change. He had to get the packing and shipping of their household belongings done as well as complete his job assignment. At this very time, however, his wife experienced a recurrence of lower-back pain. He tried but was unable to get time off; she felt that he did not make a real effort to do so, and she was left to do the packing alone. She expressed the feeling that his work was more important to him than she was. Any joy over the change in jobs was dissipated by the enormous tension and distress that surrounded their departure.

In his first session with me, Mr. Jones ruminated about the circumstances of his departure. While recognizing that he had been ignoring his wife's pain, he expected her to behave reasonably and he felt a good bit of irritation, which he did not express to her. In fact, he had fastidiously dealt with everything according to the rules and regulations.

In his first interview he detailed the onset of his obsessional difficulties, which began at a time of crisis — when he was changing jobs and moving to another city. While he related these thoughts to his relationship with his wife, it was a long time before he really understood the significance of these feelings. This feature is characteristic of all neuroses: Intellectual understanding is not necessarily accompanied by deep emotional awareness; therefore, change cannot and does not occur. Intellectual insight must be accompanied by emotional insight before change is possible.

We began a program of therapy, and for the time we remained in contact all the sessions were taped, transcribed, and stored. I have waited until now to present this detailed case to preserve the anonymity of the patient. While he is aware that it is being published, since I had a follow-up interview last year, his identity is completely disguised and is detectable only to himself.

It is very difficult and boring for a reader to have to wade through the endless details, repetitions, and recitals of banal events of a patient's existence which surface in a psychotherapeutic treatment. Occasionally, there will be a striking recall or an insightful moment after a period of intensive scrutiny and dogged persistence. This fact, more than any other, is responsible for the dearth of full treatment reports. What is generally available is a series of highlights or excerpts selected by the therapist to emphasize a point or to demonstrate some dynamic of this disorder. While such a presentation is easier to read, like the brilliant case studies that Freud published, they leave the reader dissatisfied about the validity of the process and the therapy. Since the excerpts are selected by the author to demonstrate significant elements, one can justly suspect that a degree of self-serving prejudice or preconception has influenced his choice. Unless one has trust and faith in the author's objectivity and intellectual integrity, such excerpts can be isolated confirmations of his theoretical position, neglecting those pieces of data that deny or invalidate it.

I decided to publish as much as possible of the transaction with Mr. Jones, to include the rich source of material that the analyst must work with, as well as some of the tedious, repetitive interactions involved in the process. I have included many of our exchanges in their entirety, risking criticism of my obvious errors but conveying the difficulties, complications, and requirements for skilled, warm, and empathic involvement. Some repetition, of course, has been omitted in order to make this account more readable. There is the risk of some dull reading at times but also the reward of not being subjected to the therapist's imaginative or dramatic elaborations of the material. The Hollywood version of therapy and of the dynamics of mental disorder and the colorful description of magical cures through single dramatic revivals of the past or brilliant charismatic moments of interaction with the therapist have served to distort the process and undermine the validity of psychotherapy.

It is difficult to communicate the intricacies of the actual verbal exchanges in terms of pauses, inflections, and other nuances so crucial to communication. These cannot always be indicated in the text. Moreover, long pauses — where I waited for the patient to respond before I proceeded to the next question — could not always be adequately identified. The patient must be allowed some time to respond, and only when he appears to be too tied up, or to be having difficulty acknowledging or formulating a response, should the therapist intervene with the pointed or provocative question that moves the patient along. Silences themselves are very provocative and effective facilitators when judiciously and skillfully utilized.

In general, the obsessional tolerates silences very poorly. His need for immediate solutions and his inability to tolerate anxiety lead almost immediately to defensive operations and often disrupt the therapeutic process. Therefore, it is essential not to allow silences to go on so long that the patient's anxieties increase to the point where he calls on his defenses and moves away from direct action or constructive introspective thinking. At other times it may produce a disintegration of the session and terminate whatever analytic process was set in motion. No rule can be established to deal with this eventuality. It is a matter of experience, empathy, and a willingness to intervene or to stay aloof when the situation requires it.

THEORY OF THERAPY

The therapy of the obsessional defense — whether it be a simple personality trait or an obsessional neurosis — is greatly complicated by the nature of the defense, which militates against exposure of deficits or deficiencies. Consequently, the treatment suffers from the complications that ensue from the nature of the neurotic structure. In addition, our limited knowledge and skills in dealing with these complications, which oppose the essential requirements of a therapeutic alliance, make the process extremely difficult. No wonder treatment is long, uncertain, and, too often, tediously unrewarding for both participants.

In treating the obsessional, it is very difficult to secure engagement in the therapeutic process or even a minimal commitment, and a large part of therapy is spent in the initial phases. In these therapeutic encounters treatment does not truly get going until the patient can experience, even with reluctance and many qualifications, some new understanding or an alternative hypothesis which requires a relaxation of his rigid, stubborn conviction.

The case to be presented in detail will be divided into three parts: the opening, or discovery, phase; the middle, or working-through, phase; and the termination, or behavioral alteration phase. This division coincides in many ways with the natural course of the therapeutic encounter.

Phase one lasted four months and was followed by seven months of a working through of the various insights which were developed in phase one. There was much repetition, which at times extended into phase three; trials and attempts were made to alter some of the earlier behavior and to abandon or replace the obsessional responses with more assertive, clarifying interactions with the patient's wife and colleagues. This phase terminated our work, although attempts at change usually continue indefinitely in a patient's life if treatment has been successful.

Treatment in general can be divided in this fashion, though usually the division is not completely contained and changes may occur in phase one while discoveries and new insights may take place at any time during the work. However, the tripartite division of treatment grows out of the philosophy of mental disorder according to which defenses deal with anxiety-constituting symptoms which congeal into a neurosis or character disorder which then stabilizes or becomes more or less adaptive. Treatment attempts to explore the beginning in order to understand the anxieties that required defenses; these anxieties, when explored and explicated, can be resolved, allowing for a reconstruction of the personality.

While such a division can be recognized retrospectively, it is artificial and unproductive to attempt to program it in advance. In fact, in the treatment of obsessional disorders it is particularly unproductive and antitherapeutic for the therapist to have an agenda or a fixed notion of the mechanics of the process. Such a view would tend to make the treatment itself too obsessional and would destroy the effectiveness of a spontaneous, open-ended view of human behavior.

The first phase in the therapy of Mr. Jones, which will be described in detail in chapter 12, took approximately three months. It demonstrated the difficulties of the initial involvement in therapy, highlighting many of the typical obsessional mechanisms and interpersonal gambits that require special handling and active intervention to facilitate the process. All therapists who deal with the obsessional disorder will recognize the tactics and recall the difficulties in dealing with them in their own practices.

Plan for Case Presentation

The initial session, during which the patient presented the details of his obsessions and its history, I have detailed in narrative form. The entire therapeutic process and the detailed verbal exchanges are presented unedited and unaltered except to decrease repetition. Whenever the report is altered, this will be indicated by a summary of the deleted text, so that the reader can follow the exchanges.

In presenting the interviews I will distinguish the comments and asides that I recorded in my notes at the time of the treatment from those I made subsequently in rereading and preparing the case for publication. This method will, I hope, give the reader a view of the workings of the therapist's mind as he sits listening, hypothesizing, speculating, and planning the responses to be made or notions to be stored for future use. It will reveal the strategies and understanding or lack of understanding of the therapist as he proceeds to ask questions, make interpretations, or provoke confrontations designed to enlighten the patient and promote change. It will also reveal the shortcomings and deficiencies of the therapist. Finally, it will reveal our continued state of searching and the limited understanding we have of the sources of human behavior and malfunctioning.

The comments made after the case was treated represent the view of a more experienced and, it is hoped, more competent therapist. I felt like a supervisor overseeing a student's production. The lapse of a quarter of a century makes the analogy real, since the author was at that time a young therapist who had recently emerged from training status and whose experience was limited. While the overall picture of the dynamics was recalled on rereading the sessions, many of the details of the exchanges and particularly the therapist's responses were fresh material that could be appraised and evaluated with some objectivity, almost as if it were the work of another therapist. I have included some notes which I made following each interview at that time; this summarizes what I considered to be the essential issues that were dealt with in the session, as well as recording some feelings, responses and questions that were stirred up by the session. Sharing these comments will, I hope, disparage the notion of the ideal psychoanalyst who always makes the correct moves at the right moment and will help the student to see that the supervisory process is always a more favorable situation for the supervisor than for the person being supervised. One has the opportunity to see the total interview and draw conclusions about whether it was wise to have moved in one direction or another and to speculate about alternative views and maneuvers which might have been better. One can also recognize that some issues were not touched upon that could have been dealt with effectively and see a number of needs that were overlooked at the time but which, upon reflection, can be identified and available for future use. At the time therapy is going on, one is faced with immediate decisions as to what roads to take, what observations to make, and what leads to pursue and highlight. One must also decide whether to make an interpretation or to ask a leading question, which might promote an observation by the patient and lead to insight. Should one wait on the interpretation because it is too early, too profound, too distressful, or too unlikely to be acknowledged or accepted? It is always difficult to assess whether one route is more productive than another, and one moves intuitively according to one's style in the therapeutic process. In presenting this case I hope to enlarge the understanding of the therapy of the obsessional state and to indicate that a therapeutic philosophy can allow one to be both spontaneous and useful in developing both insight and change in this very difficult disorder.

It is to be expected that every reader, as he experiences the following sessions in the quiet of his office or living room, will have his own reactions to Mr. Jones's presentation. I am certain that some of these responses will be more intuitive and the technical maneuvers that come to mind possibly more effective than what actually transpired. One of the unresolvable complications of therapy is that most of the patient's productions, both verbal and nonverbal, are open to a variety of possible interpretations or responses. During a session one is forced to make choices about which directions should be pursued and which are better left for later consideration. What is selected to be dealt with at any particular moment depends on many factors — such as the therapist's theoretical background and orientation, the major theme currently being explored; new or potentially enlightening recollections, contradictions, or substantiation of earlier material; and many others. Of the three possible determinants, — namely (1) the therapist's treatment plan, (2) the current theme being explored, and (3) the possibility of review of earlier data (the latter two being dictated by the patient's agenda) — the first is the major factor. This issue is particularly significant for the obsessional, who presents a variety of alternatives with myriads of details — which generally confuse or obfuscate matters unless the therapist is aware of what's going on, stays with the relevant and essential data, and avoids being entrapped.

The therapeutic work with Mr. Jones was of approximately fourteen-month's duration, with some interruptions because of business trips and vacations. Our work was terminated by his transfer to another town. It was an unplanned and unexpected ending of our therapeutic relationship, as sometimes happens. The length of psychoanalytic therapy often collides with other life plans and termination is not always based on theoretical grounds, as one would ideally like, which would imply either the resolution of the disorder or the achievement of maximum benefits by the patient. Nevertheless, progress and change are achieved, and one does not always need a full course of treatment to abandon destructive behavioral patterns of living. In Mr. Jones's case there was sufficient change, both in the obsessional difficulty and the character structure which supported his obsessional defense system, that it could be called a finished analysis.

LIFE HISTORY

Mr. Jones came from a fairly typical middle-class Midwestern family and grew up in a household where parental standards and demands were mainly set by his mother and either supported or silently acquiesced to by his father. The family was financially sound and Mr. Jones, the eldest of two children, was viewed and treated as a prize package. There was constant supervision by a mother who demanded proper, conventional behavior from her son. Though she was proud of him, she also was constantly critical if he did not behave in the most exemplary manner. She selected his friends carefully to meet her standards of behavior and background. Mr. Jones was prevented from having many friends, since his mother disapproved of the neighborhood in which they lived. Her unfriendliness toward her neighbors and his possible playmates made it impossible for him to fulfill his own social needs. He was a loner who lived in an adult world and was rarely allowed to be the child or the growing boy.

Mr. Jones's attitude toward his mother was that of a good boy who always tried to win her approval. His contacts with his father were minimal, though he had deep concerns about winning his approval by being manly. This produced continuing tension, since the goals of being a good boy and being manly were often contradictory. Bright, good in school, and acceptable to the grown-ups, he made his way fairly well even though there was some difficulty when he left one school to go to another. However, his knowledge in how the world operated outside of his home was very limited, particularly in regard to sex or other bodily functions.

His family had an excessive concern with and control over his activities. For example, his mother insisted that he come home immediately after school. While there were extreme expectations about his performing well in school and being independent, there was also an exaggerated tendency to keep him dependent on the family and especially on his mother. When he was five years old he attempted to be assertive by accepting the challenge of a neighborhood bully. He was quickly beaten and had to run away and hide. He was protected by a neighbor who sheltered him and who, in his own words, was a "substitute" for his mother.

These early experiences all contributed to Mr. Jones's expecting to be independent while also being uncertain and insecure. Later on he described his difficulties about pursuing jobs and his great relief when his father obtained jobs for him. It was another indication of his dependency-independency struggle, which was tied to the issue of assertiveness and the threats of danger connected with such activity.

In his early years, his anxious and fearful mother made special arrangements for his school and for all his other activities. She selected his playmates with snobbishly critical concerns. This forced him into isolation, so that he had very limited contact with peers. His skills at childhood games and boyish sports were so deficient that he avoided any opportunities for play when they did present themselves. This pattern started with baseball and stoopball and became a vicious cycle in the future, and the concerns about not performing well prevented him from improving his skills. "I was unprepared for baseball and softball because I had never done it before and I didn't know how to play athletic games. I remember when I was to come up to bat, I would purposely jockey myself further back in line to avoid coming to bat. I didn't think of it so much as being frightened but of being embarrassed at not knowing how to play, and that attitude kept me from learning. And that's the way it's been since then." While he was aware that this attitude prevented him from learning, he was unable to change it for fear of being taunted by others.

His mother escorted him to and from school until he was eleven years old. By then, he was quite self-conscious about this escort service, but he had a hard time getting his mother to discontinue it. When he was six or seven the school had a special event, and he was brought by his mother to the area in which the event took place while the rest of the students came in a group. He was embarrassed and humiliated, and his specialness became a source of concern and shame. He reported many instances in which his mother restrained and restricted his activities, so that he appeared to be a sissy and an isolate.

In the fourth grade he was transferred from the school in his district to another one that was farther away from his house. "She wanted me to go to one which she felt was in a 'higher-class' neighborhood. She persuaded the principals of both schools to allow her to make this change, and I matriculated in the 'better' school." Before school began, however, he developed an infectious disease and had to begin school several weeks late. By this time the children had already formed groups, and he was again isolated and alone.

When he was twelve, he spent much of his time riding his bike. He wanted to work before going on to college but the Depression made it difficult to find a job. At college, near his home, his attitude about socializing changed, and he joined some clubs and tried to participate in the social life of the school. "I seemed to have a feeling that my parents would have disapproved of my having any connection with any school activities. I did not do any of these things because mother and father did not understand about that, as they had both been raised in small country towns where there were no school activities." In college he even dated, and, though he felt his family would disapprove, he joined a fraternity and reported making good friends during that period. He graduated with a B.A. and took night courses to prepare himself for a career. He finally obtained a job as an insurance agent.

His work life was universally successful, and he advanced consistently in his jobs, even though his skills in relating and supervising others were constantly hampered by his need to be liked. He was unable to give orders unless he had the strength of authority behind him. There were constant unexpressed feelings of competition and rivalry with his peers; he resented any intrusion in his status. He demanded acknowledgment for his position at all times. There was a pseudodignity about him, since he himself had doubts about his status and required constant reinforcement by others. In his day-to-day life he was largely easygoing and well controlled, but he did not seem to have much, if any, fun. He was serious about his living and had a need to do the right thing without much regard as to whether he would enjoy doing it. In fact, he seemed surprised if he managed, in some accidental way, to get some fun out of going to the theater or socializing with colleagues. He was not unfriendly but certainly not warm and, in fact, had very few friends.

After a love affair which did not succeed, he married a woman much older than he was and began to live the typical suburban life. He was attentive in general to his wife's needs but was largely preoccupied with his own anxieties, which were beginning to mount. He began to feel trapped and caught by his need to satisfy his parents, who disapproved of his wife, and the needs of his wife, who thought he ought to take a stronger stand with his parents. Encounters with his wife often left him feeling annoyed and resentful; in particular, he felt he was being pushed around by his wife because of his uneasiness about confronting her. He could not manage his parents at all, and in devious ways he attempted to deal with his wife and family without alienating any of them. It was about this time that he began to notice some growing uneasiness in his relations with his wife, and their quarrels became frequent. On one or two occasions he began to have obsessional thoughts about his wife — which eventually became a total preoccupation and prevented him from concentrating on his job.

Quiet, meticulous, and proper are the words used to describe him by most of the people he knew. His view of himself, however, was that there were unexpressed yearnings, antagonisms, and resentments, which he dealt with by avoiding, overlooking, repressing or denying them or by becoming preoccupied with other matters; the latter distracted him and prevented him from focusing on his difficulties.

His sex life was characteristically proper, satisfactory, and hardly exciting. Novelty, experimentation, and variations were avoided, and there was a routinization of sex, which became less satisfying to his wife. Her reaction caused him some distress, though his implacable inability to show any feelings prevented a real showdown. He was friendly but cold, kind and decent; but in the long run he was inconsiderate of others because of his preoccupation with fulfilling his own needs.

He was a perfectionist and was critical of others, demanding perfection of them without recognizing that his standards were excessively high. He had difficulties in being decisive at all times. He put off making decisions for fear they would not be the correct ones; he could only make them when he had data and support from all sides. He had a number of minor phobias and concerns about flying and uneasiness in tunnels or on bridges; but, in general, his movements were not impeded by his anxieties, although there were constant requirements for guarantees for his technical decisions. His preoccupation with his profession led him to be a scholarly person who read all the material relating to his work and was viewed as the expert on its details. While in good physical condition, he had difficulty in accepting the weaknesses and physical incapacities in others. His impatience with and intolerance of his wife's difficulties were a source of irritation. As he became more obsessed, he experienced difficulties in concentrating; and as he found deficiencies in the work life, these reverberated into his physical life. He then became depressed and his functioning became worse. His demands on himself even during the time of his treatment did not abate.

As our work proceeded, he began to loosen up; and as his depression abated, his physical condition improved. Mr. Jones was a tall, well-built, attractive man; he spoke quietly and thoughtfully with a little stammer, being uncertain that what came out would be acceptable. There was timidity in his approach to others that bordered on detachment. While he was likable, he avoided intimacies and commitments in relationships, so that the warmth of human exchanges rarely developed — even with his wife, who had her own difficulties that in many respects were similar to his own.

Mr. Jones met and married his wife in 1944. She came from a different geographic area and had had an unsuccessful first marriage. He found it very difficult to adjust to the demands of married life. Their problems were accentuated by frequent moves while he was establishing himself professionally. His relations with his wife were also complicated by his parents' attitude toward her, which he was aware of prior to the marriage. During a visit to his parents' home without his wife, he tried to convince them that he loved her. They were not reassured, and his mother actively tried to persuade him to abandon the marriage plans. He said: "My wife was surprised that I didn't take a more definite stand about my parents' objections. While I didn't allow them to influence me, neither did I reply to their objections." During that same session: "Yes, she wondered why I didn't become more angry than I did. She said she could see how hard this experience was for me when I got letters from them, but she was surprised because I did nothing about it. I find it hard to remember just how I felt. I just pushed their objections out of my mind and pretended they didn't exist. I gave them very short answers when I wrote them but kept telling them how wonderful our love was and about our plans to get married and never acknowledged the fact that they were objecting."

His relationship to his wife was markedly ambivalent. Being dependent, insecure and uncertain about his capacity to function effectively, he was dependent on his family for decision making and support. His choice of a wife who was much older than he was and who appeared strong and effective to him was entirely consistent and comprehensible, even though it created many emotional difficulties and was the soil from which his obsessional problems erupted. While it temporarily resolved his neurotic needs, his marriage was only a temporary respite from anxiety and an ultimate stimulus for further decompensation and disorganization. She was his first real girlfriend, and their relationship, while stormy, appeared to be very effective in maintaining Mr. Jones's adjustment during the difficult early years of his professional life.

Throughout the marriage the relationship between his wife and his mother was one of mutual antagonism and hostility. Mr. Jones described innumerable instances in which he had to placate and reduce his mother's antagonism toward his wife. Since he had to be liked by everyone, he could leave no area of uncertainty open. Ultimately it was his wife who, symbolizing his mother in all respects, had to make the major compromises.

There was a mutual awareness of this hostile situation, and there were few attempts to deal with it openly. At one point, early in our work, he said: "I know what my mother's opposition was about. I think it was a feeling of possessiveness towards me and a reluctance to see anyone else have my love, or a reluctance to seeing anyone separate me from my immediate family. I know what they were opposed to. They didn't like the idea of her being older, didn't like the idea that she had been divorced, and didn't like the idea that she couldn't have children. My mother and sister, principally my sister, didn't like the idea that my wife was of a Christian sect that was different from ours."

His wife was especially resentful because she had the feeling that her husband was more concerned about his family than about her. This was especially noticeable when she was in the company of his family or in communication with them by phone or letter. At other times there were exaggerations of her own uncertain hold on Mr. Jones, who seemed not to be fully liberated from his family. She often expressed her irritability through physical complaints which focused on lower-back pains and colitis. The lower-back pain was a source of many crises during their marriage and especially at the time of the major outbreak in 1950 of Mr. Jones's obsessive ruminations about killing his wife. Her incapacity required him to be more cooperative in the household. However, his preoccupation with his job interfered, and her persistent complaining and nagging highlighted his helplessness; when he needed her support and guidance she was expecting his independent and unsolicited participation.

At this time, owing to unexpected complications, a visit to his mother in 1949 had to be canceled, and instead, they had to stay with his wife's family for a short time. This change in plans so threatened his mother that she became extremely disagreeable, and she expressed her irritation with her son in a long phone conversation, during which he tried to placate her. His wife's colitis and back pains were especially troublesome during that time, and he became uncomfortable and frightened by his wife's severe antagonism, which she freely expressed. "I can't figure any other way to describe the thing except that, knowing of my mother's disagreeable attitude toward our marriage, my wife felt that any expression of affection by my mother threatened her in some way." In trying to clarify this relationship, he continued, "When we learned of the possibility of this move we called my mother on the phone to ask her to visit us. My mother, in her effusive manner, launched into a conversation, and as I was replying I could tell that my wife was upset and displeased about the conversation, which was being diverted from the purpose of this call." He thought his wife was upset because he seemed to be getting too intimate with his mother and was expressing too much affection toward her. He could not accept her perception of the conversation and avoided any awareness of the intensity of his attachment to his mother. He was caught in a double bind which he could only resolve obsessionally. He tended to refer reactions or responses to intellectual matters; he preferred to interpret his wife's annoyance as an intellectual digression rather than as her reaction to what she considered his catering and pandering behavior with his mother. Repeatedly, the patient's tendency to confuse his wife and mother and his inability to distinguish the nature of his relationship with them needed to be identified and clarified. When this was done, Mr. Jones could identify the true nature of his involvement with these women, but the awareness was easily repressed. On one occasion he said: "After I began to realize some of the reasons for my discomfort and realize that I contributed to my wife's feeling uncomfortable, or at least not having done anything to prevent her from being uncomfortable, she began to feel better. We both began to feel better at the same time, and the long-repressed feelings of resentment against my parents could come out in the open and I could see ways in which I contributed to this feeling of insecurity on her part."

Mr. Jones hoped that in time his parents would come to like and accept his wife, but this never did happen, although there was some growing acceptance of her. He hoped that his wife would come to feel more secure with his family and be able to accept them as well. He responded to his wife's complaints with repeated requests for forgiveness and apologetic references to his family's antagonistic letters, with the hope that this would relieve his wife's uneasiness. However, during a visit, two years after they were married, the situation was inflamed anew because of his mother's expressions of resentment and hostility, which were hardly concealed from his wife. Though he was clearly aware of what was happening, he did nothing about it. He tried to enlist his father as an intermediary by telling him how happy he was with his wife and how much they loved each other, and he expressed a hope that there would be some expression of acceptance on their part. This, too, proved unsuccessful.

At that time, his mother's enthusiasm on one Sunday afternoon led them all to the backyard to take some pictures. "My mother said she wanted some pictures of just the family — the family being my mother, father, sister, and myself. My aunt took the picture. After we left I noticed that my wife was very depressed and uncommunicative, and I had no idea why. On the train, after much coaxing from me, she told me she felt like an outcast, being rejected and excluded from the group pictures. I told her she was taking it too seriously. My feelings were hurt because of her sullenness. I assured her that I loved her and that my parents would grow to love her. I had a compulsion to make them love her. I thought that as they observed that we loved each other they would gradually overcome their dislike and the reasons for their rejection of her."

However, he never argued with them or attempted to change their minds by persuasion. He hoped that a magical transformation would follow their recognition of his love and devotion. He tried to minimize his mother's display of affection for him in the presence of his wife but never communicated anything about this to his mother. He was increasingly aware of his wife's uneasiness towards his parents and she accused him of lack of vigor in settling the issue. He said, "My mother's disagreeable attitude towards our marriage threatened her [his wife] in some way, and also, I did nothing to clarify it." He wanted to be loved by all, alienating neither his wife nor his mother. Nevertheless, he regularly infuriated his wife who felt that she was entitled to his loyalty. He recognized that his mother's unduly affectionate and possessive attitude resembled the description of "Momism," about which he had been reading at that time, but he seemed curiously dense and insensitive to the reaction of his wife in these circumstances.

Transferential Distortions

At an earlier time Mr. Jones had a feeling that he had been identifying his wife with his parents all during his first obsessional illness and that he was unable to give proper recognition to each of their roles. At that time the growing difficulty with his wife was plagued by his compulsive feelings about killing her. During a severe argument with his wife, he described his obsessive feelings to her and brought up the subject of divorce. He had hoped that by expressing these obsessive thoughts they would disappear. While the disagreement was resolved, the situation continued to be inflammatory. It was about a month after this revelation that he first began to see a psychiatrist. His wife then became more understanding and he felt that the revelation might bring them closer together.

During this same period Mr. Jones was also having some difficulty with his boss, who was also seen as another authority who controlled his living and circumscribed his freedom. "I thought that he didn't assign me properly to the job I was fitted for. I thought he had to give me proper recognition and the assignment that I did want. I felt that I didn't like him and I thought he didn't like me and I was glad when he finally left. After he left I was happy and I thought the feelings of being kept under his thumb would disappear and I would be much happier. In some mysterious way these feelings that I had toward him transferred themselves also to my wife, and I began to feel these hostile feelings toward her."

Exposing the Hidden Feelings

At the third session I thought it necessary to pull together his experiences at the time of the onset of his obsessional thinking. His notion that they had some mysterious origin had to be countered by demonstrating to him that such feelings have some relationship to his thoughts and behavior and that attitudes and compulsive thoughts do not arise in some magical and mysterious way. I had to confront Mr. Jones with the notion that the hostile feelings which he was ascribing toward his wife, boss, and mother might possibly be related to the severe obsessional thoughts he was having and that they could not be eliminated by his conscious efforts. The following exchange took place at that time:

Therapist: But when you say, "mysterious," you imply that there is something kind of magical or mystical, as if the feeling that you had toward your boss was the same feeling you had toward your wife. Isn't it possible that this feeling is the same because you felt the same toward your boss and your wife?

Mr. Jones: It probably was. I probably identified both of them with my parents.

Therapist: You mean that the feeling of being under your wife's thumb is also the way you felt about your boss?

Mr. Jones: It's not only possible; it's true.

Therapist: Well, what do you think about that?

Mr. Jones: I felt that I had to please her in anything I did. And that everything I did failed to please her and she was critical and disagreeable and continually griping about what I did or did not do. It was as though she was my boss, since I was always the kind of person who was jealous of a subordinate accomplishing anything or receiving any recognition from anyone other than him. I related his attitude toward the feeling I had toward my parents as a child and adolescent — that I had to please them or I had to defer or suspend my action until they directed it.

Therapist: Was there anything else that gave you the feeling of being under your wife's thumb aside from the difficulty in pleasing her?

Mr. Jones: I felt that she was placing herself in the position of authority to approve or disapprove things I wanted to do.

Therapist: In other words, she had the final O.K.?

Mr. Jones: Well, it seemed to me then, but it doesn't anymore. She has since told me that she feels substantially the same way about me. She felt rejected and unwanted. She felt like a piece of baggage that I was directing around and had no opportunity to express her wishes. Each one of us felt the same way about the other. I have a better realization of her need for feeling secure, in wishing to have her wishes considered. Previously I merely announced that we would so and so and she finally decided that she couldn't take that kind of treatment anymore.

However, in spite of the recognition of his relationship with his parents they moved into his parents' home during a transitional period when they were looking for a house. His distress had subsided after seeing his first psychiatrist, but his dependence on his family became more severe. He felt that he could not make a decision without their help. The obsessional concerns about killing his wife, which brought him into therapy, were initiated by hostile feelings toward his wife and boss. His wife and boss were almost an exact duplication of his family situation — that is, a strong, critical, and demanding maternal figure and a paternal figure who was unaccepting and unavailable for support and encouragement. The extent of Mr. Jones's transferential confusion was manifest in the almost identical series of reactions. The attitudes towards his mother and father were the resentments that needed to be repressed in order to function effectively in a dependent relationship. The inability to do so plays a major role in the development of obsessive thoughts in many patients.

While the connections between his attitudes toward his wife and boss and those toward his parents were clearly established in the early weeks of our work, Mr. Jones had only a meager grasp of it, which he himself had sensed during his descriptions of his relationship to his wife, mother, and boss. Although I have described this in a coherent framework, the data developed over many sessions and with considerable assistance from hints, openings, and direct questions, or by my focusing on feelings, which he tended to overlook. In this way, the process of resolution of his obsessional neurosis was initiated. Now the task that followed was to gain a true understanding of the development of the feelings that needed to be defended by obsessional rituals instead of by direct expression. Skill and patience are required in trying to deal with the myriad defensive techniques — all of which are designed to prevent a real confrontation of the anxieties that pervade the life and behavior of an obsessional person. It is therefore necessary to examine the nature of these defenses in some detail as they surfaced and manifested themselves in the patient before he could acknowledge his feelings and really deal with them. This constituted the bulk of our work over the next three months. It was the exploratory phase in which data is being accumulated and patterns of functioning are illuminated and examined. While some interpretations are being made, more emphasis is placed on listening, questioning, directing the inquiry, and endlessly clarifying the obfuscations and distractions to overcome the distortions of recall and the referential descriptions of events in which the patient is the innocent victim or bystander. In this phase both the patient and the therapist are hard at work trying to discover the real from the perceived for the patient.

CHAPTER 12

The Opening Phase

Treatment began in December 1952, after the initial interview. How one proceeds to review a patient's life depends on the intensity of his present problems and the need for immediate reduction of anxiety. This will determine how quickly one can move toward an anamnestic review of the patient's past life or whether time will have to be spent on issues related to his present living. Mr. Jones, while deeply troubled by his obsessional ruminations when they recurred, and distressed by his inadequate functioning at his job, was not in any crisis. His relationship with his wife was reasonably comfortable. He therefore could move more directly into a description of his earlier life, relating it to his present complications with his wife. The therapist's role is to listen, to encourage clearer verbalizations, and to ask provocative questions that can open up potential sources of data about the personality development and early experiences related to this.

Mr. Jones described in some detail the background of his obsessional difficulties and previous therapy. At the first session he described his problems as "indefinable, very disturbing nervousness and an inadequacy to respond to a conversation." In response to my questioning, he amplified this statement and focused on his increasing distress about his inadequate and ineffective functioning, utilizing intellectually verbalized excesses that confused rather than clarified meaning. "I was experiencing a reduced vision, reasoning, and ability to concentrate or remember, both of which abilities I had had to a very high degree before that. That existed for about a month, and I was just completely at sea at what was the matter with me. After about a month, various disturbing and frightening thoughts popped into my head one morning as I was getting out of bed. I was visiting my wife's parents and suddenly the thought popped into my head 'you are going to kill your wife.'"

He related this background, describing some hostile feelings toward his wife which led to his suggesting a divorce, a notion she reacted to violently, threatening to kill herself. Instead, he went to see a psychiatrist twice a week for two or three months. "I was greatly helped by realizing that this feeling of resentment, hostile thoughts against my wife, was a cross-fire, a throwback to the feeling of unconscious resentment that I had against my parents because of excessive domination by them."

INTELLECTUAL RESISTANCES

This meaningful formulation was probably the result of his contact with psychiatry, but since it was only an intellectual understanding it seemed to have little effect on his symptom or his subsequent behavior. This occurs frequently in the therapy of mental disorders where the focal issues are emotional rather than cognitive. It is especially true in the obsessional disorders where the bright, informed, highly intellectualized patient frequently makes profound and informed statements about the psychodynaics of his pathology. The bulk of the therapeutic work then involves translating this intellectual insight into emotional understanding and a commitment to change. Mr. Jones's earliest emphasis and concern were with his impaired memory and thinking ability, the obsessional's typical displacement from the more essential issues — that is, his anger and homicidal thoughts. Recognizing this distraction from the more crucial issues, I tried to draw him back to the main problem and asked him to recall any incident in which his lack of assertion or failure to acknowledge his real feelings had occurred.

Mr. Jones: Well, an incident happened today, in which an employee prepared a letter that I sent back to him for correction. His reaction was rather surly and he said, "Well, we did it last year this way and I don't see why changes have to be made." My remarks were done with considerable hesitation and uneasiness, and I didn't feel that I could react to similar situations as spontaneously as others can.

Therapist: Is this an illustration of your lack of aggressiveness? What do you think would have been a more appropriate response?

Mr. Jones: Similar situations have occurred with the same individual before. I think it would have been appropriate if I had been able to make an aggressive stand in this case.

Therapist: You can't at the moment verbalize what you would have liked to say to him?

Mr. Jones: Well, I can't at the moment think of it.

Therapist: You were telling me some of the additional aspects of your problem as you see it, your feeling of lack of aggressiveness. Is there anything else which has concerned you?

FOCUS ON FEELINGS

In the preceding exchange I was trying to focus on his feelings, hoping to encourage a more assertive stand. But he resisted and was unable to accept my lead, so I went on with the historical presentation. He continued to describe his concerns about his memory failures and I again tried to draw him back to his account of the obsessional thoughts about his wife, encouraging him to recall by trying to set the scene and putting them into it. It is helpful to encourage recall, to replay the scenario in which each detail is filled in. Often some slight unanticipated detail may trigger the recollection because it had a direct relation to the activation of the obsessional thought. This technique is utilized in the wide range of psychotherapies, from psychodrama or role-playing to the Gestalt approaches; it depends on the factor of recall having a direct relationship to present needs. The situation proceeded in therapy in the following way:

Therapist: What were the circumstances around the beginning of the disturbing thoughts you experienced? Do you remember the actual day it first happened? Do you remember what was transpiring when you noticed them?

Mr. Jones: I can remember what actually happened. I can remember sitting in a chair and having a feeling, a feeling of helplessness ... I can't put it into words. A feeling of helplessness, nervousness ...

Therapist: What were the circumstances surrounding it? You say you were sitting in a chair. Was it morning or afternoon? What were the circumstances around it?

Mr. Jones: Well, I believe it was in the morning, before noon. I was alone, ... I can't think of any incident that, uh ... could be said to precipitate it.

Therapist: Did any incident occur around that time, whether it precipitated it or not?

Mr. Jones: No. After I had been experiencing this difficulty for two or three months. Prior to our departure I had felt nervous. However, it wasn't unduly disturbing. At the time I thought it was due to the task of packing and getting ready. At the time my wife ... was sort of irritable and critical.

Therapist: Of you?

Mr. Jones: Yes, well she was irritable because of her back bothering her.

Therapist: But it extended to everyone?

Mr. Jones: No, I realized it was due to the pain she was in, and yet when she was critical of me it did disturb me.

Therapist: What was the context of her criticism?

Mr. Jones: Well, I had intended to take time off from work to help her with packing. I had no replacement and I was kept busy right up until the last day at work before we left. Practically all the arrangements fell upon her at a time when she wasn't up to doing it.

Therapist: She implied that you were too conscientious at work but not considerate of her?

Mr. Jones: Yes, I imagine that was the way she did consider it. I kept telling her I wanted to help her, but I was needed at work. Her reaction was that I considered my work more important than I did her. I felt rather in between opposing forces. However, we did finish packing and we did leave on time. I expected that the trip would be a good rest.

The interview got sidetracked as he went on to describe his wife's physical problems. I tried to return to his reaction to her distress and the behavior which led to the following closing statement, which was so full of potentially significant revelations that I decided to allow it to stand until our next session:

Mr. Jones: I became aware of the fact that all my life I had an exacting, uncompromising attitude towards everything, everything had to be exact, perfect. Yeah. I had been trying to get rid of that attitude ever since. I've always been precise, accurate and particular about details. I realize lately that I'm too much of a stickler for adherence to the letter of any particular thing I am doing.

HOW TO DEAL WITH PREMATURE INSIGHTS

I made a mental note as well as a note on my records to pursue the preceding statement later at a suitable time. The therapist must do this often with data which cannot be handled at the time, either because it is premature for the patient's ego to handle or because time does not allow for a sufficient exploration. The therapist might comment on it by saying, for example, "This issue is too important to deal with now, as the session is ending" or "We need to deal with this later, once we get a clearer picture of what transpired." It was becoming clear, however, that Mr. Jones's critical, perfectionistic attitudes lent themselves to unsympathetic and insensitive concern for others' feelings.

During the second interview, I decided to explain to Mr. Jones how we would proceed in our work. "We want to learn all we can about you, your background, and how you came to be the kind of person you are. You can tell me about it either by starting from the present and working back or from the past working to the present. I don't know anything about you except what you have told me about yourself and your particular problem. I don't want you to be disturbed about what is pertinent and what is not but simply to say whatever comes to mind without doing any censoring of your own." I refrained from a more elaborate and intellectual discussion to avoid getting too theoretical.

It is essential that the therapist tell the patient what is to be expected of him regardless of the degree of sophistication or the past therapeutic experiences he may have had. The most common impediment to useful therapy is for the therapist to fail to inform and assist the patient in communication and verbalizing his feelings and experience. The tendency of the therapist to be passive or silent in order to avoid influencing the patient's productions or relieving his anxiety is a particularly unconstructive attitude in the therapy of obsessionals. In fact, such presumed noninterference can be extremely provocative. Silences on the part of the patient, however, can be useful and are often a rich source of data if dealt with wisely. The development of anxiety during a silence may be helpful in formulating emotional reactions, but if the silence becomes too great it can disrupt and disintegrate the situation. At an early point in therapy, the silence most often represents the patient's failure to understand the process and what is required of him. Active assistance will be most rewarding and will encourage an uncertain commitment to the therapy to be strengthened.

At the close of the second interview, the patient asked "Doctor, are we making any progress?" This statement is so typical of the obsessional that we can use it to identify such a personality structure. It refers to the extreme concern of the patient to win approval and to do the job right, and to his tendency to expect magical solutions and to attribute magical qualities to the therapist. The therapist's stock answer to this question should be: "I have no idea. We have just begun and we need to know a great deal more before we can have any notion about the question of progress." This avoids the notion of a magical therapist and conveys the therapist's reasonable concern about progress coming out of understanding and a long-term process.

NEED TO FOCUS THE INTERVIEW

It is especially important at the beginning of the therapeutic relationship with an obsessive patient to deal with specific situations and events that can be described and recalled with some clarity, in order to obviate the unusual skill such patients have to distort or misinterpret their own role in these events. This is a crucial issue, and it must be dealt with early in therapy, so that the patient is able to see how this pervasive defense operates; otherwise, the therapeutic process will become so disturbed and confused that no movement will be possible. In the absence of clarity, the patient can draw on the full range of his defensive tactics and deny or qualify his observations in his perfectionistic attempts to get the situation "exactly right." Therefore, it is necessary to focus on these distortions to educate the patient about his defensive styles and activities, while the therapist must avoid getting entangled in a tug-of-war too early in the work. Later on, as the relationship strengthens and as the therapeutic alliance becomes firm, these tug-of-wars, which result from the confrontation by the therapist of the patient's actions, should not be avoided. Thus, I intervened with this in mind when Mr. Jones related the following account in the third session:

Mr. Jones: In 1949 I called my mother to ask her to visit us. My wife was upset and displeased about the conversation being diverted from what was the purpose of my call to ... this chitchat with my mother.

Therapist: You seem to have blocked on why your wife was displeased. Do you think this has to do with diversion of conversation to chitchat, or her displeasure over what she must have concluded was a very warm and somewhat intimate conversation?

Mr. Jones: Yes, I think that's the thing that I was referring to.

Therapist: Oh, but you say it quite differently, implying that your wife was displeased because you diverted the conversation rather than the fact that you were having an intimate conversation.

Mr. Jones: I don't know, the not getting down to business was because of this intimate conversation, it delayed the purpose of the call.

Therapist: Well, what do you think your wife was displeased with, the intimacy of this call, or ...

Mr. Jones: Oh, the intimacy, of course!

This exchange led him to recall several such occasions when his inability to express his resentments toward his mother must have made his wife feel insecure. On many occasions, he noted his mother's expression "of resentment and hostility, sometimes concealed from my wife and sometimes not, but I did not do anything about it."

A striking instance of his mother's disdain of his wife had occurred one Sunday afternoon when family pictures had been taken and his wife was not included. She was very angry because he didn't protest. He said she was taking it too seriously and he resented her sullen attitude. He tried to reassure her, but he felt that he had to force his parents to love her. In fact, his parents never softened their opposition, and they could not overcome their objections to the fact that she was divorced and was unable to have children. While Mr. Jones acknowledged that some of his mother's opposition was based on her personal feelings, it required some provocative questioning to illuminate the oedipal involvements which surfaced during this hour.

Therapist: How do you understand your mother's opposition? What do you think it's about?

Mr. Jones: Well, I think it's a feeling of possessiveness towards me and a reluctance to see anyone else have my love. During a recent visit I couldn't concentrate on any conversation with them.

Therapist: Do you remember what was distracting you?

Mr. Jones: No, that's exactly what my difficulty is, that I feel distracted and unable to concentrate.

Therapist: Well, I wasn't asking you the cause, I asked if you knew what was distracting you at that time. What were you thinking about or what was in your mind at the time?

This issue is important because it was the symptom of his inability to concentrate that brought him into treatment as well as the tactic of displacement to avoid confronting the more disturbing thoughts.

Mr. Jones: My father was very free with advice and I wasn't happy about his continual interference. The feeling of distraction was a vague one rather than being any specific thing. It was a lack of concentration rather than a diversion of concentration.

Therapist: Did anything outstanding happen during that visit?

Mr. Jones: No, my mother was effusive and overly affectionate, as usual. I was anxious to demonstrate to my wife that I could dispel and combat these expressions of affection and I did so.

Therapist: How?

Mr. Jones: Oh, anytime mother would kiss or hug me or take my hand I'd hold my participation to a minimum.

Therapist: Was that because you wanted to or because you knew that you would please your wife?

Mr. Jones: I can't separate them. I'm afraid I've run out of recollections at this time.

Note the clear statement of his reluctance to continue on this theme, which was obviously very disturbing to him. However, it took only a slight nudge to get him to continue, at which time his association related to his obsessional ideas, tying them directly to the problems and conflicts with his mother.

Therapist: Just say whatever comes to mind.

Mr. Jones: Well, I've felt extremely troubled about the thoughts that I had in the fall of 1950. I finally told my wife about them. I had refrained from telling her, since they were so unpleasant and repugnant to me. I thought they would frighten her. When I finally did tell her it was on the day that we had a most unpleasant argument, when I brought up the subject of divorce. It was about a month after that that I started my visits to the psychiatrist. I learned that I had been identifying my wife with my parents during the time that I found I disliked my superior intensely. I thought that he didn't assign tasks to me properly and that he ought to give me proper recognition. In some mysterious way these feelings of resentment that I had towards him transferred themselves onto my wife and I began to feel the same hostile feelings about her I had toward him.

It later became clear that his boss and his mother stirred up similar resentments and antagonisms in areas related to authority, acceptance, and the like.

Therapist: What do you mean, "mysterious way"?

Mr. Jones: Because it was something that was unexpected by me or unknown to me until I later realized it.

Therapist: Yes, but when you say "mysterious," you imply something kind of magical or mystical, as if the feelings you had toward your superior were the same feelings you had toward your wife. Isn't it possible that they may have come from the same source?

Mr. Jones: It's not only possible, it's true.

Therapist: Well, we should give some thought to this. Do you have the same feeling of being under her thumb as you have about being under your boss's thumb?

Mr. Jones: Well, I felt that I had to please her in everything I did and that she was critical and disagreeable. The boss was always that kind of person who was jealous of a subordinate accomplishing anything or receiving any recognition. I relate this attitude toward the feeling I had about my parents as a child and adolescent, that I had to please them.

Therapist: Was there anything else that gave you the feeling of being under your wife's thumb aside from the difficulty in pleasing her?

Mr. Jones: Well, I felt at that time that she was placing herself in the position of being the authority to approve or to disapprove things I wanted to do.

Therapist: She had the final O.K., so to speak.

Mr. Jones: So it seemed to me then. It doesn't anymore. She has since told me that she felt substantially the same way about me; she felt rejected and unwanted. She felt like a piece of baggage that I was directing around and that she had no opportunity to express her wishes.

DEVELOPMENT OF THE TRANSFERENCE

The preceding exchange, which occurred in the last 15 minutes of the session, was obviously very significant. It took place when I encouraged him to explore his mother's opposition to his marriage and their relationship to each other. The existence of oedipal difficulties and transferential distortions of being bound to the unreasoning authority of maternal involvements surfaced very clearly. Yet it was still all intellectual and verbal, and in spite of the clarity of his understanding, it had only a minimal effect in liberating him from his compulsive tendencies to please. The exchange also illuminated the nature of our relationship and the expectation that he would resist and be angered by the inevitability of his viewing me, the therapist, as an authority and a manager in his life.

It might seem unusual that such profound insights can come so early in the therapeutic work. In the treatment of the obsessional this is frequently the case. Often the meaning and significance of the compulsion or obsession are apparent to the person even before the individual comes to a therapist, yet the knowledge does not enable him to change his behavior at all. It is in these instances that we note the dichotomy between knowledge and doing and the inability to overcome compulsive tendencies because the deeper, underlying, out-of-awareness conflicts and ambivalences are not understood. We will need to draw this to patients' attention repeatedly, to illuminate other disguised feelings and attitudes. The patient needs to be encouraged to probe into the deeper attitudes and feelings which trigger the compulsive symptoms.

It should also be noted that in the beginning hours of therapy the technique is geared to eliciting and illuminating data instead of making formal interpretations of the data that are revealed. Premature formulations can freeze antagonistic responses and fortify the rigidities of the already rigid and untrusting obsessional patient. The patient should be supplied with enough convincing data to enable him to arrive at his own formulation and interpretation, since, in his requirement to know everything, he will resist any knowledge from the outside and will be reluctant to accept a new thought or understanding from anyone else. It must originate in him; even when he does accept the therapist's formulation he will, at a later date, present it as his own discovery. He may either deny any understanding from others or glibly agree, in order to avoid open defiance or disapproval, while he may be covertly entertaining doubts or secret criticisms, which prevent him from using the understanding profitably.

Comments and interpretations therefore must be made in such a way that the patient will not feel coerced, intimidated, or humiliated. Although it is almost impossible to prevent the patient from feeling criticized, we must try to present our views in a way that will minimize this reaction.

During the following interview, Mr. Jones described feelings of helplessness when his wife was ill. Her deficiencies made him feel anxious and uneasy, since he demanded the same perfectionistic, superhuman qualities that he required of himself. This recognition led him to extremely interesting recollections about his compulsion to please his parents and his need to be with them all the time. He recalled his mother's perfectionistic, overly optimistic tendency to paint all her family in glowing colors, denying all evidence of strife and disorder. Yet at the same time she was critical of him, derogating him and demanding of him the same hypocritical behavior she engaged in.

Mr. Jones: I just recalled the compulsion that I had to please my parents. My mother never wanted the neighbors to know anything about our friends, relatives, my father's business. My wife has noticed the same attitude — that for my mother, life is just a perfect path of roses, and whenever anything comes up in a discussion that would mar that illusion she immediately changes the subject.

Therapist: Never had any complaints, never had any criticism?

Mr. Jones: That's almost correct. She never had any criticisms for anyone that she liked, but was very critical of those she disliked ... The situation gets more muddled up in my memory the longer I talk about it. When I was about seven or eight I remember several times one of my teachers reprimanded me for having a bragging attitude. My mother used to tell me that I shouldn't talk that way, that it was wrong to hurt people's feelings by telling them that I was better than they were.

Therapist: How did you react to this?

Mr. Jones: Well, I ... I felt confused about it but I did follow it. After I had grown up and left home I always thought that my childhood was very happy. I never remembered having had any feelings of resentment or anger towards my folks. My mother often made the statement to both my sister and me that we were an ideal family, ... we were happy in each other's company, wanted to stay home.

It became clear that his mother had severe obsessional problems which led her to make excessive demands on Mr. Jones throughout his growing years. It was just such extreme demands for exceptional performances at all levels of functioning that initiated and organized his obsessive difficulties in the earliest years, which exploded into obsessive thoughts about killing his wife in later years.

DISTORTION OF RECOLLECTIONS

The capacity to distort recollections as well as the overriding need to idealize one's past both in positive and negative terms is a well-known obsessional problem first described by Freud. As mentioned previously, the obsessional's tendency to distort the past produced the crisis in Freud's theorizing that ultimately resulted in his greatest discovery. On the basis of the accounts of his obsessional patients he realized that their recollections were fantasies rather than real events and discovered the influence of the imagination on an individual's behavior.

Mr. Jones: When I was about eleven years old my mother reprimanded me for being flippant. However, she seemed to agree with me. It was the only time that she took my side. It seemed that any time I had an argument she sided with the other person.

Therapist: On the whole your recollection is that she usually found you at fault?

Mr. Jones: Yes ... I have a vague memory of having asked her one time why she never took my part.

Having noted his mother's hypocritical and double-dealing attitude, I pursued an alternative issue at this point, instead of relating her behavior to his. This is a key issue and I presume I was waiting for enough data to document this point without his being able to quibble or qualify it. This is especially relevant with an interpretation made to an obsessional patient, however obvious or clear-cut it may be.

The picture of an obsessional mother who had perfectionistic demands and expected her children to be always pleasant, uncritical, and free of anger or irritation while she could be critical and derogatory was a significant backdrop to Mr. Jones's early need to be perfect and to deny or fail to identify feelings or attitudes that would produce negative reactions in others. The requirement to control his feelings and reactions were well installed in his early years.

Necessity for Persistent Interpretation

The next three sessions were very illuminating about the many elements of the obsessional process. On one occasion, my persistence in pursuing his associations led to a mass of detail about his sexual development. He described himself as a schoolboy who was unaggressive, shy, uneasy, and vain. However, he was also the butt of taunts and jokes because of his flapping ears, which were later operated on. He was concerned about his capacities for displacement, when he would focus on unimportant matters as a way of dealing with the deep concerns that he was having at the time (an example of classical obsessional displacement).

Mr. Jones: I can't seem to stop thinking about one thing in order to concentrate on another, and the diversion of attention is pretty serious. In fact, there is a complete lapse of attention, perhaps for a few minutes, when I come back and realize that I haven't observed what was going on in that short interval. This would happen when I was at school, and, in fact, other kids would talk about me as if I was a dreamer and out of it.

He felt isolated at school and his parents could not comprehend his dilemma. In his yearbook the class rhyme about him was that "he dreams all day and what he dreams he doesn't say." While he felt this to be very critical, his parents tried to tell him that actually it was complimentary because inventors and philosophers were also daydreamers. He was quite convinced that his parents were not aware of what he was trying to tell them, and the tendency to be diverted persisted. When he was invited to join his friends after school, he would think of some excuse to avoid a direct confrontation with his peers. This recollection led him to describe an operation on his ear.

Mr. Jones: A few times when the boys asked me to join them I would find excuses. I usually found studying very easy and my actual schoolwork enjoyable. I had a plastic operation on my ears when I was about nine; when I returned to school a boy twisted my ear and it started bleeding. I became very angry, but I couldn't say anything to him and I wanted to hit him but I couldn't do that either.

He described his ear operation and a tonsillectomy in an interesting distorted recollection.

Mr. Jones: That's the year, eight or nine, when I was in the hospital — twice for tonsil operations, as well as for the plastic operation. I'm wrong about my age; it wasn't nine — it was ten, because I remember the night my father brought me home. I had been there during the summer and my sister was then eight months old. She saw my head all bandaged and began to laugh hysterically for about half an hour.

Therapist: At eight months? And you thought she was laughing at you?

Mr. Jones: Well, I knew she was laughing about something about it that struck her funny, seeing me with a white bandage around my head.

Therapist: And the family noted that an eight-month-old baby was laughing hysterically?

Mr. Jones: Well, hysterically is not quite the correct word. Anyway, she laughed a great deal.

Therapist: This is what was told you?

Mr. Jones: No, I recall this.

Therapist: You recall?

Mr. Jones: Yes, I recollect her laughing.

Defensive Falsification of an Event

This instance throws considerable light on the memory recall process, which is a big issue in psychoanalytic reconstruction of an individual's early years. Mr. Jones recalls his eight-month-old sister laughing heartily over his bandaged head resulting from a plastic surgery operation on his ear. This is obviously a distortion or, at best, a post hoc reconstruction, in which the child attributes concepts and feelings to others that are derived from his own expectations rather than validated ideas about the other person. Mr. Jones was sensitive about his appearance and his relationships with others. The taunting of schoolmates and his expectations of being laughed at led him to recall his infant sister's reaction as one of hilarity, as if she were capable of such a complicated and mature emotional reaction. This is a serious charge against psychoanalytic reconstructions that presumes knowledge and cognitive capacity neurologically and experientially beyond an individual's capacity.

The only valid conclusion one can come to from the recollection regarding his sister is the sensitivity of the young Mr. Jones and his tendency to experience others as reflecting his thoughts and feelings. While his sister may have smiled or have been amused, she surely could not have reacted with a great belly laugh. This tendency can be considered referential and, when more fully developed and involving hostile or malevolent expectations, is labeled paranoid. Thus, much recall of the past, unless it is a true recall based on the cortical capacity for experiencing, conceptualizing, recording, and storing of an actual perception, is a reconstruction that grows out of present-day needs and interests as well as prejudices and defenses. This is the fallacy of reconstructions of events prior to ages five to six.

Therapist: How did you feel about the laughing?

Mr. Jones: I think I was amused by it. My mother had been in the same hospital seven months before when my sister was born and I felt bad during the time she was in the hospital. I couldn't go to see her and I couldn't accompany my father because they didn't allow children. My feelings were hurt because when she [my sister] came home she was put into my bed. I don't know if it's common for children to feel jealous or neglected when a younger brother or sister enters the family. I don't remember any other incident in which I felt my sister interfered with my place in the family. I do recall this one. The bed was a crib which I slept in since I was a baby and was outgrowing anyway.

His infantilization by his mother and aunt and his unique position in the family were threatened by the birth of a sister when he was nine years old. His screen memory of his eight-month-old sister laughing at him may be accounted for by his anger at her at this time. This recall led to a spontaneous review of Mr. Jones's sexual history.

Therapist: You were moved permanently?

Mr. Jones: Yes. From then until I was ... for about two years after that I slept with my aunt, who was livng with us until we moved to our new house, at which time I got a bed of my own.

Therapist: You slept in a crib until you were nine?

Mr. Jones: Yes.

Therapist: The sides and ...

Mr. Jones: No, the sides were put down. It was a kind of metal bed with sliding sides which could be raised for a small baby and lowered for an older child.

Therapist: Was it in a separate room?

Mr. Jones: No, it was in the same bedroom with my mother and father. My aunt had a separate room.

Therapist: Until you were nine you slept in the same bedroom with your parents?

Mr. Jones: During this time that I slept with my aunt I remember one occasion on which a friend of hers stayed overnight. She slept in the same bed, too. I think that I slept . . . between them. In the morning I asked her to roll over and lay on top of me.

Therapist: Your aunt, or the friend?

Mr. Jones: The friend. Why, I don't know.

Therapist: Well, what happened, did she?

Mr. Jones: I can't remember whether she did. It seems to me that she protested for a while and then she did.

Therapist: You say you don't know why you wanted her to do that?

Mr. Jones: No, I don't.

Therapist: No idea?

Mr. Jones: No. It's rather embarrassing to me to . . . tell about it.

Therapist: What is embarrassing about such an incident?

Mr. Jones: It seems embarrassing for a child to . . . tell about it.

Therapist: What is embarrassing about such an incident?

Mr. Jones: It seems embarrassing for a child to — for a ten-year-old to have such a wish.

Therapist: What are you hesitant to say?

Mr. Jones: I'm not hesitant to say anything. I'm trying to — to remember the reason why I might . . . well, ask her to do this.

Therapist: By having such a wish, you meant there's something sexual in this, didn't you?

Mr. Jones: I suppose so. Oh, nothing happened, of course!

Therapist: Why are you so hesitant to say that it was a sexual sort of play. That's what you had in mind, wasn't it?

Mr. Jones: Yes, it is.

Therapist: Uh-huh.

Mr. Jones: It's just, it always seemed odd to me . . . at that age . . . that at that age that I had any ideas of a sexual nature.

Therapist: Yeah, but I wondered why you would be hesitant in saying this here, when you certainly had it in mind. You kept calling it a wish.

Mr. Jones: Uh-huh, yes.

OVERCOMING RESISTANCES TO RECALL

Note how difficult the communication can become in the context of considerable anxiety in the patient, as in the preceding exchange. My prodding and persistence was, I believe, necessary. Otherwise, the patient would have proceeded to relate the sexual elements and avoid the awareness of what actually occurred at that time. Such active prodding is essential at times in dealing with the obsessional patient, who is controlled, reserved, and unwilling to face awkward and embarrassing situations.

Therapist: Why would you be hesitant even to say the word [sexual wish]?
Mr. Jones: It embarrasses me.
Therapist: To say the word?
Mr. Jones: Yeah.
Therapist: Sexual wish.
Mr. Jones: Well, I certainly hadn't thought of the word sexual at this — at the present moment in this connection.
Therapist: You have at other times?
Mr. Jones: I guess so.
Therapist: Uh-huh.
Mr. Jones: ...
Therapist: You were beginning to develop ...
Mr. Jones: When I started high school, I was twelve and a half and the age of most of the other boys was fourteen. The school had a swimming pool and it was the first time I had been in a swimming pool. I was ... I think it was the first time that I had even seen large numbers of boys undressed ... without any clothing on. I noticed that most of them — that their sexual organs were more developed than mine. They had hair between their legs and I didn't at that time, at twelve. I was embarrassed about that.
Therapist: Were their penises bigger than yours?
Mr. Jones: Except for that, uh, factor, why I enjoyed the pool a whole lot. But I disliked this ... period between getting undressed in the locker room and actually getting into the water. One of the instructors would inspect the whole group of boys, and they lined up after taking their showers before going into the pool. I never, never liked that. I thought he would observe how underdeveloped I was in comparison with all the others I was lined up with.
Therapist: Do you remember whether you had an erection that morning that you asked your aunt's friend to lay on you?

I asked this question to pursue the notion that the obsessional disorders were in some way related to the problem of controlling unacceptable sexual impulses. However, it is immaterial whether or not an erection did occur, since the event obviously had sexual overtones and the presence or absence of an erection might have produced too much anxiety, causing a defensive reaction instead of a process of recall. It seems to me now that this did, indeed, occur, since Mr. Jones did not respond to my question but proceeded to discuss a related, less disturbing question about his masturbation. However, this exchange permitted us to direct our attention to his sexual development, which will be presented later.

Mr. Jones: I don't remember, no ... I remember masturbating at an age earlier than that. I remember it when I was still in this bed in the room with my parents, although not while they were in there.

Therapist: You never would while they were in there.

Mr. Jones: No. The first time ... that I was old enough — fourteen — to have an issue of semen during masturbation, I was frightened at the occurrence because I thought it was blood. My mother and I had gone to her parents' home in Pennsylvania for a few weeks, and they had no electricity in their home. I was upstairs in bed when this happened. I was, uh, very frightened that I thought it was blood, so I lay there in the bed wondering what to do about it. I wanted to get up and see whether it was blood or not but I couldn't do that without going downstairs and ... my mother and her sisters were down there talking. So after about twenty minutes I called out to my mother. She heard me and came upstairs and I told her that I woke up and thought I was bleeding. She had a lamp in her hand and she asked me to see it and of course there wasn't any blood.

Note the need to be explicit — not vague or obtuse.

Therapist: See what?

Mr. Jones: To see where — where the blood was. So I took the covers off and pulled my pajamas down and naturally there wasn't any blood. So she said I must have been dreaming. Well, by that time the semen had dried up and of course I felt this stuff ... substance on my pajamas, and I wondered whether my mother had noticed it or not. She gave no inkling to me, uh ... that she thought it was anything except a dream that I had.

Therapist: You had no previous acquaintance with the idea of semen at all?

Mr. Jones: No, I never heard of it. I didn't — didn't know what was happening.

SEXUAL HISTORY

He actually had had no idea of semen or ejaculation until that experience. At age fourteen, he had no knowledge of the sexual function, the apparatus, or the activity connected with it. This was confirmed in later data with regard to the total lack of preparation for his first sexual encounter. The first ejaculation in unsophisticated and unprepared adolescents can be very traumatic and at times be a triggering event for a schizophrenic breakdown. It implies loss of bodily control, extreme guilt about one's worthlessness, sinfulness, and the like.

Therapist: A completely novel experience?

Mr. Jones: Yes. I'm trying to think how old I was then and I — I can't.

Therapist: How old do you think that would be? About thirteen or fourteen — what do you think, approximately?

Mr. Jones: I think that is about right. My father explained sexual intercourse to me, and I don't remember whether this was before or after this occurrence. The way he explained it, I never understood it very well. He never mentioned anything about an erection or any other, uh ... circumstances that would go along with sexual intercourse.

Therapist: Well, then, what did he explain?

Mr. Jones: Well, he explained that the ... Well, he asked me if I had noticed that I was built differently from my sister and I had ... So he explained how — how children were born ... and he asked me if I remembered when my sister was born, and I didn't. I'd never noticed that my mother had been carrying her. I hadn't noticed the increase in her size or anything else. When she went to the hospital I thought she was sick, and I was amazed about the existence of the baby. He told me all about this when I was nine, but he never tied it together with having intercourse or an erection. When he attempted to explain about intercourse later on, he referred to the fact as if I knew how I was born when I didn't. He told me that when he took my mother to the hospital for an operation that they were close to the baby ward and that they picked out this baby. That's all I knew. I'm reminiscing now about what he told me about the baby just a week or so after the baby was born, right at that time.

Therapist: That was his story about how you had a baby?

Mr. Jones: That was his story then. Well, I'm getting this all confused. At the time the baby was born I had no idea that my mother was having a baby or even that women had babies. They saw this baby in the hospital and liked it and brought it home. So I got some jumbled idea later than that when he was telling me about sexual intercourse. He referred to my sister being born and asked me if I knew how she was born and I hadn't. Then he explained how the baby was conceived during sexual intercourse, by the penis being inserted into the opening of the woman, but he didn't tell me anything about erection or semen and I thought that it was urine at that time, that it was urine that ... passed between man and woman.

OBSESSIONAL INNOCENCE

The need to maintain an innocence and purity with regard to sex results in such egregious distortions in educating children into the ways of man. This situation unfortunately persists to this day and it is to the glory of man's resources and intelligence that only a few suffer psychic consequences of serious proportions while almost all of us have some minor sexual dysfunctions in our adult life.

It has been my conviction for some time and I have stated it as such in many of my earlier publications that the penis is a urogenital organ, not only a genital one. Consequently, a male who uses the penis only for urinary purposes for at least the first decade of life does not know, understand, or conceptualize its genital role until he learns about it through education, contact, or the physiological developments of sperm and ejaculation. Mr. Jones demonstrated this clearly in his statement; until sperm was present and even after his ejaculation, he did not know its relation to sex or conception until the education process informed him. Rather, he thought it was urine that passed, since that was the substance he knew and was familiar with until he learned otherwise.

Mr. Jones: During the time that I was in high school, I remember having erections quite frequently during the day and during school. I would have to walk with my hand in my pocket, and I was embarrassed that that happened. I suppose anyone would be.

Therapist: By this time, knowing what they were?

Mr. Jones: Well, I seemed to know, I figured that this was ... I was confused about it in some way...I knew that was what would occur whenever I saw any women or girl that looked beautiful or interesting. I seemed to have it tied up with the fact that it was the ... preliminary to intercourse, and I never did get the connection to that until I was about twenty-two years old, after I was in the army. ... I knew what intercourse was and I knew it was a prelude to conception but I didn't tie the intercourse in with erection.

FIRST DREAM: AGGRESSIVE TENDENCIES

Following the preceding interview the patient had a two-week assignment out of town, and upon his return, he was more concerned with some disagreements which he had had on his trip and his ability to be more aggressive about his disagreements. In fact, he said that he felt that he had handled himself much better than he had at any time. He felt very good about being assertive and not allowing others to push him around. He described in detail a situation where a disagreement made him feel that his authority was being questioned, and it made him very anxious.

Mr. Jones: Perhaps I'm sensitive about not being considered respectfully. However, I know that because of my slow reactions and poor memory that perhaps people do not fully respect me. I was angry when I felt they disparaged me. I felt unhappy because I couldn't say anything.

His concerns about his passivity led to an immediate association with his aggressive dream and his lack of assertiveness in sexual situations.

Mr. Jones: I had a dream this morning before I woke up and when I did wake up it was frightening and disturbing. I was looking at a magazine or a movie, and it suddenly came to life. The situation was that a group of criminals . . . some of them evidently had an abandoned house and they were seated around a table playing cards. It seems to me that when the dream commenced I was looking at a picture; there were about twenty of them in the room, seated at various tables. One by one they started shooting each other and killing each other. That went on for several minutes and then I woke up. One by one each of them pulled a gun and would shoot someone else. The killing was still going on when I woke up. That doesn't seem to have been part of the dream. As each one got shot I don't remember his falling down. I think they were all killed.
Therapist: Does this bring anything to mind? Can you associate anything with it?
Mr. Jones: Well, it brings to mind the obsessive thoughts that I had been troubled with about my wife that were uncomfortable to me. But not in any definite way. But it was vaguely related to that.

Clearly, the patient's dream was precipitated by the events on this trip where he felt that he had to withhold his anger and irritation in the face of disrespectful behavior of some colleagues. He was unable to respond to them at an open meeting where he felt it would be discourteous and improper, so he held it all in. And it is this analogy to his holding in, to his obsessive thoughts of killing his wife, that made his associations to this dream extremely significant. We went on to discuss this dream.

Therapist: What were your thoughts about it when you woke up?

Mr. Jones: I tried to think what might have prompted it. I felt apprehensive and tense. I seemed to be an observer in the dream. I guess I was also afraid that I might be shot, but I wasn't.

Therapist: It's not an unusual role for you to be an observer while emotions are being expressed all around you. And you stay out of it.

Mr. Jones: No, I guess it's not an unusual role. I know I stay out of discussions and arguments. It reminds me about a dream I had about a year and a half ago. People were committing suicide by jumping into a body of water off a high diving board. I was standing on the pier, observing. The magazine cover I was looking at also reminds me of an experience I had in California. At that time before beginning treatment I had an emotional disturbance. I was in a bookstore at a magazine counter, looking at the cover of a detective story magazine. All the women were depicted in revealing costumes in menacing attitudes of one kind or another. I became very nervous and started to tremble and could hardly breathe. I put the magazines back and gradually calmed down. That was a wholly new experience for me.

Therapist: What disturbed you at that time?

Mr. Jones: Seemingly, the sexual implications in the way the women were depicted on the cover. Such provocative pictures have a morbid attraction for me. About that time whenever I could see pictures of an attractive woman I felt vaguely disturbed.

Therapist: Do you mean you were sexually stimulated by looking at these attractive women?

Mr. Jones: No, not exactly. Well, maybe it was sexually stimulating, accompanied by a feeling of ... I don't seem to know what it did do. It seems to me it was accompanied by a feeling of being sexually stimulated accompanied by a feeling of inability to admit it. I often seem to have a feeling of wanting to speak and become acquainted with women, but I know it's socially unacceptable and it would be aggressive.

Therapist: It is clear that you have sexual feelings that you are very reluctant to admit even to yourself.

Mr. Jones: Yeah, that's a part of it. But there are other parts to it that I can't seem to express.

Therapist: A desire to get acquainted or the inability to do so.

Mr. Jones: Yes, that sounds pretty accurate. Seemingly, a wish for someone else to be aggressive. To make the first move is the fact in this situation.

At this point the whole question of his aggressive feelings and his being stimulated by the seductive, coarse female encouraged me to try to pursue whether there were ever feelings of this kind or whether the patient had ever been aggressive or had approached girls in an aggressive way.

Therapist: What is it about aggressive women that excites you? Do they stimulate you or allow you to express your angry feelings? Have you actually been in such a situation?

Mr. Jones: Well, I'll defer a specific answer for the time being. I feel as if I would rather relate another incident which would answer the questions more completely than a yes or no would. Before I was married I was in the company of other men in town on a weekend. I saw other men picking up women, but I was unable to start this myself. Of course, if I were introduced casually I could continue the acquaintance, but I just didn't find it possible to take the initiative. After several such cases and meeting several girls and hearing my friends bragging about their sexual experiences, I found it possible to persuade the girls to have intercourse with me.

Therapist: You had intercourse with several girls?

Mr. Jones: Yes. The first time it was embarrassing to me because I mentioned it to you on my last visit that I hadn't been able to connect the significance of an erection with intercourse. It seems impossible for me to say this thing, but I just never connected it. So on this first and many other experiences I had the experience of the erection on talking and being intimate with women, such as kissing, caressing, or what not. And on the instance when I proposed intercourse, I was unable to have an erection, and yet it didn't occur to me that it precluded sex. It was a ludicrous situation. The woman thought I was nuts, of course.

Therapist: What you mean is that you tried to get in?

Mr. Jones: Yes, of course. I was unable to, and after that happened I guess I finally figured out what that was all about. I was twenty-five. So with this new knowledge, I tried and it worked.

In fact, while Mr. Jones had sexual desires when he was away from his wife, he had not succumbed to any of them and had remained faithful throughout their marriage. However, his fidelity produced rewards, as expressed in this brief encounter:

Mr. Jones: Once in a while I feel tempted or inclined to have other relations, such as when I'm out of town for an extended time and I see and hear others in similar circumstances avail themselves of casual or local acquaintances. But the knowledge of the very strong feelings that my wife had about such occurrences has always deterred me. She said she would kill herself if I ever had anything to do with another woman.

Therapist: You said she would kill herself if you ever had anything to do with another woman; one might expect she would kill you.

Mr. Jones: Well, she said that, too. I had forgotten that.

Therapist: What are you thinking of?

Mr. Jones: I'm trying to clarify this particular point. It seems to me on two occasions she said it first one way and then the other ... so, at times, I had felt that manifesto to be an uncomfortable factor.

Therapist: You mean that you didn't like it?

Mr. Jones: I mean I didn't like it.

Therapist: But you took it.

Mr. Jones: Yes. It was a feeling of anger that my wife was never quite sure whether I had been faithful to her. At times when she would read some story or hear somebody talking or bragging about all the women they slept with, she sometimes inferred that she thought I probably did too. I used to get violently disturbed about that, about the fact that I felt I had been.

Therapist: About the fact that virtue was not its own reward?

Mr. Jones: Yes, that's it, exactly.

SEXUALITY IN OBSESSIONAL STATES

The innocence and ignorance about the sexual act was characteristic of Mr. Jones's personality structure. However, with minimal opportunities for learning he seemed to perform well. In the need to do a good job and be well thought of, the obsessional male often learns the techniques for adequate sex activity, and while he proceeds with a rigid scenario, he can nevertheless be mechanically effective. To avoid rejection, sexual arrangements may be made securely in advance, preventing spontaneous sexual encounters. Sex often is more like a business arrangement, routinized and properly executed but lacking in passion.

It is extraordinary how significant such handicaps in the sexual development process can be overcome in terms of acquiring sexual techniques. The role of sex and aggression in the etiology of obsessional states has been debated since Freud's first formulations about the instinct theory. Mr. Jones's sexual development is particularly noticeable in this regard, since his innocence and ignorance of sexuality persisted until he was twenty-five years old, at which time he had his first sexual experience. However, there were few sexual difficulties in his marriage apart from some distress occasioned by his wife's complaints about his unemotional approaches; overall, this was an area in his living that seemed relatively devoid of problems, conflicts, or neurotic defensive distortions. The overbearing, demanding and controlling tendencies manifested or at least experienced by Mr. Jones did not seem to interfere with their sexual activities.

Obsessional difficulties are not necessarily accompanied by sexual difficulties, since the perfectionistic tendencies of such individuals tend to develop competent performers sexually even though feelings may be absent. They do the job well, but it is generally too mechanistic and lacking in warm, lustful desires. At other times, anxiety about performance may cause premature ejaculation or anorgasm in the female. Mr. Jones had very few sexual complaints, even though he had a surprisingly limited understanding of sex. In view of his intellectual capacities and under- standing in his professional life, his lack of knowledge of interpersonal relationships at all levels was strikingly noticeable. Cognitive deficits are sometimes seen as the core of the obsessional processes and are used to explain the inability of the obsessional to put into practice some of his presumed understanding. However, I believe that it is not a matter of cognitive innocence but of emotional avoidance of human relationships and involvements, which reduces understanding and produces failure in human relationships.

In obsessional persons, there is almost no development in the arena of emotional interaction with other humans, since this aspect of human relationship is avoided and they have no ability to look at the problem. There is, in fact, a capacity to be diverted from it, as Mr. Jones tried to do in our work whenever his sex activity was being discussed. Since violence, destruction, and unacceptable social behavior can become identified and tied in with sex, one can readily understand how a sadistic orientation toward sex or an exaggerated interest in violence in order to be sexually stimulated could occur out of a situation like this. In this regard Mr. Jones's dreams were especially interesting in that violence and destruction became involved with others, so that the safest thing was to be an onlooker or an observer who is uninvolved. As indicated, the obsessional characterological problem is in the failure to become committed because of excessive fears and concerns and the dangers implied in commitment, and the absence of such commitment explains a good deal of obsessional behavior.

ROLE OF AGGRESSIVENESS

Mr. Jones's need to be liked by everyone prevented him from fully asserting himself and taking on adult responsibility for managing and directing his life's plans. While his job required that he be a strong authority, this conflicted with his desire for universal approval. By using the rules to strengthen any position he took and living "by the book," he placed the responsibility for a decision on others, the rules, or the higher authorities over which he had no control. In succeeding interviews he gained insights into this behavior. These insights were reinforced and illuminated many times in his relationship with his mother, with whom he experienced feelings of helplessness and impotence. In the following dialogue, note the typical obtuse verbal elaborations that confuse the meaning and distort what he was trying to say — that his feelings of weakness and ineptness required constant support from outside authorities to buttress his position:

Mr. Jones: I've tried to do some mental research on this topic we were discussing on Wednesday about the reliance on some legal or regulatory authority, feeling almost like a compulsion to cite that type of authority to support any position that I might take. I don't think that the explanation is that of being afraid of being turned down, because I do use it in the context of supporting a request. Perhaps it is a way of avoiding the necessity for exerting an expression or appearance of aggressiveness. It occurred to me that other people would support their request, their stands, with mere declarations of that's that, what they wanted, and they augment that expression by various personal reasons why they needed or why they wanted something. And I consciously noted the dissimilarity between that usual or common trend of thinking and my own, which was to make a positive effort not to do that, not to base my wishes on personal convenience but on some privilege or right spelled out in the regulations.

Therapist: You mean you could never rely on your status and always had to defend it? One doesn't always have to keep proving that one has a right to do something which is within his authority.

Mr. Jones: I guess that is so. Often the stance that I would take would be questioned and, therefore, I always wanted the reinforcement of authority. In dealing with personal problems of that type mere reliance on status alone sometimes would not be appropriate, but I carried that line of reasoning even into situations where the status alone, as you say, would probably have handled it. Before I discuss their particular problem with them at all, I would look the matter up in the regulations or any other appropriate authority.

Therapist: Could you elaborate on that?

Mr. Jones: I've noticed that employees don't like it when the bosses aren't able to make a decision or tend to postpone one. If it were necessary for me to discuss some question with two or more people, each of whom had opposite ideas, I sometimes agree with each one of them — seemingly not wanting either of them to be able to cite me as opposing them.

Therapist: You wanted to avoid the possibility of each one thinking that you opposed them. Wouldn't you call that appeasement?

Mr. Jones: I always made an attempt to reconcile them. I'm just not sure exactly why I was so painstakingly careful about always wanting to rely on a regulatory authority.

Therapist: Well, speculate about it.

Mr. Jones: Well, it avoided a necessity for justification. And at that time I didn't like it when people would make a request to me supported only by the fact that they wanted something. I thought I was refraining from this objectionable quality by my always being able to be objective and support my position with some published authority. I recognize that I don't want to continue relying merely on what has already been done, and to make my own determinations. Looking at your diploma I often meant to ask you if you weren't a New Yorker. I thought that your accent reminded me somewhat of a New York accent and yet I think you have a New England accent, too.

At this juncture it is obvious that the patient was getting increasingly anxious and restless, and then he suddenly commented on a matter that he has been aware of for some time. The change of subject is a typical obsessional distracting device in the face of growing anxiety. It has also been called *substitution* or *intrusion*, when unrelated issues are introduced without conscious intent to draw the focus away from disturbing ideas. Unless the therapist is aware of this maneuver, the subject change can move the focus of inquiry away from the significant — in this instance, the growing awareness of the patient's tendency to avoid being decisive or committed or taking a stand for fear of being wrong, criticized, disapproved of, and the like. This tendency must be exposed since it is the background for feeling weak and helpless, which demands further obsessional devices that may be more extreme and severely incapacitating.

On the occasion just examined, I allowed Mr. Jones's distraction to go far enough to follow some of his unconscious associations and to tie it up with his overriding concern for status and acceptance from the world about him.

Therapist: People have a distorted notion of the New England accent.

Mr. Jones: Yes. I do not have a pronounced accent in my own speech. In fact, when I became aware of there being such a prevalent, critical attitude towards areas in our country, I felt glad that I don't have any more accent.

Therapist: So like your support with regulations, you're concerned how you would look to other people.

Even though there has been a change of subject, he was still talking about his concern with how he looked to other people. I drew this to his attention, but he moved onto the matter of his concern about always being correct and unassailable.

Mr. Jones: Yes, in both cases that was so. I think also another reason why I was so anxious to quote regulations was to impress on people the finality of what I said, hoping that there wouldn't be an argument on it. I was very conscious of how I would look to others and anxious for them to believe what I said was right.

Therapist: Or to say it another way, to avoid the possibility of their thinking you were wrong, maybe?

COUNTERTRANSFERENCE: THE THERAPIST'S OBSESSIONAL QUALITIES

My response was unfortunate in that it was evidence of *my* obsessional behavior in attempting to be precise and intellectual. What followed was essentially a quibble that the patient quickly identified. My notes at that time do not reveal that I had become aware of my intellectualizing, and Mr. Jones needed the reassurance of being right.

Mr. Jones: Well, isn't that the same thing?

Therapist: Well, not quite the same thing because you have been emphasizing your desire to avoid the argument, to avoid questions or doubts about what you say and to avoid any possibility of their having a comeback.

Mr. Jones: Exactly.

Therapist: And they would have a comeback if there were any question that you might be wrong. There's no comeback if you are right.

Mr. Jones: I was convinced of the safety of my position if I could cite adequate authority.

Therapist: So in many incidents you were inclined to deal with people by the book, not as person to person.

Mr. Jones: I think so.

Therapist: Well, let's hear more about that.

The flow of the session allowed me to get to the *real* issue — that is, Mr. Jones's greater concern for things than for people and the dehumanizing aspects of the compulsive concerns for security, safety, and status. Such a concern allows for the exposure of the self-righteous rigidity of the obsessional's notions of his own purity of motives in his living.

Mr. Jones: Well, the only thing I can think of in explanation for that is I thought it foolish of people to not support their wishes by anything other than the fact that they wanted it that way. And I thought to myself, my way is better because I can quote from authority.

Therapist: Better in what sense?

Mr. Jones: Well, I didn't think past that fact. But I suppose I thought that was such a desirable method because it was an aid in enforcing or bringing about what I wanted.

Therapist: Do you mean that you have disrespect for people who asked for what they wanted for some emotional reasons?

Mr. Jones: Well, yes. .... I recall having a verbal altercation when I felt rather good that I won because I had all these regulatory guides to support me.

Therapist: It must have happened quite often though, that, in spite of your being right, people were annoyed and antagonized.

Mr. Jones: Well, yes ... I wasn't distressed for long over that if I had some valid authority to rely on. Thinking about it now I know it's not wrong or undesirable to enforce the existing policy and yet it seems to me that maybe I overdid it. It wasn't a feeling of unimportance, it was a feeling of wanting to refrain from appearing aggressive. .... I didn't object to being aggressive, however, provided I could cite support for it.

Therapist: Uh huh.

Mr. Jones: It's complicated.

Therapist: How so? Let's hear.

Mr. Jones: In the sense of thinking that there must have been something wrong in this attitude that I had.

Therapist: Uh huh.

Mr. Jones: And yet also realizing ...there was no other way. That's what I'm confused about right now.

Therapist: You're raising the question now whether being right is always the most important thing; you're not so sure at the moment.

Mr. Jones: I always thought it was; I guess it isn't.

Therapist: Perhaps there is more in dealing with people than just the question of right and wrong.

Mr. Jones: I guess I used to think that there must be some tailor-made or available logic or solution to handle anything. And I know that there isn't. Well, I can't think ... of anything more on the subject.

Therapist: Is it disappointing or discouraging to find that out?

Mr. Jones: No, no. It isn't disappointing or discouraging ... It's rather disappointing that it took me so long to find it out.

DEVELOPING INSIGHTS AND
CORRECTING DISTORTIONS

The preceding exchange represents a rather characteristic, self-derogatory response to developing insight. Mr. Jones could not take pride in the understanding gained but berated himself for not recognizing it sooner. One must "know it all," or else be righteously critical in admitting one's deficiencies. To overcome this pattern, it is necessary to reiterate the benefits of minor achievements and minimal gains in the long, hard struggle to change one's pattern of responding. To discover that it is more fulfilling as a human being to experience feelings and the warmth of human interactions than to be right and live by the book is a step requiring enough humility to acknowledge the needs of dependent relationships in one's existence.

The theme of Mr. Jones's need to be right and to assert his needs only when he was certain was reinforced in the interview which took place several days later. Note that what he had great difficulty in accepting at the time it had been proposed was now presented as conviction that he arrived at through his own recall and rumination. This is a regular event in the therapy of the obsessional, whose first response to a new idea is to reject it — then to accept it with doubts and reservations and many qualifications, thereby preserving the illusion of intellectual honesty and independence. Later on, if the insights are valid, they will be presented by the patient as a new discovery, thus supporting his omniscience and sense of perfection. In this instance, Mr. Jones opened the session as if there had been no interval since the last session:

Mr. Jones: I tended to refrain from requests merely because of being afraid of being turned down and therefore avoided having to be aggressive or assertive about such matters. Usually in making any applications or requests if I had a lot of authority or justification on my side so that I didn't expect to meet any resistance, I would make them. Immediately after I left here the last time I was waiting for a bus; a possible explanation occurred to me for the attitude of living by the book. I think it was there all the time that I was growing up — the fact that I had so little contact or relationship with other children of my own age.

Therapist: How would that account for it?

Mr. Jones: I think that accounts for it in this way: Children playing together with others their own age over many years acquire a give-and-take spirit. And there was a sort of vacuum in my life of such give and take. There were no contacts or sports or extracurricular activities after school, and what little that there was, was limited to playing with girls who were friends of the family.

Therapist: So you are saying you never learned to give and take in the sense that with the girls you always won, you always had your way, you never had to fight.

Mr. Jones: I guess so — I guess it was easier that way. I hadn't thought of it exactly that way, but that is true.

Therapist: What else comes to mind in this connection?

Mr. Jones: Well, nothing right at the moment. . . . It seems to explain also the difficulty I experienced when my wife became ill and didn't feel like going swimming and partying. I reacted to it at that time that she was being obstinate, and my attitude was to coax and persuade her to go, ignoring the fact that she felt ill. She occasionally tearfully inquired why I couldn't be more understanding. Well, I didn't understand that . . . and the situation got worse until two years ago [in 1950] when I thought that she was trying to be the boss.

Therapist: Was that necessarily wrong? I mean your view of this.

THERAPEUTIC DILEMMAS: WHICH ROAD TO TAKE?

Rather than support a significant awareness of Mr. Jones's egocentric and somewhat paranoid view of his behavior at this time, I chose to take a stand that questioned his willingness to feel guilty and self-recriminatory, as if he were all wrong now, when before he was entirely right. It was important for him to see and avoid the extremes of reaction which often lack true conviction and sustained insight in order to bring about a more realistic awareness of the situation. It was important to emphasize his inability to empathize or become aware of another person's needs because of his narcissistic preoccupation with his desires and an unquestioned conviction of his correctness. Whether that was an appropriate response, rather than two or three others that could have been made, is uncertain. It does illustrate the therapist's dilemma in deciding which course to follow — whether to focus on the revelation of the patient who is recognizing his egocentric, selfish distortions that tend to affirm his sense of worthlessness or to minimize the effect of such revelations by supporting the positive elements in the patient's growing honesty with himself while recognizing some realities in his reaction at the time it occurs.

Mr. Jones: Yes, I think it was wrong because she didn't feel well. I don't know why I didn't realize it. I see now that probably the reason was that I didn't have a grasp of the fact that people's wants are often based on their feelings, their likes and dislikes, while mine are always based on some rule or authority.

Therapist: This is what we talked about on Monday — that you have a tendency to live by the book.

Mr. Jones: That's the point I'm getting at here. I do feel that I have a much better understanding of that subject. After I became aware and did feel more comfortable in that respect, I wondered why my understanding was so long delayed on it. It seems to me that there is a possible explanation in my lack of unrestricted association with boys my own age at the time I was growing up.

Therapist: How does that do it?

While it should be obvious to Mr. Jones, since he explained it earlier, it is crucial to encourage the patient to expand on his conception of the relationship of early experience to later pathological developments. Not only does it expand the patient's psychodynamic skills and introspective capacities, but it also adds conviction to his ability to accept and integrate the understanding. In addition, it is crucial, whenever possible, to allow the obsessional to develop such insight for himself, thereby avoiding a tussle over who is in charge and decreasing the resistances to being told something he feels he ought to know. However, this does not imply that the therapist should not suggest or amplify insights when he avoids or misses the point.

Mr. Jones: Well, in my case I did not have regular play contacts with other boys my own age. I suppose I would have learned to assert my feelings, as others were also doing the same thing. There is a certain amount of give and take or respect for the feelings of others and being able to push for your own wishes. I didn't get much of an understanding about the wants of others and neither did I learn to be aggressive about my own, as my dealings were principally with my parents rather than with boys my own age. Do you think that's a difficult or an unlikely explanation?

Therapist: No, I don't think that the explanation is unlikely; I want to avoid oversimplifying something that's considerably complex. I'm sure that what you describe had something to do with it.

In trying to avoid an inclination toward the easy answer and magical solution through omniscient intellectual capacity, I risked belittling and minimizing what was truly a valid observation. However, I believe I rescued this threat by not deprecating Mr. Jones's insight, but, rather, remarking on the complex and multiple source of his behavior.

Mr. Jones: It certainly is complex and I have been thinking about this for the last couple of days.

Therapist: There is more involved in your tendency to overlook the needs of others in a give-and-take relationship. You seem to block out awareness of what other people's needs are. I presume that still happens today, and we need to look into that in considerable detail. For example, when you are presenting your point of view by the book, you are not seeing the other fellow's point of view, which has to do with his feelings, separate from the book.

I was trying to get beyond the need to compromise and into his incapacity to become aware of the other person as a human being in his own right, with his own desires, needs, and weaknesses.

Mr. Jones: Well, I tend to think of someone else's view as not being supported by authority and thus unimportant. I didn't realize that it was an attitude; that was the only way I knew of acting.

Therapist: I still don't get the distinction that you just made.

Mr. Jones: I'm trying to make the distinction between overlooking the needs of others and not being aware of them. It seems to be the same, or maybe I misunderstood you.

COUNTERTRANSFERENCE IMPEDIMENTS

Here the therapist's obsessional need for preciseness becomes confusing to the patient and is not essential to the achievement of insight.

Therapist: I wanted to try to avoid finding pat answers to the problem which we have to solve. Your difficulty of not being aware of the other person isn't what it's all about. You do have difficulty presenting your point of view and sensing or becoming aware of what is going on in the other person's mind. When you were a child you got everything fulfilled, and we could understand that it wouldn't be necessary to consider the needs of others. Nowadays that doesn't happen.

I had added nothing to what had already been clarified, and it was therefore best left unsaid. One can see that the temptation to explain or clarify leads to the obsessional double-talk, since it is tinged with anxiety or concern to do the right thing. This is as widespread among therapists as in their patients and usually it is easier to spot in others than in oneself.

Mr. Jones: Right. Well, I was saying that having very little contact with other kids probably was the background for my lack of realization of others' needs, and of experiences in dealing with people on an equal basis. I want to be aggressive and yet I have so little experience in being or feeling that way. I didn't act that way when I was growing up since I didn't have any contacts in which there was any need for it. I tried it out occasionally on my parents or my aunts, and it didn't work.

REGRESSIVE RECALL

After the preceding session, Mr. Jones left for a two-week business trip. During this time he thought about his inability to express his feelings of rage and helplessness. The following session demonstrated many tactics which needed to be used to encourage the expression of these feelings. After a brief statement about his inability to express himself adequately on his trip and the leadership being taken away from him by a more assertive inferior, he recalled an incident when he was thirteen:

Mr. Jones: I find myself thinking of something that happened, maybe an hour ago, which reminds me of an incident that happened when I was thirteen years old, my first day or so in high school. In the gymnasium, they had two different kinds of locker rooms, a small kind and one wardrobe-size locker. The small one had locks, but I didn't understand the system about the large locker having to be kept open for others. When my gym period was over, I put my gym clothes in the big locker and put the lock on it. The next day I found that my lock had been clipped off. The gym instructor was surly and disagreeable and bawled me out for the inconvenience that was caused by my lock. I felt very angry and wanted to protest about the loss of my lock, but I wasn't able to think of anything to say. I had feelings similar to the ones that I have now — feeling a difficulty in expressing my thoughts properly.

Therapist: Which thoughts? What did you feel at the time?

Mr. Jones: Well, I felt outraged at this abrupt treatment, plus being bawled out in the bargain.

Therapist: So you couldn't express your anger and outrage?

Mr. Jones: ... Yes. I couldn't express my anger. I wasn't asked to take my lock off, and I couldn't ... express any comeback at the reprimand I received.

Therapist: How would you describe your feelings at that time? You say you were outraged.

EXPRESSION OF AFFECT

Since Mr. Jones showed no inclination to express his indignation during our session, I tried to resurrect the original situation and to encourage his expression by suggesting how unfair and outrageous the gym teacher was. I might have asked him to reenact the scene in a charade. This might get the fullness of Mr. Jones's feelings in the open and minimize his intellectualizations, which were substituted for the rich potential of an emotional reenactment. It is more convincing and therapeutically valuable to be able to demonstrate the passion of his anger as well as his strong defenses, instead of recognizing his feelings only from the substitutional and obsessional devices he uses to cover them. This could then be used to make an analogy with his behavior in the present.

Mr. Jones: Well, I felt angry and confused at not being able to protest about it.

Therapist: So in addition to your outrage, you felt helpless?

Mr. Jones: Yes ... exactly ... and ... and embarrassed at my helplessness.

Here we have a clear formulation of the universality of the obsessional defenses. They are manifested not only in extreme emotional states but also in an atmosphere of helplessness, which puts the individual entirely out of control with regard to his feelings and potential effect on others. The obsessional can only visualize the dangerous consequences and therefore must either substitute or displace such feelings by other, less dangerous thoughts (obsessions) or acts (compulsive rituals).

Therapist: Is this unfamiliar to you. Is it something that you can identify as happening often?

Mr. Jones: It happens often, currently. . . . A feeling that my reactions and responses are inadequate and . . . slow.

Therapist: That's very different from outrage or furious helplessness, isn't it?

Mr. Jones: Well, they're . . . very different situations. . . . I have this very slow, inadequate reaction to situations where no outrage or anger is involved.

Therapist: Yeah, but you said it happened often currently. I'm curious as to where it happens currently and to hear some examples.

Note the resistance to pursuing the issue of his anger and helplessness and his preference for investigating the inadequacy and slowness of his responses. While it was true, as he suggested, that they were different, the relationship between them was clear and unmistakable, particularly as they related to the extreme feelings of helplessness and anger which were the immediate precursors of his obsessional ideas about killing his wife.

RESISTANCE AND ITS RESOLUTION

Mr. Jones: Well, I was thinking of the slowness and inadequacy of the reaction rather than . . .

Therapist: Uh huh. Well, maybe they are the same. I only wanted to get it clear. Perhaps they are.

Here I was careful only to be suggestive and inquisitive instead of authoritative and insistent, in order to encourage his collaborative curiosity rather than stimulate his stubborn resistance.

Mr. Jones: No, I don't think they're the same because it isn't only when some hostility or anger or outrage is involved when I experience these slow, inadequate reactions and a feeling of distress because of them. It happens in those situations, too, where it involves anger or hostility or any sort of aggressiveness but it's not limited to that. It occurs in the most academic or technical discussions.

Therapist: Where you think there is no feeling involved.

Mr. Jones: Yes, I think that could be said.

Therapist: Do any specific instances come to mind?

Mr. Jones: Well, I think of a conversation I had with one of my colleagues. He was talking about a conversation he had had with an importer, and I asked a few questions about it, and then, after a while I didn't know what he was saying. No feeling of anger was involved there. After it happens I'm angry at myself for being that way.

It is apparent here that his free associations moved him toward an incident that documented the very issue he had just denied, that in his anger at a situation he felt helpless to deal with it. Note how I attempted to deal with it by drawing this to his attention, which brings us directly to his wife and his problems of control:

Therapist: It seems to me that in both instances you got angry when you felt helpless. What do you think?

Mr. Jones: Over the weekend I took a trip to see my wife's folks. When I got on the train, no seats were available. After a few miles I noticed several passengers who were obviously railroad employees and I thought I remembered some prohibition against railroad employees occupying seats when passengers had to stand. I wanted to point that out to the conductor, but I just had to refrain from doing it.

Therapist: Why?

Mr. Jones: I wasn't sure ... positive that I was right. It would make an unfavorable scene if an issue were made of it. I thought of writing a letter to the railway company about it, and I told my wife about it. I told her I was going to write and she urged me not to. She said it was not worth making an issue out of it.

Shades of his mother's reaction to his concern about being called sissy by his friends and the gym locker incident! However, I refrained from mentioning it here, so as not to divert his train of thought. I made a note of it, however, at the time, to be used on a more suitable occasion, in order to help him recognize his transference distortion.

Mr. Jones: I did decide at that time not to write — however, not because of her persuasion. What decided me not to was that if I was going to make an issue of it at all, I should have done so in person at the time, rather than taking refuge in writing about it.

Therapist: This is, in a sense, an instance of your outraged feeling, isn't it?

Mr. Jones: Yes.

Therapist: And feeling helpless to do anything at the time?

Mr. Jones: Well, maybe it does go back to my old habit of relying on some — some published regulation or authority. But what disturbs me is not the occurrence of these instances but my helplessness in handling them.

This was a highly significant observation and I hoped to encourage him to pursue it further by not saying anything that might increase his helplessness during our session. My response of "uh huh," however, did not seem to work very well:

Therapist: Uh-huh.

Mr. Jones: I'm trying to think of some other incidents involving this feeling pushed around. I — I don't know whether I'm unusually sensitive to that or not. A person could well be sensitive to it and yet able to . . . protest or complain about the incidents when they happen. For me it's difficult and sometimes impossible. My wife tells me that . . . sometimes I get disturbed and make issues of things that aren't worth it and that in other cases she thinks there are appropriate things to complain about which I don't.

Therapist: For example?

Mr. Jones: Well, when we bought a car. There was a continuous series of things going wrong with it. She wanted me to go to the dealer and take care of them. I was reluctant to do it. I felt incapable of taking the aggressive attitude that I wanted to. Yet on other occasions, she's told me that my attitude was unnecessarily aggressive. But about the car she was dissatisfied with my rather inconclusive efforts.

Therapist: She wasn't with you, was she?

Mr. Jones: Yes, we drove down together.

Therapist: Wanting you to do something that she couldn't achieve, huh?

Mr. Jones: Well, that was her purpose. I thought that was warranted enough in view of the circumstances — that is, the automobile in the family being more or less the husband's responsibility than the wife's. In fact, I was angry at her because of the excessive amount of interest she took in the car. I remember an occasion when a discussion got around to automobiles. She knew much more about cars than I did, and I felt foolish about that. Well, that doesn't worry me now, but I do remember that it did at the time.

This chauvinist statement conveyed a broad attitude toward the female that we needed to explore more fully. It manifested itself in subtle and manifold ways.

Therapist: How would you explain that? Why were you so sensitive then?

Mr. Jones: Well, I thought that it made me look inferior to my wife, and I felt that was the reverse of the way it ought to be ... I seem to have feelings often that I have to think of everything or at least I have to think of everything first.

Therapist: Give me some illustrations of that.

Mr. Jones: I remember many occasions when it was difficult for me to delegate my broad authority to anyone. I felt that I had to think of everything myself to prove to everyone around me that I had everything under control. I thought of myself as being on trial, so to speak. I felt that if other people had to ask me or tell me to do anything, it would be interpreted as a failure on my part for not having taken care of it.

Therapist: So that you would not only have to know everything, but even anticipate what might come up.

Mr. Jones: Yes, I tried to do that too.

Therapist: Then you needed to be omniscient, didn't you?

Mr. Jones: I guess I expected that of myself. I felt that whatever happened, that if I didn't have an immediate solution for it, I would be criticized for it.

Therapist: Did you succeed at this?

Mr. Jones: Yes, I did.

Therapist: You mean you can be perfect?

Mr. Jones: No, I didn't mean that, but ... I succeeded in having plans for most things that could occur or did occur. Many people remarked on my remarkable concentration and memory.

The perfectionistic demands of the obsessional are the hallmark of his efforts to be in absolute control of his status and situation by being beyond criticism and having mastery over his existence. To be perfect guarantees one's security and makes one impervious to danger. It is a sought-after goal for the obsessional, and it takes a fairly long time in therapy to help the patient move away from his hope that therapy will make him perfect to the realization that his drive for perfection in a compulsive, absolute way is, in fact, his problem.

USE OF SARCASM

Therapist: It must have taken enormous concentration and energy and memory and anticipating foresight and so on; it must have really been an enormous burden.

Mr. Jones: Well, I didn't think it was an enormous burden at the time; I merely thought it was what I had to do.

My comment was factual but also facetious. I was trying to highlight the absurdity of such an expectation. The use of sarcasm is extremely valuable if done warmly and with respect. It can focus effectively on an issue in a way that an intellectual discussion fails to. However, it must be used with tact and skill to prevent the development of a feeling of being mocked or poked fun at.

I tried to relate the need to be perfect with his always feeling on trial and the enormous tension and energy that was demanded of him. Such an attitude lends itself to making errors because of the anxiety involved and increases one's feeling of helplessness and worthlessness. This need produces living without joy and demands machinelike performances, making every activity an intense examination rather than a pleasure.

His awareness of how concerned he was with succeeding led him to explore his need to be liked and admired by everyone as a man who was well-informed, perfect in his behavior and demeanor, and capable of controlling his feelings. At the next session, he described an event in which he felt pushed around by his wife, and which he felt he had handled more appropriately than on other occasions:

Mr. Jones: Last night we were invited out to dinner by some friends. I was going to show them the way, but my wife supplied the directions. That irritated me quite a bit. For a while I had the same feeling of resentment that she was bossing me around which I had experienced intensely about two years ago. Those feelings have largely dissipated and seldom worry me anymore, but it did last night.

Note that at this point, after several months of therapy, his irritation and anger at his wife did not *necessarily* initiate an obsessional thought about killing her. While the inclination still continued to distress him, it did not automatically occur when he restrained his angry feelings.

Therapist: What did you do about your irritation?
Mr. Jones: I told her that she should leave the driving to me. But she insisted. I got angry and told her to take over the directions. She told me I was acting childish for protesting so much, and I told her that she was the one who was acting like a child. After I cooled down I realized it's merely her way of feeling important and participating in what we do. The realization of that usually precluded my becoming uncomfortable, but this time I did.

This comment not only demonstrates the capacity to rationalize his own petulance and his sensitivity to his status and significance as a male, but his skill in projecting and externalizing his own deficiencies. They get blamed on his wife, and in the past this served to appease his wrath so that he would not even be aware of it. As a result of our focusing on this matter, he could no longer overlook, repress or distract these feelings. To illuminate this sequence, I encouraged him to review the tendency to rationalize his reaction, based on an intellectual understanding of the situation which allowed him to cover up his irritation toward his controlling wife, who treated him like a little boy.

Therapist: Well, what has enabled you to avoid becoming irritated?

Mr. Jones: I told you that during the first few years of our marriage I felt I had to be the boss and my wife began to think I considered her unimportant. I realize now that I did tend to make her feel that she was being bypassed, and I realize now that she does need to feel important and participate in what we're doing. My initial reaction to the incident last night was that she was being too domineering.

Therapist: So in noting that in the past you overreacted, you now are wrong even when you feel your wife is taking over?

This seems to be a contradictory response from the therapist, who appears to be discouraging what is a meaningful insight on the part of the patient. Mr. Jones had recognized his excessive reaction and had become more moderate and understanding of his wife's needs. While this is clearly so, it is important not to allow him to swing to the extremes that characterize the reactions of obsessional characters. They are either all right or all wrong, and when they discover any error, however minor, they tend to feel totally incompetent. This tactic is much harder to deal with than the lack of awareness of their sensitivity to being controlled. When one points out to an obsessional patient that he is trying to be perfect, he will generally respond sharply with, "Do you want me to be an idiot?" Therefore, I tried to get Mr. Jones to recognize that while he had been overreacting, his wife did tend to be bossy and, at times, did treat him like a child.

Mr. Jones: No, that isn't the way I think of it. No, I don't feel that I was wrong last night, but I do have a better understanding of why she needs to be in on things.

At this point there was a long pause, and his associations led him to review how he handled his irritations under similar circumstances. It was an instructive and detailed account of how the distracting and substituting quality of obsessional thinking occurs, and I used the opportunity to make him fully aware of the progression of his defensive maneuvers.

Mr. Jones: Thinking last night at first I was irritated. I was so angry that it was difficult for me to think or talk properly.
Therapist: Yes. Go on.
Mr. Jones: And I remained upset during the time we were eating. I just told myself that I should tolerate this incident and not worry about it. I completely forgot about it all day today. I remembered it now because I related it to you.
Therapist: What do you do when you tell yourself to tolerate an incident? How do you manage?
Mr. Jones: I guess telling myself probably isn't an accurate way; I merely thought or reflected on it.
Therapist: Well, do you mean that you're able to simply explain away your irritation by telling yourself not to be irritated?
Mr. Jones: Sometimes it works and sometimes it doesn't. I'm sure that I felt better about it when I replied forcibly to her. Usually when my wife says something that irritates me I am able to make a comeback to her. Whereas to others, I often find myself unable to.
Therapist: Have you any notions about the difference?
Mr. Jones: No, I don't. I've thought of that question, but I don't have an answer to it.
Therapist: Would you care to speculate about why you can express your irritation to your wife but not to others?

TRANSFERENCE VERSUS REALITY

The distinction between transference and reality had to be followed up, in order to help Mr. Jones recognize the significance of transferential feelings toward his wife in contrast to others. Thus, he could recognize that it was not only the incident itself that stirred up anger and frustration but also the prevailing attitudes toward the other person, which he may have been unaware of. Making this distinction educates the patient, whatever his character structure or defensive mechanism may be, regarding the role of unconscious factors and transference attitudes in all areas of his living.

Mr. Jones: Well, in dealing with other people I seem to hesitate because of not finding the right mode of expression because I am angry. I don't seem to be getting anywhere with this thought ...

This type of blocking is not uncommon during therapy. It is clearly attributable to an accumulation of anxiety and generally produces a change of subject. It is often useful to inquire as to what is going on at that moment, so we can get some idea of what is producing the anxiety. If this tactic is successful, it can enable one to see how his thoughts and feelings affect his behavior. In this instance I chose not to interrupt his communication, in order to pursue his concern about facing hostile situations.

Mr. Jones: But when a clash of feeling is involved it's difficult for me to carry on an exchange of comments. I also fear that if I replied to some hostile statement that my response would be still more hostile and I always want to avoid such situations.

This is typical of obsessive thinking, as it relates to his concerns about losing control in dealing with his feelings. The tendency to go to extremes involves a need to control one's feelings. The need to undo and reverse an action or thought is to guarantee that it will not produce undesired effects if it were carried into action. Similarly, indecisive thinking enables an issue to be dealt with by not coming to closure and losing control.

Therapist: Are you saying that you wish to avoid hostile situations?
Mr. Jones: Yes, I wish that I didn't have the inability to function under such conditions.
Therapist: But are you also saying that you wish you could avoid hostile situations?
Mr. Jones: No, no! I'm not saying that. In the past I sidestepped them without fully realizing how much sidestepping I was doing. I wish to discontinue that condition.
Therapist: You still feel the need to sidestep them?
Mr. Jones: Well, yes, but I try to combat the need to sidestep. I was quite disturbed about the behavior of a colleague, and I asked if he would talk with me about it. I wasn't able to go over immediately and talk with him, however, since I knew I wouldn't be able to say anything.
Therapist: You were too furious?

At times the therapist must verbalize what he thinks might have gone on with the patient, since the obsessional avoids feelings. This involves activity that encourages the patient to notice his own feelings.

Mr. Jones: I certainly was. However, I talked with him about it this morning, reasonably and rationally. It was difficult for me to bring up this hostile subject, but I forced myself to do it.

Therapist: What do you think made it possible for you to do it?

Mr. Jones: Maybe I'm gradually losing some of these restraints. I know that to refrain from taking action when one feels wronged is improper.

Here he was demonstrating some cognitive understanding, but it was not yet integrated into his personality structure or manifested as a change in his behavior without prior consideration.

Therapist: Uh-huh.

Mr. Jones: When I am irritated, I try to imagine that the person didn't mean it that way and sometimes I feel satisfied and am no longer angry.... I'm still thinking about just what made it possible for me to talk to him.... Maybe the passage of time made it possible for me to do so. Is it possible that there is some connection between my uncomfortable feeling in connection with hostility and the feelings that I have for wanting to be the boss at all times? It seems odd to me to think of myself both those ways at the same time.

Therapist: What seems contradictory about them?

The patient had spontaneously posed a dilemma about two contradictory trends in his living. This is a high moment in the therapeutic process, since it indicates an awareness of the patient's behavior and an introspective willingness to entertain such unflattering views of himself. It is the most direct route to insight, since the curiosity originates in the patient and reflects on his own cognitive and emotive desire to alter his living. It also conveys some trust and positive transference to the therapist in opening himself to possible criticism. Mr. Jones's curiosity led to the clarification of a predominant trend in his neurosis — that is, a need to be liked and admired by all indiscriminately in order to feel secure and acceptable. Much of the obsessional's dynamism is directed toward that goal, which will ultimately enable him to feel safe and in control of his living.

Mr. Jones: In trying to think of myself as if I were someone else, it seems odd to find a person who wants to dominate, yet finds hostility so painful.

Therapist: You mean that it is contradictory to want to be the boss, which requires the ability to tell other employees off when necessary, and at the same time to be liked by all?

Mr. Jones: The thought I have is that it is painful for me to express myself aggressively even if there's need for it.

Therapist: Yes. What do you think is involved in this difficulty in telling someone off? Would you say that the essence of your difficulty in criticizing or in telling someone off is that they won't like you?

Mr. Jones: Yes, that is so.

ACTIVITY IN THERAPY

Since it was difficult for Mr. Jones to formulate just what was involved in his concerns about being critical in face-to-face encounters, I suggested the possibility that his uneasiness might involve the need to be loved by all, which he had already indicated in many ways. While such an action runs the risk of putting words into the patient's mouth, it is often the key to reducing the interminable treatment of obsessional disorders. To wait until the patient verbalizes his feelings, which is what the obsessional maneuver avoids, is to ask the patient to behave "normally" when he is, in fact, neurotic. The risks are slight, since if the hypothesis is correct, the patient will indicate so, even though he may be temporarily agreeing to placate the therapist. I believe this kind of activity is an essential ingredient in the therapy of the obsessional. Not only does it involve suggestions about alternative reactions, responses, or motivations, but it also leads the patient in productive ruminations, away from obsessional preoccupations. The therapist's hypotheses often mean interrupting the distracting moves of the patient and his endless stickiness to details and unrewarding narratives. Such highlighting of the data also implies direct assaults on defensive maneuvers, with humor and mild sarcasm produced by rephrasing the excesses of the obsessional views. In this instance, my suggestion seemed to be just what Mr. Jones had in mind, and it short-circuited a great deal of unnecessary verbal intellectualizations.

Mr. Jones: I do want people to like me. I wish I could liberate myself from this inability to be aggressive when the need arises for it, but I don't mean that I wish to be a belligerent, pugnacious character, always hurting people's feelings or acting like a bull in a china shop. The feeling exists whether I know the people or not.

Note how each observation requires the patient to assert that he should not go to the opposite extreme. As a defense against giving up the need for controls, the obsessional indicates that he does not wish to be entirely out of control. One must reassure the patient at such moments that moderation or balanced behavior is the goal of therapy.

Therapist: Rather interesting, isn't it, that everyone has to like you whether you know them well or not at all? The need to be liked is indiscriminate and makes it difficult to criticize or reprimand anyone.

Mr. Jones: I just don't know if that's the case or not, but why should I care if a stranger likes me or not?

Therapist: That is an unsolved puzzle, but it is important to recognize the problem before we can get at the solution. This seems to be something that you don't accept — to have everyone like you — because it seems so unreasonable. Is that why you are a little puzzled about this?

THERAPEUTIC NEED FOR CLARITY

It is often useful to slow down the pressure of global understandings, since these often serve to avoid the full and total confrontation of the real issues. Unless we are sure that the patient understands the extent of the problem and its role in his living, his impatience to resolve it may leave a false sense of understanding and then a disillusionment with the value of insight, as it leaves too many issues unresolved. The therapist should restructure the inquiry to permit a slower but clearer insight to develop. This was my purpose in insisting that the problem first be clearly acknowledged before we looked at why Mr. Jones needed to have even strangers like him and think well of him. In this instance we can see how the patient's concern with his feelings required clear and active support from the therapist. We must first bring the patient's ways of functioning to his attention and then encourage him to confront his contradictory feelings and ideas by pushing them to the limits, so that he will become aware that everyone must like him, even strangers. This serves to focus on the dilemma of how he defends against these concerns by feelings of not caring or disliking others. At this point the therapist can press for a change of behavior.

To push prematurely at a time when the patient is still too rigid will only produce more defenses and counterattacks, leading to fruitless tug-of-wars with the therapist. Should that occur it is best to say, "Let's let it rest for a while and look at it later." The pride of the obsessional in his cognitive skills must be challenged in order for him to learn that he does not think logically or consistently but in contradictory and ineffective terms. The therapist must teach the patient how to think logically by opening his awareness to feeling states.

Mr. Jones: Yes, yes! I am puzzled about it.

Therapist: But do you think you have a need for everyone to like you? Important or unimportant people, friends or strangers?

Mr. Jones: I suppose so, although I think of it more — more in the nature of having people's respect, or wanting to make an impression.

Here the patient was broadening the matter beyond mere liking, to respect and regard. He was obviously correct, but at this point I refused to be distracted and continued to stick to the matter of liking.

Therapist: Or, that they should always like you?

Mr. Jones: Well, I guess it does get down to that; I just hadn't thought of it that way.

Therapist: I wonder if there are many things that you do in order to guarantee that people will not dislike you and to guarantee that they always have respect for you?

AVOIDANCE OF PATIENT DISTRACTION

In the last few minutes of our session, the patient made moves to get away from the significant insight that had developed during this hour. Often such a tactic will tend to diffuse the core issues and leave a meaningful exchange confused, unclean, and unfocused. The therapist must guard against such a development, which is easier to note in retrospect than at the time it is occurring. Only the shortage of time prevented this session from going from his need to be liked to his need to know everything and impress others. Although the two things were clearly related, the shift would have tended to weaken his understanding of his need to be liked, of which the need to know everything was just one piece.

Mr. Jones: Well, I used to make strenuous efforts to secure people's respect for my mental ability by demonstrating a great amount of it. It's painful to me now that I find my memory poor, my concentration and my thinking ability poor.

Therapist: Do I understand you correctly? You are saying that it's painful that your memory and thinking ability are so poor that you can't guarantee that people are impressed by your brilliance.

Mr. Jones: Well, that's not the whole thing, but it is an important factor in it. I feel that people will look down upon me for the muddled way I talk and that I forget things in my daily activities.

Therapist: Do you think this goes beyond trying to show people you are smart and trying to show them you are superbright and know everything?

Mr. Jones: Well, I guess I was trying to show them I was brighter than they were. I felt a need to convince them I was always right and made excessive use of the citation of authority to prove it. Well, it's not unusual for human beings to wish to be liked. What's wrong with that?

As a final gambit Mr. Jones tried to defeat the entire insight by insisting that his behavior is reasonable and simply human. It is imperative that while we must agree with the observation, we must also demonstrate how this tendency is part of the patient's obsessional disorder. We must agree with him when he says, "There's nothing wrong with wanting to be liked." It is a universal need. The issue, however, is the way he proceeds to do this by always being correct, right, and brighter than his colleagues. It is the false assumption that he can be liked only if he is superior and a superman. This is the compulsive element that needs to be exposed and understood.

Therapist: I think that wanting to be liked is not unusual, except that we note that for you it is an indiscriminate asking for everyone to like you and be impressed with your absolute perfection.

Mr. Jones: I do want everyone to like me and I feel uncomfortable if they don't or won't.

Therapist: We must look for specific situations that come to mind which would demonstrate this, so that we can talk more about this.

At the very next session it became clear that Mr. Jones's need to be liked was intertwined with his perfectionistic drives and his meticulous, correct behavior at all times. The broadness of his obsessional process and the interrelationships of the symptomatology began to unfold.

Mr. Jones: I tried to give some thought to what we were discussing on Monday about my thinking that everyone must like me. I do feel that has been so.

There followed about twenty minutes of discussion before we could get back to the matter of "being liked." The issue involved his inattentiveness toward his wife and my observation that perhaps he couldn't tolerate any evidence of inadequate behavior.

Therapist: You started off by illustrating a situation in which you were inattentive to your wife's needs and I expected an instance of gross negligence. Instead, it's a trivial matter. It makes me wonder whether you feel you should never be inattentive at all?

Mr. Jones: I guess that's what's making it uncomfortable for me. I was seldom inattentive or wrong.

Therapist: You mean there was a time when you were perfect, or near it?

Mr. Jones: Well, I guess near it, or at least I thought I was superior to others. I am recalling something which I believe I hadn't mentioned to you.

RECALL VERSUS REGRESSION

The preceding exchange was an example of free association at its best, when recall about the past grows out of experiences in the present. Such data then serve to confirm the insight about the present as well as to illuminate possible etiological factors which produce such behavior. This type of recall stands in contrast to regression, which is a revival of earlier experiences whose painful context requires their removal from active awareness. Often the material so revived fails to relate to present experience and cannot immediately be tied to the patient's neurosis. Such revivals, because they alter the focus of inquiry, often serve as a defense against dealing with present disorders in living. They may, however, have great significance at other times in the therapeutic process and should therefore be noted, preserved, and used at a more opportune moment. The obsessional's style of displacement can effectively avoid the present anxieties and entanglements by becoming preoccupied with reconstructions of the past and referential transfers of blame onto others — mainly the parents. This can produce some insight, but rarely any change in the obsessional's style of functioning.

Mr. Jones: When I was six or seven years old I used to take pleasure in illustrating how smart I was and in ridiculing other children who couldn't keep up with me. My mother would reprimand me for showing off.

Therapist: She never encouraged you to show off, to demonstrate your skills before others?

Mr. Jones: No, she reprimanded me when I did.

I was surprised by this statement but made no move to challenge it. But, why did Mr. Jones make this recollection at this time? He seemed to reassure me and himself that he was, in fact, bright, special, and deserving of respect and admiration. By this time I had a need to hypothesis about his mother — that is, that she was very controlling and utilized her son as a source of pride in her accomplishments and would therefore be likely to encourage him to display his talents. This view was not consistent with Mr. Jones's contention that she wanted him to be modest and not show off. The contradiction was clarified when the therapist noted that his obsessional mother needed to appear modest and unassuming but was at the same time prejudiced and condemning of others. Her hypocritical and ambivalent attitudes were noted by Mr. Jones when he realized that his mother, while demanding that he be polite, derogated their neighbors. The black-white, love-hate, modest-egocentric, and too controlled-fear of loss of control dichotomies — all were apparent in Mr. Jones's mother as they were in his own personality makeup. She pushed him to excel at school and demanded that he perform exceptionally all the time.

CONCEDED MOTIVE FOR THERAPY

Mr. Jones: My grades in elementary and high school were very high for about the first four years and then there was a slump. The last two years I did much better than I expected because of this emotional difficulty — the fact that I felt inadequate coupled with the thought that others would notice and not like me. Sort of a vicious circle. Well, what does one do in a case like this?

Therapist: Are you asking me about how one makes sure that one is liked?

Mr. Jones: No, no. [laughs] I meant in eliminating the discomfort or excessive worry about whether I'm liked.

This is the familiar request: How to eliminate the anxiety about one's behavior instead of how to change the behavior. In a sense it is a request to build a better neurosis without discomfort rather than how to change and eliminate the neurotic behavior. One must demonstrate to the patient that this request is another aspect of the obsessional's need for perfection. This is also an opportunity to review the goals of therapy, stressing the concept of change rather than understanding.

The obsessional hopes that by knowing more he can control his living more effectively. He emphasizes the cognitive factors in his living, and to know all enables him to make the perfect decisions without doubts and uncertainties and guarantees that his behavior will always be absolutely right. The obsessional focuses on a knowledge of things, not of people or relationships. In therapy he hopes to accumulate the missing data to fill the gaps which are making him anxious and are producing symptoms. His goal at the outset of therapy is to gain enough understanding to overcome the deficiencies. The therapist, however, must indicate that the goal of therapy is to change his present ways of functioning without strengthening his neurosis, by demonstrating how the neurosis prevents him from functioning more effectively in his human relationships. Change requires that the patient be aware of how he really functions and how his defenses defeat his real needs. It will be hard for him to accept the goal of functioning imperfectly rather than becoming perfect, and it must be done repeatedly, since the obsessive is rigid, stubborn, and unyielding in his defensive style, which he considers lifesaving and which can only be relinquished when he can replace it with more satisfactory patterns of behavior.

Therapist: Well, that's what we're trying to do, understand the where and why of this need for excessive affection from everyone. Isn't that the problem?

Mr. Jones: Yes, that is a problem. And it seems to be tied in with this discomfort when I find it necessary to be critical of anyone.

Therapist: Uh-huh.

Mr. Jones: The thought occurred to me when I was riding down on the bus this morning that for many years I've been extremely meticulous and anxious for correctness in everything I do.

USE OF CONFRONTATION TACTICS

The preceding exchange is another example of how the obsessional, as he approaches clarity or some understanding, tends to veer off and move in other directions, which, although related, are tangential to the material under discussion. This shift reflects the increasing anxiety when he gets too close to some meaningful insight that might destroy the underpinnings of the neurotic structure early in therapy. It is necessary to allow such deviations, since they may be the source of more data; efforts to force the patient to stay on the point might disintegrate the communication even more drastically.

If confrontation is forced too early or too strongly, the obsessional's need to be right is stirred up as well as his anxiety about being controlled by others. He will then stubbornly cling to his point of view and recklessly take it to extremes, sticking his neck way out and defending his viewpoint with total abandon. He will use all his defenses to alter the focus of the issue, with increasing intellectualizations, obtuseness, and meticulous concern for details. At such times the therapist must retreat in his awareness of the obsessional's need and not expect that a more adequate or comprehensive explanation full of intellectualizations will convince the patient to relinquish his patterns. An obsessional therapist can get caught here in a tug-of-war that can only be defeating to the therapy.

Notice here how Mr. Jones continued to elucidate the obsessional's symptomatology of orderliness and meticulousness — two issues that had not yet been discussed:

Mr. Jones: Usually it shows up most in the accuracy of the statements in the reports that I write. I also make corrections of a meticulous nature on the work that others submit to me. I am afraid they think that I was being ...

Therapist: A fussbudget?

Mr. Jones: Fussbudget, exactly! And that often made some difficult situations for me. And the very thing I wanted to do was disadvantaged by the way I was doing it.

He noticed the discrepancies and contradictions in using obsessional tactics to achieve realistic goals. However, he was still unable to put them truly into practice in his living. In fact, this awareness was quite new and was stimulated by the therapeutic work as he shortly indicated.

COUNTERTRANSFERENCE: THERAPIST INEPTNESS

What follows here is a good example of how a therapist's need to make a point or to stubbornly pursue his own hypothesis may produce a confused exchange that requires some obsessional juggling on the part of the therapist. The patient tried repeatedly to bring the therapist back to the point, finally leaving him to say that he did not know where my digression had led to. The therapist tried to exit gracefully by suggesting that the digression was simply an exploration with no particular purpose. While the most useful response in such an instance might be for the therapist to admit his error, this may not be possible if he does not recognize it at the time. At a later date such an admission can be of paramount value in demonstrating that one need not be perfect or that to admit an error is not an egregious crime. It may serve to encourage the patient to acknowledge his errors and face his own rigid demands for certainty. However, during the stress of the session, if the therapist is already drawn into the patient's web or is pursuing his own particular position, the best one can hope for is to withdraw from it as quickly as possible. Such diversions are unfortunately all too frequent.

Therapist: It's what you said before, that there was a conflict between being the boss and criticizing people. Here we see a similar thing, conflict between wanting to be meticulous, doing a perfect job, and being looked upon as a fussbudget and not liked. Same problem, isn't it? Two needs get into each other's way.

Mr. Jones: Exactly. At the time that that has happened, I didn't have any mental analysis of what was going on. That just occurred to me today ... A few weeks ago I had to reprimand an employee for carelessness and inattentiveness and I experienced some discomfort in doing it. I was afraid she would think I wasn't too sure of what I was talking about and was too lenient about it, and yet I've heard from others that her reaction was the opposite, that she was taken aback by my severity.

Therapist: What do you make of that?

Mr. Jones: I recall that someone pointed out to me that I looked upon myself differently from the way that I appear to others.

Therapist: And in this instance you are thinking that you're being too lenient and the other person involved is thinking of you as being too harsh.

Mr. Jones: Yes, that's so. I suppose that involves again this feeling that I had to be perfect.

Therapist: How does that get tied in here?

Mr. Jones: Well, in this way, that I felt embarrassed by my having to grope for words instead of being in complete control of the situation without any hesitation.

Therapist: And thinking that because you were being hesitant and uneasy that actually you were being less of a disciplinarian than you should have been, is that what you mean?

Mr. Jones: Yes, that's part of it, but I didn't give you a complete picture of my thoughts when I stated that I was afraid I was getting too lenient.

Therapist: Uh huh.

Mr. Jones: But lenient isn't the proper description of what I had in mind and I'm still unable to describe it better than that.

Therapist: Well, that you were letting her off too easy or that she could have been punished even more severely if you ...

Mr. Jones: No, no! Not that, not that!

Therapist: Not what?

Mr. Jones: It was the feeling that I wasn't making a good appearance in her eyes as I could have if I were less hesitant.

Therapist: But what I was trying to bring to your attention is if you were less hesitant, it's possible that she may have felt you were even harsher, since your hesitancy usually limits or even minimizes your harshness.

Mr. Jones: Do you mean it's a self-defeating proposition?

Therapist: No, I'm suggesting at this moment it may have been self-defeating, but it may also be life-preserving. What seems to you to be easy is seen by others as harsh, and if you were not so hesitant it might even have sounded harsher.

Mr. Jones: Possibly, but I don't know where that leads us now.

At this point, I finally abandoned my attempt to enable him to see that not all his defensive efforts were maladaptive and that some were actually constructive.

After some general remarks about the need to avoid appearing harsh in order to advance one's position, he was reminded of an exchange with his wife.

Mr. Jones: Speaking of the tone of voice reminded me that my wife mentioned that a few times she has told me my tone of voice was far more severe than the circumstances warranted. That wasn't hard for me to believe because I consciously did adopt the hard tone on many occasions. I kept forgetting that she didn't feel well.

Therapist: Is it conceivable that you didn't believe that your wife was not well because your expectation was that your wife would never be sick?

Mr. Jones: Yes, yes! That's true. Also some vague idea that my wife would have experience in handling matters that would help me to get along better.

Therapist: She would be a helpmate.

Mr. Jones: Yes. And then I proceeded to remove the opportunity for her to do that by not giving her a chance to take a part in things. I remember about two months after we were married, she was all excited about a women's luncheon that she attended and that I appeared to be displeased at her doing that. She was very confused about it.

Therapist: You have no idea why you might have been displeased?

Mr. Jones: No, I don't. She was so confused that thereafter for a long time she didn't participate with others. And of course I didn't like that either, because it was something I wanted her to do or wanted us both to do.

Ambivalence and contradictory desires were evident in all areas of Mr. Jones's life — to want and not to want, to control or to be out of control. Such behavior is a way of undoing or reversing what one has thought or done, whatever side one takes or from whatever extreme one begins.

Mr. Jones: Yes, I think I had some reluctance for her to mix with the other women because ... she had been divorced and that a series of rumors or gossip would be generated because of that.

Therapist: They would disapprove of her?

Mr. Jones: Well, yes, it would amount to that. I don't feel that way now, of course. Yes, now I remember another thing — only about a week after we were married I asked her not to tell anyone she had been divorced. That hurt her feelings. She thought I was ashamed of her, not as proud of her as she wanted me to be. Well, maybe my thought was that if they wouldn't approve of her they wouldn't approve of me.

Therapist: Uh-huh. So that your wife had to assist you in getting others to have a high opinion of you.

WITHHOLDING INSIGHT

The association to his wife revealed more of his ambivalence and secret resentments of her. They appeared almost unwittingly from the context of wanting to be liked and approved of and hoping that his wife would be of some help in this regard. However, the uneasiness about her acceptability because of her divorce and other unacknowledged concerns produced a series of mixed feelings, mostly anger and resentment that she had failed him.

All of Mr. Jones's feelings added up in the final explosion of obsessional thoughts about disposing of her. It is apparent that his demands and expectations of his wife, uncommunicated and unexpressed, were issues that Mr. Jones would need to be confronted with. I made no effort to do so at this time, since it was important to encourage and develop a strong alliance first, in order to explore his explosive and highly destructive angry feelings toward her. I made a mental note of this state of affairs and later insisted on his facing this distorted notion of a marriage relationship. He would have to face his male chauvinism as well, but this was not the right time therapeutically.

Several days after the previous exchange, Mr. Jones reported an incident in which he risked displeasure in speaking harshly to a colleague:

Mr. Jones: Today I had an incident in which I found it necessary to speak in rather harsh tones and was not unduly distressed about it.

We often encounter such incidents in working with obsessionals, when they take a piece of insight, translate it into action, and report some progress in their dealing better with heretofore problem areas. We must not overvalue such events — as if they were valid and permanent characterological changes; however, neither should we minimize or fail to comment on them.

Therapist: And that was unusual?

Mr. Jones: Yes.

Therapist: Tell me about it; that's encouraging.

Mr. Jones: Well, I feel I've been too lenient in a matter for which we could be accused of stalling. I mentioned the subject to this colleague before.

Therapist: What was its effect?

Mr. Jones: Its effect was that he became, not angry, but uneasy about my attitude and left. About a minute afterward he said that he'd try to make these arrangements and proceeded to do so immediately.

Therapist: So it achieved your purpose?

Mr. Jones: Yes.

Therapist: And did it hurt too much, doing it? Have you any ideas about why you were able to do it?

Mr. Jones: No, that's why I regard it as being so unusual, because it didn't.

SUPPORTING CHANGE

In view of Mr. Jones's success in trying out his newly discovered skills, it was important to compliment him and support him as well as to get him to see that it was not necessarily accompanied by greater danger. To fix the insight and to help him to integrate validity of his change, it was most effective to explore the circumstances that enabled him to behave differently at that time.

Mr. Jones: Yes, I think I've been thinking about my unconscious need for other people to like me. I guess realizing that makes me feel not quite so compelled to please everyone. ... Well, I always feel that it is expected of me to take some action or make some comment or to be nice.

Therapist: Do you think it might have something to do with the need to be a good boy? It's being a good boy, isn't it, making the friendly comment, or appeasing others?

Again I took the active role of suggesting some reason for his anxious need to do the right thing and get approval from others. I suggested "good little boy" because much of his behavior seemed to be that of a boy seeking approval from a parent. I had accumulated enough data about him by now to feel that this notion had some validity in view of his relationship to his mother and his wife. I felt that this "little boy" attitude prevailed in all his relationships — with maternal and paternal colleagues, with superiors as well as inferiors, and with me in our relationship. It was a mode of behavior intended to win approval from all and avoid any exposure to danger. He rejected this interpretation and preferred to see his behavior as a more assertive tendency, which led to more confirmation of his inability to risk rejection by being ordinary. I followed his lead, instead of pressing him to accept my suggestion. It led directly, however, to a description of an incident with his wife where, in fact, he was talking like a little boy.

Mr. Jones: Well, maybe it is. I seem to think of it in the nature of wanting to be the leader.

Therapist: Tell me more about this. What comes to mind about this question of wanting to be the leader?

Mr. Jones: I was anxious to be a leader and to be highly regarded but often found it uncomfortable, especially in situations that conflicted with the other need that I always be liked. I was especially happy about my being able to handle this situation this morning, since I was feeling somewhat nervous early this morning as a result of an argument I had with my wife last night. We got into quite a wrangle about playing bridge. She is an excellent player and encourages me to play. I have told her many times that I don't like to play. My wife was saying that when one member of the married couple wanted to do something, the other should try to go along. That grated on me because my wife had frequently used that argument in reverse, indicating that I shouldn't press her to do things that she didn't like to do.

Therapist: And you felt that it works both ways, not just one way, huh?

Mr. Jones: Yes, exactly. But I didn't express myself until much later in the evening.

Therapist: Is that all that happened?

Mr. Jones: No, I guess I did leave out a whole lot of it. My wife indicated that even though she detested fish, she made an effort to like it because I enjoyed eating in seafood restaurants.

It wasn't clear whether he felt unhappy because of his unwillingness to make sacrifices or his wife's insistence on his always doing what she wanted. However, it was clear that he had many unexpressed expectations of his wife which he was either unaware of or else philosophically accepted. His wife was not seen as an equal partner but as a provider for some of his needs. I did not focus on these issues, since I wanted to stay with the main theme at that time — that is, his requirements for perfection and acceptance as a necessary element in his living.

Therapist: Did you play bridge?

Mr. Jones: I'm a very poor player, and I don't find it unpleasant to play for a short time.

Therapist: Is one of the reasons that you don't like to play because you're not terrific at it?

REPETITIVE RESISTANCES AS DEFENSES

So we got back to the notion again that he must be outstanding and supercompetent so as not to expose his weaknesses or deficiencies. Although he justified his lack of interest in bridge by indicating that it did not suit his temperament or he just didn't like it, he avoided it, in fact, because he couldn't master it. Playing cards was not fun for him, but instead was a serious project in which he must prove himself and impress others.

Mr. Jones: I suppose it is so. I've never seemed to be able to learn it.

Therapist: Is that important in playing the game well?

Mr. Jones: Well, I think the rules are important until a player gains considerable proficiency and familiarity with it.

Mr. Jones then tried to engage me in a discussion of bridge — the rules and the bidding — and after a brief exchange, I abruptly returned to the previous discussion to explore his usual tactics in dealing with his wife and others in controversial situations where he felt he must succumb to the demands of others in order to be viewed as a good, noncontentious fellow.

Therapist: Now in the arguments with your wife, are you the aggressor or the appeaser?

Mr. Jones: Well, in this case my wife feels strongly about bridge, and I make some effort to like it. I would like to play. But after several sporadic attempts I find it so difficult to learn that I don't enjoy it because I find the learning so unpleasant.

Note that he did not answer my question but instead focused on his behavior as the compromising, understanding husband. I brought him back to the issue by raising a question about his feelings. This is an important tactic in psychotherapy involving all varieties of symptoms and character disorders. In the obsessional disorders it is especially important, since the patient tends to intellectualize all issues and avoid feelings entirely. Although this tactic may not be successful, it is essential that the therapist constantly stress feelings and suggest that the patient must have some reaction or indicate possible responses that he might be experiencing at the moment or must have felt in the past. One must also get beyond simply asking the patient how he feels since he has developed major skills in overlooking his feelings and is quite unaware that he experiences any.

Therapist: Tell me what you're thinking?

Mr. Jones: I was thinking of some way of expressing this better.

Therapist: You weren't feeling anything?

Mr. Jones: I was trying to think of what my feelings are in connection with this problem. Well, formerly when we would have an argument I always held out without giving in or compromising my view. My wife would become so tensed up that she couldn't speak to me at all. I would try to appease her. I would plead with her not to be angry with me. I felt pain that such situations arose and I had to break through this barrier, so that we could be friendly again. That hasn't happened for a long time now.

Therapist: What you say is that you couldn't tolerate an atmosphere of antagonism for any length of time.

Mr. Jones: Yes.

Therapist: You had to terminate it.

Mr. Jones: You get the idea?

Therapist: She was sulking. And that made you terribly uncomfortable.

Mr. Jones: I must be able to find some word to express it . . . I knew she felt uncomfortable. And I dreaded the thought that I had produced it. While I did appease and apologize, I still maintained my original thoughts in the argument we were having.

Therapist: So would you say that in a sense you always lost even though you never yielded your position?

Mr. Jones: Well, sometimes the basis for these arguments involved my parents. She used to feel that she was secondary to my parents and that gave her a feeling of insecurity, and she was very unhappy about it. . . . I forgot what I was leading up to.

Therapist: About the outcome, whether you always felt that you lost.

Mr. Jones: Oh.

Therapist: Well, what was your feeling when one of these scenes was over?

Mr. Jones: Well, she would go into these tearful, emotional trances. I was so anxious to bring her into a more friendly attitude again that . . . we didn't come to any conclusion on the original argument that precipitated this situation.

INTOLERANCE OF ANXIETY

The inability to tolerate any uneasiness for any length of time characterizes the obsessional need for immediate relief of anxiety by some defensive tactic. Note that in the preceding exchange, Mr. Jones continues to avoid discussing his feelings and talks instead about his wife's action. Undoing is a magical device, giving automatic relief by its capacity for changing focus, displacing, or being inattentive to an event. The compulsion is also a ready-made, magical tactic to avoid anxiety. Rituals and phobias prevent anxiety by avoiding any situation, place, person, or thing that might produce it. The tendency for the claustrophobic to sit on the aisle or the rear of the theater, for example, is to be able to make an immediate exit if anxiety should occur. The obsessional demands immediate relief, and he cannot tolerate or sustain any waiting period. He must make immediate contact, resolve the doubt, and tolerate no uncertainties; he will try a lock a dozen times to be certain it is closed or wash his hands two dozen times to make sure they're clean. This is what Mr. Jones was trying to say in his need to make everything O.K. as soon as possible, if not sooner.

Therapist: You mean the issue would never get settled?

Mr. Jones: The issue would never get settled and after sulking she would suddenly snap out of it, and then I would feel a direct, positive sense of relief.

Therapist: Well, how did you feel about these arguments, the way they were resolved and the way they would get started?

Mr. Jones: Well, I felt that in these arguments about my parents I was in the midst of two opposing forces and that I had to placate both of them and it was impossible. I would see her side of it, but I found it impossible to visualize doing anything that would hurt my mother's feelings. My wife thought I was falling out of love with her and that I was anxious to go back to my parents. That wasn't so, but she thought it was. I thought that gradually they would come to accept her and she would feel more comfortable about them. But it was a hopeless task.

This was delivered in a painfully distraught fashion in which the helplessness and turmoil of being caught in a double bind was evident. It was also clear that his inability to deal with his mother was still greater than his capacity to deal with his wife. He could argue, confront, and deny his wife. This was not yet possible with his mother.

Mr. Jones: It's much better than it was. I felt compelled to visit my folks often and to write to them often. Now I am breaking away from this close feeling of attachment to my parents.

Therapist: In these arguments would you have the feeling of being beat down and feeling helpless?

Mr. Jones: I did feel that way. I wasn't able to realize that other people had feelings or needs that had to be satisfied. I didn't know that others could be comfortable and that I could also. I always had to push very hard on my ideas and then if I'd meet any resistance at all, I'd have to give in although I didn't want to. Those are awfully complicated things to express correctly.

Therapist: Uh-huh.

UNDOING

Mr. Jones: Sometimes I'm not sure whether I am putting my idea across to you.

Therapist: When I don't understand, I say so.

Mr. Jones: That's right. And sometimes those things are hard to remember, how I did feel.

Mr. Jones's remarks here are another example of the obsessional's tendency to undo the work of the hour by casting some doubt on whether it was accurately recalled or expressed. The preceding exchange, which occurred at the end of the session, was abruptly terminated so as not to get into a discussion that would reduce the impact of this significant session.

A very familiar tactic of undoing in connection with avoiding significant insights is the patient who, before leaving a session, asks the question, "How am I doing?" or "How is our work going?" or "Are we making any progress?" Such questions, while seemingly innocuous and relevant to the patient's interests, are actually ways of changing the focus from the work done during the session to speculation about what the therapist thinks of the patient and his efforts. This tactic can undo a meaningful session in which significant issues were raised. The therapist must deal with it directly by exploring the purpose of the question at the succeeding hour and not getting embroiled into answering it. A useful reply at the time might be, "I wonder why you ask this question now when we have just finished some important work that you might focus on?"

TESTING AND GROWTH

Following the fruitful sessions just considered, and following his return from a business trip, the patient appeared to be reflecting and testing out some of his newly discovered capacity to be assertive and to risk being disliked. This is often the case following a dramatic confrontation of an aspect of one's personality. Although the immediate effect may be to produce a strong impression, in typical obsessional style such awareness is avoided by focusing on other unrelated and perhaps less disturbing topics. However, if the impact is strong enough, the new awareness cannot be totally obliterated and will operate on a subconscious or fleetingly conscious level, simmering and stewing until it manifests itself covertly in the form of a new discovery by the patient, which he feels he has achieved through his own introspective skills. This seemed to be going on with Mr. Jones, since in a most significant exchange three weeks later, he dealt with the problem of his violence and his concern about taking strong action on any matter. While he had yet to explore with any focus or commitment his obsessive thoughts about killing his wife, this appeared to be a preliminary exploration of the fears and consequences of acknowledging his frustrated anger. Mr. Jones had been discussing his inability to express himself with subordinates and when he had to make a decisive statement.

Mr. Jones: About ten days ago we were going out to dinner with another couple who canceled at the last minute. I was dressing while my wife was talking on the phone, and when she handed me the phone I was unable to talk. I don't know what they were talking about, but it reminded me of something about my earlier years. I do remember that whenever we had company at home I had nothing to say. My father did most of the talking. I remember wishing that I could talk fluently, as he did. Sometimes when I would embark on conversations he would sort of take over. He had something to add and then he would just continue and I would be left out.

Therapist: How do you see that as related to the uneasiness about others knowing more than you?

Mr. Jones: Well, I don't have any clear idea whether there's any relation between the two ... I seem to have these feelings of distress on occasions when I think my boss may not be completely satisfied. It is comparable to my superior taking over whenever I tried to express myself ... That doesn't tie in with the situation now where I am so concerned about the impression that I make on my boss.

TRANSFERENCE PROBLEMS

Mr. Jones's comments were clearly confused, but it was clear that these recollections about his father were significant and related to his concerns about being acceptable or satisfactory. I made no observations about this matter because of my own concerns about being more fluent than Mr. Jones. I wished to avoid putting myself in the parental role of disapproving or being "smarter" than the patient. Such a countertransference reaction could only be disruptive at this time and might be usefully introduced at a later time in the therapy. Instead, I chose to explore his need to excel and win approval from his father rather than his father's competition with him. This brought us to the end of that session.

Two days later, as if there had been no time lapse at all, Mr. Jones continued to reconstruct his adolescence and his relationship with his mother and father and his need to be a good boy. His concerns about making a mistake required that he remain in a childish role, forcing his mother to make his decisions.

Mr. Jones: I tried to reflect more on the period between ages eleven and twelve, during which time my schoolwork and attentiveness slipped off. Nothing occurs to me at all as an explanation. There was another period during my second year in high school when I got rather poor grades again. My sister was two years old at that time. I don't think that had anything to do with it.

Therapist: At least the importance of which we don't, at the moment, recognize.

I had only vague notions as to the relationship of his two-year-old sister to his failing grades. However, I did not want Mr. Jones to intellectualize about it and perhaps launch into notions of sibling rivalry or displaced status in the family. In the treatment of an obsessional this is precisely the way one does *not* explore psychodynamic issues. This kind of intellectual pursuit will only increase the defensive tactics and yield no valuable insights. There are several ways to deal with such a development. One is to raise the issue of how the patient feels about the sibling or whether there are any recollections about this period of time.

Mr. Jones: I don't seem to be able to think of anything at all to talk about that we haven't already talked about.

Therapist: Just say anything that comes to mind.

USE OF SILENCE

An impasse is frequent in the course of therapy and requires some response from the therapist to get it moving again. The least manipulative approach is to simply inquire about what the patient might be thinking about at that time. It can be effective if it gets at the fleeting thoughts of the patient; these often reveal meaningful unconscious material. At other times, one can make provocative comments or express hypotheses that occur to the therapist. This may produce further thoughts or contrary opinions. Either way it can be useful in clarifying the data for the patient and the therapist.

At times, silence and the opportunity it gives for reflection can be most rewarding. Silence as a way to provoke reactions from the patient, as well as an opportunity for reflection and rumination, can be a most therapeutic tool. It must be used wisely and appropriately, however; otherwise it can produce increasing anxiety in the patient, which may result in more active defensive withdrawal or oppositional behavior. The silence may then be turned into a tug-of-war in which the rigidity and the patient's need to control can lead to an impasse. If the silence can be attributed to an indecisive uncertainty about what topic to speak about, one can use the silence as an effective demonstration to indicate the need to make some choice, rather than waiting to decide which topic is most important. This can be a valuable learning experience for noticing how the need to be correct leads to less effective living. It helps the patient see that taking active steps has fewer fearful consequences than waiting for certainty and perfection.

Silence that is the result of an inept rigid application of a therapeutic principle not to intervene can be very destructive with obsessional patients. A therapist who remains silent at a particular moment should be able to answer the question of what he has in mind in not intervening and what purpose he expects the silence to serve. It must be an active decision and not one by default or ritual. Silence creates particular stress for obsessional patients and should be used with caution and skill. The increase in anxiety during a silent period may be so oppressive as to encourage distracting and ritualized activity, thereby reducing the potential effectiveness of the session. The therapist should be sensitive to this anxiety gradient, in order to intervene before it gets severe enough to terminate useful interaction.

TRANSFERENCE ISSUES

Mr. Jones: When this emotional problem was at its worst and before I got any help for it, it seemed to be indirectly tied to other people in position of authority, as if they were my parents. I strongly resented whenever my wife complained of anything and told her that she was acting as if she were my mother.

Mr. Jones was now beginning to elaborate on the transference attitude toward his wife, which was intimately involved in his obsessional symptoms and related to his feelings of rage and helplessness in dealing with them. As this unfolds, we can see the dynamics of his neurotic behavior as it arose out of these distortions.

Therapist: Did you think that there was a basis for it?

Mr. Jones: Well, there was a basis for my thinking, but I guess there was also a basis for some of her complaints. During that time I was unable to decide anything at all and I was continually looking to her to decide trivial matters which I could have decided. I went through a period of acting like a child, practically expecting and demanding guidance.

Therapist: Let's hear some of the details about this period.

He proceeded with his account as if I had not said anything at all. This capacity to tune out someone else accounts for much of the innocence and unsophistication in the obsessional. He will rigidly pursue his line of thinking. This is not only destructive to good communication but is infuriating to the other person, who insists he has made a statement which the obsessional denies was ever made. The therapist must become aware that not everything he says is, in fact, heard by the patient and may need to be repeated many times.

Mr. Jones: When I got the guidance, of course I resented it.

Therapist: Uh huh. Now up to that point in your marriage, did you recognize anything like this happening in the relationship?

Mr. Jones: No, I didn't. Before that when my wife felt too ill to do things I wanted, I seemed to ignore the fact that she felt too ill. On one occasion I said: "I'm your husband; stop treating me as if I were your son." And she became practically hysterical at that. She said, "Stop acting as if you are a child." I came to some realization that I had been.

Therapist: Do any specific instances come to mind which would have produced such an impression?

Mr. Jones: I tried to put myself into a position inferior to other people. On one occasion, while talking to my wife's doctor, I kept repeating everything that he said and I was excessively polite and subservient. Even while I was doing it, I knew that it was unnecessary, even slightly peculiar. One night when we were visiting my sister's home I recall a vague, strange feeling I had. A thought came to me that my father who was sitting across the room from me was me or I felt as he did.

DEPERSONALIZATION

While this experience bordered on a psychotic depersonalization, it allowed us to explore his relationship with his father, which had not been touched upon so far in our work.

Therapist: Do you remember what you were thinking?
Mr. Jones: No, and I don't think it made any difference.
Therapist: What was this feeling of being like father? How were you like him?
Mr. Jones: The feeling lasted only momentarily. It was indefinite and inexplicable.
Therapist: Well, what comes to mind about that? There seems to be a connection here because you started out by telling me of the period when you were seemingly acting like a child, which brought you to this recollection of wanting to be like father, or being him, and you recognize that there is some contradiction here.
Mr. Jones: Well, I can't attribute it to a feeling of wanting to be like him; it was a mysterious feeling when I felt like him. I was always anxious to please him. When I was twelve and my schoolwork declined, he wasn't critical about it.
Therapist: He was not critical then. Was he critical at other times?
Mr. Jones: He wasn't critical, but he was sort of vaguely demanding and belittling. During any conversation with others he would take over.
Therapist: Do you think you liked him?

This question was designed not only to get at the feelings but also to congeal and strengthen any positive or negative feelings Mr. Jones had toward his father, since I had no clear picture of how he actually felt toward him.

Mr. Jones: Yes.

Therapist: Even when he was belittling?

Mr. Jones: Well, I never thought about it that way. When I was about twenty, he started including me in the distribution of cocktails when we had guests. I liked that. I took pains to act surprised when he did pass me a drink.

Therapist: Well, why was that so important to you to look surprised? Did it imply being a little boy?

Mr. Jones: ... Seems like that. I was definitely conscious of having to do this. But I can't account for it.

Therapist: Does anything else come to mind in this regard?

Mr. Jones: Well, when I was about twenty-three I went to a New Year's Eve party. I became nauseated during the party and got my clothes all dirty. I was extremely embarrassed.

Therapist: You were nauseated, or you vomited?

Mr. Jones: Vomited. I was so embarrassed that I couldn't speak to the girl for about half an hour. I was very displeased that my folks would find out about this. When they inquired I said I had had some champagne and it made me sick, but I wasn't drunk. I was distressed that she would think that I was drunk.

Therapist: So at twenty-three years you were still not able to let either your mother or father know that you were grown up enough to drink if you wanted to.

Mr. Jones: I guess that's it.

Therapist: Still sort of being the good boy?

Mr. Jones: There is another instance of that kind of thinking. When I needed a job at sixteen my father helped me but I was very careful to keep anyone from finding out that my father had been of any assistance to me.

Therapist: How did you manage to do that? Just by not mentioning it?

Mr. Jones: By not mentioning that he was in the business I was working in.

Therapist: Were you ashamed of being in need of help?

Mr. Jones: Yes, yes! Definitely.

Therapist: Having to counteract it by some exaggerated manhood, huh? Never mentioning father as a sort of helper ...

Mr. Jones: Yeah, I guess so.

The session ended on this note with the patient still being confused about his ambiguous and contradictory tendencies to need help and to deny that he received it, to be a little boy and yet try to pretend to be grown up, to be liked but also to assert himself.

DEVELOPMENT OF THE FULL OBSESSION

The preceding exchange led directly to a crucial interview ten days later, which helped to clarify the need for obsessional defenses in his attempts to cover up any feelings of strength or manliness that would be dangerous. He had to appear weak and timid, while underneath this mask he often was a fuming volcano. The session began with his description of an incident on a bus, where he identified with an abused and helpless passenger. Associated with this was his irritation at his wife, who appeared to be putting on weight. He was unable to express his irritation at her. After describing some improvement, as if to buttress himself and reassure the therapist, he detailed for the first time during our therapeutic work (aside from descriptions at the initial contact) his obsessional thoughts about killing his wife and his feeling like a little boy in dealing with her.

Mr. Jones: Right after I left here last Monday I was riding home on a bus. An incident occurred which caused me to feel upset although I had no part in it. The bus was crowded. A man who was seated in a very strong voice demanded that the standee take his newspaper out of his face. He embarked on a long and abusive harangue. The individual who was being lectured took it very quietly and made little or no protest. I recognized that I had never been able to engage in any such outburst, although I certainly didn't applaud the individual who did it. I also wondered why I was so disturbed about it.

Therapist: What comes to mind?

Mr. Jones: Before I can even start to think of what comes to mind about that I'm still trying to put into words perhaps other kinds of feelings that I had ... but it is difficult to do. It was partly embarrassment and partly a feeling of condemnation for anybody being so rude. But that doesn't explain it all.

Therapist: You sort of identified with the man who was being bawled out.

Mr. Jones: Yes, that could be so, but ... I look upon it also as an identification with the individual making this harangue.

THERAPEUTIC ERROR

Here the patient was more acutely aware of his hostile tendencies than of his compassionate ones. My immediate reaction was to feel sorry for the man being abused, and I noted that my reactions were not necessarily those of the patient. I was too quick to identify his compassionate feelings, but he didn't overlook the angry ones. In fact, his desire to harangue, abuse, and scream at his wife was such that he could identify easily with the attacker on the bus. Having made an error, I quickly withdrew and allowed the patient to explore his feelings and not my preconceptions. Too often the therapist in such a situation insists that his reactions are a true reflection of the situation and that the patient, if he disagrees, is being defensive and negativistic. We must be careful to acknowledge our preconceptions and give some credence and regard to the patient's productions. This was a striking instance of such a situation. I let Mr. Jones continue:

Mr. Jones: I would find it [such an outburst] impossible because I would be sure that everyone would condemn me for it. . . . I just recalled a feeling, when I was in high school, of my being unable to register any protests because I thought that my large size would make other people think I was taking unfair advantage.
Therapist: You had to back out because you were too strong?
Mr. Jones: That's about the synopsis for it, yes.
Therapist: To pay the penalty for being strong, you had to appear weak.
Mr. Jones: I had to take the punishment and not speak up, but . . . I don't think it's associated with any wish to appear weak. I wished to avoid appearing as a bully.

INTENT VERSUS CONSEQUENCE

The patient was making a most significant distinction, which is too often overlooked or distorted in analytic theory. He was distinguishing between intent and consequence of his behavior in contrast to the pervasive tendency in analytic practice to insist that the effect one produces is unconsciously what one desires to produce. Thus, Mr. Jones was saying that he had no wish or desire to appear weak as I had suggested; his desire was not to appear a bully. The consequence of minimizing his anger was to appear mild and weak, but that was not his intention.

Throughout the years of my practice I have often experienced the tremendous value of the distinction between intent and consequence. Such an insight helps prevent us from focusing on the wrong issues. In Mr. Jones's case the trouble was not some masochistic need to appear weak and be pushed around but rather an excessive anger and fury that must be held in check to prevent being criticized or disliked. The therapeutic efforts are dramatically different when we attempt to undo those opposing tendencies.

The wish-fulfilling concepts of psychoanalytic theory that pervade therapeutic endeavors often fail to recognize this difference. Mr. Jones clarified the difference between neurotic compulsion and the pursuit of one's needs and wishes. When we effectively pursue our needs or wishes, we are not acting in a neurotic fashion but in a healthy, constructive way. It is only when we produce opposite effects from pursuing our needs that we call such behavior neurotic. The person who strives for security or reaches for a loving relationship with such intensity and anxiety that he defeats his purpose is behaving in a neurotic fashion. He wants love and security but produces rejection and insecurity. This is neurosis. He is not looking for rejection, but for acceptance, and his efforts to achieve acceptance alienates others.

Unfortunately, the inadequately or poorly trained therapist often treats the patient as if he were a malicious, defiant, and resistant character who could behave differently if only he wished to do so, and that his behavior arises by choice. The obsessional cannot choose; he procrastinates and is indecisive until pushed by his compulsion or by external forces. He generally decides by default; since he must not make an error or act imperfectly, he postpones all action. He can be pushed by external authorities in a tug-of-war, but this is not a choice, it is an act of compulsion. Generally, however, the obsessional's rigidity and capacity to hold firm and resist change are so great that under pressure he becomes adamant and will fight to the end regardless of the consequences.

Change comes about when the obsessional abandons his compulsion and is able to make a free choice or when he develops a countercompulsion and rigidly does *not* do what heretofore he rigidly did. This occurs when the compulsive drinker (alcoholic) or compulsive eater (obesity) — because of therapy, charisma, or spiritual experience — becomes a compulsive nondrinker (total abstainer) or a compulsive noneater (anorexia nervosa). In neither choice has free will entered into such a person's life; he has simply reversed the compulsions. When the countercompulsion is more socially acceptable and sometimes less self-destructive as in the case of the alcoholic, we approve of it. When it is socially or personally destructive, as with anorexia nervosa, we do not approve of it and call it a disease. We must always be sure to distinguish intent from consequence of one's behavior.

As Mr. Jones said clearly, he wished not to appear weak but to avoid appearing as a bully. Mr. Jones continued by relating his feeling in high school to the incident on the bus.

Mr. Jones: The incident on the bus was actually a similar situation. The person making all the noise and claiming to have been abused was a small man and the individual who was waving a newspaper in his face was a large man.

Therapist: What were you thinking while watching this and afterwards? What was going on in your mind? Did you feel irritated or annoyed?

Mr. Jones: Oh, yes, I was annoyed with the party who made this unjustified outburst in public. His reaction was far out of proportion. There was also a feeling of embarrassment. The idea of comparing his outburst with my own inability to express such an aggressive response came a little later. Either that night or the night following I had a nightmare, which left me with a vague feeling of uneasiness and a fright in the morning but I recall nothing of what the dream was.

How unfortunate that these significant dreams are forgotten, never to be retrieved! I did not push or attempt any recall in this instance because I was certain it was beyond recall, particularly since I suspected it would directly relate to his own homicidal wishes, which he could not handle.

Therapist: I see.

OBSESSIONAL TRAPS FOR THE THERAPIST

Mr. Jones: The feeling wore off during the day but resumed again at night. My wife has been putting on weight which she recently lost. In the last few months she gained all the weight back.

Therapist: Do you say anything to her about it?

Notice how Mr. Jones neatly changed the subject and the focus from homicidal issues to concern about his wife's weight. Surely they were related, but the quality and quantity of anger were strikingly reduced. Also note how I was trapped and how easily it can happen without noticing it. However we shortly returned to the essential issue — that is, his rage and important feelings.

Mr. Jones: Yes, she's very conscious of the fact and mentions it quite often. I don't want her to get fat or be fat ... yet she experiences feelings of nervousness and anxiety to eat.

Therapist: Has she ever been fat?

Mr. Jones: Before we met. She was very thin when we were married, and she gained weight only about two or three years ago. I know that she has a guilty feeling about gaining weight. This morning just before I woke up I dreamed that I had been visiting a psychiatric clinic in the hospital and that each time I went I would talk to a different doctor and each time I went I had to have a lengthy discussion with the receptionist before getting an appointment. The last doctor I talked to was a woman doctor. After that the scene changed entirely and I was in a Roman city which I think I had seen in a movie. I was walking through a large, open square in the city and searching for a particular building, and that's all there was to that one.

Therapist: Yes.

Mr. Jones: I'm conscious lately of an improvement in my concentrating or thinking ability.

CHOOSING A THEME

While I had in mind to pursue the significance of Mr. Jones's dream, since it was the first one he had presented, I was quickly turned off by his statement of improvement, which led immediately into a discussion of the obsession that brought him into treatment. It seemed important to pursue this line of inquiry instead of exploring the dream, and I decided to allow that line to develop. This situation occurs frequently in the therapeutic process, and one must make a decision about what to explore when multiple themes are presented. One should generally follow any lead that directly relates to the problem for which the patient came to therapy, putting off other leads for a later time. With regard to dreams, the decision is easier to make, since the exploration of dream material is often too complex, confusing, and time-consuming, with only minimal rewards to be realized. On the preceding occasion, Mr. Jones's dream seemed clear and easily understood, although the implications might be diffuse and more complicated. The scenario clearly related to the therapy and the therapist and the difficulty the patient was having in communicating with him. He was searching and trying to be heard but was having some problems in doing so. The material that followed without interruption might have been lost, or at least unnecessarily postponed, if I had insisted on exploring his free association to his dream at that time.

Therapist: How do you mean?

Mr. Jones: Well, it's a small improvement and not nearly as much as I want or hope for, but I'm happy to notice it. I don't feel as much distraction or interference with my ability to think as I did two or three months ago. I don't have any specific explanation for it. The only thing I can think of is maybe I'm getting off my chest some of the things that have been bothering me without my knowing that they were bothering me. Does that appear logical or possible?

Therapist: Well, I presume so. I don't know whether it's the whole reason, but it is often important to get clear about the improvements as well as the difficulties. Recognizing some improvement is satisfaction in itself.

Mr. Jones: My boss praised me highly a week ago for the project I had completed and that made me happy. I still am not free from the frequent recurrence of the obsessive thoughts.

Therapist: Tell me more about it.

Mr. Jones: That I'm going to kill my wife.

Therapist: Tell me when these thoughts come. You haven't mentioned them for some time.

Mr. Jones: Well, they come often or I remember them often. They don't seem to be associated with any particular feeling or condition.

RETURN OF THE OBSESSION

In therapy it is a rare and golden opportunity to investigate the actual appearance of an obsessional thought at a particular time. If we can elicit the thoughts and feelings that precede the obsessive thought, we will have direct evidence of how thoughts or feelings that are too painful, dangerous, or humiliating need to be distorted and directed into obsessional thoughts, which are viewed as being less dangerous to the individual. Such opportunities are rare because the thoughts are often unconscious and entirely out of awareness or else so fleeting and so painful that they cannot be acknowledged and must be immediately transformed. However, the search must be made because such data are the essential links in eliminating obsessional behavior and because there is a clear relationship, which the patient cannot obfuscate, deny, doubt, or distort. Therapy can be dramatically shortened if we can move directly into such an awareness.

Therapist: Can you remember the last time it happened?

Mr. Jones: Well, just a few minutes ago, before my present mention of it.

Therapist: Can you paint a picture of what was going on in your mind? This is very useful if you can mention it when it does occur, because we can sort of get an understanding of the framework under which it occurs. Was it just before you mentioned your improvement, or what?

To achieve such recall, it is useful to ask the patient to go back into that moment to set the stage and supply all the props in order to encourage the recall. With Mr. Jones, I tried to develop the scenario, but the patient was so uneasy that our investigation became diverted and he spoke about his dream and other incidents with his wife.

Mr. Jones: Well, I think it was before that. It happens often ...

Therapist: Yes ...

Mr. Jones: I guess something else seems to be bothering me or making me uneasy. I remember those thoughts with greater frequency when I'm occupied with something enjoyable that is taking all of my attention. That, too, is in illustration of an improvement in my feelings, though. Several months ago these thoughts used to keep recurring so often that I couldn't concentrate on anything without difficulty, with a great loss of thinking power. But now I'm able to concentrate, and while I'm doing that, I don't think of that unpleasant obsessive thought.

Therapist: You can't piece together the thought you had a couple of minutes ago while you were here?

Mr. Jones: There isn't anything to ...

Therapist: I mean the moment when it occurred. It's very difficult, I know, but very useful.

Mr. Jones: I can't think of anything at all. I think it was just after I ... mentioned about the dream of being in this city in Europe.

Therapist: What's going on in your mind?

Mr. Jones: I was just thinking of Saturday. We took the trip over to see the Japanese cherry trees, which were beginning to bloom.

Therapist: What happened?

In some hope that the association would shed light on the arousal of his obsessive thought I proceeded to explore what could very well be a distraction.

Mr. Jones: On the way home the traffic was heavy. And I was changing lanes. As I did this, the man behind me blew his horn loudly and forcibly. I yelled at him. My wife was displeased. She blames me for whatever happens, regardless of whose fault it is. So we had a short exchange of ... words on that subject.

Therapist: Short exchange of words. I presume it was sort of pleasant? [sarcastically]

Mr. Jones: Oh, no! We ...

Therapist: Well, why don't you say so? You got sore at her!

EXPRESSION OF AFFECT

Efforts by the therapist to get the patient to express his feelings directly and vigorously are crucial to the success of the therapy. No such occasion must be overlooked or bypassed. The preceding exchange was the first time I had directly and sharply confronted him with his evasive tendencies in expressing his feelings. I felt our relationship was solid enough at that time to sustain a comment that had a critical ring. It was important to wait until then to be sure the relationship could handle this type of approach without it producing too much anxiety. Such confrontations are the heart and soul of the therapeutic endeavor — that is, the clarification of facts and data about feelings.

Mr. Jones: Yes, I got sore at her, and frequently do when we are driving because of her tendency to blame me for everything. She says I'm belligerent and selfish and disregard everyone's rights, but I don't think that I am and often tell her so.

Therapist: Now, on this occasion, somebody blew his horn at you?

I wanted to explore this situation in detail because what I had been anticipating was directly related to what we had been trying to explore — namely, his obsessional thoughts. He clearly got angry at his wife's reaction. I wanted to develop how he dealt with his anger clearly and unequivocally. The best way to do this was to reenact the event slowly, so as to prevent the usual uncertainties, doubts, and qualifications that plague all obsessional communications and make the understanding tentative because of the doubts that are intruded into the recollection. We may avoid or at least limit these doubts by a clear and careful reenactment of the event.

Therapist: Were you going too slow?

Mr. Jones: No, I was cutting into another lane and the car behind me was attempting to do likewise and pass me at the same time. As he passed by, I shouted at him that blowing his horn won't help.

Therapist: Do you think it was necessary to shout at him at all?

Mr. Jones: My feeling was that he was being careless and pushing himself ahead in violation of my rights.

Therapist: How was it a violation of your rights?

Mr. Jones: Well, because in order to have complied with his request, I would have had to move out of his way.

Therapist: You thought rather than blow his horn he should have waited until the opportunity presented itself and he should change lanes instead of trying to force you to change lanes. Is that it?

Mr. Jones: It's rather hard to analyze it this way.

Therapist: I'm just wondering what the situation was. Were you expected to change lanes to let him pass or was it that he wanted to pass you in the ordinary way? One doesn't necessarily expect the guy in front to pull out of a lane to let the man behind pass. I'm trying to get clear as to what provokes you or irritates you enough to yell out. This is something you just spoke of at the beginning of the hour as a rather humiliating, excessive reaction and yet you find yourself doing it.

Mr. Jones: I think that the difference between the situations would account for the difference in my feelings of ability to do it.

Therapist: Yeah.

Mr. Jones: The situation of being on the run and there being little likelihood of a continuing encounter or criticism from a bystander.

The patient was saying here that it was easier when he could get away from a situation in contrast to being shut up in the bus and having to face the other person.

Therapist: Except your wife. She was there.

Mr. Jones: Yes. I was provoked with a violent reaction from her.

Therapist: And the shouting out ...

Mr. Jones: Both the shouting out and the fact that the — that I was changing lanes. Whenever any car behind me has to blow its horn or put on its brakes or anything else, she feels that I'm in the wrong because some one else had to do something. I must drive so that no one else has to change their course on account of me.

Therapist: You should be a good boy.

Mr. Jones: It sounds like that.

The hour ended and there was still much to be done, but not all at one time. Several important issues evolved from an examination of the interview in retrospect. It is clear that while much of significance transpired and the therapy moved closer to discovery of the key elements in the development of obsessional processes, the effort was thwarted several times by the nature of the obsessional dynamism and its capacity to capture and involve the therapist in distracting maneuvers. All the attempts to explore the origins of the obsessive thoughts were fruitless and, in spite of the clarity in the therapist's program, he succumbed to the tantalizing distractions, which led to no definite etiological discovery.

REGRESSION IN THERAPY

In the preceding session, Mr. Jones appeared to be avoiding some important issues. However, two days later he confronted the issues of his childishness in a frontal fashion, producing a rich exchange. He described feeling trapped and resentful toward his mother and his wife, whom he felt maintained this bondage. A clear, direct relationship began to appear between these feelings, heretofore secret and maintained on a subconscious level, and the obsessional thoughts, which were the only ways he could discharge his strong, hostile feelings. The elucidation of these feelings and the effect they had on his relationship with his mother, wife, and other transferential figures became a major focus of the therapeutic process once they were brought into the open. The working through of these feelings gradually resolved the double binds in his interpersonal relationships, thereby loosening and ultimately eliminating the obsessive thoughts. This process began during this session, which opened with the recall of a dream Mr. Jones had had when he was twelve.

Mr. Jones: I was remembering this morning about an odd feeling which I had occasionally when I was twelve, in which sounds or noises would sound oppressively loud and frightening to me. The instance I am recalling took place one morning while I was lying in bed. My parents and my sister, who was two years old, were in one room and I was in a room by myself.

Therapist: The odd feeling consisted of what?

Mr. Jones: Consisted of noises or sounds which sounded much louder than they ordinarily were and had a frightening quality about it. It seems to me to be tied in vaguely with a dream I had several times when I was a child that I was being rolled up in a blanket, but no specific person was doing it. I struggled, but couldn't get out.

Therapist: Felt trapped?

This issue was alluded to many times in previous sessions. He could not integrate at those times, however. The feeling of being trapped, or immobilized and unable to take action to alter one's state of uneasiness, is a major aspect of the phobic and obsessional dynamism. The need to be freely mobile with an immediate access to a secure base constitutes the major element in all the phobias, whether it involves closed or open spaces, persons, things, enclosures, or specific issues. Mr. Jones's helpless feeling, which was associated with great danger and fright, was related to being under the control of others and, therefore, trapped. The phenomenon of exaggerated sounds and noises that he felt in his dream referred to his childhood, when the whole world was huge and ominous while he was small and helpless.

Mr. Jones: Yes, I'm trying to remember more about this feeling of being frightened. I don't remember anything more about it.

Note how the recall of fright, helplessness, and his inability to ask for reassurance led him directly, as he continued, into some rumination about his obsessions:

Mr. Jones: I think I have a clue on the subject of obsessive thoughts about my wife and also about the feelings I had two years ago that I was being treated as if I were a child. This morning, my wife and I were talking about putting in grass seed in the backyard. My boss offered me the loan of his seeder (on the previous Sunday) and I thought I would borrow it just to show my appreciation of his kindness. I expressed that thought to my wife and she was agreeable. But at the moment I felt a recurrence of the feelings that I had when practically anything I suggested to my wife I was sure that she was going to disapprove of.
Therapist: Uh huh.
Mr. Jones: And two years ago when I was having these feelings, I had a rather desperate attitude and expressed things so strongly and forcibly that it would practically be an ultimatum. My wife, of course, resented it. I think there's some parallel with that situation and the idea I had while I was growing up that my parents wouldn't approve of things I wanted to do unless they thought of it first.
Therapist: This morning, as you told your wife about some arrangement which you made, you had a feeling which reminded you of your parents and their inclination toward disapproval. Is that what you're saying?

I repeated it almost exactly as he had said it, in order to strengthen the awareness and to stimulate further discussion of this very important observation. In typical obsessional fashion he first objected, then qualified, and ultimately agreed. Thus, it effectively became *his* insight, initiated and developed by him. This is just what he accused his mother of doing and this is what he did with me, in the sense of having to have insight come from *his* observations.

Mr. Jones: I'm saying ... that's not quite it. I think the reason I found that uncomfortable was because it reminded me subconsciously of incidents that happened when I was growing up.

Therapist: What is there about the idea that makes you concerned about a possible rejection from your wife? What is there about your suggestion that might provoke objection?

I was trying to get him to think about some of the issues about which he felt threatened — that is, if it occurred when he took an adult position. If so, it might illuminate why the obsessional thoughts appeared in relation to some activity in which he expected some rejection and felt righteously indignant if it came.

Mr. Jones: Nothing ... I didn't even think of her possible objection until immediately after I had stated it. But two years ago I would have been prepared ... I would have been fearful and prepared.

Therapist: Yeah, but what do you think it is that stirs up some feeling of rejection?

Mr. Jones: I think it's a repetition of what I must have gone through unconsciously when I was growing up.

SIGNIFICANCE OF THE HERE AND NOW

The tendency to refer to the past without tying it clearly to the issues in the here and now is a common technique for avoiding the emotional impact of an experience. It provides a pseudosophisticated explanation that avoids the need for more intensive exploration that may be painful; if allowed to pass, this tendency can seriously impede the therapeutic process by failing to expose the emotional issues in a situation.

Although the tendency to avoid a connection to the here and now was not prominent in Mr. Jones's therapy, it nevertheless had to be dealt with when it did occur. Mr. Jones needed to be informed that his preceding statement reflected a superficial, verbal insight without the ability to initiate change. To promote change, insight must be connected to the present set of feelings and attitudes; the patient must understand how his present feelings, concerns, fears, and threats are not realistic for the present situation or relationships but are remnants of relationships out of the past and how his present reactions are mere repetitions of the past and not realistic appraisals of the present. Such a recognition then constitutes insight capable of producing and sustaining change in one's attitudes and behavior.

Therapist: Well, that's a nice, easy answer, but it must have something to do with what was going on this morning. Maybe it's a repetition of the past, but what is happening now when in your presenting an idea to your wife you are concerned about possible objections and rejections?

Mr. Jones: I cannot put my finger on anything else except a repetition of childhood experiences, and I thought that that probably was the explanation of it.

Therapist: That doesn't tell us why you still behave towards your wife as if you were going to be told off.

Mr. Jones: I thought it was the sensation that applied unconsciously to attitudes I had toward my parents. For some reason which I don't understand, it was projected into a feeling in discussing with my wife.

Therapist: Now that you think you understand it, will it stop?

Mr. Jones: I think it will diminish, since I understand it and it has diminished over what it was two years ago.

USE OF THERAPIST'S EMOTIONS

My mild impatience and irritation were manifested in my not permitting the formula of "reexperiencing childhood" to be viewed as the total explanation. The therapist's irritation and, at times, more hostile responses to the obsessional's rigidity are a continuing issue in working with these patients. The therapist must become aware of his feelings and must separate his reactions to the patient's irritating behavior from his own neurotic incapacity to tolerate ambiguity and frustration. The patient must not be attacked or criticized for behaving like an obsessional. Yet the effect of the obsessional's behavior on others must be noticed and brought to his attention. This calls for empathic awareness of the patient's anxiety in allowing some irritation to appear and be presented to the patient without stirring up too much anxiety, which would only increase the obsessional defenses.

Therapist: Why did you have to tell your wife about this arrangement [for the loan of the seeder]?

Mr. Jones: Well, we were talking at the time about planting our backyard with grass seed.

Therapist: So you weren't telling her what you were going to do. You were asking her whether it was all right to do it?

Mr. Jones: No, I don't feel that I was asking her. I felt I was telling her.

Therapist: Now if you were telling her, then why should there be a feeling of possible objection? If you said to your wife, "I'm going out to the corner for a cup of coffee," it's not a question of "May I go?" — it's "I'm going!" She might say, "Oh, please don't go." So here you're saying, "I'm going to borrow the boss's seed spreader."

Mr. Jones: Yeah, that's right.

Therapist: You're quite certain that this is the atmosphere in which it got said? "I'm going to do this." Or, are you still somewhat uncertain and querulous about it?

My continuing to press the issue was to clarify how he responded to authoritative figures like his mother and wife. The relentless quality of my exploration could easily stir up Mr. Jones's irritation. On the other hand, it was crucial to press for clarity to overcome his cloudy and diffuse thinking, sometimes at the risk of stirring up his defenses.

Mr. Jones: Apparently there was some semblance of the old hangover of that thought; otherwise I wouldn't have been thinking of all this.

Therapist: Otherwise there wouldn't be a question of objection, eh?

Mr. Jones: That's right.

Therapist: So there is still the need for permission to do something which you feel is quite appropriate?

Mr. Jones: I guess that's right.

Therapist: Do you agree, or are you simply placating me?

The obsessional has a fairly pervasive tendency to turn off pressure on him by verbal agreement even when he covertly remains in doubt or disagrees. Some patients are aware that they do this in therapeutic sessions as well as in the world at large; ackowledging it makes it less likely to occur. It also forces the patient to become aware of his other covert operations of doubting, ambivalence, rigidity, and insistence on being in control. The patient must recognize how one can control others by stubbornly insisting on one's way or, at the opposite extreme, by easy agreement while maintaining secret doubts and uncertainties. While confronting the patient with regard to these tactics may not produce the desired effect at first, it enlightens and enables the patient to notice the maneuver as it begins to develop.

Another tendency which is difficult to manage if it is not exposed early is the tendency of the obsessional to turn off and no longer be attentive to what is transpiring. Growing anxiety may initiate the process, and while the patient appears to be "with it," he is no longer listening or hearing and may be distracted or obsessing about other things. At these times he may agree with what is going on to avoid discovery. However, he will have no recollection of his agreement later on and will deny that the issue was ever presented or discussed. This phenomenon must be distinguished from deliberate evasion or falsification. It is an unconscious process, and until the patient becomes aware of its occurrence, he may fiercely deny the reality of the encounter during his withdrawn state. After several confrontations, when the therapist challenges the patient about his inattentiveness, the patient can identify these withdrawals and spot the actual moment when the turnoff took place. Not only is the moment a significant one in establishing the issue that created enough anxiety to turnoff the patient, but the awareness of it will go a long way in clarifying the obsessional's distracting techniques that produce the symptomatology of this disorder. Unless the therapist is aware of this possibility, the work seems to proceed smoothly — with the patient agreeing with and accepting the therapist's observations but without any change occurring in the patient, since nothing was truly experienced. This may be one cause of the interminable analyses of obsessional patients.

Mr. Jones: I'm agreeing with you now. I hadn't analyzed it that deeply. I thought that at first I hadn't any of these doubts. But now that I scrutinize it more closely, I realize that the doubt was occurring while I was speaking.

Therapist: So it's not simply a repetition, is it? Because as a child you had good reason to wonder whether your parents would approve of your decision. On Sunday you accepted a perfectly reasonable offer that didn't require any approval of your acceptance.

Mr. Jones: I can see no reason why I should have.

Therapist: In fact, if your wife had objected, you would probably have gotten furious.

Mr. Jones: Yes.

Therapist: Because it's a perfectly reasonable decision. So I wonder why you felt the need to get permission from your wife.

Mr. Jones: Well, the concept of getting permission was an unconscious one at the time. I didn't recognize it as that until now, when we're talking about it. Going back to my childhood again, you mentioned that I probably had good reasons to wonder whether my parents would approve. But I'm in doubt about that, too.

Therapist: I meant good reason in the sense that you were just a child and they were grown-ups, but now you are making decisions as an adult.

Mr. Jones: When I was a child, I had this semiconscious idea that my parents wouldn't want me to do anything unless they asked me to or they thought of it first.

Therapist: Uh-huh.

Mr. Jones: I can think of an application of this that bothered me when I was sixteen or so. Other boys my age were starting to smoke and I wanted to, but was afraid my parents wouldn't approve of it. I never could arrive at any suitable method of doing it or asking them, so I never did.

Therapist: How do you like the idea of always having to ask other people to approve of what you are convinced about?

Mr. Jones: Well, I have the feeling that I always had to document my request voluminously to justify it or else I wouldn't get my wish.

Therapist: Yes.

Mr. Jones: And I didn't like the idea of asking for something and being turned down.

Therapist: Well, how do you respond to the notion of having to get permission to do things which you feel fully competent to decide upon?

Mr. Jones: With resentment.

Therapist: So you must hate the business of having to present a plan in a "hoping for approval" way?

Mr. Jones: I hated it very strongly two years ago. It seemed to me then that everything I had to say was in the way of begging for approval.

Therapist: Do you think there was anything of this feeling this morning?

Mr. Jones: I think this morning there was a trace of it. There would have to be or I wouldn't have noticed anything about it.

Therapist: Did you experience a feeling of irritation about having to present it in this way even though she said yes?

Mr. Jones: The feeling wasn't dissipated when she said she was agreeable. The resentment was still there but I thought at first of the much stronger feelings two years ago when I was much more upset that I am now.

Therapist: Now you said earlier that you had some ideas about this tendency to get permission from your wife and some of the obsessive thoughts. Do you feel they were tied together?

Mr. Jones: Yes, I do.

Therapist: Let's hear what you think.

Mr. Jones: Well, merely that those thoughts occurred to me while I was analyzing this incident. It was when I had those thoughts that I wondered if there was something wrong with my mind. After I was feeling upset, these thoughts occurred to me. They were painful and distressing, and they kept recurring every second or so. I didn't — I couldn't think of anything else. Now the recurrence is not nearly that frequent when I'm not thinking about emotional difficulties as such. I may go for hours without remembering the thought.

CONFIRMING INSIGHT —
INTELLECTUAL AND EMOTIONAL

We had now established a clear, convincing connection between the obsessive thoughts and emotional states. This is essential, since patients try desperately to relate them to physical phenomena and steadfastly refuse to recognize them as their own productions. As previously discussed, prior to any psychodynamic theories, such thoughts were viewed as invasions or possession by outside forces, thereby making it impossible for the person to alter the situation except by the intervention of agents using their powers of exorcism, which were supposed to drive out these malevolent intruders. The awareness that such intrusive thoughts are of one's own making clearly allows for the possibility that one can alter or eliminate them through one's own actions.

Therapist: Can we understand anything about these obsessive thoughts in relation to the incident this morning? You already made it clear that in presenting a reasonable plan to your wife you felt some uneasiness and some irritation in having to get permission.

Mr. Jones: And the thought that she might not approve.

Therapist: And the thought that she might not approve. Well, you recognize some irritation in spite of her approval and you begin to have the obsessive thoughts about killing your wife. Do you think that there might be some relationship between anger, irritation, and frustrated fury at her that are stirred up by your having to play the role of a little boy, which gets reflected in these obsessive thoughts?

Mr. Jones: It sounds logical, but the thoughts occur at other times without any similar provocation.

This was the first time I had presented this hypothesis to Mr. Jones, and I expected that he would have some hesitation and reservation in accepting it, in spite of the careful development of data to support it. I felt no need to insist that he accept it, and, in fact, it would have been inadvisable to do so. The expected reluctance of an obsessional to accept any new explanation for his behavior requires that the therapist allow these ideas to simmer for a while so that they can be formulated and brought to the sessions as if they were the patient's own discovery.

Therapist: Maybe so, but if you had not taken this incident and kept it fresh in mind and examined it critically, we might not have seen any relationship there either.

Mr. Jones: ... I suppose so. I thought of it that way too.

He had to assume some credit for this construction, and I had to permit him to do so. The observation I made was valid, since we could not have made this association had he not recalled and related the incident. However, the following exchange became confused and blurred, and the point got lost in the patient's quibbling. I wanted to clarify why the resentment set off obsessional ideas, but I didn't quite succeed at that point. Mr. Jones's obsessional defenses blurred the distressing awareness of how he translated unexpressed anger into hostile preoccupations and compulsive thinking.

Mr. Jones: I thought it would seem logical that I would have these thoughts when some incident causing resentment or anger with my wife would occur. It would also seem logical when resentment with anybody would occur, but then it doesn't even enter my mind.

Therapist: Yes, but here it is.

Mr. Jones: I mean I just merely remember it.

Therapist: Yeah, but you've just described an incident where ordinarily there should be no resentment since she did agree.

Mr. Jones: The resentment had nothing to do with her agreeing. I felt uneasy because of the resentment I had two years ago in a similar scene.

Therapist: Possibly your resentment towards your wife two years ago had to do with a similar kind of situation?

Mr. Jones: Yes.

Therapist: So it's important to note that your resentment is not entirely due to your wife's reaction. It comes from something inside of you.

Mr. Jones: That's right, because the feeling occurred before I knew what her reaction was going to be.

Therapist: So what do you think the resentment is all about?

Mr. Jones: ... Well, I had the one hypothesis, that it's simply a hangover from childhood.

Again I wanted to avoid the oversimplified, overintellectualized explanation that merely parrots the professional explanation for all neurotic behavior as being mere remnants of childish attitudes. I therefore did not stop to explore his statement, but tried to pursue it further, examining his anxieties about approval and perfection and his feelings of threat and danger if these requirements were not fulfilled.

Therapist: Nothing else comes to mind about it?

Mr. Jones: No, it doesn't.

Therapist: What about the feeling of having to get permission to do what you want to do?

Mr. Jones: Well, I can't think what it could be.

OFFERING ALTERNATIVE HYPOTHESES

Mr. Jones's failure to pursue his feeling of having to get permission required some help from the therapist in an active way. In such an instance, one possibility would be to suggest a number of alternative hypotheses and to allow the patient to select one that appeals to him. Another way would be to suggest a likely notion that is the therapist's primary hypothesis and to see where that goes. Here I decided to propose what I thought was the most likely possibility from my understanding of what it was like to grow up in his home.

Therapist: Doesn't your concern about the need to get permission tell us something about what a bound-up individual you are? Someone who is terribly hesitant to take a step on his own, to state a position, or to take a stand?

Mr. Jones: It would seem so, and yet I often feel compelled to do exactly that.

Therapist: Well, let's hear more about it.

Mr. Jones: I'm anxious to take a positive stand and to be regarded as having authority and using it properly.

Therapist: Somewhat contradictory then, isn't it?

It is out of such contradictions that we can discover the conflicts, dilemmas, and anxiety that produce the symptoms of all neuroses.

Mr. Jones: Yes.

Therapist: What do you make of it?

Mr. Jones: I'm trying to think of — of incidents involving other people besides my wife.

Therapist: Uh huh.

Mr. Jones: And I think of the obsession I have for reinforcing all of my statements or directives with copious citations of authority.

Therapist: What about that, how does that tie in with what you say?

Mr. Jones: It ties in with your reference to being bound up, being hesitant to express wishes or desires.

Therapist: Yes, the only way you can express a wish or desire is to have it so documented that there is no possibility of it being rejected. You can't feel, "I want to do it just because I want to do it." You must first be certain that it's O.K. to do it.

Mr. Jones: I'm sure that's true.

Therapist: So although you say you like to express some authority, you feel extremely uneasy about it?

Mr. Jones: Yes.

Therapist: So much so that you expect some kind of overwhelming response even if it's a trivial matter such as accepting the offer of your colleague to borrow his seeder.

Mr. Jones: Why should I expect disapproval?

Therapist: And why do you need to get permission is an additional question we need to get answered. But at least we can make some sense as to where these obsessive thoughts come from, which in the past have seemed very mysterious to you. They don't come out of the thin air, do they? They are related to definite and pretty strong feelings of resentment.

Mr. Jones: Yes, they must . . . but they occur to me not only in situations in which resentment is present, but at other times as well.

This terminated the session, and in my notes at the end of the hour, I stated: "This was a profitable session in which the development of some insight about a very important process in the patient's life has partially occurred. The interview began with the recognition of tremendous concerns about his acceptability, expressing his own needs, desires, attitudes, and expectations of rebuff — all associated with extreme resentment, overwhelming dependency, and the reason being formalized in a sense in the obsessive thoughts. There was no introduction as he got right down to business. After about six minutes there was a drastic change in subject when he raised the question of his obsessive thoughts in relation to an incident which occurred in the morning and which he detailed in the hour. Later I tried to bring into focus his original statement of the relationship to the obsessive thought to his strong dependency and his marked resentment. The interview seemed quite meaningful to the patient in terms of understanding some of his unusual reactions and certainly clarified the development of the obsessive thought in this particular situation."

TRANSFERENCE INTERPRETATION

Five days later, at our next session, he immediately referred to the last session, raising the question of whether his need to get permission was tied to his need for being liked; but he quickly got back to the subject of his feeling angry and resentful when his wife treated him like a child, making him feel helpless and unable to assert himself. This reaction, which was directly related to his obsessive thoughts, enabled us to trace the development of his symptom from a situation that occurred at the present time. This is the essence of the value of transference in the therapeutic process, when a symptom develops during therapy and is involved in the relationship with the therapist. For Mr. Jones, it was the same symptom that had developed years earlier and was tied to feelings that were present then and were stirred up again in the therapy. In that setting, the patient had convincing evidence that his feelings and distortions produced the obsessional defensive thoughts that so disorganized his living. We could then draw inferences about his symptoms, which would allow him to change his rigid and compulsive thinking and behavior.

Mr. Jones: Do you suppose that the idea I have of having to seek permission or get approval might be related to the idea that people must like me?

Therapist: What do you think?

Mr. Jones: Well, it would seem that they ought to be related. If people have to like me then I would have to get their permission or else they might disapprove and therefore not like me.

Therapist: Have you noticed any instances of this relationship?

Mr. Jones: Well, I don't think of any specific instances immediately. There were some further events with regard to the seed spreader that I mentioned to you.

PERSISTENCE, REPETITION, AND INSIGHT

Therapy generally proceeds in this way, where recollections are not forthcoming completely at one time. As one develops understanding of an event, further recollections and insights ensue. There is much evidence that the possibility for reconstruction of an event grows out of an increasing understanding of the significance of the recall. Thus, the reconstruction of the past proceeds out of insight from present behavior, instead of insight growing out of the reconstruction of the past. To illuminate present behavior, it would therefore be more profitable to focus on present events rather than on the tedious and often questionable reconstruction of one's past life. I let Mr. Jones continue to talk about the incident with the seed spreader.

Mr. Jones: I picked up the seed spreader at my boss's home on Saturday morning and I felt uncomfortable at that time. Last week I thought that when I returned the spreader my wife and I might drop in and pay him a visit because we hadn't been out there for quite a while. She was violently opposed to that and she got very emotional. We didn't completely finish the yard yesterday. But she's had this obsession, I'll call it, of wanting to get it 100 percent completed. After we had the argument she refused to go with me.

Therapist: Even though you had made tentative arrangements to go?

Mr. Jones: Yes. I reminded her of that but she said, well, she had nothing to do with it. What upset me most of all about it is that it is similar to the episodes that occurred when my trouble began a couple of years ago. She's displeased that I haven't been able to get the yard work done before going on my trip. When we get into these arguments she gets so emotionally upset that reasoning is of no value. I told her that the yard work wasn't the only part of our life — that we had our social life and other relationships that we couldn't completely ignore.

Therapist: How did you feel when your wife refused to go and you were forced to go alone?

Mr. Jones: I felt displeased and angry and I felt mounting tension and interference with my thinking, which has been bothering me all day.

Therapist: The obsession, you mean?

Mr. Jones: Yes, recognizing that I felt resentment against her because of her uncooperative attitude. I would remind myself that resentment brings forth these obsessive thoughts. Obsessive thoughts have troubled me a few times today, which in the past few months hasn't happened too often. I noticed that interference with my thinking was intensified.

Therapist: You were saying that you had the thoughts today.

Mr. Jones: Well, I have been able to concentrate more on my work and I felt that the interference with my thinking had been lessening, but today it was bad again.

Therapist: Was it so unreasonable for you to make arrangements to visit with your wife when you returned the seeder without asking her in advance?

I wanted to get back to the main theme, which was his feelings of helplessness and uncertainty about the management of his life. He seemed to be moving away and about to take off on his somatic problems, which were responses to his anxiety. I wanted to get into the anxiety, so that we could again demonstrate how his attitudes produced anxiety — which, in turn, was manifested by somatic tension.

Mr. Jones: Sometimes she resents that and other times she's happy about it. Sometimes she tells me that I needn't feel that I have to ask her if I want to do something. I was rather surprised that she felt as hostile towards this idea as she did.

Therapist: You said that you were angry and disappointed. Would you say that you were more than angry, possibly furious, in having been put in this position of making an appointment and having to show up alone?

Mr. Jones: Yes, that displeased and disappointed me, made me angry.

Therapist: You say, angry. I don't know whether you mean angry annoyed, or angry furious, or angry boiling mad.

Mr. Jones: Making those distinctions between different shadings isn't very easy for me to do.

I was convinced as I posed this question that he had stronger feelings than he had expressed. He had to keep controls on his feelings, as well as on everything else, and therefore could not identify or experience how strongly he felt on some occasions, particularly those that would stir up strong reactions. The obsessional must be encouraged to face these feelings without expecting dramatic and cataclysmic consequences. Otherwise he remains calm or slightly annoyed, while the seething cauldron of feeling erupts in obsessional ideas in the form of murderous or destructive thoughts. We must encourage the obsessional to acknowledge his real feelings by giving him support and approval for his reactions, even though we know them to be excessive. The whole range of symptomatology in the obsessive-compulsive states is tied to their capacity to distract, substitute, displace, and defensively react to these feelings, instead of facing them directly. It is the therapist's role to assist them in changing this behavior.

Therapist: You can't remember just how you felt yesterday? With regard to your wife when she just refused to go? Did you feel she was sulking?

Mr. Jones: I felt that she was sulking and I felt rather let down about it. I was angry at having to show up alone, and I told them that she was so tired from all the work we'd done that she didn't feel like coming. Maybe being so tired brought on this demonstration. But she kept saying that it wasn't right for me to want to go and visit anyone until we had finished the work.

In her emotional distress about the yard work she launches into criticism of me for not wanting to do any work and spending time fraternizing with friends and drinking cocktails.

Therapist: That's bad? [laughter]

A light touch is crucial with the tense and intense obsessional; he has such difficulty in enjoying himself. The personality structure of Mr. Jones's wife began to emerge in his descriptions of her attitude, and I began to visualize her as an obsessional individual with perfectionistic standards and expectations paralleling those of the patient's mother.

Mr. Jones: It's bad when she thinks of it in this ultraemotional way.

Therapist: What happened when you got back?

Mr. Jones: Well, I guess she had been brooding about it all the while I'd been gone and she was still sulky. However, we tried to patch it over. This situation is quite similar to the events of two years ago. At that time there was a tremendous amount of work that had to be done and I couldn't take much time off to help her.

Therapist: You couldn't take a day off?

Mr. Jones: I couldn't readily. The work couldn't be done as well as if I were there.

It was important to get him to see how his rigidity contributed to his wife's distress, which, in turn, made her more demanding and increased the patient's anxieties about his uncooperative behavior.

Therapist: Well, isn't that always true? Does that mean that you could never take time off?

Mr. Jones: No, I could and would take time off if one or two of the three people who are now gone were present. There is quite a similarity between this situation and the one which happened two years ago.

Note that he had reported this several times as each insight stirred up further recollections that become more convincing and clarifying. Such a development is very fortuitous in the resolution of this disorder. As he moved along, he recalled still another event about the time his symptoms first appeared.

Mr. Jones: It was that that made me conscious that something was interfering with my mental ability ... Wednesday we were talking on the topic of permission. Sometimes I seek permission in the form of a question and I hope this meets with her approval or enthusiasm ... I just recalled an incident that happened on or about June 1951. We were in a restaurant and we were displeased with the service. I decided I wasn't going to leave a tip because the service was so bad. She asked me to leave a tip and I wasn't able to take that in stride at all. That upset me greatly and I became very angry at her dictating to me and it brought back these old thoughts again that she was treating me as if I were a child. She saw that I was upset and I told her that I was upset about her dictating to me.

Therapist: Did you leave a tip?

I felt the need to be sure whether he sustained his position or whether he succumbed to her demands. I anticipated the latter and wanted this additional data to strengthen my formulation about his neurotic symptoms.

Mr. Jones: Yes, I did. I didn't make any report to her of whether I did or not. Later in the car she asked me whether I did and I told her. I felt a very strange feeling coming over me that I seemed to have lost all my progress I made with my first doctor in eliminating these disturbing thoughts that were bothering me and interfering with my thinking. The whole thing seemed to break down again. I brought that out to illustrate that I had the same kind of feeling yesterday and today.

Therapist: Feel it right now?

Mr. Jones: Yes.

Therapist: Let's see if you can express it.

This was another opportunity to highlight the feeling at the present time, so that the recall might go beyond a mere intellectualization. This therapeutic tactic is essential with all patients but especially with the obsessional, who has great difficulty in expressing his feelings.

Mr. Jones: The only reason I hesitated in responding was that it seems that in the last few moments just telling that seemed to make me feel somewhat better. I have felt it all day up until now, and I still feel a good part of it.

Therapist: Just what is it you feel?

Mr. Jones: It's so vague it defied any description.

Therapist: Well, let's try to formulate it the best we can. Do you feel, as you said earlier, as if you made no progress or is it something more specific?

Mr. Jones: Well, I feel that I can't think as logically or as rapidly as I ought to or as I want to.

Therapist: Do you feel like a kid again?

I tried to keep the focus on the possible feelings of helplessness when he gets angry and cannot do anything about it except to obsess about his wife and his plans to kill her.

Mr. Jones: Well, I can't give any answer to that because I didn't have these feelings positively when I was a kid. I suppose I did unconsciously, but . . .

Therapist: No, no! That wasn't what I meant. I meant did you feel like a kid in the sense that you felt sort of helpless and weak again?

Mr. Jones: Yes, that would definitely be so. And that's frustrating because I can feel this definite obstacle in thinking constructively.

Therapist: In the last instance you spoke of you decided not to leave a tip because you were dissatisfied with the service. Your wife insisted that it would be improper not to leave a tip and you became angry at her for trying to tell you what to do. She insisted that you must behave properly. You left a tip but you began to feel helpless and experience a lost feeling.

NEED FOR REVIEW OF PROCESS

I reviewed the tip situation step by step, in order to focus on the helpless issue and to clarify the steps leading to the anger and frustration with his wife. Ordinarily the patient only recognizes the final feelings; with some help he can recall an incident that produced the feeling. However, it is the essence of the therapeutic process to enable a patient to tie his feelings to a reaction to another person or event and thereby establish without any doubt that his reactions are directly attributable to the relationship with the other person. The other person stirs up feelings and attitudes he cannot accept or tolerate, producing a reaction he is also unable to accept. This then sets off a train of neurotic defense mechanisms to avoid a direct confrontation with the events. My summary of the tip situation was designed to highlight these developments.

Mr. Jones: Exactly correct.

Therapist: What do you think produces this weak and helpless feeling? What does it have to do with?

Mr. Jones: . . . Well, maybe . . . I suppose it goes back to childhood again. I can't think of anything else.

Therapist: Let's look at the present situation. It has something to do with the way you feel at this moment.

Mr. Jones: Well, at this moment I would resent it because it implies having to take orders from my wife ... That doesn't seem to mean much though ... There is some problem involved in all of that that I can't put my finger on though.

Therapist: You think it has something to do with the fact that you had to give in?

Mr. Jones: Yes, it does, and sometimes I didn't want to give in.

Therapist: Now last night after you got home, did you give in, in a sense of trying to humor her?

Mr. Jones: Yes.

Therapist: You did. So then again it got left with the notion that you were wrong in what you did, rather than that you felt righteously indignant about her not going visiting with you.

Mr. Jones: Well, I felt righteously indignant and I still feel that I was right but I don't want to be bearing a grudge about it.

Therapist: And the way to do that is to say you were wrong?

Mr. Jones: No, I didn't say I was wrong.

Therapist: No, not in so many words — but in sort of making up, trying to do the right thing that will win her back.

Mr. Jones: Well, I knew that she was displeased and unhappy about not making as much progress with the yard as she wanted to. I didn't mind working at it again, but I was displeased that she wouldn't accompany me when I took the seed spreader back.

Therapist: So you're often left with a feeling that you always have to be the one who gives in?

Mr. Jones: Yes, yes! Often I am left with that feeling.

Therapist: Can't win ...

Mr. Jones: I'm left with that feeling when my wife is in one of these sulky and emotional moods.

This exchange ended this session. At the next session, two days later, he began to review and reappraise his relationship with his wife and mother.

Mr. Jones: I had a feeling of being very badly disturbed the other day but it passed away soon. It gave me the helpless feeling I had when I was being upset about my wife being uncooperative or unreasonable. She felt the same way and acted the same way when we had to get ready to leave two years ago. I was able to be a very limited help to her in the packing.

His view had now softened considerably, recognizing with no equivocation that he was actually uncooperative and not helpful two years ago. The two-day interval allowed him to reflect on the incident, acknowledge his role, and make gestures toward reconciliation. He was also more capable of seeing her point of view and identifying with it. This was some advance in his heretofore narcissistic viewpoint.

Mr. Jones: We had yard work to do and she thought that we were falling behind in getting the garden chores done. She was frantic and unpleasant because it is difficult for her to postpone doing something that she thought ought to be done now. On Sunday, however, I decided to go anyway because I had to. In the past such a situation caused me great distress. That happened in 1950 when we were invited to a picnic with my family. I had accepted this invitation without asking her. She didn't want to go. I didn't want to go without her and I made an excuse and didn't go. I didn't feel I was under a similar disability Sunday. I dropped in on my colleague and told him my wife wasn't feeling well.

Therapist: What made it so difficult to do in 1950?

Mr. Jones: She thought I preferred my folks to her and my mother made slurring remarks from time to time.

Therapist: You say that you think she did make some compromise in spending as much time as she did with your family?

Mr. Jones: Yes, because it was uncomfortable for her.

Therapist: Did she really want you to drop them entirely?

Mr. Jones: No, no. I don't think so. She used to feel I wanted to visit them as often as possible and I tried to show her that I cared for her by reducing the frequency of the correspondence and my visits with them.

Therapist: Was that a hard decision for you to make? Weren't you torn on both sides?

Mr. Jones: Well, yes, I suppose that's what made it so difficult. But I had the feeling that the antagonism between my wife and parents would gradually disappear and that they would get to love each other.

Therapist: Love each other? [quizzically]

He could only visualize one extreme or the other, either love or hate. No middle path of toleration, indifference, or simply liking each other was a consideration. His failure to make them love each other made him more desperately torn between them.

Mr. Jones: Yes, that's the way I felt. When I saw that that was impossible I was torn between the two and I just didn't know how to resolve this impossible situation. So I decided that, being married, my future was on her side rather than on my folks' side. And after I proved it to her time and again, she did calm down. Before that I tried to get her to be the one who would make peace with my folks.

Therapist: Why do you think your folks were antagonistic?

Mr. Jones: Well, I don't think they wanted me to get married at all. However, when we became engaged, they violently objected because she was ten years older than I and because she had been divorced and couldn't have children.

Therapist: What did you do?

Mr. Jones: I just ignored their objections and told them how nice she was and how much I loved her but I never . . . hit back at their angry statements.

Therapist: You never have yet, have you?

Mr. Jones: No.

Therapist: Has their antagonism disappeared?

Mr. Jones: The antagonism hasn't disappeared, but the outward expression of it has been muffled.

Therapist: They still think you married badly?

Mr. Jones: Yes, they do. My wife feels that my father is more pleasant toward her. I remember noticing many times during a visit last year that my mother would be belligerent or sarcastic. My mother has a habit of pretending that everything is rosy and wonderful. She would rather feel uncomfortable than say something was unpleasant or disagreeable.

Therapist: When did you first notice that about your mother?

This was the first time Mr. Jones clearly observed that his mother was extremely obsessive and hypocritical in terms of presenting a delightful picture to the world. I noted this in my summary at the end of the session, adding: "She seemed to be a person of great tolerance and sympathy while secretly having many resentments and hostilities which the patient would become belatedly aware of. Mr. Jones, like his mother, has great skills in overlooking the unpleasant issues in his life and pretending that all is well. Rather than face an issue directly, he avoids, denies, distracts, or simply covers up his deeper feelings with superficial displays."

Mr. Jones: Well, when I first started school, about the first or second grade, there was something about Negroes and Jews being in the class. She didn't like this fact. When I asked her about it, she didn't want to talk to me about it. Later I tried to tell her something about some of the Jewish kids being loud and boastful, something I didn't like, and she talked me down in a way that I knew was insincere. I knew that she had a hostile feeling, but that she didn't want me to have any hostile feelings.

Therapist: So you thought your mother was insincere? Sort of two-faced?

Mr. Jones: I didn't think of it as being insincere then. All I remember is that it made it difficult for me to tell her about anything that I didn't like because she would always debunk my ideas of not liking whatever it was.

Therapist: So, in a sense, you tended to do exactly what she did, which was to always be pleasant about what you didn't like.

Mr. Jones: That's right. She was always repressing information about the family. I had the feeling that she didn't want anybody to know or to think anything that was unpleasant or hostile about the family and that all was delightful.

Therapist: Uh-huh. She had to make the world into a never-never land, a big make-believe.

Mr. Jones: Well, often times that was true. My wife has noticed and commented on it. And it was probably some of her comments that made it easier for me to realize it.

Therapist: How did you explain these discrepancies to yourself? This business of your mother feeling one way but expressing something else? What would you think about it if you were dealing with it now, or noticed it now?

Mr. Jones: Well, if I noticed it now — I would think that's the way she had always been. If I noticed it in somebody else I suppose I would think of it as being insincere or two-faced.

Therapist: But not your mother. It would be insincere with someone else, but not your mother.

Mr. Jones: Yes, it would be insincere and two-faced of her, too. It's so confused!

Therapist: Why don't you give it some thought and let's talk about it next time.

In this exchange the patient was pressed to draw an obvious conclusion which he was reluctant to acknowledge, in spite of the abundant evidence to justify it. While making some observations, he tended to negate or undo them by talking about how confused things were, thereby reducing the impact of the awareness.

STRENGTHENING THE THERAPEUTIC ALLIANCE

Five days later, he arrived for his last session prior to a six-week trip. He had been anxious for several days in contemplating the trip and a proposed increase in responsibilities at his job.

Mr. Jones: Finding myself nervous and tense today, I think it's possible that there's some vestiges of my thinking that I must do everything perfectly. While preparing to leave and briefing my subordinates on what's to be done it distressed me that further action remains to be taken. I would feel uncomfortable that I hadn't attained perfection by finishing everything which had come up. Some of the work pertained to them and some was work which was my responsibility.

Therapist: Have you any thoughts about going off for six weeks?

Mr. Jones: No. Well, I'm hoping to be fully cured when I return. But I had begun to notice this feeling of tension on the days when I — I have to come here.

Therapist: What do you feel that is all about?

Mr. Jones: ... I think it's possible that we have begun to talk about some of the things which may really be bothering me, but it's a vague generalization.

Note his growing awareness of our approach to his problem. The trip must be an attractive escape, but he cannot yet say so.

Therapist: Uh-huh.

Mr. Jones: ... I was telling you last Wednesday about my mother's attitude — that everything was rosy and wonderful and without dissension or trouble. Well, I recall that her attitude was that anything unpleasant must be repressed.

Therapist: What do you think the effect of that has been on you that everything unpleasant should be repressed?

Mr. Jones: ... Well, apparently I had a similar attitude, illustrated by my inability to understand that my wife's health wasn't always good. I remember her saying that we had an ideal family. We all enjoyed each other's company. I have the feeling that I had some notion of not being too well pleased myself.

Therapist: So you didn't quite believe your mother?

Mr. Jones: Well, I didn't quite accept that as being the most desirable way. My mother is a very gushy talker and writer and she makes great use of superlatives in describing things as beautiful and wonderful. Well, there is one thought that comes to me on this question of the long interval which is about to take place between now and the next visit with you. I did think about whether I would have any problem in remembering some of the material that we've talked about and whether I would lose any progress as a result of there being a long interval.

The change of subject here revealed that Mr. Jones did have concerns about his absence. Note how he avoided any mention of missing me as a therapist or person.

Therapist: Uh-huh.

Mr. Jones: Sometimes I have had difficulty in remembering some of the things that we talk about that I regard as being important at the time that they occur here.

Therapist: So you have had some concern about what you might miss or lose; coming here seems more important than you indicate.

Mr. Jones: Well, I didn't think of this as being unimportant.

Therapist: No, but perhaps there is some reluctance to say it is.

Mr. Jones: No, I haven't felt that at all.

Therapist: Perhaps you haven't ever felt it?

Mr. Jones: Well, this trip is one that I, I'm being directed to make.

I was pressing for data about how he viewed our work and the possible benefits from it. My anxieties clearly intruded here, perhaps even postponing some positive emotional response he might have eventually made.

Therapist: I realize that. Since it comes only as an afterthought that possibly something important might be missed, I wonder if there is some hesitation on your part to talk about some of the benefits you have derived from our work. Isn't it difficult for you generally to be complimentary about others?

THERAPIST'S PRECONCEPTIONS AS IMPEDIMENTS

There was no basis thus far for my comment. It must have come from my training and expectations that a patient always feels bad when being away from treatment and resents the therapist if he misses a session. These ideas evolve from the intense preoccupation the therapist has with the process and his expectations that the patient also sees his whole life tied to the therapy. It took me many years to recognize that while the therapy is important even to the least committed patient, the expectation that the patient will always be devastated and angry toward the therapist because of holidays, lateness, or missed sessions is not always true. It may be true with some very dependent patients, but the obsessional patient has a stance of great independence and rarely declares or becomes aware of his dependent needs. The popular psychoanalytic notion that the patient *must* be resentful about missed sessions and vacations frequently reveals the grandiosity of the therapist and his exaggerated expectation of the value of the work. More often, patients are pleased when there is a break in therapy, since it puts off painful inquiries and may even save them some money. This attitude does not necessarily convey negative transference or poor commitment or resistance. It may simply be a feature of the patient's character style, and, therefore, he should not be pressed to discover and admit to feelings that may, in fact, not exist. Pressure from the therapist may often produce some hostile responses as to justify the therapist's original hypothesis.

Mr. Jones: No.

Therapist: It's not? Well, what do you think about it?

Mr. Jones: It's a trend of thought that hadn't occurred to me at all. No, I don't find it difficult to be complimentary, and I often am when the circumstances warrant. On two different occasions during the last two weeks I complimented my colleague on the excellent work that he has done, and I didn't find it painful.

Therapist: Isn't that what your mother's always doing?

Mr. Jones: Complimenting?

Therapist: Being effusive.

Mr. Jones: I dislike being effusive or dislike people who are effusive and I would not carry my complimenting to such ends that it would become effusive. In fact, quite the contrary. It's often been difficult for me to be critical and I would frequently wish that in situations in which I have to be critical I would rather be complimentary, in order to avoid the unpleasantness associated with being critical or reprimanding a person. What I thought you were referring to ... the possibility that I might be distressed at missing many therapy sessions.

Therapist: Aren't you?

Mr. Jones: Yes, but not to a strong degree. I mean, I thought of it more in the way of hoping it wouldn't interfere with any progress as distinguished from thinking that it probably would have a bad effect. One day last week I had another experience similar to the one today. I was asked a question and I blurted out an answer I knew wasn't right. I didn't want to say that I didn't know, so I blurted out something that was obviously not correct.

Perhaps this is a statement that my inference was correct and he could not say so. Certainly I was trying too hard to get the acknowledgment.

Therapist: Even in your nervousness you have to know the answers to everything, avoiding the possibility of recognizing that it's an imperfect world and admitting your feeling of being upset.

Mr. Jones: I suppose so. Yet I realize it more now than I had been able to up until the last year or so.

Therapist: Uh-huh.

Mr. Jones: It's during these times that I become very tense that I tend to revert to my former bad habits — that is, the thought that anyone may be displeased if I'm less than perfect all the time. It definitely still bothers me even though I realize that that's the case.

Therapist: Uh-huh. That must have something to do with your mother's attitude toward the world?

Mr. Jones: Well, I don't know.

Therapist: For some reason your mother had to present the picture of the world as a little world she lived in with her family which was just idyllic, beautiful, perfect, and nothing less than that was possible, eh?

Mr. Jones: That was usually the case.

INSIGHT THROUGH PERCEPTUAL GROWTH

When Mr. Jones returned from his six-week absence (he had attended a school during this time), we entered into a new phase of treatment. The next five sessions dealt with his growing awareness of himself and his desire to change. He became more masterful and assertive and was willing to acknowledge his own role in his living. This was highlighted by several dreams, which we examined in some detail. Mr. Jones experienced some success in his work and felt he was more in control of his future, which pleased him. There was a considerable change in his obsessional ideation and he began to raise the question of termination.

Mr. Jones: While I was at the school I felt good, but at times when I felt distressed I recognized that it was caused by some specific event. About two weeks ago I felt some interference with my thinking and concentrating, like what had been troubling me back in 1950 when this whole thing first started.

Therapist: What were the circumstances?

Mr. Jones: One factor was something in the atmosphere, which may have caused hay fever or asthma symptoms.

He still tried to assign outside factors as the cause of his symptoms. However, he rapidly got to the point of the problem — that a fellow student apparently upset him tremendously, although he had difficulty in recognizing it at the time.

Mr. Jones: In the class there was one individual who was very repulsive and repugnant to everyone because of his overbearing, insolent manner. He made a slurring remark regarding me, and I was fearful that I would be unable to come up with a suitable answer. However, on this particular day I was able to come up with a rejoinder that I felt was satisfactory.

Therapist: Did you have a problem of concentrating while at the school?

Mr. Jones: I keep thinking frequently of the obsession that I used to have that people must like me.

Therapist: Are you thinking of something specific now?

Mr. Jones: No, I don't have anything specific in mind but all of this is based on specific instances ... Oh, yes! I just thought of one now. I started to feel disturbed about a decision made in my absence which I thought I should have been consulted about first. I continue to worry about possibly failing because of the continued impairment in thinking.

Mr. Jones began to develop some insight by examining his relationship to his colleague, whose behavior was cocksure and repulsive and reminded him of his own requirements to "know it all."

Therapist: What made you feel tense?

Mr. Jones: ... Thinking about the complexity of the matter that we were discussing at the moment.

Therapist: Do you think that only you were having trouble?

Mr. Jones: Yes, I thought it applied only to me. I'm not worried over the fact that I might have missed a few points. I'm sure everybody else does, too. I think that there must be some significance in the fact that I felt distress often when I was forced to have any active contact with that one individual that I mentioned who was so repulsive to me.

Therapist: How did this dislike begin? What was it based on?

Mr. Jones: It was based on my dislike of his attitude of being cocksure about everything and that his opinion was the only possible solution to anything.

Therapist: Go on.

Mr. Jones: He was cocksure, insolent, and dogmatic.

Therapist: Uh-huh.

Mr. Jones: ... His insolence caused comment among many people, and he was so embarrassing that everyone disliked his performance. This bothered me also.

Therapist: Do you think that part of your dislike towards him might have had something to do with the recognition in him of attributes that you tend to have, such as always having to be right? You were getting a look at the way it must look to other people.

Mr. Jones: ... I don't know ...

Therapist: It is often a very strong need of yours — to always be right — isn't that so?

Mr. Jones: Yes. There's a strong need to be right which is often evidenced by a dogmatic attitude ... but I don't think I've demonstrated it in a repulsive way.

Therapist: You were wondering what there was about this fellow that annoyed you so much. Could that be one of the factors? He had dogmatic, rigid attitudes that you must recognize in yourself.

It was important to move very slowly in order to get Mr. Jones to accept an interpretation that was neither flattering nor friendly. This must be done in a way that is not experienced as derogation; otherwise the patient may become anxious and defensive, which for the obsessional means becoming evasive and distracted. One proceeds carefully, noting the degree of anxiety being stirred up and stopping short of a full confrontation. The increase in Mr. Jones's self-esteem and the feeling of achievement and development of insight over the past six weeks enabled him to accept my observation without immediate denial or contention, permitting the interpretation to proceed to a full disclosure of the problem.

Mr. Jones: Well, it's certainly possible. In fact, I did see one way in which I used to resemble him and that was in thinking that the way I thought just had to be *the* way.

Therapist: Uh-huh.

Mr. Jones: Well, why would that bother me that someone acted ... like I used to act?

Therapist: Well, I think there may be a lot of reasons why you would be upset about noticing in somebody else what is characteristic of yourself, especially noting how unpopular he was.

Mr. Jones: Well, that's a deep one.

Therapist: I don't know that it's so deep. You said earlier that you were surprised to note that the attitudes which others have about you are not always the same as the picture that you feel you are presenting to others. They saw you as someone who was efficient and effective, while you think they see you as weak and ineffective. You also had the notion that you present yourself as someone who is right, inflexible, and somewhat of a superman. You see, that doesn't often impress people in a positive way. Sometimes it alienates and even revolts people, which is apparently what they thought of this other fellow. So it wouldn't be pleasant to think that maybe you impress others this way.

Mr. Jones: That's certainly a very clear analysis of it.

Therapist: Then it's quite possible that you may impress people this way when you are insistent that your way is the only way.

Mr. Jones: Yes, definitely!

Therapist: It's much easier, of course, to see it in someone else and observe the effects it produces for him.

Mr. Jones: Well, that hadn't occurred to me nearly in that complete a fashion. I had a partial view of it.

Mr. Jones still needed to give me only partial recognition for this exposition by indicating that he had already worked on it even if not in such a total fashion. He was not yet completely willing to acknowledge the truth about his behavior; at the same time, it had begun to have a real impact on him. I continued my speculation about the defenses the other fellow must be using, in order to strengthen the interpretation that one can behave in these unfortunate ways by having illusions of one's capacities and being grandiosely unaware, indifferent or by distorting the opinion of others into admiration and respect.

Therapist: We could speculate on the possibility that this fellow is not really seeing how others thought of him and secretly thinking he's a very smart fellow.

Mr. Jones: He probably secretly thinks he's a very smart fellow, but he must wonder why he isn't more popular or why he became progressively less popular all during the time we were there. But I suppose it was impossible for him to realize the reason for his unpopularity.

Therapist: Well, if he did recognize it, maybe he explained it on the basis that he was much too smart and that the others were all jealous.

EVIDENCE OF PROGRESS

I had tried to tie together the recognition of his own tendencies to act like the other person and the need to confront the effect of his behavior on others, focusing on the possibility of functioning safely and effectively without the questionable support of grandiose ideas and unassertive catering. Mr. Jones was now well on his way to seeing himself more objectively and recognizing the basis for some of his obsessional thinking and behavior. By becoming free to recognize and express some feelings, he could test out in reality the absence of real danger to his security system. This was the real beginning of change — that is, to recognize the many pitfalls that still lie ahead and yet move into areas that require more changes in behavior.

The theme of self-awareness was continued in later sessions, when Mr. Jones described his dealings with a colleague and created an aura of pomposity because of his preciseness. He pursued the investigation without getting too defensive, and we were able to highlight his tendency to go to extremes and avoid the middle ground. Mr. Jones needed to note how his tendency toward perfection might irritate others, and at one point I asked him to look at the other person's possible reaction to him.

The obsessional patient's tendency to discount the therapist's comments even when they are identical to the patient's remarks can be very annoying. There is a constant potential for the therapist to become irritated with an obsessional patient. The patient's contentiousness, need to be on top, inability to accept new insights or be grateful for them, and need to depreciate and minimize the value of the therapist's work — all make the work often very tedious and difficult. When the time and circumstances are right, expressing these irritations to the patient can be very profitable for him. Generally they must be kept in check and noted, in order to prevent defensive or attacking behavior from the therapist. If the therapist needs verbal acknowledgment for his efforts and reassurance of his worth, he would be wise to avoid getting into intensive therapy with an obsessional. Such a patient does not express thanks or gratitude and can rarely communicate his satisfaction with the work. Instead, he will frequently complain that it is not good enough, fast enough, or comforting enough.

In working with the obsessional, the therapist must be prepared for a long, grueling struggle, in which the rewards are the satisfactions in coping with enormous therapeutic difficulties and using skills, techniques, and empathic understanding that slowly but relentlessly undo some of the rigidities and defensive patterns in the patient's behavior. The therapist who does not get irritated or who fails to notice his distress and, at times, his anger toward the patient is too obsessional himself to be useful to the patient. Recognition of such responses does not imply an incompetent or inadequate therapist but rather a human, honest, and reasonably secure one.

Mr. Jones still needed to justify his behavior, even though he felt good about himself and his attitude toward me was largely positive. I took the opportunity to explore his role in greater detail — how his needs for perfection so overshadowed his self-awareness that he tended to alienate others, instead of developing their respect and good will. The issue of timing in presenting critical or unflattering observations to a patient is an important one, as the sensitivities of the patient stimulate his defenses and cause him either to justify his actions or criticize the therapist for his, the therapist's, insensitivities. This is especially true for the obsessional, who interprets any observation as disagreement or criticism, which then stirs up anxiety because of his need to be correct and omniscient. His defensive symptoms then produce a tug-of-war or withdrawal into covert doubting and obsessional ruminations or simply tuning out the therapist. This reaction can be avoided if the therapist carefully selects the occasions for confrontation, choosing times when the patient's esteem is high and his anxieties low.

Therapist: I see something very interesting here that I want to draw your attention to. You've noted several things about this situation that have some significance in the area of your problems. You noted that your finickiness or excessive caution produces situations which are disturbing and disrupt your personal relationships. You notice that your conscientious attitude has a tendency to produce negative reactions in other people. It is clear that you were not trying to look down on your colleague in this instance.

Mr. Jones: No. I wasn't.

Therapist: But curiously enough this must be his reaction. You were actually interested in the most efficient and effective way of functioning, yet it comes out in a way that makes you look pompous and bossy. Your conscientiousness produces the very reaction you are trying to avoid.

Mr. Jones: Well, that's definitely true.

Therapist: So we can understand his reaction. You might have stirred up much stronger feelings some time ago because in your greater need to be perfect you probably stirred up more antagonism. You come across as being pompous and playing the big shot even though you don't really want to be.

Mr. Jones: No. My purpose was to show that I was not careless or slipshod.

Therapist: So your virtuous needs seem to stir up antagonistic feelings in others.

Mr. Jones: Yes.

Therapist: Could we say it this way: One of the difficulties is in your inability to be an easygoing, regular fellow instead of the serious, conscientious boss?

Mr. Jones: Would you go through that again? I seem to have missed it.

Therapist: You obviously feel good about being the boss. You have status and a feeling of prestige that goes with it and you want to continue on a friendly basis with your colleagues. Yet this tendency to alienate them creeps in just because you want to do a super job.

Mr. Jones: Well, I've had a feeling that my former colleagues, now subordinates, would wonder whether I would be pompous and overly impressed whether I would be careless and incompetent. If I have to choose between those I'd rather avoid the weak, slipshod approach at the expense of seeming pompous. At least I know that there is a conflict between the two when previously I'd be fighting the same battle, but I wouldn't have realized that there is some middle ground there.

Therapist: Yeah. But it is interesting that you still have difficulty in noting that there is a middle ground, that one doesn't have to be slipshod or weak as opposed to being pompous and rigid. There is a middle ground.

Mr. Jones: There should be.

Therapist: I'm suggesting that at the present time you have difficulty attaining it because you really don't conceive of its existence. It's hard for you to see anything but the extremes.

Mr. Jones: No, I just said that I considered the fact that there were alternatives and that some compromise had to be made.

Therapist: Yes, but don't you think your anxiety to appear strong is what gets in the way of your being human, so to speak?

Mr. Jones: A question of dominating or being dominated is one of the all-or-none issues.

Therapist: So it is very hard for you to visualize the middle ground because it's always either dominating or being dominated.

Mr. Jones: Yes, that's it. Well, do you say that there is a middle ground which can be pursued, which lies between domination and being dominated?

Therapist: I would say there usually is a middle ground; the relationship between people is not necessarily the battle between dominating or being dominated. There is a middle ground called collaboration, where one is neither dominated nor dominating.

I was trying to get Mr. Jones to recognize that his idea of being safe meant to be superman, and his attempts to be that prevented him from being merely human. The ability to accept one's humanness is the key to the resolution of an obsessive or compulsive disorder. To be human means to accept the uncertainties of existence without requiring magic guarantees and certainties to feel secure and acceptable. For the obsessional, being human means being vulnerable, weak, and under constant threat. When the patient begins to accept his fallibilities and deficiencies without going to the extreme of accepting his condition as totally helpless he has found the middle road of human functioning. When I made the observation of humanness to Mr. Jones, he did not understand it at all at the moment, so I needed to scale down my comment and tie it to the specific issues at hand.

Avoiding global generalizations and sticking to specific issues that avoid intellectual and philosophical issues are essential in the treatment of the obsessional.

The hour ended with full agreement from Mr. Jones. But five days later, in the next session, he presented a fascinating dream, in which it was apparent that the issue discussed in the preceding exchange was still troubling him.

Mr. Jones: I had a dream on Wednesday or Thursday evening that had an aspect of some behavior on my part that I don't ever remember having dreamt before — of being aggressive or argumentative in my dreams. I dreamt that I was the head of a large office with a large number of employees that had moved to a new location. The location was a dilapidated, broken-down building. Shortly after the move took place, there was considerable milling around and dissatisfaction because of being in this dilapidated building. And I noticed that several employees appeared to be leaving, so I inquired where they were going and one of them answered that Mr. So and So had told them that they could go. He was the next below me in status, and they said that he had told them they could take the rest of the day off. I was angry about his having done this without consulting me. So I looked for him to talk with him about it, and I had difficulty finding him because he was trying to stay out of my way. I finally found him talking with a group of his friends. When I asked him about this dismissal of employees without authority, he became evasive. I told him that he had no authority to do it and that he should have spoken to me about it. He, in turn, became argumentative and said that he assumed that I would want him to exercise some authority and not be a puppet. I told him that I did but that I didn't intend him to usurp my authority. In such a case as that, why even I would not have authority to give them the day off. So I began thinking in the dream of whether I should rescind his order or whether I should allow him to save face by telling him to do it, and just then I woke up. As I mentioned earlier, the significant difference was that it was the first time I ever remember being aggressive in a dream. I can remember other dreams in which other people were having arguments or fights, but I never seemed to be in it. I was always watching. I suppose it must have some relation to the situation in which I found myself in charge of a large group of people upon returning from my six weeks at school and also the verbal altercation I described a week ago.

Therapist: Well, what comes to mind about this dream? Does any of the content stir up any thoughts about yourself?

DREAM INTERPRETATION

The preceding was the second dream Mr. Jones presented for exploration. It was most interesting in that it related to some events that had occurred recently and demonstrated a change in behavior; that is, instead of being an onlooker, he was a participant and willing to engage in a minor confrontation. However, he was still indecisive, and in a typical obsessional manner, he evaded the issue by waking up.

There appear to be no special characteristics about obsessionals' dreams. All dreams reflect the life problems and the emotional relationships of the patient with the therapist and with friends and relatives. Obsessionals, in their dreams, utilize the particular techniques of defense characteristic of their waking lives. Since much of the obsessional's life is preoccupied with problems of control, it will not be surprising to find that much of his dream material concerns itself with control. The dream content should be examined in the here and now as it sheds light in the current living of the patient. To get deeply involved in understanding all the associations and every bit of detail can become a trap for the therapist and can turn into an obsessional investigation in which the ultimate effect is to lose sight of the main goals. Since dreams can be illuminating with regard to sources of unacknowledged feelings and attitudes, their use in the therapeutic process should not be discouraged. At the same time, they must be treated as simple data and dealt with in the same way as are other productions of the patient.

My own associations to Mr. Jones's dream were that it is almost an exact replay of the situation — where he was the new boss in a new job setting — discussed in the previous session. My first reaction to this dream was that it dealt with status, control, who was boss, and how to look at others in terms of power, strength, and influence. He found it necessary to criticize an employee but was uneasy lest he antagonize him. In the dream, the employee evaded him but was finally confronted, and Mr. Jones asserted his authority and told him off, even though he was in doubt as to whether he should rescind the order. At this point he woke up. There was an increased capacity in the dream to be confronting, bold, and assertive that did not exist in his waking state; the dream tended to support his growing confidence and willingness to take some risks and express his anger. I made no mention of this to him but encouraged him to associate to the dream.

Mr. Jones: Well, in actuality there is a colleague who is immediately below me who is a forceful person who uses a large amount of initiative. But it's so seldom that he misuses it that I don't often feel resentment towards him for being aggressive. I sometimes feel inadequate myself that I had not first thought of the measures that he thinks of. So it vaguely resembles that situation, although in his case, in actuality, there is no unpleasantness about it. He's not offensive about it as this person in the dream was. Also, this dream was notable because I remembered it so clearly.

Therapist: Yes.

Mr. Jones: I had another dream Sunday morning. I was in the middle of a town that was all contained in one large building. The building was mounted on a revolving mechanism, so that it was constantly turning around. Included in a group was my father. I have a vague feeling that I tried to lose him or outdistance him. I'm not certain whether I did or he just fell behind and he had difficulty in catching up with the group again. When we returned to the revolving building again, we went down in the basement to a medical laboratory. There was something peculiar about the plumbing, but that's vague. I can't describe it very well. That's all I remember of that.

It became obvious that there was a relationship between the two dreams, since in the second dream the issues of leadership, losing, outdistancing, or at least surpassing father were involved. What was the plumbing about? Perhaps associations would be enlightening.

Therapist: What does this dream bring to mind?

Mr. Jones: It doesn't.

Therapist: Well, let your mind wander and see what comes up with regard to it. What about the plumbing; what do you associate with that?

Mr. Jones: Well, on Saturday my wife wanted to show me the recreation room that one of our neighbors was building. We went in and talked with him. They were putting this recreation room in their basement. The bar he was building had one water surface line extending into the bar, but it had no drain. He was going to use a large kettle for a receptacle to catch water from washing glasses or what not. He said he would empty it once a day because he didn't feel like going to the expense of installing a drain. That's the only thing, and that didn't occur to me until just now.

How extraordinary it is that one can put such a clear association out of mind, to be resurrected only with the help of the therapist! Whether the plumbing had sexual symbolic overtones for Mr. Jones was not relevant at this point. What is striking is the degree of competence displayed by the obsessional defenses to evade such an obvious relationship!

Therapist: Well, what did you think of that?

Mr. Jones: I thought it was a sloppy arrangement, but I don't know why I should dream about it.

Therapist: We're not saying you did dream about it.

Mr. Jones: Well, I didn't dream about it. I happened to think of it now in connection with the dream.

Therapist: You thought it was a sloppy arrangement when he was telling you about it. You made no comment?

Mr. Jones: No, I didn't comment. I didn't think about it.

I was wondering whether he was assertive toward his neighbor in his waking state, since the dream dealt with his assertiveness.

Therapist: Did the visit to this basement stir up any thoughts about fixing your own plumbing or repairing your house?

What I had in mind in asking this question was the possibility that his competitiveness might have been stirred up, since he appeared to be saying something about that in regard to his father in the second dream. Also, the possible symbolism of plumbing and sexual apparatus might be an issue.

Mr. Jones: Well, we've been thinking about that, but up until now we haven't had the time or money to do anything about it ... But he had it fixed up very nice and that sort of strengthened my ideas about it. I've never had any skill in home craftsmanship or being the handyman or what not, though I wish I did. I admired the work that he was doing, being able to do most of it himself. It's far beyond what I would be able to do.

Therapist: Did it stir up any thoughts about your inadequacy or feeling ineffective in this area?

Mr. Jones: ... I don't think I thought anything except that it was nice.

Therapist: So these observations about his greater skill than yours are what you're making now, rather than what may have gone through your mind then?

Mr. Jones: Well, no, that went through my mind then, too.

Therapist: That's what I mean. Anything else?

I was pressing for some confirmation of my associations that led me to feel that such comparisons would stir up envy and competition, but none was forthcoming, and I finally abandoned this hypothesis for the moment.

Mr. Jones: I didn't feel any antagonism or envy about it.

It is interesting that I had mentioned neither envy nor competition, but he knew just what I was getting at. This suggests what many observers of the psychotherapeutic process have maintained, that the therapist does stimulate or direct the patient's ideas and thoughts through questioning that may be indirect, subtle, or open-ended. Although my questions were hardly subtle, they were clearly leading questions, even while I was avoiding a direct inquiry. At this juncture the patient overcame my distractions and returned to an exploration of the dream:

Mr. Jones: Well, this plumbing in the dream seemed vaguely located in a VD-prophylaxis station. It seemed like a laboratory and part of the time like a medical dispensary. A pipe or water faucet was protruding from the wall and I was doing something about pushing a button to control the flow of water. I don't remember what happened after that.

After a brief pause he began to describe the actual events of the evening before the dream:

Mr. Jones: We were visiting friends Saturday night and we got home rather late. I felt like intercourse, but my wife wasn't receptive to the idea. She was tired and somewhat upset by the news she had received that morning that her mother might be ill. So I didn't press the matter. I fell asleep almost immediately. I was just trying to speculate now as to whether that had any connection with the dream.
Therapist: Uh-huh.
Mr. Jones: We did have intercourse Sunday morning, however.

Obviously some connection between the dream and the plumbing had some symbolic significance in addition to representing the thing in itself. I tried again to touch a feeling, a reaction, or an emotional response. Mr. Jones might have had two elements in the dream. My hypothesis about envy got nowhere. I then tried to examine the possibility of some emotional response to being rejected.

Therapist: What is your usual reaction to being turned down?
Mr. Jones: When we were first married I just couldn't accept being turned down and usually insisted until my wife consented. She pleaded [Saturday night] that she was too tired and not feeling well but I insisted anyway. For the next few days or so she complained about it being selfish.
Therapist: Uh-huh. You wondered whether this may have had something to do with the dream, your being turned down?
Mr. Jones: No, the thought that just caused that reaction now was about some manifestations in dreams suggesting intercourse, such as the water spout or faucet.

Therapist: Which you turned on and off.
Mr. Jones: Well, I was doing something with it.
Therapist: I think you said before you were fully in charge of it.
Mr. Jones: Yes, yes!

At this point he tried to engage me in a discussion of sex and asked me a question about symbols in dreams. He was trying to intellectualize the exploration of his dream and to sidetrack some possible awareness that might be unflattering and disturbing. I resisted getting into a theoretical discussion of sexual symbolism but found myself in a tug-of-war about his evasive tactics. His defensiveness was to some degree forced by my overconcern with his tactics, and before I was fully aware of it I was drawn into a tussle with him.

Therapist: I don't want to get the subject changed. Maybe that's part of your reason for asking your question now. I wonder whether you were changing the subject perhaps because you don't like to talk about your sexual activities with your wife?

REALITY VERSUS NEUROSIS

In treating any characterological type, one should not assume that every maneuver or piece of behavior has a neurotic origin. There is an unfortunate tendency in psychodynamic theory and practice to attribute unconscious or neurotic grounds to every piece of behavior. In therapy, the behavior might be labeled resistance or neurotic, and one might overlook the constructive, even though defensive, role. In obsessional disorders it is important to draw the line between normal or obsessive, constructive or maladaptive, and healthy or neurotic behavior. Obsessional behavior generally is an extreme form of constructive or adaptive behavior, and such behavior can be salutary until it becomes excessive.

It is important that we help the patient recognize the difference between normal and obsessional behavior, so that we don't become enmeshed in a verbal hassle about whether the behavior is "good" or "bad." I felt in that position with Mr. Jones at this point. I recognized the validity of his question about symbols in dreams, but I knew I could easily be caught in his obsessional ruminations, which would become defensive and distracting. I therefore responded briefly to his valid inquiry and moved on to the issues at hand, which seemed rich in potential data and insight. My question about his uneasiness in talking about sex came from my knowledge that thus far he had never raised this question in our work.

Mr. Jones: Well, it was not an endeavor to change the subject. I happened to think of this and wondered.

Therapist: I'm not accusing you. I'm only asking whether this is something you preferred not to talk about. This is actually the first time you've ever spontaneously spoken of sex.

Mr. Jones: I guess that's true. It took me so long to either learn or find out about it.

Therapist: Let's go back to Sunday morning. Was it your impression that she was no longer tired? Why did she agree then?

Mr. Jones: Perhaps she was sorry that she had turned me down the night before or perhaps it's not complicated at all and she was just agreeable without attributing it to a complicated reason.

Therapist: Yes, our explanations don't always have to have complicated reasons. I was wondering whether it was you who initiated it again Sunday, or whether she did.

Mr. Jones: No, I did.

Therapist: And this time she was agreeable? You said that in the past you had great difficulty in accepting her refusals. Any notion as to why that changed?

Mr. Jones: Well, yes. It was a lack of understanding on my part.

Therapist: You think that's all it is — that now you understand that a woman need not always be interested and you feel less hurt about it? Do you think you have learned to deal with it better or that you learned that it's not right to complain?

It is useful to focus on this matter in order to distinguish change from the better utilization of the neurotic defenses we are trying to overcome. Here I felt there had been a real change, in view of all our work that dealt with broadening his understanding of others.

Mr. Jones: No, I think it's the former, that I understand her better now.

Therapist: So far as you can recall you had no feelings of hurt or criticism?

Mr. Jones: Well, mild disappointment, but not criticism, no.

Therapist: What do you make of the first part of the dream? In your associations to the dream, you are leading the group and showing them the sights. This idea of leadership occurred in your first and second dream.

Mr. Jones: That was a parallel situation to what actually happened. When I was at this school course, the class was divided into small groups and we traveled around and took trips to other plants.

Therapist: But you were the leader?

Mr. Jones: Well, sometimes I was and sometimes others were. Nothing of importance comes to mind about it.

Therapist: How about your father?

Mr. Jones: I don't understand his place in that dream, but he was in it.

Therapist: Nothing comes to mind about outdistancing him?

Mr. Jones: Yes, something does come to mind about that. The thought occurred to me recently, wondering whether he would be surprised at my making the progress professionally that I have.

Therapist: Tell me more about that.

Mr. Jones: I didn't think too much more about it. I wondered if my parents would be surprised about what I had done on my own!

Therapist: Was it the recent promotion that you had in mind? That your father would be surprised, meaning that he never thought you could do it?

Mr. Jones: I think I had the feeling that he would try to minimize the importance of it, and he wouldn't acknowledge fully that I could function without his helping hand.

Therapist: Do you think that visiting your neighbor's basement or recreation room had anything to do with the dream?

Mr. Jones: It did come into my mind in response to your question about plumbing.

Therapist: The visit may have had something to do with the dream when the scene shifts from showing your father and the group around. You are outdistancing him, and he can't keep up with you. He gets left behind and you get a place in the basement where there is some peculiar waterline that you have some control over.

Mr. Jones: Well, there is another connection with my father; he is handier in the home workshop.

This seemed to stir up more associations about his father, which involved competitiveness and the need to overcome earlier feelings of unworthiness and failure.

Therapist: Uh-huh. Yes.

Mr. Jones: He would try to teach me various things and I couldn't concentrate on it.

Therapist: So you never really became mechanically skilled. Your recollection about your promotion and your father minimizing it expresses your notion about your relationship with him. He doesn't quite accept the fact that you are grown-up and competent.

Mr. Jones: Yes, I just thought of another illustration of that. The first time my father visited us he was surprised that we had a nice place to live in. I noticed it and my wife mentioned it to me — about his disbelief that we could have as nice a place to live in as he did.

Therapist: Do you think this is the impression that you left with him in the sense that you have never really competed or attempted to show him what you were capable of?

Mr. Jones: No, I guess not. . . . Well, yes. I was proud to show him what I was capable of. But it wasn't in the nature of competing with him.

Therapist: You never did?

Mr. Jones: No, that isn't what I mean.

Therapist: Well, I'm asking you if you ever did compete with him.

Mr. Jones: I can't think of anything. I was proud to tell him about any advancement that I made in school. I guess it's only in the last few years that any of that could take the form of competing with him. I'm getting all mixed up.

This last statement made me aware that I had pushed this issue far enough. A statement about being confused is often a way of implying, "I have had enough and cannot absorb or pursue this line of inquiry any further." It may also imply some resistance to further inquiry, but in this instance I felt it was the former, in view of my emphasis on competition — which did not seem to be getting anywhere. Whether he was confused because my observation was involved or resistant because it touched on the truth, this was a clue to discontinue that exchange. I decided to summarize my thoughts of our dream exploration, since the session was coming to an end.

Therapist: The interesting thing about these dreams is that one seems to be simply a reenactment of a past event except that you are more aggressive. In the second dream, you are the leader and you're showing a group and your father around. This apparently is the theme of the dream, in that you are a big man who is running the show and who is the boss, so to speak; but it is contradicted by your feelings that you aren't capable of handling mechanical household things. The dream stirs up some feelings of showing your father that you're not altogether incompetent, which you feel is his view of you. Now there's something paradoxical in this, since in your waking life you are overtly reluctant to let people know about your position or your status. It is always done in a roundabout way and generally emerges twice as strong as you want it to come out. You're so concerned or anxious lest people not recognize your status that you tend to overdo it. This is what happens in the dream when you outdistance your father and leave him behind. I think you're not fully recognizing how very important it is that people see your status and prestige and position, so you frequently get caught up in excessive displays. You want to make absolutely sure.

Mr. Jones: My wife has told me that too.

Therapist: And that's because you, yourself, are still so uncertain and uneasy about it. It's as if you only half believe it.

Mr. Jones: Well, that's certainly a very clear analysis and synthesizing — probably what goes on — from just those few facts of the dreams.

This cryptic compliment was immediately followed by an awareness of a trivial aspect of the dream. It is as if he was reducing or attempting to minimize the multitude of insights that came out of the analysis.

Mr. Jones: A thought occurred to me about my ability to have a dream in which I was aggressive — that it might have some bearing on a subconscious interference with being aggressive. Consciously, I want to be.

Therapist: Uh-huh.

Mr. Jones: And yet I feel these interferences with it . . . but yet in dreams I never was that way.

Therapist: So you think this may mean that perhaps you are a little more ready to recognize your aggressiveness openly?

Mr. Jones: Well, that's certainly a better way of expressing it than I thought of, as if in some fashion that my mind was being liberated to express some. But that's the same thing.

Therapist: Uh-huh.

Mr. Jones: How did you say it?

Therapist: That you are a little freer to permit some of these aggressive feelings to come out, even if it is only in your dreams, at this time. Heretofore, they have come out in all sorts of indirect, subtle ways, which have never been noticed by you or even considered to be aggressive by you.

Mr. Jones: Some of that does explain times in which my wife has told me that I'm too aggressive and domineering at times I had thought I was being weak.

Therapist: Uh-huh.

Mr. Jones: That's exactly what you just said.

Therapist: What do you think interfered with your being recognized as more of a person by your father? Where does this conception of you come from? Why are you looked upon as someone who is likely to be incompetent?

Mr. Jones: Well, what that makes me think of is the fact that I depended on him so often. I didn't actively look for a job myself; I was anxious for him to give me a hand at it. I think I've told you that.

Therapist: Yes.

Mr. Jones: And in many instances in adolescence, I felt hesitant about doing anything unless my parents approved or suggested it. I wanted to know beforehand that they would approve of something I did before I did it. . . . But that's probably a result of my feeling dominated by my father rather than causing it.

Therapist: That's a question you want to give some thought to. Taking into account the fact that you're far from incompetent — on the contrary, you've been successful almost without exception. And in spite of this evident competence — there is great concern within yourself about your competence. This paradoxical and contradictory situation is something that we must learn more about because it could tell us a great deal about your relationship with your parents and, in particular, with your father.

Mr. Jones: Well, I don't have any present explanation for it.

Therapist: We don't want any explanation, just some thinking about it so we can explore it further.

USE OF DREAMS IN THERAPY

The preceding exchange ended the session, which I believe was a most productive one. It illustrated how a dream can be used to further the therapeutic work, but without suggesting any particular theory about the structure and interpretation of dreams. Certainly the reader will find many issues that I neglected or minimized or interpretations that he would have preferred to make. I hold no brief for the interpretation I made, nor do I suggest that deeper and more profound interpretations could not have been made. I pursued leads that came out of my involvement with Mr. Jones and the neurotic trends that surfaced in our work. I followed the data as they unfolded, but I also directed many of the associations with questions that came out of my own background, training, and preconceptions about personality development. Consequently, the summation might be dramatically different if such a dream were presented to a therapist with a different point of view. I avoided jargon, especially libidinal terms, because I find it antitherapeutic for the obsessional. My approach in dealing with dream material is to tie it directly to the work at hand, in order to advance the understanding of the transference issues and other unconscious material available around the dream material and the current therapeutic issues. I believe the value of the dream is that it advances the understanding of the work in progress.

In the next session, Mr. Jones elaborated on the gains that grew out of the analysis of his dreams and suggested additional significant material about his relationship with his father. Until this point he had dealt largely with his mother; his transference distortion of his wife; and his need to be the good, proper, controlled boy, who would be acceptable to the extent that he did not antagonize or alienate others. The awareness of his competitive strivings and the derogation by his father for his inadequate skills, which his dream scenario dealt with, opened up new possibilities for dealing with his passivity and lack of assertiveness. It also allowed him to experience anger, resentments, disappointments, and frustrated yearnings about his father. This was the phase he was now moving into.

Mr. Jones: When I came to my office this morning there was a meeting planned for 8:15. I wanted to hold a meeting with my staff to bring them up to date. My assistant seemed to imply the meeting at 8:15 interfered with other meetings. I thought he was being resistant.

Therapist: Uh-huh.

Mr. Jones: I told him that I would hold the meeting nevertheless, and I thought he was being insubordinate. I was quite upset about it.

Therapist: Did your being upset have to do with him?

Mr. Jones: Naturally. Oh yes! Last week's session described something in me that I saw an aspect of in this — namely, that aggressive or hostile thoughts get twisted up and emerge from me at strange and inappropriate times. Yesterday we were invited to a friend's house for dinner. Before dinner several of us were in the kitchen and I helped by carrying in two coffee cups. My wife cautioned me to be careful. I resented this strongly. I think I said something to the effect that she didn't have to control everything all of the time and I stared at her harshly. A few minutes later, another similar incident happened, and I barked at her again. This time I seemed to anticipate a critical remark from her before she actually said anything. I said in a sarcastic tone, "I'd thought you'd have something to say about it."

Therapist: Are you telling me this to show how you must have some feelings about her tendency to tell you how to behave all the time?

Mr. Jones: Yes, and it illustrates to me this situation of aggressive thoughts coming out sometimes at inopportune or inappropriate times. The situation was similar to those that occurred many times a day in 1950, when I first became aware of these difficulties.

Therapist: But would you do or say nothing about it then?

Mr. Jones: Uh, no. On the contrary, I, uh ...

Therapist: Then you think you were more open then?

Mr. Jones: I was even more open, but I didn't understand what was getting me so irritated, and she was at a loss to understand my belligerence — and that resulted in a sort of vicious circle in which we were snapping at each other in self-defense.

Mr. Jones's dreams and his ability to tie together meaningful insights and translate them into changes in behavior permitted me to view the first phase of treatment as ending and blurring into the second phase. Considerable data regarding his relationship to his parents, particularly his mother, have been revealed, and his compulsive needs for perfection, superiority, control, and invulnerability have been noted in many contexts. His relationship to his wife and her transferential similarity to his mother were noted and confirmed on several occasions.

The development of an obsessional thought in the course of therapy also allowed us to view its initiation, source, and function. While the possibility of further recollections will continue, insight has developed to the point that working through on repeated occasions of already discovered insights will occur as a more frequent task of therapy. This constitutes the second, or middle, phase of therapy.

CHAPTER 13

The Middle Phase

The course of an ongoing therapeutic relationship rarely follows the theoretical design outlined in textbooks. There is no clear beginning, middle, or end. Nor is there an established pattern in which a therapeutic alliance develops, followed by the exploration of the earliest experiences and parental relationships, the investigation and elucidation of the oedipal relationships, and an integration and synthesis of all the issues. Occasionally, one can move clearly from the less traumatic and most conscious level of functioning to the deeper, unconscious areas of human motivation, making the unconscious conscious.

Any outline of the therapeutic process is merely diagrammatic and theoretical and, though useful for teaching purposes, is most confusing and disconcerting for practitioners who can never fulfill the described program. All efforts to use published accounts of others as models serve only to emphasize one's own inadequacy and, ultimately, to question these case histories as artificial and contrived. Only in the broadest sense can psychotherapy be structured, programmed, predicted, and pursued according to a descriptive outline based on theoretical preconceptions. Instead, many levels of interaction are happening at once, and one must deal with the issues as they arise. The beginning of trust, positive transference, uneasiness, and a sharing of anxieties and neurotic conflicts brings into focus parental relationships, oedipal struggles, and childhood recollections, interspersed with present difficulties and crises. The therapist must sort out and select the particular lines of inquiry he wishes to pursue, leading the way for further exploration.

Accidental or serendipitous events may determine the content of the patient's presentation, which can distract us from the directions we were pursuing to alternative routes. At times we can postpone the here-and-now problems for later consideration, while at other times they must take precedence. Flexibility is an essential ingredient in all therapeutic endeavors, especially with the obsessional — who tends to be rigid and may inflexibly pursue an agenda, preventing the input of spontaneous and uncontrolled thoughts or feelings. So it was with Mr. Jones.

After a period of exploration into the relationships with Mr. Jones's wife and mother, we moved into a series of sessions that dealt with problems of authority, status, and his relationship with his father. He began to recognize his disappointments, rejections from his father, and the demands for perfection involved in his father's demands on him. I anticipated that we would follow this line until some definitive interpretations would illuminate his fear of assertion and his need to be all-knowing. Unanticipated events brought us back to his relationship with his wife, which was the predominating issue in his obsessional ideas about killing her and the difficulty in concentrating which followed these ruminations.

Several days after the last session, Mr. Jones was again discussing his difficulties with his wife, his ambivalence, his doubts about their marriage, and his anger at her maternal tendencies toward him. He hoped that in becoming more tolerant of her he could also help her mature, and, as her self-esteem grew, he would have greater respect for her. At this point in therapy he began to recognize how his need to be liked and his childish tendencies encouraged her controlling and dominating inclinations, which irritated him and revived his dependency on her. He opened this session by describing how he continued to hurt his wife's feelings:

Mr. Jones: Joan's feelings were hurt by my talking harshly to her. It was the same kind of reaction that distressed me in the past, and I had to cajole her until she became more pleasant towards me. I told her that she had a maternal attitude toward me, but she denies it and she says that she has no such intentions. I told her that the things she did irritated me and caused me to be disturbed but the reasons for it are not chargeable to her. I would explain it as a holdover of feeling inadequate that I had now buried inside of me . . . I used to think that my friends didn't like her and, well, she seemed to feel as if she were an outsider. That's disappearing. The more she participates, the more sure of herself it makes her feel . . . Some of the blame for her not participating in the past is due to me. I had conflicting feelings about her attending various parties. I wanted her to and, at the same time, I didn't want her to.

Therapist: Were you ashamed of her, perhaps?

Mr. Jones: I didn't feel ashamed of her but I felt reluctant for anyone to know that she had been divorced before we were married and that she was older than I was. Perhaps I told you all the opposition that my parents took to my marriage. I used to think that if I married a very beautiful girl I would have to be aggresive to fight off other men trying to take her away from me. She was older than I was and was not beautiful. I thought that was advantageous and would eliminate that situation coming up. I was troubled by the fact that those thoughts occurred to me. I decided that I did love her. It's rather painful to me to think of my having had such a thought.

Therapist: Why? What is painful about those thoughts?

Mr. Jones: Well . . . that's rather insulting to her that I should ever have considered such an idea as being any part of my decision to marry her. She had a feeling that other women were going to take me away from her. She was worried about it, but she finally realized that isn't going to happen. I'm glad that she's feeling more comfortable and that I don't need to feel distressed about the thought that somebody looks upon me with disapproval or displeasure. When she gets moody or angry, for forgiveness or recognition, I can wait the storm out. She even said to me a few times, "Why can't you relax and let me be mad at you?" That was incomprehensible to me. I didn't get the point at all. Now I can see how wrong I was about the compulsion that I had to seek forgiveness immediately.

Therapist: Uh-huh.

Mr. Jones: And I used to be that way toward my mother. If she was displeased about something that I had done, I had to get back in her good graces, and I just couldn't tolerate being ignored for any length of time.

Mr. Jones was referring to the obsessional's intolerance of anxiety, even momentarily. It must be immediately and magically removed and frequently this is the role of the compulsive action or the obsessional thought. The ritual that occurs without delay or deliberate intent serves to dispel the anxiety almost immediately. This incapacity to tolerate the most minimal threats, which are immediately experienced as massive and insurmountable, is characteristic of the obsessional. The danger visualized even with the slightest trauma requires extreme measures.

TERMINATION AS A DEFENSE

In the next session Mr. Jones raised the question of his reduced need for treatment. It was the first time this issue had been raised. The preceding hour had dealt with some growing acceptance of his wife, as a result of our therapy, and with his ability to respect her problems and personality after an ambivalence that had lasted for many years. However, he recognized his limitation in controlling his feelings. We can now see that the controlling pattern — a central issue in obsessional behavior — was an essential pillar in his attempt to impress others with his capacities and prevent them from seeing him as weak and deficient.

The weather had been hot and humid, and the Jones's were using their newly acquired barbecue. Some neighbors had been invited to their yard. It was a joyous occasion; however, Mr. Jones recalled being anxious. An attempt to explore the events that either produced or preceded the onset of an anxiety attack encountered typical difficulties. The nature of anxiety is such that, if severe enough, it blots out experience and prevents the exploration of the sequence of its development. It is in such situations that the technique of free association, in suggesting or pointing to clues to stimulate recall, is most effective.

Mr. Jones: I seem to be so busy and occupied during the day that I just don't have the time to think about subjects to discuss with you.

He seemed reluctant to speak about his anxiety over the visit of his neighbors. I tried to prod him on.

Therapist: Do you think that's the story, or perhaps you are reaching a plateau — feeling a little bit better and less pressure to talk about your anxieties? This hardly means there still aren't things we need to deal with.

COUNTERTRANSFERENCE RESPONSE

I reacted so precipitously to the notion that he might be withdrawing or considering withdrawing from treatment that I moved in quickly to overcome the possibility. It was manifestly a countertransference reaction and was based on my knowledge of the therapeutic process — that one does reach a plateau after a while and that there is a strong tendency to terminate after a patient experiences some benefit. Mr. Jones had supplied no clues with regard to either alternatives. I was anxious to continue our work, and I was certain that we had not reached a point of maximum benefit. I tried to overcome what I anticipated was a growing withdrawal. My move prevented further exploration of his momentary resistance and conveyed my own uneasiness about our relationship.

Mr. Jones: Well, I did think about that and I was hoping that was the state of affairs, except for the fact that I do continue to get upset with or without some definite provocation.

Therapist: Say whatever comes to mind now.

Mr. Jones: When I observe the feelings in my neighbors' children, I have all sorts of emotions and reactions. I often think that I never had such intense feelings when I was a child.

Therapist: Does this stir up any thoughts?

Mr. Jones: Well, it stirs up the recollections of having repressed my emotions when I was a child because I felt my parents didn't help me to exhibit any. It typifies my mother's behavior; she was reluctant for anyone to see her having any strong feelings.

Therapist: Did you ever see her having any?

Mr. Jones: She would express resentment by the look on her face, but she usually tried to express something favorable about everything, even though she was being insincere.

Therapist: How could you tell the difference? Would you get to know when she really didn't approve, when her response was always favorable?

Mr. Jones: I guess I just got to know that when she looked or acted that she was displeased, even though she might not say so.

Therapist: So you got the idea that someone's emotions were not proper and to be anything but charming and nice was bad?

Mr. Jones: I do remember that I was anxious not to express feelings. I can think of an example: If I was riding in a crowded subway train and anyone bumped me, I tried to avoid noticing that anything happened. If anyone said anything that was uncomplimentary to me I would try to pretend that I didn't hear.

Therapist: Trying to avoid getting angry?

Mr. Jones: I suppose that was the reason. I don't remember any conscious reasoning on my part at the time. I just seemed to have had the feeling that no one should observe me being displeased or angry or whatever.

Therapist: Why? What do you visualize as being wrong in expressing feelings and showing your feelings to others?

Mr. Jones: I'm trying to think.

Therapist: You know, you have difficulty in doing that right here, now. You tell a story as a narrative. You never tell a story about current situations with the feelings that you're experiencing. Have you noticed that?

Here was a fine opportunity to demonstrate an issue in our sessions that could not be easily distorted. This is the most effective therapeutic tool in the treatment of obsessionals who distort, deny, or cast doubt on any interpretation by insisting that it did not happen exactly as it was described. If the interpretation is not entirely palatable or comfortable, they then offer qualifications, clarifications, and additions of more and more detail (some of which are relevant and some not) — all drawn in to weaken or cast doubt on the therapist's formulations. This accounts for the endless treatment of the obsessional. The use of "maybe," "perhaps," or "yes, but" is a standard device to forego closure by a definite and committed agreement. If we can observe a piece of behavior during the session where the patient cannot introduce extraneous events to obfuscate the exploration and interpretation of the behavior, the issue is less likely to be distorted than at any other time. Such moments are rare and must always be taken advantage of when they occur. It is this feature that makes the acknowledgment of a transferential distortion, which can be demonstrated during a session, an invaluable source of insight — which has the effect of producing conviction about a matter that cannot be matched by any amount of intellectualization.

Mr. Jones: No, not specifically. But I can accept it ... I think if I show my feelings people will think I can't handle problems smoothly.

Therapist: The only reason you say you can't is not to show others that you can't handle a situation calmly. That's obviously not the whole reason, is it?

Mr. Jones: No, obviously not. I'm groping for more reasons.

Therapist: Well, instead of trying to find more reasons, let's hear about what comes to mind about this sort of thing — about the kind of situation where you find it necessary to restrain yourself, to be cautious and to choose your words carefully.

Mr. Jones: Well, what I'm thinking of now doesn't seem to have anything to do with this topic. I'm just recalling when I was eleven years old we moved into a neighborhood where there were only a few kids my age. I had hoped that I might become friends but it never worked out. I was a loner.

COUNTERTRANSFERENCE AS RESISTANCE

This hour had dealt with the following themes: his feeling of having nothing more to say; my anxious concern about it; his inability to express his feelings, supported by his mother's behavior; and his need to appear strong and in control. There was also the issue of his being a lonely adolescent, who had no chums or other relationships during this crucial era except a dominating mother and a passive father. How much of his later psychopathology was related to these factors? Did his sister and the aunt who lived in the household play a role in minimizing the potential destructiveness of this isolated, lonely, and unhappy boy? In fact, he did manage to develop with enough psychological intactness and maturity to function effectively at his job and marry and live a modestly meaningful life until his obsession became overwhelmingly disorganizing.

REALISTIC PROBLEMS OF THE THERAPIST

The uneasiness I experienced in assuming he was considering termination reflected my uncertainty about our work. I had a strong need to maintain the therapy, in order to continue the progress — which was clearly being made in a very severe obsessional. It is a well-known fact that the resolution of obsessional disorders is extremely difficult and time-consuming; yet in the short period of six months, we had made significant inroads. I wanted very much to retain him in therapy and not lose him in a transference cure or through a rapid amelioration of symptoms, which would be the rationalization to avoid further inquiry.

The need for success or professional esteem in the therapist can be an impediment in the process if it is not noticed or acknowledged. It is an indication of human fallibility in the therapist and can be a source of support and strength to a patient who is struggling to avoid recognizing his own humanness. Therefore, if the situation is right and the occasion allows it, it can be most profitable for the therapist to share these feelings with the patient. In an atmosphere of a strong, positive relationship, it can reduce the idealization of the therapist and enhance the patient's regard and respect for him. The therapist can then be viewed as competent, intelligent, but capable of making some errors.

The issues in this session could have been tied together around the notion that perhaps he had unexpressed feelings about me that he was not recognizing. These feelings could be positive as well as negative and were probably positive, since he was feeling better and was improving in his living and work life. In the more classical theoretical formulations, hostility, unexpressed rage and anger are always predominant and this case study seems to bear this out. Yet I am convinced after thirty years of dealing extensively with this disorder that the obsessive has more difficulty with handling and expressing tenderness than he does with anger, hostility, and rage.* Tender feelings imply weakness, unmanliness, and lack of control — issues that are crucial to the neurotic integration of the obsessional. Mr. Jones's obsessional thoughts illustrated an extreme instance of hateful attitudes and feelings. Warmth, tenderness, affection, trust, and dependency — all these feelings were strongly avoided and were displaced with reaction-formations.

Whenever possible, it is most beneficial to the patient to demonstrate the presence of these tender feelings in his character and behavior. This encourages the feelings of being human and compassionate, instead of being a hostile monster. This was the time to raise this matter with Mr. Jones, and I might have summarized this session by suggesting the possibility of his having warm feelings about me and letting the session end on that note, so that he could reflect on it and raise it spontaneously on another occasion. Some of these feelings must have come through in my interaction with him, in spite of my failure to raise the question specifically. The next session dealt with these issues and was replete with data about his need to recognize his feelings and human capacities for feeling dependent without threat or danger. He recognized that he depended too much on logic and denied his feelings, which at times related to his assets. He was most enthusiastic about his insights and even suggested bringing his wife to our sessions.

Although I did not see Mr. Jones's wife, it is my view that contacts with the patient's partner can be helpful and constructive in the process of therapy. While the partner's presence may introduce difficulties for the therapist, it tends to crystallize many issues and stir up others that would ordinarily be overlooked or bypassed. It can be a useful learning experience for the partner and for the therapist. It may illuminate the partner's role in sustaining the disorder in the patient and enhance the therapist's understanding of just what does go on between them. It may result in the partner's getting into therapy with either the same or another therapist. However, in terms of potential benefit for the patient, I have found it

* This conception was originally described in my earlier books: *Developments in Psychoanalysis* (New York: Grune and Stratton, 1962); *The Obsessive Personality* (New York: Jason Aronson, 1968, 1973).

generally to be most effective and productive for the same therapist to see the partners as well as other family members.

THERAPIST'S REFLECTIONS
TWENTY-FIVE YEARS LATER

It does appear as if he was ready to express positive, friendly feelings toward me at the session just discussed. The next session, five days later, reinforced his feeling that logic was no longer his best defense, although he still required perfection to keep everything under control. He opened the session by reporting an incident when his reaction of anger was appropriate, and he was grateful because he felt our work allowed him to express it.

Mr. Jones: I had a couple of more experiences with becoming angry. The first occasion was when I was riding on the bus yesterday morning. The driver deviated from the regular route and when we spoke to him about it he was obstinate and stubborn about going his way. I became so angry that after telling him that the bus was supposed to go the other route, I could hardly talk. Finally, as I was getting off the bus I did manage to make one last statement; I told him that I was going to report him and he said go ahead. At this point I feel I made progress over what my reaction would have been to that particular incident in the past. In the past any rejoinder would make me feel very uncomfortable. This time it didn't do so. I was able to report it to the bus company in a factual manner, and I didn't become excited or feel emotionally upset. The significant parts of the incident are that I have learned something about not feeling bad about people's angry retorts. But I did get so angry that I had great difficulty in speaking. I think that occurs in situations where there is always considerable embarrassment about being in the public eye in some undesirable situations.

Therapist: Why undesirable?

Mr. Jones: Looking at it logically there is nothing particularly undesirable about it; it's just that when I'm in that situation I feel that way.

Therapist: You feel it's undesirable because it is controversial.

Mr. Jones: . . . Yes, that's so. I don't know whether that's all of it or not. It may be the only reason. It seems to me that there is something else involved in this.

Therapist: Does it have something to do with the issue of dignity?

Mr. Jones: Yes, it does. It also has to do with the possibility of coming out second-best in the eyes of the observers. Yes, dignity is definitely involved.

Therapist: You view it as an indignity, but it's not necessarily viewed that way by others. You see it as not being dignified if you have to complain. When you describe some interference with your speech, don't you really mean that you were agitated and boiling with anger?

Mr. Jones: Oh, yes. Of course.

Therapist: But you indicated that there was a speech difficulty. Not that you were boiling with anger. It's important to notice that.

The therapist must try to demonstrate the defensive behavior, instead of labeling it offensive or grandiose or moralizing about the patient's disruptive and disintegrating interpersonal tendencies. It is important for the patient to see how his behavior affects others. The therapist should be neither critical nor apologetic, only descriptive.

Mr. Jones: Well, I did recognize it, but I didn't think of it that way; that is, the aspect of controversy being involved and my reluctance to enter any issue in which I'm not certain of winning . . . I think I have mentioned it to you before that when I start with an issue I always try to block any rejections with mountains of proof and evidence to eliminate any possibility of receiving unfavorable action.

Therapist: And what makes you most furious and uncomfortable is when you have to fight on some irrational grounds. You can't convince the stubborn or ignorant person with documents or evidence. The driver has to take your word. Isn't that the kind of situation that so often leaves you furious?

Mr. Jones: You hit the nail right on the head. The thought even crossed my mind that I wished I had the schedule to exhibit. I didn't.

Therapist: Why do you think that kind of situation is doubly bothersome for you?

Mr. Jones: Well, it indicates to me that my saying so, just of itself, won't be enough. Of course, the next question is, why is that?

Therapist: Do you think it leaves you with a feeling of impotence?

It is the feeling of helpless incapacity to manage or control a situation that is most difficult to deal with. I tried to forcefully emphasize this point, which produced a most enlightening exchange.

Mr. Jones: It probably does leave me with a greater feeling of impotence.

Therapist: It makes us wonder whether you don't have a tendency to depend too much on reason and logic, as if all issues could be dealt with simply by reason and logic.

Mr. Jones: On, I suppose I do ... I have a tendency to rely too much on that approach. I react by trying to show the logic of it ... I haven't had strong feelings.

Therapist: Uh-huh. And that's how you have been seeing yourself through the years? As someone who doesn't have strong feelings?

Mr. Jones: Yes, undoubtedly I have been kidding myself. I used to think that — that I just didn't have any strong feelings ... Well, I even consciously thought that I was lucky because I could act logically and coolly in situations that other people would become angry about. If these things contributed to my being in the difficulty that I'm in now, then I'm sure that they did then, when I was kidding myself.

Therapist: Not only did you think that you didn't have strong feelings, but probably you have made a virtue and a philosophy out of the fact that one shouldn't have strong feelings, that everything should be according to reason and logic.

I tried to expand the awareness and the consequences of the recognition that Mr. Jones had subdued and denied, consequently not experiencing any feelings in his relationship with others. I wanted him also to recognize how this fitted into his obsessional personality and influenced his thinking in other areas of his living. Since the problem of identifying and experiencing one's feelings and integrating them into one's interpersonal relationship is a major ingredient of the obsessional disorder, it was essential that this awareness, now that it had surfaced, be examined in detail. We can now see why the obsessional emphasizes the intellectual, philosophical and unemotional elements in his relationships. Facts made him feel safe and beyond criticism or rejection; feelings are dangerous and threatening and leave him feeling exposed. It is important to help the obsessional see that he has feelings, that they involve his relationships with others, and that they play a major role in productive living. Respecting his feelings can enable him to do what he likes and enjoys, instead of having to do the right or proper thing. It will permit him to be less rigid, demanding, perfectionistic, and intense by allowing for the responses of warmth, spontaneity and human fallibility. Note that I agreed with Mr. Jones, was silent or gave new leads to expand his insight about obsessional characteristics that I had derived from my understanding of this disorder and which the patient felt was restricted only to himself.

DEVELOPMENT OF INSIGHT

The development of insight is slow, and it emerges from different aspects of the neurotic structure, which surface at different times during the therapeutic work. One tries to tie the pieces together when associations and data allow it. The global formulations that sound so convincing to a reader are usually interpretations that the therapist makes in writing up his case history, rather than what is actually said at the time to the patient. If formulations were presented to the patient as they appear in books and journals, they would be unconvincing to him, as they would not have been integrated into the patient's actual functioning. The best we can do in the office is to attempt to assemble some of the pieces of the puzzle, recognizing that while we may see how the pieces fit together, the patient does not, nor will he necessarily accept our solution when it is put to him.

Mr. Jones: I didn't realize then that they were feelings I could have; I just knew that I didn't have them and that I reacted differently from most people. I've been trying to restrain myself from exhibiting emotions. If anyone said anything about me I ignored it if I could.

Therapist: Let's hear more about this. It wasn't only a matter of expressing feelings of being hurt; it was almost as if everything had to be controlled.

Mr. Jones: Another thing that comes to mind is that when I was an adolescent the movies and novels that were current at that time gave much attention to gangsters and criminals and bootleggers. They were played as being poker-faced, and they always had an unyielding front. I thought that was a virtuous and desirable way to act, and I tried to have a poker face.

Therapist: Because that meant what — being strong, or safe and tough?

Mr. Jones: In a way, I would put these ideas into practice. If I was in a group and some events happened that the rest of the group would be, uh, awed ... or displeased by, I would try to restrain my emotions. I always tried to cover up.

Therapist: And so you got to be known as stone face?

Mr. Jones: I don't think it had that effect. Even while I was consciously doing this, I still thought that I wasn't covering up enough, that I still appeared nervous or immature to my colleagues. This fall when I was rather nervous and having a trying time, I was amazed when one of my classmates told me he was surprised at how easygoing I was, and that I could take everything in stride and nothing bothered me. I seemed to have everything under control. That was a big surprise to me because I thought that I was just the opposite. I always had thought that others looked upon me as being inferior or inadequate.

Therapist: Was it a surprise to you that you have had difficulty seeing yourself as you were viewed by others?

Mr. Jones: Well, I have always been conscious of trying very hard to make a good impression on others, being logical and rational.

Therapist: When you started this session you said you had two instances.

I was referring here to his opening statement, of the two instances when he expressed his feelings. My comment was a maneuver to get him unstuck from his ruminations about having to present himself as tough, which I felt had gone as far as they could at that time. Obsessionals have a sticky quality in their thoughts and ruminations, and when they get on a theme they cannot get unstuck. They become repetitive and compulsively driven to go over and over the same thought or idea. This is the exact opposite of the distracting, substituting quality of not staying with anxiety, even for a moment. They both achieve the same purpose of avoiding the main issues that trouble the patient. The therapist often must take direct action to shift the needle on this broken record.

Mr. Jones: Yes, the second instance was one in which I became angry and realized I was angry and was able to express myself spontaneously. At a meeting this morning I expressed the feeling that I would not agree to the timing of another meeting. That brings up another point. I have never been able to express my feelings in words or on the spur of the moment. Usually I subdue them so that I don't think I had any feelings ...

Feelings, whether hostile or tender, are not recognized as such. They are either translated into compulsive-defensive actions such as evasion, denial, or reaction-formation, or else into obsessional thinking where anxiety and distraction-avoidance are the manifest reactions.

Mr. Jones: You have mentioned before about it being difficult for me to be complimentary. I don't agree with that.

Therapist: Uh-huh.

Mr. Jones: But it isn't that. I often am. It isn't difficult for me to be complimentary and I often am complimentary. I find it difficult only if I thought I would be forced to say something insincere.

Therapist: Uh-huh.

VALUE OF THE THERAPIST'S ERRORS

He had not forgotten my reference to his difficulties in expressing positive feelings. It arose at this point without my having any intention of discussing it. The therapist's errors can produce valuable insights. It is an enlightening experience for the patient to discover that the therapist is a fallible human and does not react to this awareness with a feeling of danger. This can be verbalized at times. Here it was apparently noted without particular focus on this matter.

Mr. Jones: About hurting the feelings of others. I often do it without realizing it or at times when I think I'm being ... too weak; I may be too harsh. Where I have realized it I would feel uncomfortable and usually try to apologize or be excessively friendly and solicitous to try and erase this injury. I've felt considerable help from the recent realization that I always had this compelling feeling that I had to please everyone. I had to look good in everyone's eyes and I realize that I did feel that way. I have made some progress in realizing that I don't please everyone and I don't have to, and if I don't, I don't always have to worry about it.

Therapist: Does it occur to you that a statement about how you feel hurt may be the kind of thing that makes others more friendly and warm toward you since it is much more human?

Now that we were on the matter of the possibility of being human, I wanted him to recognize that what he called weakness might be viewed by others as being human and considerate and what he called strength could be considered callous and indifferent.

Mr. Jones: No, that hadn't occurred to me but I certainly do think that that's so.

Therapist: Well, this is one occasion that might possibly have shocked a lot of people — that you were willing to express your feelings.

Mr. Jones: It did, as a matter of fact. There was a general giggle or laugh that went around the table when I said this.

Therapist: Sure.

Mr. Jones: I was surprised at it.

Therapist: But you are not at all a machine.

Mr. Jones: [laughs] It's uncanny the way you figure things out. One of the people who was present at this meeting expressed those very words to me a few months ago — that when he first knew me he thought that I was a machine. And, gradually, as he got to know me better, when he saw the various incidents in which I could unbend or be easygoing, he thought I was human. He told me this about six months ago.

Therapist: Uh-huh.

Mr. Jones: He used the same words, practically, that you used.

Therapist: Well, it's a curious distortion, isn't it, that when you think you are being so effective in pleasing people, it appears to be the opposite, and when you feel you are involved in displeasing them, it turns out that these may be the very elements of your being liked by them.

Mr. Jones: Exactly, except that in the latter case, I don't think it's a question of displeasing them so much as it is the question that I think I would look unfavorable in their eyes.

Therapist: I think it is useful for you to note that the human qualities, the things which in the past you have been so scared about, you are prepared to do in this instance. Your response gets a laugh out of your colleagues — a laugh which is obviously friendly.

Mr. Jones: I think the laugh was being sympathetic.

Therapist: You actually took a chance and you were willing to stick your neck out in a way that might displease someone; yet it produces an opposite reaction.

Mr. Jones: These points that come up are of such great importance to me that I realize I hadn't noticed them before and I feel very good about it. At the same time I think that there is so much to it that I hadn't realized that I'm afraid that I'll forget this new realization.

RESISTANCE TO INSIGHT

Resistance is a very familiar reaction which generally impedes the development of insight. The patient deprecates the awareness of the insight because it is viewed as not coming entirely from his own thoughts and may not be fully understood or remembered for all time. It is not enough to say, "Gosh, that's right!" The obsessional must always be able to record it indelibly and have a perfect understanding of it. The therapist must explore this notion; otherwise the search for perfection is intruded into the therapy, and the process becomes an obsessional picnic instead of a learning and changing experience.

Therapist: Well, that is a matter that we can take up at another time because you feel good about it. While you may not feel as good about it because you should have noticed it yourself and that it may not last too long, let's not worry about that now, but note your tendency to deprecate what does not come exclusively from you.

Mr. Jones: I'm not conscious of any, well, I haven't been conscious of much self-criticism about it but rather a feeling that ...

Therapist: You don't want to lose it.

Mr. Jones: That's it exactly! I don't want to lose it and I'm anxious to be able to retain all of it and make use of it.

Therapist: But that's the old story, of your trying to be perfect.

Mr. Jones: [laughs] O.K.

The session ended and a short note I wrote at the time went as follows: "A very interesting hour, especially the first twenty minutes and the last ten minutes, when the patient recognized something significant about his living. The development of insight is clearly portrayed and at the same time the feeling of having achieved something is manifested by enthusiasm and clear development of warmth in his attitude."

The following hour seemed to be involved with replaying some of the material from our last session.

Mr. Jones: We had some company last night for dinner, including a little boy about nine years old. I observed in him some behavior that is normal for most boys growing up, and yet it made a strong impression on me. Today I ran into a difficult situation that seemed to illustrate this: I was enraged at my colleague for taking a complaint to my boss, but was completely defenseless to reply. I felt that I made a very weak and ineffective stand. I've noticed this inability on my part to answer criticism effectively a long time ago. As the situation turned out today, I got even more angry after the discussion was over than when I was in the midst of it.

Therapist: Well, what happened? Could you relate that in detail? Were you bawled out?

Again I tried to tease out the details in order to discover the areas of sensitivity and neurotic needs that produced anxiety. If we could find those areas, then we could begin to explore why they were present and why they continued to disturb him at the present time.

Mr. Jones: No, I wasn't. I guess my concern was for two things: one that this complaint was off base, and secondly, I'm disturbed about my feeling of inadequacy in handling it. I guess it's difficult for me to see that all affairs or events in the world aren't determined by logic or reasoning. So it's difficult for me to reply to anything except in a logical manner or to make an attempt to be logical in places where logic won't work ... Today a quick outburst would have been far better than attempting to be logical.

Therapist: How would the quick outburst have worked? What would that have accomplished?

Mr. Jones: The accusation was not a reasonable one, and if I had been able to reply to it more or less extemporaneously, I would have felt better about it. In the past I would arrange things so as to try and attain such perfection that I would avoid criticism. Being unable to master a thing to perfection I would expect criticism, but I don't know whether this explains my inability to cope with illogical actualities. I think I've got that situation under control.

Therapist: Meaning that you can't always do that?

Mr. Jones: That I can't always do it and I don't make superhuman efforts to try to do it.

This was a major concession, and his awareness rose without fuss or fanfare. He stated matter-of-factly what we tried to get him to see for some time — that is, that logic does not always resolve problems or alleviate anxiety and that spontaneity can be most helpful at times. Also, he realized that striving for perfection in order to avoid criticism may not be the best or most pleasant way to live one's life. Such a realization is often the sign that insight has been achieved and integrated and has become a part of the changed personality of the patient. It does not call for comment or reinforcement, since it has become a part of his character structure.

SEARCH FOR CAUSES

Therapy had now clearly entered a new phase. As I indicated at the outset of this chapter the therapeutic relationship had consisted mainly of accumulating data about the patient's past and identifying the major neurotic trends and personality characteristics that distorted and interfered with his productive living. Mr. Jones felt driven to behave in ways that conformed to his concepts of duty, propriety, and drive for perfection in all areas. He could not enjoy what he was doing because he was constantly on trial to prove his adequacy and to avoid the criticism of others. While the anamestic process was proceeding, the patient was developing some trust and regard for the therapist while checking out the therapist's skill, standards, integrity, and ability to accept the patient with his defects and deficiencies. As Mr. Jones developed some insight, he began to have some feelings of gratitude and tender regard for the therapist. The therapist had come to know the patient's defenses in some detail and to formulate an hypothesis about the pathology of the patient's living. He had identified the transference distortions and some of his own countertransference attitudes.

The development of insight and the recognition of how the therapeutic process could improve his living strengthened Mr. Jones's motivations for change and his trust in the therapist's respect for his nonneurotic capacities. So far in the work with Mr. Jones, however, the exploration of the most distressing problem — his obsessional preoccupation about killing his wife — had not surfaced long enough to be examined in detail. Reference had been made to it at various times, but not until this point, when he had experienced some real benefit and developed sufficient trust, could he begin to explore the more unacceptable aspects of his behavior. We could now search for causes, origins, and the most intimate elements in Mr. Jones's thinking, feeling, and behaving about his obsession.

This search for causes followed a session in which he began to review his competitive jealousy and his need for perfection. He appeared ready to recognize his extreme pressure to win, and there was a willingness to admit error. It was as if he were making a final admission prior to a major confession, having built up enough confidence to trust the therapist's reaction.

Mr. Jones: I told you on Monday I had encounters with two people in the office in which I thought I came out second-best. There is some follow-up on that. I talked with Joan about it and her idea was that there probably was considerable jealousy among my colleagues, particularly those I suceeded when I was promoted. I had thought of that only in a vague fashion before she mentioned it, but I think that there's considerable validity to the idea. I think probably the reaction in both cases, since they were illogical, could well have been based on jealousy. I'm far younger than most of my colleagues in equivalent positions; they are fifteen years older than I. I was impressed quite strongly when Joan made this observation and said that I had been in such situations many times before and she couldn't understand why I didn't recognize it.

Therapist: What other situations, for example?

Mr. Jones: Well, I can recall two specific cases where my colleagues were somewhat older than I. In these cases it seemed to me that they were unnecessarily belligerent or uncooperative. I found it difficult to cope with such attitudes because I had to be logical.

Therapist: But one doesn't necessarily win because one is logical and correct. Does one?

Mr. Jones: Definitely not.

Therapist: It's easier to accept another person's opinion if it is logical and correct. But then it becomes a matter of winning and not a matter of settling an issue; the fight becomes more important than the issue.

Mr. Jones: Very nice way of putting it. I've heard much about the enlightened way of handling people, giving them a chance to express themselves rather than constantly ordering or directing them.

Therapist: I think you're making a very useful point here. What attitude or behavior on your part would discourage their presenting you with new ideas?

Mr. Jones: Well, I was very meticulous and I demanded perfection from them and complained a great deal when I didn't get it. Usually when some new idea was presented to me, I tried — sometimes directly, sometimes indirectly — to indicate that I had already thought of it.

Therapist: What does this remind you of?

I was hoping he would recognize how often this happened in our work; that is, when I would make some suggestions or interpretations, and he would find it necessary to imply that he had already thought about that or that it wasn't important anyway. I always wanted him to see that his perfectionistic needs discouraged activity in himself and others because of the difficulty in achieving it. It was surprising how unaware Mr. Jones appeared to be at times. He rarely took up my direct references or attempted to relate matters that were obvious and explicit. This was clearly not a cognitive problem but an overpowering tendency to avoid the awareness by perceptual distortions. At times it appeared naive, innocent, unsophisticated, or ingenuous; but it was truly a nonperceptive state of unawareness, which interfered with a reasonable inspection of the data and drawing the evident conclusions.

Mr. Jones: Well, what about it? I don't get your point. What does it remind me of?

Therapist: What are you reminded of in this connection when scrupulous adherence to detail or to proper form discourages your colleague from demonstrating any initiative?

Mr. Jones: I think I was the same way when I was growing up about my parents. I didn't want to do things unless I felt that they would approve of it or that they wanted it.

While Mr. Jones recognized the facts, it was important to notice that in spite of his superior intelligence he lacked the capacity to recognize his role and reaction to others and how he affected them. His wife had to draw his attention to the tendency of others to be jealous of him and was surprised when he missed it. Here he could not really see how his parents' demands could discourage his performance.

It is a striking phenomenon that obsessionals and some narcisstic individuals — while brilliantly capable of logical deductions and interrelations of ideas, philosophical abstractions, and such — are totally naive and unsophisticated in their interpersonal relations and are often unable to draw the simplest deductions about human exchanges. Some theorists lable this innocence. The unknowing therapist, friend, or colleague is mystified by such discrepancies and concludes that the individual is deliberately misconstruing or denying what is obvious to all. The obsessional's failure to perceive the emotional exchange between people is the cause of innumerable arguments and invalid charges against him. Being unresponsive and insensitive to his own emotional reactions, he is invariably unable to experience the subtlety of the reaction of others. Only when the other person is crudely direct or unmistakenly outspoken or rejecting will the obsessional notice. It is also easier to identify hostile or negative reactions from others and be entirely closed off from positive or tender feelings from them. Similarly, it is even more difficult for the obsessional to identify his own feelings of tenderness, in contrast to his feelings of hostility. Thus the obsessional can be skillful, informed, and even brilliant in nonhuman or technical and intellectual pursuits, while being backward and ignorant of human or interpersonal matters.

> *Therapist*: Very similar, isn't it?
> *Mr. Jones*: Well, why should that be?
> *Therapist*: Why would it be that one would be discouraged?
> *Mr. Jones*: No, why is there similarity?
> *Therapist*: Why, were you doing the same thing?
> *Mr. Jones*: Yes.
> *Therapist*: Well, what do you think?

CONFUSING THE UNWITTING
AND THE DELIBERATE

The obsessional needs to avoid clarity and to proceed along lines that will divert and distract, rather than illuminate, an issue, but the obtuseness and what appears to be deliberate confusion of the obsessional is not deliberate, conscious, willful, or resistant. More errors are made in confusing this issue by therapists and others than in any other defect in dealing with them. The obsessional is compelled to act in the way he does, and he does not willfully choose to behave that way. The essential issue in the therapy is to remove the compulsive nature of the obsessional's behavior, in order to open up the possibility of choice so that a decision can be freely made.

Mr. Jones: Maybe I was getting even for feelings that I had when my parents were doing that to me.

This was a familiar gambit. Here-and-now behavior was considered directly related to earlier experiences as a way of getting even for what had been done in the past. We mistreat others now because our parents mistreated us in the past. This is a blatant misuse of the valid concepts of personality development. The simplistic notion of repetition of childish patterns is generally an avoidance of responsibility for one's present behavior and a tendency to blame others for all one's ills.

Therapist: But this wasn't what you were trying to do — to get even. You believe that to present yourself as less than perfect or less right than they would mean to be weaker than they. How could you ever allow a subordinate to have an idea that you didn't have?
Mr. Jones: I guess that is it.
Therapist: Consequently, a guy would be afraid to present you with a new idea because he would sense that you would dislike it.
Mr. Jones: Hmm. True.
Therapist: Which is precisely what you must have sensed at home. It was dangerous to be an experimenter or a mildly aggressive guy. You often said you would try to find out what they wanted you to do and then you would do it. You tried to learn from your father what you thought he would want you to do when you finished school. You did not decide what you'd like to do.

Mr. Jones's inability to respond to my direct question often required detailed descriptions of how I viewed his development and the effect of his parents on him. These were presented as hypotheses and were designed to allow him to discuss, reject, or accept my presentation. While the insights might appear obvious to the reader, they had to be spelled out in careful detail so that they would be received and acknowledged without distortion or the need to qualify each statement. It was hoped that the expositions would stimulate some associations to reinforce my observation with additional recall and supporting data. At times this happened and enhanced the insight process immeasurably.

Mr. Jones: I can remember being in just exactly that situation when I was about sixteen and a half years old, just after I finished high school. I felt very confused and inadequate. I was waiting for them to indicate something that I should do. I wanted to be independent and yet I either was afraid to be or I didn't know how to be.

Therapist: What were the dangers involved in being independent?

Mr. Jones: I don't think my thinking went that far along.

Therapist: Well, what occurs to you now?

Mr. Jones: I felt that I would feel embarrassed in front of my parents if I looked for a job and was unable to get one.

Therapist: What do you mean, embarrassed? Let's try to pin down this feeling.

Mr. Jones: Embarrassed isn't — isn't an accurate word. I thought they would think that I was a failure if I wasn't successful.

Therapist: They would not like you?

Mr. Jones: I suppose I thought they would not like me, yet I can't remember having thought of it in those terms. Maybe it's merely a question of semantics.

Therapist: You couldn't have thought of yourself as being very likable if your acceptance depended constantly on being the perfect performer?

Here was another instance of his opacity and denseness. This led to a series of exchanges in which I assisted him directly in gaining some insight. At some points I made an interpretation or a suggestion that was productive. It was clear that he was now ready to make some connections between the past and the present with regard to his relationships and behavior. With the obsessional patient the process of slowly building up a piece of insight is the most effective way of drawing the patient into feeling that he is sponsoring and directing the process, instead of having it presented to him in a final, finished production. The latter may be impressive to the therapist or his supervisor, but it is not necessarily most useful to the patient.

Mr. Jones: I didn't get that, Doctor.

Therapist: You must not have been convinced that you were a likable person if you always had to guarantee that you'd be liked by being a perfect performer.

Mr. Jones: Well, apparently not.

Therapist: I wonder why?

Mr. Jones: That ties in directly into this idea that everything had to be determined on the basis of logic. I had to produce and I had to be right in order to be accepted. I had to excel. And I often did excel. That probably is the reason I was able to be comfortable with myself during all this time. The only long period during which I did not consistently excel was those last three years when I was getting ill. It was what I considered an improper and inferior assignment, and there were such very unsatisfactory relations whith my boss that I finally blew the fuse.

Therapist: Can you make something of that observation?

Mr. Jones: It is the reason for the disturbance that started several years ago.

Therapist: It helps us understand why it started then.

Mr. Jones: Yes.

Therapist: But hardly the cause of it.

Mr. Jones: This sounds very, very interesting; what do you see in it?

Therapist: I'm interested in what you say — that your mental health is maintained by a constant high level of performance, and if it takes the slightest drop you're a lost soul. What a demand you make that you can only be comfortable as a superman. You make enormous demands on yourself.

RESOLUTION OF RESISTANCE

I had been waiting for such an occasion for some months. I had evidence of Mr. Jones's superhuman expectations of himself and a rigidly severe superego that required absolute perfection. I had made note of this and waited until he not only was ready to accept such an interpretation but also could reinforce it with enough new and incontrovertible data to leave him convinced of the validity of the observation and unable to weaken or undo the interpretation with doubts, qualifications, or outright denial. My emphasis was intentional and was often necessary to force the patient to respond. Thus, excessive or explosive statements can be a valid technique to stimulate an emotional reaction, rather than a mild intellectual response.

Note that even at this point Mr. Jones was still unable to accept the interpretations clearly and enthusiastically, and my persistent efforts were required to prevent him from the typical obsessional defenses of distraction and obfuscation.

Mr. Jones: I — I thought so.

Therapist: Thought what?

Mr. Jones: I thought that I should have gone through all of these storms and adverse conditions and still come out on top.

Therapist: I wonder what you would think of a boss who expected that from you?

Mr. Jones: I don't see what you mean.

Note again how mildly and coolly Mr. Jones responded to such a strong presentation of how his excessive demands produced dissatisfaction in his living. It was a sympathetic presentation and was not critical or disparaging. Even this slid off his back without too much of an impact.

Therapist: Who expected of you what you expect from yourself?
Mr. Jones: I was unable to take minor setbacks, but to those I reacted by working even harder. That tided me over the minor setback.
Therapist: Yeah.
Mr. Jones: But the long-range adverse situation — that I couldn't cope with because during that time I kept trying to work harder and harder. I never got anywhere.

HUMOR IN THERAPY

I then attempted, by being sardonic and extreme, to emphasize his continued tendency to deal with all issues by greater and greater exertions that would make him a superman. I wanted to leave no doubt that he was still working toward a better neurosis, one devoid of anxiety and failure, that could be achieved only by his insisting on doing the impossible. This type of exaggeration can be successful at times if it forces the patient to see the ludicrousness of his efforts. If he has some sense of humor, which the obsessional often does not, he may smile and agree that his needs and behavior are unreasonable and inhuman. At other times, if the obsessional cannot tolerate it yet, he feels he is being derided and responds to sarcasm as being belittling and disrespectful. Then it is ineffective and the therapist must clarify his intention to assure the patient that he *is* being taken seriously and is not being derogated.

At this point Mr. Jones received my comments with good humor, and this session was quite useful as indicated by the succeeding session, five days later. It was approximately eight months since we had begun the exploration of his problem. He introduced his obsessive thoughts about killing his wife into the sessions. He was less uneasy about them and proceeded to explore the circumstances around which these thoughts developed.

Therapist: Yeah. It is unfortunate that you couldn't dig a hole through a mountain with your fingers and that you can't work twenty-eight hours a day to get it done. It's not too difficult for others to recognize why you are unable to see how you make stringent demands on the people who work under you. It doesn't seem very stringent to you because this is what you demand of yourself.
Mr. Jones: You're — you're absolutely right:

This was an unusually spirited and warm response. He finally had grasped the notion fully, as his remarks continued to demonstrate.

Mr. Jones: I remember having seen an efficiency report made out on me. It had a remark similar to that. It said that I'm far too demanding of my subordinates.
Therapist: Yeah, and it could have added that you were just as demanding of yourself.
Mr. Jones: It could have.

Our next session began with him describing his obsession but still trying to relate it to his physical state.

Mr. Jones: I've noticed that at times when I might not be physically well there's a recurrence of these obsessive thoughts that I'm going to kill my wife. They have been more active in the last few days and I was bothered with them all day yesterday and the day before. This morning, while riding on the bus, I was troubled by the recurrence of these thoughts.
Therapist: Could you detail what was going on so we can learn about what produced these thoughts?
Mr. Jones: They're accentuated whenever a situation occurs in which my wife says or does something that smacks of the maternal control that caused me lot of distress in the past. There were a few cases in the last few days when that happened.
Therapist: Let's hear about them.
Mr. Jones: Well, the first one I think I have explained to myself that she intended nothing nor had any maternal thoughts in it. We received an invitation to attend a picnic in one of our neighbor's yards. She said that because I didn't feel well she thought it would be better if we didn't go. Formerly I would have gotten very upset and I would have thought that she was overbearing, domineering and trying to run the show.
Therapist: Now you're more understanding and you're not upset about her being overbearing or dominating because you're able to see the additional element of concern for you. But the feeling of being dominated, whether your best interests are involved or not, still exists. You must still resent the fact that she didn't ask you what you want to do.
Mr. Jones: I suppose there is some resentment of that. I thought I had gotten it down to a minimum.
Therapist: How do you think you dispose of these feelings? You can't just turn them off.
Mr. Jones: Maybe I became upset at first and then when I heard that she had my needs in mind I felt less bad about it.

My activity at this time was directed at pressing him to explore his reaction, since his tendency to avoid experiencing or acknowledging his feeling prevented him from recognizing how his responses followed his feelings. His rationalizations, justifications, and excuses were efforts to be fair and decent, but they also minimized the intensity of his responses, which would then break out in opposite and extreme obsessional thoughts.

Therapist: You try to convince yourself that since she had your best interests at heart you should not get irritated or feel pushed around.

Mr. Jones: Yeah; that's certainly true.

Therapist:That's a familiar routine which says to a child: "Why should you get angry, I did it in your best interests." But that isn't the point.

Mr. Jones: No, that doesn't solve the problems. I know that at times when I strongly protest about her doing anything without asking me, then she has a tendency to get hurt. I try to take a philosophical view of these things because I know that she has those feelings. I'm being truthful when I say that it didn't irritate me much, but perhaps it was the beginning of a chain of irritation. Another expression of this maternal thing happened yesterday morning. I went out the back door of the house and crossed our neighbor's lawn. We seldom do that. This time I did it because it was hot and I wanted to make the trip to the mailbox as short as possible. Joan was standing in the backyard and as I started across their yard she said: "You be careful where you're walking." Well, that hit me very uncomfortably.

Therapist: Since you ruminated about it, could you tell me what you were thinking and feeling?

Mr. Jones: Well, I thought that this was outrageous for a wife to say to her husband unless there was a gross provocation. She know how sensitive I am about these things anyway. I had this reminder of maternal behavior again. I was thinking of whether to say something to her about the fact that it sounded like a henpecking, mothering thing to say. However, I decided not to. When I have mentioned these things to her it makes her uncomfortable. She denies it immediately.

This was another rational attempt to justify his ambivalent feelings toward his wife. But since I did not want to shift the direction of the inquiry, I avoided mentioning this association at this time and I let Mr. Jones continue.

Mr. Jones: So I said before, when these situations come up, they generally result in a recurrence or intensification of these thoughts. They trouble me greatly, these thoughts, which are unpleasant and interfere with my attention to other things.

Therapist: Well, do you remember exactly when the thoughts started again?

Mr. Jones: I remember the fact that I had these obsessive thoughts at least once, usually more than once during the day. This morning as I was riding in on the bus they were more severe.

Therapist: What were you thinking about on the bus? What was going on?

Mr. Jones: I do recall this thought to the effect that "You're going to kill you wife."

Therapist: You can't recall thinking of anything else this morning — other thoughts which perhaps were unformed, fleeting, or on the fringe of your mind:

Mr. Jones: Well, I remember thinking that when these things happen, I try to think what may have caused it and of course I thought about this mailbox situation.

Therapist: How could that cause it?

Mr. Jones: I think those situations in which there's considerable resentment are those that cause it ... There may be others, but I think that resentment is the chief cause of it.

Therapist: So it's on these occasions that you note that you have some resentment towards your wife?

Mr. Jones: Yeah.

Therapist: What do you resent?

Mr. Jones: I resent the things she may say that indicate a motherly tendency. Sometimes it's not exactly motherly but bossy.

Therapist: What about this bothers you so much?

READINESS TO ACCEPT INTERPRETATION

We had established the business of maternal elements in the behavior of others, but it was still unclear what caused him to become so infuriated. I suspected it to be a feeling of helplessness and impotence in managing his own affairs and controlling his living. It was the feeling of a "little boy" who always needs to be good and to be safe, with all the implications of this simple formula. However, this interpretation remained to be established, and I had to be careful not to intrude my hupothesis of what ailed Mr. Jones. This is a ticklish and difficult road to travel, and too often the therapist, unwittingly but with all good intentions, communicates his prejudices and preconceptions to the patient. Being aware of this possibility is the best safeguard against it but does not guarantee that it will not occur.

The element of persuasion in the subtleties of the communication process — whether by words, silences, gestures, nods, grunts, or reflections — cannot be overlooked. It is invariably present in therapeutic relationships, where the patient is already hypersensitive to the response of others or is keenly perceptive to all forms of rejecting orientations, however subtle. Although the obsessional is often obtuse and insensitive to interpersonal exchanges, his need for acceptance as an expert and the proper and perfect individual lends itself to trying to please others. In therapy it is manifested by an excessive zeal to agree when there is not complete disagreement and an exaggerated effort to read the therapist's mind to anticipate or agree with every shift or anticipated shift in his mood.

Mr. Jones: I've asked myself that but I don't have an answer for it.

Therapist: Let's see what comes to mind about it. What do you think there is about this situation that is disturbing and infuriating to you?

Mr. Jones: I think it conflicts with this rather apparently exaggerated sense I have of being dominated and the exaggerated sensitivity to it. It aggravates my feeling of resentment and sensitivity... I guess there must be some connection with the idea that my parents had to approve everything that I did and my reaction to anything that has any parental connotation as disapproval. Because I am sensitive to the disapproval of my parents, I usually didn't proceed with something until I had some sort of expression that they would approve it before I even did it.

Mr. Jones was moving away from the issue he had clearly acknowledged a few moments ago — namely, that he resented being bossed or told what to do. This is the obsessional process called displacement. From resentment to being pushed around he had come to resentment about needing parental approval — related, but hardly the same thing. As insight is built up, we come to expect this.

It's necessary to be patient and move one step at a time in trying to stay with the essentials and not be distracted by the obsessional's defensive opaqueness and meandering. Again, he is not being resistant or stupid; he is merely being obsessional. Since this is the pathology we are dealing with, we must not expect him to behave otherwise. In this instance, I tried to bring the matter back to the facts by reminding Mr. Jones of what transpired, in order to recall his actual reactions instead of encouraging philosophical speculation. We must stay with the events and the actual behavior of the participants in an exchange if we are to expect maximum understanding of the event.

Therapist: What do you make of that statement, "Watch where you're going?" When you say maternal, do you mean it's a mother talking to her young son?

Mr. Jones: Yeah.

Therapist: What is involved in this comment? Is it a bit condescending or patronizing?

Mr. Jones: Yeah, I think so. Yeah.

Therapist: Is there any notion of disapproval in that comment?

Mr. Jones: I think I find it irritating that she should even concern herself enough with some minor thing that I'm doing — concern herself enough with it to comment about it at all.

Therapist: Well, then you think it's more of a comment that a grown-up makes to a little child or to an inept or uninformed youngster.

Mr. Jones: That's right. Well, the two of them are close together — the fact that she comments at all signifies to me that she has this feeling that she's responsible for what I'm doing or that she should be watchful for what I'm doing.

Therapist: That she should be watchful or responsible because you are a little fellow who is not responsible?

Mr. Jones: Well, I guess that's implied.

Therapist: Yeah. Now you say that this is the very thing that you resented at home. Is that what you said before?

It is the therapist's task to accelerate and often initiate insight by drawing the patient's attention to data that have been revealed which tie together with other bits of data to illuminate motivation or cause. Often the therapist has held these ideas in escrow to be used at an appropriate time. He must be the facilitating agent of change by highlighting discrepancies, contradictions, and ambivalences in the patient because these are signposts for neurotic conflict and defensive formations. Yet, the patient does not necessarily accept them as valid recalls of either the patient or the therapist, since these events are often incorporated into the doubting defenses of the obsessional. At other times, there is the typical progression in the obsessional when he first responds by saying, "No, I don't think I said it," but then follows with, "Maybe I did; yes, I must have, but I have known it for a long time so there's nothing new to it."

Mr. Jones's answer to my question was typically obsessional: doubting, agreement, disagreement, doing and undoing, qualifying while agreeing because of some uncertainty, and so on and on and on.

Mr. Jones: No, I didn't make a positive statement of that. I don't think I did. Well, yes, I said I must have or probably did, and I think that must have been something like that. But at home I don't remember it happening precisely in that way, at least, not often.

Therapist: Uh-huh. Have you ever wondered why having this much deep resentment to being treated like a kid you would marry someone who has possibilities of treating you this way?

UNRESOLVED REALITIES

At this point I wanted to explore Mr. Jones's needs as well as the behavior of others, in order to emphasize that what happened was of his own doing even if he had compulsions that pushed him to behave in certain ways. The obsessional must recognize that he and he alone is responsible for his living and its complications. The therapeutic dilemma is that he is encouraged to recognize how he acts without will — under compulsion — yet we insist that he take responsibility for the consequences and decide to act to alter this. Consequently, in attempting to help the obsessional deal with those occasions where things happen that he has no control over or where his behavior is not attributable to the destructive or malevolent acts of others but to involvements growing out of his needs, we must always focus on the patient's activities, so that he can recognize the effect of his behavior. Even though Mr. Jones's capacity to influence his situation was more limited in childhood, his later behavior tended to repeat these patterns, and this was what I was trying to get Mr. Jones to recognize.

Mr. Jones: Yes, I have; it has occurred to me.

Therapist: What were your thoughts about it?

Mr. Jones: Well, I thought that I was so close to my parents when I was growing up that I had little interest or contact with others. I acquired a feeling of closeness towards people who were older than I. And I noticed that many times, both before and after I was married, that I usually felt more comfortable in the company of people who were quite a bit older than I. I could be more friendly, intimate, and comfortable with people older than myself.

Therapist: And this is another way of saying that you would be more comfortable in situations where you might possibly be treated like a younger boy as opposed to situations where you might be treated as an equal.

Mr. Jones: Well, I don't know. I thought of something that wasn't as well developed as that, but I did think of something like that. That's difficult to accept. For three years I was uncomfortable under the yoke of a superior whom I didn't like at all. I thought he looked down on me and treated me like an inferior. That was very uncomfortable.

In his literal style Mr. Jones was now questioning the issue of maternal factors by saying he felt dominated by a former boss who treated him like a little boy. The issue was not gender, but being subjugated by a dominating figure who made him feel childish and impotent. Even though he was more comfortable in the company of people older than himself because he knew how to cater and satisfy them, he was also infantilized in their presence. Mr. Jones had to recognize that we were dealing with symbols of authority who hold power over him and not with parental figures.

Mr. Jones: I suppose I did somehow accustom myself to be in situations where I was more comfortable because I was younger. I hadn't thought of it that way, could be ... Well, that would explain my feeling so uncomfortable in the company of this man. Yet I associated the recall with situations when I resent expressions of any maternal nature. How does that follow?
Therapist: It seems contradictory to you?
Mr. Jones: Yes, it does, the two must be related in some way, but the way is rather ambiguous.
Therapist: Is it possible that much of your activity with people tends to stimulate maternal feelings in them toward you?
Mr. Jones: No, I don't think so ... No, I think the actions that possibly caused these older people to be more friendly with me had to do with my greater knowledge and mature outlook on things, which has been expressed to me occasionally by different people.

How easy and insensitive was this rationalization! Mr. Jones did not even blush at the notion that he had a more "mature" outlook on things. However, he moved with no uncertainty to the next thought of his childishness.

Mr. Jones: I wonder if I sometimes may act in ways that do appear childish. I don't think I do, but nevertheless the thought occurred to me. The situation was that I had been polishing the car all afternoon. My wife helped me, and as we were nearly finished, she began talking with one of the neighbors. My wife asked me what kind of food I wanted after doing all this work or some such thing. This other woman then said something which disturbed me, to the effect that "when my little boys do some work I have to pay them first." If my neighbor had no maternal thoughts about me then she said it that way just to be mean or nasty.

Therapist: Whether it was being nasty or not, what she said stirred up the suggestion that you behave like a little boy, or Joan was treating you that way.

Mr. Jones: I think that it had no connection with me, but she may have been making a slam at my wife, who is considerably older than I am.

Therapist: Can you think of other incidents where you give the impression of behaving like a young boy?

I avoided the notion that the neighbor's remark was directed at his wife, so as not to sidetrack the exploration of his childishness.

Mr. Jones: ... Well I even had a tinge of resentment at your phrasing it that way.

ANGER AT THE THERAPIST

This is the first time in the course of our work that Mr. Jones was able to express his resentment to me directly. It was a significant development in our relationship and in his growing capacity to confront the issue about his obsessions and childishness. I moved directly into an exploration of this matter.

Therapist: Tell me about that.

Mr. Jones: It struck me that way, your phrasing it.

Therapist: Yes, tell me. What are you thinking? What comes to mind about that — your resenting it being phrased that way?

Mr. Jones: ... The thought that you, perhaps, think that, or that I impress you that way.

Therapist: That is a very unpleasant thought for you to have?

Mr. Jones: Yes, possibly.

Therapist: Why? Let's make sure about the way you feel.

Mr. Jones: Well, I don't think there are any specifics right at the moment, but another thought occurred to me. Every time anyone would call me "junior," or any other phraseology that implied my being childish, I remember resenting it.

Therapist: Is it so important for you to present yourself as a man and trying to be bigger and more serious than the other kids?

Mr. Jones: Yeah. Yes, I remember having feelings of uncertainty as to when I could dare use the word *man* rather than *boy* in referring to myself. I felt that I wanted to be a man, or at least talk as if I were. But I think when I was seventeen, eighteen, or nineteen, I had the idea that I would rather not call myself a man or people would notice and think I'm playing big shot.

Therapist: You would present yourself, then, as a boy?

Now we had a clear statement about the conflict between wanting to be the boy and dependent and safe and being the man who was not protected by the adult and who had to face the responsibilities of adulthood. The conflict was never resolved until it was raised in our work. Mr. Jones left with the suggestion that he should give further thought about the relationship of his obsessive thoughts and his concerns about being childish and dependent and his resentment when he was viewed or dealt with in this fashion.

During the next three sessions Mr. Jones dealt with the issue of his being the little boy in a variety of ways that the preceding exchange had stimulated, and he shortly came back to his obsession.

Mr. Jones: Last night a very minor incident occurred between Joan and me that I took as an indication that perhaps she does have some realization that some of her actions seem to me bossy and that she may not have intended it so. At the time when I was first having this trouble anything she said I resented as an interference and criticism. I tried to do some more thinking on this subject after we had discussed the relationship of my childishness and the obsessional thoughts about killing. At college I would sometimes avoid the use of the word boy or man in referring to myself. I didn't want to use the word boy and I was afraid if I used the word man that somebody might taunt me about it and that would make an issue of the very thing I didn't want an issue made of.

Therapist: Uh-huh. How come you didn't begin to smoke then?

I introduced the matter of smoking, which Mr. Jones had raised during previous sessions in terms of being a boy or a man. He never took up smoking because he thought his parents would object. At the time the smoking issue was first raised, there was no opportunity to relate it to the issue of his needing permission to engage in activities that were appropriate to his age, so I made a mental note of it for use at a later time. It seemed to me the time was now, when I could emphasize the dependent relationship which he had established.

The clearer the data are and the less room there is for obsessional maneuvering, the greater is the conviction for the insight that results. This is a constant goal in the therapeutic process, where emotional commitment to a viewpoint or interpretation enables the patient to get beyond mere verbal or intellectual agreement. The introduction of Mr. Jones's smoking was used in this fashion.

Mr. Jones: I wanted to but I was afraid my parents wouldn't like it.

Therapist: You never smoked on the sly either?

Mr. Jones: Yes, once or twice. I used to think of various ways I could either talk with them about it or appear with a cigarette in their presence, but I never could bring myself to do it. Well, I just remembered something not directly related to it, something that worried me a great deal when I was about seventeen. My aunt lived with us at this time. One night my aunt and I were at home and we each went to bed in our own rooms. I asked her to come into my room, which she did, and she got into my bed while we continued talking. I got close to her and got an erection. I don't know whether she felt it or not, but anyway she went back to her own bed. My knowledge of the facts of life was so rudimentary that I became worried for months after that — that she would become pregnant. There was no intercourse whatever, but I didn't know enough at that time about what intercourse consisted of. This doubt persisted in my mind for many months.

Therapist: What did you think of that episode then, and now?

Mr. Jones: I worried about all sorts of things, but I was so embarrassed and puzzled that I didn't talk to anyone or do anything about it except worry. It did make me feel resentful of my father for not having acquainted me better with sexual intercourse. There was an incident when I first started in high school before he told me anything about it which embarrassed me greatly.

The association to childishness and immaturity had led him to discuss the gross deficiencies in his sex education. The naiveté and lack of information about sexuality and his manliness were the cause of many embarrassing moments, which confirmed his feelings of inadequacy and immaturity.

Therapist: What was that about?

Mr. Jones: When I was thirteen, I asked my biology teacher what the difference was between a mammal and an animal. She gave an explanation which I didn't understand very well, but I could see she was embarrassed and she became rather angry. Sometime later my father did make an explanation about sex, and as he did this, then this incident in high school became clearer. I felt that if he had told me about sex at an earlier date I would not have been embarrassed in that matter. His explanation was a fragmentary one; about all he told me was that babies were formed by intercourse between men and women. I didn't even know enough to ask him about how or when it took place. He didn't even tell me anything about semen; I didn't know about that at all. I thought the fluid of intercourse was urine.

Therapist: This incident with your aunt was later then, after the explanation?

Mr. Jones: Yes, much later, three or four years later. Maybe I felt embarrassed and uncomfortable that being a child or being an adolescent, that I was experiencing a man's reactions.

Therapist: Were you having any contact with girls during this time?

This was also the first time that he directly discussed his relations with the opposite sex and how this phase of his development was also tied to his pleasing his parents and being the good boy.

Mr. Jones: No, the first date I ever had was when I was seventeen, I think. That was arranged by my mother and aunt. And gradually I made dates with other girls. In a vague sort of way I blamed my parents that I was so far behind other people my age in having dates and going to dances.

Therapist: How did they come to be blamed?

Mr. Jones: It's rather nebulous to me, but I guess it was something like smoking. I thought that they wouldn't approve of it.

Therapist: Did you show some interest in dating?

Mr. Jones: No, I don't think so.

Therapist: You just assumed that they wouldn't like the idea?

Mr. Jones: I assumed that they wouldn't like it and I felt that I had to go through some ritual of obtaining their permission . . . During high school I wanted to go to a dance, but I didn't know how to ask a girl, or how I was going to ask my parents about it, and so I just didn't do anything about it.

Therapist: You had to ask your parents' permission to do everything?

Mr. Jones: I felt so.

Therapist: Any notion as to what gave you that feeling?

Mr. Jones: No, I certainly tried to think many times on that. I rarely talked with my parents about events that happened, day-to-day events. If I did tell them something, it was always in brief, summarized form. They had both attended country schools in a small town and I thought they wouldn't understand anything about a school in a big city.

This session ended with no summary statement because I did not want any closure on this question. By leaving it open-ended, I wanted to maintain enough curiosity and tension so that he would ruminate about it until our next session.

TERMINATING INDIVIDUAL SESSIONS

The issue of terminating individual sessions is a complicated and important matter, and although no rules can be laid down, some general principles are operative: (1) A summary is a useful way of tying together the various strands and issues that are raised during a session, but this summary should not close off further introspection. (2) Provocative and challenging statements or silences can be used to stimulate recall of confirming or associated data to the material at hand. (3) A session can be abruptly terminated by a question which demands an answer but not at that time, in order to stimulate thinking in the interval. (4) Actual suggestions or assignments can be made to ruminate on certain matters. (5) If a pressing matter is still being considered, the session should be extended to reduce serious anxieties. (6) Closure by a formulation or interpretation may be the need of the therapist, to appease his anxiety. (7) Brief notes of the major directions and trends of the session could be jotted down by the therapist, and references to significant data could be recorded. (8) If issues are left for further discussion, it is essential that they be raised or continued in succeeding sessions, either by the patient or, if the patient fails to do so, by the therapist.

The following session with Mr. Jones picked up the themes of the last one.

Mr. Jones: I had an experience last Thursday and I had a very strong reaction that I don't understand very well. My wife came to my office unexpectedly. I was speechless ... She noticed it. I recovered in a few minutes and introduced her to my secretary and my chief, who was talking with me. I was so excited over this that it took me about three hours to quiet down.

Therapist: What was the excitement all about?

Mr. Jones: My secretary is very beautiful, and I detected a feeling of jealousy on my wife's part. It reminded me of a previous situation when Joan thought one of the women in my office was making up to me. At that time I recognized that Joan was exhibiting unreasonable jealousy.

Mr. Jones's wife demonstrated her own doubts and insecurities on many occasions. Her jealousies were only manifest evidence of her own feelings of uncertainty about her husband because of the age difference and her appearance. At times these doubts took on paranoid proportions, which Mr. Jones had difficulty handling because of his righteous and prudish attitude and his inability to entertain notions of infidelity, let alone to actually express them. Therefore, he was indignant and insulted when any suggestion of infidelity was raised by Joan.

He continued to recall the previous situation.

Mr. Jones: Joan thought I was being too friendly during office hours. We had an extensive argument over that, so I think I may have subconsciously remembered that situation last Thursday when Joan came in unexpectedly. My secretary was in the office and I reacted as if I had been caught in the act of doing something improper.

Therapist: Like a little boy?

Mr. Jones: Yes. I remember when I was in school ... my parents were invited to come to the school. I wanted my parents to come and I didn't want them to come at the same time.

Therapist: Why wouldn't you want them to come? Was it shame?

Mr. Jones: I don't know that I can say that. I remember wondering whether my father ... ever felt ashamed of my mother. He would attend social functions from time to time that related to his business, but he never included her in, although other men did have their wives there. I used to wonder why that was ... I think I asked mother about it one time, and a tight expression came over her face which I could observe.

I tried to clarify my picture of his mother by asking some direct questions, so that I could properly evaluate the transference distortions if they were present. This is an essential aspect of the therapeutic process. To clarify a patient's perceptual distortion we must have enough data to rule out reality factors. It's important to know, for instance, whether a particular relationship is damaged by a patient's neurotic traits or because, in fact, the participants have lost interest in each other. In working with an obsessional it is even more critical to distinguish reality from fantasy, as the obsessional's perfectionistic need for precise accuracy can lead to a series of denials or doubts about the clarity of the therapist's interpretation. He must therefore have a definitive statement supported by agreed-upon observations, in order to lessen the patient's doubts and contentious need to be right.

Mr. Jones: My mother was rather tall and built large, although not fat. I wouldn't say she was unattractive, yet in my memory, however, she never seemed attractive.

Therapist: Was she older than your father or younger?

Mr. Jones: Younger.

Therapist: Was your father inclined to be ashamed of her in that she was not bright enough or had no social graces? Just what do you think?

Mr. Jones: I don't know.

Therapist: So that raises an interesting question, doesn't it — that either your mother never put pressure on your father to participate or else he was strong enough to put down any desire on her part to participate. Either he had a way of making it perfectly clear that he didn't want her or she was just unable to force him to include her in.

TESTING HYPOTHESES

Upon rereading my question I can't recall just what I had in mind or hoped to communicate about his parental relationships. I may have been testing my hypothesis that his mother was the active, aggressive, dominating figure in the household. Yet his account at this point contradicted this. Such contradictions are valuable signals of underlying anxiety and may reveal unconscious tendencies of great significance. On the other hand, the hypothesis might need to be abandoned if the data did not support it.

Mr. Jones: Both of them had, in my opinion, strong personalities. I felt uncertain for some indefinite time as to whether they loved each other and whether I loved my mother as much as I did him. I remember there was a strange atmosphere between them that lasted about two years.

Therapist: What were the details about this?

Mr. Jones: I could tell that there was a definite feeling of strain or tenseness.

Therapist: Since you have described that in your household there wasn't any real display of affection between your father and mother, I wonder what you had noticed.

Mr. Jones: There was no show of feelings between them in any romantic sense.

Therapist: At any time?

Mr. Jones: There was a kiss; there was that, but I think it was limited to that in a perfunctory way.

Therapist: To recapitulate — you started the hour by telling me of an incident which was peculiarly upsetting. You had invited your wife to come to your office when she showed up unexpectedly. You have a good job; you have status in your office. You aren't quite clear about the peculiar reaction which is stirred up. You don't know whether it's like being caught at having done something wrong. And it reminds you then of the situation five years ago when Joan made a big deal out of a relationship with your secretary. You felt her reaction was rather silly because there was nothing actually going on and that your intimacy was in a friendly sense, not in any sexual sense.

Mr. Jones: That is difficult for her to accept.

Therapist: Now in thinking about that you sensed the similarity in terms of feeling caught, as if Joan would again be accusing you. There is the same feeling of being the little boy which reminded you of school where for some reason you preferred your parents not to make an appearance one day. And so I raised the question of whether there possibly was some shame with regard to your parents. Many kids are ashamed of their parents when they come from a different culture. In speaking of your father's feeling of shame about your mother, we recognize that we know little of what actually went on in your household. Today we learn that your father, either out of shame or for some other reason, preferred going to certain business affairs alone, even though other people brought their wives. It's interesting that your father had some feelings about your mother which made it difficult for him to expose her to his business associates. And then I raised the question of how you noticed a definite change in the relationship between your mother and father when you were fourteen to sixteen since their relationship was only a formal, pleasant, and conventional one. There didn't seem to be any exchanges of warmth publicly or privately. You say that you noticed the difference because it was a cutting down even of these minimal contacts.

Mr. Jones: Yeah.

Therapist: So that there were only the required exchanges. Isn't it extraordinary how little you knew about your father's feelings toward your mother and her feelings toward your father? Feelings seemed to be absolutely taboo in your household.

Finally, I was led to discuss the paucity of expression of feelings in the household and between members of the family!

Mr. Jones: I guess so. It's difficult for me to describe them to you. No picture comes to my mind to bring out the details of their feelings and relationships to each other. I can't recall any romantic demonstrativeness between them ever. They did kiss, probably on departing, but nothing else. They never used any endearing terms such as my wife and I do — for instance, honey, or what not.

Therapist: Do you think there was much love between them?

Mr. Jones: Well, I don't know.

Therapist: Then it was a cold atmosphere that you grew up in? Were there any playful activities, humor, anything like that?

Mr. Jones: There was some. My mother is exceptionally demonstrative. At least, she is now; maybe she wasn't then. Now she is excessively demonstrative toward me by hugging and kissing when it embarrasses me. I didn't realize that until just this minute. Although mother is now excessively clinging to her children, both my sister and me, I don't think she was that way before.

This session ended with Mr. Jones trying to clarify his perception of others and, in this instance, his family.

Two days later, in the dialogue that follows, we moved right back to the little boy problem. This was the last session before we both took a month's vacation, and in my note at the end of the session I indicated that he was clumsy and uneasy in expressing some feelings of affection toward me. The patient was reluctant to go, and he told me about his skin lesion, which he asked me to look at. I explained that I didn't know much about skin diseases but that I would have a look and I did. He had some hesitation in leaving, finally putting out his hand to shake mine, and in that embarrassed way he wished me a very good trip. The situation was uncomfortable, but he was obviously expressing warmth toward me.

Mr. Jones: Hello, Doctor. There was another occasion yesterday of an exhibition of jealousy on Joan's part towards my secretary. Joan called, and my secretary told her I was busy. She was quite put out at my inaccessibility.

Therapist: Were you angry?

Mr. Jones: She was angry and frustrated that my secretary made her wait. She said she didn't like the idea of my secretary setting herself up as a barrier, and I told her that is what a secretary is supposed to do. She said, "I'm more important than they are." I said that she was more important, but I didn't think we were engaged in a contest of determining relative importance.

Therapist: You put your finger right on it.

Mr. Jones: Well, I don't know whether that places the finger on what it is that is making her uncomfortable. I tried to stick to the facts rather than getting into an emotional battle over it. I didn't indicate to her that I was distressed or uncomfortable about our situation.

Therapist: You didn't want her to know that?

Mr. Jones: That's not quite the way I looked at it. I felt that it might be babyish or weak if I told her that her attitude upset me emotionally.

Therapist: You did tell her that she was childish to insist the secretary disturb you just because she called.

Mr. Jones: Yes, that's the gist of what I told her.

Therapist: Your wife put you in a real double bind with your secretary. If it is an emergency, that might be quite different from interrupting what may be an important conference.

Mr. Jones: Very true, but I just seemed unable to say it.

Therapist: Because it would be critical of Joan?

Mr. Jones: Well, probably because it would amount to a positive establishment of the kind of barrier that Joan was complaining about.

Therapist: Oh, you mean it wouldn't have clarified it, only made it worse?

Mr. Jones: No, no. That isn't what I meant. I haven't been able to get my ideas across to you.

Mr. Jones was clear and direct. It was a recent event, and it was possible for him to be this direct with me, because our relationship had become warmer, more trusting and respectful. In fact, this clear criticism of my ability to understand him came at a time when he felt very good about our relationship, a feeling he expressed during this session.

Mr. Jones: What I was trying to say is that probably my inability to tell the secretary that she had done the proper thing was because if I did, I'd be setting up a situation which was the opposite of what Joan wanted or what Joan had been complaining about.

Therapist: You found yourself wanting to do something opposite to what Joan wanted you to do.

Mr. Jones: Yes. Now you have it.

Therapist: Why should that be so difficult for you?

Mr. Jones: It's the little boy business again.

Therapist: Really ties you up, doesn't it?

At this point, the session ended and the patient reluctantly set out to leave on his vacation.

THERAPIST'S TECHNIQUE: COUNTERTRANSFERENCE

In the first session following his return, Mr. Jones described reactions of surprise and concern over an incident with his neighbor. I interpreted his behavior in terms of his embarrassment when there was some indication of his being liked. We got into a brief tug-of-war when my insistence produced a flat rejection of my interpretation from him. I persisted in my view, with the support of some previous data that suggested that he had some difficulty handling tenderness.

My persistence was undoubtedly a response to my concern about our relationship following his absence. His ability to disagree in a forthright manner was evidence of his growing self-esteem and assertiveness, which began to be manifested. The obsessional patient has a distinct tendency, because of his stubborn need to be right and to know the right answers, to stir up counterrigidities in the therapist. Therefore, when he is in error, he can be as persistent as when he is correct, and the therapist must be sensitive and comfortable enough to accept some of the patient's rigidities and must not fall into the obsessional trap of trying to have the last word and to be correct all the time.

Mr. Jones: Yesterday my wife arranged to play bridge with a neighbor. I told her to ask her friend to bring her husband along. When he arrived, I blurted out, "Your wife said you were going bowling," in such a way that he probably interpreted it to mean that I was annoyed about him being there.
Therapist: What do you think that was about?

At this point I had no idea at all about his curious reaction at seeing the friend who arrived earlier than he was expected. I would have assumed that he would be pleased. Since he became anxious, I suggested that the uneasiness was a response to his not being ready and that the early arrival stirred up the typical obsessional uneasiness about the unexpected and unplanned — which can be threatening or anxiety-provoking because the individual is momentarily out of control.

However, I assumed that Mr. Jones's reaction was attributable to the repression of his pleasurable feelings. Could this assumption have stemmed from my concern about what seemed to be an unenthusiastic reaction to our renewed sessions which he had repressed? There was no warmth or expression of pleasure at resuming our sessions. Was I looking for some recognition and decided that if it wasn't expressed it was because of his difficulty in expressing tenderness? I could have interpreted his coolness as evidence of some underlying hostility provoked by the vacation. This would have been a conventional expectation, based on the assumption that the patient would feel abandoned or rejected. I do not accept this point of view unless there is clear evidence to support the notion that any absence of the therapist is viewed with hostility and resentment on the part of the patient. We both had vacations, and I was firmly convinced that we were both pleased to be away and to be back. But my subsequent pressure to get him to accept my interpretation that he was covering up his enthusiasm was indirect evidence of my concern, especially after he indicated that he wished to continue our work.

This interview was rich with data of the subtlety of countertransference feelings and the extent to which they can intrude and influence the therapeutic process. While rationalizing his interpretations and using formulations that can be supported by the data, the therapist can overlook his own needs for acceptance and recognition.

Mr. Jones: I don't know.

Therapist: Well, see what comes to mind.

Mr. Jones: I was just wondering whether there will be a change in our working relationship. My thought is that it's helping me, but I see the need for more ... a continuation of it.

Therapist: Helping you, but?

Mr. Jones: I guess the "but" was just a conjunction. I meant that it's helping me but I think I need more of it.

Therapist: Tell me more about the evening you spent with your neighbor. You found yourself for some peculiar reason blurting out something about his bowling. Then what happened, how did it go?

Mr. Jones: I was expecting him, there he was, I was glad to see him, I like him, and yet I became ...

Therapist: That is what is so interesting about this. You were expecting him; he came? You like him, yet you were surprised. Is it possible that what was involved here was a simple feeling of being pleased that he really came? When you blurted out that his wife said he was out bowling you might have been overwhelmed by the possibility that someone likes you enough and actually shows it.

Mr. Jones: Well, that's very interesting, but I don't really think it was a feeling of joy or a pleasant feeling.

Therapist: Well, maybe not. Your expectations are that people don't like you but they do.

Mr. Jones: Well, in that case too, I had an inadequate feeling which was immediately followed by this uneasy feeling. I am having difficulty in going ahead.

No wonder. I had misled him to a point of confusion, and he was unable to understand where I was going. I tried a new approach. Clearly my anxiety was operating here.

Therapist: Yes, we are curious about your reactions when people like you and are friendly. You are more used to being in a situation where you are ready to fight.

I had now raised a matter totally unrelated to the present discussion which indicated most clearly that my disorganization was distracting and confusing him.

Mr. Jones: That's quite complicated, being in a situation where I have to fight.
Therapist: It is complicated; the first thing you blurted out was "Your wife said you were bowling!" almost as if you were astonished that he should come here instead of being at the bowling alley.
Mr. Jones: Well, I think I was surprised that he was there that early. I don't think that I was surprised that he came at all.

I was still insistently trying to get him to agree with my formulation. He again responded with a simple statement with no neurotic defensive distortions. Why was it so difficult for me to see that he was surprised that the man came early instead of surprised that he came at all? Probably, I was on an entirely different tack, determined to pursue my view and stimulated by my own anxieties of not being sufficiently acknowledged. I was closed off to the simple, obvious truth and was instead exploring the unconscious, deeper truths — which I was sure conveyed his real feelings.

Therapist: I was suggesting that you were surprised at the fact that he came. You think of yourself as undesirable.
Mr. Jones: I can see that that's a wrong attitude, that it probably does happen. It's just a little difficult for me to think of my reacting that way with this person because I do think that he does like me.
Therapist: That's probably why you were so shocked. Don't you think that maybe you share this idea as well — that this sudden, curious uneasiness was a feeling of being embarrassed, so that you blurted out? Embarrassment and uneasiness are closer then.

How stilted and garbled was my retort! It demonstrated how the therapist's anxiety can be disruptive when his defensiveness is thwarted. This can lead to more confusion and ultimately to a disintegration of the therapeutic process. Such sessions seem disastrous in retrospect, but they may often mirror events in which the patient sees his therapist as human and infallible. If the therapist becomes aware of this early enough, it can be used as a most effective therapeutic tool for focusing on this issue — emphasizing that even if one is anxious, stubborn, or wrong, it does not mean total disaster.

Mr. Jones: Terror of this thing; it's hard — it's difficult to put an adjective on it. But I have noticed that in many ways I didn't expect people to like me and I was afraid that they would not and I strived desperately that they should.
Therapist: Oh, really?
Mr. Jones: Even knowing that, there are times when I see myself making unusual efforts to be liked, doing things so that I will be well received. When anyone compliments or praises me, it makes me feel very good.
Therapist: Doesn't it embarrass you?
Mr. Jones: Yes, it embarrasses me, and I'm at a loss for words.
Therapist: Maybe even blurting out things? . . . Deep down it's still hard for you to believe that people do like you.

I seem to have finally forced him to some acceptance of my point of view. But the foregoing discussion was entirely valid, since this session was one in which I tried repeatedly to force some recognition of a tendency that *I* insisted was present. It demonstrated that the patient who wants to be liked and accepted will ultimately accept an interpretation to placate the therapist, even though he resists it and it may not be valid. It demonstrates how subtle and insidiously the therapeutic process may force an insight and stimulate behavior that derive from the therapist's needs, rather than from the patient's own requirements.

Mr. Jones: I guess it is. I often think of the times that I was desperately seeking for people to like me. I thought that everyone had to like me. Now I see that it's impossible and unnecessary. It's a slow process to completely eliminate, but I can at least recognize some of the effects of it. I think I profitted with some insight of the incident which happened today.

At this point our session ended.

CHAPTER 14

The Working Through

The process of therapy involves a tedious examination and exposure of the patient's patterns of behavior, which he compulsively maintains and reluctantly alters. The therapist's task is to review and strengthen the patient's awareness of these patterns and to assist him in acknowledging the destructive role they play in his life. Before any moves can be made to change one's behavior, the individual must have a strong conviction about the need to change and a trust in the understanding derived from collaboration with the therapist. This is especially true with the obsessional, who clings rigidly and tenaciously to his behavioral patterns and to his rationalizations for his behavior.

The strength of the obsessional's defenses rests on a strict, rigid, compulsive adherence to them, since the dangers which would unfold if he didn't would be severe and dramatic. The obsessional's stickiness, persistent intellectual defiance, and resistance to seeing his behavior in alternative ways are intense and stubborn. His views and attitudes are firmly embedded and are defended by barricades that must be slowly eroded, piece by piece and inch by inch. This requires patience, tolerance, and the ability to sustain a continuous interest in the patient in spite of the boring, repetitive behavior — which persists in spite of the clarification of its destructive, negative quality. The compulsive behavior continues in spite of the knowledge of its lack of validity and its destructive potential.

Thus, a large part of the therapeutic process is concerned with a review and reexamination of issues that are dealt with over and over again. The therapeutic task lies in the therapist's ability to see the same issues in a new light, adding an additional piece of insight here and reviving an additional recollection there, in order to strengthen and fortify the patient's conviction about the understanding so that it becomes so intrinsic a part of himself that he finally sees it as if he discovered it alone. Familiar neurotic tendencies must be explored from the fresh perspective of different events that include new pieces of data and add additional insights. This also relieves the monotonous refrain of the patient who says, "We went through that already." The therapist must become reconciled to the awareness that a single clarification is rarely followed by a change in behavior. Working through must be seen as a necessary ingredient for change. This process can provide conviction and trust for risking a new and untried approach to living that the patient previously considered dangerous.

The next three sessions with Mr. Jones demonstrated the working-through process. At times the therapist must take the lead and push the awareness to the fore by introducing new questions and new directions for inquiry and suggesting alternative explanations to clarify the patient's reaction. This activity, however, cannot take place until mutually accepted pieces of data have been presented by the patient, so that an hypothesis suggested by the therapist does not come wholly out of his theoretical preconceptions. The therapeutic relationship must have proceeded to a point where the patient has developed enough trust and respect for the therapist that he can disagree and reject some interpretations while accepting others with conviction and commitment.

In the following sessions, I tenaciously pursued a point that needed to be clarified. As one gets nearer to strongly defended fears and anxieties, the resistances are greater and the therapist's pressures must equal or surpass the patient's rigidities. This looks like a tug-of-war and frequently becomes one. However, for the therapist, it must be an issue of clarity and validity — not power; for the patient, it may continue to be overwhelmingly a matter of control and principle. In spite of the therapist's perception and discernment, he will often lose the tug-of-war because of the patient's exceedingly capable tactics of obscuring, distraction, and misleading.

The following account details how the working-through process developed with Mr. Jones in three sessions twelve months after therapy began. The patient opened this hour, his second since returning from his vacation, with a report of an incident in which he felt a good deal of esteem and didn't need to push for recognition.

Mr. Jones: I attended two different meetings yesterday on rather complex subjects in which there was considerable heated discussion, and I felt very pleased with the way I was able to respond to the points that came up. There were many times when I was able to take the initiative without feelings of discomfort or loss of memory.

Therapist: You mean, you didn't feel the pressure to look good?

Mr. Jones: Well, I felt that I did look good, and I wasn't worried about it. I remained silent to protect my boss, who wasn't yet familiar with all the issues.

Therapist: So life is not only a battle between people to get to the top of the ladder.

Mr. Jones: I could see that aspect of it — more of a competition between organizations rather than the need that I had personally to either be at the top of the heap or else at the bottom.

EXTREMES

The issue of extremes is what lies beyond the compulsive need to push, to be on top in spite of the risks and dangers, because the alternative is to be on the bottom. It's either all or nothing, with no capacity to see any middle course because of the threat of total extinction.

Following a short pause, Mr. Jones returned to his obsessive thoughts. It seemed that he couldn't tolerate any awareness of some decency or warm concern for his boss, which surfaced in this brief exchange; he immediately needed to undo any possibility of being viewed as soft or tender. This is frequently the essence of the compulsive symptom or ritual, which attempts to deal with uneasiness about one's tender, human concerns as being dangerous or threatening. These are immediately displaced by obsessive thoughts of being fierce or hostile, giving the individual the illusion of strength and power.

As mentioned earlier, the psychoanalytic theories about the obsessive-compulsive neurosis rest heavily on the issue of unexpressed sex and aggression. This was an outgrowth of Freud's instinct theories, which viewed sex and aggression as pressing for fulfillment and needing to be restrained. The data accumulated about this disorder since Freud's great contributions seem to confirm this formulation. It has been my experience, however, that the obsessional's manifest content and much of the compulsive ritual — while rich in data suggesting hostility and violence — are, in fact, displacements for the underlying, threatening feelings of tenderness, concern, love, and simple humanity. Although Mr. Jones seemed to support the more traditional dynamic explanation of the obsessions, we did have to deal with his tender feelings and disappoint—ments in his mother, wife, and other transferential figures from whom he had strong tender needs — which would have been dangerous to acknowledge.

Mr. Jones: The recurrence or repetition of unpleasant obsessive thoughts, particularly hostility to my wife, still continues.

Therapist: When did they come up and why are you reminded of it just now, in the context of your considerate behavior toward your boss?

Mr. Jones: It comes quite often, and I can't assign definite reasons to what brings it up. If I'm having an argument with my wife, it seems to accentuate or intensify it. It recurs if I'm having any difficulty with other people. I think it usually occurs when I'm having an argument with someone else and when I don't feel well able to hold up my end.

Therapist: Does any particular incident come to mind?

It is essential in pursuing any issue with an obsessional patient to get to the particulars and avoid the generalizations, which become clouded in intellectual verbiage. A specific incident can be dissected in detail, and the therapist can help the patient view each step, noticing his reactions and emotional responses to each event. He will thereby discover what it is that sets the anxiety into motion and requires obsessive mechanisms to cover up and give the illusion of strength. While this is difficult to do under most circumstances, since the anxiety often blots out the recall, the possibility of such recovery does exist and, if it can be produced, may result in profound illumination.

Mr. Jones: Well, an incident where I was not troubled by it for several hours at a time was the long session we had yesterday in which I was able to concentrate and perform very satisfactorily. I wasn't troubled by any memory or recurrence of the obsessive thoughts for several hours. I was having a discussion a few weeks ago with one of the men in my office on a matter which he is quite familiar with and I am unfamiliar. I felt uncomfortable and I found my mind slipping and I was not able to concentrate at all on what he was saying.

Therapist: What were you concentrating on?

Mr. Jones: I can't recall whether I was thinking about something else specifically.

Therapist: Perhaps you were concentrating on the humiliation and feeling of failure and defeat because you didn't know as much about this as you should know.

Mr. Jones: That may be so, but I wasn't recognizing that consciously....

I'd be trying to listen to him and for a time I'd find my attention wandering and unable to concentrate, and then I would recall these obsessive thoughts. Then I would really try and get back into the trend of thought, which was partially successful; then I'd drift off again, remembering obsessive thoughts again, trying to get back on the track again, and so on. That would repeat itself, maybe in a three-minute interval, something like that.

Therapist: Yes, but you make a very important observation when you recognize that, in those situations where you do not know as much as you think you should know or as you are expected to know, you become distracted, begin to obsess, and miss what is going on and fail to learn from your colleagues.

Mr. Jones: Yes, I don't often profit by my contacts.

Therapist: Or from your experiences.

FAILURE TO LEARN FROM EXPERIENCE

It is axiomatic that obsessionals cannot learn from their experiences, since they are unavailable to totally participate in a situation because they are distracted by obsessional thinking or they attempt to surmount a new situation by means of a pseudoknowledge of the event. Not knowing, being uninformed, or being in a situation they have not mastered stirs up great anxiety — which takes the focus of their interest and activity, making them unable to become immersed and involved in the issues going on at the time. One can often find an obsessional patient wandering off as the therapist is talking to him in a face-to-face encounter. The patient may be able to admit it if the relationship is a good one. Sometimes he will even admit that he turned off in a discussion and had not heard anything that transpired in the exchange. It is a great advance when the patient can recognize this as it is happening or is able to admit to the therapist that it had, in fact, happened.

Therapy can stir up much anxiety in the obsessional because he is involved in a process where he is initially in the dark and not in control; searching for an understanding that must come from the help of the therapist. He must acknowledge not knowing the answers and be open to learning more about himself. The therapist must understand the obsessional's difficulties in learning in spite of his cognititive capacities and recognize the therapeutic requirements of repetition of the same insights.

Mr. Jones: That's quite annoying.

Therapist: We need to get clear about your difficulty in concentrating, which you tend to think is a mysterious business where you suddenly find you can't concentrate. Sometimes your difficulty in concentrating has to do with the fact that you're preoccupied with other things, how you look, how much you know, how much you should know, and why others know more than you. You can't learn if you should already know everything and you certainly can't learn from others if you are supposed to know more than they do.

Mr. Jones: Yes, that's true.

An interesting exchange followed my suggestion that we drop the question of status. I recognized that I had introduced a matter for which we were not prepared at this point. However, he would not let me drop it, as if, having caught me in error or without sufficient background, he focused on this to the detriment of the essential issue. This is a distracting technique. The obsessional avoids the essential, crucial issue and gets bogged down in side issues, where he is surer and more in control. Once one gets caught in this situation, it is extremely difficult to get out of, and the efforts to get out of it often produce even more complications. In this instance, I had considerable difficulty, as will be seen, in withdrawing my notion of hierarchies as a reason for Mr. Jones's obsessional avoidance.

Mr. Jones: It has some, but the inability to concentrate on an unfamiliar subject would exist just as much if it were someone superior to me who was talking.

Therapist: Well, I was incorrect to introduce it; let's not get sidetracked. It's not an essential thing.

Mr. Jones: That's right, yeah. I don't think it's too important. In a case of a person below me it would have the effect, but it would disturb me.

Therapist: O.K.

Mr. Jones: It would disturb me because I ought to know as much or more. If it was a person superior to me it would disturb me, however. Well, I just experienced a similar sequence of thought.

OBSESSIONAL DEVELOPMENT
DURING A SESSION

The development of a neurotic thought or obsessional idea in the midst of a therapeutic hour is a laboratory situation full of great potential for learning. It must always take precedence in the session, since it can be the most illuminating of all reconstructive endeavors. As there is no distortion of time possible and no other parties to complicate the investigation, we can frequently trace an event just as it occurred. The transference phenomenon is most clearly highlighted, and the patient's conviction about an interpretation is intense.

Therapist: Let's hear it.

Mr. Jones: I found my attention wandering to some extent, the obsessive thoughts recurring again, and I found myself thinking, "This is important; I want to be sure and remember it," and yet the very fact that I was concentrating on my wish to remember it somewhat interfered with — interfered with my assembling what we were talking about.

Therapist: What do you make of that?

Mr. Jones: Well, it illustrates perfectly your description of a vicious circle. It's sort of like a person being so anxious that he trips over himself.

Therapist: Why do you think it happened at that particular time?

Mr. Jones: ... Well, I don't know whether it describes any particular reason at that particular time because it happens often.

Therapist: Yes, but here we have one in camera, so to speak, right before us. What else were you thinking as I was talking? See if we can get some picture of what else might have been going on.

Mr. Jones: Only those two sets of thoughts that I was conscious of — one, the obsessive thoughts, and two, my need to remember and profit by these observations.

Therapist: Words of wisdom, eh?

Mr. Jones: Well, yeah.

Therapist: Uh-huh. I'm being facetious.

Mr. Jones: Yes, I think you are.

Therapist: I'm being facetious because I think other things go on that you don't quite grab hold of, yet say that you must catch these magical words and make sure not to miss anything. It is a slight exaggeration of what I have to offer.

Mr. Jones: No, I don't think that's it. I find that I do profit by the insight or realization that results from many of these things that we discuss. And this seemed to be relevant and therefore I wish to remember it.

Therapist: I'm not quibbling with that. I think that's very understandable, but we also have to understand how, in the process of trying to understand, you trip over yourself.

Mr. Jones: Yeah, that's interesting and baffling.

Therapist: You say you feel good in getting some information, and I seriously wonder whether it's all good feeling.

When I tried to stir up any mixed feelings he might have had about my "pearls of wisdom," he responded only intellectually, and my sarcasm was lost in the reasonable appraisal of my observations. I tried again, convinced that, in fact, he didn't always receive my correct interpretations with unmixed joy, since I knew how difficult it was for him to acknowledge the truth of his not knowing everything. Such an awareness would threaten his omniscient illusions, so he would either need to deny it or insist that it was something he already knew. If he could do neither he might depreciate its significance. I continued my attempt to explore this issue.

Therapist: You have just told me that you don't feel good when you find yourself in a situation where somebody knows more than you do. I wonder whether you don't have some of that feeling now, here, that never gets expressed — that there is some uneasiness and resentment about finding someone telling you about things which you feel you should have been able to notice yourself? I wonder how often you resent the fact that I do say things that are a profit to you?

Mr. Jones: Oh, you're pointing that out regarding the present situation?

Therapist: Yes.

Mr. Jones: I think it's surprising that it hadn't occurred to me before. Surely that can't be the same as resentment? The subject yesterday [his difficulty in learning from others], for example, was intensely interesting to me, but because I'm so concerned about my status, I found the other matter uninteresting.

Therapist: So that you couldn't listen to that?

Mr. Jones: Well, that's why it's a problem. It's something that I ought to know about and I want to, and yet something trips me up.

Therapist: Well, I'd like for us not to get too far away from the experience that you have right here, when it's fresh in your memory.

Mr. Jones: O.K.

Therapist: Have you any other feelings while I'm talking? It's hard for me to imagine that the only feeling is one of satisfaction with the gems that are going to be offered.

I continued to be facetious, hoping to stir up some of his anticipated annoyance or distress at my statement.

Mr. Jones: ... Well, that's pretty much true, however. I'm able to feel comfortable in talking with you. I haven't any resentment against you as a person.

Therapist: Uh-huh.

Mr. Jones: With our relationship or what you say.

Therapist: Uh-huh. But having no resentment toward me as a person or what I say doesn't preclude the possibility that you would respond to me in pretty much the way you respond to other people, without it being anything personal.

Mr. Jones: I respond to you as I do to other people whom I like ... There are some people that I find difficulty in talking with, in making contact with.

Therapist: Yes.

Mr. Jones: I don't find that with you. With you I do find difficulty in talking about some of the subjects that we talk about.

Therapist: Well, I think this is a good opportunity to point out the tremendous importance of your not only being aware of your feelings but also communicating them in the course of the work. This is especially true of feelings you have during our sessions and the development of these feelings in the course of our interview. To increase our understanding about where these responses come from, it is most important that you be able to present these feelings or attitudes which develop when they occur.

Mr. Jones: Well, I forgot to, that the specific thoughts herein [his feelings that I insist he talk about] generally are on the importance of recognizing thoughts and impressions that come to me while I'm here or while we're talking.

What a beautiful obsessional statement. Note how he uses the word *herein* and the awkward way it is presented — like a legal report rather than a personal statement.

Therapist: I was trying to direct your attention to something you've already noticed: That in the process of attempting to get something that is important and useful to you, something seems to go on that interrupts the process and you get caught in a vicious circle.

Mr. Jones: That's exactly right!

DISTRACTION AS A DEFENSE

Therapist: Thus, in the course of my presenting some observation, the same thing may happen; your machine begins to dysfunction and, instead of moving forward, it stops dead. We are very curious about what goes on at that time. You note that the more you tell yourself that this is important, the more you are unable to listen. Your difficulty in concentrating may have been due to the fact that you get more preoccupied with how you stand in a situation than with what is happening.

Mr. Jones: I think that's it. I feel much more comfortable in a situation where I know more than the persons I'm talking to than if I am the one who knows less.

Therapist: So there's a question of being at a disadvantage in knowing less to start with.

Mr. Jones: Yes, of course. There's the vicious circle again.

Therapist: Yeah. You note that that is one of the factors that occurs if you know less than the other person. You've also noted many times in the past that you feel uneasy, annoyed, or resentful at being told what you feel you should have known. I wonder if you could recognize some of it going on in our relationship — that is, that you feel a resentment or resistance in a situation where I know more than you.

Mr. Jones: Of course if that exists at all, it's unconscious.

Therapist: Yes, perhaps so, and I want to direct your attention to it so that when you have some fleeting thoughts or fringe feelings like this, we can talk about it.

Mr. Jones: All right, I'll try.

Therapist: It wouldn't be unexpected that you might resent being told many things here. We would expect it because one doesn't suddenly change when one comes to this office from when one is at one's own office.

Mr. Jones: No, that's interesting. I hadn't expected or hadn't thought of that condition.

Therapist: Why should you be better able to accept what I have to offer you than what anyone else has to offer you? You're not a different person when you come in here then when you are outside, are you?

Mr. Jones: No. There are ...

Therapist: In the sense that you are on good behavior here, it may be different?

Mr. Jones: No, no. That isn't what I was thinking ... Well, I don't know if it's possible to express, but I'll try.

Therapist: Sure.

Mr. Jones: There are different feelings of contact between different people. You notice it as well as I do, probably much better than I do. With some people I feel at ease and can exchange information; with others there's a barrier.

Therapist: Are you saying that you feel much less of a barrier with me than you do with some other people?

Mr. Jones: Yes.

Therapist: While we take that into account, it's not the whole answer that you feel so comfortable here that you throw away all your defenses.

Mr. Jones: I don't seem to grasp that part of it.

Therapist: We would expect that you try to look good here and to impress me, but that you would also feel uncomfortable if you were caught not knowing something that you should know.

Mr. Jones: It's probably so, and yet I'm trying to tell you about it rather than conceal it.

Therapist: Exactly, that's the point. In other situations it becomes important to conceal it. Here it's very important to do the opposite.

Mr. Jones: Well, I recognized that a long time ago. It occurred to me that it was ridiculous to feel distressed at not making a good impression, since that's the reason that I'm having to go to a doctor in the first place.

Therapist: Yes, and I would suggest that when the feeling arises here we need to talk about it.

Mr. Jones: O.K.

Therapist: Because it will always tell us something about your anxiety, about how you look to another person or what he thinks of you.

Mr. Jones: Oh, yes. Definitely.

Therapist: Anxiety is the problem when you find yourself unable to listen.

Mr. Jones: Yes, I can feel it in my stomach right now and also a light sensation in my head.

Therapist: I wonder if you could think of why you might be feeling it now?

Mr. Jones: Well, I mostly think it's just a hangover from the tension that accumulates during the day.

Even at this juncture and after a lengthy explanation of anxiety and its role in his disorder and the value of understanding it, he still tended to refer its presence to some hangovers accumulated during the day, instead of looking for some present issues that might have produced it.

Therapist: You see, I'm raising a serious question about why you should have so much faith in me.

Mr. Jones: ... Well, I'd like to think it's based on results, that I have felt some beneficial results ...

Therapist: Uh-huh. Do you think that is the main reason? Or does it have to do with your great expectations? I'm also wondering whether such faith might not be related to your great need and hope of some relief.

ACTIVE AND PERSISTENT PRESSURE

I have begun to press hard to get Mr. Jones's attitudes and feelings toward me into the open. Up to this point, our relationship had been friendly, sometimes mildly contentious, but always reasonable and calm. In my presumption that he had some doubts and criticism of me, I tried to encourage this communication. Otherwise it would remain hidden, covertly sabotaging any progress or commitment to change. It was necessary to push for a clear statement of the patient's feelings because of his overpowering need to be a good, acceptable boy.

Mr. Jones: I wasn't thinking of sticking my neck out but when I said "strong expectations," it was in the context of strong expectations for improvement and my pulling out of these difficulties that are bothering me.

Therapist: But your expectations are based on a limited knowledge of whether I can fulfill them?

Mr. Jones: ... Well, you can put it that way.

Therapist: Isn't that sticking your neck out?

Mr. Jones: ... Well, to get back to the terminology that I used, in which you said it was important, why I said "strong expectations of improvement." And although at that time I wasn't thinking of ... well, I better say, say what I was thinking of ... I was thinking of my strong wish.

Therapist: To get well?

Mr. Jones: To get well and I wasn't thinking of you specifically at that moment. I can't milk anything more out of it. I said that I was intensely anxious to get better and to be freed of these thoughts.

Therapist: I'm not trying to milk any more out of that except to say the very strength of the expectations may interfere with the results. I'm trying to draw on the two which we talked about today. This may be one of the things that gets you all tensed up. In fact, in your intense desire to hear well, for example, you invariably hear less.

Mr. Jones: Well, that could be.

Therapist: It's important to see how often you put obstacles in your own way.

Mr. Jones: Caused by zeal?

Therapist: Call it zeal if you like; I would much prefer to call it your great ambitiousness, not in any derogatory sense. By having to know everything, to get all there is to offer, you often miss a lot that you could get.

Mr. Jones: That's exactly it, but the reasons for it I don't know.

At this point we had concluded the three sessions referred to earlier as demonstrating the working-through process.

VALUE OF DETAILED DATA

It is important for the therapist to realize that the patient often eliminates feelings and reactions before they reach awareness. If the therapist assumes that the patient must have the same, or even more extreme, reactions as the therapist has, he may accuse the patient of holding back, resisting, deceiving, or what not. He insists that the patient feels anger or resentment but is holding back. At times the pressure gets strong enough for the patient to get angry at the therapist for what he perceives as the therapist's insensitivity and authoritarian, overbearing presumption. At this point the patient may express some anger but withholds his contemptuous feelings of superiority toward the therapist, thereby creating even greater obstacles later on.

The obsessional patient must first learn to recognize the existence of feelings before he can discover their presence. What he generally experiences is the immediate displacement and conversion of the anxiety into a typical obsessional symptom. As the anxiety is altered before there is any conscious awareness of it, the patient only experiences the defensive alteration, not the underlying emotion that sets it into action. A minute dissection of the events in which defenses are manifested helps the patient recognize the momentary, fleeting fringe thought or feeling that immediately sets the neurotic process into motion, producing the obsessional symptom. When that recognition is achieved, it is then possible to help the patient search for these emotional responses.

The following two sessions began with Mr. Jones describing an incident with one of his colleagues during a conference.

Mr. Jones: This afternoon I had a brush with a colleague who has a rather brusque manner which to me seems discourteous. He seems generally disrespectful and does not acknowledge my status.

Therapist: He doesn't have enough respect?

Mr. Jones: I suppose that this business today is another manifestation of some sensitivity that I have when people don't respect me, even though I don't think of myself as any god that people have to go on bowing down to.

Therapist: You don't?

Mr. Jones: No, but there's these certain situations when I feel ...

Therapist: But it's a reasonable conjecture. We'll agree that you don't feel like a god that people have to bow down to, but doesn't it sometimes seem that way, that you're very careful about measuring someone's behavior toward you in terms of whether it is deferential enough?

Mr. Jones: Well, putting it in those terms, I have a tendency to do that. But isn't it normal for other people to like or dislike certain people whether there's a logical basis for it or not?

Therapist: Sure, but you are trying to justify your feelings, which I don't think you have to do. It's not a question of justifying your feelings as much as trying to understand them. Are you responding as if I had just said you were a bad boy, and you would have to justify it?

I felt my inquiry was conveying some disapproval of his behavior, which was not intended but was experienced this way by the patient. The same sensitivity he had experienced with his colleague was now being played out in our session, and he felt a need to apologize or defend himself. It was essential that the therapist clarify this point, so that his negative, hostile, or unfriendly feelings might be openly expressed without concerns about disapproval. Therefore, I stated directly that I was not being critical but exploratory, and I tried to tie this up to his need to be the good guy all the time.

Mr. Jones: My reaction to him made me look peculiar because I wasn't facing up to my dislike of him. Thus, I get in my own way, but I realized it immediately afterwards.

The issue here was his inability to experience a feeling when it was occurring. Such an awareness must be developed if the patient is ever to see how he immediately transforms feelings that might produce anxiety into displaced obsessional symptoms. I was still carrying out the same thesis I was pursuing in the previous session — that is, his tendency to get involved in a self-destructive vicious circle because he failed to identify his feelings. He was pointing up clearly how, in fact, he didn't become aware of the feeling and therefore could not respond reasonably or directly to a colleague.

Therapist: Well, this says something about your inability to deal with people about whom you have some strong feelings.
Mr. Jones: You're correct in the statement that my not liking him complicates dealing with him.
Therapist: Does this, then, help us understand why you are reluctant to take your dislike of someone into account?
Mr. Jones: Well, I suppose so, but it's difficult for me to even conceive how to do that, since the words are not available to take the dislike of someone into account.
Therapist: What comes to mind about this difficulty in dealing with people whom you might not like?
Mr. Jones: A thought just crossed my mind which I think of every once in

a while. It's so vague that I can't draw much from it — that it was difficult for me to ever tell my mother that I didn't like anyone or to say anything critical. She was critical, but she never allowed me to express any criticism or dislike of anyone.

Therapist: What was her attitude towards that? Did she love everybody?

RECALL IN RESPONSE TO INSIGHT

This discussion had produced an association with a memory out of the past. This often happens during psychotherapy, and it can be most illuminating in supplying data about a person's developmental patterns. The recollections may be vague but must be viewed with serious interest. Here it was clear that Mr. Jones's mother had hypocritically discouraged or disapproved of his disliking or criticizing others while she had been pervasively critical of everyone, especially her son. She posed as a devout Christian, full of brotherly love, but she disapproved of her husband and son for being human, thereby pushing them to make superhuman demands of themselves in order to win her approval.

Mr. Jones: Well, a Pollyanna attitude, and even then I recognized that it was insincere, but I couldn't do much about it. I do remember having a feeling of resentment that whenever there was some disagreement between me and some other child, she always sided against me. I remember feeling unjustly treated, and I compared myself with other kids whose mothers stuck up for them. I felt that — I don't know what I felt.

Note the typical ambivalence and procrastinating before accepting the notion that he was angry at his mother for not supporting him. Also note how he tried to dislodge this recall from the issue to which it was tied — namely, that it was her disapproval that had made it difficult for him to acknowledge all feelings: postive and tender, negative and hostile.

Therapist: But did you ever permit yourself to have any strong feelings about someone or to express them directly?

Mr. Jones: ... I don't know. ... Apparently my feelings towards them had an effect. How to take my feelings of dislike or resentment towards a matter into account when dealing with them presents rather a difficult question to me.

Therapist: Let's hear your thoughts about it.

Mr. Jones: As to how I do that ... I'm puzzled about that myself. Being belligerent isn't the answer because that produces unrealistic results. This was an ordinary question my colleague asked me and should not have produced even a ripple. Yet it did. I'm pretty sure that it was because it's the person whom I resent asking the question which caused this unusual reaction.

Therapist: Uh-huh.

Mr. Jones: I think if it was someone else, that it would have been a purely routine situation, and I would have been able to answer it. I have a feeling that I'm just not getting anywhere in trying to figure this one out.

This was an interesting comment in view of the fact that he had figured it out and that earlier he related his reaction to the question of status and recalled incidents in his childhood where he had been reprimanded for expressing hostile thoughts. In fact, he had a second recall about an earlier occasion when he was unable to express feelings toward someone he disliked. Yet in the face of the obvious connections, he said that he was not getting anywhere when he was, in fact, getting close to the whole truth. Moves toward clarity in the obsessional frequently produce confusion or doubt, since he prefers to keep matters muddled and unclear. Therefore, when some clarity is a potential in the therapeutic process, the patient often tries to distract or cloud the issue by introducing new data, which are presented as exceptions or qualifications about the point being made. Or the obsessional may claim to be tired or bored or unable to follow the therapist's reasoning. This state of affairs demands that the therapist restate the matter simply and clearly and try to get on with the exploration.

Therapist: Just say what comes to mind. You raised the question of how one can take into account one's feelings in dealing with another person. You come up with nothing about how you have done it in the past.

Mr. Jones: Well, I don't remember any such reactions of this sort up until recently or at any rate until I noted that I was having some emotional difficulties. Before that I can't recall any parallel to this. I guess up to that time, if anyone I really didn't like asked me something and it was a person with whom I thought I could get away with a harsh answer, I would give one. If it was not such a person, then I would probably give them a meek answer. Well, there's another aspect from this that had some bearing on my feeling of importance. This individual tended to make me feel unimportant and made me feel that my status or significance is open to question. Perhaps it's that they make me think they don't like me that gives rise to my feelings of dislike for them.

Therapist: An incident of that comes to mind in this regard?

Mr. Jones: I'm trying to think of some right now. I'm unable to reminisce too clearly tonight.

Therapist: Well, how do you think that might work, that sort of thing where other people not liking you might set up some dislike in you for them?

Mr. Jones: ... Well, because it's difficult for me to express my feelings, and perhaps that has been one of the few ways that I could even acknowledge what I thought was some feeling on their part — that is, to have a feeling of dislike for them but not to be able to do much about it.

He has indicated that his inability to acknowledge his feelings toward others often got expressed as feelings of dislike because of his assumption that they didn't like him. But note that he was again trying to avoid the issue by continuing to talk about being muddled.

Mr. Jones: This issue gets more muddled up whenever we talk about it.

Therapist: Is it so muddled up?

Again I tried to make sure that we did not lose the significance of these exchanges. However, we never returned to the issue of his mother, which got put on the shelf to be used at some other appropriate time. This is often the dilemma in dealing with obsessionals: Too many issues get put on the table, and the effect of exploring them all would be to lose the impact of any discovery that might have been made. We must therefore select and pursue one issue, in the attempt to achieve clarity, and neglect the others. Which one is selected depends on a number of factors, including the degree of understanding, the level of anxiety and defensiveness surrounding certain issues, and the patient's ability to deal with some issues better than others. I therefore continued to pursue the incident with Mr. Jones's colleague.

Therapist: You're telling me first about the situation in which you make a very inadequate reply to a simple, direct question. It isn't a simple, direct response and you wonder why. You recognize that for some reason you have difficulty in communicating directly with people you don't like. We were also suggesting that perhaps your feeling toward this man comes out in the way you deal with him because you somehow don't take into account your feelings toward him. That's the point we were trying to get at. It's possible to dislike people and still have contact with them. You find that you have never settled on how one does that, as if it's a completely new phenomenon. Perhaps you are not recognizing some of your resentments to people because if you were to recognize your resentments, you couldn't deal with them. Therefore, it's quite possible that, more often than you know, you don't let yourself take account of your antagonistic feelings.

Mr. Jones: Well, that's certainly interesting. What difference should it make to me what someone does or thinks of me?

Therapist: Oh, it makes a lot of difference what people think of you. No one wants to be disliked. Certainly it makes a difference, but you don't get it down to that. You skip that and say, "He's not treating me respectfully," which is different.

Mr. Jones: A normal person doesn't like to be disliked. But do you think that should cause them so much pain?

Therapist: You're evading the question. When you say that it shouldn't make any difference to me whether I'm liked or disliked, I try to point out that it makes a lot of difference to people whether they're liked or disliked.

The expressed notion that one should not be concerned about whether one is liked or not expresses the typical tendency of one extreme or the other. Because of the obsessional's overwhelming need to be accepted or approved of, his conception of change is to go to the opposite extreme and be totally unconcerned about it. The therapist must help the patient recognize the in between — where being liked is human and understandable while not being compulsively caught in the necessity to be liked by everyone. The middle of the spectrum is lacking in every aspect of the obsessional's living, and he generally deprecates such issues as mediocrity, normality, average, or similar deprecating labels. It is imperative to deal with each such issue as it arises, in order to slowly integrate the notion that reasonable moderation is not mediocrity or dull normality.

Mr. Jones: I felt perhaps it made too much difference to me whether people like me or not.

Therapist: It certainly does, and yet you said just a few minutes ago, "Why should it make any difference to me whether people like me or not?" It must make a difference since you're only human.

Mr. Jones: Yes, of course, but I was doing that to illustrate that I thought that it probably did make more difference than it ought to.

Therapist: If you say you are too dependent on the business of being liked and that becomes a major consideration, then it is clear. You're always thinking in those terms.

Mr. Jones: One ought to be concerned about it.

Here again appeared the ought, should, must, etc., even when seconds before had we noted its inappropriateness.

Therapist: I am concerned more than one is supposed to be. It's always the business of what is proper, or what is correct, or what does everyone else get.

Mr. Jones: It may be normal for a person who does not experience undue stress in such cases.

Therapist: No, I think you said it right when you said that you are too much concerned with that issue, as opposed to many other issues that can come between people. Often you stress whether a person likes you or not, and you're not even giving any consideration to whether you like them. That's not even taken into acount.

Mr. Jones: That's true! That's true. That doesn't — that hasn't seemed to alter the situation or even be considered by me!

Therapist: Yes. And in that sense you are indiscriminate in wanting to be liked.

Mr. Jones: Everybody must like me, and if there is someone who doesn't, I am uncomfortable about it.

Therapist: Yes, whether it's a kind of person you want to like or not doesn't matter.

These five sessions dealt with the problem of the need to be liked, approved of, and viewed as the "good boy." Mr. Jones acknowledged his inability to express negative feelings, which also impeded his expression of positive feelings. The hypocritical attitudes of his mother served as the model for appearing friendly when, covertly, there might be resentments and antagonisms. Ths is the dynamic in obsessive-compulsive states where unexpressed feelings, both positive and negative, need to be avoided and unacknowledged through a variety of defensive devices — often through obsessive thoughts that divert the individual.

Mr. Jones in these sessions was prevented from moving away from the central issue and thereby from obfuscating and distracting from a clear understanding of his behavior, its sources, and its outcome. Thus he can confront the issues and begin to change his behavior. This working through of an insight many times over, using new data as it unfolds in his present living, is the essence of the working-through process that leads to firm insights and ultimate characterological change.

THERAPY AS REITERATION

The process of working through — or the massive reiteration and repetition that characterizes the psychotherapeutic process — can again be observed in the following session. There was another review of Mr. Jones's defenses and the way he used them to confuse and be confused as his needs for perfection and his resistance to being criticized again appeared. He was able to confront some of these attitudes and to recognize that he need not always live up to the demands of others or be perfect and beyond human fallibility. He was then able to view the way he lived in the extremes of right and wrong, and good and bad. He was expanding his insight with increasing conviction, which was manifested in later interviews.

The session opened with a frank admission of his reluctance to come to the session — something he could not have done or felt before, since that would have meant he was an imperfect and resistant child.

Mr. Jones: I didn't feel much like coming tonight. I've been sort of tired and upset all day long. I almost considered the idea of calling and telling you that I didn't feel like coming, but I decided to come anyway.

Therapist: Uh-huh. Let's hear what you were thinking and feeling about this.

Mr. Jones: I decided to come when I became aware of being nervous this morning after an argument with a colleague. I discussed a point with him, and his attitude was that it was inconsequential and that it really didn't matter whether it was right or wrong. I realized that this might have been one of the cases in which I put too much emphasis on unimportant points.

Mr. Jones's nit-picking, overly precise, and perfectionistic attitude, which serves both as a rationalization for responsible behavior and a claim for special distinction, is expressed in this statement. Yet it was rarely recognized as an issue that was alienating and put distance between himself and others. He did recognize that he might be putting too much emphasis on unimportant points. This insight was incomplete and was not necessarily reflected in behavior change, for he continued to get hung up in these petty concerns.

Mr. Jones: However, I was unable to express my annoyance. He inferred that I was spending too much time on minor points. I didn't acknowledge my own protest against his talking that way. The next contact was a few minutes later, on another matter, and I acted rather cool toward him and had an idea that he did cool off a bit. He perhaps regretted that outburst because he made a mild response on another point — sort of a conciliatory attitude. I just accepted that as if nothing had ever happened, and I made no show of treating it as an apology. All of that left me with a rather nervous and upset condition.

PARANOID DEVELOPMENT

Mr. Jones's exposition of his ruminations following an instance of anxiety is most revealing of how paranoid ideation develops and alienation follows when the incident is viewed and documented entirely on the subjective responses of the individual concerned. The motivation was as follows: Mr. Jones was caught in an "unworthy" act (his view), which he considered worthy until others rejected it. He failed to respond appropriately with anger or admission but instead responded with passive acquiescence. He then viewed the other person as critical and rejecting, and he reacted cooly toward him. The other person probably thought nothing more about the incident and came to no conclusions with regard to Mr. Jones. He approached Mr. Jones hours later in a friendly way, which Mr. Jones interpreted as conciliatory on the assumption that the other person felt guilty and regretful about his response. Mr. Jones accepted it this way and got on with the relationship. However, had Mr. Jones been more sensitive and less introspective and insightful, he might have been very angry at the other person, avoiding him or insulting him and being met with a counterassault that would confirm his feelings. A true rejection by the other person would then have been precipitated as a result of Mr. Jones's expectant and entirely subjective response. It was Mr. Jones's hypersensitivity to being imperfect, fallible, and human that initiated this event. Subsequent events with Mr. Jones's colleague bore out this interpretation.

Mr. Jones: This morning my two colleagues and I were discussing another matter. One of them wanted to let things drift along, and I had a rather frustrated feeling. It occurred to me that I probably had a greater feeling of frustration than I realized. And that made me realize that my picayune attitude, plus his belligerent reception of it, may have been due to this mutual frustration that we both experienced at the hands of a superior. The conciliatory attitude tended to confirm that he was blowing off steam, rather than being too genuinely upset about what I was doing.

Mr. Jones was now able to recognize some earlier aspects of his referential tendencies. He then assumed that his colleague, instead of being annoyed at him, felt frustrated, and he concluded that the other person's conciliatory attitude was because he had been in the wrong. Mr. Jones had moved beyond the feelings of certain rejection and hostility to a recognition of his own hostility. This was the beginning of the clarification of a paranoid referential tendency and the awareness that the need to put oneself in the center of other people's reactions may reflect anxiety within oneself. It is the ability to unravel such a distortion that can illuminate the development of a paranoid idea.

The therapist must help the patient develop more awareness and insight into his referential tendencies. This can only be done by a careful, detailed review of an event, focusing on the patient's feelings, how he viewed the other person's feelings, what he thought the other person felt, and how he attributed attitudes to the other person that grew out of his own expectations rather than from the manifest behavior of the other person. The unravelling of even one development of this kind may be the beginning of the resolution of more severe paranoid ideas in all types of personality disorders. It demonstrates to the patient with utmost clarity how such ideas originate entirely within oneself, based on unrecognized and unacknowledged feelings.

Therapist: Perhaps he's right in his observations that you do have a tendency to be petty.

Mr. Jones: I think that's so. I try to consider it. If I take issue with what appears to be a petty matter, I usually don't require that the work be done over, but rather I try to make it a point to remember in the future so as not to repeat the error.

Therapist: So that you're not all bad, just half-bad, and you're not that petty.

I was trying to indicate that he was, in fact, being petty then and with me now and that he was trying to modify and minimize this tendency by saying that he was not so petty as to demand that the work be done over. He was unable to accept his behavior because he himself was critical and dissatisfied with it, and so he tried to get out of the dilemma by being the "nice guy."

Therapist: Our interest is in trying to understand the tendency to get caught in this kind of petty detail, which doesn't utilize your best skills. It is sort of bookkeeper stuff rather than ...

Mr. Jones: It's just that kind of feeling that it gives me too.

SELECTIVE INATTENTION

The preceding exchange is a striking example of the obsessional's tendency to distort and accuse the other of the very tendency he manifests himself, and at the same time he seeks credit for his tolerance and decency.

It is astonishing that he fails to see this and selectively inattends to the fact that only fifteen minutes earlier he indicated his displeasure and intolerance at being corrected. I did not take up this lead with Mr. Jones, in order to avoid being sidetracked. I was in pursuit of one insight and did not want to weaken or deflate this search by going off in another direction, even though it was a significant one.

Mr. Jones: I perceive something that's incorrect, and yet I have the frustrated feeling if I try to get this corrected, I'll be considered a fussbudget and people will resent it and an argument will ensue.

Therapist: So one of the difficulties you have is in knowing where you've gone to the extreme and when it's justified, when it's a fussbudget attitude and when it's a serious concern for the job, eh?

Now I felt we were getting close to a significant issue in discovering that his perfectionistic tendencies were designed to avoid anxiety by being beyond criticism instead of trying to do a better job. The fact that this tendency could be annoying to others was not as essential an issue at this point as getting Mr. Jones to clearly observe his perfectionistic drives.

Mr. Jones: Yes, that's about right. My own attitude when anyone brings my attention to some error in work that I've done is to regret that I made an error, and I'm anxious to correct it as soon as possible or even to apologize for the error having occurred. But I observe that other people don't react in that way. When I bring errors to their attention they're mad that I'm showing it to them. I find it rather hard to understand.

Therapist: Do you think you have some tendency to be fussy in the area of preciseness and certainty?

Mr. Jones: From the way others react to it, yes, apparently it is too fussy. It's merely that I am more precise than others. I am forced to conclude that it's offensive to be that way.

Therapist: To be which way?

Mr. Jones: Well, if being precise and meticulous is being too fussy, I'd have to acknowledge that I am.

Therapist: I don't think that helps our understanding, when you say that if being precise and meticulous is being excessively fussy then you must acknowledge it. There's surely a difference between being precise and meticulous and being so preoccupied with preciseness that other things are overlooked or it becomes the main issue and overwhelming concern. Perhaps it's not your preciseness, but the emphasis you put on being meticulous and perfect?

I was trying with some difficulty to help him see that the intensity of his compulsive needs, which derived from anxiety, stirred up resentment in others. This is a most difficult insight for an obsessional and must be approached from many directions in a simple, clear, and emphatic way before it can be accepted.

Mr. Jones: Yes, that's true and it leads to these, uh, undesirable arguments and feelings.

Therapist: Are you agreeing with me?

Mr. Jones: Well, it seems to make a virtue of a sin, in that it stirs up hard feelings which do more harm than the fact that the error is corrected or not.

Therapist: Yes. Now let's get back to what you said in the beginning of the hour.

I wanted to review where we have been because I felt that our discussion had become too diffuse and undirected. I wanted to pull it together to make a clear, unambiguous statement about this behavioral tendency.

Therapist: You felt sufficiently upset and you wondered about whether you would come to this session. What was this upset feeling about?

Mr. Jones: Well, the manifestations of it were that I felt nervous in my stomach and in my head. This disturbing incident occurred just before lunchtime, and I had lunch with my boss but I just didn't feel like talking.

Therapist: What do you think was upsetting?

Mr. Jones: Well, I've outlined the incident, but you're asking for an analysis about it.

Therapist: Yes, I'm asking you to give some thought to what in that incident might have upset you.

Mr. Jones: I think it was the feeling that he was making this veiled attack on me. I was unable to reply with some force to it.

Therapist: By making a veiled attack, you mean he had found you to be imperfect?

Mr. Jones: Well, yes, that is a good way of saying that I thought he found me to be imperfect. And his inference was that I was being too picky about it.

Therapist: So you responded with anxiety because you were found to be somewhat imperfect and feeling that you've been criticized.

Mr. Jones: Well, a feeling that I've been criticized by an individual somewhat below me — in the hierarchy.

Therapist: Yes.

Mr. Jones: So it was like a mild case of insubordination, and I was unable to react to that.

Therapist: So that is insubordination! That's a new one; when someone disagrees with you and he's a rank lower than you, that's insubordination?

Mr. Jones: No, no!

Therapist: That's an interesting way of putting it, isn't it?

Mr. Jones: No, you're misinterpreting it. I'm not basing it on the fact that he disagreed, but because he said I had no business wasting his time on this matter.

Therapist: Yeah, you mean he disagreed in an improper way.

Mr. Jones: Well, you're at least showing me that there's more than one way to look at this situation.

Therapist: I think we ought to go back to what you said at the beginning of the hour when we were discussing a particular tendency of yours — namely, why your precise and meticulous attitude should produce difficulties. I am curious why you get so upset because someone didn't find you meticulously correct.

Mr. Jones: You're right, you're right! Because he didn't accept the corrections that I wanted to make indicates that he thought I was being incorrect in raising the issue!

Therapist: Uh-huh.

Mr. Jones: You're correct. I hadn't looked at it that way, but I can see it now. So it changes the situation from one in which I'm doing the correcting to one in which I'm being criticized.

Therapist: Yeah, and in addition you are angry at someone who doesn't make as much of a virtue of perfection as you do.

Mr. Jones: Uh-huh.

Therapist: I wasn't there, but the sense of the situation as I get it is that you don't have to get too fussed about everything. Some things don't make enough difference, and perhaps he wasn't criticizing you at all. Maybe he was trying to get some balance. What is more important at the moment, is it meticulousness, or getting a job done? You think meticulousness, he thinks it's the job.

Mr. Jones: Well, that's right, and since he thought I was being too meticulous it made him irritated.

Therapist: Or it made him disagree with your values at the moment.

Mr. Jones: Well, yes, that's right. He did disagree. I thought he seemed especially irritated due to this issue.

Therapist: Do you mean that people shouldn't get irritated at you?

Mr. Jones: I used to think so. And there's this lingering hangover that it's still difficult for me to accept it. I used to think that if others didn't like my way of operating, that I had to change — I had to apologize. Yet in matters of precision and meticulousness it has been difficult for me to change. I'm doing much better at it than I used to. I used to be much more precise and meticulous than I am now, and I used to require every error, no matter how small, to be corrected.

Therapist: This raises a significant question. There's nothing wrong with being meticulous. You're still very confused about this notion of whether it is a virtue or a sin, but *that* isn't the point. It's not that you have to change from being meticulous, as much as recognizing that being meticulous may have some benefits as well as deficits.

I wanted to be sure that we didn't move from one extreme to the other, or from one obsession or compulsion to its opposite, like moving from absolute cleanliness to total sloppiness — both compulsive qualities. It is therefore essential that it not become a matter of right or wrong, good or bad, but that we note the issue as one of extremes, compulsions, and need for certainty that is the expected return from the compulsions. Therefore we needed to reiterate this issue again and again.

Therapist: It's a flexible situation and has its disadvantages. If you're making a gun you better be meticulous about the bore and the bullets that go in it; on the other hand, if you're weeding a garden and leave a few weeds, it won't destroy the whole garden.

Mr. Jones: I can profit from that. I'll have to use more care in when it's necessary to be meticulous and when it doesn't matter.

AVOIDING THE COUNTERCOMPULSION

The notion that our exchange was directed at telling him what's right and what's wrong and how to learn new and better compulsions was just what I wanted to avoid — that is, a compulsion not to be meticulous. In some disorders, like alcoholism and drug addiction, a compulsion *not* to drink or take drugs may be a major alteration with beneficial results. However, the countercompulsion, like counterphobic behavior in general, has its own deficits and destructive potential. It may seem effective to the patient for the moment, but in the long run it will be counterproductive. This must be clarified in the therapy of every obsessional, whose goal is generally to discover newer and better compulsions than the ones that failed and brought him into therapy.

Therapist: I want to be clear that this isn't what I'm trying to say. I'm not giving you a lecture on how or when to be meticulous. I'm simply raising the question which has to do with your responses to those situations where you react to an observation with the feeling that you're being criticized or even being rejected and that people won't like you or accept you because you're not altogether perfect. You react as if a criticism is a total denunciation. You assume that if there is some disagreement then there's an overwhelming rejection of you. The issue of your meticulousness is also looked at in the extremes. There's either meticulousness or complete sloppiness. It is very difficult for you to see that the other fellow has his weaknesses and assets and can still be a functioning human being. He can disagree with you without criticizing you or throwing you overboard. You were making these demands on yourself. Not only were you saying the job had to be meticulous, but you were also saying, "I must be entirely beyond reproach."

Mr. Jones: Uh-huh. I was telling myself that I must be wrong for having made an issue of this, since the reaction to it is different from what I would hope for. Well, we go round and round on this, and I'm still confused about it.

We can now understand the role of confusion in the obsessional's psychology. He does not understand the issue clearly because he keeps mixing up the issues, instead of separating them for clarity and preciseness. Confusion is an ally in not facing an issue directly, as is every other defense of the obsessional. Confusion is designed to avoid directness and clarity.

Therapist: I wonder if we can clarify what your confusion is about?

Mr. Jones: Well, it might be that the question is what the dividing line is between meticulosity and valid areas for correction.

Therapist: Do you recognize something familiar about your question?

Mr. Jones: Well, yes. How can I find a way so that I can point out somebody's error and yet still have them like me?

Therapist: Or, how can I find a way of doing the right thing? Some magic way of knowing what is excessive and what isn't so I can do the right thing. I say it a little differently to focus it differently, but it's the same story all over again. You want to learn how to do the right thing, but it's confusing because the issue has nothing to do with right or wrong.

Mr. Jones: Ummm.

Therapist: The issue has to do with a capacity to recognize that there are various points of view. If the one you present is not accepted, it doesn't mean that you've disgraced yourself.

Mr. Jones: And yet it usually has that effect on me. If there's less than complete agreement with what I'm saying, I think that I'm looked down upon or disliked.

Therapist: That's what we need to understand, isn't it?

Mr. Jones: I guess we do.

Therapist: And your insistent tendency to look for an ultimate or ideal solution. You automatically and unconsciously get attracted to the idea that "I must find the right and perfect way."

Mr. Jones: That's right. I almost regularly become involved in this maze. It's even difficult to talk about it. It's hard for me to identify what the different reactions are of myself and others.

Therapist: Quite the contrary. You don't have difficulty identifying reactions: You are highly skilled at that. The difficulty is in being sidetracked by this question of always being right and perfect, so that it's hard to see what else is going on. In the past you talked about being confused and that confusion was one of the problems that brought you to therapy. This is a good opportunity for us to examine what this confusion is about.

RELATING SYMPTOM TO INSIGHT

Whenever the therapist can relate the insight to the problem the patient brought in initially, it should be done. This increases the value of the interpretation and emphasizes the value of the therapeutic process. It is a major factor in increasing the patient's conviction and remaining doubts about the therapeutic process. Doubting is a key issue in the dynamics of the obsessional, and it must be dealt with before change can occur. It cannot be approached directly and can only be reduced by a continuing display of adequacy on the part of the therapist and a growing self-esteem on the part of the patient. The conviction develops from the therapist's skill in illuminating an issue or identifying a feeling that the patient can recognize and accept, after having kept it hidden and repressed. This is not only a demonstration of the value of the therapy but also a striking illustration of the patient's defensive system. Repeated examples of this as they occur during therapy are the most effective means of overcoming the doubts that help sustain the obsessional avoidance and substitutive capacities.

Therapist: You are confused in the situation today because you cannot understand why somebody should get irritated at your being meticulous and careful and wanting to do a good job. But you're also confused because trying to do a good job isn't what produces the arguments or disagreements.

Mr. Jones: Well, what then?

Therapist: We're trying to get clear about your extreme reactions. If someone disagrees with a minor point, then you feel that they have said that you are utterly incompetent.

Mr. Jones: Well, I agree with that.

Therapist: Yeah, but you see it differently deep down. He not only disagreed, but he really slapped you hard in the face. You tense up; your stomach gets tight; you find yourself having difficulty in dealing with the fellow.

Mr. Jones: I felt rejected and I felt that my importance or status was being seriously undermined.

Therapist: Rather an extreme reaction, isn't it? The confusion in these situations is often a question of your seeing only a very small part of it.

Mr. Jones: Attributing far more to some person's statement than they mean it to have.

Last week you asked me if I could think of any instances in which I tried very hard to secure my parents' approval and I wasn't able to think of examples of it. But a couple of days ago, I did remember something that might be a clue toward it — that was one summer when my confusion was about at its worst. I had a frantic feeling that I had to get my wife's approval as to everything that I did or said, and I would look intriguingly at her for some outward expression of approval as if I were a small boy. Since I've realized other ways in which I was placing her in the status of one of my parents at that time, it occurs to me that this may be an example of something that I may have done or may have felt toward my parents.

What appears to have been a change of subject was actually an association to the idea of wanting to be liked and approved of, as well as being the good boy. It is a good example of how the therapeutic process initiates recall and serves to reinforce insights about present behavior.

Therapist: It would not be farfetched to assume that you may have had this same response as a youngster, when to do anything wrong meant total rejection?

Mr. Jones: I suppose it did because whenever my parents, or at least my mother, were displeased with me, it was intolerable and I was devastated. So I would beg her for her forgiveness and write notes telling her that I was going to do better and I wouldn't be bad anymore. I can remember such an incident when I wrote her a note and apologized.

Therapist: Wasn't this an instance where you were pleading for your parents' acceptance?

Mr. Jones: This is a good example of it. I thought I had told you this incident. I brought that up as an illustration that I couldn't tolerate their disapproval. I was putting my wife in that category and pleading for her recognition and approval at the very time she was so upset about other things. She would usually react in a negative manner, and that was difficult for me to bear.

Therapist: Made you push all the harder, eh?

Mr. Jones: That's it, exactly!

Therapist: Now that's what you had reference to at our last hour when you were talking about the unsuccessful attempts to win favor from those people with whom you felt your position was in doubt. You would get apologetic and you would have to find out what they wanted so you could do the right thing. And you usually succeeded in achieving the opposite.

Mr. Jones: Yes.

Therapist: Now I think we can see something about this from the incident today. This incident doesn't call for the recognition that you were wrong and therefore had to apologize and start on a campaign to win his favor. It wasn't a question of right or wrong. You feel that you must either be apologetic or you tell the other guy off.

Mr. Jones: And that was the way I saw it.

Therapist: Always dealing in extremes.

Mr. Jones: All during our discussion, I was confused and the confusion kept getting worse. I think it is somewhat clearer now . . . and I was able to get some more . . .

Therapist: Well, I hope you don't feel that it is totally clear because if you did, then I would know that you are still engaged in the same extremes.

So ended the session on a note of clear insightful recognition that extreme reactions are the problem and that the goal in productive and nonstressful living is a balanced effort to do what one can in the best possible way rather than to be perfect or totally ineffective.

MAGIC AND COINCIDENCE

I tried to emphasize to Mr. Jones in this context of mutual acceptance and good will that the tendency to jump to either extreme has too many pitfalls. I didn't want to disparage his insight, only to avoid its being dealt with in the usual obsessional way of making it a magical formula. The notion of magic is so pervasive with the obsessional defense that it surfaces all the time.

The following session dealt with Mr. Jones's ability to express himself more openly, noting that it could have positive consequences. He became aware that a lessening of anxiety about feeling accepted and worthy enabled him to express his opinions without fear of criticism or rejection.

Mr. Jones: I felt that everything had to be perfect because anything in which I have a connection would reflect unfavorably on me.

This was a striking instance of the demand for perfection and the requirements of extreme or absolute certainty before he could feel assured by his status and acceptability. Mr. Jones tended to explain his success in terms of good luck, accident, or coincidence, or his perfection and omniscience. It was crucial that he recognize that he got support and acknowledgment because he was acting in the general interest, based on a reasonable amount of competence. The magic of the extreme did not account for his success (a superman performing miracles) but the mundane benefits of a reasonable performance. This required a clarification of the events involved in his feeling of achievement.

Mr. Jones: I thought that if any instances occurred in which my boss would criticize, then I would be in danger of losing my status.

The pervasive pattern of encouraging and determining one's perceptions of others based on one's expectations is a well-understood concept called the *wish-fulfilling prophecy*. Seeing it work beyond a mere concept has convincing value when it is traced step by step in the patient's recent adventures. Patients are often astonished to note that their behavior and feelings have created responses in others and that they are not always the passive recipient of the malevolence of others toward them because they view themselves as being weak or unworthy of a more respectful relationship. When Mr. Jones felt that he was unworthy or inadequate, he perceived the behavior of his boss as potentially rejecting and critical.

Therapist: Maybe your feeling that people won't support you or that your boss won't support you has something to do with some doubts about whether you're worthy of their support.
Mr. Jones: That's probably so.
Therapist: I was raising the question at the moment about the kind of expectations you have from people and how, at times, they must have been

confirmed. It's quite conceivable, isn't it, that you felt you wouldn't be supported on many occasions because there was no reason why you should be?

Mr. Jones: You mean my demands were based on petulance alone?

Therapist: Yes. You have had many experiences in the past where you haven't been backed up, and we were wondering whether these experiences have arisen out of your concern about status rather than the job itself. That's where the petulance comes in — when the insistence is, "Look! I'm a big shot!" and not "Look, there's a job to be done about which I have some interest and concern." Isn't that really what we're talking about? It's been your insistence that you be seen as the big shot, as if the important element was that everyone should recognize that you're their boss.

Mr. Jones: No, it's deeper than that.

Again notice the unwitting and automatic distracting tendencies in Mr. Jones. In spite of the prior agreements about why his boss supported him, he still had to explain it in terms of his correctness and perfectionistic tendencies, underwriting his position that acceptability is based on strength alone. Although this factor must be acknowledged or else the patient can get stuck in an endless debate of how important strength is in all human affairs, the therapist must skillfully get beyond that matter to explore the neurotic doubts and uncertainties that produce excessive demands for superhuman powers. In this exchange Mr. Jones had sufficient self-esteem and assertiveness, which was growing stronger all the time, to disagree with me — real progress!

Therapist: Uh-huh.

Mr. Jones: I think that would be sort of an intermediate step. But it was distasteful to me to be bypassed because I was afraid the boss would think I wasn't strong enough to be able to defeat such an invasion. I can remember as a child, whenever there was an argument between myself and some other child, my mother would apologize to the other child's mother. She would indicate that I was wrong. Now that seems to me to be a probable antecedent of feelings that I wouldn't be supported.

Therapist: Uh-huh.

Mr. Jones: I don't think that the major issue is one of insistence on my status. It's the fact that the status exists that makes it more irritating when it is violated. I get so tangled up in questions of status that I don't see other issues. When status is involved, there are other fears that arise in my mind. I would be afraid that he would see me as being a dispensable person — just in the way — and therefore if I brought up this point that I had been bypassed, he might say, "Well, we got along without you; I guess we don't need you." It was half-conscious feelings like these that would get me all steamed up. The outward appearance of it was that I was concerned over status. I remember instances in which my mother did not support me in cases somewhat analogous to this.

Therapist: Why, were you *always* wrong?

Mr. Jones: No, I felt uncomfortable that she acted as if I were wrong.

Therapist: Yeah, you were uncomfortable that she always acted as if you were wrong.

Mr. Jones: No, no. I didn't decide that I was wrong, but I never got any satisfactory solution of the problem.

LATE RESISTANCES

Mr. Jones was still forcefully defending his position and not simply accepting my formulations. I encouraged him to pursue this issue more intensively by silence or grunts, which often serve as strong impetus to further introspection. As long as it continues, the therapist should not intervene; only if it is clearly becoming irrelevant or sharply altering the focus should the therapist pull the inquiry back into some productive direction.

Therapist: Uh-huh.

Mr. Jones: I spoke to her about it one day, and the answer was that it was the polite thing to do. That didn't satisfy me, but that still ended it.

Therapist: Main thing is to be polite ...

Mr. Jones: Well, no, no. I was even less satisfied with it than that. I thought that I was still being unjustly or unfairly treated. I guess it looked as if their attitude was that it was more important to be polite than what I thought.

Therapist: Hmm. Yeah.

Mr. Jones: So if they could give that answer to me, why I unconsciously inferred from that, that I was wrong to even bring it up. As I see it now, even if a person's petulance is based on violation of status alone, he still has a justifiable gripe if it's a bad enough case.

This was a strong show of feelings, and it deserved support and recognition.

Therapist: Are you saying that regardless of what provoked your grievances, whether it was petulance or an insistence upon your rights, you had a right to express them?

Mr. Jones: Yes.

Therapist: And one of the situations that you seemed to have faced so much in your childhood was that expressing any grievance was wrong?

Mr. Jones: Yes, definitely.

Therapist: You were always wrong to do so?

Mr. Jones: I was always wrong if things didn't go very smoothly. In the past, even though I would be in situations where my superiors were highly pleased with me, I always regarded that as very transitory, so that if the least thing happened they'd become dissatisfied with me. So it was a continual struggle to impress them with my efficiency and a continual struggle to prevent anything from coming up which I thought would reflect unfavorably on me. If I had a complaint about somebody, I couldn't bring that up because I thought I would be regarded as incompetent for having allowed anything to happen to disturb this perfect situation.

Mr. Jones was describing the fragile security the obsessional has and how he feels constantly threatened. Even though Mr. Jones had just received some acknowledgment that should enhance his secure position, it might be shattered a minute later. The obsessional has no ongoing feelings of acceptance, and every event is a new trial of success or failure, acceptance or condemnation. He therefore has great difficulty in learning from experience and recognizing any carry over of his acceptability. His repeated complaint is, "Well, it's all right now, but how can I be sure it will be all right the next time?" He wants a guarantee that can be achieved only through perfection and omniscient and omnipotent capacities. This element is a serious obstacle to change in the obsessional, since he has no carry-over of success or achievement and does not benefit from the esteem achieved by the last success. He is reluctant to test out new discoveries or anticipate rewards, which would come from his increasing capacities. The beginning of a slow growth of self-worth, with increasing convictions about his real strength and value, enables the obsessional to move onward against great obstacles and doubts about himself. The therapist must be sensitively aware of this handicap throughout the treatment process.

Therapist: Hmm. The goal was for complete harmony between everyone, everything moving smoothly.

Mr. Jones: Well, that was one of the goals, yeah, — complete harmony between everyone, everything working smoothly. And if it was something for which I was responsible, I mustn't allow anything to happen that would indicate there was any imperfection. And I thought if there was any reason for anybody to have any comment or notice anything other than perfection that I would be severely criticized.

Therapist: As you have noted time and again, expressing your feelings, doubts, criticisms and enthusiasms does in fact improve your situation rather than harming it. It is difficult, because of your past experiences, both while you were growing into adulthood and in your recent living, to observe this. Your expectation was always that you would be disapproved of. When you are open and secure enough to observe the effect of your behavior, you see that the results tend to be constructive.

Mr. Jones seemed to have interpreted friction, disagreements, feelings, and the like as dangerous and disruptive and to be avoided at all cost. I wanted to strengthen his awareness, in order to highlight his own fears of confrontation in the adult world — where the consequences of abandonment do not necessarily follow. This ended the session.

Mr. Jones: Well, I think I'm finding out that a person disagreeing with me doesn't mean that I have to interpret it as an attack on me.

Therapist: Can you elaborate?

Mr. Jones: I took a paper that I had prepared for my boss to a colleague. He didn't like it. I thought he became belligerent, and I answered that he had failed to notice that he was criticizing me prematurely. I felt myself getting upset at this time, but then I realized that I didn't necessarily have to get upset. I sensed that this was the kind of situation that I formerly would get real upset about and sometimes couldn't even figure out why I was so upset.

CHAPTER 15

Termination

Five days later Mr. Jones returned for his next session, enthused by a number of discoveries. Some of these discoveries had been integrated into his living and manifested in some encounters with his colleagues, which demonstrated that they had clearly altered his philosophy and attitude toward himself and others. These changes demonstrated both intellectual and emotional understanding and he felt assured that they would survive. He was almost garrulous in his presentation, and I rarely interrupted except to highlight some issues and emphasize others.

His increased self-esteem permitted him to raise the matter of his obsessional thoughts — which were still continuing, although somewhat reduced in their intensity and impact on him. For the first time, he offered some speculations about their function in his relationship with his wife. These speculations were entirely his own and were not initiated or directed by my questioning. Finally, he felt enough self-assurance to counter my request for a change in our schedule and did not immediately comply to avoid irritating me. He asserted his views and we arrived at a compromise solution without his feeling anxious or concerned about my not liking him. It was a significant session in enhancing his feelings of worthiness and presaged our moving into the third phase of therapy, in which insights and understandings are translated into behavioral change. In this phase support and encouragement are essential in order to minimize the difficulties in trying out new behavior. The therapist should be an ally and friend as well as leader as the patient attempts to put into use insights he has achieved through his therapeutic work. Approval for such moves and support for minimal gains are essential in the terminal phase of treatment.

OMNIPOTENCE OF THINKING

Mr. Jones: Formerly, when a person disagreed with me, I just couldn't tolerate it and I had to rush to prove that I was right. It's a new way for me to be able to look at things.

It was important to help Mr. Jones recognize that the reaction of others does not necessarily come out of the awareness of their behavior toward him but may derive from their appraisal of their own behavior. The idea that the obsessional have such undue influence on others and that his thoughts or behavior has such an effect on others derives from his grandiose notion of his omnipotence and singular significance. It produces the familiar problem of the magical effect their omnipotent wishes and thinking lead them to feel; that is, that their thoughts can produce dramatic effects on others. A wish becomes equivalent to a deed and is a source of enormous distress when the obsessional assumes responsibility for multiple effects because he has had a thought about it. The obsessional may attribute the accidental injury or death of a person to his dislike of that person. The obsessional's preoccupation with major catastrophes as a result of some minor or insignificant act leads to obsessive doubting and endless rituals and is another instance of the tendency for referential thinking. The throwing away of a match or stepping on an unknown object and the like may produce endless preoccupation about whether he may have started a major fire or killed someone, requiring repeated reexaminations and visits to make certain this has not happened. The extremes in behavior producing these bizarre rituals stem from the obsessional's omnipotent grandiosity, when he assumes major responsibility for all events in which he is involved. This produces the magical expectations and the undoing ritual to counteract any disaster he thinks he has produced. It also accounts for the ritualization and ultimately, the paranoid misinterpretation, since the obsessional has distorted expectations of the criticism or disapproval of others.

Mr. Jones: I had a disagreement with a colleague and about an hour later I passed him again in the hall and he said, "I hope you and I can disagree on something every now and then without it becoming a personal matter." I said, "Yes, we certainly can. I didn't take it personally at all." While it wasn't completely true, I still thought it was the thing to say, and I also could feel that there was some sincerity on his part; whereas in the past, if that happened, (a) I wouldn't be able to reply to a statement like that at all, and (b) I would think that he was still trying to undermine my importance and I would think he was way off base for disagreeing with me. Now I can see that there is another side to it. . . . I've probably got some more seeing to do before I reach the point when that won't get me riled up even to the extent that it did today.

Therapist: Was it something he did that permitted you to react somewhat differently? What do you think was involved?

Mr. Jones: No, I don't think so. He was quite belligerent for the moment. I think it was my realizing that a disagreement, even a violent one, doesn't necessarily mean that I'm being violently attacked. . . . I haven't had an experience for quite a while of being completely unable to concentrate on something because of my attention being diverted. I don't think that's happened within the past month or so. Even shortly after this incident today my boss called me in and we were discussing rather complicated matters, and I found myself able to pay attention to what he was talking about and reply when necessary.

Therapist: You mean you could recover more quickly from an upset?

Mr. Jones: Right! . . . I used to prepare myself for some unfavorable situation in which I would be in danger of losing an argument. I thought I had to be on top all the time and had to have the right answer or had to look good. Any contemplation of my being stumped or outtalked was painful to me to think of . . . Well, I just remembered something that might illustrate that.

Therapist: Uh-huh.

Mr. Jones: In the early part of 1946 I was worried that some people might make sneering remarks about me. That worried me quite a bit. I visualized myself being put into a situation where I was being ridiculed, and I didn't know how I'd be able to react to it.

This was anticipatory anxiety — which plays a major role in phobic states, although it is universally present in those individuals who always feel on trial and must guarantee their performance. They therefore attempt to control all the factors that might be involved in an event and write the entire scenario. This tendency has great dangers, since if any factors are altered, even minor ones, they are unprepared and inflexible and may collapse completely. It is the need for absolute control that requires the obsessional to consider all the possibilities in advance to be able to confront the issue. Since this is rarely possible, the individual invariably feels unprepared, anxious, and distraught; thus, he prejudices his performance at the outset, thereby confirming his fears that unless he knows it all, it is best to avoid the event in the first place. The participatory anxiety may be so great that the individual prefers not to face the situation at all. This produces the avoidance reaction called a phobia.

Therapist: Uh-huh.

Mr. Jones: No strong incident along those lines ever came up. I'm just recalling how worried I was even at the prospect, in advance. When others would tell of experiences along that line that they had had, I would become rather uncomfortable and would always be anxious to ask them what they did about it, looking for some kind of clue as to how to handle it — looking for some regulation or formula to lean on.

My impression was that Mr. Jones was having a flood of recalls during this insightful period and was unable to isolate them at the moment. He was also trying too hard to document his new insights, and the tension prevented the recall instead of expediting it. It is a commonplace but profound truth that the intensity of the desire to achieve something produces a state of tension, which prevents the effort. Only when one can relax and stop trying does the event materialize or the recall occur. Only in a state of relaxation can one carry out an action that involves a clear focus, since the anxiety involved in trying to arrive at a focus tends instead to focus on the tension and not the activity to be accomplished.

Therapist: Uh-huh. What do you make of that?

Mr. Jones: I wanted to set the stage in advance for everything that I did so I could keep everything under control with no surprises and uncertainties. I utilized that technique in looking for a job. I was afraid to go for an interview unless I had thought for days what I might possibly be asked and how I should answer certain questions.

Therapist: What made it seem so important to have the stage set?

Mr. Jones: . . . I don't know.

Therapist: Does anything come to mind about it?

Mr. Jones: . . . I seem to think I wouldn't be able to reply spontaneously, but I don't know why I thought so.

Therapist: That you wouldn't be able to reply spontaneously?

Mr. Jones: Well, in the connection of interviews for getting a job, I felt the more preparation that I made, the better my chance of success.

Therapist: Preparation is a good rule, but that isn't the issue here, is it?

Mr. Jones: No, it isn't.

Therapist: You are talking about your need to have the situation laid out for you in advance, so nothing unexpected could happen.

Mr. Jones: That's what I'm talking about. You're saying why, and I'm puzzled.

Therapist: It's not a question of preparation, is it? It's very good to be well prepared, naturally. The issue was having to have the situation laid out all in advance, so nothing unexpected could happen — so there could be no surprises.

Mr. Jones had introduced this crucial issue in obsessional thinking and behavior — that is, to achieve certainty and guaranteed success in every endeavor. This means controlling every situation and every outcome by writing the script or knowing in advance what might happen. This requires one to be omniscient and to know everything, so that one can plan or anticipate everything. It avoids spontaneous, unexpected events and has prescribed formulas and rigid compliance in all eventualities. Most of all, to know everything is to be able to predict and thus to be totally prepared. The unexpected sometimes produces disorganization and panic.

Mr. Jones: Yeah.

Therapist: What you wanted to do was control the future.

Mr. Jones: I practically wanted to have the blueprint, so it would go through automatically.

Therapist: You're really saying that you want the situation laid out for you in advance — meaning, you want a guarantee.

Mr. Jones: ... Yeah, that would be the case.

Therapist: That's a pretty extravagant demand, isn't it? The only time you can be comfortable is if you can control the whole situation so that nothing unexpected would happen, isn't it?

Mr. Jones: Well, that's it. That certainly puts it in a ridiculous light.

Therapist: I wasn't thinking of it as ridiculous but as a demand which would make your life pretty threatening, since there's no possibility of guaranteed living.

Mr. Jones: That's what I had in mind.

Therapist: I wonder whether this operates in other areas of your living?

Mr. Jones: I think I've gotten away from some of that in the last two years. I can't think of a parallel. I remember it happening fifteen years ago or so in connection with looking for a job. I remember thinking along those lines again in the summer of 1950, when I was so confused I didn't know which way to turn. My wife and I were always bickering. I didn't like that, and yet I constantly felt so much under attack and being submerged by her; I was putting her in the place of my parents. I remember a discussion I had with her, in which I made the proposition whereby we could eliminate this bickering if she would always allow me to have the final decision.

This was just the situation that we had uncovered earlier, in which he resented being treated like a little boy, and that had produced the obsessional thought about killing his wife. It is most instructive to note that, while he was reviewing it here, in a few moments he spontaneously commented on his obsessive thoughts, indicating that they were still present and disturbing. This association is a striking illustration of the free-association process and evidence that it functions actively in man. At a level of awareness and without any deliberate, contrived direction, Mr. Jones made the association in his mind between his obsession and the circumstances and psychological dynamics that had produced it.

Mr. Jones: It was my idea that we would have an initial discussion and she could say what she thought, and if there was any controversy why I was the boss and it had to be done my way.

Therapist: Well, that is a certain way to avoid difficulty, isn't it? You can say what you want, but I'll make the decisions. That being known in advance, feel free to say anything you want. [Mr. Jones laughs] It's rather interesting, isn't it? That seems to you to be the prescription for good adjustment, as long as the control is left in your hand.

Mr. Jones: Well, it did. It did then. I was pretty badly upset at that time. And I was frantically searching for some way of eliminating this bickering.

Therapist: But wasn't that precisely the cause of the bickering, the fact that you were insisting on having the last word?

Mr. Jones: Yes, certainly that was responsible for a good share of it. Another thing which accounted for it was that I visualized myself then as having to submit things for my wife's approval. I was then acting as the little boy.

Therapist: Uh-huh.

Mr. Jones: But of course those two ideas were always in violent opposition. But that's the last I can recall having that kind of idea. I had to set the stage thoroughly in advance, and nothing out of the ordinary should come up.

Therapist: Isn't that what you're talking about today? You sense a little less of it, perhaps, but isn't that one of the unspoken demands which you still make on your subordinates or your colleagues?

Again it was necessary to acknowledge Mr. Jones's progress, while keeping it in perspective and avoiding the extreme of thinking the issue was settled because some movement toward change had occurred.

Therapist: It has to be guaranteed in advance, nobody will disagree. The shock, concern, and irritation come with the fact that sometimes they do disagree. Isn't that still the way you react?

Mr. Jones: That's right. I guess so.

Therapist: You're still asking for a guarantee; that everyone should know if you do or say something, it is correct and perfect.

Mr. Jones: Uh-huh. Yes, it sounds like you have something there. I always regarded situations in which people disagree with me as being unpleasant and undesirable situations. I wondered how I would distinguish disagreement from a situation in which there actually was a belligerent attack on me. I didn't know any way of distinguishing between those two if there is a distinction. So I had to assume that all of them were trying to beat me down and either take vigorous countermeasures when they occurred or try to prevent such things from happening. These obsessive thoughts are still painful and troublesome.

Therapist: When have you noticed them coming up?

Mr. Jones: Well, usually still without anything definite that I can tie it to. But in cases where I am having some issue with something my wife does that I don't like or if we're having an argument, then the thoughts accentuate at that time. I somehow got in the habit that when these thoughts would pop into my head I would tell myself not to worry about it, that I wasn't going to kill my wife and that the reason those thoughts existed at all was because of the resentment that I had against her and for the excessive domination over me by my parents. The time that those thoughts first came to me, I was putting my relationship between us in the status of my being a little boy under my parents' domination. I told myself not to worry about those thoughts; they're due to the overdomination by my parents.

Therapist: And that's what controls them?

Mr. Jones: Uh, it seems to be of some value.

We had reached the end of the session, and I preferred to close it rather than to suggest some very crucial additions to his views about his obsessional ideas. This situation frequently arises in long-term treatment situations.

With an obsessional patient, it is best not to introduce new ideas near the close of the session, since they will be dealt with largely as distractions and will take the focus away from material dealt with earlier. It is best to postpone it until the next session, but the therapist must make a mental note to raise it in the next session if the patient fails to do so. Otherwise, it will be lost and will be viewed by the patient as the therapist's device to avoid dealing with important issues.

PREPARATION FOR TERMINATION

By now, it was becoming increasingly apparent in the therapy that Mr. Jones had developed considerable insight into his behavior, which was manifested in changes in his living. The symptoms that brought him to therapy had begun to diminish, and he was more self-respectful. His work performance had improved, and his relationship with his wife was slowly improving. After one of the sessions, I noted that improvement led me to begin to consider termination; however, I took no initiative toward that goal. Nevertheless, therapy was terminated three weeks later when he moved because he had to take an assignment in another city. Because of the sudden and unanticipated termination, we could not approach the end of therapy with an organized plan — which would have included a review of the problem, the insights achieved, and the tasks that still needed to be done. The last three or four sessions would have concerned themselves with these questions, as well as with a summary statement of the dynamics of the disorder.

In the last few sessions we continued to focus on some of his remaining problems.

Mr. Jones: Well, I feel all tensed up again tonight and nothing to attribute to it. . . . Yesterday I was sort of an arbiter in a violent vocal bout in my office. My colleague became violently upset about some errors his secretary brought to his attention and was abusive to her.

Therapist: How did you handle it?

Mr. Jones: Well, reasonably well, I think . . . it could have been better.

Therapist: You felt you should have been able to handle it better?

Mr. Jones: He got to the point that there was no way of dealing with such matters without yelling. I had to deal with her feelings, and also I didn't want to depreciate his importance.

Therapist: It wasn't easy, was it?

Mr. Jones: No, it wasn't.

Therapist: Think it's easy for anyone?

Mr. Jones: No, no! I'm getting to another point. Looking back on the thing as a whole I think I handled it quite well, but what I was agitated about at the time and still am ... is the inability to get started without a few unsuccessful attempts.

Mr. Jones was still hanging on to his unrealistic expectations of perfection. We needed to try to pin it down firmly, since the issue arose at a time when he clearly functioned well, and I could forcefully present the issue without his becoming too defensive and therefore unable to integrate the insight. I used an approach that can be effective in getting past pure intellectual formulations. I exaggerated his own demands in pointing out his unrealistic expectations by being mildly sardonic — which caught his attention and tended to mobilize his focus to respond.

Therapist: If we pinpoint this, we hear something that sounds like an old story. You describe a tough situation in which an executive is acting with lack of dignity toward an employee who is emotionally upset because of his brutality. Each has to be handled, and each may be right. Whoever is right is not the issue, since you come out with the feeling that in the overall sense it went pretty well, but you are agitated now because it didn't go off perfectly. You should have been able to go in there like a seasoned mediator and resolve the situation to everyone's satisfaction. Well, it generally doesn't happen that way except in the dreams of Walter Mitty — dreams of glory. This isn't to belittle the fact that you have trouble getting started. We recognize that. But notice how you emphasize the wrong things. You emphasize the difficulty in getting started, rather than the fact that it was a damn tough situation for anyone to handle.

Mr. Jones: I emphasized that only to the extent that I wanted to bring out what it was that caused me to feel uneasy and inadequate.

Therapist: You know it takes considerable maturity to settle this kind of dispute. Most people prefer not to get involved.

Mr. Jones: I didn't think of that at all, but I recognize it immediately now that you mention it.

Therapist: You were very vulnerable in such a situation, each person feeling that you sided with the other.

Mr. Jones: I was very conscious of both, having to walk a tightrope.

Therapist: So that if you try to do a perfect job in an area that not even God can do, it would tend to make you uneasy.

Mr. Jones: ... Yes. Probably most people would run from such a situation.

Therapist: But when you get more occupied with your deficiencies in dealing with it, you are not sufficiently aware of the elements which are required to handle it.

Mr. Jones: Yes. I do have a feeling of inadequacy and that threw me off the track.

Therapist: Why is it always there?

Mr. Jones: Well, you suggested a few minutes ago that it takes place because my initial thought is that I must have the perfect solution.

Therapist: You did the only thing possible. But you hoped you could come up with the perfect retort.

Mr. Jones: Yes, I did hope so.

Therapist: That's superman stuff.

Mr. Jones: Yes, it is ... but in such cases a sort of quick daydream comes into mind. If Mr. So-and-so were handling this, he'd have just the right thing to say. I frantically tried to be Mr. So-and-so at that time and have just the right way of handling it. He is my boss.

This had a familiar ring for those who think the grass is always greener in someone else's yard. For Mr. Jones, there still was a perfect solution and someone else could produce it. It was the idealization he attributed to others that maintained the desire and expectation that he could achieve it.

Therapist: What would he do that you so desperately want to be able to do?

Mr. Jones: He would be able to come out with some definite statement which would hush them both up and answer the specific questions they were raising. I think the reason why it was impossible for me to reply had something to do with their angry tones, the excessive atmosphere of belligerence. In fact, each of them was able to keep up this crossfire to the other's charges far better than I was able to intercede. I rather admired the secretary's ability to talk back to someone far above her.

Therapist: Uh-huh. Your picture of the person who was able to do this, your boss, includes that of a powerful being who always has the correct solution in his control?

Mr. Jones: Well, maybe I do, maybe I always pick out some person who would have a good solution to the problem. I would pick out different people according to what the problem is.

Therapist: That's a very useful insight, isn't it?

Mr. Jones: A very recent one, too. I just thought of it now.

Therapist: Which tells us why you expect that you can be all things to all people.

Mr. Jones: I did used to expect myself to be all things to all people.

Another aspect of this problem that I think I handled much better than I formerly would have been able to is that I didn't make a big project out of this. I listened to each of them, then after I finished with them I talked briefly to each separately. I then took no further action. I let them unburden themselves. Formerly, I would have made a big project about it. A big deal.

Therapist: Hmm. How was that possible? You have something rather meaningful there, always making a big deal out of everything. Here you feel you didn't have to. And evidently you had less anxiety about it. I imagine that making a big deal and getting in touch with the boss usually gets involved with status and being afraid that unless you did something he would think poorly of you.

Mr. Jones: You're right! Absolutely right, that would be the thing — that would have occurred to me. But there are many times lately in which I'm able to recognize situations of the type that you just mentioned. It isn't necessary, and I have to make conscious efforts to, to keep myself from doing it, correcting it immediately.

Therapist: Previously you would do just the opposite because of your uneasiness.

Mr. Jones: Everything had to be covered up. I was always plugging up holes, potential holes.

Therapist: It took a hell of a lot of energy, didn't it?

Mr. Jones: Yes! [laughs]

Therapist: But I'm still curious as to what gets involved in your difficulty in recognizing your ability to handle these situations?

Mr. Jones: If there's any tension involved it is difficult.

It is just as important to understand the anxieties that prevent one from recognizing one's assets as those which distort one's behavior. They are undoubtedly closely related. The tendency to focus on deficits, defenses, and distorted behavior — which is the presumed role of the therapist — often gets overdone so that one fails to notice the positive, creative aspects of the neurotic's behavior. This tendency is further extended in the prevailing psychoanalytic tendency to view all behavior as derived from defensive sources and to question all feelings as if they were defenses against some anxiety. Thus, tender feelings, instead of being viewed as spontaneous, could be analyzed a defensive reaction formation against hostility. While this may be the case, it is not necessarily so.

Therapist: When you easily overcome obstacles, you imply that they weren't very difficult ones.

Mr. Jones: Yes, that's true. Oh, in the past it would imply that I used far more force and far more reliance on some established authority than I needed to have. I would take pleasure in being able to cite some established authority and bring about the solution to the problem without inserting myself personally or relying on my own status.

Therapist: So there wasn't any real pride in the achievement because it was always somebody else who did it, or because they were scared of your status.

Mr. Jones: I used to always be striving with a drastic compulsion to keep explaining and to keep showing why my way was right, because I always wanted the opponent to say, "Oh yes! You're right!" Of course, I was usually disappointed.

Therapist: They rarely said you were right. Besides, people who are defeated generally are not able to withdraw gracefully.

Mr. Jones: And yet, I tried to do that myself. In situations where I would see I was wrong, I always made quite a show of admitting it — maybe because that was the action I hoped I would get from others.

Therapist: It must have been very hard to get people to like you; you were either excessively obsequious or you were being so defensive making certain that they didn't hold anything against you that you would overwhelm them with explanations. This must have made people uncomfortable.

Mr. Jones: I suppose. I never could rely on my own status to say no and let it go at that; whether the person liked it or not, I always had to try to prove to them why it was necessary for me to do that. I always hoped that they would say, "Oh yes. I see." Nobody ever did that, but I kept on looking for it. I guess I ... the corollary to that was ... if I just took a definite stand without the detailed explanations, I thought that they would think I was being unreasonable. I also thought that it took these explanations backed up with lots of authority to make them accept what I told them.

Therapist: Which is another way of saying you never really believed that people could accept your authority, that everyone somehow knew you were a little guy masquerading as a big man.

Mr. Jones: Yes, I did sort of think that.

Therapist: Well, let's see — what comes to mind about that?

Mr. Jones: Well, that did use to concern me quite a bit during the first seven or eight years that I was an executive. I thought that my youthful appearance combined with my high status would cause people to resent me. Every now and then an incident would happen which confirmed that.

Therapist: Why should you be exempt from expressions of resentment?

Mr. Jones: That's a good question; that thought hadn't occurred to me.

Therapist: The notion about masquerading, did you have a feeling that they thought you were too young or didn't deserve the status? That you were there under false pretenses?

Mr. Jones: No, none of these.

Therapist: Does the notion strike home that you often go around with the secret feeling that people have some contempt for you?

Mr. Jones: Yes, it does strike home.

Therapist: And subsequently what you have to offer needs all kinds of protection, support, and fortification for your position.

Mr. Jones: Exactly. In most cases I tried to ... I would try to cite this authority in such a way that it would be absolutely final and no one would have any possibility of contesting it. But at the same time I wanted to avoid anybody thinking that I was leaning on my superior.

Therapist: You wanted to be the final authority.

Mr. Jones: I guess that's it.

This ended the session.

HOMEWORK IN THERAPY

The next hour began with references to the issues we had discussed at the last session, after which he described some recollections of his mother that had a direct relevance to the matter of not being viewed as a grown man or taken seriously. Mr. Jones was clear that the beginnings of this tendency to doubt his acceptability arose in his uneasy relationship with his mother, whom he felt he could not please or impress with his achievements. He had done his homework well, and his insights were growing more profound.

Ruminating about the therapy outside of the therapeutic sessions is the key ingredient in the development of insight. Occasionally, awareness does develop during a session. However, most often the insight will develop in the intervening hours and days between sessions, when the patient ruminates, introspects, and translates some understanding into his current living. Thus, good therapy should provide material for consideration and rumination between sessions. This can be done by leaving important questions unresolved or open or by posing a question or assignment for consideration during the intervals.

Mr. Jones: My wife and I visited a government building today. She struck up a conversation with one of the guards. When I saw her I felt that I had just slipped into one of these conditions in which I was putting her in the place of my mother.

Therapist: What happened? What are you thinking?

Mr. Jones: I'm trying to think of some way of expressing this. It just reminded me in an uncomfortable way of having gone to a museum or a zoo or something of the sort with my mother and feeling some sort of unpleasant restraint. You suggested last week that I try to recall some instances in which I thought others doubted what I did, that they may have been a source of my doubting myself. I haven't thought of anything very specific. I did recall an incident on a holiday that happened when I was about eight or nine. We went with friends and there was a girl about my age with whom I quarreled frequently. This other woman complained to my mother that she allowed me to hurt her daughter and my mother apologized and reprimanded me for it. I was very resentful of that. Later on she did change her approach somewhat and said I probably couldn't help it because this girl was disobedient. I felt good that she made that statement because there had been other incidents in which I always felt that I didn't get any support and I was blamed for whatever I or the other kid might have done.

Therapist: This was one occasion where you did get support.

Mr. Jones: Yes. Support was a funny thing. When I thought I needed support I didn't get it, and yet there were other times when I didn't want very close guidance that my folks were right there practically holding my hand.

This morning before we left home I remembered another incident which seems totally unrelated to this subject. It seems to be the reverse, illustrating how I am trying to push myself into people's attention. When I was thirteen or so, the first year I was in high school, we were reading a book and I recognized the names of many towns. I would raise my hand to say that I knew about that or I'd tell something that I knew about it. The teacher just tolerated me in a sort of good-humored way, but occasionally, she would try to quiet me down. I think I was just seeking some kind of attention or recognition, which I wasn't getting otherwise, since I never participated with any group or in after-school activities. I remember this incident about the book and my shouting out in class because it's rather unusual for me to behave in that manner.

Therapist: Inappropriate for a kid?

Mr. Jones: Yes, I think so, under those circumstances.

Therapist: It was different then, in that you were always a well-behaved boy.

Mr. Jones: Yes, I was well behaved, and when I deviated from good behavior, it was very painful to me if my mother became displeased. As soon as I recognized it, I would try to rectify whatever I was doing and I would be profuse with apologies.

Therapist: What disturbed you at the building when you saw your wife talking to a guard? Do you think she was talking about you?

Mr. Jones: Well, it was something like that. It was very mild; I certainly didn't resent it that she bragged about me.

Therapist: Why do you immediately jump to that?

I was surprised that he assumed that the conversation his wife was having with the guard was about him and perhaps flattering. I pressed him to pursue that line of inquiry, which had the "little boy" flavor.

Mr. Jones: I just happened to think of it.

Therapist: Was someone bragging about you familiar?

Mr. Jones: No, that is not a particular characteristic of my parents. Somewhat the reverse. My mother was always afraid that I would be conceited and if I displayed more knowledge than others had, she thought I was acting conceited.

Therapist: You mean the idea was always to be modest, even though you knew more? Your mother didn't want you to be conceited, but in a sense encouraged you to be special and different?

Mr. Jones: Well, no, I wouldn't say she encouraged me to be special and different, but, yes, that's true [ambivalence]. In respect to other kids, she did want me to be special and different. Whenever any innoculations or vaccinations were given at school she never allowed me to take them along with the rest of the class. She always took me to the family doctor.

Therapist: Why was that?

Mr. Jones: Just a peculiar attitude she had. I remember one case in which the doctor bawled her out and told her that there was no need to pay him four or five dollars for a vaccination, that I could have gotten it for nothing at school.

Therapist: Yeah, but you were special. The school doctors weren't good enough for her son.

Mr. Jones: That must have been her attitude. It wasn't mine. I didn't like this idea of being segregated.

Therapist: So your mother would be critical if you were conceited and she worked awful hard to make you look special and different.

Mr. Jones: Hmm, that's interesting. ... Yeah, both of those were true.

This is the typical double bind that is the obsessional's despair — the tendency to operate in the extremes which characterizes the attitude of others toward them and, consequently, their attitude toward themselves. Mr. Jones was supposed to feel modest and never behave improperly at the same time that he was superspecial and different. He could not have a valid feeling of being worthwhile without feeling split and ambiguous because feeling worthwhile was unworthy and feeling special was improper. He could not believe either one or accept either view.

Therapist: So it wouldn't be a surprise that you might have become conceited, eh?

Mr. Jones: No, I didn't regard these things as sources of conceit. I didn't like them. It isn't wrong to be conceited. I guess you might say it's regarded as mildly disapproving.

Therapist: This is something you have very mixed feelings about, isn't it? You always seem to want to be considered special and different and perfect and beyond reproach and beyond any critical evaluation.

Mr. Jones: Hmm ...

Therapist: Then, on the other hand, you feel very uneasy when you are put in a special role and treated as a special individual. Three or four incidents you've related from your early years imply a very confused atmosphere where on the one hand you are encouraged to be different and isolated from other kids while on the other hand you are told you should appear smarter and different. It's all right to be different, it's all right not to be like other boys, but don't let them find that out because if they do they will not like you for it.

Mr. Jones: Something like that.

Therapist: One of the important problems in your living is that you do consider yourself different or special. And yet you don't want to be.

Mr. Jones: That's kind of hard to grasp. How do I consider myself different?

Therapist: Well, you ponder over that for a minute and see.

I felt that the exposition was clear enough for him to grasp and I wanted him to establish the connection and fortify the insight that came out of his feeling, instead of from an intellectual exercise. Only this could be the prelude to attempts to alter his living.

Mr. Jones: Well, perhaps my habit of making too strong demands on myself, of thinking that nothing less than perfection was even passable.

Therapist: Yeah. That's what we're talking about.

Mr. Jones: I guess that would be considering myself different, but at the time I didn't look at it that way.

Therapist: That's not considering yourself different, that's considering yourself superhuman.

Mr. Jones: But I wasn't considering myself superhuman. I just thought that I had to be that way in order to be even passable.

Therapist: That's a contradiction, isn't it?

Mr. Jones: Yes, it is. I can clearly see others who are mediocre, happy-go-lucky, didn't care, fairly good, and yet I thought I had to be perfect. It was rather painful when I wasn't.

The preceding is a characteristic obsessional exchange and is invariably presented to justify grandiose or perfectionistic attitudes. When the patient is forced to acknowledge his superhuman propensities, he tries to deal with it in one of two ways: First, he might say that, in fact, he is only trying to be acceptable, not perfect, and that he has difficulty in performing at all and he just wants to be able to survive. This argument is thin and specious, since he has already indicated that being mediocre, ordinary, or average is totally unacceptable to him. He is special, with high values and expectations, and nothing else will receive the acclaim and admiration of others. Second, when he senses that this attitude is present, he will take the opposite tack and insist that if he is being asked not to be perfect, then he cannot function at all. The obsessional makes extreme contradictory claims, and he requires that both be acknowledged at the same time.

Here Mr. Jones was denying that he wanted to be superman when he had clearly made the statement just one moment earlier that perhaps in making too strong demands on himself he was thinking that nothing less than perfection was even passable! The demand for certain acceptability was responsible for his ambivalent, totally dichotomous split in his expectations of himself.

Mr. Jones: The subject of conceit reminds me of an incident when I was sixteen or so. I was looking in the mirror and tying my tie, and my mother said something like: "Do you think you're good-looking? You're spending so much time looking in the mirror. Actually you aren't nearly as good-looking as your father was when he was a young man." Well, I felt quite confused at that time because actually I was entertaining such a thought. I thought I was good-looking, and to have her contradict that, an unspoken thought of mine, left me rather confused.

Therapist: Why should she immediately compare you with your father?

Mr. Jones: Well, I do resemble him somewhat. However, her method of comparison just follows a pattern that she often followed, that I mustn't hurt people's feelings by acting as if I'm better.

Therapist: And how would it hurt people's feelings if you had a good impression of yourself?

Mr. Jones: Well, I can't conceive of any way that it would.

Therapist: So your mother not only didn't brag about you, but apparently she took pains to pull you down to size.

Mr. Jones: Well, she did on that occasion, at any rate.

The next session dealt directly with the obsessional problem and his experiences with his wife when he returned from a week's vacation. He began describing it at once.

Mr. Jones: My wife and I had a violent argument on Friday morning. I was going to help her with the washing, and just about the time we were ready to start she got a telephone call. I filled the washer, put the soap in, and started the wash. When she came downstairs she was enraged, saying I had put too much water in the washer, too much soap — and that the suds were drooling over the top. I was sort of taken off balance by the violent, emotional, illogical reaction she had.

Therapist: Are you saying that all that happened was that you started the laundry and then the outburst came as a result of noticing that you had, perhaps, not done it properly?

Mr. Jones: Yeah!

Therapist: Nothing else transpired?

Mr. Jones: Nothing else transpired! The probable background of it is that she was upset about her mother.

Therapist: What goes on in your mind while she's carrying on this way, what do you think?

Mr. Jones: At first I tolerate it, but in this case she kept getting more and more hysterical. At that time she burst out with a statement that I'm always trying to take things over, and she didn't like the way I did it. I did reply to that by telling her that she was basing her tantrum on her imagination and that she was building up her anger on an imaginary sequence of undesirable events which she visualized and which weren't consistent with the facts.

This was a classical obsessional statement, devoid of feeling and worded with excessive care: "weren't consistent with the facts" — meaning she was wrong.

Mr. Jones: And I became rather heated myself. I told her that my purpose in starting this was purely to help her and had no idea it would cause her any displeasure.

Therapist: What goes on inside of you while this is going on?

Mr. Jones: Well, it brings these obsessive thoughts more into being, makes them more disturbing.

Therapist: That's what we want to talk about, because obviously something is going on inside of you. You must be thoroughly fed up or disgusted. However, you present it as if you're standing there calmly and cooly.

Mr. Jones: No, that's not so. Except for the outset of it, I try to remain calm.

Therapist: That's what I'm trying to get at. Something goes on inside of you during such an episode, even though you try to remain calm.

Mr. Jones: Well, I was disgusted, fed up, with the absurdity and unfairness of this emotional tantrum. I did think it was childish and said so.

Therapist: And at the same time the obsessive thoughts get more insistent?

Mr. Jones: Hmm, yes.

Therapist: Then, or afterwards?

Mr. Jones: Well, I guess it is afterward more so than at the time.

UNDERSTANDING THE OBSESSION TO KILL

Now we were approaching the end of our work in trying to fully understand the obsessions. Mr. Jones presented a clear picture of the development of the obsessive thoughts at a time when he was angry, confused, and helpless to do anything, since he could not control or influence his wife's behavior. It was the feeling of impotent rage, which was not manifest in any outward reaction. Instead, he tried to be cool and calm, while inwardly the obsessive thoughts were becoming stronger and more persistent.

Therapist: At the time you're also angry, eh?

Mr. Jones: Yes, I was angry. Although I was angry I realized it was one of these outbursts that she goes through which I have tried to take less seriously than I used to. I used to take it very seriously. I used to regard it as being strongly disapproving of what I was doing and that I had caused it. I was frantic to get her to come out of her mood. I'm able now to react in some positive fashion such as telling her that she's behaving childishly in an illogical emotional fashion which previously I couldn't seem to do.

Therapist: Do you think you did something so awfully wrong?

Mr. Jones: I don't think that what I did was wrong at all.

While he evidenced much growth in his ability to handle these moments with greater ease and less obsequiousness, I wanted him to become more aware of the helpless capacity to experience his feelings at such times, in order to tie in the obsessional thoughts with his feelings of lack of control of the situation. I was not trying to show him that his reactions were unjustified or excessive or that he was an innocent bystander.

Mr. Jones: Later she started in on this tirade of abuse all over again, so I did become very heated, but I can't remember what I said. I replied forcefully to everything she said.

Therapist: Do you have any idea as to why she was so angry?

Mr. Jones: Well, I'll try to give you her side of it. She said that I was blundering ahead doing the thing improperly and that I was taking over. A thought that ran through my mind at the outset of this episode was that even if I had done it differently than she would have done, it didn't seem to be important enough to make such a fuss about. I wasn't able exactly to put that into words. In fact, I hadn't remembered it at all until right now.

Therapist: So it was as if she was angry about something other than that you were doing anything wrong?

Mr. Jones: I wouldn't say there was anything that she was angry about. I think that she was very nervous and on edge about her mother being sick. That causes her a great amount of distress.

It was fascinating to notice how even at this stage of our work and his understanding of the situation with his wife and the relationship of his obsessional thoughts to her behavior, he still tried to tie emotional reactions to mysterious or physical origins and avoid the manifest evidence of the interpersonal effects of his behavior on others. He still could not clearly indicate that her reaction, surely aggravated by outside forces such as her mother's illness and her lower-back pain, could be attributed to his tendency to take control and give her a feeling of being pushed out. He could not acknowledge that what he did affected others; at least, he was still most reluctant to do so.

Therapist: Well, I'm sure it does, but you cannot explain everything with this magic formula. First she's on edge because she has a sore back, then it's her mother, and next week it can be something else. But it's more than that. Yes, she's distressed about these things, but there's something about this particular kind of dealing with you and how she reacts to your behavior that turns it on.

I waited until this point to indicate that, in fact, he was taking over without asking for her agreement to carry out a task that he knew was usually done by her. Even though he tried to be helpful, she perceived it as her being left out. He had difficulty in collaborating. My tactic was to help him recognize his anger and disappointment in his wife's failure to acknowledge feeling justified and his helplessness before I highlighted his taking-over role, which would tend to make him guilty and cover up the strong feelings he experienced. In dealing with feelings, whether they are justified or not, we recognize that a person is freer to express negative feelings if he feels justified than if he realizes that the feelings are irrational or neurotic.

Mr. Jones: Yes, I suppose so.

Therapist: Do you have any notions about what that could be? Could we say that here you were trying to help your wife out, trying to ease her work?

Mr. Jones: Yeah. I wasn't feeling like a martyr about it. I was happy enough to do it.

Therapist: Yes. And you felt you were doing her a good turn, weren't you?

Mr. Jones: Yes.

Therapist: And look what comes out of it! Does this seem familiar to other aspects of your living?

Mr. Jones: It does right at the moment; it hasn't up until now.

Therapist: Uh-huh. Let's hear.

Mr. Jones: Well, it strikes me as being similar to the reactions that I generate in other people when I think I'm doing my job properly. I will do or say things that cause resentment, usually because I'm overly meticulous and have this exaggerated sense that everything must be perfect. That causes me to take issue with people on things that probably would be just as well if it was done their way rather than with the corrections I suggest. But getting back to this incident with my wife. There is a rather contradictory thing. Whenever we do things together or I help her with something, she is dissatisfied that I don't help her more. But when I do help her on those things she thinks I'm "taking over." And I usually don't agree with her. I don't feel that I have had ideas of taking it over or that I've acted that way.

Therapist: By taking it over, I guess she means that whenever you come in to do a job you push her out?

Mr. Jones: Well, yes. I usually counter her statement by telling her that no two people have the same way of doing things, and I can't possibly do or act exactly as she would.

Therapist: Yeah, but I wonder whether the focus of the trouble is that you don't do it the way she wants you to do it. Isn't it more in the nature of her feeling that when you do it, there is something you communicate about that being the only way to do it? Isn't there something about this that is reflected in your office activity? Don't you sometimes have the feeling that if you could do it all then it would really come out well?

Mr. Jones: Umm.

Therapist: Which sometimes must make other people feel that they are of little use to you, or they are just there by virtue of the fact that you can't do everything. They don't get that feeling of really being useful.

Mr. Jones: Well, maybe it is that. It's awfully hard for me to think that she could have a logical basis for thinking that though; maybe I should say it's hard for me to think that she could have *any* basis for thinking that.

Therapist: As I talked, you smiled, with some feeling of recognition, as if what I was saying really . . .

Mr. Jones: Well, I was recognizing it as it applies to my daily work, rather than recognizing it as applying to her.

Therapist: Do you recognize that you must communicate to others a kind of subtle, unspoken criticism? This occurs with regard to your wife as well as others and is not necessarily a question of whether you think you could do the laundry better than she.

Mr. Jones: That's ridiculous. Of course I don't think that.

Therapist: No, you actually don't think that, and yet . . .

Mr. Jones: I had no thoughts of there being any contest to see who could do it better.

Therapist: Yeah. But even where your intentions are well meant, where you're really trying to help someone out, for some reason this attitude creeps in.

Mr. Jones: Yeah, and that similar attitude crept in Saturday night; I was helping her make a fruitcake, and we were getting along very well. She was doing most of it, and I was doing things of an apprentice nature. I finished what I was doing and she asked me "Well, what's next on the recipe?" and I read, "creaming the butter and sugar," and asked her how to do that. She then started out after me. I got the idea immediately. I did push in and take over in that aspect of it.

Therapist: She resented that?

Mr. Jones: She resented that and walked out. She said, "When you get through taking over, why don't you let me know and I'll come back and finish the cake," and I wasn't completely surprised at that. And I intended not to take over the whole project, but merely take over that particular portion of it.

Therapist: Does it occur to you to tell her that maybe you do have problems with your tendency to take over, since she interprets your behavior as always taking over? Does it occur to you to tell her that because you have trouble cooperating and she is unwilling to accept your cooperation when you are cooperating, you're also being a bad boy by taking over too much?

This was the familiar double bind that had plagued Mr. Jones all his life. Its earliest beginnings with his mother were almost identical to his present difficulty with his wife. He tried to be helpful and cooperative, but in doing so, he pushed in and took over, alienating the other person, who then abandoned the project. He did not want to appear uncooperative and bad, but when he was good he was also "bad." This dilemma could be terminated when he could recognize his tendencies to go the extreme in whatever direction he took.

Mr. Jones: Well, I told her something like that, not precisely that way.

Therapist: I'm not suggesting that you tell her precisely as we formulate it. I'm only raising the question whether this comes into your mind in these situations. You feel guilty, as if you've taken over or have done something wrong, as well as being irritated and disgusted because of her contemptuous way of reacting towards you.

Mr. Jones: Oh, I think it's much more the latter. I have no intention of being offensive. Therefore, when someone is offended, I'm at a loss.

Therapist: Well, it's not that you intend to be offensive but that apparently you communicate to others some sort of feeling that you're the only one who can really do it well.

Mr. Jones: . . . That's probably a very accurate way of putting it. I guess I do . . . I guess I communicate such an expression even though I'm trying to create just the opposite impression.

Therapist: Yes. I'm saying that possibly this impression gets communicated because you still have a reluctance to recognize that deep down this operates in your personality. You can't see it as an element in your relations with people, something you have to deal with. In the past it's a matter of feeling guilty because you recognize it and condemn yourself for it. Most of the time, however, you do not sense it at all and just react with indignant fury at being falsely accused.

Mr. Jones: Yeah. There is also the reaction that people don't like me.

Therapist: That could be the explanation to it all, but there's more to you than just that.

Mr. Jones: What do you mean by that?

Therapist: Only when you are willing to recognize that this is something that you do will you be able to acknowledge that you were doing more than just being cooperative or bossy and taking over. In fact, you enjoy helping with the wash and making a cake, and it's not simply a matter of managing everything.

Mr. Jones: Yeah.

Therapist: But you respond as if everyone is falsely accusing you and being mean and vindictive and not recognizing your goodwill.

Mr. Jones: Well . . .

Therapist: So that you can't really get a kick out of that aspect of being cooperative because you don't recognize your tendency to take over.

THE PATIENT'S ASSETS

Realizing his assets was essential to the final integration of Mr. Jones's tendencies, as it was not a matter of just eliminating his undesirable tactics. He also had to recognize that some aspects of his behavior were a source of pride and enjoyment to him. It was the excessive, compulsive, unaware quality of his behavior that alienated others. Mr. Jones was, in fact, a helpful and curious man who enjoyed participating in many activities with his wife. He enjoyed the housework and was helpful to his wife, who would certainly acknowledge this if she were asked. It was his excessive, controlling tendencies that she objected to and not his interest and desire to collaborate with her.

The dilemma of Mr. Jones raises the question of the value of seeing couples together and perhaps helping them to clarify these dilemmas and double binds. Had there been time, I would have encouraged Mr. Jones's wife to come in and be seen, either alone or with her husband. It would probably have been very useful in his treatment and would have illuminated some of her distress with him. This would not be just to have her accommodate herself to him, but more as a way of clarifying the effect each had on the other and thereby clarifying his pathology.

Mr. Jones: No, I haven't recognized the other. The only aspect of it that I've recognized is that people are bound to dislike me.

Therapist: But they don't, do they? They're only bound to dislike you because even your own attempts at being cooperative and friendly get caught up with this other unconscious tendency.

Mr. Jones: They certainly do. That's a hard nut to crack. Surely the answer isn't being meek and retiring and to wait for invitations to do or say anything!

Therapist: Certainly not.

Mr. Jones: So the key must be in the way of taking initiatives, rather than any indications that I should never take the initiative.

Now he caught on completely to what was required for him to change. It was not a matter of going to the opposite extreme but of altering the assertive way he functioned. It was not a matter of shifting from one compulsion to do, to another compulsion *not* to do. The solution was to find a way of functioning in which he could do what he wished to do without the insistent tendency to overwhelm others with his own requirements.

Therapist: Well, you might go a little further and say that the key lies somewhere in being willing to see yourself as you really are and not as you would like yourself to be.

Mr. Jones: Well, I've been making efforts to soft-pedal my former tendencies to demand perfection and absolute correctness, or demand that these be expressed exactly the way I would. I'm getting away from that.

Therapist: Uh-huh.

Mr. Jones: I have recognized that the making of corrections, or taking issue with people on rather minor things, can create resentment. Because it hadn't occurred to me until now, I'm still puzzling about it — that my way of bringing things up may be a cause of resentment.

The last two interviews with Mr. Jones pursued major issues that had not yet been dealt with adequately, particularly that of displaying his feelings as an indication of weakness. We had been building up insights in rapid succession, and many of his symptoms were now becoming more comprehensible to him. He demonstrated more awareness of his need to play the manly role when he confronted his wife about her tendency to mother him and of his reluctance to be the grown-up, which required him to be perfect. This insight was yet to be fully integrated, but he began to allow himself to be wrong and to leave some arguments unsettled.

The first of these sessions dealt with Mr. Jones's primary difficulties in expressing his feelings of anger and resentment, which left him feeling impotent rage. The awareness of this emerged slowly, with some provocative and pointed observations by the therapist. It was a significant hour, since it dealt directly with the obsessional problem. In the preceding session, the same problem was elaborated but only partially integrated.

CONSOLIDATION OF INSIGHT

The following exchange illustrates the slowly emerging quality of an insight in dealing with mundane issues, rather than the sudden, magical illumination that comes from a brilliant interpretation by the therapist. Generally, a patient resists and defends himself against each slowly developing idea, and the therapist must assist him in a persistent and dogged examination of the data until a clear illumination of the issue is achieved. This is the essence of the role of the therapist — to guide and assist the patient in becoming aware of what the patient does not see. This enables the patient to put the pieces together and realize what he has been avoiding and why. He can then recognize how his symptoms have been maintaining the misperceptions.

Mr. Jones: I remembered another incident much the same as the one I was telling you about on Monday, in which it's difficult for me to handle anyone who's prying into my affairs or asking me something that I don't care to answer.

He was referring to a patient of my colleague who was talkative and intrusive and who tried to question him while they were in the waiting room.

Mr. Jones: When I was on the train with my boss, we went into the club car, and another passenger sat down next to me. He was not drunk yet, but on the road to becoming so. He was behaving in a rather belittling and derogatory fashion. He was asking me all sorts of questions, and I found it difficult to cope with the situation.
Therapist: What was the difficulty?
Mr. Jones: I wanted to cut off further questions but I couldn't. Finally, after many questions, he said, "You probably object to answering this, but I'm curious as to how old your are." To that I was able to reply, "I don't think that has any interest to you at all."
Therapist: Rather a nice way of saying, "It's none of your goddamned business!"
Mr. Jones: Well, that did the trick momentarily, but he started in again.
Therapist: What is it that gets in the way of your doing what you would like to do?
Mr. Jones: I wouldn't want a scene to develop, and I considered it likely to develop in view of the guy's abusive drunk stage.
Therapist: And that's the only alternative. As you see it, if you were to handle the situation, it would be to develop a scene. To avoid a scene you must be silent or agreeable.
Mr. Jones: Yes. Well, I did make some sort of countermeasure.
Therapist: Yeah, but we're curious as to why it couldn't have been handled more comfortably, and that you are put on the defensive when it should be the other way around.
Mr. Jones: I don't know. Something's even getting in the way of my talking about it now.

Therapist: Is it because you're presenting yourself in a bad light, as some weakling pushed around by this fellow? Is that what's getting in the way now?

Mr. Jones: I don't think so.

Note that he felt comfortable and free enough to express his disagreement clearly and affirmatively without being defensive and with no alternative explanation. I recognized his disagreement and altered my hypothesis, which involved the notion that he was being defensive because he couldn't aggressively handle the intrusive drunk. He thought he appeared unmanly and weak in the eyes of his boss and was therefore anxious, tense, and defensive.

Therapist: You don't think that's getting in your way now?

Mr. Jones: No, no. It isn't that.

Therapist: O.K. If we look at the situation on the train for a minute we find you trying to deal in a serious, dignified way with an undignified individual.

Mr. Jones: Yes, I was giving him serious answers, being unable to tell him off or kid along or ignore it. Also, I was trying to imply by the brevity of my answers that I didn't care to make a long conversation out of it.

Therapist: Uh-huh. Yeah. Very familiar technique for you. You hope the person will understand that you don't want to talk to him by giving him brief answers.

Mr. Jones: I don't like the idea that things happen that way, but your description is accurate.

Therapist: You notice that you don't like the situation on the train and are getting irritated with it and you want it to end. Yet you feel trapped and helpless to do anything. Why? Do you think it has something to do with your being forced to maintain or present some picture of yourself?

Mr. Jones: Yes, it must.

Therapist: Because you feel that you are supposed to behave in some acceptable way. You can't respond to your irritation as a human being, but must behave as a dignified executive in some stereotyped way.

Mr. Jones: Yes, that's all true.

Therapist: That's what traps you, having to play a role, whether at the office or not. It would be a difficult situation for anyone, but you find yourself being so tied down by the role that you can't do anything else. For you, everything must have a beautiful outcome and resolve itself in the most ideal way.

Mr. Jones: That's all true and it's pretty uncomfortable.

Therapist: Yeah, I'm sure it is. I'm sure it's as uncomfortable as the situation you described during our last hour — that is, the situation with your wife. But you must also realize how you take yourself so seriously that it distorts your behavior. You begin to see yourself as having been singled out by this fellow for abuse instead of seeing him as just a plain, pesty drunk that anyone might run into.

Mr. Jones: Well, I don't agree with the part of that that implies that I visualize myself as having been singled out for special abuse by this individual.

He picked the one unnecessary but correct assessment of the paranoid element in this situation, and I withdrew it. I believe it was probably accurate, but to have maintained my view would have distracted us from the major focus, which was his feeling of impotent rage.

Therapist: No, I don't mean that you were singled out for special abuse by this individual, but you're taking the whole thing so seriously, as if this is something of greater significance than a drunk who is a pain in the ass.

Mr. Jones: Well, the thing of greater moment was that I wasn't able to handle it to my satisfaction.

Therapist: But you can't handle it to your satisfaction partly because you're taking it so damned seriously.

Mr. Jones: Perhaps.

Therapist: You have a lot of difficulty taking things lightly. People must wonder if you have a sense of humor, which I'm sure is there.

Mr. Jones: It is there. I ... it seldom comes up in our discussions. I think of myself as being pleasant and agreeable enough.

Therapist: Oh, that was never the problem, about your being pleasant and agreeable.

Mr. Jones: Well ... also having a sense of humor, too. [laughs]

Therapist: This drunk becomes an issue of great significance instead of just an unpleasant experience on a train.

Mr. Jones: A peculiar postscript to this is that this guy finally did leave. My boss remarked that this guy sure was a nuisance and said that whenever he met a bastard like that he lost his temper and told him off. He thought I was very tolerant to put up with him.

Therapist: He thought you were tolerant; he didn't know ...

Mr. Jones: That's what I was about to say. That was the ironic feature about this, that I was being good and I was complimented for something that I thought I handled poorly. And I also thought about whether my boss thought that I had handled it in a weak manner, rather than in a tolerant manner. I wondered if he was being sarcastic about it.

Therapist: Those are the alternatives as you see them?

Mr. Jones: The alternatives are that I'm catching the shitty end of it regardless of what happens.

Therapist: Regardless of what happens, exactly. You either are supposed to smash him or cut him sharply, in which case others will think you're strong, or if you do what you did, then your boss will think that you're weak. [patient is laughing]

Mr. Jones: That never occurred to me, about this striving to maintain some model or ideal sort of appearance.

Therapist: That's involved in it, isn't it?

Mr. Jones: Of course.

Therapist: We see this interesting contradiction again and again.

Mr. Jones: Situations like these are what I get disturbed about. In a period of calm reflection, I can think of a lot of alternatives, but when faced with this problem I can't think of one.

I wanted Mr. Jones to understand that I was not suggesting that he behave like his friend or like me. What he needed to recognize was that there were alternatives available to him and suitable to his personality. Too often the therapist unwittingly serves as a model for the patient, who may be so different from him that it becomes an instance of role-playing, rather than acting as oneself. The therapist must keep such transferential matters clearly in mind to forestall or reduce this, so that the changes we hope will take place in the patient's life will indeed occur. The patient must utilize his own capacities, talents, and background instead of trying to imitate the therapist, who may be viewed as his ideal.

Therapist: We want to see what makes it so necessary for you to maintain this picture of yourself.

Mr. Jones: I've got to preserve this image or else I will be viewed in a poor light. I'll be criticized, despised, ridiculed, derided, or what have you.

Therapist: So the only alternative you see in these situations is that, if you let yourself do what you want to do, there would be a show of violence that might be infinitely worse than what happens, eh?

Mr. Jones: No, I ... no, it isn't — it's ... no. I have no picture of myself being excessively violent. But rather that if I got on my high horse at all, that this other character would create a scene which would be hard for me to handle and still maintain the dignity of my position.

Therapist: He'd create a scene which would then force you to use some violence, or else look like a fool.

Mr. Jones: Well, I guess so. Yep, that's right, too. Yes, and I guess I could recognize that phase of it, if I were not so formal and didn't have that worry. Then I probably would have the other worry that he will create a scene which will force me to use some degree of violence which is lurking in the background. I'll be the goat no matter what happens.

Therapist: And do you think it's possible that you were restraining yourself from being angry and assaultive to this guy on the train?

Mr. Jones: No, that doesn't seem like it.

Therapist: Isn't that what you feel like doing, sort of eliminating him? If you could make him disappear, that would be the solution?

Mr. Jones: Well, it would be easy to say yes to that. I actually would be saying that I would prefer that the situation hadn't arisen at all. I can't say that I was conscious of an impulse to slug him.

Therapist: No, not quite as crude as that. That isn't really what I mean — physically slugging him. I would imagine that you don't allow yourself to recognize the same kind of impulse that your boss expressed when he said he would have lost his temper.

Mr. Jones: Something to that effect.

Therapist: You deny that possibly that feeling might come into your mind. I don't see why it's so unthinkable, that if it occurs to your boss, it could also occur to others.

Mr. Jones: No, I wasn't busy trying to deny it. I was trying to be truthful about it.

I wanted to make certain that the point about his strong feelings was clearly understood, knowing how easily he could undermine or distort an awareness moments after it had been established. It was crucial that he be able to recognize the association of suppression of violent feelings to his obsessional preoccupations about his wife. The tactics involved not only highlighting how human and understandable such a reaction might be but also pointing out that others, including his boss, would experience such feelings. Finally, he had to recognize why, in order to maintain some idealization, he might deny, repress, or distort some reactions and be unaware of them.

Therapist: Of course, and you don't have to get busy trying to defend yourself since you're not being attacked. I said that you have great hesitation in coming to grips with certain feelings within yourself. You find it easier to talk about the guy being a nuisance and making you feel anxious and you being unable to cope with the situation. You can recognize those aspects as well as the feeling of inadequacy that gets stirred up. You can also recognize how you're made to feel defensive and how you come out the ass end of the deal. All these things you can grasp quickly. But it is with the greatest difficulty that you grasp how you are feeling at the time it's going on.

Mr. Jones: I guess it's so obscure that it didn't occur to me.

Therapist: Because it's quite conceivable, isn't it, that much of your behavior, especially this appeasing behavior, comes from your concern about what you might do?

Mr. Jones: You mean some unconscious, hostile feelings?

He had said it himself. Whether it was merely a refrain from what he has guessed the therapist was trying to get across or whether he truly recognized it to be the issue remained to be seen. What follows will give us some clues as to how deep the understanding went and whether it would have any prolonged effect on his behavior.

Therapist: Unconscious or out of awareness — hostile feelings, especially hostile feelings that must arise when a person makes you feel impotent, helpless, and trapped.

Mr. Jones: It sounds logical that that's so.

This was just what we did not want to happen in the sense that it was an intellectual understanding and a cognitive agreement. Therefore, I challenged his statement that it must be so because I said it was or else logically it should have been there.

Mr. Jones: I can only say it was unconscious or obscure and I didn't realize that such feelings were there.

Therapist: You mean, you're saying they were there? Or are you just saying that because I say they must be there?

Mr. Jones: I'm not saying it for the purpose of being agreeable with you, I'm saying it because it sounds logical and there's something . . . there must be some solution to the problem and perhaps that's it. But I'm saying I can't remember that I actually had such a thought.

Therapist: What I hear is some reasonable, rational explanation of how you might feel in the situation. I don't hear you saying, "That drunken sot, I wish to hell he would leave me alone!"

Mr. Jones: I think I know what you mean and it occurred to me momentarily to express it in that manner but I rejected that method because it would appear to you as if I was using you for assistance in it.

He was saying that he avoided using this type of language for fear I would think it was only to use me to help him express it. Such patients must avoid the show of needing help, which is viewed as a weakness. Therefore, even if Mr. Jones really did experience a need or a reaction, he would have to cover it up. This also interfered with his ability to express his anger at others.

Mr. Jones: That would be asking you to handle my problems.

Therapist: That would be weak! That's an interesting notion, isn't it? It would be weak to say to your boss that this drunk is a pain in the ass. You have to handle it in this proper, dignified way. Yes, it is very interesting that you consider an expression of feeling a weakness.

This idea is most important for the obsessional, who already tends to keep his feelings under control in his need to control all elements in his living. In addition, the need to be omnipotent, independent, safe, and secure will be threatened by the awareness of feelings or the expression of them if they are viewed as evidence of weakness. This not only complicates the issue of openness to feelings but also further impedes the expression of them once they are acknowledged to exist. I reached that impasse with Mr. Jones, who was nearly ready to identify his feelings but still felt it unsafe and unwise to express them if, if so doing, he would be viewed as a weak, ineffective person.

Mr. Jones: That's true. I was able to express that to my boss after we were in the dining car, but I wasn't able to turn to the drunk and say it to him. No, I didn't do that.

Therapist: You expect now that you should be a superman and be like your boss.

Mr. Jones: I thought that you thought I wasn't even able to express any hostility toward the guy to my boss at all. Yes, I agree that he was a son of a bitch.

Therapist: I mean it's very difficult for you to express feelings and you have felt that it's a weakness to do it even here. Probably, therefore, when you felt this momentary urge or thought, you cast it aside, since it is sensed by you as a weakness. That goes on a great deal, doesn't it?

Mr. Jones: Yes, it goes on all the time. When I would observe some irrational, emotional, or angry, unreasonable behavior in others, that seemed very undesirable to me and something I should strive not to do — not to appear in that way.

Therapist: Uh-huh, that was a weakness.

Mr. Jones: That was a weakness, or so I interpreted it.

Therapist: And the great goal became expressed in terms of being a machine that was always in control and in strict conformity to what was required and what was proper.

Mr. Jones: It sure did.

Therapist: Hmm. Now can you recall an incident sometime back when one of your employees wanted you to take up an item of business that you just weren't interested in pursuing and you announced to the committee that you were taking the afternoon off?

Mr. Jones: Yes, yes. I remember.

Therapist: And you had some good feeling because one of the group suggested that, "Well, that's pretty good," implying that you were able to operate on the basis of a feeling. You wanted to take the day off and you were not being hemmed in by requirements and the demands and the schedules. You took the day off. Now was this an expression of weakness? Was this interpreted as weakness by others?

Mr. Jones: No.

Therapist: I can't possibly see how it could be.

Mr. Jones: Well, it wasn't. It was probably realizing that that gave me a comfortable feeling about it.

Therapist: Sure. The reaction was along the lines of "We hardly expected you to ever do something like that; it's so human."

This recollection of mine was introduced to strengthen his recognition that the expression of feelings was not necessarily viewed by others as weakness and might, in fact, have been viewed as strength.

Mr. Jones: That's right. Now you're hitting it exactly right.

Therapist: That you are really human.

Mr. Jones: That's it exactly.

Therapist: How does this situation relate to the situation with the drunk? What about that could be interpreted as weak? You also said that in telling this to me you had the feeling that you were asking me to relieve you of this unpleasantness.

Mr. Jones: I was afraid that you would think I was asking you to help me out on something that I ought to handle.

Therapist: You think I would interpret what you said as a request to do something about it.

Mr. Jones: I was afraid you would think that I thought that way.

Therapist: Now that strikes me as a very interesting thought. Why should I interpret an incident which is of inconvenience to you as a demand or an order to get busy easing the situation for you?

Mr. Jones: You shouldn't, but I was afraid that you would think that I was asking you to.

Therapist: Now I'm asking you to think about why I or anyone else would interpret it that way. I think you are saying that if you complain about something, you have an uneasy feeling that the other person is going to interpret this as a request.

Mr. Jones: That I'm weak.

Therapist: Yeah, as a request to come in and help you out.

Mr. Jones: But I'm afraid that the other person will think that I'm so weak that I have to ask them for help. It seemed axiomatic that that would be the reaction of others.

Therapist: Hmm. I think that merits a good bit of thought, that it is axiomatic that if one complains to another person, that is tantamount to a request for alleviation of the nuisance.

Mr. Jones: I never thought of there being any other interpretation.

The transferential issue here was patent and obvious. Since we were at the end of the session I chose to do nothing more with it at this point. Now it seemed to me that it was an expedient decision and a wise one as well, since I left him pondering on this curious transformation of his automatic expectation of fulfillment or relief of uneasiness when he experienced any problems. It related to his grandiose feelings of childish privileges and magical expectations as well as the readiness to feel judged as weak and ineffective.

In the next session, the last recorded one even though I saw Mr. Jones on two other occasions, we pursued the issue of his being hostile when he felt weak and helpless.

Mr. Jones: Did I ever mention to you that it's uncomfortable to me for anyone to call me Junior?

Therapist: Yes, you mentioned it, but I would have presumed as much. [patient laughs] Did something come up in this connection?

Mr. Jones: Yes. I was going to relate an incident that happened last week when my neighbor called me Junior. I was sizzling about that, but my wife felt that I was oversensitive to feel that way.

Therapist: She felt the woman was just being cute?

Mr. Jones: Something like that. She said the woman didn't mean to hurt my feelings at all. My wife told me that I was being childish taking offense at harmless remarks. I would only cause people to think that I was neurotic.

Therapist: That would be a crime worse than death! For people to think you're neurotic! [patient laughs]

Mr. Jones: Well, I told her that I didn't think there were enough occasions on which I took offense that they would think anything particular about it. I told her I didn't like this Junior business and sometime I might tell this woman that I didn't like it. Well, of course she was against my doing that. Then she said, "I'm not going to say anything to her about it for you." I said I certainly didn't want her to, that I didn't expect her to. If there is to be anything said to her at all, then I'll certainly do it. And that was rather interesting to me as being one example of my thinking that in expressing a complaint against someone to a third person, I give the impression to the person that I was asking for the person's assistance.

Therapist: And here it happened.

Mr. Jones: And here it happened. And I remember well the discussion we had on that point.

Therapist: How do you account for that? How do you account for the fact that you think that others seem to respond to some complaint that you make in terms of offers of assistance? It certainly isn't what generally happens.

Mr. Jones: I am not conscious of having led her to that. I said or implied nothing to lead her to it.

Therapist: Uh-huh. Nothing in your relationship with Joan at any time would lead her to feel that you are asking for help? I'm wondering whether you have had some way of presenting yourself in a pitiful sort of way that encourages people to want to help you?

Mr. Jones: No, I don't think so. I presented it that I was mad about this business of being called Junior. Whether or not I liked it depended on whether the person had some malice in mind. I told her that I was sure that she didn't have any malice in mind but I still didn't like it. Well, I think that it's possible that in the past I might have presented something in a pitiful way. Well, I do know that back in 1950 I was most confused and tended to think of my wife in terms of a parent-child relationship, rather than a wife-husband relationship. I sometimes sounded as if I was whining about something.

Therapist: Uh-huh.

Mr. Jones: But I'm certain that I didn't present that aspect this time. It's possible that she had the same thoughts in mind, though, but it's puzzling to me because of knowing how seldom I do express feelings and yet here was a case where I did take the occasion to express them and this peculiar result happened.

Therapist: Uh-huh.

Mr. Jones: Well, another reason which might account for her having that thought may be . . . as I was telling her this she might have been reluctant for me to bring it up to the neighbor. Maybe she entertained the thought for a moment that she might do it. However, she might have concluded that she didn't want to do it and expressed that.

Therapist: Why should she do it?

Mr. Jones: She shouldn't. I have never, as long as I can remember, liked situations in which it looked as if I was being thought of as a child.

The patient's name was, in fact, Mr. Jones, Jr. Although he rarely informed others, he signed his name this way.

Mr. Jones: Possibly the reason that I find expressions of that kind offensive is because they conflict with my need to think that I always have to behave and appear to others in a certain model way. Do you think that is possible?

He had clearly learned the matter of his tendency to behave in some idealized way.

Therapist: Well, it may be, but it may also have something to do with the fact that you're working so hard at trying to play *senior*, because you seem so very much afraid people might think of you as junior. All these things that you talked about — namely, dignity, status, and having to be right — is playacting the grown-up rather than really being the grown-up. The grown-up doesn't have to go around demanding status and respect; he just gets it.

Mr. Jones: Hmm. Could be. Well, and yet it seems to me that in order to get it there's a certain demeanor or impression that must be presented.

Therapist: It certainly has seemed so to you; as a matter of fact it has seemed to you so strongly that most of the time you had the demeanor but not the status. You walk around trying to appear like a grown-up, while you're afraid to take a step without asking Daddy if it was all right.

Mr. Jones: Well, that's true, although that's fifteen years ago. And I had that attitude also three years ago when I was putting Joan in the place of my parents. It was hard for her to realize exactly what was happening. It irritated her.

Therapist: It must have been disturbing in recognizing how much you were the little boy. Don't you think one of the reasons you're so sensitive about being called Junior is that you must often have the suspicion that you are still too much the junior?

Mr. Jones: Well, yes ...

Therapist: The thing you don't like in yourself. So much of your being grown-up has been playacting grown-up — insisting, in a sense, that you are grown-up because you were with grown-ups; insisting that you get the same kind of status that they get even though you are younger.

Mr. Jones: I insisted on it because my status or position indicated that I ought to have it and that if I didn't have it, it might indicate I wasn't the proper person to be in that place.

Therapist: Yeah, it's what we said a few minutes ago, isn't it? It's all backwards. If people called you grown-up that meant you were, so the way to become grown-up is to put on long pants and have everybody call you Mister, rather than by your first name. Yes, you thought that the way to be grown-up is to demand that people acknowledge that you are grown-up, not taking into account the fact that people who are grown-up don't need to demand or force the acknowledgment. They don't even require that people call them by their last names and bow in respect. As a matter of fact, I'm sure you have noted that the people who are really comfortable are the ones who are least demanding with regard to status.

Mr. Jones: Yes, I suppose that's true.

Therapist: The guys who really have arrived are the ones who make the least fuss about form.

Mr. Jones: And yet I occasionally get remarks from Joan that I'm acting too childish — "be more grown-up" — and that gets me mad as hell.

Therapist: What do you mean, is that so surprising? Is it so surprising that your wife notes that you act childish at times?

Mr. Jones: It's rather confusing to me right at the moment to think of all of those same conflicting things.

Therapist: But they're not so conflicting. It is acting childish to demand that one respect one's status because grown-ups demand it. The insistence that others recognize your status is not necessarily grown-up. It is often quite the opposite.

Mr. Jones: O.K. I wasn't thinking of that kind of incident, however, as prompting her opinion that I was childish. I can agree or acknowledge that I often spent a lot of time playing the part.

Therapist: Yeah, it's important to see that because then you can have the opportunity to get clearer about the elements of childishness in your behavior, so that you can do something about it.

Mr. Jones: After we knew each other only two months or so, she said some of the things I do are rather childish while other things are actions of people much older than I am.

Therapist: Hmm. Sort of having to be a superman to overcome all the notions of your childishness. She thinks sometimes you're childish, but the minute you try to step out of the role and be really grown-up she says, "Watch out, you might step on someone's toes," huh? Isn't this like mother again?

Mr. Jones: Yeah, exactly.

Therapist: So she says, be grown-up, but in fact, doesn't let you.

Mr. Jones: Yeah.

Therapist: I think that's something you need to face pretty squarely.

Mr. Jones: Well, I think I did in this case, in telling her I didn't like it and that my purpose in discussing this wasn't to solicit her intervention. In no way did I back down in insisting that I didn't like this. She kept trying to show me the neighbor didn't mean any harm, and it is perfectly true.

Therapist: That's right. Because people don't intentionally kick you, does that mean it shouldn't hurt? [patient laughs] What I was implying about recognizing Joan's role is in noticing that you say Joan takes this or that point of view on the assumption of what's best for you. You seem to automatically accept it as so, not taking into account that perhaps her point of view is often what is best for her. She has her own problems. It's conceivable, isn't it, that at times she would prefer that you were not completely the man?

Mr. Jones: Yes, that is entirely possible and it's probably the reason that I find some of her attitudes unpleasant. I have told her at times that she's treating me as if she was my mother and I the child. Usually she gets enraged at that and insists that she isn't. Sometimes, though, she says, "Most women have a mother complex, so maybe I do, too." I've answered that by saying, "Well, probably they do, but I find it very unpleasant when you exhibit it so strongly."

Therapist: Meaning that it's all right to treat you like a child when she wants to, but then when you catch her at it you should be an adult and not hold it against her. You should be both. She's kind of mixed up herself in what she expects.

Mr. Jones: Yes, I think she is.

Therapist: And you're very mixed up about this whole problem, aren't you, about what is grown-up and what is adult and what is not?

Mr. Jones: Yes, I suppose I am.

Therapist: Because the notion that I think you are trying to talk about today was that grown-ups don't complain or gripe, only children do that. Complaining always means asking for someone else's help in your way of thinking. Adults should not criticize or find fault.

Mr. Jones: Finding fault would be interpreted as whining.

Therapist: Finding fault is interpreted as whining; criticizing is interpreted as appeals for help; complaining is interpreted as "please get me out of this terrible situation." Now that has gotten in the way of any situation where your assessment may have been correct in finding the situation needing correction. You could only deal with it in a pseudo-grown-up way by being so correct and so proper that no one could ever possibly accuse you of being critical or whining or complaining. And your notion of handling the situation in a grown-up way is to be so absolutely pure and correct that no one could find anything wrong.

Mr. Jones: It still left me without any means of expressing wrongs that I found others doing.

Therapist: Of course, because it still left you with the impossible position of trying to be grown-up by being superman, which means that you couldn't simply be human.

Mr. Jones: Well, when there's differences of opinion between me and Joan, I often now can leave it on an unfinished note. I can leave it that she's disagreeing with me. I never could do that. I always had to either knuckle down to an agreement with Joan's opinion or keep agitating the same thing over and over again until she would agree with me.

Therapist: Force her to knuckle under. That's grown-up.

Mr. Jones: No, but I don't think I really was doing that. I think I was agitating and pleading for her to see it my way.

Therapist: Let's face it. You had the greatest difficulty in being wrong or admitting that you were wrong. Now you're saying that you are better able to let discussions go. This is another way of saying you don't have to have it immediately settled, that you have to be right, or the grown-up.

Mr. Jones: Right.

EVIDENCE OF CHANGE

Here was clear evidence of a change in his behavior, as well as in his thinking, and clear progress in his dealings with his wife. It could now be assumed that the obsessional thoughts had clearly decreased and had much less significance in his dealings with her and in fact had less presence in his ruminations.

Therapist: And you can tolerate the possibility that you may be wrong. You couldn't be wrong in the past. You had to force agreement.

Mr. Jones: I couldn't be wrong in the past because nothing could be left unsettled. It had to be decided. One way or the other. Either the person had to agree with me or I'd have to keep prodding until they did, or else I would have to be the one to knuckle under. I don't think that deep down I thought of it as forcing the other guy to knuckle under, that was the more outward appearance of it. I think it was that they wouldn't like me or they won't want to do it my way unless I can prove to them that that really is the right way.

Therapist: But why did they have to do it your way?

Mr. Jones: Well, under my old system of operating, it was because that was the way I conceived that laws and regulations ordained it and everything had to be orderly and correct.

Therapist: What is the danger as you see it in having someone disagree with you? Some people conceivably could say that if one is always orderly and correct, the possibilities for creative ability are lost. That is, you don't let anything new enter the situation.

Mr. Jones: Yeah.

Therapist: Is there something in this that you're afraid of?

Mr. Jones: Well, I was afraid that I might be wrong and if I didn't convince them that I was right, I was afraid that they wouldn't like me. There seems to be something else involved in there that I can't get a hold of. I wish I could think of some reason for this playacting. I told you how nervous and shocked I was when Joan dropped in to visit me in my office. I suppose that was something to do with the playacting and stage setting.

Therapist: Yeah. What comes to mind?

Mr. Jones: Well, it could have been more comfortable to me if I had known she was coming at this exact time. I wasn't adverse to her coming — in fact I told her that I wanted her to come — but I wasn't expecting her that day. That seemed to make all the difference in the world. I felt as if I was caught in the act of doing something wrong.

Therapist: Sort of playacting the big shot?

Mr. Jones: No ... I don't know what caused me to be so shocked.

Therapist: But I think you're right; I think it does have something to do with this business of playacting, because we know that you do this a lot in spite of your status. There's some tendency still to deal with yourself as if you really weren't the successful executive.

Mr. Jones: That's definitely true.

This preceding exchange was from the last tape recording I have of our sessions. My notebook contained some brief comments, as follows: November 4: "Relates progress in all areas of his living and in our analysis." November 30: "Got into a situation of open conflict. Developed some awareness of his aggressiveness at the job and raised questions about his intense hostility which he can now recognize and acknowledge." December 6: "First instance in our sessions of strong feelings which he feels and admits but still needs to hold back somewhat. Very upset, terribly distressed, and repeating over and over how much he has been helped and how upset he is at our having to stop."

SUMMATION

Many changes had occurred and the symptoms that brought Mr. Jones into treatment had improved, as had the relationship with his wife. Although his obsession seemed to be less pervasive and persistent, only time could tell how often and to what extent it would reappear on unfavorable occasions in his day-to-day life. His capacity to relate to colleagues, friends, and his own family were enhanced as his self-esteem grew.

Ideally, treatment would have continued for some time to consolidate the gains and integrate the insights more solidly in Mr. Jones's living. Perhaps more aspects of his obsessional tendencies would have emerged, and we would have explored his sexual adjustment with his wife, although practically nothing had been raised about this during the year and two months of our work together. With further therapy, I would hope that the gains would be sustained and would perhaps become more solid.

It is abundantly clear that the psychodynamics of Mr. Jones's behavior was closely related to his inability to express or deal with his hostile feelings. These feelings were held in check or controlled by a variety of defenses — displacement, reaction-formation, and ritualization — all described and detailed as they occurred throughout the sessions. I disagree with Freud's emphasis on the anal-erotic aspects of such formulations. In addition to the conflicting evidence over the bowel-training struggle, there are many obsessionals in whom all the elements of control seemingly affect all areas of their living except the anal function. The widespread prevalence of obsessive behavior in children can be readily understood as a factor of the child's helplessness and vulnerability and the need for order and control in dealing with insecurities. The child is also engaged in a struggle for self-expression and in maintaining an identity. This struggle takes place on all fronts and in relation to problems of acculturation as well as to toilet training. While the factors suggested by many theorists can be identified in the obsessive-compulsive mechanisms, the overriding purpose of the behavior is to attempt to achieve some security and certainty for the person who feels threatened and insecure in an uncertain world. The possibility of controlling oneself and the forces outside oneself by assuming omniscience and omnipotence can give one a false illusion of certainty. Therefore, the main ingredient is one of control.

Freud saw the obsessional symptom as a device for dealing with unacceptable hostile or sexual impulses. He felt that such people control the expression of these impulses by using displacement and symbolization as defenses against them. The symptom, he thought, was a compromise of "doing" the forbidden wish and at the same time "undoing" it. However, the obsessional needs to control not only sexual or hostile impulses but also the tender, friendly, stupid, and unworthy thoughts and feelings. In my view, the obsessive-compulsive dynamism is a device for preventing any feeling or thought that might produce shame, loss of pride or status, or a feeling of weakness or deficiency — whether such feelings are hostile, sexual, or otherwise. I see the obsessional maneuver as an adaptive technique to protect the person from the exposure of any thought or feeling that will endanger his physical or psychological existence. This extends Freud's views and does not require the postulate of an instinct theory or a libido theory.

The case of Mr. Jones supplies ample data to support the hypothesis that obsessive-compulsive behavior is a technique for the control of unacceptable, hostile impulses. However, I believe that this formulation is not a complete description of what, in fact, constitutes the essence of this disorder. One can recognize and acknowledge the need for the control of hostile impulses in relationships that are necessary and essential to a person. The consequences of the overt expression of these feelings could jeopardize the relationship and security of the person. Yet the individual anticipates a greater tragedy and a more fearsome outcome if he were to communicate his feelings to the other person. However, we must still account for the anger and hostility unless we accept this as a given, genetic quality that the traditional analyst would call an instinct.

There is an undeniable quality of dependence in the relationships of the obsessional seen in Mr. Jones's relationship to his wife and mother. This will help us understand not only the anger but also the need for certainty and absolute control in order to feel safe and secure in the world. Mr. Jones had intense needs for intimacy and acceptance in a tender, loving relationship. While his mother was devoted, loving in her demanding way and prideful in her son, her inability to be physically close and tender was very apparent to him. She rarely kissed him or her husband, and there were no warm or empathic exchanges or manifestations of tenderness except in an intellectual way. This is what Mr. Jones wanted and tried to obtain with his proper, catering, "good boy" behavior. However, his mother was ambivalent and contradictory and impossible to please. He lived in a chaotic, uncertain world in which only the perfect, absolute, omniscient, and omnipotent person could feel safe. If one could not be omnipotent, the illusion of omnipotence could be sustained by magic rituals — which, if properly carried out, guaranteed one's status. This is the essence of the obsesssional or compulsive ritual. So the development of the obsessional character structure is an effort to assure one's security and acceptance in human relationships. The anger is a response to the ambivalent, contradictory, unstable, and uncertain expectations from those persons on whom one's security rests. One is disappointed and feels cheated in one's desperate need. Then anger follows, but such anger must be subdued and repressed. What we are dealing with is not the frustration of an aggressive instinct, but the frustration of the need for tenderness from someone whose affection and acceptance seem to be essential for survival. That is why the obsessional neurosis is a false, illusionary feeling of security, which requires extreme measures to feel minimal trust and safety. The scaffolding of certainty is required, since the obsessional is unable to sustain doubts, errors, failures, and ambiguities because of a basic lack of esteem and warm acceptance from those on whom survival depends.

This is what I believe Mr. Jones was trying to deal with. His anger was secondary. His need for tenderness and interpersonal intimacy was the primary factor. What must be achieved in therapy to overcome this fearful, uncertain, threatened state? Therapy of the obsessional state involves illuminating and exposing the patient's extreme feelings of insecurity and uncertainty. As he comes to understand his neurotic structure as a defense against recognizing these weaknesses, he can begin to build a new security system. At therapy's inception the obsessional defense cannot be abandoned because the individual is afraid of the consequences. As his esteem grows and the awareness of his strength increases he can slowly risk abandoning these patterns and be freed to function on a more productive level. The goal is to move from superhuman expectations to human productiveness — which can reach whatever limits the individual is capable of. When he discovers that the impossible goals have left him disappointed, he will abandon them. An awareness of his valid capacities to produce may actually stimulate greater activity. In essence, the obsessional must learn that in abandoning rigid, inflexible patterns of behavior designed to control and protect himself, he can actually feel more secure and more capable and be more productive as well.

TWENTY-THREE YEAR FOLLOW-UP

In 1975, I was able to locate Mr. Jones, with whom I had had no contact since 1953 when our incomplete therapeutic relationship was interrupted. I found myself anxious about my first call and increasingly concerned about our face-to-face meeting despite his cordial agreement to meet with me. I wanted his permission to publish the material in this volume, but I was also very curious about a twenty-three year follow-up of a treatment problem that generally has a very poor prognosis. Was his wife alive? Did the marriage continue? Did he receive any further help with his obsessional ideas? Did he have a severe mid-life experience? What happened when he retired? Had he benefitted from our work together or did it only have a temporary effect with a more severe recurrence? I was flooded with questions and curiosity as I awaited his visit in my office.

I recognized Mr. Jones with some difficulty as he entered my office, while he recognized me as if we'd seen each other only last week. He looked very well and greeted me warmly. I informed him of the purpose of my call and my hope that he would agree to permit publication of the material, provided, of course, that I would alter any identifying data. I assured him I could do so without changing any of the transcripts, and since the Nixon tapes were then in the news, we shared a laugh about the possible gaps and alterations.

I was eager to hear about his life over the past years and he brought me up to date. His wife was alive and well. Their marriage had continued and was satisfactory; in fact, it was much improved since he became more assertive as well as more considerate and aware of her needs. She, in turn, became less demanding and critical. There were occasions when she irritated him and sometimes infuriated him. He became aware of these feelings quickly as they were accompanied by reflections about his obsessional ideas in the past. In general, his obsessional thoughts had not troubled him, since they had not persisted or preoccupied him. His capacities to concentrate and be effective at his job had been greatly enhanced, and, until his retirement, he felt he had performed more effectively than at any time in his life. Work had gone well and he had enjoyed life; he felt he had become less rigid and intense and more capable of easygoing fun.

Over these twenty years, he felt the need to see a psychiatrist on one occasion for only three sessions after he retired and began feeling depressed, lost, and uncertain of himself. He felt the therapeutic work he and I had done had given him sufficient insight and capacity to introspect, looking at himself with perspective so that he could handle the immediate consequences of the retirement quickly and effectively.

The interview was warm and friendly. He was curious as to what had happened to me, and we shared some of our experiences. He expressed the feeling that he had been greatly influenced by our work and was deeply grateful for the changes he felt had taken place in his life as a result of it. He felt it had helped restructure his living, so that he was a more effective, happier, social being, even though he indicated that he and his wife were still inclined to be loners with few friends. After I promised to send him a copy of the book when it was published, he took his leave and we both felt a warmth and fellowship.

I was surprised when he called a week later to tell me how pleased he had been to see me and wished me well with the book, but that he preferred I did not send him a copy of it as he was not sure his wife could handle it, since she would know it was about him. I agreed.

I reflected on that and wondered what it was all about. I could only conjecture that he had not resolved some of his difficulties with his wife and still felt uneasy at the prospect of revealing his thoughts and feelings to her of twenty-three years ago because some of them might still be present today. It might have been unwise at this time in his life for him to stir up these old irritations, disagreements, and hostile feelings which had prevailed during all those years; it might stir up dissatisfactions and open old wounds. Perhaps it was wise and mature not to reintroduce these issues. His decision also suggested that he had sufficient interest and tender regard for her not to remind her of how severe and extreme his resentments of her had been. While he was more assertive, he probably still felt like he needed to be a good boy, and, though their communication had dramatically improved, it still might be difficult to handle such a damaging attack on her personality. He dealt with life still in his characteristic style — agreeing and, perhaps, even catering and then having second thoughts and doubts and playing it safe. This was an obsessional style with certain ramifications but not necessarily neurotic or destructive ones. He preferred to maintain peace at home and forego whatever static the book might bring.

I never got to know his wife as a person, nor did I see her in my office as a partner of my patient in his struggle to liberate himself from the oppressive symptoms he was experiencing. I was surprised in reading the transcript to find that I had never made inquiries about her first marriage, nor did I know much about her background and her assets. She was an important person in his life and in his neurosis, but we did not deal with her as a person in her own right.

When psychodynamic theory hypothesizes that neurotic difficulties stem from internal sources related to the individual's inability to deal with his libidinal energies, then the therapeutic work needs to concern itself with the vicissitudes of the libido and the outside world as an accidental or coincidental arena in which such a development takes place. Currently, there is a greater tendency to view the external world as a prime mover in neuroses; such developments are viewed as disturbances of ego function and the ego interacts with the environment as it develops. My therapeutic approach in the 1950s was not strictly classical or orthodox, but I did follow the technical rule of not seeing both husband and wife even for limited or occasional contact. At that time, mothers were not seen by therapists treating the child and these rules were amply supported by tendentious rationale and theoretical "musts." I would now consider it valid and necessary to see the partner of a patient or the parents of a patient or whoever could provide any clues to the patient's problems, if the patient agreed, and whoever could play a role in the reorganization of the patient's life. My experience has amply supported this point of view, and the development of group and family therapy is an outgrowth of this viewpoint. Seeing parents, wives or husbands, relatives, and friends, when appropriate and with the patient's consent, is a useful and time-saving technique. If it creates difficulties, these can be dealt with when they occur. The therapist, in his effort to be useful to the patient, must assume this burden.

EPILOGUE

Man lives in a world in which he is only part master. While knowledge and the advances of science have broadened his command over nature, he is still unable to completely control either himself or his environment. He remains dependent on his fellow man and their benevolent concern for his survival, as well as on the impersonal forces of nature that are entirely outside his control. Uncertainties and insecurities pursue his everyday existence, and he has had to settle for some absolutes (such as death) over which he has no influence whatsoever. In more limited ways, he has had to acknowledge his own inability to completely control his own functioning — especially in those areas of physiology and psychology that are outside his awareness.

From the earliest records of human behavior it is evident that much activity has been devoted to attempts to control, influence, and guarantee those forces that are beyond man's immediate access. The major content of all the primitive religions was devoted to rituals and devices designed to curry favor with the gods, in order to prevail upon them for some favorable influence. There were endless ritualistic practices inside and outside of religious systems, in which the goal was to increase man's authority in matters over which he recognized he had no direct control. These practices were neither subtle nor devious. They were simple "bargains" in which it was hoped that fair exchange could be obtained through such performances. As man's grasp of nature increased and as he developed a growing confidence in his own strength and powers, he developed more subtle religious practices and more devious devices to guarantee his living. Monotheism replaced polytheism, and man did not apply for direct aid but hoped that in his overall devoutness and dedication, God would know and minister to his needs. Later on, he introduced a ministry that interposed with God for him. He made his religion less a commercial transaction and more a moral commitment. Instead of mere exchange in the form of sacrifices or gifts, he offered a total devotion in the form of worship. However, when it came to death — which he could never deny or overcome no matter how powerful or influential he might be — he required a different tactic. As death could not be overcome, he developed an endless variety of placating illusions and soporific fantasies of an existence beyond death that was to be even more glorious and fulfilling than the existence on earth. This folklore served many purposes, but among them was an evasion of the final acknowledgment of man's limited meaningfulness in a physical sense and his utter incapacity to overcome finiteness. It was an evasion of his powerlessness, and Christian eschatology became a social tranquilizer designed to deal with man's inability to accept the finality of his biological existence. This type of security operation represented an advance in his intellectual capacities for conceptualization.

When we translate these oversimplified and broad notions of the role of ritual, religion, and fantasy into the language of the obsessive-compulsive defense, we can recognize many parallels. The obsessive defenses are attempts to deal with feelings of powerlessness and helplessness in a broad, as well as in a limited, sense. They represent a private and personal religion in which the ritual attempts to gain a measure of guaranteed living by preventing any possibility of loss of control. As opposed to the ritual designed to influence or control an outer force such as a god, the obsessive ritual is intended to control an inner force that the individual feels he has no capacity to manage. The obsessive device — through its aspects such as procrastination, distraction, indecision, and preoccupation with the need to know everything — is used to establish guarantees and certainties about the future.

What guarantees and certainties were necessary for Mr. Jones to function without anxiety or threat? Because of his overriding need for approval and acceptance he was required to be good — a perfect, flawless, and faultless superman. This impossible goal demanded that he hide from his human fallibilities and be the controlled, unmoved, unemotional robot. He needed to restrain his tender as well as his hostile feelings. When pressed by his ambivalent desires to be both safe and effective, he was able to restrain his impulses by using obsessional ruminations which kept him severely controlled. He manifested almost every type of obsessional symptom except phobia.

The phobia achieves its results by forbidding any possibility of loss of control in a particular area of living by removing that area from the individual's existence. It is the ultimate weapon in the struggle to maintain the illusion of control when the fear of loss of control leaves us in danger, either because of what we might do or because of our inability to control what others might do. However, to be effective the phobia must not eliminate too many areas of functioning or it will defeat its purpose and produce a living death, that is, a total isolation from all living.

The attempts at omniscience and omnipotence that are demanded of the obsessional individual frequently lead to grandiose conceptions of himself with consequent expectations of special privilege and exemption from human limitations. This explains much of the behavior of those individuals who are compulsively driven to overeat or who are addicted to drugs or alcohol. The feeling of exemption leads them to deny the inevitable consequences of their compulsions. Their expectations of being exempt from the effects of the drug, alcohol, or food lead them to believe that they can take them with impunity, or they assume they can control their intake. When trapped in excessive intake, they have grandiose conceptions of their capacity for future control. Thus, addiction results from these magical expectations, which also account for these people's inability to profit and learn from their last debauch. Likewise, the psychopath or sociopath — who appears to learn nothing from his previous misadventures and always expects to escape the consequences of his next one — is driven by grandiose conceptions of his invulnerability and exemption from natural laws and cause-and-effect relationships. The grandiosity that accompanies the attempts at obsessional perfection also participates in the delusional processes of the schizophrenic and the paranoid states.

As much of the social and community law that regulates all society requires controls over the participants, the problem of compulsions becomes intimately related to the legal processes as well as to social practices in general. Exemptions, special privileges, and immunity from the laws of man are not available to any person except perhaps the rulers, be they kings or presidents. Consequently, any psychological development that either encourages or sustains a belief in such exemption must inevitably lead the individual into conflict with society in one form or another. In individual terms, it interferes with adequate interpersonal relations and produces gross disturbances in the individual's capacities to sustain fruitful relationships at work, in marriage, in sex, and in other areas. Such difficulties characterize the living of the obsessional. Mr. Jones, although effective in his work situation, was concentrating poorly, as his obsessional ruminations began to preoccupy him. Not only was his relationship with his colleagues deteriorating, but his marital situation was becoming desperate. Yet he was not behaving in such extreme ways that his social adjustments led him to antisocial acts. However, in the more extreme situations, when loss of control and grandiose expectations produce antisocial or asocial behavior, the presence of pathological changes or disease must be taken into account when assessing guilt and punishment. Such interpretations must consider not only psychological or dynamic intrapersonal forces but also the social system itself. Because the obsessional mechanism is triggered not solely by internal forces but is also greatly dependent on the external situation, the political, economic, and social structure of the society must be taken into account as well. It is not a question of "who is to blame," but rather an issue of recognizing causes in order to prescribe adequate remedies. In such an instance, we see in clear terms the intricate relationship of the internal and external environment in producing neurosis. The cultural nature of neurosis is exemplified in the obsessional neurosis — wherein the individual utilizes his psychological resources to counter insecurities and uncertainties imposed on him by cultural restrictions as well as by his own physiological limitations. Thus, the valid administration of justice and the proper use of the legal processes to sanction behavior as well as to eliminate crime and special offenses must incorporate this understanding in all its considerations.

Finally, the full and productive use of man's resources requires that he use the free and fertile skills that he possesses. Freedom has long been recognized as the sod from which the human potentialities can grow fully and mature. While this is widely acknowledged in a political sense, it is only beginning to be understood in a personal and psychological sense. It was not too long ago that the existential and realistic insecurities drove individuals to "escape from freedom" into a false security of obsessional dictates. This is still largely true today. Lack of clarity about the role of compulsions has nurtured the curious but popular notion that creativity or genius springs from neurotic sources and may even be the cause or result of disease. This view is still widely shared by psychologists and writers who draw the inference that since creativity frequently coexists with neurosis, the elements are related in a cause-and-effect manner. However, there are considerable data to suggest that while neurosis and creativity can coexist, the neurotic elements limit and often destroy an individual's creative capacities. In his persistent preoccupation, the obsessional individual often manages great accumulations of knowledge and know-how and can be a first-rate craftsman. However, his rigidity and unwillingness to take intellectual as well as physical risks and his insistence on guaranteed certainties interfere with the novelty and spontaneity so crucial to a truly creative achievement. Compulsions resemble dedication, but they lack the freedom of choice and the spontaneous readiness to change direction that lead to discovery.

Creativity is a complex process about which very little is known psychologically. Freud speculated about its relationship to mature sexuality, and others have proposed a variety of explanations, including genetic factors. Dedication, hard work, scholarship, and innate talent appear to be critical factors. However, an additional dimension once such a combination of elements is present is an inner freedom to be open to new experiences without fear or resistance. It is this factor that is lacking in obsessional individuals in spite of their extraordinary capacity for devoted and sustained effort. Their compulsive tendencies limit their openness and curiosity, and, consequently, they are unavailable for new insights and combinations of experience. In a lesser degree, we find the precise situation present in all obsessionals whose capacities are seriously limited by their defensive maneuvers. In all such instances, the individual's capacities to produce and to enjoy life's potentialities for joy, discovery, and novelty are restricted.

This feature was amply documented in Mr. Jones's living. He was tight, restricted, unspontaneous and formal. He had trouble having "fun" — relaxing, enjoying the lightness and frivolities that relieve the burden of much of our mundane living. He was too serious, too controlled and too rigid; he had difficulty laughing and playing with the light touch of one who was secure in his acceptance and status. As treatment became more effective, these positive qualities in Mr. Jones became more evident. He could laugh more easily and be more playful with his wife and associates. He was easier to get on with, and others noted that he was less tight and more available.

The treatment of obsessionals, while difficult, is often very successful. It results in a freer, less restricted, and less rigid individual who is no longer tied to "shoulds" — that is, to absolute and impossible demands. A capacity to accept the limitations of one's powers and to recognize the impossibility of overcoming certain existential uncertainties tends to enhance and stimulate activity in the areas of attainable goals. It is not wrong to strive for perfection or to attempt to encompass all that is knowable. It is not arrogant to defy and attempt to overcome the forces of nature both inside and outside the individual. The danger and the disease rest on the *absolute* need to do so and the inability to compromise once we have discovered that the goal is impossible. The unwillingness to do one's best because it is never perfect (and therefore not good enough) is a disease, whereas the recognition that one can do only that which one is capable of may stimulate the individual toward heroic efforts to fulfill all his capacities and potentialities. An unwillingness to enter the race because there is no guarantee of winning does not develop a champion but an obsessional neurotic. Only taking the risk of losing permits one to win. Only the readiness for defeat and failure allows an individual to perform in a manner that may ultimately prove successful. This is the difference between functioning at one's best and being *driven* to a kind of "perfection" that makes the individual avoid encounters and contests.

Life is a series of risks, uncertainties, and gambles. There are no guarantees and no predictable consequences of our behavior. In the face of a consistency in regard to the universe's major laws, we confront numerous possibilities in regard to its minor principles. To function effectively and productively, we must be satisfied with being able to do the best we can — provided we exert the effort to do just that.

In these many respects Mr. Jones showed considerable improvement in his living. He was less driven and more the driver. He could assert himself with less concern about the consequences and therefore was less timid at his office and in his home. He felt more the man and less the boy, and therefore could behave more like the man.

The obsessional demand for guarantees does not indicate a higher virtue or a more dedicated conviction; rather it shows an unwillingness to face life with all its possibilities. The existential dilemma which has confused our generation deals precisely with this matter. To be happy, one must risk unhappiness; to live fully, one must risk death and accept its ultimate decision.

INDEX